INTERNATIONAL TRADE
Theory and Evidence

INTERNATIONAL TRADE
Theory and Evidence

James R. Markusen
University of Colorado, Boulder

James R. Melvin
University of Waterloo

William H. Kaempfer
University of Colorado, Boulder

Keith E. Maskus
University of Colorado, Boulder

McGraw-Hill, Inc.
New York St. Louis San Francisco Auckland Bogotá Caracas
Lisbon London Madrid Mexico City Milan Montreal
New Delhi San Juan Singapore Sydney Tokyo Toronto

This book was set in New Century Schoolbook by Publication Services, Inc.
The editors were Scott D. Stratford and Lucille H. Sutton;
the production supervisor was Louise Karam.
The cover was designed by Joseph Gillians.
Project supervision was done by Publication Services, Inc.
R. R. Donnelley & Sons Company was printer and binder.

INTERNATIONAL TRADE
Theory and Evidence

This book is printed on acid-free paper.

2 3 4 5 6 7 8 9 0 DOC DOC 9 0 9 8 7 6 5

ISBN 0-07-040447-X

Library of Congress Cataloging-in-Publication Data

International trade: theory and evidence / James R. Markusen . . . [et
    al.].—International ed.
        p.   cm.
    Includes bibliographical references and index.
    ISBN 0-07-040447-X
    1. International trade.   I. Markusen, James R., (date).
HF1379.I5848   1995
382—dc20   94-24782

ABOUT THE AUTHORS

James R. Markusen was raised in Minneapolis and earned his B.A. and Ph.D. degrees in economics from Boston College. He spent 18 years in Canada at the University of Western Ontario, interspersed with visiting appointments in Ghana, Australia, New Zealand, and Israel. In addition, he has lectured and studied in a number of other countries including Ireland, Sweden, England, Mexico, Spain, Norway, and Fiji.

Markusen's principal interests are in the field of international trade. His research for the last 10 years has concentrated on multinational corporations and the industrial-organization approach to trade theory. He has worked both on theoretical models and on numerical, applied general-equilibrium models. This latter work empirically estimates the production and location effects of various government policies, including reductions in trade barriers, and the imposition of environmental controls. He has published widely in such journals as *The American Economic Review, The International Economic Review, the Journal of Political Economy,* and *The Journal of International Economics.*

Markusen is a research associate of the National Bureau of Economic Research and has recently completed a National Science Foundation grant to study the effects of trade and environmental policies on plant location decisions. A dedicated bicyclist and skier, Professor Markusen moved to the University of Colorado, Boulder, in July 1990.

James R. Melvin was raised on a farm in southern Manitoba and completed an undergraduate science degree at the University of Manitoba. He received his M.A. degree at the University of Alberta, then attended the University of Minnesota, where he earned his Ph.D. in economics in 1966. He took a job as faculty member at the University of Western Ontario, where he remained for 24 years, including a five-year stint as department chairperson. He moved to the University of Waterloo in 1990, where he also is chair of the economics department. He has been a visiting professor at the

University of New South Wales in Australia, the University of California at San Diego, and the University of California at Santa Barbara. He was named Fellow of the Royal Canadian Society in 1982 and served as President of the Canadian Economic Association during 1988 and 1989.

Melvin's main areas of research have been international trade theory and regional economics, focussing on the determinants of trade and extensions of the basic trade model. He has published important articles on trade in intermediate goods, increasing returns to scale, and, more recently, on demand conditions in trade and trade in services. His papers have appeared in such journals as *The American Economic Review, The Journal of Political Economy,* and *The Quarterly Journal of Economics.* He has also completed funded research projects for the Ontario Economic Council, the Economic Council of Canada, and the U.S. Treasury Department.

Jim is a committed amateur naturalist who enjoys planting trees, identifying native plant and animal species, and improving the natural environment at his cottage property on Lake Huron.

William H. Kaempfer earned his B.A. from The College of Wooster in Ohio and his Ph.D. from Duke University. His initial academic appointment was at the University of Washington in Seattle. He moved to the University of Colorado, Boulder, in August 1981, where he teaches international trade and financial theory and economic theory. Kaempfer has been a visiting professor at the Claremont Colleges and also has lectured in Indonesia, among other places.

Professor Kaempfer's primary research interests are in public-choice theory as applied to international trade policy. His research largely has been devoted to the political determinants of the choice of trade policies by self-interested government actors, one important example being his work on the choice of economic sanctions applied to South Africa. He has also written extensively about various effects of different trade policies under alternative market structures, and the endogeneity of trade policy. His articles have appeared in such journals as *The American Economic Review, The Quarterly Journal of Economics, The World Economy,* and *International Organization.*

Professor Kaempfer is an ardent naturalist, conservationist, and bird-watcher who will travel anywhere if the visit promises to increase the length of his bird lifelist.

Keith E. Maskus earned his B.A. from Knox College in Illinois and his Ph.D. from the University of Michigan, Ann Arbor. He came directly from graduate school to the faculty at the University of Colorado, Boulder, in August 1981. He teaches international trade theory, economic theory, and econometrics. He has lectured in Indonesia, the Republic of Korea, Japan, the United Kingdom, and Belgium, among other countries. He has been a visiting research scholar at the Federal Reserve Bank of Kansas City and at the U.S. Department of State, where he served as chief trade economist.

Maskus' main research interests are in the empirical determination of the sources of comparative advantage and in the economics of international technology policies, including intellectual property rights. He has published numerous papers on the Uruguay Round negotiations among the world's nations covering issues such as investment regulations, patent policies, and services trade. His articles have appeared in such journals as *The Journal of International Economics, The Review of Economics and Statistics,* and *The World Economy.* He is currently completing a research grant from the National Science Foundation to study the effects of international patent policies on foreign trade flows.

Professor Maskus is a frequent participant at meetings of the National Bureau of Economic Research. He enjoys bicycling, hiking, and playing tennis. He gets additional exercise by running regressions and jumping to conclusions.

CONTENTS

4 General Equilibrium in Open and Closed Economies

Part II Cause and Consequences of Trade

14   Empirical Studies of Comparative Advantage Models   216

Part III   Trade Policy

15   Tariffs   245

Part IV Factor Trade, Growth, and the Theory of Direct Foreign Investment

PREFACE

This book is intended primarily for a conventional one-semester or one-quarter course in international trade for undergraduate economics majors. It is most suitable for a course with a one-semester intermediate-microeconomics prerequisite, but we have not assumed that students will have had such a course. The book is not well suited to a course which covers both international trade and finance in one semester or quarter, and not well suited to a course for non-majors. The book also serves as a background text in graduate courses, giving students the basic theory before they plunge into journal articles.

Our interest in producing such a book was born from the frustration derived from the fact that virtually all alternative texts are simplified versions of what most instructors would prefer for a semester course in trade for economics majors. Competing books are tightly clustered in the center of a linear Hotelling-Lancaster characteristic space, trying to be suitable for combined trade-and-finance courses for non-majors at one end of the spectrum, to trade-only courses for majors at the other end. We are entering at the upper end of the characteristic line, hoping to carve out that market niche.

Having defined the market, we should quickly indicate the analytical level of the book lest we scare off the faint of heart. The analytical exposition is largely in terms of geometry, with the necessary tools being developed up front in Chapters 2–4. Relatively simple algebra is used, and when more advanced methods are applied, we are careful to place the material in sections that can be skipped without loss of continuity. The use of calculus is quite minimal, even in the more advanced sections.

Indeed, the book uses few analytical methods more advanced than competing texts. What distinguishes the book is partly its analytical approach, but more importantly the breadth and depth of its coverage. We have tried to maintain a uniform level of analysis throughout the book, and the same basic "tool kit" developed in Chapters 2–4 is used over and over to avoid the costs of developing and learning new analytical constructions for each new topic. Our perception of standard texts is that they tend to treat one topic on a fairly formal level, such as the Heckscher-Ohlin model, and then resort to anecdotes about other topics, such as the industrial-organization approach to trade. Our analysis of the Heckscher-Ohlin model is not more advanced than that found in the more advanced of the competing texts, but our analysis of other equally important topics maintains approximately the same level and depth of presentation.

This new book is a much revised version of an old Markusen and Melvin text. The book has been greatly strengthened by the addition of two new authors, Bill Kaempfer and Keith Maskus. Maskus is widely known and respected for his papers on empirical trade and policy issues. He brings strengths that are complementary to those of the original theory-oriented authors, and has improved the book both in its coverage of empirical evidence and in its exposition of the subtleties of modern trade policy. Kaempfer has written extensively on the political economy of trade policy, ranging from analyses of sanctions to the choice of policy instruments, and determinants of the pattern of protection. It is essential that trade theory texts move on from simply analyzing the effects on tariffs and quotas to analyzing why they arise in equilibrium. Kaempfer's efforts also have strengthened the book.

Key features of the book are as follows:

1. Part 1 of the book (Chapters 1–5) introduces the microeconomic foundations of the theory, and develops almost all of the tools which are used subsequently. By popular demand, offer curves are avoided in favor of excess demand curves. Offer curves are covered in an appendix. Chapter 5 analyzes the gains from trade, laying a foundation which is used repeatedly throughout the book.

2. Part 2 (Chapters 6–14) develops the positive theory of trade and considers empirical tests of those theories. Our world view is that many things cause trade, and each deserves an analysis in isolation from the others. Accordingly, Part 2 follows a methodology in which two economies are identical in every respect except one. These "bases for trade" include differences in technology, differences in relative factor endowments, government policies including taxes and subsidies, imperfect competition, scale economies, and demand factors, such as non-identical and non-homogeneous preferences and preferences for diversity.

3. Part 3 (Chapters 15–20) turns to trade policy, considering the various consequences of tariffs, quotas, and voluntary export restraints. In line with current research interests, a major chapter is devoted to strategic trade policy. Two other "non-traditional" chapters include one on the political economy of trade policy and one on administered protection. The

former analyzes ways to endogenize protection, while the latter discusses institutions, rules, contingent protection, and major features of trade law and surrounding controversies.

4. Part 4 (Chapters 21–23) reverts to positive theory, analyzing factor trade, multinational firms, and growth. These chapters incorporate a great deal of research undertaken since the old Markusen and Melvin book was drafted almost a decade ago.

Thanks are due to many individuals. Our editor, Scott Stratford at McGraw-Hill, put a great deal of effort into the project, and in particular organized the most thorough and constructive set of reviews we have ever seen. We thus wish to express great appreciation to those reviewers for their significant contributions to the book. Ex post facto, we learned that they were James Cassing, University of Pittsburgh; Eric Fisher, The Ohio State University; Craig Schulman, University of Arkansas; and Nicolas Schmitt, Simon Fraser University. Carsten Kowalczyk read several chapters and gave us a number of valuable suggestions. If readers find something particularly objectionable about the book, there is a good chance that one of these five pointed it out, and for one reason or another we did not make the change. Veta Hartman, Jim Markusen's administrative assistant, ably performed many departmental functions so that he had time to work on the manuscript. Laura Langhoff composed all of the figures in electronic medium, rendering the ruler and flex-curve additional obsolete parts of trade theory.

James R. Markusen
James R. Melvin
William H. Kaempfer
Keith E. Maskus

PART
I

TECHNICAL
CONCEPTS
AND THE
GAINS
FROM TRADE

CHAPTER
1

INTRODUCTION

1.1 THE GLOBAL ECONOMY

In recent years international economic issues have taken center stage in the news. For example, on January 1, 1994, the United States, Canada, and Mexico entered into a joint compact, called the North American Free Trade Area (NAFTA), that would gradually reduce trade barriers among them. As readers may recall, negotiation of NAFTA was heavily controversial in all three nations, and its passage was anything but certain. Some people in the United States were worried about the impact of freer trade with Mexico on the living standards of lower-skilled Americans, while others had concerns about the potential effects of NAFTA on environmental standards in the region. On the other hand, U.S. advocates of the agreement proclaimed its potential to raise incomes overall through greater trade and investment flows. Canadians had the same concerns and hopes about the potential effects of NAFTA, with further worries about safeguarding the security of their supplies of oil and natural gas. For their part, many Mexicans were wary of closer competition with the United States' high productivity standards and advanced technologies, expressing particular concern about the fate of traditional Mexican agriculture and peasant cultures.

The countries of the world are also moving toward closer trade integration through acceptance of the Uruguay Round Agreement in the General Agreement on Tariffs and Trade (GATT). The GATT agreement would set out broad rules governing national policies that influence international competition, including tariffs, quotas, foreign investment regulations, agricultural subsidies, and patents and copyrights, among other practices. Because different countries have conflicting interests in these areas, negotiation of the Uruguay Round accords was also quite contentious. Nonetheless, most economists argue that its passage will represent a valuable step forward for global trading relations, bearing the potential for expanding trade and world incomes by hundreds of billions of dollars per year.

As nations have become more interdependent in recent decades through growth in international trade and investment, episodes of trade conflict have become more evident and interesting to the public. An obvious example is the continuous effort by the United States and Japan to manage their bilateral trade relationship, which involves a significant American trade deficit with Japan. Many American critics claim that the Japanese market is effectively closed to foreign firms, while a standard Japanese response is that foreign firms do not try hard enough to penetrate the market. Japan is hardly unique in this regard, of course. There are loud complaints from numerous countries about protectionism and arbitrary government interference with trade in the United States, Canada, South Korea, India, China, and the European Community, among other nations and areas.[1] Unquestionably, there are significant pressures in the world economy for nations to interfere with the free exchange of goods in order to limit the negative effects trade may have on some groups and industries.

A major component of this growing international interdependence is the phenomenal growth of multinational enterprises (MNEs), firms that have production and marketing facilities in numerous countries. Many global corporations have become absolutely huge in terms of world sales, assets, and employment, and their international operations have significant effects on both host and home nations. Accordingly, these firms are highly controversial in a number of dimensions, with some people blaming them for shifting jobs out of high-wage countries to low-wage countries and others claiming that they change locations in response to differences in environmental or business regulations. On the other hand, most economists tend to view MNEs as conduits for efficient global allocation of capital.

This brief review suggests that international economic problems will continue to gain prominence in debates over public policy. While hundreds of interesting questions on this subject could be posed, obviously important ones include the following: Should countries continue to work toward global free trade, or are particular nations better off with regional free trade arrangements? When might it be sensible to place quantitative restrictions on imports of particular goods? What are the connections between the need for business regulations and the operation of trade policies? Should nations interfere with the free flow of capital and labor? These kinds of questions, which are both positive and normative in nature, concern us in this book.

1.2 PERSPECTIVE ON THE THEORY OF INTERNATIONAL TRADE

In this text we study both international trade, which is the exchange across national borders of goods, services, and factors, and the impacts of this trade on domestic and global economies.

The economic unit under study in this text is the nation. We will study decision-making in a national context and examine whether nations can work to maximize some measure of collective well-being. In doing so, we will consider decisions at both the individual and the governmental levels.

Within each nation is an aggregate of individuals acting in the economic arena. International trade results from the interactions among those individuals and with persons in other nations. Thus, understanding the theory of the firm and the theory of consumer behavior is important in studying this level of international economics.

Different nations arise largely because of historical, political, and geographical factors. In practical terms, however, nations are identified with their governments, which take actions that affect the domestic and global economies. This level of decision-making is one feature that distinguishes the study of international trade from the study of traditional economics. Our usual presumption is that governments act in order to maximize the overall income and welfare of the economy. As we will see, however, this presumption is often untrue.

International economics can be divided conveniently into two parts: *real analysis* or trade theory, and *monetary analysis* or international finance. Real analysis studies the reasons that trade takes place, the implications for commodity and factor prices of changes in real variables (such as the stock of capital and the supply of labor), the benefits that accrue from international trade, and the effects of trade restrictions on the welfare of the economy. Because its focus is equilibrium determination of real trade flows and welfare, trade theory generally analyzes barter exchange expressed in terms of a numeraire good. It ignores macroeconomic disequilibrium problems by assuming the existence of full employment and aggregate trade balance. Monetary analysis, on the other hand, is concerned with such issues as the determination of exchange rates and the international transmission of unemployment and inflation. Often the two branches of international economics use different methodologies, with trade theory using market-clearing microeconomic equilibrium processes and international finance using macroeconomic concepts such as a single aggregate output and price level, in which there can be short-run fluctuations. However, this distinction can easily be overdrawn. In recent years economists have made great strides in integrating the two approaches by modelling aspects of international finance, such as the existence of an aggregate trade deficit, as the result of microeconomic equilibrium processes in which agents trade goods both across borders and over time. We incorporate this approach into the final chapter of the text.

The subject matter of this book concerns the trade in commodities and factors that takes place among nations. One question naturally arises: why is it necessary to distinguish trade between nations from trade between regions, and even from trade between individual consumers? The basic motivations for all such exchanges are similar, including differences in tastes and factor endowments. However, there are some unique features of international trade. First, though it is reasonable to assume that labor is completely mobile *within* a country, labor mobility *among* countries is severely restricted because of government regulation and differences in such things as language, religion, and social customs. Indeed, it is usually assumed in trade theory that labor is completely immobile among countries. Much of the theory of international trade also assumes capital to be immobile among countries, though we thoroughly analyze the implications of capital mobility in later chapters. Differences in the degree of factor mobility are important because they help govern the incentives for and the implications of trade in commodities.

A second distinguishing feature of international trade is the governmental regulatory power that does not exist in individual or interregional trade. Countries impose tariffs and nontariff barriers against imports. They limit the free flow of factors of production among countries and even adjust domestic policies so as to change the pattern of international trade. Such activities are virtually unknown among regions within the same country and in many countries are actually against the law. For example, the U.S. Constitution reserves to Congress the right to regulate interstate commerce, implying that individual states cannot erect barriers against imports from other states.

This dichotomy between interregional and international trade policies is quite interesting. In part, it reflects a popular, though flawed, view that trade among agents within a country is beneficial while international trade may be costly. People in wealthier nations often argue that trade with poorer nations is harmful because it invites competition from low-wage foreign labor, while people in poorer countries make the opposite case that trade with countries with high-level technologies is unfair. These two views are fundamentally *mercantilist* in nature, in that they see international trade as taking place within a fixed-sum game. The gains to one country are accompanied by losses to another country. This view is wrong because international exchange, like trade among domestic agents, tends to expand aggregate incomes in all countries. Indeed, a substantial point of inquiry in our book will be to investigate the nature of the *gains from trade,* or the benefits from international commerce.

To gain a basic understanding of this question, however, note that countries would be worse off if they were precluded from trading. For example, if Canada were not able to export commodities such as wheat and other grains and natural resources, Canadians could not enjoy their present high standard of living. Japan imports raw materials and exports final products; without such trade the real incomes of workers in Japan would be significantly lower. Even large and diverse economies such as that of the United States depend on foreign trade to supply a significant proportion of essential commodities such as petroleum and automobiles. Attaining self-sufficiency at the national level is no more feasible than it would be for a single family to produce all the goods it must consume.

1.3 THE IMPORTANCE OF INTERNATIONAL TRADE

To justify a careful examination of international trade it is important to demonstrate that such trade is an important part of the overall economic activity of nations. There are numerous dimensions to this issue, including the growth, levels, and structure of trade in relation to domestic production.

Trade, Growth, and Economic Interrelatedness

Globally, international trade has grown considerably in recent decades. For example, over the period between 1963 and 1979, the rate of expansion of real merchandise exports (that is, the value of exports deflated by changes in export prices) in the world averaged 11.8 percent per year, a remarkably high growth rate by historical standards.[2] Indeed, this figure likely underestimates the true growth in the real volume of exports because available price data do not adequately account for the marked improvements in product quality in recent years. At the same time, global growth in real output, measured by gross domestic product (GDP) in each country, averaged 6.1 percent per year, also high by historical standards. Thus, during that period, the world experienced a rapidly rising effective integration among countries as they became more closely interrelated through international trade in goods. This trend continued after 1979, though economic activity grew at markedly slower rates. Over the period between 1979 and 1991, real export growth averaged 4.4 percent per year, while real output expansion averaged 2.9 percent per year.

This increasing interrelatedness among countries may be observed for specific nations as well. Table 1.1 lists a selected set of countries at different levels of economic development. The first two columns of figures show per-capita gross national product (GNP) in 1990, measured in U.S. dollars, and the average annual growth rate in this variable between 1965 and 1990.[3] Clearly there is wide variation in international living standards, as measured by per-capita GNP. While there are problems in constructing such measures, it appears that there may be as much as a one hundred-fold difference in per-capita incomes between the poorest and wealthiest countries of the world.

Looking at per-capita incomes in a particular year provides only a snapshot of the relative positions among nations. Over time, some countries tend to grow faster than others, as noted in the second column of figures. Overall, it seems that poorer countries tend to grow somewhat faster than richer countries, though this relationship is weakly reflected in these data. Indeed, in some nations, such as Uganda, measured standards of living have actually deteriorated in the last 25 years. One clear suggestion from the data is that between 1965 and 1990 the nations of East Asia (China, Indonesia, the Republic of Korea, Singapore, and Japan as shown in Table

TABLE 1.1
Measures of national incomes and trade for selected countries

Country	GNP per Capita 1990 ($)	Average Annual Growth 1965–90 (%)	Exports 1991 ($b)	Imports 1991 ($b)	Exports/GDP 1970 (%)	Exports/GDP 1991 (%)
Uganda	236	−2.4	0.2	0.6	16.7	7.9
India	350	1.9	17.7	20.4	3.8	7.8
China	370	5.8	72.1	63.8	1.8	19.5
Indonesia	570	4.5	29.0	25.9	12.4	24.9
Turkey	1630	2.6	13.6	21.0	5.3	14.2
Mexico	2490	2.8	27.1	38.2	3.4	9.6
Brazil	2680	3.3	31.6	23.0	7.6	7.6
Rep. of Korea	5400	7.1	71.7	81.3	9.0	25.3
Singapore	11160	6.5	58.9	66.0	84.2	147.3
EC-12[a]	17334	2.5	1366.0	1447.1	16.5	22.4
Spain	11020	2.4	60.1	93.1	6.3	11.4
U.K.	16100	2.0	185.1	210.0	18.2	21.1
Germany[b]	22320	2.4	401.8	387.9	18.5	22.4
Canada	20470	2.7	124.8	117.6	22.6	24.4
U.S.	21790	1.7	397.7	506.2	4.3	7.1
Japan	25430	4.1	314.4	234.1	9.5	9.4
Switzerland	32680	1.4	61.5	66.3	25.1	26.5
World	4010	1.5	3336.6	3508.2	10.1	15.4

Sources: Calculated by the authors using the World Bank, *World Development Report*, and the International Monetary Fund, *Direction of Trade Statistics Yearbook*.

[a] EC-12 refers to the current twelve members of the European Community. Though not all of these countries were members in 1965, the data for all twelve are included here. For the EC, figures on GNP per capita in 1990 and average annual growth rates were weighted by national populations.

[b] Data for Germany exclude figures for former East Germany.

[handwritten margin note: Is int'l trade a cause or a consequence of ec. growth?]

1.1) registered the strongest economic growth among regions of the world. Thus, two important questions for study, to which we will turn in Chapters 13 and 23, are how international trade is related to economic growth and whether trade should be considered a cause or a consequence of growth.

Suggestive evidence in answer to these questions exists. Consider the data in the final two columns of Table 1.1, which show the ratios of merchandise exports to GDP in 1970 and 1991. These ratios are often considered to be measures of a nation's "openness" to international trade, though it is more appropriate to interpret them straightforwardly as indications of the share of national production that is exported.[4] Thus, they provide rough suggestions of the relative importance of international trade in aggregate output. In Uganda, as in some other very poor nations, this export share has fallen considerably over the last 25 years, because of a dramatic decline in Uganda's merchandise exports. On the other hand, with the exception of Japan, the East Asian economies in our table registered marked increases in the contribution of their exports to GDP. Most striking is the experience of China, whose exports rose explosively from 1.8 percent of GDP to 19.5 percent of GDP. That Japan's share was relatively static does not mean that export growth was unimportant. To the contrary, Japan's merchandise exports rose sixteen-fold over the period, as did its GDP. No other developed nation experienced such rapid increases in economic activity. Thus, at this level it appears that rapid trade growth is positively related to rapid economic growth.

Trade and National Characteristics

Some particular features of the data are worth mentioning. Note that Singapore's exports were almost half again as large as its GDP in 1991. This fact reflects Singapore's status as a center for *entrepot trade,* involving the provision of warehousing, transport facilities, and services in transshipping goods from one market to another. For example, much of Malaysia's exports are processed through Singapore to their ultimate destinations elsewhere. In principle, it is possible for any nation to have a level of exports greater than GDP, though this is unusual in practice. Note also that Canada has long had a high proportion of its GDP devoted to exports, with a slight rise to nearly one quarter by 1991. Canada is an excellent example of a nation that economists regard as "open," in the sense that international transactions represent a highly significant proportion of overall activity. For example, in Canada exports now tend to comprise a larger component of national demand than investment.

The United States has slowly but steadily seen the importance of exports in GDP rise over time. Over seven percent of U.S. GDP in 1991 was produced for export, a figure that amounted to some $398 billion. While this is a substantial sum, the United States retains the lowest export-to-GDP ratio among the major industrialized nations. The primary reason for this is simply that the United States is such a large country that relatively little of its output needs to be produced for the foreign sector. Most of its output may be sold in the huge domestic market with its diversified tastes.

The European Community (EC) provides a good example of a set of countries that are intimately interrelated through international transactions. The EC is an example of a *customs union,* in which the member countries erect no barriers to imports from the other members while adopting a common set of restrictions on imports from outside the union. This structure provides a strong measure of economic integration among the participating nations. Accordingly, over 22 percent of the total GDP in these economies is exported, much of it to other countries within the Community. Over time, each of the twelve countries has become more open in the sense considered here, in large part because of the integration of their economies through trade. Spain, for example, joined the EC in 1986 and has seen its trade with other EC members rise rapidly.

An additional factor in the strength of trade among the EC nations is simply their proximity to one another, which limits associated transport costs. This element is an equally strong consideration in the trade behavior of other Western European countries. Switzerland has long had a strong export component in GDP, reflecting its close trading relationships with the EC and other Western European countries. Similarly, the marked growth in Turkey's export position reflects its proximity to Europe. In contrast, the relatively small ratio of exports to GDP in Japan reflects in some part the geographical isolation of that country from the other industrialized markets.

Note finally that the world as a whole also experienced a marked rise in the importance of exports relative to production, with the ratio rising from 10.1 percent to 15.4 percent between 1970 and 1991. This reaffirms our earlier observation that the globe has become more economically interrelated in recent decades.

Of course, exports are only one part of this story. The middle two columns of Table 1.1 list the values of both exports and imports of merchandise in 1991 for our set of countries. Exports may not equal imports in a particular year for any country, reflecting the existence of merchandise trade deficits or surpluses.[5] Of more interest here is that imports tend to rise along with exports over time as countries become more integrated. Thus, for example, if we were to compute for a given country the ratio of imports to GNP (a rough measure of the importance of foreign sources of consumption goods and intermediate products), we would likely find that it has risen in relationship to the rise in the exports-to-GDP ratio. In 1991 this ratio would have been 8.9 percent for the United States, 22.5 percent for Germany, and 6.4 percent for Japan.

Despite the fact that in some countries, such as the United States and Japan, trade is relatively less important than in others, international transactions still have an extremely important influence on the overall level of economic activity. This point was clearly emphasized by the mid-1970s energy crisis in the United States. Although at the time, less than five percent of the United States' consumption of petroleum products originated in the OPEC countries, those countries' restrictions on supply and the resulting increases in energy prices brought about significant disruptions in the American economy. The impact was even more dramatic in Japan, where nearly all petroleum products must be imported. The oil price increases of the 1970s hastened Japan's shift into alternative energy sources, including nuclear power.

The Sectoral Structure of Trade

Levels of trade can be significant in particular sectors of the economy even if the overall trade ratios are modest. For instance, the United States imports all of its consumption of certain tropical products, such as cocoa. Looking at two major domestic sectors, in 1990 the United States exported over 45 percent of its agricultural production and imported over 43 percent of its consumption of motor vehicles and automobile parts.[6] Clearly, changes in the international economy that affect these sectors bear potentially significant impacts on domestic prices, output, and employment. Further, such impacts can spill over into other portions of the economy through their effects on consumer demand and input purchases.

A fundamental concept in international trade theory is *comparative advantage*. As will be made clearer in later chapters, the economic characteristics of nations and commodities combine to explain the pattern of international trade. To introduce the reader to this concept, we will describe briefly the structure of trade in major commodities for particular countries. In Table 1.2 we have classified six major trade categories, which are really aggregations of numerous detailed commodities, into sectors in which our countries exhibit a strong excess of exports over imports, a strong excess of imports over exports, or a near balance between exports and imports. (The "+" and "−" signs after the entries in the final column indicate whether there was a small trade surplus or deficit in the sector.) This classification is based on actual trade flows in 1990, with sectoral trade balances adjusted to account for the fact that each country had an aggregate trade imbalance

TABLE 1.2
Classification of major sectors by 1990 trade orientation for selected countries*

Country	Strong Net Exports	Strong Net Imports	Near Balance
India	CLOTH	FUEL, CHEM, OFFTEL	FOOD(+), AUTO(+)
China	FOOD, FUEL, CLOTH	CHEM, OFFTEL, AUTO	
Indonesia	FUEL, CLOTH	CHEM, OFFTEL, AUTO	FOOD(+)
Turkey	CLOTH	FUEL, CHEM, OFFTEL	FOOD(+), AUTO(+)
Mexico	FUEL	OFFTEL	FOOD(−), CHEM(−) AUTO(+), CLOTH(−)
Brazil	FOOD, AUTO	FUEL, CHEM, OFFTEL	CLOTH(+)
Korea	OFFTEL, CLOTH	FOOD, FUEL, CHEM	AUTO(+)
Singapore	OFFTEL, CLOTH	CHEM	FOOD(−), FUEL(+), AUTO(+)
EC-12	AUTO	FUEL, CLOTH	FOOD(−), CHEM(+) OFFTEL(−)
Spain	AUTO	FUEL, OFFTEL, CLOTH	FOOD(+), CHEM(−)
Germany	CHEM, AUTO	FOOD, FUEL, CLOTH	OFFTEL(−)
U.K.	CHEM	FOOD, CLOTH	FUEL(+), OFFTEL(−) AUTO(+)
Canada	FOOD, FUEL	OFFTEL, CLOTH	CHEM(−), AUTO(+)
U.S.	FOOD, CHEM	FUEL, AUTO, CLOTH	OFFTEL(+)
Japan	OFFTEL, AUTO	FOOD, FUEL, CLOTH	CHEM(−)
Switzerland	CHEM	FOOD, FUEL AUTO, CLOTH	OFFTEL(−)

Sources: Calculated by the authors using General Agreement on Tariffs and Trade, *International Trade*, 1990–91, and United Nations, *Yearbook of International Trade Statistics, Vol. I,* 1990.

*FOOD: food and live animals; FUEL: fuels and fuel products; CHEM: chemicals and chemical products; OFFTEL: office machines and telecommunications equipment; AUTO: motor vehicles and automotive parts; CLOTH: clothing.

in that year. The calculations are designed to reveal a rough measure of comparative advantage by sector in each country.[7]

Some brief comments about the sectors in this table are in order. It is evident that export strength in food is related to the existence of abundant supplies of agricultural land, as is found in China, Canada, and the United States. Correspondingly, countries with limited land supplies, such as Korea, Japan, and Switzerland, tend to import food. Similar statements can be made about the determination of exporters and importers of fuel. The United States is noteworthy in that although it is one of the largest petroleum producers in the world, it remains a major importer because of its huge demand for energy. In general, however, it is clear that relatively greater supplies of natural resources are a major determinant of comparative advantage.

Clothing represents a strong net-export good for nearly all the developing economies and a strong net-import good for all the developed economies. Clothing is the best example of a good that is produced cheaply with relatively abundant supplies of lower-skilled labor. Thus, it appears that the technological characteristics of production functions interact with factor supplies to help determine comparative advantage.

The remaining three sectors—chemicals, automotive products, and office machines and telecommunications equipment—all represent relatively sophisticated manufacturing products. In addition to standard inputs in production, these goods tend to require substantial scale, innovation, and product differentiation for export success. The developed countries compete among themselves in the latter dimensions, so that there is no obvious pattern of comparative advantage for these goods within that group. For example, Germany, the United Kingdom, the United States, and Switzerland are all major exporters of chemicals, while Canada and Japan tend to import them, as do the developing countries. Germany, Japan, and Spain are successful exporters of automotive products, while the United States and Switzerland are major net importers. Comparative advantage in office machines and telecommunications equipment is similarly mixed, with Korea and Singapore having broken into the ranks of net exporting countries.

In truth, if we were to break up these broad categories of manufactures into small components, we would find that each of the developed countries would be net exporters of some goods, such as fax machines, and net importers of other similar goods, such as computer modems. Among the industrialized countries, this trade in similar goods, which economists term *intra-industry trade*, is prevalent. One of our challenges will be to explain this phenomenon theoretically.

Other international transactions. International trade in merchandise has provided one source of significant growth in economic interrelations among nations. Here, we briefly note that other significant forms of international transactions, including trade in services and foreign direct investment (FDI), have also risen rapidly in recent years.

In principle, trade in services should be treated no differently from trade in goods. Some countries, depending on their factor supplies, technology, and tastes, have a comparative advantage in providing certain services to international customers, just as some countries have a comparative advantage in certain goods. Major traded services include financial or management expertise, insurance underwriting, transport, tourism, construction, and numerous other professional services. Nonetheless, some important distinctions between trade in goods and services arise. For example, sometimes foreign purchasers come to the domestic economy to consume a service, such as a medical procedure or a vacation. These transactions are properly regarded as exports for the providing country. On the other hand, to provide banking services in a foreign market typically requires establishing facilities there instead of exporting some tangible commodity. Because the banking services are produced in the foreign market using primarily foreign inputs we would not count them as exports for the country undertaking the investment.

While it is clearly difficult to get a comprehensive measure of trade in services, it is possible to get rough measures from the balance-of-payments statistics of particular countries. We present data on exports and imports of services for a smaller set of countries in Table 1.3. Note that trade in services is nearly as important quantitatively as trade in merchandise as reported in Table 1.1. Indonesia and Mexico are fairly typical among developing countries in being net importers of services. In part this reflects

TABLE 1.3
Trade in services, stocks of foreign direct investment, and workers' remittances in selected countries, 1991*

Country	Service Exports ($b)	Service Imports ($b)	Stocks of FDI ($b) Host	Source	Net Workers' Remittances and Migrants' Transfers ($b)
Indonesia	3.4	12.6	NA	NA	NA
Turkey	9.3	6.8	NA	NA	2.8
Mexico	16.4	20.9	NA	NA	1.9
Rep. of Korea	15.5	17.1	5.9	3.5	−0.3
EC-12	813.4	851.9	NA	NA	NA
Spain	38.2	30.2	55.8	20.8	1.5
Germany	142.5	149.1	61.1	148.2	−4.2
U.K.	194.2	183.2	237.6	242.4	NA
Canada	25.1	56.2	112.7	80.1	0.9
U.S.	289.0	227.2	487.0	655.3	−7.3
Japan	188.6	206.2	12.3	231.8	NA
Switzerland	46.6	30.2	44.2	75.4	−2.1

Sources: Calculated by the authors using International Monetary Fund, *Balance of Payments Statistics Yearbook*, 1992.

*Services trade includes investment income. Stocks of foreign direct investment are in current values.

the need for these countries to import foreign management techniques and commercial expertise. It also reflects the fact that developing nations tend to pay substantial amounts of interest, dividends, and profits on the foreign investments in their economies. They also pay significant royalties for imported technological information. These payments are included in service imports because, effectively, the developing countries import the services of foreign capital and technology. In any event, trade in services, capital, and technology are all important and growing forms of international transactions in the modern world economy.

Foreign direct investment results when multinational enterprises choose to operate facilities in different countries. We will present a rigorous analysis of this phenomenon in Chapter 22. At present, however, note in Table 1.3 that the magnitude of such foreign investments is remarkably high, at least in the developed economies. For example, MNEs headquartered in the United States own approximately $655 billion in foreign producing facilities, while foreign MNEs own $487 billion worth of production operations in the United States. The United Kingdom is both host to and source of over $200 billion in foreign investments. Spain has seen rapidly expanding FDI in its economy, particularly from MNEs in other EC members, since its accession to the Community. Switzerland and Germany are also major participants in both inward and outward FDI. Japan is unique among developed countries in being the source of massive amounts of investment while relatively little FDI has found its way into that country.

This examination of FDI demonstrates that, despite the standard assumption in trade theory that factors are immobile across countries, it is possible for capital (as opposed to exchange in capital goods, which is considered merchandise trade) to move across borders. The final column of Table 1.3 shows that labor, too, can flow internationally. Like FDI, international labor migration is a complicated topic that we must treat theoretically in a later chapter. However, we observe in Table 1.3 that workers and migrants often transfer a portion of their incomes earned in a host country back to their home countries. For example, in 1991, Turkish citizens working abroad repatriated some $2.8 billion back to Turkey, while Mexican workers abroad sent back $1.9 billion. This finding suggests that developing countries tend to be net suppliers of labor internationally. Correspondingly, considerable sums were transferred out of Germany, the United States, and Switzerland by resident foreign workers. Spain tends to provide labor to the rest of the EC, while Canada also receives remittances on net, mainly from the United States.

1.4   PLAN OF THE BOOK

Our brief review of aspects of international trade outlines the course of study we undertake in this text. In the first part we provide a rigorous analysis of the theoretical microeconomic concepts we need for developing trade theory. These concepts include factor endowments, production functions and production frontiers, returns to scale on the supply side, and utility and preference aggregation on the demand side (Chapters 2 and 3). From these models we develop the notion of general equilibrium with and without trade, which allows us to consider aspects of the gains from trade and how they are distributed (Chapters 4 and 5). A unifying feature of the text is its use of theorems about the gains from trade under various circumstances.

In Part 2 we go on to develop specific theories of why countries trade with one another. The prevailing challenge is to explain the determinants of national comparative advantage. After making some methodological points, we consider first the major traditional theories, including relative differences in labor productivity, the interaction of factor endowments and production functions, and short-run factor specificity (Chapters 6–9). However, we go far beyond these standard theories by developing full general-equilibrium theories of several other potential determinants of trade. These include the issue of how government taxes and subsidies influence trade patterns and the gains from trade, the effects of imperfect competition, and increasing returns to scale (Chapters 10–12). These treatments strongly distinguish our text from others. We further discuss the theory of differences in demand among nations and how these influence trade (Chapter 13). We then integrate preferences, returns to scale, and product differentiation to explain in a consistent fashion the phenomenon of intra-industry trade. We also consider simple dynamic models of the evolution of comparative advantage. A final chapter in Part 2 provides a thorough review of the empirical literature on these various theories in order to place each in perspective (Chapter 14).

Part 3 is devoted to the analysis of government trade policies. We first consider aspects of tariffs in general equilibrium, including welfare effects, the optimal tariff, and effective rates of protection (Chapter 15). Many of these concepts are applied to quantitative trade restrictions in the next chapter on quotas (Chapter 16). We next turn to a comprehensive examination of trade policy under imperfect competition and increasing returns (Chapter 17). A series of models is advanced to demonstrate the implications of different features of market structure for the effects of trade and industrial policies. Prominently featured in that treatment is a full discussion of strategic trade policy. This comprehensive treatment of trade policy in imperfect markets constitutes another significant distinguishing feature of the text. The next chapter examines the theory of preferential trade areas, such as customs unions (Chapter 18). The following chapter provides a theoretical discussion of the politics of protectionism, considering the interplay between voter preferences and biases toward the imposition of tariffs and quotas (Chapter 19). We supplement all of this theoretical treatment by discussing policy-related aspects of the world trading system (Chapter 20). Important topics include world and national trade rules, the mechanisms by which countries protect their industries from imports, and the relationship between trade policies and environmental regulations.

Part 4 concludes the text with theoretical treatments of trade in factors and international trade in the context of economic growth. The first chapter considers models of trade in labor and capital in neoclassical models with differences in endowments, the existence of market distortions, and related issues (Chapter 21). The next chapter extends this work to an explicit treatment of the theory of direct foreign investment and the creation of multinational enterprises (Chapter 22). Finally, the last chapter analyzes several sources of economic growth and their relations to international trade (Chapter 23).

NOTES

1. Throughout this book we use the phrase "European Community" to refer to the nations of Western Europe that are allied economically in what is variously called the Common Market, the European Economic Community, and, most recently, the European Union.
2. These data exclude certain nations that had been closely associated with the former Soviet Union, including that country itself. The source for these figures is the International Monetary Fund (1992).
3. Gross national product measures the value of all final goods and services produced by citizens of a particular country, including income earned abroad through providing labor and capital services. For our purposes it is best thought of as national income, which is why we select it as our indicator of international income levels. Gross domestic product, on the other hand, excludes receipts for income earned abroad. It is a better measure of the actual gross production activity in an economy.
4. There is no necessary relationship between a country's restrictions on trade and its aggregate level of exports or imports. Far more important in explaining these latter variables are an economy's size, its factor supplies, and, over time, its saving rate, as we will see in later chapters.
5. It is curious that the world showed a trade deficit in total in 1991. One reason for this is that not all countries are included in the total (it excludes countries formerly in the Soviet bloc). More fundamentally, this global deficit is a common phenomenon simply because countries tend to undercount their exports relative to their imports. The latter flows are measured more accurately because tariff receipts are collected on them.
6. The source for these figures is Council of Economic Advisors (1992).
7. There are numerous conceptual difficulties in such calculations. For further information see Ballance, Forstner, and Murray (1987).

REFERENCES

Ballance, R. H., Forstner, H., and Murray, T. (1987). "Consistency Tests of Alternative Measures of Comparative Advantage." *Review of Economics and Statistics* 69: 157–161.

Council of Economic Advisors (1992). *Economic Report of the President.* Washington, D.C.: Government Printing Office.

International Monetary Fund (1992). *International Finance Statistics Yearbook.* Washington, D.C.: International Monetary Fund.

CHAPTER
2

SUPPLY
AND PRODUCTION
POSSIBILITIES

2.1 PRODUCTION FUNCTIONS

Many of the *causes* of international trade are found in countries' differing abilities to produce certain goods. These varying abilities are in turn related to underlying aspects of production such as technologies, factor endowments, competitive conditions, government taxes and subsidies, and returns to scale. An understanding of these considerations will ultimately help explain why the United States exports aircraft and cereal grains and imports clothing. These same considerations will help us understand the *consequences* of trade, including overall welfare gains and the distribution of those gains among the members of a society.

An understanding of trade requires an understanding of complex and indirect relationships, such as how a country's endowments of capital and labor determine its optimal pattern of trade. Before we can grasp the whole picture, we need to establish an understanding of the individual pieces of the puzzle, and that will be the task of Chapters 2–4. In this chapter, we will develop the tools of production theory and producer equilibrium. Many of you will be familiar with the basic ideas from intermediate microeconomics or principles of economics. For those of you who are relatively unfamiliar with these technical constructions, we urge you to work through them slowly and carefully. We hope that your patience in this and the next two chapters will be rewarded. The ideas developed here will be used repeatedly throughout the book, so your investment should pay off. The puzzle is assembled in Chapter 5.

17

The basic building block of the supply side of our model will be the production function,

$$X = F(K, L) \tag{2.1}$$

This equation is the algebraic representation of the fact that commodities are produced with certain primary factors and certain technical knowledge or technology. Thus, Eq. (2.1) is simply a shorthand way of saying that, given a certain technology as represented by the function F, an amount of capital represented by K and an amount of labor services represented by L can be combined to produce some quantity of output represented by X.

The production relation described by Eq. (2.1) contains three variables: the levels of input of capital and labor and the level of output. Geometrically, it could be represented by a three-dimensional surface; diagrammatically, it can be illustrated as in Fig. 2.1. The production surface can be thought of as a hill, with the origin representing the ground level. At the origin there is neither labor input nor capital input, and therefore, there is no output. With positive amounts of both capital and labor, there will be a positive level of output of X, and as we add more of either capital or labor or both, the output of X increases.

Three-dimensional diagrams are awkward to draw and are not very useful in illustrating economic phenomena. Economists have traditionally found it more useful to convert three-dimensional diagrams, such as the one shown in Fig. 2.1, to two dimensions by considering one of the three variables as fixed. Reexamining Eq. (2.1), we see that there are three possibilities available; we could fix X, L, or K. First, suppose we fixed the level of output at some amount $\overline{X}$ and considered the combinations of K and L that are consistent with this level of output. Looking at Fig. 2.1, we can imagine taking a slice through the production hill at a height $\overline{X}$ above

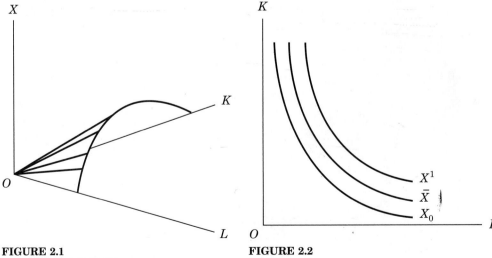

FIGURE 2.1
The production surface.

FIGURE 2.2
Isoquants.

the plane KL. Looking down on the plane KL from above, as in Fig. 2.2, the edge of the slice could be represented by the line $\overline{X}$. Note that this line $\overline{X}$ is completely analogous to a contour line in a topographical map. It represents the locus of points of equal height above some arbitrarily chosen reference plane. In terms of our production model, it represents the locus of output points distance $\overline{X}$ above the origin.

Loci such as $\overline{X}$ of Fig. 2.2 are called *isoquants,* and show all possible combinations of capital and labor that could be used to produce the level of output $\overline{X}$. There are, of course, many such loci, and indeed, one such locus can be drawn for every possible level of output. In Fig. 2.2 the locus X_o represents a level of output $X_0 < \overline{X}$, while X' represents a constant level of output greater than $\overline{X}$.

Now, suppose that rather than fixing the level of output in Eq. (2.1), we fix the level of one of the inputs. In particular, suppose we assume that the level of input of capital is fixed at the level $\overline{K}_0$, and investigate the relationship between varying amounts of the input L and the output X. This would give the locus $F(K_0, L)$ shown in the upper panel of Fig. 2.3, which represents the *total product curve.* There are several characteristics of this curve that are of interest. Note first that we have drawn the curve starting at the origin. This implies that no output is possible unless there is a positive amount of labor used as an input; although not necessary for our analysis, this assumption seems quite reasonable. It will also be noted that the total product curve of Fig. 2.3 has been drawn to curve toward the labor axis. Thus, although additional units of labor input are assumed to result in additional units of output, the rate of increase of output is assumed to diminish as more and more labor is added. This is an illustration of the *law of diminishing returns,* which we define as follows:

> **Definition.** Fix the inputs of all but one factor of production. Increase the amount of that factor. Do this for each factor of production in turn. If the result in every case is that output increases at a decreasing rate, the production function exhibits diminishing returns.

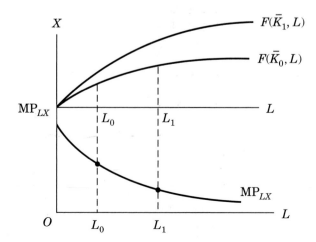

FIGURE 2.3
Total and marginal product curves.

The additional unit of output associated with adding one more unit of an input (holding other inputs constant) is called the *marginal product*, which we will denote by MP. In Fig. 2.3, the marginal product of labor in X is the *slope* of the total product curve: the change in X divided by the change in L. The lower panel of Fig. 2.3 accordingly plots the marginal product of labor in X, MP_{LX} against L. Another way of stating the law of diminishing returns is to say that the marginal product of labor is falling, holding other factors fixed. The fact that the MP_{LX} is less at input level L_1 than at input level L_0 corresponds to the fact that the slope of the total product curve $F(\overline{K}_0, L)$ is less at L_1 than at L_0.

The top panel of Fig. 2.3 shows only one total product curve, but it is clear that there will be a different total product curve for every different level of capital stock that is assumed. For capital $\overline{K}_1 > \overline{K}_0$, the total product curve will lie everywhere above the one shown in Fig. 2.3, while for smaller capital stocks the total product curve will lie everywhere below the one shown. It is also clear that rather than fixing the amount of capital, we could have fixed the labor supply and drawn the relationship between X and K. This would have given a figure completely analogous to Fig. 2.3, and again, of course, a whole family of curves could be drawn, depending on the quantity of labor assumed. Note that just as the isoquants of Fig. 2.2 can be thought of as the loci formed by taking a slice through the production hill parallel to the KL plane, so the total product curve of Fig. 2.3 can be thought of as the locus of the production hill found by taking a slice parallel to the XL plane.

Although Eq. (2.1) is a convenient algebraic summary of production conditions, it is a very general expression. To make it useful for economic analysis, we must impose several restrictions on it. Such restrictions have been implicitly assumed in drawing Figs. 2.2 and 2.3, and before proceeding, we must state these explicitly. Specifically, it is assumed that all isoquants are smooth and that, for any level of output, the set of all combinations of capital and labor that would yield at least that much output is convex.[1] It should also be noted that the law of diminishing returns, referred to in the last section, is assumed. Although this last assumption will be made throughout most of our analysis, production functions in which this condition is not satisfied are easily constructed.

2.2   RETURNS TO SCALE

Another particularly important characteristic of production functions such as that represented by Eq. (2.1) relates to the response of output to equiproportional changes in *both* of the inputs. A very common assumption in economics is that of *constant returns to scale*, the assumption that proportional changes in all inputs lead to the same proportional change in output. This assumption is referred to somewhat more formally as *homogeneity of the first degree.* It is such an important concept in economics and in the discussion of this book that a formal definition seems worthwhile.

Definition. Let $\lambda > 0$. The function $X = F(K, L)$ is said to be homogeneous of degree k if $\lambda^k X = F(\lambda K, \lambda L)$. If $k = 1$, the function is said to be homogeneous of degree 1, and production is characterized by constant returns to scale.

This definition is easy to interpret. Suppose, for example, we double both K and $L(\lambda = 2)$. If the function is homogeneous and if k is equal to 1, then the output will also double. With k greater than 1, called *increasing returns to scale,* a doubling of both factors will result in more than the doubling of the output. Similarly, for $k < 1$, called *decreasing returns to scale,* a doubling of both inputs will result in output less than double.

The returns-to-scale assumption can be illustrated by the isoquant diagram of Fig. 2.4. Consider first the isoquant X_0 where it has been assumed that the level of output is equal to 10. All the points on the curve X_0 represent the infinite number of combinations of capital and labor that, when combined with the assumed technology, would give this level of output. One such point, A, shows that 10 units of output can be produced using 6 units of labor and 7 units of capital. Suppose we now double the inputs of both factors and move to point B. Since the capital/labor space is "full" of isoquants, there must be one that passes through point B. The question now is: What is the level of output associated with that particular isoquant? Clearly, the answer depends on the assumption we make about the degree of homogeneity of the production function. If k is equal to 1, yielding constant returns to scale, then it is clear that the level of output associated with point B must be 20 units, twice that associated with point A. If, on the other hand, k is greater than 1, implying increasing returns to scale, then although we do not know the precise number to be attached to isoquant X_1, we know that it will be greater than 20. Similarly, for decreasing returns to scale, where k is less than 1, the level of output associated with X_1 would be less than 20.

Another characteristic associated with the concept of homogeneity relates to the slopes of the isoquants as we move along a ray from the origin, as in K/L of Fig. 2.4. It can be shown that for any such ray, and for

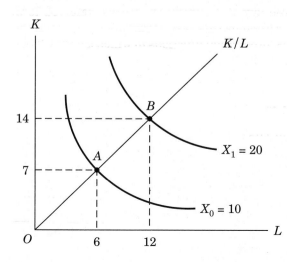

FIGURE 2.4

Constant returns to scale.

production functions that are homogeneous of any degree, the slopes of the isoquants at all points such as A and B are identical. This characteristic will be very important in the analysis, for it means that once one isoquant is known, all other isoquants can be derived. In terms of Fig. 2.4, if isoquant X_0 is known, then at point B, where $OB = 2OA$, there will be another isoquant with exactly the same slope. For any other ray, other points on this new isoquant can be found in the same way. Furthermore, since $OA = AB$, and since this production function has been assumed to be homogeneous of the first degree, the level of output associated with this isoquant will be equal to 20, twice that associated with X_0.

Note that there are two important characteristics associated with the preceding assumption of homogeneity. First, the slopes of the isoquants along any ray from the origin are equal. This is true regardless of the degree of homogeneity. The second characteristic, regarding the degree to which the functions are assumed to be homogeneous, is that the value of k determines the spacing of the isoquant in Fig. 2.4.

Note that there is an important difference between the law of diminishing returns discussed in the last section and returns to scale discussed here. With the law of diminishing returns, we fixed the input of one of two factors and varied the input of the other to observe how this changes output. For returns to scale we varied *both* factors in the same proportion and examined how this changes output. It should be noted that there is no conflict between the assumption of constant returns to scale and the law of diminishing returns; indeed, many of the production functions that we use in this book will be assumed to satisfy both conditions.

2.3 EQUILIBRIUM FOR A SINGLE PRODUCER

To this point, attention has been focused entirely on the physical characteristics of the production functions; no behavioral assumptions of any kind have been made about our producers. This section presents a very brief summary of those parts of production theory that will be central to our discussion of competitive models. The behavioral assumptions for an individual producer can be stated in either of two entirely equivalent ways: The producer can be thought of as maximizing output subject to a cost constraint or as minimizing costs subject to a production constraint. We will employ the first approach, but the equivalence of the two will become obvious as we proceed.

It is assumed that producers, having access to technology represented by Eq. (2.1), wish to maximize output, subject to the condition that they must spend no more on inputs than an amount C_0. It is assumed that the wage rate, w, and the rental on capital equipment, r, are known to the producers. It is further assumed that each individual producer is too small to have any influence on the price of his or her inputs, so that w and r can be treated as constants regardless of the level of output. The first task is to describe all possible combinations of K and L that a producer could purchase

Iso cost line; Combinations of k+L that a producer can purchase for a given cost.

2: Supply and Production Possibilities **23**

with the fixed amount of money represented by C_0. The set of combinations of K and L that can be purchased for a cost of C_0 is referred to as an *isocost line*, given by

$$C_0 = wL + rK \tag{2.2}$$

This can also be rewritten in the conventional form for the equation of the budget line in Fig. 2.5.

$$K = \left[\frac{C_0}{r}\right] - \left[\frac{w}{r}\right]L \quad \text{—slope} \tag{2.3}$$

C_0/r is the intercept of the budget line on the vertical (K) axis in Fig. 2.5, a point we denote by K_0. $-(w/r)$ is the slope of the budget line. In general, we will ignore the negative sign throughout the book and refer to the slope simply as (w/r).

To produce efficiently, a producer of X must maximize the output of X for any given level of cost expenditure, C_0. In more formal language, the producer solves the following optimization problem:

Maximize $X = F(K, L)$ subject to $C_0 \geq wL + rK$

We can understand the solution to this optimization problem by imposing on Fig. 2.5 two representative isoquants from Eq. (2.1). The producer could either produce a quantity of output X_0 by allocating expenditures between labor and capital as represented by point B or produce the same quantity by purchasing the capital and labor services associated with point C; but it is clear that neither of these allocations would be efficient. For the same expenditure, the larger output associated with X_1 could be achieved by producing at point A. It is thus evident that output is maximized by producing at point A, the point at which the highest isoquant is tangent to the cost constraint.

An individual firm is thus optimizing when the wage-rental ratio is equal to the slope of an isoquant. It is also possible to derive an expression for the slope of an isoquant. Consider moving between any two points in

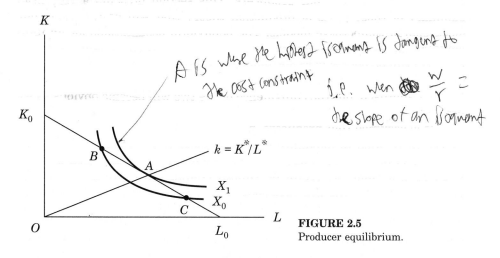

A is where the highest isoquant is tangent to the cost constraint i.e. when $\frac{w}{r} =$ the slope of an isoquant

$k = K^*/L^*$

FIGURE 2.5
Producer equilibrium.

the (K,L) space of Fig. 2.5. We can express the change in the output of X as the additional output of X obtained from an additional unit of L times the change in L, plus the additional output of X associated with an additional unit of K times the change in K. The additional unit of output associated with adding one more unit of an input is called the *marginal product*, as previously noted, and is written as MP. Thus, our expression for the total change in X can be more formally written as

$$\Delta X = (MP_L)\Delta L + (MP_K)\Delta K \tag{2.4}$$

where Δ is defined as the change in a variable. Now suppose that both points are on the same isoquant. From the definition of an isoquant, this means that $\Delta X = 0$, and thus, Eq. (2.2) becomes

$$0 = (MP_L)\Delta L + (MP_K)\Delta K \tag{2.5}$$

Rearranging, we obtain

$$-\frac{\Delta K}{\Delta L} = \frac{MP_L}{MP_K} \tag{2.6}$$

where the right-hand side is positive since ΔK and ΔL have the opposite sign. But as we consider two points on the same isoquant, and as these two points become closer and closer together, it is clear that $\Delta K/\Delta L$ becomes a closer and closer approximation to the slope of the isoquant. Indeed, in the limit $\Delta K/\Delta L$ is the slope, and thus the slope of any isoquant is equal to MP_L/MP_K, the ratio of the marginal products. We showed that the slope of the isocost line is w/r, and thus the condition for output maximization, namely that the slope of the isocost line be equal to the slope of the highest attainable isoquant, is given by the *production efficiency condition* (2.7):

$$\frac{w}{r} = \frac{MP_L}{MP_K} \tag{2.7}$$

In the last section it was noted that for production functions that are homogeneous, all isoquants have the same slope along any capital-labor ratio. This implies that for a given wage-rental ratio, the optimal capital-labor ratio will be constant regardless of the level of output. Thus for any wage-rental ratio, all production points will lie along a line such as QA of Fig. 2.5. The capital-labor ratio is thus a function of the wage-rental ratio only and does not depend on the level of output. An even stronger condition can be derived when production functions are homogeneous of degree one; that is, when production functions exhibit constant returns to scale. Not only the *ratio* of marginal products but also the individual marginal products are constant for any capital-labor ratio. These results will prove to be useful in Chapters 8 and 9.

2.4 THE TWO-GOOD, TWO-FACTOR MODEL

In this section we will develop the simple general-equilibrium model that will be used throughout much of the book. We assume that two commodities,

X and Y, are produced using two factors, capital and labor, with technologies described by the production functions shown in Eqs. (2.8).

$$X = F_x(K_x, L_x)$$
$$Y = F_y(K_y, L_y)$$

(2.8)

Note that subscripts are now being used to distinguish the two production functions and the inputs used by each. These production functions are assumed to be homogeneous of the first degree and are assumed to be increasing functions of both inputs. It is further assumed that positive outputs imply positive inputs of both factors. The economy is assumed to have fixed total supplies of both capital and labor, and these two constraints are represented by Eqs. (2.9):

$$\overline{K} = K_x + K_y$$
$$\overline{L} = L_x + L_y$$

(2.9)

fixed supplies of K + L are available
K and are used

As well as showing the allocation of the two factors between the two production processes, the equality sign in these two equations implies that these two processes use all the available $\overline{K}$ and $\overline{L}$. Full employment is, therefore, implicitly assumed. Also implicit in our analysis is the assumption that both factors of production are completely divisible and are homogeneous in the sense that all units are identical.

An assumption central to the analysis is that the commodities, X and Y, differ in the sense that the production functions differ. Representative isoquants Y_0 and X_0 for the two industries are shown in Fig. 2.6. While it is clear from the diagram that these two isoquants have been derived from different production functions, it will be useful to describe the differences in a somewhat more formal manner. Consider an arbitrary wage-rental ratio equal to the slope of the line K_0L_0. With these relative factor prices, production in industry Y would take place somewhere along the line OA, and production in industry X somewhere along the line OB, these being the points where the wage-rental ratios are tangent to the respective isoquants.

k_Y (which is K/L) is > k_X → k_Y is relatively cap.- int.

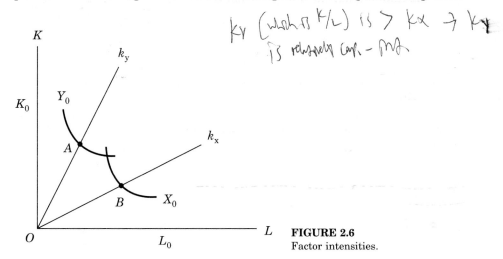

FIGURE 2.6
Factor intensities.

It is clear that the capital-labor ratios $k = K/L$ for industries Y and X, represented in the figure by k_y and k_x respectively, differ. We thus have the following definition.

> **Definition.** Consider fixed factor prices. If $k_y > k_x$ at those factor prices, Y is said to be *capital intensive* and X is said to be *labor intensive.*

From Fig. 2.6 it is evident that k_y is greater than k_x, and thus commodity Y is said to be capital-intensive relative to commodity X as noted in the definition. Of course, a completely equivalent statement is that commodity X is labor-intensive relative to commodity Y. For the remainder of the book, we assume that commodity Y is capital-intensive relative to commodity X for all wage-rental ratios. This is known as the *strong factor intensity hypothesis.*

2.5 THE SHAPE OF THE PRODUCTION POSSIBILITY FRONTIER

The *production possibility frontier,* as its name implies, is a locus that shows all possible efficient production points. It is important to note that two kinds of efficiency are being assumed here. The first, which we might call *engineering efficiency,* implies simply that for either of the production functions and for any bundle of inputs, output is as large as it could possibly be. In other words, we are assuming that there is no waste involved in the production process. The second kind of efficiency, which we could call *market efficiency,* is concerned with the way in which factors are combined in the production processes.

The specific task now faced is to construct, from the technological information given by the production functions in Eqs. (2.8), and the constraints on factor use given by Eqs. (2.9), the production possibility frontier. This locus is also called the *transformation curve.* Two points on this locus are easy to find. Suppose that all the labor and all the capital were allocated to the production of commodity Y, so that in Eqs. (2.8), K_y and L_y are replaced by $\overline{K}$ and $\overline{L}$. This will give us a well-defined level of output for Y, which we can call $\overline{Y}$, as shown in Fig. 2.7. Note that since all factors are being used to produce Y, the output of X must be zero. Similarly, allocating all of the capital and all of the labor to the production of X would give a point such as $\overline{X}$ in Fig. 2.7.

A slightly more difficult task is to find the various points on the production possibility frontier that allow some output of both commodities. To obtain some idea of where this curve might be, construct the straight line joining $\overline{Y}$ and $\overline{X}$ and consider whether points on this line are possible production points. Recalling the assumption of constant returns to scale, we see that all such points are indeed possible. Suppose, for example, that one-half $\overline{L}$ and one-half $\overline{K}$ are allocated to both production functions. Because of constant returns to scale, half the inputs results in half the output, so we

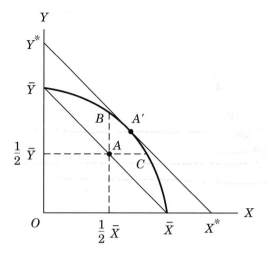

FIGURE 2.7
The production frontier.

have the two points $\frac{1}{2}\overline{Y}$ and $\frac{1}{2}\overline{X}$ shown in Fig. 2.7. This gives point A in output space, and it is obvious that this point lies on the straight line $\overline{YX}$. All other points on the line $\overline{YX}$ could be generated in a similar fashion, so all points on this line are *feasible* production points.

We have shown that points such as A in Fig. 2.7 are possible production points. The important question, however, is whether these points are efficient or, in other words, whether there are possible production points outside the line $\overline{YX}$ yielding larger outputs of both commodities than those implied by points such as A. It is important to remember here that we have assumed different production functions for the two industries. Recall from Fig. 2.6 that for a given wage-rental ratio, the capital-labor ratios in the two industries differ, which suggests that simply dividing the two factors proportionally between the two industries will not result in the maximum output. If the two outputs were guns and butter, it would not make much sense to allocate half of the farmland to the production of guns. Thus, in Fig. 2.7, a reallocation of factors between the two industries, in particular a shift of more K to the production of Y and more L to the production of X, will result in a larger output of both commodities than that associated with points such as A on the line $\overline{YX}$. After the reallocation of factors, a production point such as A' could be possible. The same argument will apply to all points on the line $\overline{YX}$, with the obvious exception of the two points $\overline{Y}$ and $\overline{X}$, and the resulting production possibility locus would be $\overline{Y}A'\overline{X}$.

The preceding argument has presented an intuitive reason for believing that the production possibility frontier lies everywhere above the equiproportions line $\overline{YX}$. Curves having this shape are said to be concave to the origin, while the set of feasible production points is said to be convex, admittedly causing some confusion. We will need to use both terms, referring to the production frontier in Fig. 2.7 as concave and to the set of feasible production points (*production set* for short) as convex.[2]

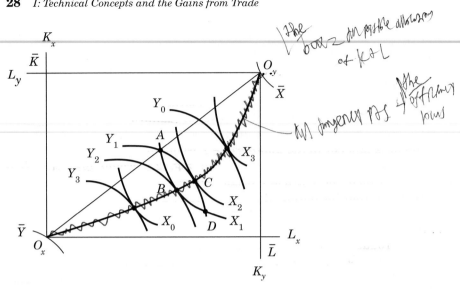

The handwritten annotations on the figure read: "The box is all possible allocations of K & L", "All tangency pts is the efficient locus".

FIGURE 2.8
The Edgeworth-Bowley box.

A more rigorous demonstration of this curvature is required, effected by a construction known as the Edgeworth-Bowley box diagram. This construction, shown in Fig. 2.8, gives a concise representation of the information obtained in Eqs. (2.8) and (2.9) and demonstrates precisely what is meant by market efficiency.

In Fig. 2.8 several representatives of the isoquants for the X industry have been plotted from origin O_x. The total available quantities of capital and labor, $\overline{K}$ and $\overline{L}$, are also shown in the diagram, and it is clear that the maximum amount of X that could be produced when all factors are allocated to the production of X is $\overline{X}$. This is the same $\overline{X}$ as shown in Fig. 2.7. The same procedure is now employed for the Y industry, except that in this case the isoquant diagram is turned upside down and plotted from O_y. Note that the output of Y increases as one moves from O_y toward O_x. From the point of view of the Y industry, O_x on isoquant $\overline{Y}$ represents the maximum possible amount of commodity Y that can be produced, for it represents the total allocation of $\overline{K}$ and $\overline{L}$ to the production of commodity Y. The isoquant $\overline{Y}$ thus gives the point $\overline{Y}$ of Fig. 2.7.

All possible allocations of capital and labor between the two industries are represented by the points in the production box $O_x\overline{K}O_y\overline{L}$. Among these possible production points we seek a locus of points that is efficient in the sense that, for a given output of one commodity, the output of the other commodity is maximized. To take a specific example, suppose an output Y_1 of commodity Y is chosen, and that we seek to maximize X subject to this constraint. A possible allocation of factors between the two industries is now represented by all points along the isoquant Y_1 in Fig. 2.8, and we want to find the particular point along this curve that maximizes the output of X. First, suppose that production were to take place at point A, halfway between O_x and O_y. Such a production point is clearly feasible, for it exactly exhausts the total available supply of capital and labor, and such an allocation results in the outputs of Y_1 and X_1 for industries Y and X, respectively. But while this production point is possible, it is clearly not efficient. Any movement along the isoquant Y_1 from A toward point C, although not reducing the output of Y, will clearly increase the output of X. Point C is the tangency point for the two isoquants Y_1 and X_2, and, for a given quantity of Y, output of X is maximized at the point where the highest X isoquant is tangent to the appropriate Y isoquant.

Joining all the tangency points in Fig. 2.8 would give the locus $O_x B C O_y$, called the *efficiency locus*. All points on this locus have the characteristic that the output of one commodity cannot be increased without reducing the output of the other. It is precisely this criterion that describes the market efficiency referred to previously.[3]

The production possibility frontier can now be derived quite easily from the information given in Fig. 2.8. With each point on the efficiency locus there is associated an output of X and an output of Y, and these points, when plotted in XY space, give us the production frontier of Fig. 2.7. Figure 2.8 allows a more rigorous demonstration of the fact that the production possibility curve has the shape shown in Fig. 2.7. Point A in Fig. 2.8, in which half the factor endowment is allocated to each industry, corresponds exactly to point A in Fig. 2.7. This follows from constant returns to scale: if half of the total factor endowment is allocated to each industry, then each industry will produce exactly half the output that it would produce if the entire factor endowment were allocated to that industry.

Furthermore, point B in Fig. 2.7 corresponds exactly to the factor allocation at point B in Fig. 2.8. Point B in Fig. 2.8 has the same output of X as point A but a greater output of Y, which corresponds to the relationship between A and B in Fig. 2.7. Similarly, point C in Fig. 2.8 has the same output of Y as point A but a higher output of X, which corresponds to the relationship between points A and C in Fig. 2.7. Thus, the efficiency locus $O_x B C O_y$ in Fig. 2.8 maps into the concave production frontier $\overline{Y} B C \overline{X}$ in Fig. 2.7.

The concave production frontier shown in Fig. 2.7 is basically a result of the fact that factors of production are not equally suited to different industries; this is the fact of differences in optimal factor intensities between industries. Point A' is feasible, but as we transfer factors from Y to X, we are transferring factors that are useful in Y but much less useful in producing X. Beginning at A' and transferring factors to Y has the same effect. To put it slightly differently, we cannot produce twice as much X or twice as much Y as at A' in Fig. 2.7 because when we shut down the other industry, we are releasing the "wrong" factors. Thus, while point A' in Fig. 2.7 is feasible, Y^* and X^* are not.

2.6 COMPETITIVE EQUILIBRIUM

Now we turn to the questions of (1) whether or not production will actually take place on the production frontier and (2) if so, at what point on the transformation frontier production will take place. It has been shown that

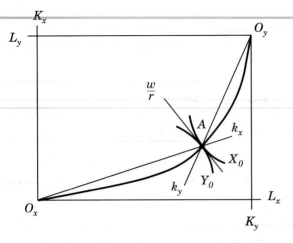

FIGURE 2.9
Competitive equilibrium in input markets.

the efficient allocation of resources requires that production take place at a point where an isoquant from one industry is tangent to an isoquant from the other. It has also been shown that, for the individual producer, the maximization of production subject to the cost constraint requires that the ratio of factor prices be equal to the slope of the isoquants. Since this condition is true for both industries, the isoquants for the two industries will be tangent to each other if the two industries face the same factor prices for w and r. This outcome is illustrated in Fig. 2.9. At point A, the isoquants X_0 and Y_0 are both tangent to the wage-rental ratio w/r and hence are tangent to each other. In answer to question (1), *if industries are competitive and face the same factor prices, production is efficient and will occur on the production frontier.*

We are now in a position to answer the second question, concerning *where* on the production frontier the economy will produce for a given set of prices. First, we note that a condition for profit maximization for a competitive industry is that firms hire factors up to the point where the value of the marginal product contributed by an additional unit of the factor hired equals the price of that factor. The *value* of the marginal product of a factor is the price of the good times the "physical" marginal product of the factor we discussed earlier in the chapter. Competitive equilibrium involves four of these conditions, two factors for each of two industries. Let MP_{LX} denote the marginal product of labor in the production of X, and define other marginal products similarly. The four value-of-marginal-product conditions are given by:

$$p_x MP_{LX} = w \qquad p_x MP_{KX} = r$$
$$p_y MP_{LY} = w \qquad p_y MP_{KY} = r \tag{2.10}$$

By dividing the top equations by the lower equations and rearranging, we can express Eqs. (2.10) as

$$\frac{p_x}{p_y} = \frac{MP_{LY}}{MP_{LX}} = \frac{MP_{KY}}{MP_{KX}} \tag{2.11}$$

The marginal products in Eqs. (2.10) and (2.11) are the change in the relevant output divided by the change in the relevant input so, for example, $MP_{LX} = \Delta X/\Delta L_x$, etc. Using these relationships, we can rewrite Eqs. (2.11) as

$$\frac{p_x}{p_y} = \frac{\Delta Y/\Delta L_y}{\Delta X/\Delta L_x} = \frac{\Delta Y/\Delta K_y}{\Delta X/\Delta K_x} \qquad (2.12)$$

But because factors are in fixed total supply, represented by Eqs. (2.9), $\Delta L_x = -\Delta L_y$ and $\Delta K_x = -\Delta K_y$. Using these relationships to cancel denominators we can reduce Eqs. (2.12) to a simple expression:

$$\frac{p_x}{p_y} = -\frac{\Delta Y}{\Delta X} = \text{MRT} \qquad (2.13)$$

[handwritten: Marg Rate of Transformation]

where MRT stands for the slope of the production frontier, the *marginal rate of transformation*: $-\Delta Y/\Delta X$ (note that ΔY and ΔX must have opposite signs, so the MRT is positive). Production occurs where the price ratio is tangent to the production frontier. This result is illustrated in Fig. 2.10 where p is used as shorthand for the price ratio: $p = p_x/p_y$.

We now have a key result regarding the efficiency of competitive, undistorted markets which will be used many times throughout the book: *if factor and commodity markets are competitive and if industries face the same factor prices, then production will occur at a point where the commodity price ratio $p = p_x/p_y$ is tangent to the production frontier.*

If world prices are given by p, then an economy will select production point A in Fig. 2.10. Note for future reference that this will in turn lead to factor market allocation at point A in Fig.2.9. This in turn determines factor prices as w/r in Fig. 2.9. Thus, in a trading economy, commodity prices on world markets will determine commodity supplies, which will in turn determine factor demands and hence factor prices. Some popular arguments reverse this causality and assert that the price of labor, for

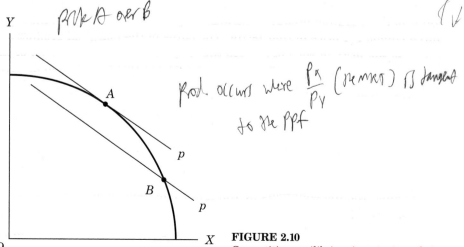

FIGURE 2.10
Competitive equilibrium in output markets.

example, determines commodity supplies and prices. This is not the case if a country faces fixed world commodity prices.

The result shown in Fig. 2.10 has an implication that will be important in subsequent sections. We can think of the price line through the production point A as a "national budget line" in the sense that all points on that line have the same value of consumption. The tangency property of competitive equilibrium implies that the economy attains the highest budget line at the given price ratio p: *in competitive equilibrium, the value of output is maximized at equilibrium prices.* To help understand this point, consider an alternative production point B in Fig. 2.10. At price ratio p, the economy would be on a lower national budget line if it produced at B; national income would be lower.

One final point should be noted for future reference, and indeed it will come up in the next section: *If there is only one factor of production and there are constant returns in both industries, then the production frontier is linear.* If labor, for example, is the only factor, the marginal product of labor is constant in both industries. Each unit of labor moved out of Y and into X generates the same negative ΔY and the same positive ΔX. Thus, the slope of the production frontier is constant. It is the addition of factor-intensity effects, which shift "inappropriate" mixes of factors from one industry to the other, that leads to the concavity in the two-factor case.

2.7 INCREASING RETURNS TO SCALE

Many industries are characterized by increasing returns to scale. Although these scale economies may eventually diminish, they can be very important relative to the size of the market in small economies, and even in the United States' very large economy, they are important for a few industries including aircraft and mainframe computers. There are many respects in which economies of scale in an industry lead to important differences relative to the constant-returns case that we have been discussing. Therefore, this book will spend considerable time discussing technologies of both constant and increasing returns.

As we showed in the previous section, differences in factor intensities between industries tend to make the production frontier concave or "bowed out" (the set of feasible production points is convex). Here we will show that scale economies make the production frontier convex or "bowed in" (the production set is non-convex). An analysis including both scale economies and factor-intensity effects thus tends to get messy, with the former tugging the production frontier in and the latter tending to pull it out. Therefore, from this section forward we will present a simplified analysis of scale economies in which there is only a single factor of production, which we will call labor. Suppose that the production functions and labor supply constraint are given as follows:

$$Y = L_y \qquad X = L_x^k \qquad k > 1.$$
$$\overline{L} = L_x + L_y$$

$$(2.14)$$

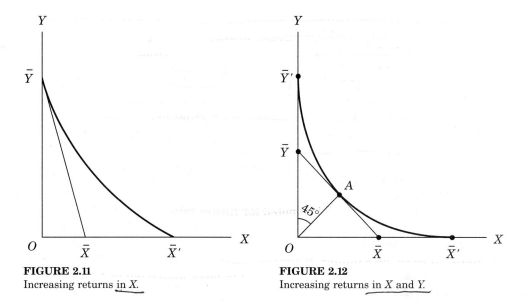

FIGURE 2.11
Increasing returns in X.

FIGURE 2.12
Increasing returns in X and Y.

The definition in section 2.2 of this chapter can be used to show that the production function for X is homogeneous of degree $k > 1$. A doubling of the labor allocated to X more than doubles the output of X. The production frontier for this economy is shown in Fig. 2.11. $\bar{Y}$ can be produced by allocating all labor to Y. If X is characterized by constant returns to scale, then shifting labor from Y to X generates the linear production frontier $\overline{YX}$ in Fig. 2.11: each unit of labor transferred generates the same ΔY and ΔX and so MRT $= -\Delta Y/\Delta X$ is constant, as we noted in the previous section. But with increasing returns to scale in X, each additional unit of labor transferred from Y to X generates a larger ΔX than the previous unit. Thus MRT $= -\Delta Y/\Delta X$ must *fall* (the production frontier becomes flatter) as we move down from $\bar{Y}$. We have drawn the production frontier corresponding to the technology in Eqs. (2.14) as $\overline{YX}'$ in Fig. 2.11.

The convexity of the production frontier is reinforced if *both* industries have increasing returns. Suppose in Fig. 2.12 that we know that A on the 45° line ($X = Y$) is on the production frontier. If both industries have constant returns and there are no factor-intensity effects, then we know that the production frontier is the linear segment $\overline{YX}$: relative to A, doubling the labor input to either industry merely doubles output. But if both industries have increasing returns, then doubling the labor allocation to either industry more than doubles the output of that industry. Thus the true production frontier will be given by $\overline{Y'X}'$ in Fig. 2.12.

Another type of technology is often used to represent scale economies. Suppose that production of X requires a fixed amount of labor F as an up-front fixed cost, but thereafter requires one unit of labor per unit of X. We can write the production function for X in "inverse" form, indicating the

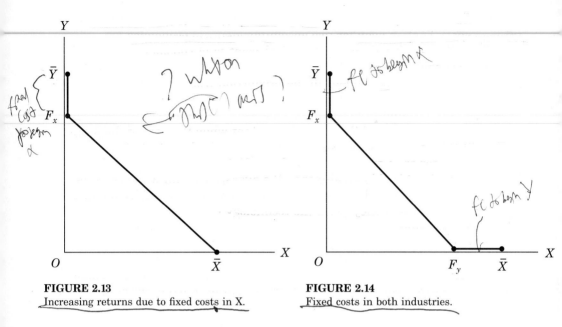

FIGURE 2.13
Increasing returns due to fixed costs in X.

FIGURE 2.14
Fixed costs in both industries.

amount of labor L_x needed to produce a given amount of X. Instead of Eqs. (2.14), we now have:

$$Y = L_y \qquad L_x = X + F$$
$$\overline{L} = L_x + L_y \qquad\qquad (2.15)$$

L_x can be thought of as the real cost of X in units of labor. The technology in Eqs. (2.15) gives rise to the production frontier shown in Fig. 2.13. $\overline{Y}$ is the maximum output of Y. But before we can get any actual output of X, we must withdraw labor equal to the fixed cost F from Y. This is given by the vertical distance $\overline{Y}F_x$ in Fig. 2.13. Thereafter, we can move labor between Y and X so as to generate the linear segment of the production frontier $F_x\overline{X}$. Thus the production frontier is given by $\overline{Y}F_x\overline{X}$ in Fig. 2.13. When both goods have increasing returns, we get the production frontier $\overline{Y}F_xF_y\overline{X}$ in Fig. 2.14, where $\overline{Y}F_x$ denotes the fixed cost of labor needed to begin X production and $\overline{X}F_y$ denotes the fixed cost of labor needed to begin Y production.

Although Figs. 2.13 and 2.14 have linear segments in the production frontiers, they share an important property with Figs. 2.11 and 2.12 whose production frontiers have smooth curvature. In all four diagrams, the production sets are non-convex; that is, the sets of feasible production points are not convex sets. In all these cases, for example, points on a line joining the end points of the production frontiers are not feasible production points. You can produce two cars or two stereos, but you cannot produce one of each with the same amount of labor (although with constant returns you can). While this may appear to be a minor technical point at this time, we will show in subsequent chapters that the non-convexity of the production set is of considerable importance. It can, for example, lead to gains from trade through specialization even for two absolutely identical economies.

One other seemingly minor technical point is of considerable significance, as we shall see later in the book. With increasing returns to scale, prices are generally not tangent to the production frontier. The reason for this has to do with the fact that, as we increase the output of an increasing-returns good, marginal products of factors rise when production functions are of the form in Eqs. (2.14) or remain constant when they are of the form in Eqs. (2.15). In the case of Eqs. (2.14), the *marginal* product of labor in X is then greater than the *average* product of labor. The amount produced by the last worker hired is greater than the average over all workers. If the firm paid all labor the value of the marginal product produced by the last worker, it would lose money. With the technology in Eqs. (2.15), if the firm paid labor the value of its (constant) marginal product, the firm would fail to cover its fixed costs. Therefore, the analysis of Eqs. (2.10) to (2.13) is not valid with increasing returns to scale. In general, increasing returns must involve imperfect competition or externalities, and for producer equilibrium, the price line will have to cut the production frontier. Further discussion of this point is postponed until later chapters.

2.8 CONCLUDING REMARKS

The purposes of this chapter were to discuss (1) the properties of production functions, (2) producer equilibrium in a competitive setting, (3) the shape of the production frontier and (4) the point chosen on the production frontier in relation to commodity prices when production is competitive. You should have an understanding of the key points in the following list, which you can use to help guide your review.

1. When production is competitive, producers will choose a capital-labor ratio such that the marginal rate of substitution (slope of an isoquant) is equal to the wage-rental ratio w/r.
2. If in both industries there are constant returns to scale and only one factor, then the production frontier is linear.
3. Factor intensities refer to the capital-labor ratios used in different industries at a common set of factor prices. If there are constant returns to scale in both industries and (with two factors) factor intensities differ, then the production frontier will be concave (the production set will be convex).
4. If production is competitive and producers in different industries face the same prices for capital and labor, then production will take place on the production frontier.
5. For given commodity prices, competitive producers maximize profits by producing at the point where the price ratio is tangent to the production frontier. This in turn implies that the value of national output is maximized in competitive equilibrium.

6. Commodity prices determine commodity outputs, which determine factor demands, which determine factor prices and hence the distribution of income between factors.

7. With one factor of production and increasing returns to scale in one or both industries, the production frontier is convex, or more generally, the production set is non-convex. Specifically, points on a line joining the end points of the production frontier are not feasible production points.

8. With increasing returns to scale, equilibrium generally does not involve a tangency between the production frontier and the price ratio. Such an outcome would in general imply that firms are losing money.

PROBLEMS

1. Suppose the production functions for commodities X and Y are identical. How will this affect the shape of the efficiency locus? What will the production possibility curve look like for the case of (a) constant returns to scale and (b) increasing returns to scale. How will the efficiency loci differ for these two cases?

2. Suppose that the total available quantity of labor increases and that the available quantity of capital decreases. How will this affect the shape and position of the production possibility curve?

3. In terms of Fig. 2.8, show that the equilibrium wage-rental ratio increases as one moves from O_x to O_y along the efficiency locus. (Hint: begin by asking how k_x and k_y change as the economy moves along the efficiency locus.)

4. Suppose that there are increasing returns in both industries and that $\overline{Y}$ and $\overline{X}$ are the end points of the production frontier. Write out an explanation of why $(\overline{Y}/2, \overline{X}/2)$ cannot be a feasible production point.

*5. Show that for production functions homogeneous of any degree, the efficiency locus cannot cross the diagonal of the factor box.

*6. Suppose that in a figure such as Fig. 2.9, the wage-rental ratios for the two industries differ. This could come about, for example, if one factor were taxed in one industry but not in the other. How would this affect the production possibility curve?

*7. Draw representative isoquants for the X industry and the Y industry such that, while k_x is less than k_y for some wage-rental ratios, k_x is greater than k_y for other wage-rental ratios. (This is referred to as *factor intensity reversal*.)

NOTES

1. A set is said to be convex if, for any two points A and B in the set, all points on a line joining A and B are also in the set. Note that in Fig. 2.2, the set of all points on and above the isoquant X' (or any isoquant) satisfies this condition.

2. Using the proper mathematical terminology, the production frontier in Fig. 2.7 is a strictly concave function and the production set is strictly convex (e.g., a linear function is concave,

---

*Denotes difficult questions.

but not strictly concave). In order to avoid repeating the word "strictly" countless times, we henceforth note that concave and convex should be taken to mean "strictly concave" and "strictly convex" respectively. Linear functions will be referred to as "linear." As we noted earlier in defining a convex set, such a set has the property that, for any two points in the set, all points on a line segment joining those two points are also in the set.

3. It can be shown that if both production functions are homogeneous, then the efficiency locus lies either everywhere on only one side of the diagonal of the Edgeworth-Bowley box or directly on it. For a single country, either $k_y > k_x$ at all production points, or the opposite holds, or $k_x = k_y$ (the efficiency locus is the diagonal). You are asked to prove this in question 5. [Hint: prove that if one point on the efficiency locus (with $X, Y > 0$) lies on the diagonal, all efficient points lie on the diagonal.] Two countries may however have opposite factor intensity rankings (i.e., $k_y > k_x$ in one country and $k_y < k_x$ in the other), a phenomenon known as factor-intensity reversal. This topic is considered in Appendix 3.

4. We could also define production functions with decreasing returns to scale. However, many economists feel that what may appear to be decreasing returns are actually diminishing marginal products: increases in outputs are diminishing because one or more factors are fixed as in Fig. 2.3. In addition, decreasing returns are simply not very important in the analysis of international trade and thus will not be discussed.

REFERENCES

Melvin, J. R. (1971). "On the Derivation of the Production Possibility Curve." *Economica* 39: 287–294.

Savosnick, K. M. (1958). "The Box Diagram and the Production Possibility Curve." *Swedish Economic Journal* 60: 183–197.

CHAPTER
3

PREFERENCES,
DEMAND,
AND WELFARE

3.1 THE UTILITY FUNCTION

The previous chapter described the production or supply side of the traditional international trade model; in this chapter attention is focused on the demand side. Fundamental to the notion of a representable demand relationship is the assumption that consumers buy commodities because these commodities provide satisfaction, or *utility*. The relationship between the utility derived from such consumption and the quantities of the commodities consumed is summarized in a utility function of the form

$$U = U(X, Y) \tag{3.1}$$

This three-dimensional relationship has an obvious similarity to the production functions of Chapter 2, and, indeed, several of the characteristics of the production functions described in Chapter 2 will be assumed to apply to the utility function as well. One assumption that production and utility functions have in common is that both are assumed to be increasing functions of both inputs. For the utility function this implies that a little more of either commodity always increases a commodity bundle's utility, or in other words, that a consumer is never satiated with a particular commodity. Thus, the utility function, like the production function, can be thought of as a three-dimensional hill such that for any point on this hill, a larger amount of either or both of the two inputs will yield higher utility.

There is, however, one important distinction between the production function and the utility function. For production functions it is possible to calculate the specific level of output of a particular commodity that will result from a specific bundle of factor inputs. In contrast, it is not possible to assign a specific, numerical value to the utility level that will be associated with a specific commodity bundle. However, levels of utility associated with different commodity bundles can be compared. A consumer decides either that one commodity bundle is preferable to another or that the two yield equal satisfaction. In the latter case, we say that the consumer is "indifferent."

If we think again of the three-dimensional utility hill and imagine ourselves at some point on that hill, it is clear that the various points on the surface of the hill can be compared, even if we have no information about actual elevations above the ground level. Some points will be higher on the surface, some lower on the surface, and some at the same level. If points at the same level are traced out and projected on the YX plain, a locus such as U_0 of Fig. 3.1 results. This is a contour line of the utility hill, and it therefore represents the locus of all combinations of commodities X and Y that would yield a constant level of utility. Because the individual consumer is assumed to be indifferent at all points on this locus, any such locus is referred to as an *indifference curve.* These indifference curves are obviously analogous to the isoquants of Chapter 2. Of course, since an indifference curve can be drawn for any level of utility, there is an infinite number of such indifference curves, only three of which are shown in Fig. 3.1. In this figure, higher indifference curves represent higher levels of utility, since higher indifference curves represent contour lines that are farther up the utility surface. Note, however, that from a utility point of view, no significance can be attached to the distances between any two indifference curves.

While it has been convenient to describe the indifference curves in terms of the utility surface, it is worthwhile observing that indifference curves can be derived quite independently of the concept of the utility function. To illustrate, consider point A of Fig. 3.1, containing 10 units

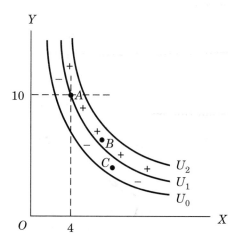

FIGURE 3.1
Indifference curves.

of Y and 4 units of X. To construct a set of indifference curves for a certain individual, we could ask a consumer to compare the utility received from other bundles of X and Y with the utility received from point A. It is first of all clear that, given the assumption that both goods yield positive utility, any point below and to the left of point A would yield less utility than A. Similarly, any point above and to the right of A would yield more utility and would therefore be preferred. A point such as B, however, contains more X but less Y, and thus no predictions can be made on the relative merits of this point as compared to A. To find out whether or not B is preferred to A, we ask whether the individual would be willing to give up A in exchange for B. If the answer is yes, then B must be preferred to A. For a point such as C, the consumer might respond negatively to the trade offer, indicating that A is preferred to C. If the individual is asked to compare a large number of commodity bundles, and if a positive sign is attached to every point at which the individual agrees to exchange and a negative sign to every point at which the individual declines to exchange, a line separating the pluses from the minuses can be drawn. This line would include all those points at which the individual is indifferent, producing an indifference curve such as U_1 in Fig. 3.1.

3.2 CHARACTERISTICS OF INDIFFERENCE CURVES

Several characteristics of the indifference curves for individuals are of interest in the subsequent analysis. First, the indifference curves are assumed to be convex to the origin, as illustrated in Figs. 3.1 and 3.2. As we will see later on, this characteristic is important in determining the equilibrium position for an individual consumer. The economic rationale for this assumption can be seen by considering points A, B, C, and D in Fig. 3.2. Since these points are all on the indifference curve U_0, the individual is, by definition, completely indifferent as to which of these bundles of commodities he or she

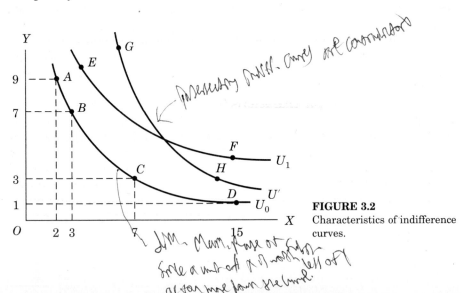

FIGURE 3.2
Characteristics of indifference curves.

Marg. Rate of subst. = Slope of Indiff. curve at a Pt. = ratio of mar'l util'es of 2 comms.

3: Preferences, Demand, and Welfare   **41**

consumes. The four points have been chosen so that the movement from A to B and the movement from C to D both represent a reduction of two units of commodity Y. The increase in the amount of X needed to persuade this individual to give up these two units of Y varies significantly between these two sets of points. To persuade the individual to move from A to B, only one unit of X is required, while the movement from C to D requires an additional 8 units of X. The economic argument underlying this assumption is that, for commodity bundles with relatively large quantities of Y and small quantities of X, the reduction in the utility associated with giving up a unit of Y, the plentiful commodity, is much smaller than the increase in utility associated with receiving an extra unit of X, the scarce commodity. Thus, at A in Fig. 3.2, the individual is prepared to give up 2 units of Y to obtain one additional unit of X. Moving down the indifference curve, however, the individual receives more X and less Y, and as this movement takes place, the extra utility associated with an additional unit of X will fall relative to the reduction in utility associated with relinquishing a unit of Y. At point C, we must offer 8 units of X to persuade the individual to give up 2 units of Y. The slope of an indifference curve at any point is equal to the ratio of the marginal utilities of the two commodities and is called the *marginal rate of substitution in consumption*. Indifference curves shaped like those in Fig. 3.2 are said to exhibit a diminishing marginal rate of substitution, referring to the fact that the utility associated with a unit of X falls relative to the utility associated with a unit of Y as one moves down the indifference curve from A to D.

The second important characteristic of indifference curves is that utility increases as the individual moves to higher indifference curves. Consider, for example, the two indifference curves U_0 and U_1. (Ignore for the moment the indifference curve through points G and H.) Because we have assumed that additional amounts of either commodity increase utility, it is clear that point E on indifference curve U_1 is preferred to point A on indifference curve U_0. But how can we compare points F and A when point F contains more X but less Y than point A? The answer to this follows directly from the definition of an indifference curve. Because E and F are both on the indifference curve U_1, they are equivalent from the individual consumer's point of view, and thus because E is preferred to A, F must also be preferred to A. Therefore, all points on the higher of two indifference curves are preferred to all points on the lower one.

The final important characteristic of indifference curves is the fact that no two indifference curves for the same individual can intersect. This fact is most easily demonstrated by drawing two intersecting indifference curves and then examining the inherent contractions that result. In Fig. 3.2 the indifference curve through points G and H has been drawn to intersect the indifference curve U_1. Consider points G and E. Because G contains a larger quantity of both Y and X, it is clear that the individual would prefer G to E. Now, points E and F are on the same indifference curve, meaning that the individual is indifferent between them. Similarly, the individual is indifferent between G and H on the indifference curve U'. Thus, because H is indifferent to G, because G is preferred to E, and because F is indifferent to E, it must follow that H is preferred to F. But because F contains more of both X and Y than does H, this is impossible. The intersection of the two indifference curves contradicts the basic assumption that more of both commodities is preferred. Therefore, it can be concluded that indifference curves cannot intersect.

3.3   THE MAXIMIZATION OF UTILITY

Up to this point, the discussion of utility has been confined to the consideration of individual tastes, or relative preferences for various commodity bundles. The actual choices that the consumers make, however, depend also on their incomes and on the prices of the commodities. To create a working equation that includes these additional factors, we assume that the prices of the two commodities, p_x and p_y, and that income, I, are given. Assuming for the sake of simplicity that the individual's entire income is spent on purchases of the two commodities, it is clear that the total expenditure on X plus the total expenditure on Y must equal I. This gives the budget constraint that can be written as

$$I = p_x X + p_y Y \tag{3.2}$$

To depict this budget constraint geometrically, or, in other words, to illustrate the set of possible consumption points, suppose that all income is spent on commodity Y. In terms of Eq. (3.2), this implies that $X = 0$, and solving for Y, we obtain $Y = I/p_y$. This point, shown in Fig. 3.3, represents the maximum amount of Y that could be purchased if all income were spent on this commodity. Similarly, if all income were spent on commodity X, consumption would take place at I/p_x in Fig. 3.3. Income can be divided between the two goods to allow the consumer to reach any point on the line connecting these two endpoints.

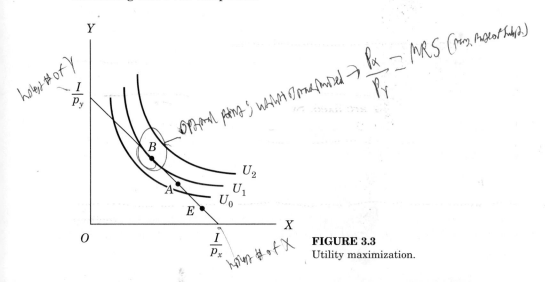

FIGURE 3.3
Utility maximization.

An alternative method of plotting this budget constraint would be to solve Eq. (3.2) for Y to obtain

$$Y = \left[\frac{I}{p_y}\right] - \left[\frac{p_x}{p_y}\right]X \qquad (3.3)$$

This is a standard form of the equation of a straight line, where I/p_y is the intercept on the Y axis, and where $-p_x/p_y$ is the slope of the line. The budget line is thus analogous to the isocost line for the firm in Eq. (2.3).

The indifference curve map can now be combined with the budget constraint to illustrate how the equilibrium position for an individual consumer is determined. In Fig. 3.3, three representative indifference curves for an individual are shown. In order to maximize his or her welfare, the individual will purchase at the highest level of utility possible within the budget constraint. Of all possible choices along the budget line, one such as point E is not optimal. Moving up the budget line to A increases the individual's welfare by crossing higher indifference curves. Welfare is maximized at point B, the highest level of utility attainable within the budget constraint. Because point B represents the tangency between the budget constraint and the highest indifference curve, *utility is maximized by setting the marginal rate of substitution equal to the ratio of commodity prices.*

$$\frac{p_x}{p_y} = \text{MRS} \qquad (3.4)$$

Because international trade is concerned with general equilibrium questions, we are interested not so much in the maximization of *individual* utility as in the conditions that characterize equilibrium for the *entire community*. To consider the simplest such case, suppose that the quantities of X and Y are fixed at $\overline{X}$ and $\overline{Y}$ and that the economy consists of two individuals. The locus of possible equilibrium points for this simple society is derived in the same way as was the efficiency locus in Chapter 2. In the box diagram of Fig. 3.4, we have plotted the indifference curves for the first individual from O_1 and the indifference curves for the second individual from O_2. Note that in terms of O_1, point O_2 represents the total available quantities of commodities X and Y. Superscripts have been used to distinguish the two sets of indifference curves.

One method of deriving the locus of equilibrium points for the two individuals is to maximize the utility for one individual, subject to some fixed level of utility for the other individual and to the constraint that the quantities of X and Y are fixed. Suppose that we constrain the second individual to consume somewhere along the indifference curve U_1^2 and maximize the utility of the first individual subject to this constraint and to the constraint that $Y = \overline{Y}$ and $X = \overline{X}$. Would it be optimal for consumption to take place at a point such as B? The answer is clearly no, for movements from B toward A, while leaving the second individual at the same utility level, would result in higher and higher levels of utility for the first individual. It can also be seen that at point A, the utility of the first individual is maximized subject to the constraints we have imposed. While points on higher indifference curves would be preferred, no such points can be achieved

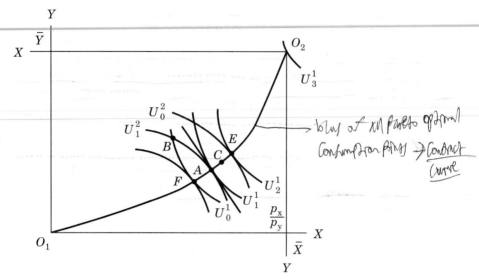

FIGURE 3.4
The contract curve.

because they would require the total consumption of more commodities than exist in the economy. Thus, although the first individual would clearly prefer to be at a point such as C, this could be achieved only by reducing the consumption of the second individual, moving that individual's purchase to a lower indifference curve. Therefore, point A is optimal in the sense that the utility of one individual's choice cannot be increased without reducing the utility of the other individual's choice. This is the *Pareto criterion* of optimality (named for the Italian economist, Vilfredo Pareto), and a point such as A is said to be *Pareto optimal.*

Of course, the choice of indifference curve U_1^2 was arbitrary, and the same argument applies equally to any other indifference curve. Suppose we choose indifference curve U_0^2 and maximize the utility for the first individual subject to this constraint. In this case the Pareto optimal point is E, the point where U_0^2 is tangent to the highest indifference curve for the first individual. By choosing various indifference curves for the second individual and maximizing utility for the first individual subject to each of these curves, the locus O_1AEO_2 can be traced out. This is the locus of all Pareto optimal consumption points and is called the *contract curve.*

It is important to note that the criterion of Pareto optimality is strictly an efficiency condition and has nothing to do with equity. Movements such as those from B to A or B to F are desirable because they increase the utility for one individual without reducing the utility for the other. The Pareto criterion does not rank points such as F and E, however, because one individual is made better off and one is made worse off by moving from F to E. Point O_2 on indifference curve U_3^1 is Pareto optimal, even though it implies that the first individual receives the entire available quantity of both X and Y while the second individual receives nothing.

From Fig. 3.4 we see that the contract curve is the locus of Pareto optimal tangency points between the indifference curves for the two individuals. It was previously shown that a consumer is in equilibrium where the commodity price ratio line is tangent to one of that individual's indifference curves. It follows that, at any point on the contract curve, the equilibrium commodity price ratio line must be tangent to indifference curves for both individuals, as is p_x/p_y at point A. Therefore, *a requirement for Pareto optimality is that both consumers face the same commodity price ratio.* Note that this condition is similar to the condition in the previous chapter that producers face the same factor prices. That condition ensures that a fixed supply of factors is allocated efficiently. The condition discussed here ensures that a fixed supply of commodities is allocated efficiently (in the Pareto sense) although not necessarily equitably.

3.4 AGGREGATING INDIVIDUAL PREFERENCES

As noted in the previous section, we are concerned not only with individual preferences and demands but also with those of entire countries. Unfortunately, it turns out that only under special assumptions can the preferences of individuals be aggregated together to get national or "community" indifference curves.

Suppose that all individuals have preferences of the type described in the preceding sections, giving rise to demand functions that depend on prices and incomes. Assume that there are only two goods and that the price ratio is denoted p. The income of individual J is denoted by I_j. If all individuals in the economy face the same price ratio but generally have different incomes, then the total demand for the good X can be written as the function D:

$$X = D(p, I_1, I_2, \ldots, I_n) \tag{3.5}$$

where it is assumed that there are n individuals in the country. The question of whether or not community indifference curves exist is essentially the same as the question of whether or not the demand function in Eq. (3.5) can be written as a function of aggregate income (the sum of the individuals' incomes)—that is, whether or not the distribution of income affects total demand.[1] The intuition here is that when we draw community indifference curves, we are saying that the country has preferences over aggregate bundles of goods that depend only on prices (the slope of the price line) and total income (the distance to the price line from the origin). Preferences, hence, demands, are independent of how that aggregate income is distributed. In short, we can write Eq. (3.5) as

$$X = D(p, I) \qquad I = \sum_{j=1}^{n} I_j \tag{3.6}$$

Special assumptions are necessary for demand to be independent of the distribution of income and, hence, for Eq. (3.6) to be valid. One problem that arises in aggregation is shown in Fig. 3.5, where we have two consumers with identical but nonhomothetic tastes.[2] In other words, at constant relative prices, the ratio of Y/X consumed is not independent of income. Specifically, consumers desire more X relative to Y as income increases at constant prices.

Suppose that we have two individuals initially consuming at point A in Fig. 3.5 and that we give some of consumer 1's income to consumer 2 so that they adjust to consuming at points B and C, respectively. The chord AB is steeper than the chord AC, and so the changes in the consumption of the two individuals do not balance. Even though we have changed neither the prices nor the aggregate income, there will now be a higher aggregate demand for X and a lower aggregate demand for Y. Aggregate demand depends on the distribution of income; therefore, community indifference curves do not exist in this situation.

Now consider homothetic but nonidentical tastes. This situation is shown in Fig. 3.6. Consumer 1, who has a relatively strong preference for Y, is initially at A_1, while consumer 2, who has a strong preference for X, is initially at A_2. Now take income away from consumer 1 and give it to consumer 2, holding prices constant. Consumer 1 moves to point B_1, while consumer 2 moves to point B_2. Again, the changes in consumption are inequivalent (more X and less Y will be demanded), even though prices and total income are constant. Community indifference curves do not exist when preferences differ.

This analysis suggests the fact that community indifference curves will exist if all consumers have identical and homothetic tastes (and if they face the same prices). This is, however, a somewhat stronger assumption than we need, and we use a slightly weaker one at several points in later

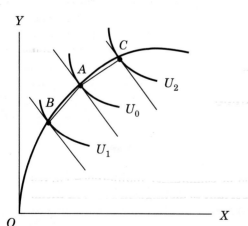

FIGURE 3.5
Aggregation problems with
non-homothetic tastes.

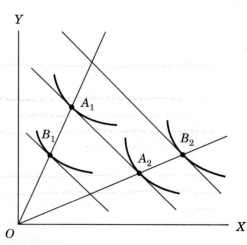

FIGURE 3.6
Aggregation problems with non-identical tastes.

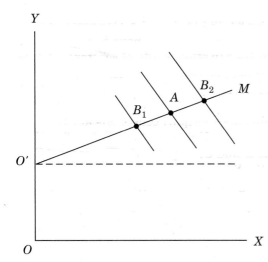

FIGURE 3.7

Aggregation with quasi-homothetic tastes.

chapters. An alternative condition is shown in Fig. 3.7, where consumers are assumed to have identical but nonhomothetic tastes. The income expansion path, shown as $O'M$, does not go through the origin, but it is linear.

Assume that two consumers are initially at point A in Fig. 3.7. Now take income away from consumer 1 and give it to consumer 2 so that they move to points B_1 and B_2, respectively. Note that the changes in their consumption levels cancel so that there is no change in aggregate demand. This type of preference, sometimes called *quasi-homotheticity*, does imply the existence of community indifference curves. As we will see in later chapters, these preferences are useful for dealing with differences in per capita income across countries. Note in Fig. 3.7 that the ratio of Y to X consumed depends on income (per capita income for a country) at constant prices. In the case shown, the share spent on X increases with income.

Throughout most of the book we will assume that preferences can be aggregated into community indifference curves. This permits an easy exposition of many points that do not rely on this assumption but that cannot be shown graphically without it.

3.5 INTERPRETING COMMUNITY INDIFFERENCE CURVES: AGGREGATE DEMAND VERSUS INDIVIDUAL WELFARE

There are two different interpretations of community indifference curves (assuming they exist), and it is very important to distinguish between them. One is what economists call a *positive* interpretation. Under this interpretation, the community indifference curves simply tell us what the country will demand under various price and aggregate income combinations. That is, if we pick income and prices so as to determine an aggregate budget line like the one in Eq. (3.3), we can find the quantities demanded by the intersection of the highest community indifference curve and the budget constraint. The positive interpretation of community indifference curves does not necessarily attach any welfare significance to the indifference curves.

The *normative* interpretation of community indifference curves does attach a positive welfare significance to moving from a lower indifference curve to a higher indifference curve (or even to moving along one indifference curve) in the same way that we would interpret that move for an individual. If a trade policy can lead to such a movement, we say that a country will be better off (or equally well off) under that policy.

The pitfalls in the second interpretation are illustrated in Fig. 3.8, where A and B are two aggregate commodity bundles and U_a and U_b are two community indifference curves. Under the normative interpretation of community indifference curves, national welfare clearly increases in a move from A to B. However, suppose that the country is composed of two individuals, denoted by superscripts 1 and 2, with identical, homothetic preferences. In the initial situation A, measure the consumption of individual 1 from the origin O and that of individual 2 in the opposite direction beginning at A as in the Edgeworth-Bowley box. As drawn in Fig. 3.8, individual 1 has initial consumption OA', and individual 2 has consumption $A'A$. Suppose that the move from A to B somehow redistributes income from individual 2 to individual 1. This is of no consequence for the community indifference curves. However, the move from A to B clearly has the effect of greatly helping individual 1 while harming individual 2, whose consumption is reduced from $A'A$ to $B'B$. The point to remember in making normative interpretations of community indifference curves is that *a movement to a higher community indifference curve does not mean that the welfare of all individuals in society has increased*. Similarly, moving along a single community indifference curve does not mean that the welfare of all individuals is being held constant.

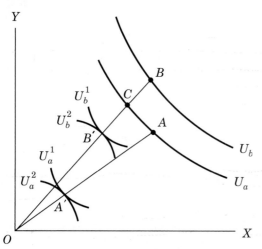

FIGURE 3.8

Contrasting community to individual welfare.

In later chapters we will present cases in which aggregate welfare increases while leaving some individuals worse off. Indeed, this is a relatively common problem with trade policy, and it is one of the points of departure in what is called the political-economy approach to trade policy. Throughout the book, we will often make normative interpretations of community indifference curves, but we must keep the caveat just mentioned in mind. One traditional way of avoiding difficulties is to say that if preferences are indeed identical and homothetic, then there will always exist some domestic redistribution of income or other compensation that will make all individuals better off when the economy moves to a higher indifference curve. The existence of such possible compensations implies that all individuals are *potentially* better off. This is not entirely satisfactory, however, since in the absence of actual redistributions, the individuals who are made worse off are not at all happy with the potential-improvement argument. We will deal explicitly with the income-distribution problem at a number of points in the book; at other points we will simply attach normative significance to community indifference curves.[3]

3.6 CONCLUDING REMARKS

This chapter develops the tools for analyzing consumer demand and for making welfare interpretations of trade policies. As was the case in the previous chapter, these tools will be used repeatedly throughout the remainder of the book. You should leave this chapter with a good understanding of the following points.

1. For given commodity prices, consumers will pick commodities such that their marginal rate of substitution in consumption (the slope of an indifference curve) is equal to the commodity price ratio.
2. If all consumers face the same commodity prices, then the allocation of commodities across individuals will be Pareto optimal; that is, it will not be possible to redistribute the commodities so as to make one individual better off without making another individual worse off.
3. In general, it is problematic to aggregate individual preferences into community indifference curves. The difficulty is that aggregate demands generally depend on the *distribution* of income among individuals, not just on prices and aggregate income.
4. Special restrictions can be imposed to produce community indifference curves. A positive interpretation of these curves will tell us what commodity bundles will be demanded at various combinations of prices and aggregate income.
5. Community indifference curves can also be interpreted in the normative sense, in which the movement from a lower indifference curve to a higher indifference curve is said to improve welfare. The problem with this interpretation is that such a move does not assure an increase in the welfare of all individuals in society. If individuals have identical and

homothetic (or quasi-homothetic) tastes, a move to a higher community indifference curve does mean at least that all individuals are *potentially* better off with an appropriate domestic redistribution scheme.

6. Throughout the book, we will often give normative interpretations of community indifference curves, but the reader must remember the distributional problem regarding individual welfare. This will be brought to the forefront at several points in the book. Because of distributional problems, we cannot automatically assume that governments set policy to attain the highest community indifference curve.

PROBLEMS

1. Show that, for an individual consumer maximizing utility subject to the budget constraint, the equilibrium position will not necessarily be unique unless the indifference curves are convex to the origin.
2. Refer back to our discussion in Chapter 2 of how commodity prices determine factor prices. Why might changes in commodity prices change the distribution of income among consumers?
3. In Fig. 3.3, trace out a locus of consumption points as the price of X falls.
4. Consider the two individuals with the preferences shown in Fig. 3.6. How might each consumer feel about a proposed policy that would raise the price of X but lower the price of Y?
5. What sort of redistribution policy might ensure that all consumers are individually better off under a trade policy that moves the economy to a higher community indifference curve?

NOTES

1. This statement is somewhat inaccurate. The existence of community indifference curves and the ability to write demand as a function of aggregate income are not quite the same. In particular, an aggregate demand function exists but community indifference curves do not when consumers have heterogeneous tastes but each consumer has a fixed share of income. For the purposes of this book, we have decided to avoid a lengthy discussion of the fine points. The analysis that follows presents restrictions on preferences that guarantee the existence of both community indifference curves and aggregate demand functions. Relatively simple discussions of aggregation can be found in Green (1976) or Deaton and Muellbauer (1980).
2. The assumption of homothetic tastes is similar to but slightly more general than the assumption of homogeneous production functions made in Chapter 2. Specifically, any monotonic transformation of a homogeneous function is homothetic. Because for preferences we assume only that more of a commodity is preferred to less without determining by how much more it is preferred, the weaker and more general homothetic assumption is sufficient for our uses. For practical purposes, assuming homothetic tastes implies that, as we increase income but hold prices constant, a consumer will hold constant the ratio of goods consumed; that is, the consumer will increase consumption of all goods by the same proportion.
3. A method of aggregating individual preferences is shown in Appendix 1.

REFERENCES

Chipman, J. S. (1965). "A Survey of the Theory of International Trade: Part 2, The Neo-Classical Theory." *Econometrica* 33, 685–760.

Deaton, A. and Muellbauer, J. (1980). *Economics and Consumer Behaviour*. London: Cambridge University Press.

Green, H. A. J. (1976). *Consumer Theory*. London: Macmillan.

Melvin, J. R. (1975). "On the Equivalence of Community Indifference and the Aggregate Consumption Function." *Economica* 42: 442–445.

Samuelson, P. A. (1956). "Social Indifference Curves." *Quarterly Journal of Economics* 64: 264–289.

Scitovsky, T. (1942). "A Reconsideration of the Theory of Tariffs." *Review of Economic Studies* 9: 89–110.

CHAPTER
4

GENERAL EQUILIBRIUM IN OPEN AND CLOSED ECONOMIES

4.1 GENERAL EQUILIBRIUM IN THE CLOSED (AUTARKY) ECONOMY

The two previous chapters developed the tools of production and consumption theories. The purpose of this chapter is to combine the production and demand sides of the economy to arrive at an overall or *general* equilibrium analysis. This section considers general equilibrium in a closed economy, one that is self-sufficient and does not trade. Such an economy is said to be in *autarky*.

Throughout this chapter producers and consumers are assumed to be competitive. In later chapters we will consider many cases of imperfect competition and other distortions. Of the three conditions that determine general equilibrium in a closed economy, the first two are *optimization* conditions for producers and consumers: (1) Competitive, profit-maximizing producers pick outputs such that, at given commodity prices, the marginal rate of transformation is equal to the producer price ratio; this condition was given in Eq. (2.13) as p_x/p_y = MRT. (2) Consumers pick commodities such that, at given commodity prices, their marginal rate of substitution in consumption is equal to the consumer price ratio; assuming that consumer and producer prices are the same, this condition was given in Eq. (3.4) as p_x/p_y = MRS. The third condition is a _market clearing_ condition: (3) The supply and demand for each commodity must be equal; let subscript c denote consumption of a commodity and subscript p denote production of a commodity. Our three conditions for general equilibrium are summarized by

$$\frac{p_x}{p_y} = \text{MRT} \qquad \text{producer optimization}$$

$$\frac{p_x}{p_y} = \text{MRS} \qquad \text{consumer optimization} \qquad (4.1)$$

$$X_c = X_p \qquad Y_c = Y_p \qquad \text{market clearing}$$

Figure 4.1 shows an equilibrium for a closed economy that satisfies these three conditions. Producers produce optimally at point A, where the slope of the production frontier is tangent to the price ratio, p_a. Similarly, consumers consume optimally at point A, where the slope of their indifference curve is tangent to the price ratio. And finally, markets clear because the production and consumption points are the same. Note also that the equilibrium at A is *optimal* in the sense that the economy consumes on the highest possible community indifference curve at which production is feasible (i.e., where the production point is on or interior to the production frontier $\overline{XY}$). This is a property that goes back to Adam Smith's "invisible hand," in which decentralized decision-making by optimizing, self-interested producers and consumers leads the economy to an efficient outcome.

Note for future reference that the equilibrium at point A determines a factor allocation in the Edgeworth-Bowley box in Fig. 2.8 (if indeed the two-factor model is the underlying production structure). Thus, factor prices are also determined in general equilibrium. To the extent that consumers have different factor endowments, the factor prices determine the distribution of income among consumers.

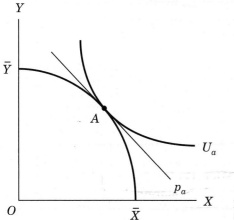

FIGURE 4.1
Closed-economy general equilibrium.

4.2   GENERAL EQUILIBRIUM IN THE OPEN (TRADING) ECONOMY

Now assume that an economy can engage in trade at a fixed world price ratio, which we will denote by $p^* = p_x^*/p_y^*$. The first two optimization conditions mentioned in the previous section remain unchanged. The only difference is that world prices will generally be different from the prices determined in autarky. Producers optimize by equating the marginal rate of transformation to whatever prices prevail, and, similarly, consumers optimize by equating their marginal rate of substitution to those prices.

The difference in equilibrium between the closed and the open economy lies in the third condition, market clearing. With international trade, an economy is no longer constrained to consume only what it can produce. The loosening of this constraint is the very source of gains from trade, as we shall see. A trading economy is able to sell some of one good at world prices and use the proceeds to buy the other commodity. Instead of market clearing, we have what we call a *trade balance* condition: the value of what a country sells on world markets must be equal to what it buys. We can define the *excess demand* for goods X and Y as $(X_c - X_p)$ and $(Y_c - Y_p)$ respectively. If excess demand is positive, the economy is consuming more than it is producing, which corresponds to demand for an import good. If excess demand is negative, an economy is consuming less than it is producing, resulting in an export good. The trade balance constraint requires that the value of all imports be equal to the value of all exports. An alternative way of saying this is that the sum of the value of the country's excess demands must equal zero: the positive excess demand for the import good must equal the negative excess demand for the export good.[1] The trade balance condition is given by

$$p_x^*(X_c - X_p) + p_y^*(Y_c - Y_p) = 0 \qquad (4.2)$$

Note that this condition is completely general and does not depend on which good happens to be the import good and which happens to be the export good.

We can rearrange the terms in Eq. (4.2) to rewrite the equation in a different way.

$$p_x^*X_p + p_y^*Y_p = p_x^*X_c + p_y^*Y_c \qquad (4.3)$$

The left-hand side of this equation is the value of production at world prices, while the right-hand side is the value of consumption at world prices. Thus, equivalent to the trade balance condition is the requirement that *the value of production must equal the value of consumption.*

We can think of the value of production as the income of the country. By placing a line with the slope of the world price ratio p^* through the production point, we derive the "national budget line." As explained in Chapter 2, this budget line defines national income by evaluating domestic output at world prices. Consumers are then free to choose any point on this budget line, because the value of consumption will be equal to the

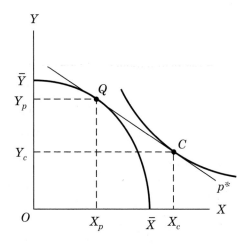

FIGURE 4.2
Open-economy general equilibrium.

value of production. This is shown in Fig. 4.2, where the fixed world price ratio is given by p^*. Producers optimize by choosing production at point Q. Consumers optimize by choosing consumption at point C. In the particular case shown, the country imports X ($X_c > X_p$) and exports Y ($Y_c < Y_p$). Trade will balance insofar as the value of production at world prices equals the value of consumption. To summarize, the conditions for general equilibrium are given as follows.

$$\frac{p_x^*}{p_y^*} = \text{MRT} \qquad\qquad \text{producer optimization}$$

$$\frac{p_x^*}{p_y^*} = \text{MRS} \qquad\qquad \text{consumer optimization} \quad (4.4)$$

$$p_x^*(X_c - X_p) + p_y^*(Y_c - Y_p) = 0 \qquad \text{trade balance}$$

Note finally that the autarky market clearing condition is a special case of trade balance. It satisfies the trade balance condition in that both terms in parentheses are zero. If world prices happened to be the same as the country's autarky prices, then the trading equilibrium would be identical to the autarky equilibrium.

4.3   THE EXCESS DEMAND FUNCTION

We now turn to the larger question of the determination of world prices and an international general equilibrium (our world will consist of two countries). Consider Fig. 4.3. The autarky price ratio p_a is shown for reference. At the price ratio $p_1^* < p_a$, the country produces at Q_1 and consumes at C_1. Excess demand for good X is positive; i.e., X is imported. This makes economic sense, recalling that $p^* = p_x^*/p_y^*$. If the relative price of X is lower on the world markets than on the domestic market, then buying from the low-cost source would mean importing the good. Similarly, if Y is relatively more

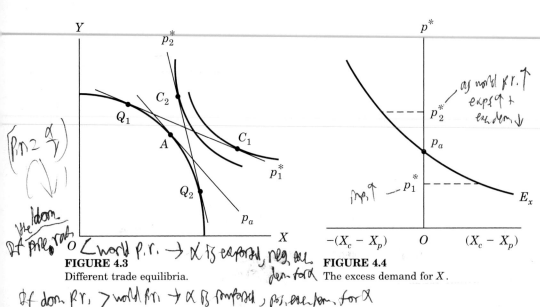

FIGURE 4.3
Different trade equilibria.

FIGURE 4.4 The excess demand for X.

[handwritten margin notes: $(Pn_2 \frac{\alpha}{\gamma})$; the Idam, of price ratio ; $\mathcal{L}$ world P.r. → X is export, neg ex. dem for X ; as world P.r. ↑ exps↑ + ex dem ↓ ; mp↑ ; If dom. P.r. > world P.r → X is import, pos. ex. dem for X]

valuable on the world market than at home, then exports of Y are in order. At the price ratio $p_2^* > p_a$ in Fig. 4.3, producers pick point Q_2 and consumers pick point C_2. <u>With the price ratio greater than the autarky price ratio, the home country exports X (the relatively valuable good on the world markets) and imports Y (the relatively cheap good on the world market).</u>

This is a general result. If the world price ratio exceeds the domestic price ratio ($p^* > p_a$), then X is exported and there is a negative excess demand for X. If the world price ratio is less than the autarky price ratio ($p^* < p_a$), then X is imported and there is a positive excess demand for X. In Fig. 4.4, we construct an excess demand curve for good X for the country. <u>At the autarky price ratio p_a, there is zero excess demand.</u> Price ratios p_1^* and p_2^* in Fig. 4.4 correspond to the similarly labelled price ratios in Fig. 4.3. Excess demand for X becomes increasingly negative (exports of X becomes increasingly positive) as the world price ratio increases above p_a. Excess demand becomes increasingly positive (imports of X become increasingly positive) as the world price ratio falls below p_a. The excess demand curve for X, labeled E_x in Fig. 4.4, is much like a conventional demand curve, except that the quantity demanded may be either positive or negative. A negative excess demand is simply a desire to supply (export) the good to the world market at that price.

4.4 THE SHAPE OF EXCESS DEMAND CURVES

What are the factors leading to the specific shape that an excess demand curve assumes? Essentially, the excess demand curve takes its shape from the reactions of producers and consumers to new prices. Any price movement away from p_a will elicit a response from producers and consumers.

The production effect is the most straightforward. Suppose $p^* < p_a$. Producers will choose to move resources out of the production of X and into the production of Y. This will exacerbate any given excess demand for X at $p^* < p_a$, leading to the negative slope of the excess demand curve. Similarly, $p^* < p_a$ leads to a substitution effect in consumption. The falling price of X makes consumers willing and able to buy more of it, and again the excess demand for X grows as its price falls. Furthermore, the concavity of the production possibilities curve and the concavity of community indifference curves will combine to ensure that the excess demand function will itself be convex.

A subtlety in constructing the excess demand curve may arise when $p^* > p_a$. In this case, the curve may bend backward (take a positive slope) in the exporting section (negative excess demand) of the curve. As the price of the export good continues to increase, the country gets richer from the sales of that good. This leads consumers to want to devote some of their additional income to purchases of that good. At some point, this *income effect*, which leads consumers to demand more of the export good, may outweigh the substitution effect, which leads consumers to want less of a good when its price rises. Consequently, exports may fall with a further increase in price. We have elected not to pursue this possibility here, but it is discussed in Appendix A, containing the derivation of offer curves. In any event, the position of the excess demand curve is ultimately determined by the resources the country has available to produce X even if it chooses not to consume it at all.

Finally, movement along the excess demand curve away from p_a in either direction is welfare-improving because any change in price leads to an increase in the consumption choices for consumers. As prices fall from p_a, for instance, consumers who could still afford the previous combination of X and Y choose a preferred combination instead. Similarly, as the price of an export good rises, consumers can either maintain their consumption levels of the export or buy more imports as an alternative.

4.5 INTERNATIONAL GENERAL EQUILIBRIUM

Now introduce a second country, referring to it as Country F, and call the original Country H. Fig. 4.5 shows an excess demand curve for Country F, E_x^*, placed arbitrarily above the excess demand curve for Country H, E_x. The autarky price ratio in Country F is p_a^*, greater than Country H's autarky price ratio, p_a.

General equilibrium in the world economy is then determined at an international price ratio where the excess demands of the two countries are equal and opposite. In Fig. 4.5, this occurs at price ratio p^*. At that price, the positive excess demand (imports) of the Foreign country are equal to the negative excess demand (exports) of the Home country. The market for X clears, which is a condition for international equilibrium: $E_x + E_x^* = 0$.[2]

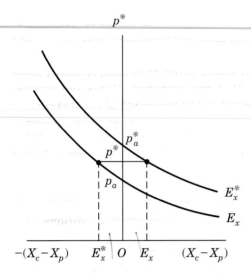

FIGURE 4.5
International general equilibrium.

Note for future reference that the equilibrium price lies between the autarky prices of the two countries.[3] This is a general result, at least in competitive models, and it makes economic sense. When two countries are combined through trade, X becomes relatively less scarce in the country with the initially high price because that country can now obtain the good through trade. Producers in the country in which X has the low price initially can now find additional buyers of their good through exports.

What about the market for Y? When we have only two goods and we impose a trade balance condition, we need examine only one market to find international equilibrium. If Country H is satisfying its trade balance condition, then $p_x^* E_x = -p_y^* E_y$ where the latter is the excess demand for Y by H. Similarly, if Country F is satisfying its trade balance, then $p_x^* E_x^* = -p_y^* E_y^*$. Thus, if $E_x = -E_x^*$, then $E_y = -E_y^*$. The need to find equilibrium in only one market is known as Walras' Law in economics.

The direction of trade at this equilibrium in Fig. 4.5 makes economic sense. With the relative autarky price of X higher in Country F, F will import X and H will export X in international equilibrium. We will see many times in the chapters that follow that differences in autarky prices are the key to determining the *direction of trade,* or which countries import and export which goods. A major topic of Part II of this book is determining how underlying characteristics of economies, such as technologies and factor endowments, lead to differences in autarky prices.

4.6 CONCLUDING REMARKS

This chapter draws on the tools of production and consumption theories developed in the previous two chapters and combines them to determine general equilibrium in closed and open economies. The following points summarize the key results of the chapter. You can use them as a review list.

1. Equilibrium in a closed economy is determined by three conditions: (*a*) producer optimization, (*b*) consumer optimization, and (*c*) market clearing.

2. If production and consumption are competitive, the closed economy equilibrium is efficient in the sense that the economy attains the highest community indifference curve subject to the feasibility of production.

3. International trade removes the constraint that an economy consumes only what it produces. It also replaces the market clearing condition for equilibrium with the much weaker condition that the value of total production must equal the value of total consumption. We show that this restriction is exactly equivalent to the restriction that the value of imports must equal the value of exports. Open economy equilibrium is determined by the producer and consumer optimization conditions plus the trade balance condition.

4. A country's willingness to trade with the rest of the world can be summarized by an excess demand function for one of the two goods (we chose X). This function gives the country's desired imports or exports at all possible price ratios. This curve slopes downward like a conventional demand curve, except that the quantity demanded can be either positive or negative. A negative excess demand simply means that the country wishes to export at a given price. Excess demand is zero at the country's autarky price, and movement away from autarky is welfare-improving.

5. A second country can be introduced and its excess demand curve derived. International equilibrium is found at the price where the exports of one country match the imports of the other country. This price is between the autarky price levels of the two countries. The autarky price differences determine the direction of trade, with the low-price country exporting the good and the high-price country importing the good.

6. We noted that, because of the trade balance restrictions, we need consider only one market to determine general equilibrium. If that market clears, so does the other market.

PROBLEMS

1. Suppose that the production frontier for a country is linear. Construct its excess demand curve.

2. Assume that a single consumer has an initial endowment of good X rather than a money income. Show the consumer's desired consumption bundles (and therefore desired trades) as the price ratio changes. Is it possible that the consumer may wish to sell less X as the relative price of X rises? (This is the "backward bending" issue.)

3. If you succeed in answering question 2, can you show that less X will be supplied as its price rises because the income effect of the price increase outweighs the substitution effect?

4. Suppose that the country in Fig. 4.1 grows in a "neutral" fashion such that its production frontier shifts out and the autarky price ratio remains unchanged. What happens to the country's excess demand curve in Fig. 4.4?

5. How will the growth described in question 4 change the equilibrium world price ratio in Fig. 4.5?

NOTES

1. In a dynamic model with many time periods, trade need not balance in any one time period. A country can consume more than it produces by selling *assets,* which can be thought of as claims to future consumption. The United States has been in a position of *trade deficit* for years, indicating that foreigners are accumulating United States assets and hence have a claim on future United States production. This is an important topic in international finance, but we will also discuss it in the last chapter of the book.
2. Because of the possibility of backward-bending sections of excess demand curves in the exporting region (i.e., negative excess demand) mentioned in the previous section, there is a possibility of multiple equilibria. This is also discussed in Appendix A on offer curves.
3. Later in the book we show that with imperfect competition, the free trade price for a good need not lie between the autarky prices of the two countries. Additional competition induced by trade may lead to a fall in the price of the good in both countries.

REFERENCES

Chipman, J. S. (1965). "A Survey of the Theory of International Trade: Part 2, The Neo-Classical Theory." *Econometrica* 33: 685–760.

Johnson, H. G. (1959). "International Trade, Income Distribution and the Offer Curve." *Manchester School* 27: 241–260.

Lerner, A. P. (1953). *Essays in Economic Analysis.* London: Macmillan.

Meade, J. E. (1952). *A Geometry of International Trade.* London: Allen & Unwin.

Melvin, J. R. (1985). "Domestic Taste Differences, Transportation Costs and International Trade." *Journal of International Economics* 18: 65–82.

CHAPTER
5

THE GAINS
FROM TRADE

5.1 GAINS FROM TRADE

We are now in a position to address one of the most fundamental issues in the study of international trade: the gains from trade. We will be able to show that under certain circumstances, a country's overall welfare is in some sense improved by international trade, which should thus be viewed as desirable. Yet the popular press often seems to assert that imports and trade are not beneficial for the national economy. Another popular view is that if one country gains though trade, the other country must lose. This is what economists would call a "zero-sum game": the gains to one player equal the losses to the other player. We will show that there is a wide range of circumstances in which all countries gain mutually from trade, circumstances in which trade is a "positive-sum game."

However, we will also show that not all individuals within a country will necessarily benefit from trade. In other words, while a country's total income is increased by trade, these gains may be very unevenly distributed to the point where some individuals or groups are worse off. A solid academic understanding of the gains from trade will have practical applications in evaluating various anti-trade arguments put forward by business, labor, and even government groups.

Figure 5.1 shows the production frontier and indifference curves for a single country. Autarky equilibrium occurs at point A, with the economy reaching utility level U_a.[1] Figure 5.1 also shows two alternative world trading price ratios, p_1^* and p_2^*. We have deliberately constructed the diagram so that these two world price ratios both lead to the same free trade utility

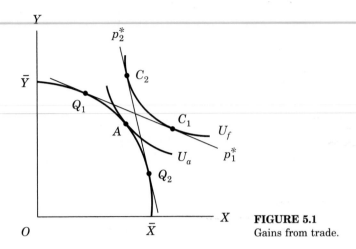

FIGURE 5.1
Gains from trade.

level, U_f. Figure 5.1 is not a formal proof, but it illustrates a result that can be proved more rigorously: *the ability of a country to trade at any price ratio other than its autarky prices must make the country better off.* Note also that if the world price ratio happens to equal the autarky price ratio, the country is no worse off. We encourage you to draw a few diagrams like Fig. 5.1 in order to convince yourself that any world price ratio other than the autarky ratio leads to gains. The result does require that the conditions of Eq. (4.4) hold; for example, the price ratio must be tangent to the production frontier. We will have more to say about this in the next section and in chapters to come.

Another thing to note in Fig. 5.1 is that the *direction* of trade is of no particular welfare significance. The utility level U_f can be achieved either through the export of Y in the case of world price ratio p_1^* or through the export of X in the case of world price ratio p_2^*. The only condition is that the world price ratio must differ from the domestic autarky ratio. Given any such difference, the country gains by exporting what is more valuable on world markets than at home and by importing from the rest of the world what is more costly to produce at home than abroad. This point is important in answering the many arguments that attach particular significance to what goods a country imports or exports. For example, you will hear arguments in the United States and Canada that it is good to export computers and bad to export agricultural and forestry products. But both countries have a huge comparative advantage in such products over countries in Europe and the Far East where land and resources are scarce. Figure 5.1 emphasizes that there is no significance to the direction of trade per se, and that arguments to the contrary should be greeted with great skepticism.

Returning to a point made in the first paragraph of this section, it also follows that two countries enjoy *mutual* gains from trade. Figure 4.5 of the previous chapter depicts a situation in which the equilibrium world price

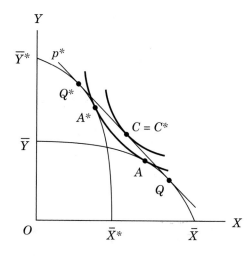

FIGURE 5.2
Mutual gains from trade.

ratio lies between the different autarky price ratios of two countries. In equilibrium, the world price ratio at which the countries trade is different from the autarky price ratio for each of them. It follows from our analysis of Fig. 5.1 that *both countries are made better off by trade.* Each country sells the product that it produces relatively cheaply and imports the product that is relatively costly to produce at home.

By constructing a very special case, Fig. 5.2 illustrates mutual gains and also makes the point that the direction of trade is of no significance. The two countries have identical preferences but different production frontiers. The production frontiers for Home and Foreign are given by $\overline{X}\,\overline{Y}$ and $\overline{X}^*\overline{Y}^*$, respectively. Home is relatively good at producing X, while Foreign is relatively good at producing Y. This difference is then reflected in their autarky price ratios, Home consuming at A and Foreign at A^* in Fig. 5.2. Free trade allows both of them to reach the same point $C = C^*$ at price ratio p^*, with Home producing at Q and Foreign producing at Q^*.

We emphasize that this is a very special case; in general there is no presumption that two countries will reach the same utility level through trade or that the gains from trade will be shared equally. The latter point will be made many times throughout the book. But the points that both countries do gain and that the direction of trade is not necessarily of any significance are general results.

5.2 THE GAINS-FROM-TRADE THEOREM[2]

We will now present a somewhat more formal treatment of the gains from trade. In particular we present a simple proof of what is called the gains-from-trade theorem. This helps make clear the assumptions necessary to ensure that a country gains from trade.

The diagrams that we have presented up to this point make use of the result from Chapter 2 that, in competitive equilibrium, the economy maximizes the value of production at equilibrium prices. That is, the economy attains the highest possible national budget line at equilibrium prices.[3] In Fig. 5.3, world prices p^* result in production at point Q for reasons discussed earlier. The value of production resulting from producing at any other point in the production set at price ratio p^* must be less than or equal to the value of producing at Q. In particular, we see that the value of production at Q is greater than the value of production at A, the autarky equilibrium.

Let superscript f denote quantities produced in free trade and superscript a denote the quantities produced in autarky. Subscript p denotes production as in Chapter 4. When the value of production is maximized at free trade prices, we have the following inequality:

$$p_x^* X_p^f + p_y^* Y_p^f \geq p_x^* X_p^a + p_y^* Y_p^a \tag{5.1}$$

In words, the value of free trade production at free trade prices exceeds the value of autarky production at free trade prices. This is the result shown in Fig. 5.3. In autarky we must have market clearing as noted in Eq. (4.1) of the previous chapter, while in free trade we must have trade balance as noted in Eq. (4.2) or Eq. (4.3). Using the latter form of the balance-of-trade equation, Eqs. (4.2) and (4.3) are rewritten here.

$$X_p^a = X_c^a, \qquad Y_p^a = Y_c^a, \qquad p_x^* X_p^f + p_y^* Y_p^f = p_x^* X_c^f + p_y^* Y_c^f \tag{5.2}$$

Now substitute the market clearing conditions into the right-hand side of Eq. (5.1), changing production quantities to consumption quantities. Similarly, substitute the trade balance equation in Eq. (5.2) into the left-hand side of Eq. (5.1), changing production quantities to consumption quantities. This transforms Eq. (5.1) into the following inequality.

$$p_x^* X_c^f + p_y^* Y_c^f \geq p_x^* X_c^a + p_y^* Y_c^a \tag{5.3}$$

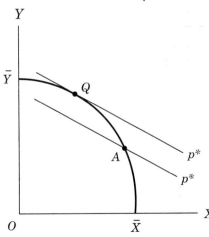

Y

$\bar{Y}$

Q

A

p^*

p^*

O $\bar{X}$ X

FIGURE 5.3
Maximization of the value of output at world prices.

This inequality states that the value of free trade consumption evaluated at free trade prices exceeds the value of autarky consumption evaluated at free trade prices. This means that in free trade, where consumers can choose the autarky consumption bundle (X_c^a, Y_c^a), they instead choose the free trade consumption bundle (X_c^f, Y_c^f), which costs at least as much. In Fig. 5.3 the autarky bundle lies on a lower national budget line; therefore, Eq. (5.3) holds as a *strict* inequality. Because the autarky bundle costs less, consumers would choose it if they preferred it to the free trade bundle. This means that the free trade consumption bundle is preferred to the autarky consumption bundle.[4] This result is known as the *Gains-from-Trade theorem.*

> **The Gains-from-Trade theorem.** Suppose that the value of production is maximized at free trade prices. Then the value of free trade consumption at free trade prices exceeds the value of autarky consumption at free trade prices. The free trade consumption bundle must thus be preferred to the autarky bundle, because if it were not, consumers would pick the cheaper autarky bundle.

It is extremely important to understand that this theorem is not trivial and also that there are many situations in which it fails to hold. In order to appreciate this, we need to examine more critically the result seen in Chapter 2 that the value of production is maximized at free trade prices. While this property may hold in ideal cases such as the simple competitive model of Chapter 2, it need not hold in more complex cases. Figures 5.4 and 5.5 illustrate two situations in which it does *not* hold. In Fig. 5.4 there is some distortion in the economy such that the world price ratio is not tangent to the production frontier. In such a situation, it is possible that

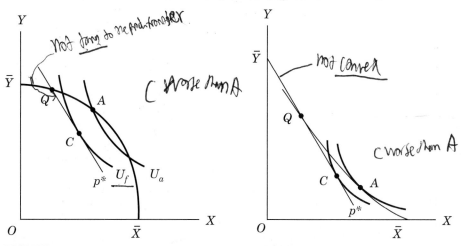

FIGURE 5.4
Failure of the "tangency condition."

FIGURE 5.5
Failure of the "convexity condition."

autarky consumption at *A* is superior to free trade consumption at *C*. The inequality in Eq. (5.1) does not hold, so neither does the one in Eq. (5.3). These inequalities thus require that the free trade price ratio be tangent to the production frontier when both goods are produced. (If only one good is produced, the price ratio must not pass inside the production set.) We can refer to this as the *tangency condition:* the free trade price ratio must be tangent to the production frontier in order to guarantee that the value of production is maximized at free trade prices.

Figure 5.5 illustrates the other key assumption, convexity of the production set. Figure 5.5 depicts free trade production at *Q* and consumption at *C*. This is inferior to autarky consumption at *A*. Again, the inequality in Eq. (5.1) does not hold. We can refer to this as the *convexity condition:* the production set must be convex in order to guarantee that the value of production is maximized at free trade prices.

We have seen that the tangency and convexity conditions are sufficient to ensure that the value of production is maximized at free trade prices. These conditions will generally hold in economies that have (1) constant returns to scale, (2) perfect competition, and (3) no other distortions such as certain production or factor taxes. The production set will be convex, and prices will be tangent to the production frontier, with the corresponding restriction holding when the economy is specialized. Later in the book we will see that difficulties arise when there are production taxes or imperfect competition. These can lead to a failure of the tangency condition. With increasing returns to scale or factor market distortions, the convexity condition may fail. We already noted the non-convexity in the presence of scale economies in Chapter 2.

We would like to close this section by strongly emphasizing that the existence of distortions or increasing returns does not mean that losses from trade are *likely;* it means only that they are *possible.* Indeed, scale economies and imperfect competition are major sources of gains from trade, as we shall show later.

5.3   THE GAINS FROM EXCHANGE

It turns out that the gains from trade can be conveniently broken down into gains from two distinct sources: gains from exchange and gains from specialization. The gains from exchange refer to the fact that if individuals or countries are endowed with different amounts of goods or have different preferences, they can both gain by trading with each other.

Suppose we have two individuals, Jim and Janet, and that Jim has six bottles of beer and no bags of peanuts, while Janet has five bags of peanuts but no beers. As shown in Fig. 5.6, Janet and Jim will both attain utility level U_a in their respective diagrams. But various possibilities exist for mutual gains. For example, Janet could give Jim three bags of peanuts for two beers. They would then move to point *C* in their respective diagrams, each attaining a utility level of U_f. An implicit trading price is established,

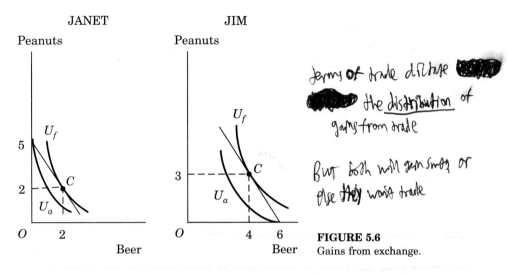

FIGURE 5.6
Gains from exchange.

Handwritten margin notes: terms of trade affect the distribution of gains from trade. But both will gain something or else they won't trade.

insofar as three bags of peanuts are deemed to be equal in value to two beers. Beer is relatively more valuable; the price of beer in terms of peanuts is $3/2 = 1.5$.

Other trades could have been arranged, such as two bags of peanuts for two beers, establishing a price ratio of 1. Obviously, Janet would prefer this trade, while Jim would prefer the one mentioned in the previous paragraph. Different trades affect the *distribution* of gains between the traders, and stronger or smarter traders will tend to move the terms of trade to their advantage, as we will discuss in later chapters. The important point here is that both individuals will gain something from voluntary trade (otherwise they would not trade); that is, voluntary trade is mutually beneficial. As we discussed at the outset of the chapter, this point is extremely important in countering the popular opinion that any gain from trade by one country must be another's loss. It is not true that a consumption gain by Japan or the United States in trading with Canada must mean an equivalent loss for someone in Canada. Trade results in mutual gains, as we have just shown.

This result can be demonstrated more formally with the kind of box diagram shown in Fig. 5.7 (similar to the box diagrams in Chapter 3). The two goods are again X and Y, and the two individuals are 1 and 2. The initial endowment point is point E. The welfare levels of 1 and 2 at this endowment point are given by U_a^1 and U_a^2, respectively. You should be able to convince yourself that moving from E to any point in the interior of the "lens" formed by U_a^1 and U_a^2 will make both individuals better off. But not all of the possible moves are Pareto optimal—that is, moves after which we could not make one individual better off without making the other one worse off. Beginning at E in Fig. 5.7, the set of Pareto optimal trades is given by the segment of the contract curve between A and A', where indifference curves are tangent. Point F illustrates one possible Pareto optimal trading equilibrium between A and A' at which gains are shared fairly equally. As

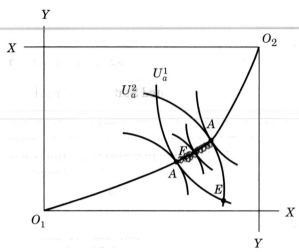

FIGURE 5.7
Cooperation and conflict.

discussed earlier, in other trades between A and A' the gains shift more toward one trader or the other, but both still do gain. The existence of many possible beneficial trades, differing in the distribution of gains, implies that there is some element of conflict as well as an element of cooperation in trade.

5.4   THE GAINS FROM SPECIALIZATION

The previous section assumed that the total quantities of all goods were fixed. In fact, individuals or countries can generally increase total production and realize additional gains by specializing in the goods they produce most efficiently. This proposition is usually fairly obvious in the case of individuals. In modern society no one is self-sufficient, and indeed, most people engage in an extremely narrow range of work activities in order to earn income to buy a wide range of goods and services. Everyone seems to grasp the idea that we would have a much lower standard of living if people all tried to grow their own food, make their own clothes, build their own houses, and so forth. Specialization in a narrow range of activities is efficient.

The same principle holds true for countries, although people seem to lose sight of this fact. One frequently hears arguments in the United States to the effect that we should be producing a certain good rather than importing it from abroad. Consider a simple example in which we have two countries, the United States and Japan, that produce two goods, wheat and steel. Suppose that the number of tons of wheat or steel that one person can produce per year in each country is given in Table 5.1. One labor-year devoted to wheat production in the United States results in 30 tons of wheat, and so forth.

The United States is relatively more productive in wheat, and Japan is relatively more productive in steel. Using terminology familiar to most readers, the *opportunity cost* of producing one more ton of steel is three tons of wheat in the United States, but only 1 ton of wheat in Japan. Japan has an advantage in steel in the sense of being the *low opportunity cost* producer of steel. Suppose we now move one worker in the United States out of steel production and into wheat production. Similarly, we move one Japanese worker out of wheat production and into steel production. Changes in outputs following this reallocation are given in Table 5.2. The table shows that simply moving workers in each country into the industry in which the country has the advantage (its low opportunity-cost industry) results in an increase in the world outputs of *both* goods. The countries may then engage in trade that leaves both better off.

Now suppose that Japan is more productive in both goods. Do gains from specialization still exist? The answer is a definite yes, as was first pointed out by the 19-century British economist David Ricardo. Let us double the productivities of Japanese workers shown in Table 5.1. We will now have the situation in Table 5.3. In this example Japan is said to have an *absolute advantage* in both goods, whereas in Table 5.1 the United States had an absolute advantage in wheat and Japan an absolute advantage in steel. But in both cases the United States is said to have a *comparative advantage* in wheat, meaning that the American economy is *relatively* more productive in wheat; the United States can produce 1 ton of wheat at an opportunity cost of $\frac{1}{3}$ ton of steel, whereas in Japan the opportunity cost of 1 ton of wheat is 1 ton of steel.

> **Definition.** A country has an *absolute advantage* in good X if one unit of labor produces more X than is produced by one unit of labor in the other country. A country has a *comparative advantage* in X if its opportunity cost of X in terms of Y is less than in the other country.

Ricardo noted that as long as some pattern of comparative advantage exists, there will be gains from trade, regardless of whether one country has an absolute advantage in all goods. To see this, suppose we now reallocate two workers in the United States from steel to wheat and one worker in Japan from wheat to steel. The resulting changes in outputs

TABLE 5.1
One labor-year of production

	U.S.	Japan
Wheat	30	20
Steel	10	20

TABLE 5.2
Changes in outputs due to reallocation of one worker

	U.S.	Japan	Total
Wheat	+30	−20	+10
Steel	−10	+20	+10

TABLE 5.3
One labor-year of production

	U.S.	Japan
Wheat	30	40
Steel	10	40

TABLE 5.4
Changes in outputs due to reallocation of two workers in United States, one in Japan

	U.S.	Japan	Total
Wheat	+60	−40	+20
Steel	−20	+40	+20

are given in Table 5.4. Once again, we see that the total outputs of both goods can be increased if both countries specialize according to their patterns of comparative advantage. Gains from specialization will always exist if countries have different opportunity costs (i.e., if there exists some pattern of comparative advantage).

Figure 5.8 summarizes our discussion by showing how the total gains from trade can be decomposed into gains from exchange and gains from specialization. Point A gives the autarky production/consumption point, and U_a gives the autarky utility level. Suppose the economy can now trade at prices p^*, and suppose that the economy cannot change its output levels (production is fixed at A). Gains from exchange can still be realized by trading to point E. The movement from A to E and the increase in utility from U_a to U_e illustrate the gains from exchange. But further gains can be realized if we move the production point to Q, showing relatively more specialization in good X. The movement from E to C and the increase in utility from U_e to U_f illustrate the gains from specialization.

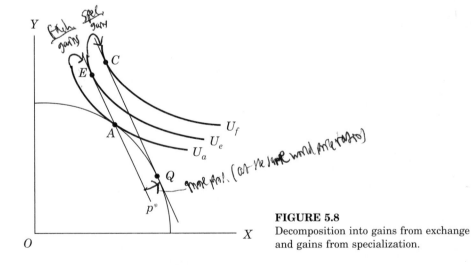

FIGURE 5.8
Decomposition into gains from exchange and gains from specialization.

5.5 THE DISTRIBUTION OF GAINS
WITH HETEROGENEOUS TASTES[5]

The preceding sections have shown that a country will gain from international trade in the sense that it can potentially consume more of both goods. The gains were illustrated with the use of community indifference curves, although the main argument can be made without them. But while trade may result in aggregate consumption gains, these gains are not necessarily distributed evenly among the members of a society. Indeed, it is possible that certain groups will actually be worse off in a situation of free trade than in an autarky or a restricted trade situation. These possibilities must be understood when you are evaluating certain trade policy questions.

One possibility occurs when individuals in a society have very different tastes. Suppose that all individuals in the society have identical factor endowments and therefore identical incomes and budget lines. Suppose that the world price ratio exceeds the price ratio that would prevail in autarky $(p^* > p_a)$ so that the country exports X and imports Y (as in Fig. 5.1 with $p^* = p_2^*$). Now consider two individuals with different tastes (but identical incomes). Let AA' in Fig. 5.9 be the identical autarky budget line for both individuals. Individual 1 has a high preference for Y and so chooses autarky consumption bundle A_1. Individual 2 has a high preference for X and therefore chooses bundle A_2. Their utility levels are given by U_a^1 and U_a^2, respectively.

As was shown in Fig. 5.1 $(p^* = p_2^*)$, trade has the effect of raising the relative price of X, which we illustrate in Fig. 5.9 by rotating the budget line to TT'. Individual 1 increases her consumption from A_1 to T_1 and experiences an increase in welfare from U_a^1 to U_f^1. But the increased price for X has affected individual 2 so adversely that his consumption falls from A_2 to T_2 and his welfare from U_a^2 to U_f^2. Thus, when individuals have heterogeneous tastes, the gains from trade will be distributed unevenly, and some groups may indeed become worse off.

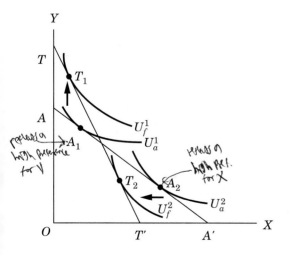

FIGURE 5.9
Distribution of gains with heterogeneous preferences.

One example of this problem was the entry of Great Britain into the European Economic Community (EEC) in the early 1970s. Prior to entering, Great Britain had imported inexpensive food from countries such as New Zealand and Australia. After entering, the British were forced to pay much higher European prices for many foods, especially meat. In exchange for this, the British were able to purchase a wider range of manufactured goods at cheaper prices. The net benefit to a household would surely depend on the household's income, number of children, and so on. It is likely that some large families with low incomes that were spending a large fraction of family income on food were made worse off by entering the EEC.

5.6 THE DISTRIBUTION OF GAINS WITH HETEROGENEOUS ENDOWMENTS

A second example of uneven distribution of gains from trade occurs when individuals differ widely in their factor endowments. Suppose that society is comprised of two distinct groups, capitalists and laborers, and that laborers own no capital and capitalists perform no labor. Assume also that X is labor-intensive and that Y is capital-intensive.

Budget lines for laborers and capitalists are shown in Fig. 5.10, with each group's initial autarky income constraint given by AA' and each group's initial welfare level by U_a. Now assume that trade raises the price of X as in Fig. 5.1 from p_a to p_2^*. The economy responds to this change by shifting resources out of Y production and into X production. The outputs of the economy move from point A in Fig. 5.1 to point Q_2.

In a later chapter, we will show that this increase in the output of X, the labor-intensive good, leads to an increase in the demand for and price of

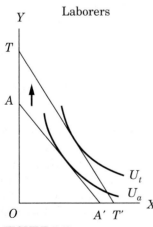

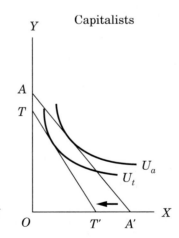

FIGURE 5.10
Distribution of gains with heterogeneous endowments.

labor. Similarly, the decrease in the production of Y, the capital-intensive good, leads to an overall decrease in the demand for and price of capital. The commodity price changes caused by trade in turn cause factor price changes. In these circumstances the budget line of laborers will shift out everywhere as in Fig. 5.10. Laborers will be better off even if they wish to consume only X, the good whose price has risen with trade. Conversely, the budget line of capitalists may shift in everywhere because of the decrease in the price of capital and the subsequent decreases in capitalists' incomes. Capitalists thus lose from the income redistribution caused by trade.

A good example of income redistribution caused by international price changes occurred in the United States during the 1970s. The redistribution among states and among economic groups resulted from the oil price increases that occurred during that decade. The energy-producing states realized huge gains from the price changes, while the energy-consuming states were certainly much worse off.

5.7 CONCLUDING REMARKS

This chapter develops one of the most important ideas of international trade theory, the proposition that countries can benefit mutually from free trade. You should now be able to counter many of the anti-trade arguments you read in the press (which is often simply reporting the speeches of politicians and labor and business leaders). Nevertheless, some arguments may raise valid concerns about free trade. Gains from trade can be distributed very unevenly and, in the absence of some redistribution plan, some groups within society have legitimate fears. The following points summarize the principal concepts of the chapter.

1. Countries can gain from trade if they can trade at any prices different from their autarky prices. Any price difference allows a country to gain by selling what is relatively more valuable on world markets and buying on world markets what is relatively more costly to produce at home.

2. There is no particular welfare significance to the direction of trade. International price differences determine the most efficient direction of trade. Canada and the United States gain from exporting primary products because they are very efficient at producing them.

3. Gains from trade are mutual. The gains by one country are not at the expense of other countries. As we noted in Fig. 5.7, there are generally many trades that can leave both parties better off. Each possible trade leads to a different distribution of the gains, with the result that there is some element of conflict as well as an element of cooperation in international trade.

4. We emphasized that there are certain assumptions needed to prove the gains-from-trade theorem. When there are various distortions such as taxes or imperfect competition, or when there are non-convexities due to scale economies, gains cannot be guaranteed. On the other hand,

we will argue later in the book that scale economies and imperfect competition are nevertheless likely to be very important sources of gains from trade. Thus, these problems do not argue against trade; they simply emphasize that corrective domestic policies may need to accompany free trade agreements. Much more will be said in later chapters.

5. The gains from trade can be broken down into gains from exchange and gains from specialization. Exchange allows consumers to exploit the differences in their endowments or preferences. Specialization allows the world to produce more of all goods by allowing each country to concentrate on what it does best (produce goods for which it has a low opportunity cost).

6. The gains from trade will not be shared equally by all citizens of a country. Because individuals have different tastes or different endowments (recall that trade changes factor prices), some individuals may even be worse off. In the absence of income redistribution to compensate the losers, some groups will rationally oppose any move to free trade or lobby hard for protection. This will be a key point in our discussions of the political economy of trade policy in later chapters.

PROBLEMS

1. Show that a country gains increasingly from trade as the world price ratio departs further from the autarky price ratio.
2. Derive the inequality in Eq. (5.3) using Eqs. (5.1) and (5.2).
3. Suppose that we change Fig. 5.2, making preferences different in the two countries such that Home has an autarky equilibrium at Q and Foreign has an autarky equilibrium at Q^*. Is it possible for the countries to gain from trade?
4. Use the Jim and Janet example of Fig. 5.6 to prove that if three bags of peanuts trade for two beers, the price of beer in terms of peanuts is $3/2 = 1.5$, not $2/3 = .67$.
5. With reference to Section 5.4, show that if there is no pattern of comparative advantage (the ratios of wheat to steel production are the same in the two countries), then no gains from specialization exist.
6. Redraw Fig. 5.8 for the case in which the world price ratio is less than the autarky price ratio. (If you can't do this, you don't really understand the diagrams.)
7. Suppose we know that with trade the total amounts of both goods consumed exceed the amounts consumed in autarky. With reference to either Section 5.5 or 5.6, can you prove that the group that is better off with trade could compensate the losers so that both groups end up better off relative to autarky?

NOTES

1. Note that we never observe an autarky equilibrium in the "real world" (although trade is severely restricted in many countries). We use the autarky equilibrium as a conceptual device: in order to understand the effects of trade, we consider what would happen in the complete absence of trade.

2. This section is more advanced and can be skipped without loss of continuity. However, the same methodology will be used often in more advanced sections of the book. An investment in time at this point could have a payoff later in the book.
3. To use more technical terminology, in competitive equilibrium the world price ratio is *supporting* to the production set. Basically, this just means that the set of all feasible production points lies on, or on the same side of, the world price ratio. (If you turn Fig. 5.3 over, you see that the production set sits on the price ratio; i.e., the price ratio "supports" the production set.)
4. Some readers will recognize this as a *revealed preference* argument: the consumers could have chosen the autarky bundle, but instead chose the more expensive free trade bundle, thus revealing that they prefer the free trade consumption bundle.
5. A more advanced analysis of the distribution of gains among individuals is given by Chacholiades (1978), Chapter 12.

REFERENCES

Chacholiades, M. (1978). *International Trade Theory and Policy*. New York: McGraw-Hill.

Kemp, M. C. (1969). *The Pure Theory of International Trade and Investment*. Englewood Cliffs, N.J.: Prentice-Hall.

Markusen, J. R. and Melvin, J. R. (1985). "The Gains-from-Trade Theorem with Increasing Returns to Scale", in H. Kierzkowski (editor), *Monopolistic Competition in International Trade*. London: Oxford University Press.

Samuelson, P. A. (1939). "The Gains from International Trade." *Canadian Journal of Economics and Political Science* 5: 195–205.

———. (1962). "The Gains from International Trade Once Again." *Economic Journal* 72: 820–829.

PART
II

CAUSES AND CONSEQUENCES OF TRADE

CHAPTER
6

THE CAUSES OF
INTERNATIONAL
TRADE

no trade → 1) all autarky price ratios identical
2) no scale economies

6.1 THE NO-TRADE MODEL

In the previous chapter, we emphasized that countries gain from trade by importing what is relatively costly to produce at home and by exporting what is produced relatively cheaply (efficiently) at home. But what are the underlying characteristics of an economy that give it its pattern of comparative advantage? Part 2 of this book, comprised of Chapters 6–13, turns to this question. These chapters, with the exception of Chapter 12, examine alternative sources of national differences that can give rise to trade. Chapter 12 focuses on scale economies, which can give rise to trade even between identical economies. Part 2 of the book is thus concerned with the determinants of the direction of trade, those characteristics that determine the pattern of imports and exports by particular countries.

In fact, the trade of any country is a complex outcome of many causes all operating at the same time. There is generally no single cause of trade, but in order to understand the overall picture, we need to study how each possible cause of trade operates in isolation. The empirical question of which particular determinant of trade is the most important for a particular country is addressed in Chapter 14.

A convenient method of examining the causes of trade is to first imagine a world in which there is no trade. In terms of our simple model, this would be true if all autarky price ratios were identical and there were no scale economies. Thus, we begin by imagining a situation in which all countries have identical, convex production sets and in which the same set

Prod. Pos. curve is determined by: 1) homogeneity
2) factor endowments
3) production functions

of community indifference curves prevails in all countries. We are assuming that any two countries can be represented by the situation shown in Fig. 6.1.

What assumptions are necessary to ensure that the demand and supply situations in all countries are identical? This question is easily answered by recalling from Chapters 2 and 3 the underlying assumptions that were made in deriving the production possibility curve and the community indifference curves. On the demand side it is sufficient to assume that identical and homogeneous tastes exist throughout the world. On the production side three conditions determine the position and shape of the production possibility curve: degree of homogeneity, factor endowments, and production functions. Thus, to achieve identical production possibility curves in all countries, it is sufficient to assume that all countries have the same constant-returns production functions and that all countries have the same factor endowments. These assumptions will give the same aggregate demand and supply relationships in all countries, but there is one further restriction that we must impose. We are seeking conditions that will make commodity price ratios the same in all countries, and this will be the case only if commodity prices are determined by aggregate demand and supply. We must, in other words, ensure that equilibrium prices are determined by the tangency between the highest community indifference curve and the production possibility curve as shown in Fig. 6.1, and to ensure this we assume that there are no distortions in the model. Distortions include taxes, subsidies, and imperfect competition. We can write down a set of five conditions that together guarantee the no-trade situation. These are

1. Identical production functions among countries
2. The same relative endowments in all countries

[margin notes: Thus to get identical supply & demand conditions. Shape + homogeneity types exist in the world. — 1) Same constant returns prod. functions. 2) Same factor endowments]

[margin: assuming no distortions in comm. prices (taxes, subs, etc.)]

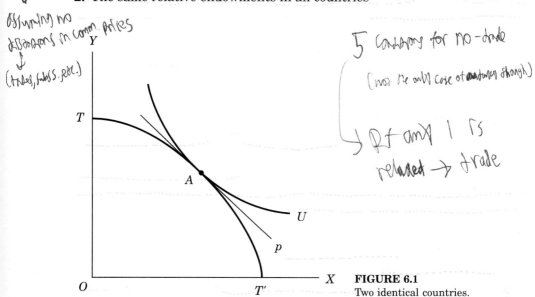

[handwritten: 5 conditions for no-trade (not the only case of autarky though) → But any 1 is relaxed → trade]

FIGURE 6.1
Two identical countries.

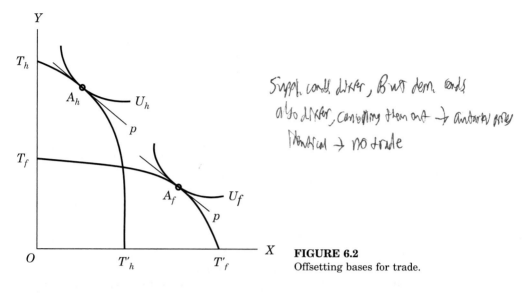

Suppl. cond. differ, But dem. ends also differ, canceling them out → autarky price. Identical → no trade

FIGURE 6.2
Offsetting bases for trade.

3. Constant returns to scale
4. Identical and homogeneous tastes in all countries
5. The absence of distortions (e.g., taxes, subsidies, imperfect competition)

While these five conditions are sufficient to imply that there will be no trade, there are obviously many other models that could be invented in which autarky prices would be identical so that no trade would take place. In other words, while this set of assumptions will guarantee no trade, it is not the only set of assumptions that will do so. This is illustrated in Fig. 6.2, where subscripts h and f refer to the countries H and F, respectively. Production conditions are clearly different in the two countries, with H producing relatively more Y and F relatively more X at any common price ratio. Demand conditions also differ, however, and in the situation shown, these differences are just enough to offset the production conditions, leaving autarky prices identical.

The real importance of these five conditions is not that they describe a world in which there will be no trade, for such a situation is not of much interest, but that they summarize the various things that can *cause* trade. If any one of the five conditions is relaxed, a situation will arise in which trade will be possible. These five conditions can therefore be thought of as the five broadly defined determinants of, or *bases* for, trade. The next seven chapters will investigate how the relaxation of each of these five assumptions can give rise to international trade and will discuss the implications of the models derived in each situation.

6.2 SOME METHODOLOGICAL CONSIDERATIONS

In the last section it was argued that the relaxation of any one of the five assumptions listed will give rise to a situation in which international trade can take place. To illustrate this, we will relax each of the assumptions in turn, maintaining all four of the others, and examine the implications for international trade. This approach is sometimes criticized as being unrealistic in the sense that the models generated do not accurately describe the real world. To assess the relevance of this criticism, we must understand precisely why this approach is being employed and what kinds of conclusions we expect to draw from the analysis.

It is clear that no conclusions about a specific cause of trade can be derived unless we can be sure that no other things are causing trade at the same time. For example, we could not identify the effects of demand differences in a model in which endowments were also different, for it would generally be impossible to separate the effects of these two variables. This is the situation of Fig. 6.2, where the two conditions are offsetting, resulting in identical autarky prices. Our analysis can be thought of as a kind of theoretical experiment in which, in order to study the effects of one variable, all other variables are neutralized.

At this stage of the analysis, then, the question of whether the model is "realistic" is not a relevant one, for no claim has been made about its predictive powers. In each of the models developed in subsequent chapters, the strict assumptions made are necessary in order to isolate the effects of the particular determinant being examined. The assumptions of no distortions, identical production functions, and so on, are made not to describe the real world but to allow individual determinants to be considered in isolation.

While developing realistic models is not necessary for the kind of *theoretical* experiments that we have just described, it is the principal focus of *empirical* analysis. If we were interested in empirical tests of trade models, we would be faced with determining a set of assumptions appropriate for a model used to explain real-world trade flows. If the implications of the various determinants of trade models are different, then we would ideally include any variable that can cause trade. In practice, of course, some simplification is necessary, and each investigator has to decide which variables are important and how the model should be constructed.

To strengthen this last point, consider the fact that *none* of the five conditions holds between any two countries in the world (although in some cases, a condition can be "close" to holding). In comparing the characteristics of North America, the European Union, and Africa, for example, we would find that the United States and Canada have a higher ratio of land endowment to labor endowment relative to Europe. North America and Europe have superior technology and higher endowments of physical and human capital relative to unskilled labor when compared to Africa. We would find that many important industries such as aircraft, autos, and chemicals have strong scale economies. We would find that tastes differ across countries and are far from homogeneous in any one country. (For example, the share of income spent on food declines steadily with per capita income.) Countries have tax systems that differ significantly from one another, and many industries (generally those with strong scale economies) are characterized by small numbers of firms and significant imperfect competition.

The assumption that two countries have only one basis for trade (only one of the five conditions fails to hold) is made for the purposes of understanding that basis' individual contributions to determining trade. It is the job of empirical analysis to determine the quantitative importance of the five bases for trade.

CHAPTER
7

DIFFERENCES
IN TECHNOLOGY

7.1 A SIMPLE MODEL OF PRODUCTION FUNCTION DIFFERENCES

→ i.e. tech.: amount of output derived from input factors

The determinants-of-trade question will be analyzed in the next seven chapters by relaxing, in turn, each of the five assumptions from Chapter 6 and examining the implications for international trade. The first model we consider is one in which production functions (technologies) differ across countries. This model is often associated with 19th-century British economist David Ricardo. In order to keep the model simple and the focus as clear as possible, we will assume that labor is the only factor of production. By differences in technology, we mean that the amount of output that can be obtained from one unit of labor differs across countries. The one-factor model can be thought of as a special case of condition 2 of the previous chapter: with one factor, the issue of differences in relative endowments does not arise.[1]

Constant returns to scale are assumed. In terms of the production functions of Chapter 2, a one-factor model with constant returns will have a linear production possibility frontier. As we will see later, this assumption significantly simplifies the analysis. We also impose the remaining conditions of Chapter 6: there are no distortions such as imperfect competition or taxes, and tastes are identical and homogeneous (the last assumption is not actually needed for any of the principal results).

84

7.2 ABSOLUTE AND COMPARATIVE ADVANTAGE

The Ricardian model assumes that labor is the only constraint on the production process. Thus, assuming that two goods, X and Y, are produced, the production functions and the labor constraint can be written as

$$X = F_x(L_x) \tag{7.1}$$
$$Y = F_y(L_y) \tag{7.2}$$
$$\overline{L} = L_x + L_y \tag{7.3}$$

We assume that the production functions are characterized by constant returns to scale, and this implies that Eqs. (7.1) and (7.2) take the simple forms

$$X = \alpha L_x \tag{7.4}$$
$$Y = \beta L_y \tag{7.5}$$

where α and β are some positive constants. The assumption that production functions differ between countries implies that the values of α and β will be different in the two countries. Note that α and β are the *marginal products of labor* in industries X and Y respectively: α and β give the additional outputs obtained from one unit of labor.

The Ricardian approach is illustrated in Table 7.1 (similar to Table 5.1), where we show the outputs of X and Y produced from one unit of labor in two countries, H and F. It is assumed that in Country H, 20 units of X are produced from one unit of labor, whereas $30\,X$ can be produced in Country F with one unit of labor. Home produces $20\ Y$ from one unit of labor, while Foreign produces $10\ Y$ from one unit of labor.

It can be shown that in this situation, profitable production specialization is possible for both countries. Country F has an advantage in the production of X, while Country H has an advantage in the production of Y. We can imagine a situation in which Country F specializes in X and Country H specializes in Y and in which consumers in both countries maximize their welfare through international trade. Using the terminology of Chapter 5, F is said to have an *absolute advantage* in the production of X: $\alpha_h < \alpha_f$. H is said to have an absolute advantage in the production of Y: $\beta_h > \beta_f$.

TABLE 7.1
Marginal products of labor

	Home	Foreign
X	$\alpha_h = 20$	$\alpha_f = 30$
Y	$\beta_h = 20$	$\beta_f = 10$

TABLE 7.2
Changes in outputs due to labor reallocation of one worker from X to Y in Country H and one worker from Y to X in Country F

	Home	Foreign	Total
X	-20	$+30$	$+10$
Y	$+20$	-10	$+10$

Table 7.2 shows the possibility of increasing world production of *both* commodities through specialization. If we move one worker from X to Y in Home and one worker from Y to X in Foreign, the total world production of each commodity rises by 10 units.

Now consider Table 7.3, where we again show the outputs of X and Y produced from one unit of labor in two countries, but where we have changed the marginal products of labor in X and Y in Country H from 20 to 5. Now Country F is more efficient in the production of both commodities, so it is said to have an absolute advantage in the production of both X and Y. The question that now arises is whether profitable trade is still possible in this situation. The same type of exercise we performed in Chapter 5 will convince us that it is, for we observe that while Country H has an absolute disadvantage in the production of both commodities, there is a *comparative advantage* for H in the production of commodity Y : $\beta_h/\alpha_h > \beta_f/\alpha_f$. In Country F, three units of X must be sacrificed to produce one unit of Y, but in Country H, only one unit of X must be sacrificed to produce a unit of Y. The opportunity cost to Country F of producing a unit of Y is three times as much as in Country H.

Table 7.4 illustrates that there are still production efficiency gains to be captured by the two countries. In Table 7.4, we perform an experiment similar to that in Table 7.2, except that we move four workers from X to Y in Country H and one worker from Y to X in Country F. The total world outputs of both goods rise, demonstrating that there are still gains from specialization to be captured even if one country is more efficient at producing both goods. Table 7.4 illustrates the principle of comparative advantage, which we defined in Chapter 5. What is needed to ensure gains from specialization is

TABLE 7.3
Marginal products of labor

	Home	Foreign
X	$\alpha_h = 5$	$\alpha_f = 30$
Y	$\beta_h = 5$	$\beta_f = 10$

TABLE 7.4
Changes in outputs due to labor reallocation of four workers from X to Y in Country H and one worker from Y to X in Country F

	Home	Foreign	Total
X	-20	$+30$	$+10$
Y	$+20$	-10	$+10$

a pattern of comparative advantage, by which we mean that the *ratios* of the marginal products of labor differ in the two countries.

7.3 THE PRODUCTION POSSIBILITY FRONTIER

Figure 7.1 illustrates the production frontiers for countries H and F based on the pattern of comparative advantage indicated in Table 7.1. Let $\bar{L}_h$ and $\bar{L}_f$ denote the labor endowments of countries H and F, respectively. The production frontier for Country H, HH', has a maximum X output of $\alpha_h \bar{L}_h$ and a maximum Y output of $\beta_h \bar{L}_h$. The production frontier for Country F, FF', has a maximum X output of $\alpha_f \bar{L}_f$ and a maximum Y output of $\beta_f \bar{L}_f$. The distance of a country's production frontier from the origin depends on the absolute levels of its labor productivity coefficients (α, β) and on its labor endowment $(\bar{L})$.

    The slope of a country's production frontier is simply the ratio of that country's labor productivity coefficients: $-\Delta Y / \Delta X = \beta / \alpha$. In autarky, Home and Foreign are in equilibrium at points A_h and A_f, respectively. This simple Ricardian model with linear production frontiers has the property that a country's autarky price ratio is given by the slope of its production frontier.[2] Because the slope of the production frontier reflects a country's comparative

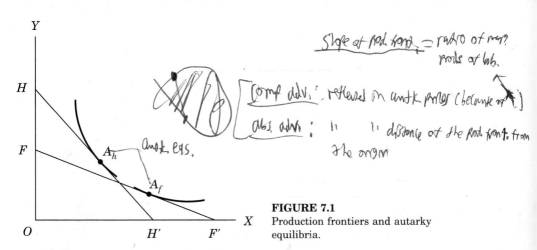

FIGURE 7.1
Production frontiers and autarky equilibria.

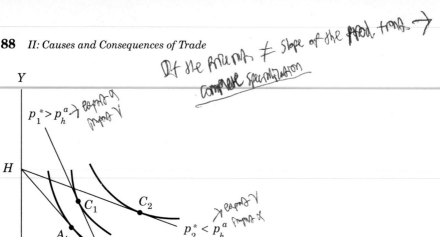

[handwritten annotations: "Df the return rate ≠ slope of the prod trans →", "complete specialization", "$p_1^* > p_h^a$ → export Y, import Y", "export Y, import X", "$p_2^* < p_h^a$"]

FIGURE 7.2
Specialization at alternative world price
ratios.

advantage, *autarky prices reflect comparative advantage.* Absolute advantage is reflected in the distance of the production frontier from the origin, as
just noted.

Figure 7.2 considers how Country H will respond to the possibility of
trade. The first important point is that if the world price ratio p^* happens to
equal the domestic autarky price ratio p_h^a, then H will wish to consume at
A_h but will be indifferent to producing at any point between and including
H and H' on the production frontier. For example, H could specialize in
Y and produce at H in Fig. 7.2, exporting Y and importing X to reach
consumption point A_h. Or it could just as well specialize in X at point H' in
Fig. 7.2, exporting X and importing Y.

What about trade at world price ratios that differ from the autarky
price ratios? At any price ratio p^* that differs from the slope of the production
frontier, a country will specialize completely. At the world price ratio $p_1^* > p_h^a$
in Fig. 7.2, H will specialize in X at point H', exporting X and importing
Y to reach consumption point C_1. At the world price ratio $p_2^* < p_h^a$, H will
specialize in Y at point H in Fig. 7.2, exporting Y and importing X to reach
consumption point C_2. In order to see that specialization is an equilibrium
when p^* differs from p_h^a, recall from Eq. (2.12) of Chapter 2 that the slope
of the production frontier is the ratio of the marginal products of labor in
the two industries: MRT = $\text{MP}_{LY}/\text{MP}_{LX}$ = β/α. Thus, if the price ratio is
steeper than the production frontier, as it is in the case of p_1^* in Fig. 7.2,
then we must have

$$\frac{p_x^*}{p_y^*} > \text{MRT} = \frac{\beta}{\alpha} \Rightarrow p_x^* \alpha > p_y^* \beta \qquad (7.6)$$

The value of the marginal product of labor in X is greater than the value
of the marginal product of labor in Y. The only way to ensure equilibrium
is to produce X with the equilibrium wage w equal to the value of labor's
marginal product in X. Y is then unprofitable and is not produced. It cannot be the other way around, because if w were equal to $p_y \beta$, then $p_x \alpha$ would

exceed w, and it would be profitable for a firm to enter the X industry. Equilibrium with $p^* > p^a$ is thus given by

$$p_x^* \alpha = w > p_y^* \beta \Rightarrow X = \overline{X}, \qquad Y = 0 \qquad (7.7)$$

where $\overline{X}$ is the economy's maximum output of X (H' in Fig. 7.2).

7.4 EXCESS DEMAND AND INTERNATIONAL EQUILIBRIUM

The fact that countries *can* potentially gain from trade does not necessarily ensure that they *will* in fact capture these gains. The purpose of this section is to examine a competitive equilibrium between two countries and show that in general, both gain. As we will show in the next section, the worst outcome for one country is for it to capture zero gains, but it cannot be made worse off through trade in a competitive, distortion-free world.

Results from the previous section are transferred to an excess demand diagram in Fig. 7.3. The "flat" section of Country H's excess demand curve at its autarky price ratio p_h^a corresponds to the results discussed in connection with Fig. 7.2: at the autarky price ratio, H will consume at A_h but will be indifferent to producing at any point on its production frontier HH'. The distance OH' in Fig. 7.2 thus corresponds to the distance $H'H$ in Fig. 7.3. This horizontal section of the excess demand curve is of some interest, as we shall see shortly.

At world price ratios p^* greater than p_h^a, H will wish to export X. p_1^* in Fig. 7.3 corresponds to p_1^* in Fig. 7.2. At world price ratios p^* less than p_h^a, H will wish to import X. p_2^* in Fig. 7.3 corresponds to p_2^* in Fig. 7.2.

Figure 7.4 presents the excess demand curves for both countries based on their production frontiers in Fig. 7.1. Each excess demand curve has a flat

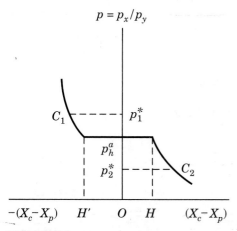

FIGURE 7.3
Country H's excess demand curve.

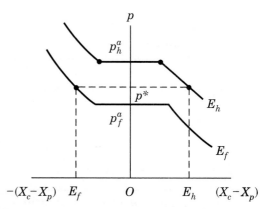

FIGURE 7.4
International equilibrium.

section at that country's autarky price. In the situation shown in Fig. 7.4, international equilibrium occurs at price ratio p^* at which the import demand of H $(E_h > 0)$ matches the export supply $(E_f < 0)$ of Country F. As we discussed earlier in the book, the equilibrium world price ratio falls between the autarky price ratios of the two countries. If this were not the case, then both countries would want either to import or export the same good. For example, if $p^* > p_h^a$, then both countries would wish to export X, which cannot result in an equilibrium.

We know from Chapter 5 that when the free trade price ratio differs from each country's autarky price ratio, as in Fig. 7.4, both countries must gain from trade. However, the gains from trade are not necessarily distributed "evenly" (whatever that might mean), and the country that trades farther away from its autarky price ratio gains more than the other.

7.5 THE ROLE OF WAGES

We have shown that in the Ricardian model, comparative advantage is determined simply by the relative productivity of labor in producing commodities, or, equivalently, by international differences in production functions. It may seem surprising that wage rates did not enter the discussion. After all, there has been much concern expressed in high-income economies about the possible effects of competition from low-wage workers in developing countries. In this section we examine the role of wages in the Ricardian framework. We will show that in this model, international differences must adjust to reflect underlying real productivity differences, but that all workers gain real income in moving from autarky to free trade. However, more productive economies do enjoy higher real wages in equilibrium.

Begin with a simple observation about wages in autarky in the Home country, for example. Because of perfect competition, the value of the marginal product of labor must equal the wage rate in each sector, as we have discussed before.

$$p_x^a \alpha_h = w_h \qquad p_y^a \beta_h = w_h \qquad (7.8)$$

Here, α and β are the marginal products of labor in goods X and Y. It immediately follows that the *relative* price in autarky is independent of the wage rate:

$$p_h^a = \beta_h / \alpha_h \qquad (7.9)$$

This equation reflects what Ricardo referred to as the *Labor Theory of Value*. Relative prices must equal relative real costs in terms of labor inputs. Here, if sector Y has a relatively low marginal product and sector X has a relatively high marginal product, the home country is likely to have its comparative advantage in good X. The wage rate, which is the nominal price of labor, has no effect on relative commodity prices as long as it is the same in both sectors.

real wages = Marg. labr Productivity

The wage rate is relevant for determining real wages, or the living standards of laborers. Note from Eqs. (7.8) that real wage rates equal marginal labor productivities:

$$w_h/p_x^a = \alpha_h \qquad w_h/p_y^a = \beta_h \qquad (7.10)$$

These "real wages" can be interpreted graphically as the end points on the budget line of an individual worker. Assume that 1 worker owns 1 unit of labor. β is the maximum amount of Y that can be purchased if all income is spent on Y; similarly, α is the maximum amount of X that can be purchased if all income is spent on X. An individual worker's budget line is given in Fig. 7.5.

Consider again the movement from autarky to free trade. This change will alter nominal wages in both countries, generating wage rates w_h and w_f. To determine the impacts on real wages, note that in free trade the home country exports good Y and the foreign country exports good X. Since the free trade prices of each good must equal the average cost of producing them, we know that real wages for a home laborer are constant in terms of good Y. However, the worker can now purchase good X at price ratio $p^* < \beta_h/\alpha_h$. Because the price ratio p^* is the vertical intercept of the budget line (β_h) over the horizontal distance, the horizontal intercept (i.e., the real wage w_h/p_x^*) must be $\beta_h/p^* > \alpha_h$. The intercepts of the consumer's budget line in free trade are now given by

$$w_h/p_x^* = \beta_h/p^* > \alpha_h \qquad w_h/p_y^* = \beta_h \qquad (7.11)$$

Thus, trade does not alter the home country's real wage in terms of its export good, but it does change the real wage in terms of its import good. The free trade budget line is shown in Fig. 7.5, where we see that the welfare of an individual worker rises from U_a to U_f. A corresponding argument can be made about the welfare of an individual worker in Country F, whose income is fixed in terms of good X but rises in terms of Y.

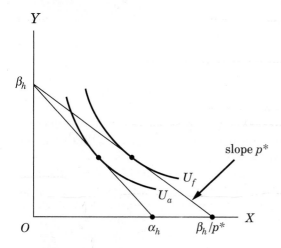

FIGURE 7.5
Budget line of an individual worker in Country H.

There is an important final point to make. It is quite possible that in free trade, real wages are higher in one country than in the other. We can show that if the home country, for example, has an *absolute advantage in both goods,* it will necessarily have a higher real wage than does the foreign country. In such a situation, we have $\alpha_h > \alpha_f$, where α_f is a worker in Country F's real wage in terms of X. Using $\alpha_h > \alpha_f$ together with Eqs. (7.11), we have

$$w_h/p_x^* > \alpha_h > \alpha_f = w_f/p_x^* \tag{7.12}$$

We can similarly show that a worker in Country H earns a higher wage in terms of good Y when H has this absolute advantage in both goods. In summary, absolute advantage is important for determining differences in real wages (per capita incomes) across countries, but comparative advantage determines the direction of trade.

7.6   THE DISTRIBUTION OF GAINS FROM TRADE: BIG VERSUS SMALL COUNTRIES

The purpose of this section is to use the Ricardian model to discuss the division of gains from trade between two countries. One principal determinant of this division is the economic size of countries, measured in terms of either their factor endowments or their productivity levels. In other words, a country grows "bigger" economically as its production frontier moves farther from the origin. Let us conduct a thought experiment with our two countries in which we make Country F bigger by shifting its production frontier in a parallel fashion farther out from the origin. This can be accomplished either by increasing F's endowment of labor or by improving its technology: increasing α and β in the same proportion.

The effect of this is shown in Fig. 7.6, where F_0F_0' is the initial production frontier and F_1F_1' is the expanded frontier. This expansion will leave F's autarky price ratio unchanged and increase the length of the horizontal segment of its excess demand curve (equal to Country F's maximum output of X, OF_1'). Suppose that p_0^* in Fig. 7.6 is the initial world equilibrium price ratio, so that F specializes in the production of X and consumes at point C_0. Now expand the production frontier to F_1F_1'. If we hold the world price ratio constant at p_0^*, F will now wish to produce at F_1' and consume at C_1. Provided that Country F wishes to spend some of its increased income on Y (homogeneous demand may exist, but it is not necessary), then Country F will wish to export more X and import more Y at the existing equilibrium price ratio p_0^*.

The same argument can be made for any price ratio. The expansion of the production frontier will lead Country F to wish to trade more at any world price ratio. The effect on Country F's excess demand curve is shown in Fig. 7.7. E_fE_f is F's initial excess demand curve. The new excess demand curve is shown by $E_f'E_f'$. The horizontal segment, corresponding to the

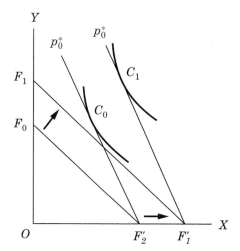

FIGURE 7.6
Growth in Country F.

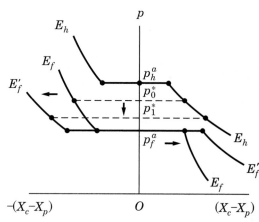

FIGURE 7.7
Expansion in Country F's excess demand.

distance OF'_1 in Fig. 7.5, expands; therefore, the country now desires to trade more at any price ratio other than its autarky price ratio.

Assuming that nothing has happened in Country H, p_0^* can no longer be an equilibrium price ratio. Country H wants to import the same amount of X that it did previously, but Country F now wants to export more X. There is an excess supply of X, so the world price ratio must fall to reestablish equilibrium. This is shown in Fig. 7.7 as a fall in the price ratio from p_0^* to p_1^*.

The change in the world price ratio due to the increase in Country F's size (productivity) has important implications for the gains from trade. First, Fig. 7.6 could be used to show that Country F gains less by growth than if the price ratio had stayed constant at p_0^* (try to redraw Fig. 7.6 with the price ratio falling from p_0^* to p_1^*). In technical language we say that F's _terms of trade have deteriorated:_ the equilibrating price change involves a fall in the relative price of F's export good. For Country H, on the other hand, the price change due to F's growth is beneficial. *H's terms of trade have improved:* the price change involves an increase in the relative price of H's export good (fall in the relative price of H's import good). This is shown in Fig. 7.8, where the price change from p_0^* to p_1^* leads to a consumption and welfare increase from C_0 to C_1.

An extreme case of unequal distribution of the gains from trade between countries is shown in Fig. 7.9. In this case, Country F is sufficiently larger than H so that the equilibrium occurs at Country F's autarky price ratio p_f^a. The equilibrium world price ratio is at one extreme of the feasible spectrum between the two autarky prices. Country H imports the quantity E_h, while Country F exports E_f of good X. In this case, Country F captures no gains, although it is not worse off with trade. All gains from trade are captured by the smaller Country H. Country F is indifferent to trade.

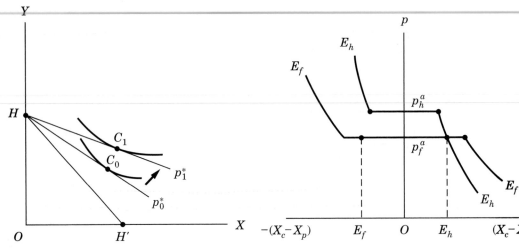

FIGURE 7.8
Effect of growth in Country F on
Country H.

FIGURE 7.9
Equilibrium world price equal to Country F's autarky
price.

Two things can be learned from this exercise. First, smaller countries are likely to be major gainers from free trade. This result is of considerable importance insofar as some smaller countries worry about their positions vis-a-vis large countries. Many Canadians, for example, worry about whether Canada gets a "good deal" in trade with the United States, whose economy is approximately 10 times larger. But the analysis we have just made suggests that, in a free trade situation, Canada may be doing very well indeed. At the same time, it does not follow that the United States does not gain from trade. Although not small compared to Canada, the United States is certainly small compared to the world as a whole and can therefore expect significant gains from trade. (Later in the book, we will discuss the ability of large countries to use tariffs to extract more gains from trade.)

The second thing to learn from this analysis is that a country may benefit from productivity growth in its trading partner. Trade is not warfare, as we have noted, and productivity growth in a trading partner should not be likened to increasing arsenals in an enemy country. Figures 7.6 to 7.9 illustrate that Country F passes on the benefits of its productivity growth to Country H in the form of a lower price for its import good.[3] Indeed, it is theoretically possible that the deterioration in the terms of trade may be so severe for Country F that it is made worse off by its productivity growth (although it still gains from trade relative to autarky). This possibility is referred to as *immiserizing growth* and will be discussed in the final chapter of the book. American consumers have benefitted from the tremendous productivity growth in Japanese consumer electronics, and Japanese have similarly benefitted from the great improvement in many American exports such as aircraft.

7.7 CONCLUDING REMARKS

This chapter is the first of several that explain the underlying differences between economies that can lead to differences in autarky price ratios, thereby leading to trade. Here we focus on differences in production functions or technologies between two countries. Countries can exploit these differences, with each country specializing in the good in which it has a *comparatively* better technology and exporting that good in exchange for the good in which is has a comparatively poorer technology. The principal results of the chapter are summarized here.

1. The slope of a country's production frontier reflects its *relative* abilities to produce X and Y. If these relative abilities differ between two countries, a pattern of *comparative advantage* exists. The two countries will then have different autarky prices, which creates the potential for gains from trade. Having a comparative advantage and the potential of gains from trade is comparable to having an *absolute advantage* in producing both goods: a country in this situation can still benefit from trade.

2. The fact that potential gains from trade exist for both countries does not guarantee that these gains are captured in free trade. After constructing the production frontiers for the two countries, we construct excess demand curves for the two countries. The equilibrium free trade price ratio must lie between the autarky price ratios for the two countries. This implies that the countries specialize according to their comparative advantages and that both countries capture gains from trade. Further, every individual worker in each country gains from trade by having an improved standard of living relative to autarky. Real wages can be different in the two countries, however, and a country with an absolute advantage necessarily has the higher real wages. Absolute (productivity) advantage is thus important for international real wage comparisons but does not affect the direction of trade.

3. The distribution of gains from trade between the two countries depends on several factors, but one important factor is each country's absolute "economic size," by which we mean the distance of its production frontier from the origin. A country is better off as it trades farther away from its own autarky price ratio and closer to the other country's autarky price ratio. We showed that when a country becomes bigger or more productive, its terms of trade tend to deteriorate (the equilibrium world price ratio moves closer to that country's autarky price ratio). This transfers some of the benefits of the productivity growth to the other country.

4. An implication of the previous point is that small countries are likely to be major gainers from international trade. A second implication is that countries benefit from productivity growth in trading partners, although in more general models this requires that the productivity growth be either neutral between exports and imports or concentrated in export sectors. The price mechanism allows a country to benefit from its partner's growth through the decrease in prices for import goods.

PROBLEMS

1. Can the notion of comparative advantage apply to trade between individuals? Suppose a lawyer is a better typist than his or her secretary. Who should do the typing? Why?

2. Interpret Table 7.3 as the maximum feasible outputs of X and Y for countries H and F (i.e., each has one unit of labor). Draw the production possibility sets for both and find the possible range of equilibrium commodity prices.

3. Does it make any difference to anything whether we double Country H's maximum outputs of X and Y by (a) doubling H's labor supply or by (b) doubling α and β for Country H? (Hint: what about per capita income?)

4. Does the manner in which Country H doubles its maximum feasible outputs (in question 3) make any difference to Country F?

5. Suppose that in free trade, the wage rate in Country H is $10 per unit of labor, while the wage in Country F is $100 per unit of labor. Using the data in Table 7.3, compute the average costs of production of both goods in both countries. Indicate why this cannot be an equilibrium set of wages and describe what must happen to these wages. What are the limits to the relative wage ratio in this case?

6. Is the horizontal section of Country H's excess demand curve necessarily symmetric around zero? That is, are OH and $H'O$ of equal length in Fig. 7.3? Under what special circumstance are they of equal length? (Hint: the answer has something to do with preferences.)

7. If the growth in Country F shown in Figs. 7.6 and 7.7 is due solely to growth in labor supply, what is the implication of the deterioration in the terms of trade for the real income of labor (or per capita consumption)? (Hint: begin with Eq. (7.7))

8. With reference to Figs. 7.6 and 7.7, what would happen instead if the productivity growth in Country F were in only the Y industry? Show how F's excess demand curve shifts.

NOTES

1. In more formal terms, we could show that the assumption of one factor is equivalent to a special case of the two-factor model: countries have identical relative factor endowments, and both goods use factors in the same proportions (the goods have identical relative factor intensities). The latter assumption is somewhat stronger than condition 2 of Chapter 6.

2. An exception could occur if there were no tangency between an indifference curve and the production frontier, or alternatively, if the highest feasible indifference curve were reached at a corner on the Y or X axis. In this case, the country specializes in autarky. We will not discuss this case here, but it is of some importance with increasing returns to scale, in which it is very costly for a small country to produce a wide range of goods in autarky. This will be discussed in Chapter 12.

3. This is not a completely general result. When production frontiers are concave ("bowed out"), as they will be in the next chapter, countries will generally not specialize completely. Thus, if a country achieves a productivity improvement in an import-competing industry, it will wish to import less, and the terms of trade will move against its trading partner. In general, productivity improvements in a country's export industries are partially passed on to trading partners through lower prices.

REFERENCES

Chipman, J. S. (1965). "A Survey of the Theory of International Trade: Part 1, The Classical Theory." *Econometrica* 33: 477–519.

Dornbusch, R., Fischer, S., and Samuelson, P. A. (1977). "Comparative Advantage, Trade, and Payments in a Ricardian Model with a Continuum of Goods." *American Economic Review* 65: 297–308.

Graham, F. D. (1948). *The Theory of International Value.* Princeton: Princeton University Press.

Haberler, A. C. (1950). "Some Problems in the Pure Theory of International Trade." *Economic Journal* 70: 215–240.

Jones, R. W. and Neary, J. P. (1984). "The Positive Theory of International Trade." In R. W. Jones and P. Kenen (editors), *Handbook of International Economics, Volume 1.* Amsterdam: North Holland, 1–62.

Melvin, J. R. (1969). "On a Demand Assumption Made by Graham." *Southern Economic Journal* 36: 36–43.

Melvin, J. R. (1969). "Mill's Law of International Value." *Southern Economic Journal* 36: 107–16.

Ricardo, D. (1817). *On the Principles of Political Economy and Taxation.* London: John Murray.

Ruffin, R. J. (1988). "The Missing Link: The Ricardian Approach to the Factor Endowments Theory of Trade." *American Economic Review* 78: 759–772.

CHAPTER
8

THE HECKSCHER-OHLIN MODEL

Handwritten margin notes:
Concave prod. fct.
2 factors
identical prod. fcts.
focuses on lab. + cap. diffs' effects on trade
No complete specialization
Redist. btw. cap. + lab. with f.t.
importance of natural fact. endowments for comp. adv.

8.1 INTRODUCTION

In the previous chapter we analyzed the effects of international differences in technologies on trade and welfare. A number of powerful conclusions were drawn about the concepts of comparative advantage and the gains from trade. However, the Ricardian theory employed presents a highly stylized model of technological differences. It assumes the existence of a single factor of production, labor, that exhibits constant productivities in generating commodity outputs. This simple specification led our analysis to some sharp theoretical predictions, including constant opportunity costs, the likelihood of complete specialization in trade, and the existence of positive income gains from trade for all workers in both countries (unless one country is much larger than the other and does not specialize completely). In practice, of course, we rarely observe such outcomes from trade. As a simple example, it surely cannot be true that all workers are made better off by engaging in international trade, for we observe that representatives of labor interests tend to oppose freer trade in the United States and other high-wage economies. Thus, we need to move beyond the Ricardian theory to develop models that make more realistic predictions about trade.

In this chapter we make a substantial move in that direction by presenting the famous Heckscher-Ohlin model, which has served as the pre-eminent trade theory in the 20th century. The Heckscher-Ohlin model, which was named for the two Swedish economists who developed its essentials, departs from the Ricardian model in two fundamental ways. First, it assumes the existence of a second factor, which we will call capital, allowing for a much richer specification of production functions. Second, rather than assuming different technologies, the model rests on the notion of identical production functions in both nations. This assumption is made explicitly to neutralize the important possibility that trade is based on international technological

98

variations in favor of the possibility that trade is based solely on differences in supplies of capital and labor.

As we will show, adding a second factor to the analysis yields richer and more realistic explanations of trade and its effects. First, the production frontier becomes concave, reflecting rising opportunity costs, as discussed in Chapter 2. This means that countries will tend to produce both goods in free trade rather than specializing completely. Rarely do we see a country devote most of its resources to the production of a particular commodity.[1] Rather, countries tend to be diversified in production across a broad range of goods, even though they do not typically produce all possible goods. Second, even though countries enjoy aggregate gains from trade in this model, free trade causes a redistribution of real income between capital and labor in comparison with autarky. This redistribution effect will help explain some of the reasons that certain factors oppose free trade.

In the Heckscher-Ohlin model, comparative advantage and trade are determined by national differences in factor endowments. Upon even casual consideration, this observation makes sense. Countries that have abundant supplies of agricultural land, for example, tend to be net exporters of grains and food. Developing nations with abundant endowments of low-skilled labor tend to export labor-intensive goods such as clothing, footwear, and consumer electronics. While there are certain technical difficulties in achieving unambiguous evidence on this model in the real world, the consensus among trade economists is that factor endowments provide one of the most important explanations for observed international trade patterns.[2] Thus, the evident empirical relevance of the model provides a strong motivation for its study as well.

8.2 THE EFFECTS OF ENDOWMENT DIFFERENCES

The Heckscher-Ohlin trade model builds on the neoclassical supply-side theories developed in Chapter 2. It adopts and maintains three assumptions about production characteristics in each country. First, the production functions for goods X and Y exhibit constant returns to scale. These production functions, which are the same in both countries, differ in relative usage of capital and labor. Specifically, we will always take good X to be labor-intensive and good Y to be capital-intensive. Second, there are fixed total supplies of the two factors, labor and capital, which are homogeneous and perfectly mobile between industries within each country. Thus, a single wage rate and a single rental rate on capital prevail within each economy. However, labor and capital are assumed to be perfectly immobile between countries. Third, there are no market distortions such as imperfect competition, labor unions, or taxes that would influence production or consumption decisions. Note that these assumptions guarantee that factors are fully employed.

When expanding the model to allow for trade, two additional assumptions are required. First, preferences in both countries are taken to be identical and homogeneous. This assumption eliminates the possibility that comparative advantage can be based on differences in demand behavior. We will relax this assumption in Chapter 13.

The last assumption is the defining characteristic of the Heckscher-Ohlin model. Countries are assumed to differ in their *relative* factor endowments. Because the model assumes identical technologies, constant returns to scale, and common tastes, this is the only meaningful difference between the countries. Of the five conditions in Chapter 6, the Heckscher-Ohlin model relaxes assumption 2, that of identical relative endowments, while maintaining the others.

Factor Endowments

We need to be clear on the meaning of factor abundance and factor scarcity in this relative sense. We define factor endowments specifically in terms of the ratios between capital stocks and labor forces in the two countries. Thus, if the capitol-labor ratio in Country H is greater than it is in Country F, we say that Country H is relatively capital-abundant (and labor-scarce) while Country F is relatively labor-abundant (and capital-scarce). This *physical definition* gives Eq. (8.1):

$$(K/L)_h > (K/L)_f \tag{8.1}$$

To understand the concept of relative factor endowments, consider the estimates of real capital endowments and labor forces presented in Table 8.1. Capital stocks were computed as the cumulative sum of gross fixed capital formation in the 15-year period through 1984, corrected for depreciation and inflation, and converted to U.S. dollars using a consistent set of international price and exchange rate comparisons.[3] Thus, capital stocks are in billions of 1984 dollars. The labor force in each country is defined to be the economically active population (that is, those employed and those looking for work) in

TABLE 8.1
Capital and labor endowments for selected countries, 1984

Country	Capital stock ($b)	Labor force (m)	Capital per worker ($)
India	482	254	1,898
Brazil	507	53	9,566
Rep. of Korea	204	14	14,571
Mexico	353	23	15,348
U.S.	3,696	116	32,421
Canada	419	12	34,917
Germany[a]	1,018	26	39,154
Japan	2,336	59	39,593
Switzerland	120	3	40,000

Sources: Compiled from International Monetary Fund, *International Financial Statistics Yearbook*, Summers and Heston (1988), and International Labor Organization, *Yearbook of Labor Statistics*.

[a] Data for Germany exclude former East Germany

millions of workers. The final column shows the ratios of capital to labor. Several features of these data are worth discussing. First, note that it is relative endowments that affect the measurement of factor abundance. For example, although the United States has a larger labor force than either Brazil or Mexico, it is capital-abundant and labor-scarce because it has a comparatively larger capital supply. Switzerland has the smallest absolute capital stock, but it is the most capital-abundant country in the group. Second, while the Heckscher-Ohlin theory assumes these factor endowments to be fixed, it should be clear that capital and labor supplies depend to some degree on economic conditions. For example, the size of the aggregate labor force may well depend on the wage rate and on the attractiveness of working conditions. This explains why different countries have different participation rates by workers in the labor force, ranging from 34 percent in India to 50 percent in the United States.[4] Third, endowments data for a particular year present only a snapshot in the evolution of factor supplies over time. Japan and Korea, for example, have invested in capital at very high rates in recent decades, with a consequent rise in their capital-labor ratios. Factor growth is an important feature of the world economy, and we consider its implications in Chapter 23. In the present chapter, however, we restrict ourselves to the focus of the Heckscher-Ohlin model on fixed endowments. In effect, this theory takes a long-run perspective in which there are no changes in relative endowments among nations.

We note an important implication of differences in physical endowments for autarky factor prices. For two countries with identical demand patterns, we would expect relative factor prices to reflect factor endowments. Thus, in autarky, Country F would have relatively inexpensive labor and Country H would have relatively inexpensive capital. We prove this proposition in Section 8.5.

minimize fact. prices
(w/r)

Factor Intensities

It is useful to reintroduce the concept of factor intensities discussed in Chapter 2, because they also play a central role in the Heckscher-Ohlin theory. Good Y is relatively capital-intensive and good X is relatively labor-intensive if the capital-labor ratio used in production is higher in the former sector:

$$(K/L)_y > (K/L)_x \tag{8.2}$$

Recall that in equilibrium both sectors choose capital-labor ratios that minimize costs for the prevailing relative factor price, $\omega = w/r$, where w is the wage rate and r is the rental rate on a unit of capital. In principle, it is possible that at different relative factor prices, the rankings in Eq. (8.2) can be reversed if one industry finds it technically easier to substitute capital for labor along an isoquant than does the other. This possibility, termed a *factor-intensity reversal* (FIR), poses certain problems for the Heckscher-Ohlin trade theory, which we will note briefly as we proceed.[5]

The model must therefore make the further assumption that there are no
factor-intensity reversals.

Table 8.2 presents estimates of capital-labor ratios in certain U.S.
manufacturing industries in 1984. Again, capital stocks were computed
as the real value of accumulated capital, accounting for depreciation. Our
selected industries represent wide disparities in factor intensities, ranging
from the most capital-intensive industries (petroleum refining and paper
products) to the most labor-intensive industries (footwear and wearing
apparel).[6]

Implications

To illustrate the effect of endowment differences we begin by considering
the case in which endowments are the same for two countries, H and
F. This level of endowment is represented by point E of Fig. 8.1, with
endowments $\overline{L}$ and $\overline{K}$. For this point, the maximum producible quantities
of X and Y are $\overline{X}$ and $\overline{Y}$. These two maximum output points are shown
in Fig. 8.2, where the corresponding production possibility curve is $\overline{Y}\,\overline{X}$.
Now consider the effect of changing the endowment point for one of the
two countries. Specifically, assume that the endowment point for Country
H is E_h. Note that, because we have increased the capital endowment and
reduced the labor endowment for Country H, points E_h and $E = E_f$ satisfy
Eq. (8.1). The isoquants passing through point E_h give the maximum levels
of output of the two commodities in H. The diagram is drawn so that the
isoquant through E_h for commodity Y lies above $\overline{Y}$, whereas the isoquant
for commodity X lies below $\overline{X}$. These new isoquants are represented by $\overline{Y}_h$
and $\overline{X}_h$, respectively, and produce the two endpoints $\overline{Y}_h$ and $\overline{X}_h$ of Fig.
8.2. Here, the increase in the endowment of capital and the reduction in
the endowment of labor result in a rise in the maximum output of Y, the
capital-intensive commodity, and a reduction in the maximum output of X,
the labor-intensive commodity. As one would expect, the production frontier

TABLE 8.2
**Capital-labor ratios used in selected U.S. manufacturing
industries, 1984**

Industry	Capital stock ($m)	Employment (th)	Capital per worker ($)
Petroleum Refineries	27,005	95	284,263
Paper Products	33,007	613	53,845
Iron and Steel	25,607	505	50,707
Transport Equipment	51,635	1,849	27,926
Food Products	31,758	1,263	25,145
Footwear	514	107	4,804
Wearing Apparel	3,416	978	3,493

Sources: Compiled from United Nations, *Yearbook of Industrial Statistics*, and Summers and Heston
(1988).

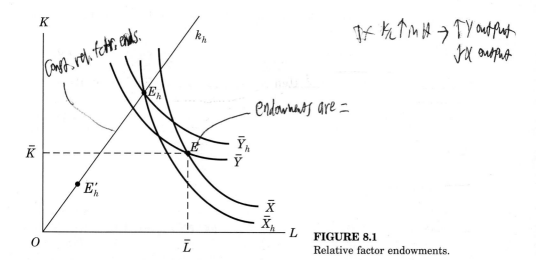

FIGURE 8.1
Relative factor endowments.

for the labor-abundant Country F is biased toward the X axis, and the production frontier for the capital-abundant Country H is biased toward the Y axis.

This result holds, regardless of the sizes of the two economies. Note that the endowment point for Country H, E_h, lies on the ray Ok_h, along which relative endowments are the same at any point. Because of constant returns to scale, isoquants for goods X and Y are homogeneous. Thus, for any endowment point on the ray, a corresponding pair of maximum-output isoquants intersect at that point, meaning that the production frontier for Country H shrinks in or grows out in a parallel fashion. For example, if endowments at point E_h' are one-third those of the original point, the new production frontier will be precisely one-third as far from the origin as the original frontier. For any ray from the origin in Fig. 8.2, the marginal rates of transformation along production frontiers Y_hX_h and Y_hX_h are the same.

In Fig. 8.3 we have reproduced the original production possibility curves for the two countries (now placing f subscripts on F's curve) and

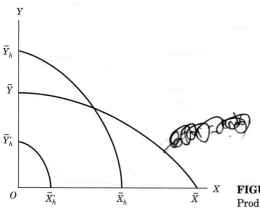

FIGURE 8.2
Production possibility frontiers.

(handwritten at top: $(p = P_x/P_y)$)

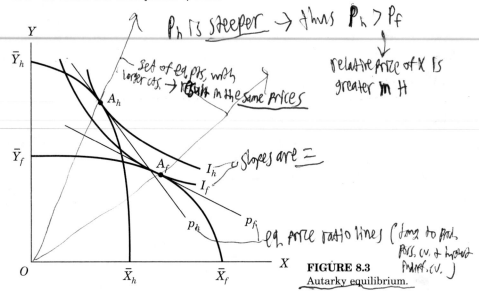

(handwritten annotations around figure: "P_h is steeper → thus $P_h > P_f$", "set of eq. pts. with larger cars → result in the same prices", "relative price of X is greater in H", "slopes are =", "eq. price ratio lines (tang. to prod. poss. cv. + highest prod. cv.)")

FIGURE 8.3
Autarky equilibrium.

added two community indifference curves, reflecting identical and homogeneous preferences, that determine the autarky equilibrium points. For Country F, the highest community indifference curve is tangent at A_f, while A_h is the autarky equilibrium point for Country H. Because the slopes of the indifference curves are the same along any ray from the origin, in autarky the equilibrium price ratio line will be steeper in Country H than in Country F. These autarky price ratios, the price ratio line simultaneously tangent to the production possibility curve and the highest community indifference curve at the autarky point, are p_f and p_h for countries F and H, respectively. Thus, in autarky we have

(handwritten left margin: "Absolute size is irrelevant because of consi. reas. + identical, homogeneous tastes")

$$p_h > p_f \tag{8.3}$$

Recall that p is defined to be p_x/p_y. Finally, because of the homogeneity of production frontiers and community indifference curves, these relative autarky prices would be the same regardless of country sizes. The equilibrium points would lie along rays OA_h and OA_f, generating the same prices. Thus, absolute size is irrelevant for the determination of comparative advantage in the Heckscher-Ohlin model by virtue of the assumptions of constant returns and identical, homogeneous tastes. What matters are relative endowments and factor intensities, which is why this theory is often called the *factor-proportions model*.

(handwritten left margin: "factor proportions model")

8.3   THE HECKSCHER-OHLIN THEOREM[7]

Figure 8.4 reproduces the autarky equilibrium point for the two countries of our model. We now want to examine the implications of opening up the model to allow international trade. From Eq. (8.3) we see that in autarky the relative price of X is higher in Country H than it is in Country F. When international trade is permitted, the residents of Country H will observe that the price of commodity X is cheaper in the other country than it is at

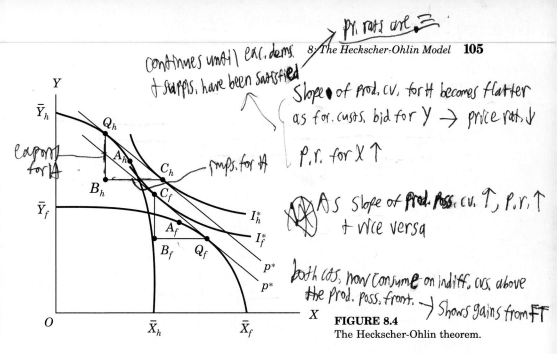

(handwritten annotations on figure)

Pri rats are ⩵

continues until exc. dems + supps. have been satisfied

Slope of prod. cv. for H becomes flatter as for. custs. bid for Y → price rat. ↓

P.r. for X ↑

mps. for H

As slope of prod. poss. cv. ↑, P.r. ↑ + vice versa

both c/s. now consume on indiff. cvs. above the prod. poss. front. → Shows gains from FT

export for H

FIGURE 8.4
The Heckscher-Ohlin theorem.

home; likewise the residents of Country F will observe that the price of Y is cheaper in H than it is in F. Thus, there will be an incentive for residents of H to make some of their purchases of commodity X in F and an incentive for residents of Country F to purchase commodity Y in H. As long as the price of a commodity is lower in one country than it is in another, consumers will continue to shift from purchasing goods in the higher-priced market to purchasing them in the market where prices are lower.

This change in demand that results from free trade also implies a shift in production. Consumers in Country F now bid for some of the domestic output of commodity Y in H, and consumers in H purchase some X in F. Therefore, the production point in Country H will shift toward the Y axis. Because the slope of the production possibility curve becomes flatter as the economy moves toward the Y axis, this shift in production implies that in Country H the price ratio will fall. The analogous argument can be made for Country F. Because there is an overall increase in the demand for commodity X and an overall decrease in the demand for commodity Y, the production point in Country F will shift toward the X axis. Because such movements imply an increase in the slope of the production possibility curve, the result will be an increase in the slope of the price ratio line.

Assuming that there are no impediments to international trade, this process will continue until the excess demands and supplies for both commodities in both countries have been satisfied. Production will continue to change until trade has equalized price ratios in the two countries at some intermediate level p^*. Thus, the first important point to be observed is that trade will result in the equalization of commodity prices in the two countries. This price equalization happens at points of equal slope (marginal rates of transformation) on both production possibility curves. These points, which are labelled Q_h and Q_f, demonstrate that in free trade, countries will generally produce both goods.

The equality of relative prices in the two countries does not, by itself, imply that a new equilibrium position has been reached. Also required is the condition that world excess demands and supplies of the two countries be zero, or in other words, that the amount that one country wants to export will be exactly equal to the amount the other country wants to import. This situation is illustrated in Fig. 8.4, where we have depicted an equilibrium with equal trade triangles. Notice that both nations now consume on community indifference curves that lie outside their production frontiers. We therefore conclude that free trade in the Heckscher-Ohlin model provides aggregate gains from trade for each country.

We also show the free trade situation in Fig. 8.5, which demonstrates equilibrium using excess-demand curves. Free trade establishes relative price ratio p^*, with Country H importing quantity $OX_h (= B_h C_h$ in Fig. 8.4) of good X and Country F exporting the same quantity. This trade pattern is consistent with comparative advantage. The labor-abundant Country F exports the labor-intensive commodity X, and the capital-abundant Country H exports the capital-intensive good Y. This is an illustration of the Heckscher-Ohlin theorem, which we now state:

> **The Heckscher-Ohlin theorem.** Given the assumptions of the model, a country will export the commodity that intensively uses its relatively abundant factor.

Note carefully the implication of this theorem. The important characteristics distinguishing each country are its relative supplies of capital and labor. By virtue of exporting the capital-intensive good and importing the labor-intensive good, Country H implicitly exports the services of capital, its abundant factor, and imports the services of labor, its scarce factor. Thus, international trade in commodities accomplishes the task of exchanging surplus factor services between countries. This is an important phenomenon for understanding the effects of trade on factor incomes, as we discuss in Sections 8.4 and 8.5.

An interesting question regarding the Heckscher-Ohlin theorem relates to how far we can relax the underlying assumptions and still ensure

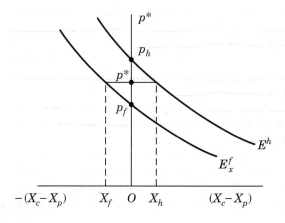

FIGURE 8.5
Free trade equilibrium.

that the result holds. Non-constant returns to scale would clearly invalidate the notion that country size is irrelevant for trade patterns, and allowing arbitrary international differences in technology would also render the theorem generally invalid. If factors were not homogeneous, meaning that labor was distinguished by skills and that capital came in different types, the simple two-factor theorem would no longer be relevant. However, as we discuss in Section 8.6, an important variant of the fundamental message of the model—that countries export the services of their abundant factors—is still valid. If factors are not mobile between industries but instead must remain fixed in employment for some period of time, the model must depart from the long-run nature of the Heckscher-Ohlin theorem in favor of a short-run view. This last possibility is clearly important and will be analyzed in the next chapter.

A further assumption is that labor and capital are immobile internationally. This assumption is made to allow investigation of the effects of commodity trade without also worrying about trade in factors. However, if factors could migrate internationally, they would do so to take advantage of differences in factor returns. Such trade in factors would tend to supplant trade in goods, inasmuch as both flows would exist to compensate for differences in relative endowments. In an extreme situation, factor movements could eliminate the need for commodity trade, though we would generally expect both kinds of trade to occur simultaneously. The Heckscher-Ohlin theorem would remain valid. The effects of factor mobility are examined in detail in Chapter 21.

The existence of some market distortions, such as monopoly and export subsidies, can overturn the Heckscher-Ohlin theorem if their effects are powerful enough to offset the influence of endowments. However, the most common distortions we consider in trade models are import restrictions such as tariffs, quotas, and transport costs, which we analyze in later chapters. These barriers can reduce or even eliminate trade in goods, but any remaining trade would obey the pattern generated by the Heckscher-Ohlin model. Thus, the theorem is still applicable when trade restrictions are allowed.

It is also possible to allow moderate differences in demand patterns between countries, provided these differences are not so great as to overcome the effects of endowments, a possibility we illustrate in Chapter 13. Finally, it is theoretically possible for a factor-intensity reversal to occur between countries. That is, given the differences in relative factor prices between nations, product Y could be capital-intensive in capital-abundant Country H and yet be labor-intensive in labor-abundant Country F in autarky. In this case, the Heckscher-Ohlin theorem would predict that both countries would export the same good, a practical impossibility. Appendix 3 considers the case of factor intensity reversals.

It might appear from this review that the Heckscher-Ohlin model is fairly fragile in the sense that it may not survive departures from its underlying assumptions. Of course, this is a feature of any theoretical model embodying simplifying assumptions. The important question relates to the practical importance of the model's insights. In this regard, the notion that differences in factor endowments provide a significant explanation for comparative advantage and global trade patterns is undeniable. It is clear that a substantial portion of world trade involves the implicit exchange of factor services through trade in natural resource-intensive items such as raw materials, labor-intensive items such as clothing, and capital-intensive items such as machinery.[8] It is important to point out that international exchange of this type is likely to be most prevalent between nations with widely differing factor endowments. Thus, we would expect endowments-based trade to be most evident between developed countries, such as the United States, and developing countries, such as Mexico. Note also that such trade involves exchanging the products of one distinct industry, such as agriculture, for those of another, such as clothing. Thus, Heckscher-Ohlin-based exchange is often termed *inter-industry trade.*

8.4   THE FACTOR-PRICE-EQUALIZATION THEOREM

The Heckscher-Ohlin theorem demonstrates the possibility that the pattern of comparative advantage and international trade is determined by national differences in relative factor endowments. It should be evident that trade must, as a result, influence the prices of productive factors. For example, if a nation exports the services of its abundant factor, there must be an implicit increase in demand for that factor, thereby raising its price. The factor-price-equalization (FPE) theorem investigates this relationship in detail.

Before stating the theorem, we must develop a fundamental relationship between relative commodity prices, p, and relative factor prices, ω, in an economy. In Fig. 8.6, p_a is the initial equilibrium commodity price ratio giving rise to production at point A with quantities Y_a and X_a. In the Edgeworth-Bowley box diagram of Fig. 8.7, the corresponding production point is again A, which, of course, is the point of tangency between the X_a

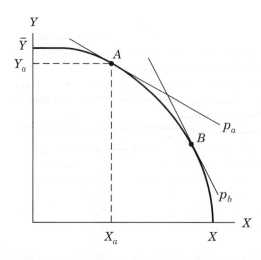

FIGURE 8.6
Changes in commodity prices and outputs.

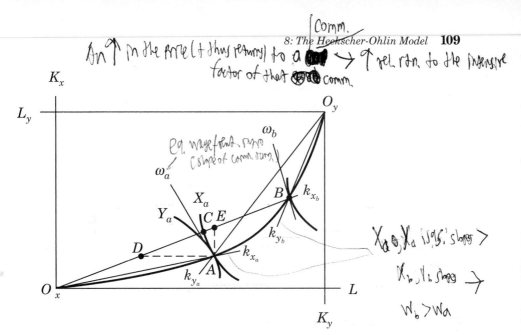

Comm.

An ↑ in the price (+ thus returns) to a [●] → ↑ rel. rtn. to the intensive factor of that [●] comm.

eq. wage-rent ratio
(slope of comm. turn.)

X_a, Y_a isoq. slopes >
X_b, Y_b slopes →
$W_b > W_a$

FIGURE 8.7
Changes in outputs and factor prices.

and Y_a isoquants. The slope of the common tangent at point A is ω_a, the equilibrium wage-rental ratio. Thus, for any point on the production frontier there is a corresponding point on the efficiency locus. We wish to show that under constant returns to scale there is a unique ω for each p for which some of both goods are produced.

Suppose there is a relative increase in the price of commodity X to p_b, leading to production at point B. The outputs of X will rise, and those of Y will fall. The corresponding point in the factor box diagram will be B. The question now is how the wage-rental ratio at B will compare to ω_a. Recall that for constant-returns-to-scale production functions, all isoquants have a constant slope along any ray from the origin. Thus, the slope of X_b, the X-isoquant through point B, must be the same as the slope of X_a at C. It follows that the common slopes of the X and Y isoquants at B exceed their slopes at A and that $\omega_b > \omega_a$.

In Fig. 8.7, we have assumed that commodity X is labor-intensive. Recalling that $\omega = w/r$, we see that an increase in the relative price of a commodity (in this case, X) will increase the relative return to the factor used intensively in that industry (in this case, labor). This result clearly works in both directions, meaning that an increase in the relative price of good Y would raise the relative return to capital. The economic logic behind this effect is straightforward. Given a rise in the price of the labor-intensive good, the economy would move to produce more X and less Y. During this adjustment, the capital-intensive sector Y would release resources in a bundle involving a higher ratio of capital to labor than the labor-intensive sector X would choose to employ at initial factor prices. Accordingly, there would emerge an excess demand for labor and an excess supply of capital, causing a rise in ω sufficient to establish a new equilibrium.

Thus, we have demonstrated that there is a unique relationship between relative factor prices and commodity prices, so long as both goods are produced. This relationship may be written as

$$w/r = G(p_x/p_y). \qquad (8.4)$$

Here, G is a function that depends only on the production functions for the two commodities. With production functions assumed to be identical between countries, G would also be identical.[9] There are two immediate implications. First, because $p_f < p_h$ in autarky by virtue of the Heckscher-Ohlin theorem, it must be that $\omega_f < \omega_h$ in autarky as well.[10] Second, given the fact that free trade equalizes the commodity price ratio between countries, the wage-rental ratio will also be equalized. The equalization of these factor returns means that the relative wage must rise in F and fall in H in the movement to free trade.

Let us state this result clearly. Returning to our trade model, let there be two countries, Country H being relatively capital-abundant and Country F being relatively labor-abundant. With identical, constant-returns production functions and identical and homogeneous tastes, in autarky H will have a higher wage-rental ratio than will F. The factor-price-eqalization theorem then states that, given certain assumptions, the equalization of commodity prices in both nations through trade will result in the equalization of relative factor returns. In other words, if the ratio of commodity prices is equal in two countries, then the wage-rental ratio will also be equal.

The factor-price-equalization theorem is most easily demonstrated by introducing the concept of the *unit-value isoquant,* which also allows us to provide further perspective on the model. In Fig. 8.8 we have chosen an isoquant for each industry such that the value of output for each industry is exactly one dollar. Thus the output of X times the price of X equals the output of Y times the price of Y, both of which equal one dollar:

$$X_o p_x = Y_o p_y = \$1 \qquad (8.5)$$

Thus, given a set of commodity prices, we simply choose the levels of output for X and Y that will satisfy Eq. (8.5). The resulting unit-value isoquants are labelled $X_{(\$1)}$ and $Y_{(\$1)}$. Note that because of the assumption of constant returns to scale, it makes no difference for the relative positions and shapes of the isoquants what value of output is chosen as long as $X p_x = Y p_y$.

In Fig. 8.8 we have also included the unit isocost line for an arbitrarily chosen pair of factor prices. The intercepts of this line are the inverses of the factor prices, $1/w_a$ and $1/r_a$. Given relative factor prices ω_a, the slope of the isocost line is determined, and the condition for cost minimization is that the isocost line be tangent to both isoquants. Note that this tangency is required for an equilibrium in which both goods are produced. For example, if the unit-value isoquant for good Y were to lie outside the unit isocost line, then it would cost more than a dollar to produce one dollar's worth of Y, and no firm would produce it. Alternatively, if the unit-value isoquant for Y were to lie inside the unit isocost line, then economic profits would be made in sector Y, which is inconsistent with perfect competition. It can thus be seen

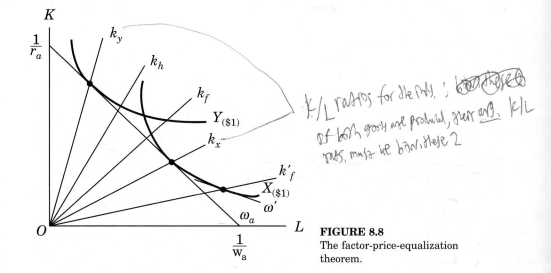

FIGURE 8.8
The factor-price-equalization theorem.

that an equilibrium in which both commodities are being produced and in which total revenue is just equal to total cost in both industries requires that the same unit isocost line be tangent to both unit-value isoquants. As shown in Fig. 8.8, the points of tangency between the two unit-value isoquants and the isocost line give the capital-labor ratios for the two industries, k_x and k_y. The capital-labor ratios shown in Fig. 8.8 are the same capital-labor ratios shown in the box diagram of Fig. 8.7 at point A.

Observe that if both goods are produced, it must be that the *average* capital-labor ratio for the two commodities lies between k_y and k_x. Furthermore, this average capital-labor ratio must be the exact endowment ratio for the economy as a whole.[11] Thus, if both goods are produced, the economy-wide capital-labor ratio must lie between k_y and k_x. Putting it the other way around, if the overall endowment ratio lies between k_y and k_x, the economy produces some of both goods. If the endowment ratio just equals k_x or k_y, the economy specializes in X or Y, respectively. Thus, the region between k_x and k_y in Figure 8.8 is often called the *cone of diversification,* indicating that for wage-rental ratio ω_a, if the economy's relative endowment ratio lies within the cone, both goods will be produced.

Figure 8.8 thus illustrates one of the conditions required for the equalization of commodity prices to result in the equalization of wage-rental ratios. Under the assumptions of the Heckscher-Ohlin model, production functions between countries are identical; therefore, if trade equalizes commodity prices, then unit-value isoquants for both countries must also be identical. In our two-country model, isoquants $Y_{(\$1)}$ and $X_{(\$1)}$ represent the unit-value isoquants for both Country H and Country F. Now suppose k_h is the overall capital-labor ratio for Country H and k_f is the capital-labor endowment ratio for Country F. Because both overall endowment ratios are within the cone of diversification, both countries face the same wage-rental ratio, namely, ω_a. Thus, with the same production functions, if trade equalizes commodity prices and if both countries produce both goods, then wage-rental ratios will be equalized as a result. This is the essence of the FPE theorem. Notice that if the endowment of one country lies outside the cone of diversification (at k_f' for example), then although commodity prices might well be equalized by trade, wage-rental ratios will not be. In this case, we would find instead that $\omega_a > \omega'$. In an equilibrium like this, Country F would specialize in good X, while Country H would produce both goods. One interesting implication of this analysis is that factor price equalization becomes more likely as the endowment ratios of nations approach each other.[12]

From the preceding discussion we can state the factor-price-equalization theorem.

> ***The factor-price-equalization theorem.*** Under identical constant-returns-to-scale production technologies, free trade in commodities will equalize relative factor prices through the equalization of relative commodity prices, so long as both countries produce both goods.

In fact, an even stronger result can be stated. If *relative* factor prices are equalized by free trade, the capital-labor ratios employed in industries X and Y will be the same in both countries as well. As we will show in the next section, this result implies that the marginal products of labor and capital will be equalized in both nations. It follows that *real* factor prices will be equalized by trade as well.

These powerful predictions deserve further comment. The fact that relative and real factor prices are equalized by trade in goods has the fundamental implication that laborers and capital owners would have identical living standards in all countries. In turn, there would be no economic incentives for factors to migrate, as we noted earlier. In short, commodity trade acts as a complete *substitute* for trade in factors if it results in factor-price equalization.

In the real world, of course, we do not observe workers enjoying identical living standards in all nations. Rather, there are huge disparities in labor incomes and returns to capital. This fact suggests that the special assumptions of the FPE theorem must fail to be true in important dimensions. Transport costs are significant in numerous commodities, meaning that even free trade will not result in identical commodity prices. Trade restrictions such as tariffs and import quotas have an important influence on world trade and help prevent the equalization of factor prices, even as they limit access to full gains from trade. There are also numerous market distortions that sustain differences in international factor prices, such as monopolies that generate rents for their owners and employees or labor unions that sustain real wages in excess of marginal labor products (perhaps at the expense of higher unemployment). A related issue is that production functions may likely fail to exhibit constant returns to scale. In this event, comparative advantage may be related to factors such as country size and product differentiation, elements that do not appear in the Heckscher-Ohlin world. We analyze these issues at length in other chapters of this book, where we will show that in such models, trade in goods and factors may be *complements* rather than substitutes. Also significant are government policy distortions, such as production taxes on manufactures or price supports that maintain differences between world and domestic prices for agricultural commodities.

Perhaps the most significant point to remember is the falsehood of the basic assumption that technologies are the same everywhere. We should be careful in making such a statement. In principle, it is not difficult for technological information to flow easily across borders, so in well-functioning markets for information it may be true that technical knowledge is broadly similar everywhere. However, the efficiency with which this knowledge is translated into outputs is a function of the quality of inputs, along with management and entrepreneurship. There is substantial evidence that countries vary markedly in this efficiency, though growing international trade has caused some convergence in technologies.[13]

Another significant issue is that the assumption that workers are homogeneous is questionable. Within any economy workers may be differentiated by their skills, especially skills acquired by education and training. Further, natural resources, land, and capital may be distinguished in terms of their economic characteristics. This observation points to the importance of analyzing international trade theories when there are many factors, which we do in the last section of this chapter and again in Chapter 14. For now, however, note the important implication that a nation like the United States may well be scarce in unskilled labor but abundant in technologically skilled labor, implying that these sectors will have opposing viewpoints on the desirability of free trade. Unskilled workers will find their real incomes falling as they compete with labor-intensive imports from abroad. The real wages of technical workers will rise, however, as their services are exported on net. Note that this observation helps explain the fact that in the industrialized nations, wages in the export sectors tend to be significantly higher than wages in the sectors that compete with imports.

While there are strong reasons to doubt that international trade can result in equal real factor prices internationally, it is clear that trade can result in strong tendencies in that direction. This is true especially when trade is of the Heckscher-Ohlin type, where it compensates for differences in relative factor endowments. This interindustry trade tends to be prevalent between the developed countries, on one hand, and the developing countries, on the other hand, where there are marked differences in factor supplies and factor prices. In this context, trade tends to equalize real incomes of similar workers and capital owners. Accordingly, we can point to trade as an important source of the growth in real wages in countries such as Korea relative to that in the United States. It also helps explain the preferences of labor interests in the United States and other high-wage economies for protection against labor-intensive imports. Finally, a corollary result is that if barriers to trade prevent the equalization of real incomes, there will be incentives for labor and capital to migrate internationally. Thus, if an unskilled-labor-scarce nation truly wishes to protect the incomes of its workers, it will require barriers to both trade and immigration.

8.5   THE STOLPER-SAMUELSON AND RYBCZYNSKI THEOREMS

The Heckscher-Ohlin and FPE theorems we have just discussed seem simple, yet their proofs rest on complex notions about the operation of an economy with two factors producing two goods under constant returns to scale. Numerous features of such an economy were developed in Chapter 2, but it is important at this point to specify further results that are critically related to the trade theories. We now analyze the effects of changes in commodity prices on real factor prices and the effects of changes in factor endowments on commodity outputs. Note that because these theories relate to the inner workings of the economy, the analysis will focus on a single country. We will then relate the theories to certain trade issues.

Two fundamental observations about relationships in the economy should be kept in mind. First, factors are fully employed in producing outputs in sectors X and Y. It follows that any change in the available supply of factors will affect commodity outputs. Second, the presence of perfect competition means that the price of a product is comprised strictly of payments to labor and capital. Changes in commodity prices must influence factor prices accordingly. These are the relationships we wish to study.[14]

The Stolper-Samuelson Theorem

The first fundamental theorem about the internal functioning of the economy pertains to the relationship between commodity prices and real factor incomes. We demonstrated previously that there is a unique relationship between changes in relative commodity prices and relative factor returns and that this relationship depends on technology. However, there is an even stronger theorem, which was first proven by two American economists, Wolfgang Stolper and Paul Samuelson. The principal purpose of their theorem is to show that changes in commodity prices have determinate effects on real factor rewards. That is, movements in the prices of goods change the distribution of real incomes between capital and labor, which is an extremely important element in the economy.

In particular, a relative increase in the price of the labor-intensive good X causes the real wage rate, measured in terms of the price of either X or Y, to rise, whereas the real return on capital, measured in terms of either commodity price, must fall. In other words, a rise in the price of the labor-intensive good leads to an increase in real wages and a decrease in real returns to capital. To demonstrate this, we must show that both w/p_x and w/p_y increase and that both r/p_x and r/p_y decrease when p_x/p_y increases.

Recall from Eq. (2.10) in Chapter 2 that one condition for profit maximization is that firms pay each productive factor the value of its marginal product. Thus, for labor and capital in the X industry we must have, respectively, that $p_x \text{MP}_{LX} = w$ and $p_x \text{MP}_{KX} = r$. A similar pair of conditions hold for the Y industry. We reproduce these eqations below by stating them in terms of marginal products:

$$\text{MP}_{LX} = w/p_x \qquad \text{MP}_{KX} = r/p_x$$
$$\text{MP}_{LY} = w/p_y \qquad \text{MP}_{KY} = r/p_y \tag{8.6}$$

Since these equations must hold in equilibrium, it is clear that if the marginal products of labor in both industries rise, both w/p_x and w/p_y increase as well. Similarly, r/p_x and r/p_y will both decrease if, and only if, the marginal products of capital fall in both sectors. That marginal products behave in this fashion follows from two additional properties of our production functions. First, consider again Fig. 8.7. The slopes of the rays emanating from origins O_x and O_y through point A represent the capital-labor ratios chosen in sectors X and Y in the initial equilibrium. At point B both of these rays are steeper than at point A, demonstrating that the rise in the wage-rental ratio induces *both* goods to be produced with relatively more capital and relatively less labor than before. Of course, given fixed factor endowments, this is possible only because output of X rises and output of Y falls.

Second, the higher capital-labor ratios raise the marginal products of labor and reduce the marginal products of capital in both industries. To establish this fact we simply recall the result from Chapter 2 that for constant-returns-to-scale production functions, the slopes of isoquants, and thus the marginal products of both factors, are constant along any ray from the origin. Consider again the movement from A to B in Fig. 8.7. How does this change affect the marginal product of labor in X and Y? Because the marginal products are constant along the line $O_x C B$, any point on this line can be used to find the answer. Consider point D, where the line AD is parallel to the L_x axis. The movement from A to D involves a reduction in the amount of labor used in the production of X, while the input of capital remains constant. Recall from Chapter 2 that the law of diminishing returns applies to this kind of movement, in which the shift from A to D corresponds to a movement down the total-product curve for labor. We reproduce a typical total-product curve in Fig. 8.9, with points A and D corresponding to those in Fig. 8.7. The slope of this curve is, of course, the marginal product of labor in sector X, and thus we see that the MP_{LX} at D is higher than the MP_{LX} at A. But from the point of view of the marginal products, the movement from A to D is equivalent to a movement from A

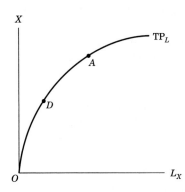

FIGURE 8.9
Total-product curve for labor.

to B. Thus, we have demonstrated that the relative increase in the price of X (A to B in Figs. 8.6 and 8.7) has increased the marginal product of labor. It follows from Equation (8.6) that w/p_x has risen as well.

Now consider the vertical movement from A to E in Fig. 8.7, which represents an increase in the use of capital in industry X with an unchanged labor input. This would imply a movement to the right along a total-product curve for capital (which we do not draw), implying, by the law of diminishing returns, a reduction in the MP_{KX} and, in turn from Eq. (8.6), a fall in r/p_x. This result is equally true at any point along ray O_xB, including the new equilibrium at point B. Thus, we have demonstrated the desired results for both factors in the X industry.

We could reconstruct all the steps in the previous demonstration for factors in the Y industry, but fortunately, a shortcut to this proof is available. Our proof for sector X relied on the increase in the capital-labor ratio associated with the movement from point A to point B. Indeed, it can be shown that *any* increase in the capital-labor ratio must reduce the real return to capital and raise the real wage of labor. But this same movement from A to B also implied a rise in the capital-labor ratio in industry Y. Thus, there results a rise in the marginal product of labor and a fall in the marginal product of capital in Y, with corresponding changes in the real returns to those factors.

Note that these results are true only as long as the economy remains incompletely specialized, for as soon as all capital and labor are allocated to a particular good, no increase in its price can change marginal products in producing that good. We have thus established the Stolper-Samuelson theorem.

> **The Stolper-Samuelson theorem.** If there are constant returns to scale and if both goods continue to be produced, a relative increase in the price of a commodity will increase the real return to the factor used intensively in that industry and reduce the real return to the other factor.

It is important to examine this result further. The Stolper-Samuelson model holds factor endowments fixed while allowing commodity prices to change, which shifts the demands for factors, thereby changing real factor incomes. This is not overly restrictive, for it seems reasonable to suppose that factor supplies are exogenously given. However, as we suggested earlier, there may be some question about this if, for example, laborers are able to choose between work and leisure.

The Stolper-Samuelson theorem embodies an interesting implication. An increase in the relative price of good X may be equivalently stated as a larger percentage increase in the price of X than of Y when both nominal prices are subject to change. The theorem assures us that this change will result in a percentage rise in the wage that is larger still than the higher price increase (because w/p_x must increase) and a percentage rise in the nominal price of capital that is smaller than the lower price increase (because r/p_y must fall; of course, it is possible that r could actually decline).

Thus, in relative terms, factor prices change *more* than commodity prices in order to get determinate effects on real factor incomes. This outcome is called the *magnification effect* in trade theory.[15] We know that an increase in the relative price of good X raises the wage rate and reduces the return to capital compared to the prices of both goods. This effect can be written as follows:

$$\%\Delta r < \%\Delta p_y < \%\Delta p_x < \%\Delta w \qquad (8.7)$$

The Stolper-Samuelson theorem as presented here is not really a theorem about international trade, for no mention has been made of trade flows or other nations. Although changes in domestic commodity prices could result from shifts in world prices in an open economy, they could just as likely result from internal changes in a closed economy. Changes in commodity taxes or fundamental shifts in consumer preferences, for example, could cause movements in commodity prices, thereby affecting the distribution of real incomes between capital and labor.

However, we can use the Stolper-samuelson theorem to investigate our primary interest in the effects of international trade on factor incomes. Suppose that labor-abundant Country F enters free trade with capital-abundant Country H. We know that this will raise the relative price of X in F and lower it in H as the countries import the relatively cheaper good. It follows immediately that labor is made better off and capital worse off in Country F, the reverse being true in Country H. Put differently, the abundant factor in each nation is made better off by free trade, and the scarce factor is made worse off. The reason for this outcome is that trade in goods compensates for national scarcities in factor supplies. In general, each country exports the services of its abundant factor, resulting in a higher demand for that factor, while it imports the services of its scarce factor, generating a fall in demand for that factor.

Each country must make aggregate gains in welfare, as we demonstrated in Fig. 8.4 (note also that the gains-from-trade theorem in Chapter 5 is fully applicable here). However, there is now a *redistribution effect* from free trade: the abundant factor earns more than the total gains from trade, making the scarce factor worse off. In principle, an appropriate compensation uses some of the gains to nullify any losses.

Thus, there is another important difference between trade based on differences in technology with a single factor of production (the Ricardian model) and trade based on different endowments with equal technologies. In the former case, all workers are identical and share equally in the gains from trade. In the latter case, only the abundant factors gain directly from free trade.

It should be noted that our statement of the theorem is not exactly the same as its original presentation. Stolper and Samuelson were concerned with the effects of tariffs on real factor rewards. A tariff, which is a tax on imports, would generally be expected to raise the domestic relative price of the importable good and thereby the real income of the scarce factor, which is used intensively in that good. Put differently, a tariff moves a country back toward autarky and helps protect the incomes of scarce factors from import competition. We now have an explanation for why different factors of production lobby for import protection while others lobby for free trade. For example, the United States is relatively scarce in laborers with limited skills, as we will show in Chapter 14. Representatives of labor interests, such as labor unions, may therefore be expected to argue against reductions in American tariffs; this was certainly the case in the political discussions surrounding the recent negotiation of the North American Free Trade Agreement with Mexico and Canada. Similarly, Japan is quite scarce in agricultural land, and the owners of this land, rice farmers for example, argue vehemently for the continuation of strict controls on food imports. This topic will be taken up again in the discussion of tariffs.

The Rybczynski Theorem

The Rybczynski theorem describes the second fundamental relationship in the economy. Named for the British economist who developed it, the theorem is concerned with the relationship between changes in factor endowments and changes in the outputs of the two commodities when commodity prices are assumed to be given. Suppose that an economy experiences a rise in its labor endowment through labor immigration. One might expect this change to raise the outputs of both X and Y because it would expand the production possibility frontier. Holding prices fixed, however, this turns out to be false, because the expansion of the labor-intensive good X draws capital and additional labor from good Y, causing Y to contract. The theorem states that, given unchanged relative commodity prices and assuming that both commodities continue to be produced, an increase in the endowment of one factor will increase the output of the commodity that uses that factor intensively and will reduce the output of the other commodity.

This theorem is most easily demonstrated through the use of the Edgeworth-Bowley box diagram of Fig. 8.10. With origins O_x and O_y, it reproduces Fig. 2.9, except that the efficiency locus has been omitted. Recall that point A represents the common tangency between isoquants from both industries. The factor-intensity rays k_y and k_x represent the capital-labor ratios for industries Y and X, respectively. Note that good Y is capital-intensive and good X is labor-intensive.

Now assume that the endowment of labor is increased by the amount ΔL. We represent this change by shifting the origin for commodity Y from O_y to O_y'. We are interested in how this change in endowments will affect the outputs of the two commodities, holding relative commodity prices constant. Recall again that as long as both goods are produced, relative commodity prices and relative factor prices bear a one-to-one relationship with each other. Thus, because commodity prices are unchanged, factor prices are unchanged; therefore, the capital-labor ratios in the two industries remain unaffected. In terms of Fig. 8.10, this result implies that, even though the endowment of labor has increased, the ray k_x is unaffected and the

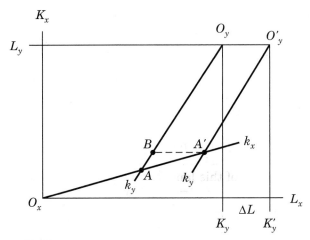

FIGURE 8.10
Changes in endowments and output.

ray k_y shifts in a parallel fashion as the origin O_y shifts to O'_y. Thus, line AO_y is parallel to line $A'O'_y$. Note that point A' must be the new equilibrium position along a new efficiency locus $O_x A'O'_y$ (not shown).

The effects of the increase in the labor supply on outputs are easily seen. Because point A' is farther from origin O_x than is point A, it follows that the output of commodity X increases. Further, output of commodity Y must decrease, which may be seen by drawing a horizontal line from A' to B. Because the length of BO_y is equal to the length of $A'O'_y$, we know that AO_y is longer than $A'O'_y$. This fact implies that point A' is on a lower Y isoquant than is point A and that the output of Y is lower. We can thus state the theorem:

> **The Rybczynski theorem.** If relative commodity prices are constant and if both commodities continue to be produced, an increase in the supply of a factor will lead to an increase in the output of the commodity using that factor intensively and a decrease in the output of the other commodity.

The Rybczynski theorem has important implications for the effects of changes in endowments on production possibility curves. Consider the production frontier $\overline{YX}$ in Fig. 8.11. An increase in the endowment of labor will shift this curve out to $\overline{Y'X'}$. Because good X is labor-intensive, we would expect that the maximum producible quantity of X would increase more than the maximum producible quantity of Y, or that the curve would experience a shift biased toward the X axis. The Rybczynski theorem may be used to demonstrate this result, holding prices fixed at ratio p. The equilibrium production point in the initial situation is A, the point where the price line p is tangent to the production possibility curve. After the increase in the labor supply, the new equilibrium position will be A', where there is a larger output of X but a smaller output of Y. This is true for any price ratio involving incomplete specialization, so that the new frontier is

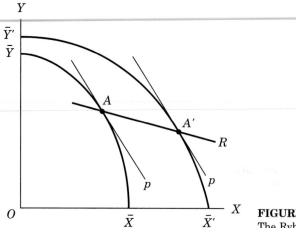

FIGURE 8.11
The Rybczynski line.

biased toward good X throughout its length. The locus R through points A and A' is called the *Rybczynski line*. It shows how output changes as one factor endowment changes with given commodity prices. A similar line for increases in the capital endowment could be constructed that would show increases in Y output and reductions in X output as the production frontier grows in a direction biased toward good Y. The Rybczynski lines are in fact linear if constant returns to scale exist in both industries.[16]

The Rybczynski theorem allows one factor endowment to change while the other is held constant. This model is easily generalized by allowing both factor endowments to change. Suppose, for example, that the capital stock rises by 10 percent and the labor force by 15 percent. We may decompose this change into an identical 10-percent rise in both factors and the additional 5-percent rise in labor. With constant returns to scale, the joint increase simply shifts out the production frontier in a parallel fashion. The Rybczynski theorem then ensures that the additional labor force causes a further biased shift in the production possibility curve. Thus, if both factor endowments are changing, the PPF shifts in a biased direction toward the good that is intensive in the faster-growing factor. An immediate implication is that countries with different relative factor endowments will have production frontiers with biased shapes as discussed in Fig. 8.2. Therefore, the Rybczynski theorem is an important building block for proving the Heckscher-Ohlin theorem.

An additional implication of this decomposition relates to output changes. Holding relative prices fixed, a balanced 10-percent increase in labor and capital would expand output of both goods X and Y by ten percent. Adding further growth of 5 percent in the labor force then reduces output of Y and raises output of X from that point. The additional expansion in X must exceed 5 percent, because further labor and capital are absorbed from sector Y. The overall result is that production of Y rises by less than 10 percent (or even falls) and output of X rises by more than 15 percent. We have demonstrated a generalized version of the Rybczynski theorem, which is also a magnification effect: at given commodity prices, changes in relative factor endowments result in magnified shifts in outputs, in that the percentage changes in commodities lie outside the percentage changes in endowments. In this example, we would write:

$$\%\Delta Y < \%\Delta \overline{K} < \%\Delta \overline{L} < \%\Delta X \tag{8.8}$$

Notice that the Rybczynski theorem itself is a special case of this result. In our example, the percentage change in the capital stock was zero (capital was held fixed), implying that the percentage change in output of good Y must be negative, that is, its output must fall.

We make some final observations about the Rybczynski theorem. Because the theorem holds relative commodity prices constant, it is only a partial exercise in comparative-static analysis. In a full general-equilibrium analysis, we would expect prices to change within an economy as outputs of goods X and Y shift, though the precise effects would depend on demand characteristics. However, this simple theorem is most useful for understanding the effects of endowments on production frontiers, as we have seen. Moreover, it is directly applicable in one important scenario. Consider a small economy that is open to international trade, implying that its relative goods prices are determined by international markets. If those relative prices are stable over time, changes in endowments in the small economy will dictate growth in its outputs and trade patterns. It is quite possible, for example, for an initially labor-abundant economy that experiences comparatively rapid accumulation in its capital stock to find its trade pattern shifting toward exports of capital-intensive goods and imports of labor-intensive goods. That is, differential rates of growth in factor supplies are consistent with changing comparative advantage, which lends an added dynamic to the Heckscher-Ohlin theory. We consider these kinds of issues more fully in Chapter 23. For now, however, note that this observation helps explain the transition of the Japanese economy. In the early 1960s, Japan was a labor-abundant net exporter of labor-intensive goods, such as textiles and simple consumer electronics. Today it is a capital-abundant net exporter of sophisticated capital-intensive goods, such as machinery and transport equipment. Japanese savings and investment rates over the last three decades were substantially higher than those in most other industrialized nations. A similar process is currently happening in the rapidly industrializing nations of Asia, including Singapore, Hong Kong, and Korea, where investment rates are also very high.

8.6 TRADE THEORY WITH MANY GOODS AND FACTORS

Throughout our analysis we have assumed that there are only two goods and two factors. The question naturally arises as to whether and to what extent the model can be generalized to higher dimensions. One possible generalization assumes that products X and Y are *groups* of products, such as all manufactures or all agricultural products. If it is then assumed that relative commodity prices within the two groups are unchanged at all times, all the preceding conclusions will hold as relative prices and outputs of the two groups change.

If there are more than two distinct commodities, however, difficulties arise even with only two factors of production. In simplest terms, this is because the factor-intensity ratios employed earlier need not produce unique results in this scenario. Suppose a third good, Z, is added to the model and that $K_y/L_y > K_x/L_x > K_z/L_z$. What would be the pattern of trade in a two-country world? One might expect that the country well-endowed with capital would export Y, the country well-endowed with labor would export Z, and some indeterminacy could exist about good X. However, this is not necessarily true. It is possible for either country to export *both* Y and Z and import X. What can be shown is that the bundle of commodities exported by the capital-abundant country will be capital-intensive in the sense of embodying a higher ratio of capital to labor than its import bundle; the corresponding situation will hold for the labor-abundant nation. However, the capital-abundant country's export bundle could consist either of some of both Y and Z, the two extreme goods, or of good X, the good of intermediate capital intensity.

With more than two factors, additional problems arise if we insist on ranking pairs of factor intensities. For example, with a third factor of natural resources, called R, it is possible to have $K_x/L_x > K_y/L_y$ but $K_x/R_x < K_y/R_y$. Which good is capital-intensive in a case like this? It obviously depends on how the comparison is made. Bilateral comparisons do not have much meaning in a world with more than two factors. Results such as those given by the Stolper-Samuelson theorem and the Rybczynski theorem, which make use of bilateral comparisons, do not easily generalize to higher dimensions.[17]

The Heckscher-Ohlin theorem does generalize in an important way, however, if we modify our definition of relative factor endowments. Suppose we can define products and factors so that there is an equal number of each, as in the two-by-two model, though the number can be anything larger than one. There can be any number of countries. We retain the assumptions of identical constant-returns technologies, identical homogeneous preferences, and the absence of distortions. It is possible to rank the endowments of any country by computing its share of each endowment in the global supply, with the most abundant factor being the one with the highest relative share and the most scarce factor the one with the lowest relative share.[18] In general, any factor in which a country's share of the global supply exceeds that country's share of global income is ranked as abundant, and others are ranked as scarce. If we then compute the amounts of each factor that are used to produce the bundle of exports, imports, and gross national product, we can derive a theorem about the *factor content* of each nation's trade:

> **The factor-content theorem.** For an arbitrary but equal number of goods and factors, a ranking of the content of any factor in net exports (that is, exports minus imports) divided by its content in total output will duplicate the ranking of relative factor endowments.

This theorem is often called the Heckscher-Ohlin-Vanek theorem because of the contribution of Jaroslev Vanek to the basic trade theory.[19] Its practical importance is in showing that, under reasonably general circumstances, differences in relative endowments still determine comparative advantage. However, comparative advantage in this sense refers to the pattern of trade in factor services rather than in goods. Indeed, it does not really matter that we cannot predict whether a country will export or import a particular commodity, because commodity trade is merely the means for implicitly trading factors.

The factor-price-equalization theorem also generalizes for any number of factors and goods as long as the number of goods is equal to the number of factors and all countries produce all these goods (that is, they are "incompletely specialized"). More generally, both the factor-price-equalization theorem and the factor-content theorem hold if there are more goods than factors, so long as the number of goods produced in common by each nation is at least as large as the number of factors.[20] For example, it can easily be shown to hold for three commodities and two factors.

8.7   CONCLUDING REMARKS

This chapter has considered a model in which the only important difference between countries is in relative factor endowments. We assume that economies are alike in all other respects, including having equal access to constant-returns-to-scale technologies, sharing homogeneous preferences, and exhibiting no market or policy distortions. Thus, the model differs importantly from the technology-based theory of trade in the prior chapter. Using this model we made several important predictions about economic structure and trade patterns.

1. A country will export the commodity that uses the well-endowed factor more intensively, which is the prediction of the Heckscher-Ohlin theorem. Thus, comparative advantage is determined by the structure of factor endowments (or autarky factor prices) in conjunction with relative factor intensities of commodities.

2. The factor-price-equalization theorem makes the powerful prediction that free trade in goods actually equalizes the relative and absolute prices of homogeneous factors internationally. The essential reason for this is that trade in goods can substitute for trade in factors. There are numerous reasons why we do not observe such equalization in practice, but there are important tendencies in that direction to the extent that international trade is the result of variations in factor endowments.

3. The Stolper-Samuelson theorem, which relates changes in commodity prices to changes in real factor prices, provides a fundamental prediction about the effects of trade (or impediments to trade) on the distribution of real incomes between capital and labor. Because free trade causes exports and imports to rise, it follows that the relatively abundant factor gains real income in each country and the scarce factor loses real income.

However, the gains-from-trade theorem is relevant here, in that the economy enjoys an overall rise in welfare by moving from autarky to free trade.

4. The Rybczynski theorem, which relates changes in factor endowments to changes in commodity outputs, assuming constant commodity and factor prices, provides the theoretical basis for the Heckscher-Ohlin model. This theorem is also important for understanding the effects of factor growth on the evolution of comparative advantage.

5. It is possible to extend the Heckscher-Ohlin theory to the case of large numbers of goods and factors. The factor-content theorem predicts that the implicit trade in factor services depends on rankings of factors, even if the trade patterns for particular commodities are not determinate.

PROBLEMS

1. Show that, in a two-country model, increasing the size of one country (increasing both K and L in the same proportions) will change commodity prices, factor prices, outputs, and the volume of trade in both countries, but will not change the pattern of trade.

2. How will the production possibility curves of Fig. 8.2 differ if in Fig. 8.1, Country H has more K but the same amount of L as Country F?

3. In Fig. 8.4, why must the consumption points for both countries lie on a common ray from the origin?

4. Illustrate a case in which either or both countries could specialize completely in the presence of free trade. Does this possibility invalidate the Heckscher-Ohlin theorem? What about the factor-price-equalization theorem?

*5. The factor-price-equalization theorem makes no assumption about demand. Nevertheless, demand conditions may well determine whether or not factor prices are equalized. Explain this seemingly paradoxical result.

6. Show that factor prices will be unequal if the technologies in the two countries differ for industry X (or Y).

7. Show that an increase in the labor supply of a small country could either increase or decrease the volume of trade.

*8. How will an increase in the supply of labor affect the terms of trade in the two-country model (recall Problem 7)?

NOTES

1. One exception might be a country that is largely specialized in the production of a primary commodity such as petroleum. However, this kind of specialization is related to the overwhelming endowment of natural reserves rather than to any relative labor productivity, so the Heckscher-Ohlin model is the more appropriate view here as well.

2. We review these issues thoroughly in Chapter 14.

3. See Maskus (1991) for details on the construction of these variables.

4. This difference is largely a result of the fact that a significant portion of the Indian population works in the so-called "informal" sector, where economic activity is unmeasured. Theoretically, the existence of factor endowments that are variable rather than fixed does

not change the fundamental conclusions of the Heckscher-Ohlin theory, as shown in Martin (1976).

5. Technically, an FIR is possible between two constant-returns-to-scale production functions if the elasticity of substitution is higher in one of the functions. Note, however, that an FIR cannot happen within a single country because the contract curve in the Edgeworth-Bowley Box cannot cross the diagonal (see Problem 5 in Chapter 2). Thus, the issue arises in comparisons of factor-intensity rankings in different countries.

6. As discussed by Maskus (1991), there is great similarity in these rankings across a large group of developed and developing countries. Thus, in practice, factor-intensity reversals seem to be unimportant empirically.

7. Professor Paul A. Samuelson made so many contributions to this model that it is often called the Heckscher-Ohlin-Samuelson theorem. We have chosen to use the original title.

8. We review formal empirical studies of this question in Chapter 14.

9. The countries would differ only in the relative prices at which they become specialized in X or Y, given the endowment-based differences in their production frontiers. Once a country becomes completely specialized in a good, say X, further increases in its price cannot attract any further resources, so both r and w rise in proportion to p_x, keeping ω constant.

10. This statement vividly illustrates the danger of treating specific variables as exogenous in a general-equilibrium model. We could have stated instead that different autarky factor prices are the source of different autarky goods prices, which seems logical. Indeed, some trade theorists define factor abundance in the Heckscher-Ohlin model in terms of relative factor prices in autarky.

11. Strictly speaking, the endowment ratio must be a *weighted average* of the capital-labor ratios in X and Y, with the weights given by the proportion of the total labor force allocated to each sector.

12. An additional theoretical requirement for factor price equalization is that there be no factor-intensity reversal between countries H and F. Suppose, for example, that in H at autarky, good X is capital-intensive, while in F, good X is labor-intensive, with $\omega_h > \omega_f$ due to factor endowments. In free trade, let Country H export Y and Country F export X. In this case, the wage-rental ratios in both nations would rise from free trade, and there is no clear presumption toward their convergence.

13. See Dollar and Wolff (1993) and Maskus (1991).

14. In methodological terms, trade economists thus view endowments and commodity prices as *exogenous variables* that determine outputs and factor prices, the *endogenous variables*. This interpretation should be treated cautiously, however, as all these elements contain some degree of endogeneity.

15. The magnification effect and other aspects of the general equilibrium two-sector model are developed in Jones (1965). A simple proof that a rise in the relative price of X is equivalent to a larger percentage rise in its price is as follows:
Let both p_x and p_y rise but $(p_x^1/p_y^1) > (p_x^0/p_y^0)$. Rearranging this inequality and subtracting 1 from each side, it follows immediately that $[(p_x^1 - p_x^0)/p_x^0] > [(p_y^1 - p_y^0)/p_y^0]$.

16. To see this, recall that with fixed p, each commodity retains the same capital-labor ratio. Thus, a given increase in labor use in sector X after a rise in the labor supply must call a proportional amount of capital from sector Y, yielding a linear increase in X output. Similarly, the proportional reduction in capital and labor used in Y results in a linear reduction in that sector's output.

17. For a full treatment of these issues, see Ethier (1984).

18. We present computations of this nature for actual countries and endowments in Chapter 14.

19. See Vanek (1968). Credit should also be given to Melvin (1968) and Leamer (1980).

20. Mathematically inclined students will recognize this as a statement from linear algebra in which we need enough information on common commodity prices to determine common factor prices in a system of linear equations. If there are more factors than goods (a case that is most unlikely), there will be no presumption of any kind toward equalization of global factor prices.

REFERENCES

Chipman, J. S. (1966). "A Survey of the Theory of International Trade: Part 3, The Modern Theory." *Econometrica* 34: 18–76.

Dollar, D. and Wolff, E. N. (1993). *Competitiveness, Convergence, and International Specialization.* Chicago: University of Chicago Press.

Ethier, W. J. (1984). "Higher Dimensional Issues in Trade Theory." in R. W. Jones and P. B. Kenen, eds. *Handbook of International Economics.* Amsterdam, North-Holland: 131–184.

Johnson, H. G. (1961). "Factor Endowments, International Trade and Factor Prices." in H. G. Johnson, ed., *International Trade and Economic Growth.* Cambridge, Mass.: Harvard University Press, 17–30.

Jones, R. W. (1965). "The Structure of Simple General Equilibrium Models." *Journal of Political Economy* 73: 557–572.

Jones, R. W. (1956-57). "Factor Proportions and the Heckscher-Ohlin Theorem." *Review of Economic Studies* 24: 1–10.

Leamer, E. E. (1980). "The Leontief Paradox Reconsidered." *Journal of Political Economy* 88: 495–503.

Martin, J. (1976). "Variable Factor Supplies and the Heckscher-Ohlin-Samuelson Model." *Economic Journal* 86: 820–831.

Maskus, K. E. (1991). "Comparing International Trade Data and Product and National Characteristics Data for the Analysis of Trade Models." in P. Hooper and J. D. Richardson, eds., *International Economic Transactions: Issues in Measurement and Empirical Research.* Chicago: University of Chicago Press, 17–56.

Melvin J. R. (1968). "Production and Trade with Two Factors and Three Goods." *American Economic Review* 63: 1249–1268.

Metzler, L. A. (1949). "Tariff, the Terms of Trade and the Distribution of National Income." *Journal of Political Economy* 57: 1–29.

Rybczynski, T. N. (1955). "Factor Endowments and Relative Commodity Prices." *Economica* 22: 336–341.

Samuelson, P. A. (1948). "International Trade and the Equalization of Factor Prices." *Economic Journal* 58; 163–184.

Samuelson, P. A. (1949). "International Factor Price Equalization Once Again." *Economic Journal* 59: 181–197.

Samuelson, P. A. (1953). "Price of Factors and Goods in General Equilibrium." *Review of Economic Studies* 21: 1–20.

Stolper, W. F. and Samuelson, P. A. (1941). "Protection and Real Wages." *Review of Economic Studies* 9: 58–73.

Summers, R. and Heston, A. (1988). "A New Set of International Comparisons of Real Product and Price Levels: Estimates for 130 Countries, 1950–1985." *Review of Income and Wealth* 34: 1–25.

Vanek, J. (1968). "The Factor Proportions Theory: the n-Factor Case." *Kyklos* 21: 749–756.

CHAPTER
9

THE SPECIFIC-FACTORS MODEL

9.1 INTRODUCTION

Chapter 8 considered the Heckscher-Ohlin model where two factors of production, capital and labor, were used to produce two outputs, and where both factors were perfectly mobile between the two industries. This model has formed the central structure for most of the theoretical international trade literature that has developed in the last four decades. Recently, however, international trade economists have become interested in models that go beyond the assumptions of the Heckscher-Ohlin model. The remaining chapters in this part of the text will consider a variety of models that relax central assumptions of that framework. In the present chapter we remove the assumption that both factors are perfectly mobile between the two industries.

It is important to understand that the Heckscher-Ohlin assumption of free factor mobility between industries describes a state at which an economy can arrive only in the long run. The assumption of perfect mobility of capital implies an economy in which industries can convert one kind of capital into another. In many circumstances, this process may require a considerable time period. For example, the capital used to produce automobiles is much different from that required to produce wheat or textiles. Capital mobility between such diverse industries requires time for physical capital to depreciate in some uses and for new investment to take place in others.

It is perhaps most natural to consider capital to be fixed in its sectoral usage for some time, and this is the basic approach we adopt. However, we note that labor could also be characterized similarly to the extent that skills are particular to specific tasks. Individuals skilled in the operation of textile looms, for example, require some retraining before becoming proficient at computer programming. Thus, for short time periods, factor specificity is common. Some factors, such as agricultural land, are quite specific in their use even for long time periods.

Economists make a logical distinction between time periods that is implicit in our discussion. The *long run* is defined as a period of time sufficient to allow all factors to be in variable use in production functions, which corresponds here to free intersectoral factor mobility. The *short run* is defined as a period of time in which at least one factor is fixed in production functions, corresponding to capital specificity. This is the fundamental distinction we maintain in this chapter.

Clearly, the long run is important and deserves analysis. However, many economic changes have important short-run consequences. The imposition of tariffs or changes in the terms of trade may have significant effects on the economy in a shorter time period than would allow for the complete mobility of capital between industries. We may also be interested in whether the short-run effects of such changes are the same as the long-run consequences discussed in Chapter 8. For example, will we expect factor prices in different countries to be equalized in the short run if the other conditions for equalization described in Chapter 8 are maintained? Will the Rybczynski theorem and the Stolper- Samuelson theorem derived for the long-run conditions of the endowment model also apply in the short run? Also important is whether the basic Heckscher-Ohlin prediction of trade flows based on given factor endowments holds in a short-run version of this model. Thus, even though the theories are identical in the long run, there are important differences in our theoretical predictions in the short run, when capital is sector-specific. Indeed, these differences are so striking that it is natural to consider the specific-factors model as an important theory of trade and income distribution in its own right. We will investigate these questions in this chapter.

The model employed here is similar to the Heckscher-Ohlin model except that one factor, capital, is assumed to be useful for the production of only one commodity. For example, automobiles require one kind of capital and textiles another, and in the short run the amount of capital allocated to each industry is fixed. No substitution of capital between industries can take place, though labor is mobile. Because capital is specific to a particular industry, the model we describe has become known as the specific-factors model. It has a long history in the economic literature, but recent interest in the model dates from the work of Jones (1971) and Samuelson (1971). Other key contributions were made by Mayer (1974) and Mussa (1974).

It should also be noted that although we are considering the specific-factors model as a short-run version of the Heckscher-Ohlin model, the specific-factors model has other interpretations. In particular, we can consider the specific factors to be quite distinct kinds of inputs, such as different natural resources. The analysis can be used to develop a model in which these resources form the basis for comparative advantage and international trade.

9.2 THE SPECIFIC-FACTORS MODEL

In many respects, the specific-factors model is similar to the model used for the Heckscher-Ohlin analysis of Chapter 8. We assume that two commodities are produced with production functions that exhibit constant returns to scale. We also assume that two factors of production are required for both production functions. As usual, tastes are assumed to be homogeneous and identical for all consumers, allowing the representation of preferences by a set of community indifference curves.

The essential difference betwen the Heckscher-Ohlin model and the specific-factors model is that in the latter theory, only labor is homogeneous and common to the two production functions. Capital is fixed by industry in the short run. Therefore, instead of the production functions in Eqs. (2.8) of Chapter 2, we have the production functions shown below: *2 diff. types of cap., specific to diff. sectors*

$$X = F_x(R_x, L_x)$$
$$Y = F_y(S_y, L_Y) \tag{9.1}$$

R_x and S_y represent types of capital that are specific to sectors X and Y, respectively. Corresponding to the factor-supply constraints of Eqs. (2.9) of Chapter 2, we have the following equations:

$$\overline{R} = R_x$$
$$\overline{S} = S_y \tag{9.2}$$
$$\overline{L} = L_x + L_y$$

Equations (9.2) simply show that the entire available stock of factor R is used to produce commodity X and the entire endowment of factor S is used to produce commodity Y. Note that again we are assuming that all factors of production are fully employed. The return to labor (the wage rate) is defined to be w, which is the same in both industries by virtue of the free mobility of workers. The returns to R and S will be defined to be r and s, respectively. Thus, the specificity of capital allows the returns to capital to differ across industries in the short run. This fact points out that in the short run, the two capital stocks are different inputs and that the model may also be interpreted as a theory with two goods and three factors.

It is useful at this point to review certain properties of production functions that have constant returns to scale. In Chapter 2 we discussed the notion of the total product curve for labor. This curve depicts the response of output in an industry to increases in a variable factor, holding constant the input of a fixed factor. This construction, reproduced in Fig. 9.1, is directly applicable to the specific-factors model. In the top panel we show that the total product of labor in sector X rises as more labor is added to the fixed

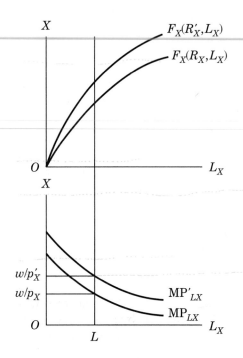

FIGURE 9.1
Total product and marginal product curves for labor.

stock of R_x, but it does so at a diminishing rate (indeed, at some point, the total product could fall). In the bottom panel we depict the marginal product of labor in industry X, which is the slope of the total product curve. Because of diminishing returns, the marginal product declines as employment in X rises. A similar construction applies to good Y, given the fixed stock of S_y.

These results hold in a more general sense. As described in Chapter 8, the marginal product of labor in either sector is an increasing function of the capital-labor ratio used in that sector. Consider, for example, an increase in capital usage of 10 percent and an increase in labor usage of 5 percent in industry X. We may decompose this change into, first, an identical 5 percent rise in R and L and, second, an additional rise in R. With constant returns to scale, the first component has no impact on the marginal product of labor. However, the second component raises the marginal product of labor for any given level of employment. Indeed, as depicted in Fig. 9.1, an increase in the endowment of R_X will shift up both the total product and marginal product curves for labor.

Analogous conclusions hold for the determination of the marginal products of capital, which are declining functions of the capital-labor ratios in each industry. Finally, under constant returns to scale, the marginal products of each factor depend only on these capital-labor ratios and not on the level of production.

We retain the assumption that factor markets are perfectly competitive, implying that firms pay each factor the value of its marginal product. Thus, in the X industry we have:

$$\text{VMP}_{LX} = \text{MP}_{LX}p_x = w$$
$$\text{VMP}_{KX} = \text{MP}_{KX}p_x = r \tag{9.3}$$

Similar equations characterize factor-market equilibrium conditions with respect to industry Y. Note that from these conditions we can specify that the real returns to labor and capital in terms of commodity X are equivalent to their marginal products: $w/p_x = \text{MP}_{LX}$ and $r/p_x = \text{MP}_{KX}$, respectively. This result means that changes in real returns to factors are known as soon as changes in capital-labor ratios are determined. For example, in Fig. 9.1, a rise in the capital stock for a given level of employment generates a higher real wage. Moreover, because marginal products are functions of only the capital-labor ratios, if we know how one marginal product changes, we immediately know that the other marginal product has changed in the opposite direction. Thus, an increase in the marginal product of labor implies a decrease in the marginal product of capital in the same sector. In other words, if we find that w/p_x rises, we know that r/p_x must necessarily fall. These relationships hold regardless of what is happening to outputs or endowments in the economy.

Completing the model requires linking sectors X and Y together in a short-run general equilibrium framework. This is done by noting that inter-industry labor mobility must establish a common wage in both industries, generating an equal value of marginal product of labor in equilibrium. This feature allows us to determine the allocation of labor between X and Y in each equilibrium, as depicted in Fig. 9.2.

Employment in sector X is indicated from left to right, relative to origin O_x. Suppose that p_x is given and that the capital stock in industry X is held fixed. As more labor is employed in this sector, the marginal product of labor declines, causing the value of labor's marginal product, or VMP_{LX}, to be a downward-sloping curve. Because equilibrium requires the equality of

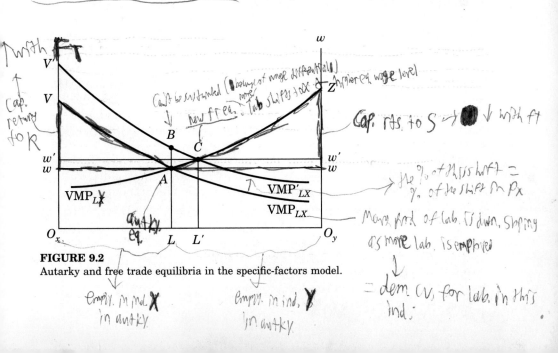

FIGURE 9.2
Autarky and free trade equilibria in the specific-factors model.

VMP_{LX} and w, it is possible to interpret this schedule as the demand curve for labor in industry X. Note that a rise in either p_x or R_x would shift the VMP_{LX} curve upward.

The demand for labor in sector Y is represented by the VMP_{LY} schedule, which is drawn from right to left relative to origin O_y. Thus, movements to the left represent larger employment in Y and correspond to declines in the marginal product and in the value of the marginal product of labor for a given endowment of S_y and a fixed p_y.

Suppose point A represents autarky equilibrium in this economy. Accordingly, the distance O_xL measures employment in industry X, the distance O_yL measures employment in industry Y, and labor is fully utilized. It is convenient to characterize income distribution in this equilibrium. There is a common wage w paid in both industries. Total labor income paid to workers in sector X is the area wO_xLA, while that in sector Y is wO_yLA. The remaining income generated in each sector represents nominal total returns to each capital stock. Thus, in autarky, factor R earns the area VwA and factor S earns the area ZwA.

9.3   COMMODITY PRICES AND FACTOR PRICES

We are now in a position to consider how price changes will affect factor prices and income distribution in this model. Because only relative price changes matter in general equilibrium, let us suppose that p_y remains fixed at some arbitrary level and consider the effects of a change in p_x. A natural supposition in this scenario is that our closed economy is small and that, upon entering into free trade, it faces a higher world price for good X. Thus, the economy would choose to export good X as its price rises to the world level.

In Fig. 9.2, the higher p_x would shift up the value of marginal product schedule for good X as shown. Note that the ratio of distances, BA/AL, measures the *proportional* increase in the price of X by virtue of the fact that VMP_{LX} is the product of the marginal product of labor and the commodity price. For example, a 20 percent rise in p_x results in a 20 percent shift upwards in the value of marginal product curve throughout its length.

Consider the adjustment to the new equilibrium under free trade. Point B cannot be an equilibrium because it corresponds to a higher wage in sector X than in sector Y. Thus, labor moves from Y to X, which provides the additional resources to expand output of the latter commodity and allow for its export. This labor mobility lowers the marginal product of labor in industry X and raises it in industry Y, moving the economy along the relevant VMP_L curves to the free trade equilibrium at point C. There is a higher allocation of labor to good X and a higher nominal wage rate in both industries.

Our primary interest is in the effect of the higher price of good X on real factor returns. Inspection of Fig. 9.2 demonstrates that both the total income paid to R, which is the specific capital stock in X, and the total wages paid in the economy are larger in free trade. Total income for S, the specific capital stock in Y, is smaller. Thus, the nominal factor prices r and w are higher, but s is lower. We conclude that laborers and owners of the capital stock in industry X enjoy higher real returns measured in terms of their ability to purchase good Y, the price of which has remained constant, while owners of the capital stock in industry Y receive a lower real return.

The latter capital owners also suffer a lower real return in terms of good X, the price of which is now higher. It follows that owners of the specific capital stock in the declining industry are made worse off by the price change induced by the entry into free trade.

To reach precise conclusions about the real returns to owners of R and to laborers relative to the higher-priced good, we consider the changes in marginal products. The labor influx lowers the capital-labor ratio in use in industry X, thereby raising the marginal productivity of the fixed capital stock as well as its real price, r/p_x. Thus, owners of the specific capital stock in the expanding industry unambiguously gain real income from the price change.

Finally, the fact that the capital-labor ratio falls in sector X and rises in sector Y as a result of the interindustry employment shift from point A to point C implies that the real wage falls in the expanding sector and rises in the declining sector. Indeed, it is this decline in the real wage that supports the expansion of output in industry X. Each laborer is better off in terms of ability to consume good Y but worse off in terms of ability to consume good X. Whether workers gain or lose welfare depends on their preferences for the two commodities. This result has been termed the *neoclassical ambiguity* in trade theory. We have proven the following proposition.

> **Commodity prices and factor prices.** A relative price increase of a good benefits the specific factor used in that industry, reduces the real income of the other specific factor, and has an ambiguous effect on the mobile factor.

It is useful to provide further perspective on this result. This proposition is in sharp contrast to the Stolper-Samuelson theorem discussed in Chapter 8. The Stolper-Samuelson theorem, which is based on the long-run supposition that both factors are costlessly mobile between industries, predicts that the effect of a relative change in commodity prices on real factor prices depends on the factor intensities of the commodities. Thus, a rise in the price of the labor-intensive good, for example, draws both labor and capital from the capital-intensive good and results in both goods being produced with higher capital-labor ratios. As a result, real wages rise in terms of both goods, while real capital incomes fall in terms of both goods. In Fig. 9.2, a long-run equilibrium would exist at a point to the right of C (because the induced capital flow would further raise output of X) and higher than B (because the nominal wage must rise in comparison with the price of X). Note carefully the implication that in the long run, output responses in the economy are *more elastic* with respect to price changes than in the short run. This fact merely reflects the inability of capital to move in the specific-factors model.

In the specific-factors model, on the other hand, the relevant characteristic in the short run is not factor intensities but the identity of mobile factors and specific factors. Our description of the movement from autarky to free trade made no mention of factor intensities. This is hardly surprising because the notion of factor intensities makes little sense in the specific-factors model. It would be meaningless to compare the ratios of capital to labor in sectors X and Y because the capital stocks are not comparable. Mobility is important, however. Indeed, had we constructed our model economy with mobile capital and fixed labor forces, the impact of trade on capital real income would have been ambiguous, while the laborers would have gained or lost, depending on the sector of employment.

Returning to the short-run model, the economic intuition behind the impacts of commodity price changes on the prices of specific factors is straightforward. The rise in p_x induces firms to wish to produce more X, raising the demand for the services of R. Because no additional supplies of R are available to satisfy this demand, the factor experiences a substantial rise in its real price. In effect, capital owners in this industry gain both from the influx of labor and from receiving a share of the higher price of X. Indeed, because the wage rises by proportionally *less* than the price increase, the price of capital must rise by proportionally *more*. To return to our example, a 20 percent rise in the price of good X emanating from free trade results in an increase in the return to R of more than 20 percent. The opposite effects occur for owners of S as output of good Y declines in the short run. That is, there is a decline in demand for S-capital, reducing its price. Notice that this logic implies a variant of the long-run magnification effect we identified in Chapter 8. In the present case we would write

$$\%\Delta s < \%\Delta p_y < \%\Delta w < \%\Delta p_x < \%\Delta r \tag{9.4}$$

Again, keep in mind that the ranking here depends on factor mobility (or homogeneity) and not on factor intensities.

It is also interesting to note the difference between this model and the Ricardian model for the implications of free trade and incomes. In the Ricardian model each worker is identical and each gains equally from the entry into free trade by virtue of specialization at improved terms of trade. Here there are three distinct factors, and trade has ambiguous impacts on workers' real incomes.

The specific-factors model provides a powerful basis for understanding the interests of different factor owners in supporting or opposing government policy changes, such as trade protection, that influence relative prices. Factors employed solely in sectors that will enjoy a price increase would strongly support such measures, while factors employed in other sectors would oppose them. Mobile factors may be relatively unaffected by such policy changes and may avoid expressing opinions through voting or lobbying. Accordingly, the model helps explain the observed phenomenon that lobbying for and against protective barriers against imports tends to be done by coalitions of specific factors in particular sectors (Magee, 1978). In contrast, the Stolper-Samuelson theorem would frame such behavior as a conflict between abundant and scarce factors.

9.4 ENDOWMENT CHANGES, FACTOR PRICES, AND OUTPUTS

Two central features of the endowment model in Chapter 8 were the factor-price-equalization theorem and the Rybczynski theorem. We now show that the predictions of these models do not generally hold in the specific-factors model.

Factor Price Equalization

The factor-price-equalization theorem stated that in free trade with equalized commodity prices, if two countries produce both goods in common, real factor prices will become identical as well. The existence of different factor endowments does not change this result as long as countries are incompletely specialized. The theory relies on the assumption that there are at least as many goods as factors so that equalized goods prices would be sufficient to determine equalized factor prices. In this context, it is no surprise that factor price equalization does not hold in the specific-factors model, because it embodies three factors and only two goods. To make the point more concrete, simply imagine countries H and F moving from autarky to free trade. If H exports good X, then the real income of R-capital will rise and that of S-capital will fall, as we demonstrated. In F the real income of S-capital will rise and that of R-capital will fall as that country exports good Y. Labor will have a higher real wage with respect to good Y in H but a lower real wage with respect to good Y in F (and the opposite effects would manifest with respect to good X). There is clearly no presumption toward equalization of real factor prices in the short run.

We provide a more formal demonstration by showing that in free trade, countries will experience different real factor incomes. Consider the effects of endowment changes on real incomes, as depicted in Fig. 9.3, where we take as the initial situation the free trade equilibrium at point C. To simplify matters, we suppose that the diagram refers to a small open economy that continually faces fixed international prices, thereby holding both domestic prices fixed throughout.

Consider first an increase in the endowment of S, the specific capital stock in sector Y. Clearly, all of the new capital stock must be employed in industry Y, and this infusion of capital increases the marginal product of labor in that industry. In Fig. 9.3, this outcome is represented by the upward shift in the VMP_{LY} schedule. The higher wage induces labor to flow from sector X to sector Y until the wage is again equalized at point T. Output of good Y goes up, drawing labor from good X, the output of which declines.

Implications for factor incomes are clear. With a higher wage and fixed commodity prices, all laborers enjoy higher real earnings. This is a result of the rising capital-labor ratio in *both* industries (recall that good X loses labor

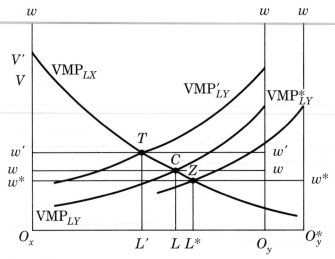

FIGURE 9.3
Endowment changes in the specific-factors model.

to good Y) and the consequent increases in marginal products of labor. We also conclude immediately that the real returns to *both* specific factors are reduced by virtue of the higher capital-labor ratios. Again, with unchanged goods prices but a higher wage, the nominal returns to both capital stocks must be lower, causing an unambiguous decline in the real incomes of their owners. Thus, an increase in the endowment of S reduces the return to both specific factors and increases labor's real income. It is easily seen that the same result will hold for a rise in the supply of R, for the effects of increases in the specific factors are symmetrical. In general, then, any expansion of the endowment of a specific factor at constant commodity prices will lower the real return to both specific factors and raise the real return to the mobile factor.

Next consider the effects of an increase in the endowment of labor. This change is represented in Fig. 9.3 by an enlargement of the labor force, shifting the origin for sector Y to O_y^*. In turn, the VMP_{LY} schedule is displaced to the right by the same amount. Thus, the curve VMP_{LY}^* contains information equivalent to that in curve VMP_{LY}, but with reference to the new origin.

The rise in the labor endowment causes the economy to move from the initial free trade equilibrium at point C to a new equilibrium at point Z. The immediate implication is that the additional labor supply reduces the nominal wage rate from w to w^*. With fixed commodity prices, laborers are made worse off. It is also clear that total capital income in sector X is higher, implying higher nominal and real returns for owners of R. Implications for owners of S are unclear from Fig. 9.3. To reach precise conclusions, note that the increase in the labor endowment is divided between sectors X and Y, causing both outputs to rise in the short run. This follows from the fact that distance $O_x L^*$ exceeds distance $O_x L$, while distance $O_y^* L^*$ similarly exceeds distance $O_y L$.[1] Thus, the increased labor force results in a lower capital-labor ratio in both sectors, raising the real returns to both specific factors and lowering the real wages of labor. We have proven the following proposition.

> ***Factor endowments and factor prices.*** At constant commodity prices, any increase in the endowment of a specific factor will increase the real returns to the mobile factor and lower the real returns to both specific factors. An increase in the endowment of the mobile factor will reduce its own real income and increase the real income of both specific factors.

Again, to make the contrast to the factor-price-equalization theorem, recall that in that model, any endowment change resulted in no impacts on the real returns to any factor as long as the economy remained incompletely specialized. In the specific-factors model, however, endowment shifts have sharp impacts on real factor incomes, whether or not the economy is specialized.

To make the comparison to the factor-price-equalization theorem fully explicit, the rise in the endowment of the specific factor S in the small open economy of Fig. 9.3 cannot have an impact on commodity prices or factor prices in the rest of the world. Thus, this economy would have higher real wages and lower real returns to its specific factors than would exist elsewhere in the short-run equilibrium. This absence of factor price equalization carries over to the case of two large countries who trade with each other. Suppose, for example, that Fig. 9.3 represents Country H and that in the initial equilibrium at point C, H is exporting good Y. The expansion in Y output after the rise in the endowment of S should, under most circumstances, result in greater exports of good Y and a fall in its relative price. In the foreign country this change would tend to raise the relative return to the specific factor in sector X and lower the relative return to the specific factor in sector Y with an ambiguous impact on the real wage. While these effects would pertain also to the home country, they only partially offset the initial impacts of the endowment change. Thus, there is no presumption toward factor price equalization in the short run. We can, therefore, add the following theorem.

> ***Trade and factor prices.*** In the specific-factors model, the equalization of commodity prices by international trade does not equalize factor prices.

An important implication of this finding is that free trade in goods does not fully exhaust the available gains from trade, in the sense that productive factors have an incentive to migrate in such an equilibrium. Even in the absence of any impediments to trade, if factors are intersectorally immobile, there will be international differences in their real returns. Factors may be too impatient to wait for the long-run equalization of their returns (assuming such equalization were even possible in practical terms) and may prefer to move to the other country to find employment in their specific sectors.

Again, trade in factors is a significant phenomenon, and we will analyze it in Chapter 21.

Endowment Changes and Outputs

Turning to the Rybczynski theorem, the discussion in Chapter 8 demonstrated that under constant commodity prices, an increase in the endowment of a particular factor raises the output of the good intensive in that factor and lowers the output of the other good. In the specific-factors model, where factor intensity is less important than factor specificity, the predictions about endowment changes and outputs are again quite different, as we have already demonstrated.

Specifically, we have shown that an increase in the endowment of a specific factor increases the output of the good that uses that factor and must lower the output of the other good by pulling labor from it. This is similar to the Rybczynski prediction, but it depends on the sectoral specificity of the expanding factor rather than on factor intensities in production. We have also demonstrated that a rise in the labor endowment expands *both* outputs as the new labor force is divided between the sectors. Again, this is due to the mobility of labor rather than to the labor intensity of production. Thus, we can state the following proposition.

> ***Factor endowments and outputs.*** An increase in one specific factor increases the output of the commodity that uses that factor and reduces the output of the other industry. Increases in the supply of the mobile factor will expand both outputs.

We note in passing that the impacts of endowment changes in the specific-factors model suggest that different groups of factors will have different incentives to lobby for or against international factor migration. It is clear from our discussion that mobile factors would oppose policies allowing freer immigration of competing mobile factors, while owners of specific factors would favor them. Again, this is a result of factor *mobility* rather than factor *scarcity,* as in the Heckscher-Ohlin model.

9.5   THE PATTERN OF TRADE

One of the principal results of the Heckscher-Ohlin theorem described in Chapter 8 is that we can predict trade patterns from the knowledge of technology and factor endowments. In particular, we found that a country will export the commodity that uses its abundant factor most intensively. We now want to investigate whether a similar property holds for the specific-factors model. To facilitate comparison, we depart from the small open economy notion and assume, as before, that there are two countries, H and F. We begin by assuming that H and F have identical endowments of labor and *total* capital in the long run. As we know, in this case, with preferences assumed to be identical in both countries, the two economies will be identical in every respect and there will be no possibility of international trade.

While there are identical long-run endowments, suppose that in the short run the capital in the two countries is allocated differently between the two industries. Specifically, assume that in Country H there is more capital in the Y industry and that in Country F there is more capital in the X industry. In economic terms this would mean that Country H has a greater stock of specific factor S and a lower stock of specific factor R than does Country F. As we have seen in Fig. 9.3, this structure of capital endowments would generate a higher output of good Y and a lower output of good X in H than in F for any common relative commodity prices.

The economies are no longer identical and will find it advantageous to trade. With identical preferences, it follows that the home country will export good Y and the foreign country will export good X. Thus, in the short run, each country will export the commodity that is produced with the relatively abundant specific factor. While this outcome sounds much like the Heckscher-Ohlin theorem, it relies on the existence of specific factors and not on relative factor intensities. Had we assumed that Country H had a larger initial stock of R-capital, then we would have expected H to export good X.

Now suppose we return to the situation of identical long-run factor supplies and no trade initially. Allow Country F to experience a rise in its labor endowment. In the Heckscher-Ohlin model, Country F necessarily would export X, the long-run labor-intensive commodity. However, in the specific-factors model, the rise in the labor supply would generate an increase in the output of both goods X and Y in Country F. In general it is impossible to predict which of these commodities will be exported without more information on production technologies. Referring back to Fig. 9.3, the relative increases in outputs depend on the slopes of the VMP_{LX} and VMP_{LY} schedules, which depend on the underlying production functions and on how capital is allocated between the two industries. Suppose, for example, that the VMP_{LX} curve is quite flat but the VMP_{LY} curve is quite steep.[2] This configuration would mean that the short-run changes in outputs would favor a larger rise in X, suggesting that it would be exported. These relative slopes could be different, however. We thus have the following proposition.

> *The pattern of trade.* In the specific-factors model, each country will export the good with the absolutely abundant stock of specific capital, assuming identical endowments of labor, the mobile factor. With differences in labor endowments, trade patterns will depend on the nature of the production functions and on the allocation of capital (that is, on the stocks of specific factors).

9.6 CONCLUDING REMARKS

In our discussion we have interpreted the specific-factors model as a short-run version of the Heckscher-Ohlin model discussed in Chapter 8.[3] This approach is useful, for it allows an easy comparison of the principal results of these two models. The specific-factors model has a much broader interpretation, however. The specific factors need not be different kinds of capital but instead could be capital and land. In this case the model could be used to consider the production and trade of two commodities whose outputs are closely tied to the specific factors. Examples would include manufactures and food: where manufactured goods use capital and labor as inputs, and food uses land and labor. Alternatively, where the specific factors are resources such as iron or timber, a model of trade for resource-rich economies would be considered. The conclusions we have reached in terms of the relationship between commodity prices and factor prices and between endowments and outputs would remain unaffected, and these alternative models could be constructed simply by renaming the variables in the earlier sections of this chapter. In any case, many trade economists agree that the effects of specific factors have a powerful impact on global trade.

The specific-factors model provides an interesting contrast to the Heckscher-Ohlin model described in Chapter 8. In particular, we have seen that the theorems associated with the endowment model do not carry over to the specific-factors framework. Our major conclusions may be listed as follows.

1. In the specific-factors model, the primary technological characteristic is factor mobility versus factor specificity, rather than factor intensities as in the Heckscher-Ohlin model. It is on this basis that factors are identified. The presence of specific factors means that they will have different prices within the economy.

2. In the Heckscher-Ohlin model, factor prices are uniquely determined by commodity prices, and real factor rewards change in a predictable way when commodity prices change. In the specific-factors model, although the returns to the specific factors are unambiguously related to commodity price changes, such is not the case for the return to labor, the mobile factor. Whether labor loses or gains from a price change depends on the consumption pattern of the representative worker.

3. Trade does not equalize factor prices across countries in the specific-factors model. In simplest terms, this is because there are two goods but three factors, so equalized commodity prices do not imply the necessity of equal factor returns, even if both countries produce both goods.

4. Differences in factor endowments also have somewhat different effects in the specific-factors model. Increases in a *specific* factor will necessarily increase the output of the commodity using this factor. However, an increase in the *mobile* factor will raise the output of both commodities; the nature of production functions and the endowments of specific factors will determine which output increases by more.

PROBLEMS

1. Describe obvious situations in which the need to produce different sectoral outputs, such as wheat, iron ore, machinery, textiles, computer programs, and

legal services, renders certain productive factors sector-specific. Which factors may be reasonably characterized as intersectorally mobile?

2. Suppose that unskilled workers cannot easily move from one industry to another because of geographical or market frictions, such as the need to sell a home or the requirement for union membership. Should these frictions be considered a source of sector specificity of labor? Why or why not?

3. Figure 9.2 described the adjustment from the short-run equilibrium at point A to a new short-run equilibrium at point C. Continue the analysis by analyzing the further adjustment to some new long-run equilibrium in terms of effects on outputs and real factor prices. (Hint: consider the effects on the VMP_L curves.)

4. Repeat the analysis in Fig. 9.3 for an increase in the endowment of R rather than in S.

5. Figure 9.3 shows a short-run adjustment to an increase in the supply of specific factor S. Describe the further adjustment to the long-run equilibrium with unchanged commodity and factor prices, as in the Rybczynski theorem. Do the same for the increase in the labor endowment.

*6. Show in a diagram like Fig. 9.2 that a rise in the relative price of good Y has an ambiguous impact on real returns to labor in the short run. For a representative laborer (as consumer), develop a budget constraint before and after this price change and show that whether the laborer is better or worse off depends on whether his or her tastes are biased toward good X or good Y.

7. Show that if the real return to labor in free trade is relatively higher in Country H, then the real return to both specific factors must be relatively higher in Country F.

NOTES

1. Another way to see this is that at the new wage w^*, sector Y would find itself further down its original VMP_{LY}, implying that there must be more labor in that industry.
2. Technically these slopes would correspond to a high elasticity of substitution in sector X, implying a large expansion in output there, and a low elasticity of substitution in sector Y, implying a small expansion.
3. See Neary (1978) for a full theoretical treatment of the specific-factors model as a short-run version of the Heckscher-Ohlin model.

REFERENCES

Jones, R. W. (1971). "A Three-Factor Model in Theory, Trade, and History." In J. Bhagwati et al., eds., *Trade, Balance of Payments, and Growth,* Chapter 1. Amsterdam: North–Holland.

Magee, S. P. (1978). "Three Simple Tests of the Stolper-Samuelson Theorem." In P. Oppenheimer, ed., *Issues in International Economics,* Chapter 10. Stocksfield, England: Oriel Press.

Mayer, W. (1974). "Short Run and Long Run Equilibrium for a Small Open Economy." *Journal of Political Economy* 82: 955–967.

Mussa, M. (1974). "Tariffs and the Distribution of Income: The Importance of Factor Specificity and Substitutability and Intensity in the Short and Long Run." *Journal of Political Economy* 82: 1191–1204.

Neary, J. P. (1978). "Short-run Capital Specificity and the Pure Theory of International Trade." *Economic Journal* 88: 477–510.

Samuelson, P. A. (1971). "Ohlin was Right." *Swedish Journal of Economics* 73: 365–384.

10

GOVERNMENT POLICIES AS DETERMINANTS OF TRADE

10.1 INTRODUCTION

Chapters 7, 8, and 9 discussed in some detail two of the five determinants of trade described in Chapter 6, production function (technology) differences and endowment differences. In this chapter we will discuss domestic distortions as a determinant of trade, focusing in particular on taxes and subsidies. The examination of taxes and subsidies is intended as an example of the effects that a wide range of government policies can have on trade. For example, environmental policies and regulations impact on firms' costs, therefore having effects on outputs and trade similar to those produced by taxes.

We are not asserting that commodity and factor taxes rank with factor endowments as a cause of trade, but we do believe that collectively, government policies have a much more profound impact on trade than is suggested in most international trade textbooks. One theme of this chapter is that government policies can generate trade but that this trade is not necessarily beneficial.

As before, the approach will be to neutralize other factors so that a clear understanding of the specific effects of each can be obtained. Throughout the chapter we will assume either a single country facing fixed world prices, or two countries that are identical in all respects (technologies, factor endowments, homogeneous utility functions), with constant returns and perfect competition in production. In the absence of the distortions we will introduce, the two countries would have no incentive to trade; the free trade equilibrium would be identical to autarky.

10.2 DISTINGUISHING AMONG CONSUMER, PRODUCER, AND WORLD PRICES

When we introduce taxes and subsidies into the analysis, it becomes important to distinguish prices paid by consumers from prices received by producers. Once we introduce trade, consumer and producer prices must be distinguished from world prices, the prices at which the country can trade. Throughout this chapter, we will use the notation q to represent consumer prices, p to represent producer prices, and p^* to represent world prices. This notation will also be used in later chapters, particularly the chapter on tariffs.

In order to focus on trade issues, we will also make the assumption throughout the chapter that there is no government sector per se; the government returns all tax collections to consumers in lump-sum fashion and/or raises all subsidies by lump-sum taxation. We implicitly assume a very large number of consumers, with each consumer getting a check or a bill which gives to (or takes from) the consumer his or her share of taxes (subsidies). Consumers regard their bills or checks as being unaffected by their own purchases. For example, if a consumer pays $1 in sales tax, the consumer gets a refund of only $1/N of that amount where N is the number of consumers (consider the refund if there are 100 million consumers). Thus, each consumer does indeed regard the tax as raising prices, even though the tax is returned to all consumers collectively. Similar comments apply to subsidies.

Throughout the chapter we will specify taxes and subsidies in an *ad valorem* (percentage of value) form rather than in specific form. t will denote a tax and s a subsidy. Ad valorem taxes are quoted as rates. A sales tax of 5 percent, for example, would mean a tax rate of $t = .05$ in this context. (*Specific* taxes, on the other hand, are quoted in monetary units per unit of the good: the US gasoline tax is quoted in cents per gallon.) Thus the relationship between consumer and producer prices with a tax or subsidy is given as follows.

$$q = p(1+t) > p \quad \text{tax}$$
$$q = p(1-s) < p \quad \text{subsidy} \qquad (10.1)$$

A tax raises the consumer price above the producer price, while a subsidy lowers the consumer price below the producer price. A tax rate $t = .05$ raises the consumer price 5 percent above the producer price: $q = p(1.05)$. When there are only two goods, the effects of a tax on one good are equivalent to a subsidy on the other good. In order to see this, consider the commodity price ratios resulting from a tax on Y versus a subsidy to X.

$$\frac{q_x}{q_y} = \frac{p_x}{p_y(1+t)} < \frac{p_x}{p_y} \qquad \text{tax on } Y$$

$$\frac{q_x}{q_y} = \frac{p_x(1-s)}{p_y} < \frac{p_x}{p_y} \qquad \text{subsidy on } X \qquad (10.2)$$

We see from Eqs. (10.2) that a subsidy to X and a tax on Y induce the same "wedge" between the consumer and producer price ratios.

Figure 10.1 gives autarky equilibrium at point E when there is *either* a tax on Y or a subsidy on X, assuming that the tax revenue is redistributed in lump sum fashion and the subsidy is raised by a lump sum tax. These latter assumptions are reflected in the fact the consumption and production bundles are the same even though, in the case of a tax, for example, the consumption bundle costs more than the value of those goods at producer prices. The consumers pay more than the producers receive because of the tax, but then they receive an income in excess of the value of production because they receive the tax refund. Let subscripts c and p denote consumption and production quantities, respectively. For a tax on Y,

$$q_x X_c + q_y Y_c = p_x X_c + p_y(1+t)Y_c = [p_x X_c + p_y Y_c] + [p_y t Y_c] \qquad (10.3)$$

The left-hand side of Eq. (10.3) is consumer expenditure at consumer prices. The first bracketed term on the right-hand side is income received from production (payments to factors of production), while the second term on the right-hand side is redistributed tax revenue. Thus, consumer expenditure equals consumer income. A similar analysis of a subsidy requires only that we change the sign of t.

Figure 10.1 illustrates the distortionary effect of the tax on Y or the subsidy on X. Welfare is lower at E than at the undistorted competitive equilibrium at A. The producer price ratio p is tangent to the production

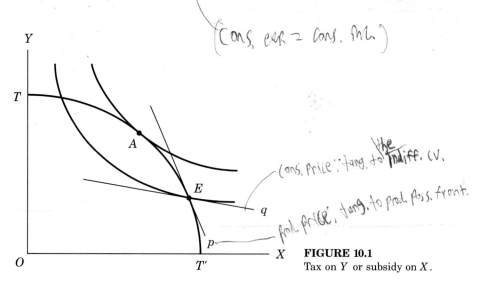

FIGURE 10.1
Tax on Y or subsidy on X.

frontier TT', while the consumer price ratio q is tangent to the indifference curve through E. The tax causes the consumers to perceive Y as more expensive than its actual production cost, or a subsidy to X causes consumers to perceive X as relatively cheaper than its actual production cost.

The previous paragraph should not be taken to suggest that all taxes or subsidies are bad. First, governments usually raise revenues in order to provide public goods that are not or cannot be provided by markets. This analysis takes no account of public goods. Second, not all taxes are distortionary or as distortionary as the commodity tax shown here. For example, in the present model, an equal ad valorem tax on both goods would leave the relative consumer and producer prices equal. Such a *set* of taxes is non-distortionary. We will return to this point in discussing factor taxes later in the chapter.

Finally, some government policies are imposed to correct an *existing* distortion in the economy, such as an environmental externality. In such a situation, Fig. 10.1 might accurately depict the effects of a pollution tax (on Y) on production and trade, but the indifference curves no longer accurately indicate welfare changes. Welfare may be improving due to lower pollution (i.e., there is actually a third good, environmental quality, not shown in the diagram). More will be said about taxes in the presence of existing distortions later in the book.

10.3 TAXES AND SUBSIDIES AS DETERMINANTS OF TRADE: A SMALL OPEN ECONOMY

Suppose that Country H faces fixed world prices. Assume also that these prices happen to be equal to H's autarky price ratio so that H does not choose to trade at these prices. This is completely unlikely, but we are simply following the strategy outlined in Chapter 6: "neutralize" all causes of trade except the one which we wish to examine. The situation is shown in Figs. 10.2 and 10.3, where the autarky equilibrium A is also the free trade equilibrium at price ratio p^*.

Once we introduce trade, we have to keep track of not only consumer and producer prices, but also world prices. This in turn means that we have to specify whether a tax or subsidy is assessed on consumption or production. In the closed economy it does not matter, because production and consumption of each good are equal. But with trade, consumption and production are generally not equal, so it matters which one we are taxing. With a consumption tax, consumers pay a tax on both domestic and imported goods. Alternatively, if the good is exported, then the tax is paid only on the part of domestic production that stays in the country. Producers can trade at world prices. The relationships among consumer, producer and world prices with a *consumption* tax on Y are given by

$$\frac{q_x}{q_y} = \frac{p_x}{p_y(1+t)} = \frac{p_x^*}{p_y^*(1+t)} \quad \text{or} \quad (1+t)\frac{q_x}{q_y} = \frac{p_x}{p_y} = \frac{p_x^*}{p_y^*} \qquad (10.4)$$

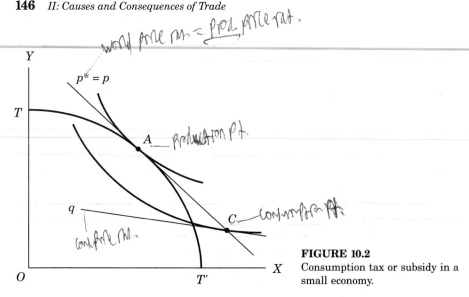

[handwritten: world price rat = prod. price rat.]

[handwritten annotations: p* = p; A — production pt.; C — consumption pt.; consmptn rat; cons price rat.]

FIGURE 10.2
Consumption tax or subsidy in a small economy.

The second equation emphasizes that producers in H face world prices. The consumption tax on *Y* (consumption subsidy on *X*) is shown in Fig. 10.2. When the tax is levied, producers will continue to produce at *A* where the world price ratio, equal to the producer price ratio, is tangent to the production frontier. The balance-of-trade constraint requires trade to balance at world prices, so we know that the consumption point must be on *p** through *A*. The consumption point is given by the point on that "national budget line" through *A* where the slope of an indifference curve is equal to the consumer price ratio. We show this in Fig. 10.2 as point *C* and label the consumer price ratio as *q*.

Economic intuition would lead to the result shown for the consumption tax in Fig. 10.2 even without the formal analysis. We see that, given fixed

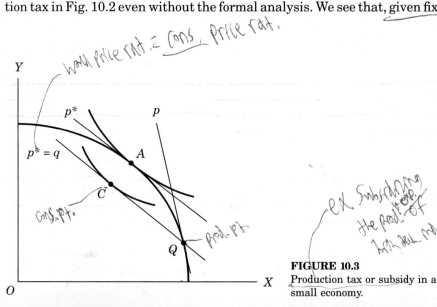

[handwritten: world price rat = cons. price rat.]

[handwritten annotations: p*; p; p* = q; A; C; Cons. pt.; prod pt; Q; ex. subsidizing the prod. of the X. gd. incr.]

FIGURE 10.3
Production tax or subsidy in a small economy.

[handwritten margin notes: tax on cons. → produces true world prices; " prod. → cons's]

world prices, the tax has no effect on production but that consumption of Y is discouraged. Consumers substitute away from the expensive commodity and in favor of the relatively cheaper commodity, X.

Welfare is reduced by this distortion, because consumers make inefficient choices when they do not face the true costs of producing the commodities. But again, we should separate this welfare result from the results concerning consumption and trade, because not all consumption taxes must be welfare-reducing. Most countries have gasoline (petrol) taxes, for example, which have the beneficial effects of reducing pollution and traffic congestion.

Now consider a tax on the *production* of Y or a subsidy on the production of X. In this case, consumers, not producers, face world prices. The relationships among the three price ratios are given by

$$\frac{p_x}{p_y(1+t)} = \frac{q_x}{q_y} = \frac{p_x^*}{p_y^*} \tag{10.5}$$

The relationships in Eq. (10.5) are shown in Fig. 10.3. The producer price ratio is now greater than the consumer and world price ratios, so production is shown as taking place at point Q in Fig. 10.3. Consumption must take place along the world price ratio through Q, and consumers now face world prices. Thus, the consumption point is given by the tangency between an indifference curve and the price line p^* through point Q. We show the consumption point as C in Fig. 10.3. The production tax discourages production of Y and leads to a substitution in production toward good X.

Several important results are shown in Figs. 10.2 and 10.3. First, they clearly demonstrate that government policies such as taxes and subsidies can generate trade. However, they show equally clearly that *trade induced by the introduction of distortions is not beneficial trade.* In both Figs. 10.2 and 10.3, H receives a welfare loss as a consequence of distortion-induced trade. This is a very important result insofar as governments decide that it would be a good thing if the country produced and exported more of a certain good (e.g., "high tech" goods). We could think of Fig. 10.3 as a situation generated by a government's decision that it must be good to produce and export X. By subsidizing the production of X, we do indeed get exports of X, and the government congratulates itself on the success of its project. However, exports generated by distortions are welfare-reducing (put differently, the initial level of exports, zero, is optimal).

The second thing that Figs. 10.2 and 10.3 help to emphasize is that production and consumption taxes/subsidies are very different from each other in the open economy. For example, they have opposite effects on the direction of trade. A consumption tax on Y discourages consumption and therefore tends to lead to *exports* of Y (production minus consumption). A production tax on Y discourages production and therefore tends to lead to *imports* of Y (consumption minus production). Governments must therefore be careful about where they levy a tax when assessing its likely effects.

[handwritten margin notes: Cons. tax ↑ leads to exps.   Prod. tax → leads to imps.]

10.4 TAXES AND SUBSIDIES AS DETERMINANTS OF TRADE: TWO IDENTICAL COUNTRIES

Now we introduce a second country and explicitly return to our concept of the two-country, no-trade model. Suppose that we have two identical countries, both with production frontiers TT' in Fig. 10.1, such that the point A in Fig. 10.1 represents both the free trade and autarky equilibria for both of the countries. Now Country H imposes a consumption tax on Y or a consumption subsidy on X. At the initial free trade price ratio p^*, Country F will wish to continue to produce and consume at A in Fig. 10.2 (the same as A in Fig. 10.1), while Country H will wish to consume at point C in Fig. 10.2.

This cannot be an equilibrium, because there will be excess demand for X and excess supply of Y at the initial prices. The price ratio p^* must rise until excess supplies and demands balance. The outcome is shown in Fig. 10.4, where both countries produce at point Q because they are identical and face the same producer prices, $p = p^*$. Country F consumes at C_f and Country H consumes at C_h. We now have the same result that we had in Fig. 10.2: Country H creates trade by its tax or subsidy, but the trade is not beneficial.

The other interesting result we get from Fig. 10.4 is that *Country F is made better off* by H's tax or subsidy. Recall from Chapter 5 that the ability of a country to trade at any prices other than its autarky prices can make it better off (and *will* make it better off if it has no distortions). The institution of the tax or subsidy in H now allows F an opportunity to trade at prices different than its autarky prices. This might also help us understand why H has to be worse off. With the countries absolutely identical, there are no opportunities for mutual gains from trade. If the distortion makes F better off, it must make H worse off.

A very different question can also be asked. Suppose that H has the tax or subsidy in autarky and now opens itself to trade. Is H better off in

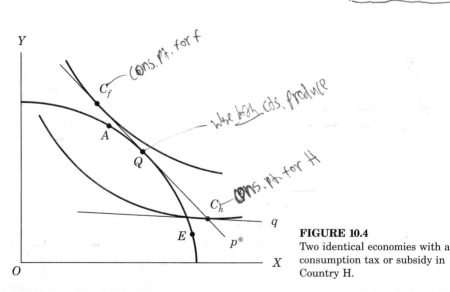

FIGURE 10.4
Two identical economies with a consumption tax or subsidy in Country H.

trade with the distortion than it was in autarky with the distortion? In other words, we are now asking whether point E in Fig. 10.1 is on a higher or lower indifference curve than point C (Fig. 10.2) or point C_h (Fig. 10.4). In general, the answer is that these points cannot be welfare-ranked, or alternatively that introducing free trade in the presence of an existing distortion may make the country worse off. This is an application of what is known as the *theory of the second best.*

> **An application of the theory of the second best.** Removing one distortion (trade barriers) in the presence of a second distortion (taxes or subsidies) does not necessarily make the country better off. Conversely, introducing a second distortion (trade barriers) in the presence of existing distortions (taxes and subsidies) might make the country better off.

In Fig. 10.4, we show point E (corresponding to E in Fig. 10.1) as being on a lower indifference curve than C_h, but this need not be the case. This topic will be pursued more formally in the next section for those willing to work through the algebra.

Now suppose that the tax on Y is collected from its producers in Country H (or that a subsidy on X is paid to its producers in Country H). The situation at initial prices is shown in Fig. 10.3. Country F wishes to continue to consume and produce at A, while Country H wishes to produce at Q and consume at C. This cannot be an equilibrium, because there will be excess supply of X and excess demand for Y. The price ratio p^* must fall, giving us a new equilibrium as shown in Fig. 10.5. The fall in p^* induces Country F to export Y and import X, producing at Q and consuming at C_f in Fig. 10.5. Country H produces at R and consumes at C_h. As in the case of Fig. 10.3, we see that a production tax on Y or subsidy on X can indeed generate exports of X, but this is not welfare-improving trade. Similar to the result for the consumption tax/subsidy, the beneficiary is Country F, which can now gain by trading at prices other than its autarky prices.

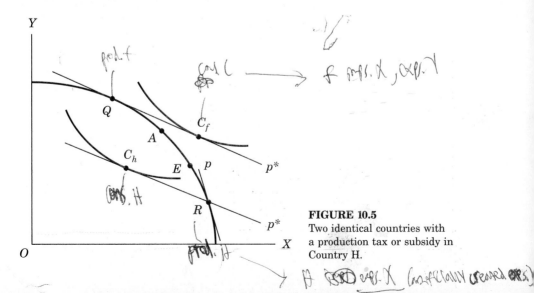

FIGURE 10.5
Two identical countries with a production tax or subsidy in Country H.

If we now compare a distorted autarky equilibrium for Country H at E in Fig. 10.5 to the distorted free trade equilibrium at C_h, advanced analysis will show that these points cannot be welfare-ranked. We have drawn a case in which E is welfare-superior to C_h, but this is not a general result. Introducing trade in the presence of a distortion is certainly not guaranteed to make a country worse off; rather, it cannot be proved that it will make the country better off. Again, the following section presents a more formal analysis.

Comparing Fig. 10.5 with Fig. 10.4, we see that the direction of trade is opposite in the two cases, even though the tax is on Y (or the subsidy is on X) in both cases. This result can be intuitively predicted and is the same as the result in the previous section. The consumption tax discourages consumption of Y by domestic consumers but reduces the price foreigners pay, and therefore the home country will export Y in the absence of other causes of trade (Fig. 10.4). The production tax discourages production of Y and permits foreign consumers to buy X at the lower tax-distorted price, so the home country exports X and imports Y (Fig. 10.5).

10.5 GAINS FROM TRADE: A FORMAL ANALYSIS*

In this section, we will use the formal analysis developed in Chapter 5 in order to more fully understand the problem of introducing trade into a distorted economy. Let superscripts f and a denote quantities evaluated in free trade and in autarky, respectively. A subscript p denotes production quantities, and a subscript c denotes consumption quantities, as in Chapter 5. In the consumption tax case, Fig. 10.4 shows that the value of free-trade production (Q) at free-trade prices (p^*) is higher than the value of any other feasible production point at those prices.

$$p_x^* X_p^f + p_y^* Y_p^f > p_x^* X_p^a + p_y^* Y_p^a \tag{10.6}$$

Now substitute the balance-of-trade constraint into the left-hand side of Eq. (10.6) and the autarky market clearing conditions into the right-hand side as we did in Chapter 5, section 5.2. This has the effect of converting all production quantities in Eq. (10.6) into consumption quantities.

$$p_x^* X_c^f + p_y^* Y_c^f > p_x^* X_c^a + p_y^* Y_c^a \tag{10.7}$$

But in order to evaluate welfare, we need to have consumption at *consumer* prices, not producer prices. This can be accomplished by adding several

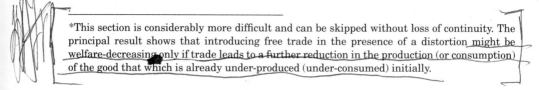

*This section is considerably more difficult and can be skipped without loss of continuity. The principal result shows that introducing free trade in the presence of a distortion might be welfare-decreasing only if trade leads to a further reduction in the production (or consumption) of the good that which is already under-produced (under-consumed) initially.

terms to both sides of the inequality in Eq. (10.7) such that the inequality must continue to hold.

$$p_x^* X_c^f + p_y^* Y_c^f + p_y^* t Y_c^f - p_y^* t Y_c^a > p_x^* X_c^a + p_y^* Y_c^a + p_y^* t Y_c^f - p_y^* t Y_c^a \quad (10.8)$$

The inequality in Eq. (10.8) can be rearranged to yield

$$p_x^* X_c^f + p_y^*(1 + t) Y_c^f > p_x^* X_c^a + p_y^*(1 + t) Y_c^a + p_y^* t \left(Y_c^f - Y_c^a \right) \quad (10.9)$$

Using our definition of consumer prices, this simplifies to

$$\left[q_x X_c^f + q_y Y_c^f \right] > \left[q_x X_c^a + q_y Y_c^a \right] + \left[p_y^* t \left(Y_c^f - Y_c^a \right) \right] \quad (10.10)$$

The term to the left of the inequality sign of Eq. (10.10) is the value of free trade consumption at free trade prices, while the first term to the right of the inequality sign is autarky consumption at free trade prices. The right-most term is positive if trade increases the value of Y consumption. Thus we see that free trade consumption is preferred to autarky consumption if Y consumption increases. A sufficient condition for gains from trade is that consumption of the tax-distorted good increases. To put the matter the other way around, a country may fail to gain from trade when trade further reduces the consumption of a taxed good (or increases consumption of a subsidized good).

Comparing the *undistorted* autarky equilibrium at A in Fig. 10.2 to distorted free trade consumption at C, the sufficient condition clearly fails. Consumption of the taxed good Y is lower in free trade. Comparing the *distorted* autarky equilibrium E in Fig. 10.4 to the distorted free trade equilibrium C_h, the comparison is uncertain. The diagram is drawn to show consumption of Y increasing with trade, but this is entirely arbitrary.[1]

The same type of analysis can be applied to the production tax or subsidy. In Fig. 10.5 we see that the value of free trade production (point R) evaluated at the producer price ratio p, is greater than the value of any other feasible production bundle evaluated at these prices.

$$p_x X_p^f + p_y Y_p^f > p_x X_p^a + p_y Y_p^a \quad (10.11)$$

Recalling that $p_y(1 + t) = p_y^*$, we can write the producer price of Y as $p_y = p_y^* - p_y t$. The consumer price of X equals the world price of X. The inequality in Eq. (10.11) becomes

$$p_x^* X_p^f + p_y^* Y_p^f - p_y t Y_p^f > p_x^* X_p^a + p_y^* Y_p^a - p_y t Y_p^a \quad (10.12)$$

Rearranging terms, this becomes

$$p_x^* X_p^f + p_y^* Y_p^f > p_x^* X_p^a + p_y^* Y_p^a + p_y t \left(Y_p^f - Y_p^a \right) \quad (10.13)$$

As before, use the balance-of-trade constraint to replace the left-hand side of Eq. (10.13) with the value of consumption, and use the autarky market clearing conditions to replace the production quantities on the right-hand side with consumption quantities. Eq. (10.13) then becomes

$$\left[p_x^* X_c^f + p_y^* Y_c^f \right] > \left[p_x^* X_c^a + p_y^* Y_c^a \right] + \left[p_y t \left(Y_p^f - Y_p^a \right) \right] \quad (10.14)$$

The left-hand side of Eq. (10.14) is the value of free trade consumption at free trade prices, while the first term on the right-hand side of Eq. (10.14) is the value of autarky consumption at free trade prices. A sufficient condition for free trade consumption to be preferred over autarky consumption is that the second term on the right-hand side of Eq. (10.14) be positive. This term is positive if trade expands the production of Y, the tax-distorted production sector.

Comparing the undistorted autarky equilibrium A in Fig. 10.3 to the distorted free-trade production point at Q, we see that the sufficient condition fails: trade reduces production of the taxed good Y. Comparing the distorted autarky equilibrium at E in Fig. 10.5 to the free trade production point R, we do get a stronger result than in the consumption tax case. When trade is opened up, the relative consumer price of X is lower in Country H than in Country F: $q_h < q_f$ (see Fig. 10.1). The consumer price ratio $q_h = p^*$ must rise in H, so the producer price of X rises as well. Production of X is increased, and point E must lie above point R in Fig. 10.5. The sufficient condition for gains from trade fails, so Country H may be worse off opening up to trade.

10.6   FACTOR MARKET DISTORTIONS

In this section we consider the effects on international trade and welfare of a factor market distortion. The particular distortion we choose is motivated by the corporate income tax. The effects of this tax are significantly different from those of a commodity tax, for the corporate income tax applies to factor returns, which introduces a distortion into the production side of the model as well as changing relative commodity prices. In the following discussion we assume a two-good, two-factor, Heckscher-Ohlin-type model, and we assume that the tax is imposed on one of the factors (capital) in one of the two industries (the corporate sector).

Three main effects of the corporate income tax are of interest. First, the corporate income tax, by creating a divergence between the factor-price ratios faced by producers in the two sectors, will result in production inside the production possibilities frontier. Second, the new distorted production "frontier" no longer must be concave to the origin but could be convex or could alternate between being concave and convex. Third, equilibrium price lines will generally not be tangent to the distorted production frontier. This third effect is familiar from the production tax case discussed in the previous section.

Suppose the tax on capital is in the Y industry. X producers pay r for capital, while Y producers pay $r(1 + t)$ for capital where t is the tax. The factor-price ratios faced by the X and Y industries will then bear the relationship

$$\left[\frac{w}{r}\right]_x > \left[\frac{w}{r(1 + t)}\right]_y \tag{10.15}$$

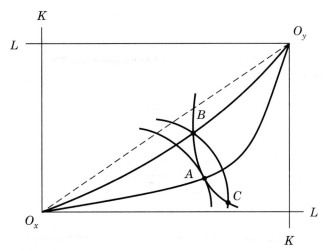

FIGURE 10.6
Production inefficiency induced by a factor tax in one industry.

Figure 10.6 shows the factor market allocation in an Edgeworth-Bowley box. A is an initial equilibrium on the contract curve O_xAO_y. When the tax is introduced, the two industries will face different factor-price ratios, with that faced by the X industry being steeper than the factor-price ratio in the Y industry (Eq. (10.15)). A new equilibrium point must be a point like B in Fig. 10.6 where the X isoquants are steeper than the Y isoquants. But note that B is not an efficient production point. At B the same amount of X is produced, but less Y is produced than at A. B must, therefore, correspond to a point that is interior to the efficient production frontier.

We can find all of the points in Fig. 10.6 where the difference in the slopes of the X and Y isoquants is the same as at point B. Linking these distorted allocations, we have a distorted contract curve given by O_xBO_y in Fig. 10.6. (A larger tax could mean that the distorted contract curve lies on the other side of the diagonal, but the distorted contract curve cannot intersect the diagonal, though it can lie exactly on it; these issues are not important for our purposes.)

Figure 10.7 shows the corresponding output diagram with TAT' giving the efficient production frontier. TBT' in Fig. 10.7 is the distorted production frontier corresponding to the distorted contract curve in Fig. 10.6. The distorted frontier need not be strictly concave as shown, but this is not particularly relevant for our purposes. The corporate income tax thus leads to production interior to the efficient production frontier. Note that point B in Fig. 10.7 corresponds to B in Fig. 10.6.

The movement from A to a point on TBT' in Fig. 10.7 does not complete the analysis, for the final equilibrium will not be a tangency solution. The proof is difficult, but the rationale is as follows. The slope of the distorted production frontier at a point such as B is equal to the ratio

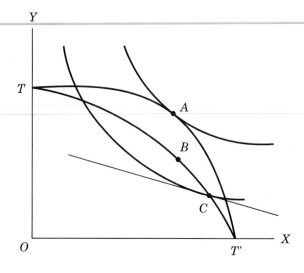

FIGURE 10.7
Distorted production frontier
and autarky equilibrium with
a factor tax.

of the "true" or "social" marginal costs of producing X versus Y. But the "private" marginal cost of producing Y is greater than the true marginal cost because Y producers must pay the tax on capital. The private and social marginal costs of producing X are the same because there is no tax in that industry. Let MRT_d be the marginal rate of transformation along the distorted production frontier TBT' in Fig. 10.7. Let MC^* denote the true or social marginal cost and MC denote the private marginal cost of producing a good. The tax on capital in Y leads to the relationship

$$\text{MRT}_d = \frac{\text{MC}^*_x}{\text{MC}^*_y} > \frac{\text{MC}_x}{\text{MC}_y} = \frac{p_x}{p_y} \tag{10.16}$$

since

$$\text{MC}^*_x = \text{MC}_x, \qquad \text{MC}^*_y < \text{MC}_y \tag{10.17}$$

In competitive equilibrium, the ratio of private marginal costs is equal to the competitive price ratio. The inequality in Eq. (10.16) therefore implies that $\text{MRT}_d > p$ where p is the producer price ratio. This price ratio is equal to the consumer price ratio if there are no taxes on outputs. The distorted autarky equilibrium must be at a point like C in Fig. 10.7, where the indifference curve is flatter than the distorted production frontier. This non-tangency is very much like the result obtained from the production tax case considered in the previous section. The difference here is that the non-tangency is along the distorted production frontier. The factor market distortion thus involves two distortions. One distortion can be thought of as the movement inside the efficient production frontier and the other as the movement along the distorted frontier.

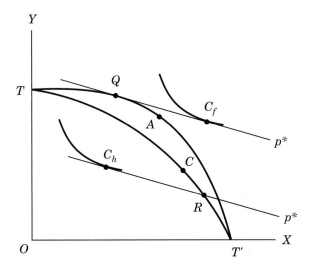

FIGURE 10.8
Two identical countries with a factor tax in Country H.

Figure 10.8 shows the implications of the corporate income tax for the international trading equilibrium, again under the assumption that we begin with two identical countries. The initial production frontiers are given by TAT' with autarky equilibrium at A for each of the two countries. Country H imposes the corporate income tax with the consequences described in Fig. 10.7 and in autarky consumes and produces at C. The tax discourages production of Y in Country H, thus raising its price. Country F benefits from this price change, moving production to Q and exporting Y to H. Country H shifts production to R and imports Y to reach the consumption point C_h. H clearly loses relative to the *undistorted* autarky (and free trade) equilibrium at A. H may either gain or lose from trade relative to the *distorted* autarky equilibrium at C, depending on whether the indifference curve through C_h passes above or below point C in Fig. 10.8. Note that this diagram looks very similar to the production tax diagram in Fig. 10.5, except for the addition of the distorted production frontier. These diagrams are indeed conceptually similar in that both taxes discourage production of Y in Country H. And as before, the effect of the distortion is to create trade, but this trade is not necessarily beneficial for the country with the distortion.

Factor market distortions are a complex topic; their various types have very different effects. Other factor market distortions include the effects of unions and minimum wage laws. The preceding analysis of the corporate income tax is only one of many interesting situations. But some of the specific results we have obtained can be generalized to cases involving other distortions. First, factor market distortions generally result in production interior to the efficient production frontier. Second, the production of disadvantaged goods (e.g., goods bearing taxes) is reduced. Third, the trade generated by the distortion is not necessarily beneficial for the country with the distortion.

10.7 CONCLUDING REMARKS

This chapter has turned our attention away from underlying production differences between countries, principally differences in technologies and factor endowments. Governments have taken active and major roles in most economies. Our discussion of tax and subsidy distortions is intended to provide some insight as to how various government policies can affect trade and the gains from trade, even if their intended purpose is unrelated to trade (e.g., the corporate income tax is not instituted to affect trade). One important general lesson from our analysis is that exports should never be confused with welfare. We showed cases in which exports generated by a subsidy reduced the country's welfare. The principal findings of the chapter can be summarized as follows.

1. A commodity tax or subsidy induces a distortion in the economy that prevents welfare maximization in competitive equilibrium, even if the tax revenue is returned (or subsidy costs are raised) by lump-sum redistribution (or taxation). Because consumers and producers do not face the same prices, consumers do not face the "true" costs of goods in making their consumption decisions. This certainly does not imply that all taxes are bad. Governments must use taxes to pay for public goods, which have no role in our analysis here. In some cases, taxes or regulations are introduced to counteract existing external distortions, such as pollution. In such cases, instead of being a distortion, the tax is correcting a distortion. More will be said about this later in the book.

2. Trade induced by the introduction of a distortion such as a commodity tax or subsidy is welfare-reducing trade.[2] Governments must be careful not to confuse exports with welfare. Government policies can induce the export of a good, but such exports are welfare-reducing in an initially competitive, distortion-free economy.

3. Consumption and production taxes or subsidies are quite different from each other in an open economy. In particular, they have opposite effects on the direction of trade. A consumption tax decreases the consumption of a good, leading to increased exports or decreased imports. A production tax decreases the production of the good, leading to decreased exports or increased imports.

4. If an economy with an existing distortion is opened to trade, the resulting trade might not improve welfare. The possibility of welfare-reducing trade occurs when the distortion is made "worse" by the introduction of trade. For example, if the economy initially has a production tax on Y, then the economy is underproducing Y in autarky. If trade leads to a further reduction in the production of Y, then trade may reduce welfare. A sufficient but not necessary condition for gains from trade is that trade lead to an increase in the production (consumption) of a good that is initially being underproduced (underconsumed).

5. The preceding point is an example of the *theory of the second best*. If one distortion (barriers to trade) is removed when other distortions exist (domestic taxes and subsidies), then welfare may fall. Note that this is not an argument against free trade; it is better interpreted as an argument against domestic distortions.

PROBLEMS

1. Illustrate the case (similar to Fig. 10.4) in which, with a consumption tax in Country H, trade reduces welfare (relative to E).

2. Use the gains-from-trade argument to show that Country F will always be made better off by a tax in H (when the two countries are initially identical), regardless of whether the tax in H is a consumption or a production tax.

3. Is it true or false that, in a small open economy, a consumption subsidy cannot affect the production of a good? Explain your answer.

4. Is it true or false that, in a small open economy, a production subsidy cannot affect the consumption of a good? Explain your answer.

5. Suggest how our analysis of commodity taxes would change if the tax were collected by tax collectors who would have been producing X or Y in the absence of the tax (i.e., the institution of the tax reduces the effective labor supply to X and Y production). Do you have a guess as to what an economist might mean by "cost of revenue-raising?"

6. With reference to Fig. 10.6, suppose that the capital tax is so large that the distorted contract curve lies above the diagonal. Can you prove that the resulting distorted production possibility curve is now convex (i.e., the distorted production frontier lies below the diagonal connecting the endpoints of the distorted production frontier)?

NOTES

1. Essentially, there are income and substitution effects working in opposite directions. Trade increases the value of production, which tends to increase the consumption of Y. But in this case, trade leads to an increase in the relative price of Y. (Note in Fig. 10.1 that the producer price in Country H is greater than that in Country F. Trade equalizes the producer prices, implying that p_h falls, implying that q_h falls.) This causes consumers to substitute away from Y, the good that is already being underconsumed. It is not clear whether the consumption of Y is higher or lower at point C_h relative to the distorted autarky equilibrium.
2. Possible exceptions to this statement are presented in later chapters. First, if the country has some monopoly power in trade, then free trade may not maximize welfare. Second, if there are existing distortions in the economy, the introduction of a counter-balancing distortion can improve welfare. Section 10.3 of this chapter assumes fixed world prices (no monopoly power) and no existing distortions in the economy.

REFERENCES

Bhagwati, J. and Srinivasan, T. N. (1983). *Lectures on International Trade.* Cambridge: MIT Press, Chapters 20–23.

Brecher, R. A. (1974). "Optimal Commercial Policy for a Minimum-Wage Economy." *Journal of International Economics* 4: 139–149.

Feenstra, R. C. (1980). "Monopsony Distortions in an Open Economy: A Theoretical Analysis." *Journal of International Economics* 10: 213–236.

Friedlaender, A., and Vandendorpe, A. (1968). "Excise Taxes and Gains from Trade." *Journal of Political Economy* 76: 1058–1068.

Herberg, H., Kemp, M. C., and Magee, S. P. (1971). "Factor Market Distortions, the Reversal of Factor Intensities, and the Relation between Product Prices and Equilibrium Outputs." *Economic Record* 47: 518–530.

Kemp, M. C., and Herberg, H. (1971). "Factor Market Distortions, the Shape of the Locus of Competitive Outputs, and the Relation between Product Prices and Equilibrium Outputs." In J. Bhagwati et al., eds., *Trade, Balance of Payments and Growth.* Amsterdam: North–Holland.

Magee, S. R. (1971). "Factor Market Distortions, Production, Distribution and the Pure Theory of International Trade." *Quarterly Journal of Economics* 85: 623–643.

Melvin, J. R. (1970). "Commodity Taxation as a Determinant of Trade." *Canadian Journal of Economics* 3: 62–78.

——. (1979). "Short-Run Price Effects of the Corporate Income Tax and Implications for International Trade." *American Economic Review* 69: 765–774.

——. (1982). "The Corporate Income Tax in an Open Economy." *Journal of Public Economics* 17: 393–403.

CHAPTER
11

IMPERFECT COMPETITION AS A DETERMINANT OF TRADE AND THE GAINS FROM TRADE

11.1 AUTARKY EQUILIBRIUM WITH A MONOPOLIZED SECTOR

The presence of monopoly in one or more of the industries in the basic model provides another type of distortion. Monopoly can arise for a variety of reasons. In free market economies, the most typical reason is the existence of scale economies in production. High costs of producing small outputs may mean that only a small number of firms (a single firm in the extreme) can survive in equilibrium. In some countries, there are licenses and other restrictions that prevent entry of additional firms even though profits are positive. A firm may possess a technology that other firms are prevented from obtaining, either through secrecy or through perfectly legal means such as patents. But in the modern world, imperfect competition in some industries is an issue for even the largest economies. Wide-bodied commercial aircraft, for example, are produced by only three firms: Boeing, Airbus, and McDonnell-Douglas. The American firms Intel and Microsoft have dominant market shares in personal computer micro-processors and operating systems, respectively.

In this chapter, we will abstract from the reasons for the existence of monopoly. We will assume constant returns to scale. In the next chapter, we will turn to scale economies and consider them as a determinant of trade along with the market power that scale economies typically imply. We feel that it is helpful to introduce monopoly by itself first, in order to avoid introducing both scale economies and monopoly at the same time. As will be seen, the results for one of the simple cases to be discussed here are quite similar, from the point of view of trade effects, to the case of a commodity tax in one industry. In both cases, prices are not tangent to the production frontier, and so the conditions that guarantee gains from trade are not satisfied. At the same time, we will argue that the existence of monopoly makes it likely that countries will benefit or that they will benefit more from trade relative to a situation where markets are perfectly competitive. The reason is that trade tends to induce a *pro-competitive effect* that can reinforce the usual comparative-advantage sources of gains from trade.

There is a variety of ways in which monopoly could be introduced. One could assume that both industries in one country were monopolized, or that monopolized industries existed in both countries. This section will begin with perhaps the simplest case, in which the home country has a monopoly producer of X in autarky. To keep things simple, we make the assumption that the monopolist has no *monopsony* (a single buyer) power in factor markets. Finally, note that the price paid by the consumer and the price received by the producer are the same throughout this chapter, so we will denote both q and p by p.

The profit-maximizing rule for a producer is to increase production up to the point where the revenue gained from an additional unit sold (marginal revenue, MR) is just equal to the cost of producing that additional unit (marginal cost, MC). Small competitive firms are assumed to face fixed prices, and so marginal revenue is just the price of the good: MR $= p$. The profit-maximizing rule MR $=$ MC then becomes

$$p = \text{MC} \tag{11.1}$$

With perfect competition in both industries, Eq. (11.1) holds for both X and Y, and dividing one by the other, we have

$$\frac{p_x}{p_y} = \frac{\text{MC}_x}{\text{MC}_y} = \text{MRT} \tag{11.2}$$

In order to see that the slope of the production frontier MRT is the ratio of marginal costs, think of a simple model with one factor, labor. The marginal cost of producing X is the wage rate w times the change in labor input needed, ΔL_x, to produce a given increase in X, ΔX: $\text{MC}_x = w\,\Delta L_x/\Delta X$. The marginal cost of Y is given by a similar expression, so the ratio of marginal costs in Eq. (11.2) is given by

$$\frac{\text{MC}_x}{\text{MC}_y} = \frac{w\,\Delta L_x/\Delta X}{w\,\Delta L_y/\Delta Y} = -\frac{\Delta Y}{\Delta X} = \text{MRT} \qquad \text{given that } \Delta L_x = -\Delta L_y \tag{11.3}$$

Equation (11.2) gives the efficient outcome we discussed in Chapter 2 and again in Chapter 5. With competition in both sectors, producers choose

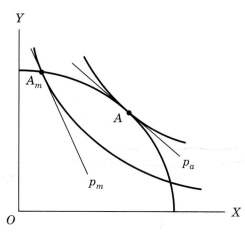

FIGURE 11.1
Autarky equilibrium with monopoly in X.

outputs efficiently such that the price ratio is tangent to the production frontier in competitive equilibrium. This is the condition that prevails in the autarky equilibrium at point A in Fig. 11.1.

With monopoly in industry X, however, the condition in Eq. (11.1) is no longer appropriate. The monopolist faces the entire market and hence faces a downward-sloping demand curve. It is not possible to sell all he wants at a fixed price. After a point, to sell more units of his good, the monopolist must reduce the price charged on all units (we assume that all sales are at the same price). The marginal revenue received from selling an additional unit of X must be less than the actual price of X because the price must be reduced on other units sold. Marginal revenue will consist of two terms: the price of the last unit sold, minus the reduced revenue on the other units sold as a consequence of the price reduction needed to sell the last unit.

The relationship between price and marginal revenue is derived as follows. Total revenue (TR) for the monopolist can be written as price times quantity:

$$TR = p_x X \qquad (11.4)$$

The change in the monopolist's total revenue can be derived from Eq. (11.4):

$$\Delta TR = p_x \Delta X + X \Delta p_x \qquad (11.5)$$

The first term in Eq. (11.5) is the change in revenue due to the change in output, holding price constant. The second term is the loss in revenue on existing sales caused by the fact that price must be lowered ($\Delta p_x < 0$) in order to sell an additional unit of X.[1] Divide Eq. (11.5) by ΔX to get marginal revenue MR_x: the change in revenue from the sale of one additional unit.

$$MR_x = \frac{\Delta TR}{\Delta X} = p_x + X \frac{\Delta p_x}{\Delta X} < p_x \qquad \text{given that } \Delta p_x / \Delta X < 0 \qquad (11.6)$$

As we mentioned, marginal revenue is composed of two terms: the price of the last unit sold plus the revenue lost by lowering the price on all units in order to sell the last unit. This second term is negative, so marginal revenue is less than price for the monopolist.

Now multiply the second term of the MR expression in Eq. (10.9) by p_x/p_x and factor out a p_x from both terms:

$$MR_x = p_x \left[1 + \frac{\Delta p_x/p_x}{\Delta X/X} \right] \tag{11.7}$$

The quotient in the square brackets in Eq. (11.7) has a relatively simple interpretation. The price elasticity of demand for X is defined as the proportional change in X, $\Delta X/X$, in response to a given proportional change in $p_x : \Delta p_x/p_x$. Often the price elasticity of demand is defined as minus this ratio in order to make it positive, and we will adopt this convention, defining the price elasticity of demand as

$$e_x = -\frac{\Delta X/X}{\Delta p_x/p_x} > 0 \tag{11.8}$$

Substituting the result in Eq. (11.8), the monopolist's profit maximization rule MR = MC becomes:[2]

$$MR_x = p_x \left[1 - \frac{1}{e_x} \right] = MC_x \qquad e_x = -\frac{\Delta X/X}{\Delta p_x/p_x} \tag{11.9}$$

One way to interpret Eq. (11.9) is to think of $1/e_x$ as the firm's optimal markup rate, $m_x = 1/e_x$, which it sets on its output: $p_x(1 - m_x) = MC_x$. The markup rate m_x is thus very much like an ad valorem tax, assessed as a percentage of the consumer price. To put it slightly differently, the price received by the producer p_x equals marginal cost MC_x plus markup revenue (akin to tax revenue), $p_x m_x : p_x = MC_x + p_x m_x$.[3]

Figure 11.2 illustrates the standard profit-maximization condition for a monopolist as it would appear in an intermediate microeconomics textbook. With a linear demand curve D, the marginal revenue curve (MR) is also linear and is steeper than D (recall that MR must be less than price at any

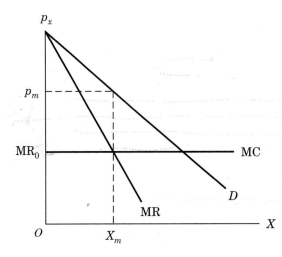

FIGURE 11.2
Partial equilibrium diagram.

given quantity). With marginal cost MC, the profit-maximizing output is X_m, and this can be sold at price p_m. Price is clearly higher than marginal revenue MR_0. Note that perfect competition is a special case of the general formula in Eq. (11.9). Perfect competition refers to a situation in which the demand facing an individual producer is perfectly elastic; that is, competition is perfect when e facing an individual producer is infinite, and so $1/e = 0$.

Price is assumed to equal marginal cost in the Y industry. The monopoly in X (Eq. (11.9)) means that the economy's equilibrium condition changes from Eq. (11.2) to

$$\frac{p_x \left(1 - 1/e_x\right)}{p_y} = \frac{MC_x}{MC_y} = MRT < \frac{p_x}{p_y} \qquad (11.10)$$

The fact that $p_x > MC_x$ implies that the equilibrium price ratio p_x/p_y is greater than the slope of the production frontier (MRT) at the equilibrium point. This is shown in Fig. 11.1, where A_m is the autarky equilibrium for the home country and p_m is the home country's autarky price ratio.

Three facts should be noted about the monopoly equilibrium A_m relative to the competitive equilibrium at A in Fig. 11.1. First, the monopolist restricts the output of X below its competitive level at A. Second, the monopolist raises the relative price of X above its competitive level p_a. Both effects should be familiar to students from standard partial equilibrium analysis such as that in Fig. 11.2. Third, welfare is reduced by the monopoly below the competitive level at A in Fig. 11.1.

The equilibrium described by Eq. (11.10) and Fig. 11.1 looks similar to our analysis of the production tax in the previous chapter. The only major difference between the distortion induced by imperfect competition and that induced by a production tax is that the monopoly distortion is *endogenous*; that is, the monopoly distortion can change as a consequence of the introduction of international trade. That is the subject to which we now turn.

11.2   PRO-COMPETITIVE GAINS FROM TRADE

As just noted, the imperfect competition distortion is more complicated than the tax distortion in that its degree of distortion is endogenous. This significant complication means that trade may well have additional benefits when there is imperfect competition in an economy. We will refer to any such gains as "pro-competitive gains from trade." This section presents a simple case, whereas the next section presents a more difficult situation.

Suppose that the economy has a monopoly producer of X and so has an autarky equilibrium at A in Fig. 11.3. The competitive equilibrium would be at B in that same diagram. To keep the example very simple, suppose that this is a small country in a very large world. Assume, in fact, that when trade is permitted, the country (and its producers) will face fixed world prices. In line with our no-trade model, assume that these fixed world prices happen to equal the undistorted autarky price ratio p^* in Fig. 11.3.

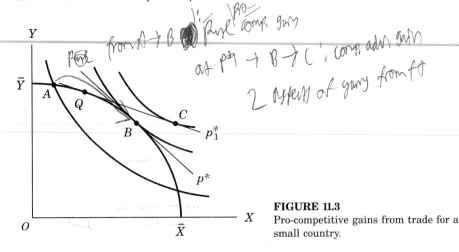

FIGURE 11.3
Pro-competitive gains from trade for a small country.

With trade, the domestic monopolist (or former monopolist) will now face a constant p_x^*, and so MR $= p_x^*$. Alternatively, the elasticity of demand "perceived" by the monopolist is now infinite, and the monopoly distortion (markup) goes to zero. The equality between the price ratio and the MRT will be restored. At the world price ratio p^* in Fig. 11.3, the country will produce and consume at B.

The movement from A to B in Fig. 11.3 is what we will refer to as a pure, *pro-competitive gain from trade*. This gain is equal to the gain that could be achieved in the closed economy by eliminating the monopoly distortion. An interesting feature of this special case with p^* equalling the undistorted autarky price ratio is that there is a gain from trade, but no trade actually occurs. The *ability* of domestic consumers to buy and sell at the undistorted autarky price ratio leads to the beneficial elimination of the monopoly distortion.

Of course, a pro-competitive gain from trade will typically be accompanied by gains from trade because of the existence of comparative advantage. Suppose that the fixed world price ratio is p_1^* in Fig. 11.3. Under the "small-country assumption," trade takes the economy from A to C in Fig. 11.3. This gain from trade can be decomposed into two separate moves: A to B and B to C. The movement from B to C is the normal comparative-advantage gain from trade for a distortion-free economy that we have discussed throughout this book. But now we have an additional gain from trade, which is the movement from A to B. The pro-competitive gain adds to (rather than replaces in some sense) the usual comparative-advantage gain from trade.

It must be admitted that the small-country assumption (fixed world prices) in Fig. 11.3 is rather special. Nevertheless, there is a general argument in favor of the view that procompetitive gains from trade are likely to exist. This argument was outlined earlier. When trade is permitted, there will be a larger number of X producers in competition with any single producer. Any individual producer will now have proportionately less influence over the price of the good, and will therefore benefit less from restricting output. In technical terms, the individual producer usually faces a more elastic demand curve with trade. The situation shown in Fig. 11.3 is the extreme case of this more general result.

11.3 COURNOT-NASH COMPETITION

The purpose of this section is to present another example of pro-competitive gains from trade. The model given in this section is also quite restrictive, but it will help to make the point about pro-competitive gains in a more general fashion. We assume two identical countries, each with a single monopoly producer of X. The motivation for this example is that monopoly power often arises from the existence of scale economies, as we indicated earlier, and so the same industry is likely to be imperfectly competitive in all countries. Scale economies are defined and analyzed in the next chapter.

The initial autarky equilibrium for both of the identical countries is given by point A in Fig. 11.4. Now suppose that we open the economies to trade and assume that each monopolist (now more properly called "duopolist") picks the best output, given the output of the other firm. In other words, each firm makes a *best response* to the output of the other firm. This assumption is known as Cournot-Nash behavior. A Cournot-Nash equilibrium is a situation in which each firm is producing its best-response output given the output of the other firm.

Now refer back to the marginal revenue expression in Eq. (11.6) and consider the X producer in Country H. The relevant X in this equation is no longer the combined output of both producers but rather the output of only the home firm. (The corresponding situation holds for the foreign producer.)

Let X_h and X_f denote the outputs of the home and foreign firms, respectively. We assume that with free trade, the world is "integrated" so that the single world price of X is a function of the total supply of both firms: $p = p(X)$, where $X = X_h + X_f$. The "perceived" marginal revenue, MR_{xh}, for the home producer should now be written as

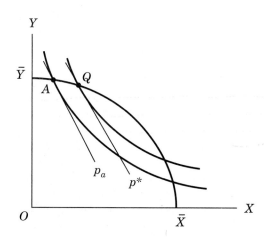

FIGURE 11.4
Cournot competition: pro-competitive gains for two identical countries.

$$\text{MR}_{xh} = p_x + X_h \frac{\Delta p_x}{\Delta X} \frac{\Delta X}{\Delta X_h} = p_x + X_h \frac{\Delta p_x}{\Delta X}$$

$$\text{given that } \frac{\Delta X}{\Delta X_h} = 1 \text{ (Cournot)} \qquad (11.11)$$

The change in the "world" price of X depends on how the total supply of both firms changes when the home firm changes its output. The Cournot assumption is that the home firm chooses its best output *given* the level of the foreign firm. Thus, $\Delta X/\Delta X_h = 1$: the home firm takes the foreign firm's output as fixed, and so the total change in X output is equal to the change in its own output, X_h.

We can now multiply the term, $X_h \Delta p_x/\Delta X$, of Eq. (11.11) by X/X and then by p_x/p_x to transform Eq. (11.11) as follows.

$$\text{MR}_{xh} = p_x + \frac{X_h}{X}\left[X \frac{\Delta p_x}{\Delta X}\right] = p_x + p_x \frac{X_h}{X}\left[\frac{\Delta p_x/p_x}{\Delta X/X}\right] \qquad (11.12)$$

The expression in Eq. (11.12) is similar to the monopoly formula in Eq. (11.10) except for the term X_h/X, which is the share of the home firm in total sales. We will denote this share as $s_h = X_h/X$. Continuing to denote the market price elasticity of demand for X as e_x, Eq. (11.12) can be written in a form comparable to the monopoly (autarky) formula in Eq. (11.9).

$$\text{MR}_{xh} = p_x\left[1 - \frac{s_h}{e_x}\right] = \text{MC}_{xh} \quad s_h = \frac{X_h}{X} \qquad (11.13)$$

In the Cournot equilibrium, the home firm's markup, m_x, is given by $m_x = (s_h/e_x)$ and now diminishes with the firm's market share. The reason is that when the home firm increases its output by one unit, the revenues lost by the price reduction needed to sell the additional unit are now shared between the two firms. The share of this revenue loss borne by the home firm is simply its share in the market. The home firm does not take into account the revenue loss to the foreign firm when it considers increasing sales by one unit. The same is true for the foreign firm.

Equation (11.13) gives a formal demonstration of our earlier assertion. Adding producers through trade makes the demand facing any individual producer more elastic. Consider opening trade between two absolutely identical economies when each is at the initial autarky equilibrium A in Fig. 11.4. Can A still be an equilibrium? If both X producers continue to produce at A, the equilibrium price p_a will remain unchanged as will the market elasticity of demand e_x. But with reference to Eq. (11.13), each firm's share of the market will fall from 1 (when it is a monopolist in autarky) to $\frac{1}{2}$ (when it is a duopolist with trade). Recalling that the e_x is positive, the fall in s_h (and s_f) means that marginal revenue in Eq. (11.13) rises. If one firm increases output believing that the other firm will hold its output constant, some of the costs in terms of reduced price for previous units sold is borne by the rival firm as just noted. Thus, the firm that is increasing its output perceives marginal revenue to be greater than if it were a monopolist bearing all of the cost of a price reduction.

When trade is opened up, each firm perceives MR to be in excess of MC. Each firm will thus increase output until the MR = MC equality is reestablished. This could be at a point such as Q in Fig. 11.4, with a price ratio p^*. In this particular situation, there will be no net trade, as each country consumes and produces the same amounts of X and Y. (With no trade barriers, some consumers could be buying from the foreign producer and vice versa, but this trade balances exactly.) Yet there is clearly a gain from the removal of trade barriers as the competition between the two X producers generates an increase in X production in each country. The increase in welfare shown in Fig. 11.4 could be termed a "pure" pro-competitive gain from trade. Note that, because the countries are identical in all respects, there is no pattern of comparative advantage in this example. Yet there is a "gain from trade," which means that a pattern of comparative advantage is not a necessary condition for gains from trade. Much more will be said about "non-comparative-advantage trade" in the next chapter on scale economies.

11.4 GAINS FROM TRADE: THE PRODUCTION-EXPANSION CONDITION*

How should we think about the pro-competitive gain in more basic economic terms? The basic difficulty induced by monopoly is seen in Fig. 11.1: the economy produces too little of the monopolized good. The gains from trade shown in Fig. 11.4 are due to the fact that the economy is induced to produce more of the good that is undersupplied initially. We will refer to this as the *production expansion condition* for gains from trade. Another way to think about this comes from more standard microeconomic welfare analysis. The price of a good reflects the marginal value to consumers of an additional unit of the good, whereas the marginal cost of production reflects the opportunity cost of the resources needed to produce an additional unit of the good. Welfare is maximized when the two are equal. When price exceeds the marginal cost of production, as it does in the case of monopoly, too little of the good is being produced. Alternatively, one additional unit of the good generates a benefit (price) that exceeds the resource cost of producing it (marginal cost).

In this section, we will use the formal analysis developed in Chapter 5 and used in the previous chapter in order to understand the production expansion condition more fully. If the production set is convex, as it is in the diagrams of this chapter, then the free trade production point evaluated at the "price ratio" tangent to the production frontier yields a higher value of output than does any other feasible production point. But in the present

---

*This section is more difficult and may be skipped without loss of continuity. The principal conclusion is similar to that in Section 10.5 of the previous chapter. Introducing free trade in the presence of a domestic monopoly distortion is welfare-decreasing only if trade leads to a further reduction in the production of the monopolized good.

chapter, the "prices" tangent to the production frontier are generally not the consumer prices, but rather the marginal costs of production as indicated in Eq. (11.3). The value of free trade production evaluated at free trade marginal costs is higher than the value of any other production bundle at those marginal costs. Let superscripts f and a denote quantities evaluated at free trade point Q and autarky point A in Fig. 11.4, respectively. Comparing these points at the marginal costs (slope of the production frontier) at Q yields

$$\left(\text{MC}_x^f\right)X_p^f + \left(\text{MC}_y^f\right)Y_p^f > \left(\text{MC}_x^f\right)X_p^a + \left(\text{MC}_y^f\right)Y_p^a \qquad (11.14)$$

where subscript p denotes production quantities. The marginal cost of X is equal to $p(1 - m_x)$, where m_x is the markup (not necessarily the Cournot formula), and the marginal cost of Y is p_y. Substituting these into Eq. (11.14) gives us

$$p_x^*(1 - m_x)X_p^f + p_y^* Y_p^f > p_x^*(1 - m_x)X_p^a + p_y^* Y_p^a \qquad (11.15)$$

Now rearrange terms as follows.

$$\left[p_x^* X_p^f + p_y^* Y_p^f\right] > \left[p_x^* X_p^a + p_y^* Y_p^a\right] + p_x^* m_x\left(X_p^f - X_p^a\right) \qquad (11.16)$$

The term in square brackets on the left-hand side of the inequality in Eq. (11.16) can be replaced by the value of consumption via the balance-of-trade equation as we did in Chapter 5. For the term in square brackets on the right-hand side of the inequality, the production quantities can be replaced by consumption quantities, because in autarky the production of a good is equal to the consumption of that good. These substitutions convert all the production quantities in the terms in square brackets to consumption quantities (subscript c).

$$\left[p_x^* X_c^f + p_y^* Y_c^f\right] > \left[p_x^* X_c^a + p_y^* Y_c^a\right] + p_x^* m_x\left(X_p^f - X_p^a\right) \qquad (11.17)$$

The term in square brackets on the left-hand side of Eq. (11.17) is the value of free trade consumption at free trade prices, while the term in square brackets on the right-hand side of Eq. (11.17) is the value of autarky consumption at free trade prices. A sufficient condition for free trade consumption to be revealed preferred over autarky consumption is that the right-hand term in Eq. (11.17) be positive; this occurs when free trade production of X exceeds autarky production. In other words, the *production-expansion condition is a sufficient condition for gains from trade*. Furthermore, from the definition of m_x, note that $p_x m_x$ is simply price minus marginal cost:

$$p_x^* m_x\left(X_p^f - X_p^a\right) = \left(p_x^* - \text{MC}_x^f\right)\left(X_p^f - X_p^a\right) \qquad (11.18)$$

Here we see the price-minus-marginal-cost term that we talked about earlier. Trade has a beneficial effect if it expands production of the sector that is initially underproducing—that is, the sector with price in excess of marginal cost.

How likely is it that the production-expansion condition will be met in practice? The answer is that it may not be, and that is the subject of the

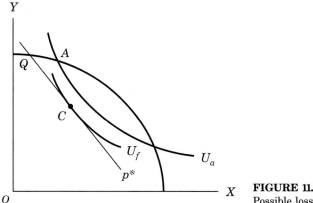

FIGURE 11.5
Possible losses from trade.

next chapter. However, the pro-competitive effect of trade liberalization that we have just discussed generates some *presumption* toward the existence of pro-competitive gains through production expansion. It is only if firms in different countries are somehow able to collude following liberalization that we will not get some type of aggregate pro-competitive gains, and such collusion is very hard to sustain.

11.5 QUALIFICATIONS

It is possible that some countries will experience no expansion of underproducing sectors when trade is introduced. When this occurs, the country may fail to gain from trade. The purpose of this section is to briefly introduce a few possibilities discussed in the broader trade-theoretic literature.

Different Costs

Suppose that the X producers in home and foreign have very different costs, and assume in particular that home is the high-cost producer. When trade is introduced, two opposing effects will occur. First, we will have a comparative-advantage effect that will reduce production of X in H. Second, unless the firms are able to collude, we will have a pro-competitive expansion of X production in both countries. If the first effect dominates, then X production falls in H, which may experience negative gains from trade. This is illustrated in Fig. 11.5 where A is the autarky equilibrium and Q and C are the free trade production and consumption points, respectively. Trade reduces the production of X and Country H loses.

Figure 11.6, however, emphasizes that expansion of X production is a *sufficient* but not a *necessary* condition for gains from trade. Again, A is the autarky equilibrium, generating a welfare level of U_a. Q and C are the free trade production and consumption points, respectively, and the free trade utility level is U_f. Note also that if the world price ratio continues to fall in Fig. 11.6, it is likely that the country will specialize in Y (the monopoly

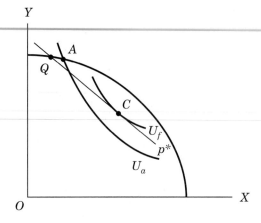

FIGURE 11.6
Expansion of the distorted sector as a sufficient but not necessary condition for gains.

X producer is driven out completely). This is likely to generate significant welfare gains, but it is also likely that the *X* producer will lobby fiercely against trade liberalization.

Different Size Countries

Suppose that two countries are identical except for size and that both have a single *X* monopolist in autarky. This is a bit hard to imagine; for example, if scale economies are limiting entry, then the large country should have more firms. In this admittedly implausibile situation, there will again be two effects working in opposite directions. Suppose that Country H is much larger than Country F. First, the home firm will find that it suddenly has a rival when trade is introduced, yet from its point of view, there has been only a very small expansion in the total market. It is almost as if a second firm has been introduced into the home market. Thus, it is possible that the home firm's output contracts. The foreign firm now has a rival also, but from its point of view, the total market has greatly expanded (much more than doubled in size). Working against this first effect, which tends to contract production in home, is the pro-competitive effect, which works in the direction of increasing the outputs of both firms.

In both the cases mentioned, it is possible to construct numerical examples where the large or high-cost country is worse off with trade. But the differences in size or cost have to be relatively extreme to overcome the effects of the pro-competitive effect in a Cournot model. In addition, these possibilities ignore the crucial role of scale economies, which are what typically give rise to imperfect competition (at least in free market economies) in the first place.

11.7   CONCLUDING REMARKS

This chapter has deviated substantially from traditional trade theory, which often presents only the Ricardian and Heckscher-Ohlin models as determinants of trade. These two models typically assume perfect competition, involving situations in which underlying differences between countries produce trade and gains from trade. These models are in no sense incorrect, and indeed, most international trade economists believe that they continue to explain a major proportion of international trade. Different models are not substitutes for one another. Each model presented in this section of the book explains some proportion of trade. Trade has many causes, and each chapter isolates only one cause.

There have been a few systematic attempts to understand how much of international trade is related to the existence of imperfect competition. Some of these will be summarized in Chapter 14. The existing evidence does suggest that imperfect competition produces significantly larger gains from trade for small economies than for large ones. We observe that trade by large firms accounts for a significant proportion of trade in many industries, and we also observe that a very large proportion of trade is carried on intra-firm by multinational enterprises. These firms will be the subject of Chapter 21.

The following points summarize the findings of this chapter.

1. If there is a monopoly producer in one sector of an economy in autarky, equilibrium is not given by a tangency between the production frontier and an indifference curve. The monopoly leads to a reduction in the production and consumption of that good relative to the efficient competitive outcome and also to a reduction in welfare. The monopoly equilibrium leaves the price of the good (the benefit from one additional unit) higher than the marginal cost of the good (the resources needed to produce one more unit); therefore, the good is being "underproduced" in autarky.

2. Trade can be beneficial in exposing monopoly firms to foreign competition. The increased competitive environment in the larger world market leads to what we call pro-competitive gains from trade. These gains from trade do not rely on the existence of differences between countries, and hence they are "non-comparative advantage" gains from trade.

3. The simplest case to consider is when a small economy with a single firm in one sector is integrated into a large world, such that the (former) monopolist now faces a fixed world price. In such a situation, Fig. 11.3 showed how the gains from trade could be decomposed into comparative advantage gains and pro-competitive gains from trade.

4. Section 11.3 considers a situation in which two identical economies, each with a single X producer, are integrated through trade. We defined a concept called Cournot-Nash behavior, in which each firm picks a best response output given its rival's output. Integration through trade raises each firm's "perceived" marginal revenue. When a firm sells one more unit of X, part of the lost revenue on other sales caused by the price reduction needed to sell the additional unit is borne by the other firm. Thus, trade causes each firm to increase output above the autarky monopoly level, and the result is gains from trade for both countries. This is both a pro-competitive and a non-comparative-advantage gain from trade.

5. Section 11.4 relates the results of the previous two section to basic welfare economics. As noted above, monopoly leads a good to be underproduced in autarky. Trade is guaranteed to improve welfare if it leads to an expansion of production of the underproduced good. This is a sufficient condition for gains from trade, but it is not necessary, as illustrated in Fig. 11.6.

6. The final analytical section of the chapter offers some comments about possible situations in which a country could lose from trade in the presence of monopoly (Fig. 11.5). If a country's monopoly firm is a high-cost producer or if the country is very large, it is possible that trade could lead to a contraction in production, thus worsening the distortion (the underproduction of the good). For this to happen, a comparative disadvantage in the production of the good must outweigh the pro-competitive effect.

7. As a closing thought, note that there is nothing said here to indicate that a country should refuse to trade with a foreign monopoly supplier. The possibility of losing from trade comes from the existence of a *domestic* distortion, not a foreign distortion. Recall from Chapter 5 that the gains-from-trade theorem does not rely on any assumption about whether or not the foreign country has competitive firms. The home country might gain more if the foreign firms are competitive, but a country cannot be worse off by trading with a foreign monopolist than it is by not trading at all.

PROBLEMS

1. With monopoly in both industries, would it be possible to have the price line tangent to the production possibility curve? What condition would this require?

2. Redraw Fig. 11.3 so that free trade leads to a smaller production of X than at the autarky equilibrium. Production of X is contracting, yet the country definitely gains from trade. Why is this? (Hint: with reference to Eq. (11.17), what is happening to the distortion in this case? m_x in Eq. (11.17) is the value at the free trade equilibrium.)

3. Redraw Fig. 11.3 so that the country exports X in free trade. Compare this diagram to Fig. 11.3. Does the difference between the autarky monopoly price and the world price necessarily tell us whether X will be imported or exported in free trade?

4. Assuming that one of two otherwise identical countries has a monopoly producer of X, could trade result in factor-price equalization?

5. With imperfect competition and/or commodity taxes, do the differences in autarky factor prices across countries necessarily imply anything about differences in factor endowments?

6. What happens to markups in the Cournot model as we continue to add firms to the market (assuming that the market elasticity of demand remains constant)?

NOTES

1. Students of calculus will recognize Eq. (11.5) as the rule for differentiation of a product, in this case the product of p_x and X. Strictly speaking, Eq. (11.5) is exactly correct only as Δ goes to zero (Δ becomes d in calculus).
2. A monopolist will produce only where marginal revenue is positive, which restricts equilibrium to sections of the demand curve where e is greater than 1. Demand in this region is said to be "elastic."
3. There is some possible confusion here in relating the optimal markup to the production tax of the previous chapter. In Chapter 11, the production tax was defined as a proportional markup on marginal cost (equal to the producer price): $q = MC(1 + t)$. This is the standard convention in economics. But monopoly markups, as in the case of this chapter, are usually defined in terms of a proportion of the *consumer price* (which in this case is equal to the producer price). Thus, the monopoly markup is usually written such that $q(1 - m) = MC$. The reason for this is that, when the markup is expressed as a proportion of the consumer price rather than as a proportion of marginal cost, it takes the very simple form given in Eq. (11.9). We apologize for the inconvenience, but we are using fairly standard terminology.

REFERENCES

Brander, J. A. (1981). "Intra-Industry Trade in Identical Commodities." *Journal of International Economics* 11: 1–14.

Brander, J. A., and Krugman, P. R. (1983). "A 'Reciprocal Dumping' Model of International Trade," *Journal of International Economics* 15: 313–323. Reprinted in G. Grossman, ed., *Imperfect Competition and International Trade.* Cambridge: MIT Press, 1993.

Grossman, G. M., ed. (1992). *Imperfect Competition and International Trade.* Cambridge: MIT Press.

Helpman, E., and Krugman, P. A. (1985). *Market Structure and Foreign Trade.* Cambridge: MIT Press.

Markusen, J. R. (1981). "Trade and the Gains from Trade with Imperfect Competition." *Journal of International Economics* 11: 531–551. Reprinted in G. Grossman, ed., *Imperfect Competition and International Trade.* Cambridge: MIT Press, 1993.

Melvin, J. R., and Warne, R. D. (1973). "Monopoly and the Theory of International Trade." *Journal of International Economics* 3: 117–134.

Venables, A. J. (1990). "The Economic Integration of Oligopolistic Markets." *European Economic Review* 34: 753–773.

CHAPTER
12

INCREASING
RETURNS
TO SCALE

12.1 INTRODUCTION

It has long been recognized that economies of scale provide an opportunity for trade and gains from trade. Yet very little theoretical research has been done on scale economies until recently. This is in spite of the fact that empirical research in countries as large as Canada and the Western European nations has emphasized the benefits when trade allows domestic firms to rationalize production. High protective tariffs in some of these countries have encouraged the manufacturing industries to produce a wide range of goods in small production runs rather than concentrating on larger and more efficient production of a narrower range of commodities. The more recent view is that even countries as large as the United States have not exhausted scale economies in the domestic market in some industries. Commercial aircraft and computers are two examples. United States consumers benefit from lower prices and higher quality in these industries because companies like Boeing and Intel can spread very high fixed costs over foreign as well as domestic sales.

The gains from trade due to scale economies can be understood fairly intuitively. Suppose, for example, that the cities and towns across the United States could not trade with one another. What do you suppose automobiles would cost if each town had to produce its own? The disadvantages of small-scale production would likely make automobiles prohibitively expensive in all but the largest cities. Trade allows production to be concentrated in a few large factories that ship to all parts of the nation. In fact, even a country as large as Canada is too small to fully reap the scale economies inherent in automobile production. Canada entered into the Auto Pact of 1965 with the United States in order to achieve further scale economies. As a result of the increased trade permitted by the pact, plants in both countries (but especially Canada) produced fewer varieties of cars and increased the length of production runs, thereby lowering costs.

Scale economies are generally difficult to incorporate into general equilibrium models. They are usually inconsistent with perfect competition in production, for reasons discussed in the next section. Therefore, some of the techniques used in earlier chapters to analyze trade are no longer useful; a more complex analysis involving imperfect competition must be used.

12.2 EXTERNAL ECONOMIES

One exception to this problem of analyzing scale economies in general equilibrium occurs when they are external to individual firms, occuring instead at the industry level or at the level of industry groups (e.g., the manufacturing sector). Individual firms remain "small" so that the tools of competitive general equilibrium theory can still be used. It should be emphasized that this is not just a technical convenience. In the very first formal analysis of international trade, Adam Smith emphasized that increasing the size of the market permits a greater degree of specialization and therefore a higher level of productivity. It was only some time later that Ricardo introduced the notion of comparative advantage that became the cornerstone of international trade theory. Adam Smith's view was largely forgotten until recently.

Take agriculture, for example. Economies of scale for individual farms run out at a very small level of production, relative to the size of the market. Yet, as the size of the agricultural sector has grown, it has become profitable to produce specialized machinery and fertilizer, build railroads and handling facilities, conduct research into better seed varieties, and so forth. These developments have led to increasing production at decreasing cost while the industry as a whole captures scale economies, even though each individual producer may have constant returns to scale and may face fixed prices.

Let us return to the no-trade model and assume that all conditions of Chapter 6 hold, except that there are increasing returns to scale in one or both sectors. Suppose we have two absolutely identical economies whose production frontiers are both given by TT' in Fig. 12.1. The production frontier is bowed in (the production set is non-convex), under the assumption (as discussed in Chapter 2) that scale economies in X and/or Y outweigh any factor-intensity effects. Assume that the autarky consumption and production point for both countries is given by point A in Fig. 12.1.[1] It is interesting and important to note that in this case, no pattern of comparative advantage exists (autarky prices are equal), and yet there are potential gains to be had from specialization and trade. Suppose that Country H specializes

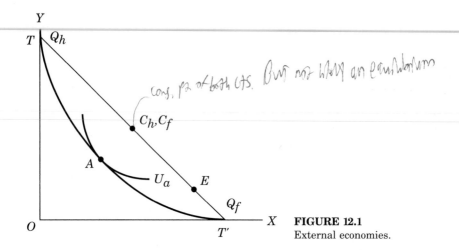

Cons. p2 of both c/s. But not likely an equilibrium (handwritten)

FIGURE 12.1
External economies.

in Y and Country F specializes in X, so that they produce at Q_h and Q_f, respectively, in Fig. 12.1. Each country can now trade half of its output for half of the other country's output, so that each country will consume at $C_h = C_f$. The utility level in each country will increase. Both countries will thus be better off, even though they were absolutely identical to start with. It is in this sense that scale economies offer gains from specialization above and beyond those obtained from any pattern of comparative advantage.

Although the consumption point $C_f = C_h$ in Fig. 12.1 could be an equilibrium, this is unlikely. An indifference curve for each country could be tangent to the cord TT' exactly at the midpoint, but only by chance.

Suppose that when the countries in Fig. 12.1 specialize, each wishes to consume at point E. This cannot be a trading equilibrium because the desired exports and imports of Country H exceed the desired exports and imports of Country F. In order to balance trade, the price of X will have to rise and the price of Y will have to fall. An equilibrium will eventually be reached as in Fig. 12.2, where Country H consumes at C_h and Country F consumes at C_f. The gains from trade are shared unequally even though the countries are identical. In fact, it is just possible that in equilibrium the price of Y is so low that the price line from Q_h passes below A, resulting in losses for Country H.

If Country H were a dictatorship, an all-knowing leader would naturally refuse to allow the country to specialize in Y in the case of Fig. 12.2. This could be accomplished by restricting the sale of Y to keep its price higher, for example. But the problem is that in a highly decentralized economy with external economies or imperfect competition (discussed subsequently), there is no mechanism to ensure that the country will not inadvertently end up as bad as or worse off than Country H in Fig. 12.2. The equilibrium in Fig. 12.2 is stable. In Country H the relative price of X in terms of Y (the slope of the price line) is less than the relative cost of producing X in terms of

(handwritten bottom notes) In terms of Y (for c/h H); Price of X (slope of price line) < Cost of producing X (Prod. faster) — Thus need an EA.

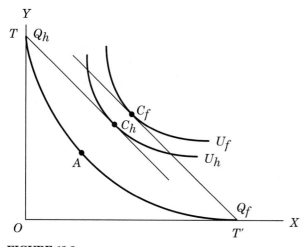

FIGURE 12.2
Uneven gains from trade.

Y (the slope of the production frontier). Thus H is in equilibrium specializing in *Y.* This demonstrates that with scale economies it is possible for the significant gains from trade to be very unevenly distributed and for one country to actually lose from trade.

This simple model of scale economies provides an interesting contrast to the Heckscher-Ohlin model with respect to the effects of trade on factor prices. Suppose the underlying production structure is Heckscher-Ohlin: there are two factors of production, and the factor intensities differ between industries. In the situation shown in Figs. 12.1 and 12.2, not only are factor prices not equalized by trade, but they are actually driven apart by trade. At the autarky equilibrium *A* in Fig. 12.1, the factor prices in the two identical countries must be equalized. With trade, one country specializes in *Y* and the other in *X*. Now because the two countries have the same technologies and factor endowments by the assumption that they are identical, each has the same total bundle of factors allocated to the good that it is producing. But if *X* is labor-intensive relative to *Y*, for example, the slope of an *X* isoquant through a given factor bundle must be steeper than the *Y* isoquant through that same factor bundle (e.g., refer back to Fig. 8.1). In each country, the factor price ratio w/r will be the slope of the isoquant of its good through the endowment point. Taken together, these arguments imply that if *X* is labor intensive, then the country specializing in *X* in Fig. 12.1 or Fig. 12.2 will have a higher w/r ratio than the country specializing in *Y*. The factor-price ratios, which are equal in the absence of trade, are driven apart by trade.

Two final points should be mentioned. First, note that this last example implies that each country in Figs. 12.1 and 12.2 has a relatively high price for the factor used intensively in its export industry. This has some very important implications for the effects of factor mobility, which we will discuss in a later chapter. Second, note that although *relative* factor prices change with the introduction of trade, this does not imply that one factor is necessarily worse off with trade as it would in the case of the constant-returns Heckscher-Ohlin model. In the present case, the capture of scale economies in the good in which the country specializes means that the absolute productivities of both factors may rise at the same time that their relative productivities change. In the case in which both factors are better off (even if unequally so), there will be less opposition to trade liberalization.

12.3   INTERNAL ECONOMIES OF SCALE

We will now consider economies of scale that are internal to the individual firm. This applies to many manufacturing firms that obtain advantages from large-scale production. It is also often the case for some extractive industries such as mining and petroleum. Internal economies may also characterize some service industries such as banking, finance, and insurance.

The problem with internal economies of scale is that they are generally inconsistent with perfect competition and competitive equilibrium. The problem is examined in Fig. 12.3. Suppose a firm must incur some large fixed cost in plant or equipment in order to start production but can thereafter produce with constant returns to scale, or more precisely, at a constant marginal cost. Total cost will be given by

$$\text{TC}_x = F + (\text{MC}_x)X; \qquad \text{AC}_x = F/X + \text{MC}_x \qquad (12.1)$$

where F is fixed cost, MC_x is marginal cost, and X is output. Average cost is equal to TC/X and is given by $\text{AC}_x = F/X + \text{MC}_x$. The situation is shown in Fig. 12.3 where MC_x is constant. AC_x falls steadily as the fixed cost is spread over a larger and larger output. AC_x approaches but never actually touches MC_x.

In this situation, could we have a competitive equilibrium in which price equals marginal cost? The answer is no, as we can show in a simple proof by contradiction. Suppose that the current market price is given by $p = p_c = \text{MC}_x$ in Fig. 12.3, and that each firm perceives this price to be constant. At any output, each firm will lose money by virtue of the fact that $\text{AC}_x > \text{MC}_x = p_c$ or that the average cost exceeds price, no matter how much the firm produces. Therefore, price cannot equal marginal cost in equilibrium. If, for example, the firm produces at X_c in Fig. 12.3 where demand cuts the marginal cost curve, the firm's losses (negative profits) are given by the vertically hatched rectangle. This area is the per-unit loss of price minus the average cost $(p_c - \text{AC}_c)$ times the number of units produced (X_c) or $(p_c - \text{AC}_c)X_c$.

Suppose instead that the current price exceeds marginal cost and that each firm believes it can sell all it wants to at this price. In this case, each firm will attempt to produce an infinitely large output, because at some point AC will fall below price and then keep falling. Thus, no competitive equilibrium exists with internal increasing returns since either (1) the price is equal to (or below) marginal cost, in which case no firm will wish to

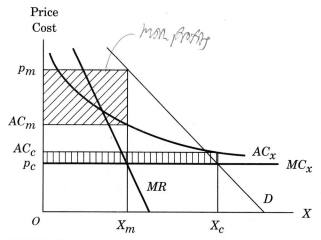

FIGURE 12.3
Partial equilibrium analysis of monopoly.

produce anything, or (2) the price is above marginal cost, in which case each firm will attempt to produce an infinite amount.

One feasible solution to this dilemma is for one large firm to monopolize the industry and to somehow prevent the entry of other firms (e.g., a second firm might calculate that if it enters, it will incur losses). We then have the standard monopoly outcome shown in Fig. 12.3 where MR is the marginal revenue curve drawn with respect to the demand curve D. Monopoly output and price are given by X_m and p_m, respectively, where MR = MC. Profits are given by the diagonally hatched rectangle, $(p_m - AC_m)X_m$, or unit profit times output.

Alternatively, we could allow for free entry of firms until the demand curve facing each firm is driven down to tangency to the AC curve at one point. But in this and all possible equilibria we must be left with the situation that price exceeds marginal cost ($p >$ MC). This is the key result for our purposes: price must exceed MC or the firms will be losing money.

Figure 12.4 gives a general equilibrium representation of this fixed cost plus constant marginal-cost technology, which we will use for the remainder of the chapter. Suppose that X and Y are produced from a single factor, labor (L), which is in fixed supply ($\overline{L} = L_x + L_y$). Assume further that Y is produced with constant returns to scale by a competitive industry so that units can be chosen such that $Y = L_y$. If Y is chosen as *numeraire* ($p_y = 1$), the wage rate in terms of Y will also equal 1. p will denote the price of X in terms of Y, with the cost of producing X given by L_x.

It is assumed that the production of X requires an initial fixed cost, given by F, and then a constant marginal cost, MC_x, as in the preceding example. The total cost of labor required to produce X is then $L_x = F + (MC_x)X$. The production frontier for this economy is shown in Fig. 12.4 as TFT'. $T = \overline{L}$ is the maximum output of Y when $X = 0$. To begin

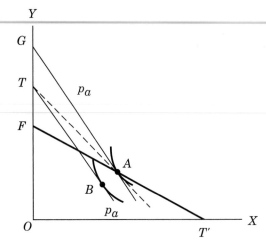

FIGURE 12.4
Monopoly equilibrium and the distribution of income.

producing X, the fixed cost TF must be invested before any output is realized. Thereafter, the constant marginal cost of producing X gives the linear segment FT', which has a slope equal to MC_x. This "kinked" production frontier is just a special case of the non-convex production set shown in Figs. 2.13 and 2.14 in Chapter 2. Note that although the production frontier in Fig. 12.4 is composed of linear segments, it has a property similar to those in Figs. 12.1 and 12.2 in that it lies everywhere below the diagonal connecting its endpoints T and T'.

The average cost of producing X is total cost (L_x) divided by output, or

$$\text{AC}_x = \frac{L_x}{X} = \frac{(\bar{L} - L_y)}{X} = \frac{(T - Y)}{X} \tag{12.2}$$

Consider point A in Fig. 12.4. Equation (11.2) shows, for example, that the average cost of producing the amount of X at A is simply the slope of the line passing through T and A (the dashed line in Fig. 12.4). As we move along the linear segment FT', we see that the average cost of X is everywhere decreasing in the output of X, or alternatively, that production of X is characterized by increasing returns to scale. The equilibrium price ratio must cut the production frontier if positive X is produced at non-negative profits. This result is simply the general equilibrium representation of the result in Fig. 12.3 that price must exceed marginal cost. In Fig. 12.4, the slope of the price ratio must exceed the slope of the production frontier along FT', which is equal to MC_x, the marginal cost of production.

An autarky equilibrium with strictly positive profits for a monopoly producer of X is shown in Fig. 12.4, where the price ratio p_a through equilibrium point A is steeper than the average cost of X, given again by the slope of the dashed line TA. Point G in Fig. 12.4 gives the GNP of the country in terms of good Y. Workers are paid a wage of 1 in terms of Y (because the marginal product of labor in Y is 1), and so total wage income is given by $\bar{L} = \bar{Y}$ or OT in Fig. 12.4. GNP is thus composed of wage income in terms of $Y(OT)$ and profits in terms of $Y(TG)$. The budget line of wage earners is given by a line with slope p_a through $T = \overline{L}$ as shown in Fig. 12.4.

Point B on the wage earners' budget line represents the consumption budget of labor in Fig. 12.4. Therefore, the difference between the consumption bundles B and A is consumption out of profit income. Since wage earners' income is fixed at $T = \overline{L}$ in terms of Y, a decrease in p always increases wage earners' utility or real income (their budget line rotates around the fixed point T). Wage income equals GNP if profits are zero (e.g., if the price ratio is given by the dashed line TA in Fig. 12.4). Trade will change GNP through changes in workers' utilities and/or changes in monopoly profits. These two components of GNP may, of course, change in opposite directions.

12.4 SOURCES OF GAINS FROM TRADE WITH INCREASING RETURNS

Although there is always a *possibility* that a country could lose from trade when there are distortions, there are several conceptually separate sources of gains from trade in the presence of increasing returns and the associated imperfect competition. Which of these are captured depends on the given situation. For example, the pro-competitive effects of trade may lead to the exit of some firms and the consequent savings of fixed costs.

Pro-Competitive Gains

This was discussed in the previous chapter, so we will repeat the point only briefly here. Scale economies imply that the market can support only a limited number of firms, which will consequently be imperfectly competitive. Trade creates a larger market that can support a larger number of firms and the resulting greater level of competition. The pro-competitive effect of trade has been defined and measured in two ways in the economics literature. One way is to define it as a lowering of the markup on a firm's output. The other is to define it as the expansion of a firm's output (the product-expansion effect), with the resulting capture of price over marginal cost. There are technical inaccuracies in both definitions. Lowering the markup while holding the firm's output constant yields ambiguous welfare results. An expansion of output that captures the excess of price over marginal cost can occur in an external-economies model with no imperfect competition at all. These two effects are often inseparable. In the case of Cournot competition in Section 11.3 and Figure 11.4, the fall in the markup and the expansion of production occur together. *Both* are caused simultaneously by the perception of more elastic demand.

As in most of the literature, it is more convenient for our purposes to define the pro-competitive effect as identical to the product expansion effect of Chapter 11. When we do this, the pro-competitive effect can be decomposed into the sum of two separate components. Recall from the previous chapter that welfare is affected by a change in the output of X when X is priced above marginal cost by the amount

$$(p - \text{MC}_x)\Delta X \tag{12.3}$$

An increase in the output of X is beneficial in that the economy captures the excess of price (the value of an additional unit in consumption) minus marginal cost (the value of the resources needed to produce an additional unit). Now write the total cost of producing X, TC_x, as average cost times output (since average cost is just total cost divided by output).

$$TC_x = X(AC_x) \qquad \Delta TC_x = AC_x \Delta X + X \Delta AC_x \qquad (12.4)$$

Now divide the change in total cost in Eq. (12.4) by the change in output to get marginal cost.[2]

$$MC_x = \frac{\Delta TC_x}{\Delta X} = AC_x + X \left[\frac{\Delta AC_x}{\Delta X} \right] \qquad (12.5)$$

Substitute the right-hand equation in Eq. (12.5) into Eq. (12.3) for MC_x.

$$(p - MC_x)\Delta X = (p - AC_x)\Delta X - X \left[\frac{\Delta AC_x}{\Delta X} \right] \Delta X \qquad (12.6)$$

The pro-competitive (product-expansion) effect $(p - MC_x)\Delta X$ thus decomposes into two effects. The first term on the right-hand side of Eq. (12.6) can be called the *profit effect*. If price exceeds average cost (it need not always do so), then an increase in output generates a surplus of price over average cost on the additional output. This surplus is part of national income, although it may be very unevenly distributed. The second term can be called the *decreasing-average-cost* effect. With increasing returns, the change in average cost with respect to output is *negative*: $\Delta AC_x / \Delta X < 0$. Thus, when we include the minus sign in Eq. (12.6), we see that an increase in output improves welfare in that the average cost of producing the initial output X falls. When more output is produced, the initial output requires fewer resources.

The profit effect. We have just explained how a country can gain from trade when its firm expands output, capturing the excess of price over average cost on incremental output. Note that a gain here is not inconsistent with a fall in profit to zero as a consequence of trade, which is why the term *profit effect* is not a perfect one. Trade may lead the price of the product to fall so much that, in the new equilibrium, price is equal to average cost and profits are zero. But in the process of moving from autarky to free trade, the economy captures the excess of price over average cost (even if that difference is shrinking) on each additional unit of output produced. In a model with external economies of scale where price is equal to average cost for each firm, the profit effect is zero.

The decreasing-average-cost effect. The second effect in the decomposition of the pro-competitive (or product-expansion) effect derives from the fall in the average cost of producing the initial output when the firm expands its output. This is a savings in real resources, whereas the profit effect arises from the imperfect competition that generally accompanies scale economies. This effect can occur only with increasing-returns technologies. If we had

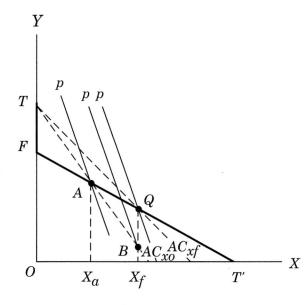

FIGURE 12.5
Decomposing the pro-
competitive gain from trade.

imperfect competition with constant returns to scale, average and marginal cost would be the same, and we would have only the profit effect.

These two effects are separated in Fig. 12.5. Point A shows the initial equilibrium at price ratio p. Suppose that p stays the same with the introduction of trade (not very likely) but that the X producer expands output to point Q in Fig. 12.5. Now the country is clearly on a higher budget line. The movement from A to Q can be broken down into two components: A to B, and B to Q. First, consider the same expansion of X output from X_a to X_f, but holding average production costs constant at their initial level, AC_{x_0}. The latter is given by the slope of the dashed line through points T and A. Therefore, the movement from A to B is the profit effect as defined above. The movement from B to Q is the decreasing-average-cost effect. We can produce more Y at Q than at B because the average cost of production has fallen from AC_{x_0} to AC_{x_f}.

Figure 12.5 also shows two special cases we have mentioned. First, if the price ratio p equals the initial average cost AC_{x_0}, then there is no profit effect (the economy does not move to a higher budget line). The entire movement from A to Q would be the decreasing-average-cost effect. Second, if there were constant returns to scale (no fixed cost), then average costs would coincide with the slope of the production frontier and there would be no decreasing-average-cost effect. The entire effect of moving from A to Q would be due to the profit effect.

Figure 12.6 shows a possible outcome of trade in which two identical countries are combined, very much like the Cournot case of Fig. 11.4. The autarky equilibrium of both countries is at point A, with price ratio p_a. When trade is open, we assume that the two monopoly exporters behave according to the Cournot pricing rule discussed in Section 11.3 of the previous chapter.

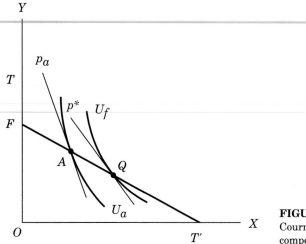

FIGURE 12.6
Cournot competition and pro-competitive gains from trade.

Each producer now views demand as more elastic and increases output. The final equilibrium could be at a point like Q at price ratio p^* in Fig. 12.6, with no net trade between the two identical countries but a gain from trade, nevertheless. Utility rises from U_a to U_f. This pro-competitive gain is due to both a profit effect and a decreasing-average-cost effect as defined above.

Firm Exit Effect

The gain from trade described in the preceding section resulted when the two existing firms increased their outputs in response to a perceived increase in the elasticity of demand. But what if the initial situation were characterized by the entry of firms up to the point where profits are zero? Then the increased competition induced by trade might lead to losses and to the exit of some firms.

Scale economies pose something of a dilemma with respect to the number of firms in an industry. On the one hand, it is desirable in terms of technical efficiency that there be a small number of firms. If the average-cost curve is everywhere downward-sloping (as in our current example), it is desirable to have the entire industry output produced by a single firm. But a small number of firms generally implies greater market power and correspondingly greater monopoly output restriction. This trade-off for a single economy gives rise to a third source of gains from trade. With trade we can increase the total number of firms in competition while reducing the number of firms in each individual country. For example, suppose two countries with 10 firms each enter into trade with each other and that the resulting competition drives out three firms in each country. The number of firms in each country has decreased, but the total number competing with one another is now 14, an increase over the 10 that were competing in each country in autarky.

More advanced theoretical treatments have shown that this is exactly the kind of outcome we will get if there is Cournot-Nash competition and free entry of firms in each country. Free entry drives profits down to zero in each country in autarky. But the opening of trade causes each firm to perceive demand as more elastic, as was discussed in the previous chapter. Generally, firms will increase output, and some firms will then exit as profits are initially negative. The trading equilibrium will have fewer firms in each country, with each firm producing a higher level of output at lower average cost. Empirical analyses for Canada have confirmed that trade liberalization has this rationalizing effect on manufacturing firms.

The situation is illustrated in Fig. 12.7, where A is the autarky equilibrium for each of two identical countries. Free entry has forced price down to average cost, and the vertical distance TF' is now interpreted as the combined fixed costs of the existing firms. Trade causes each Cournot-Nash firm to perceive its demand curve as more elastic and therefore to increase output. But this leads to negative profits and the exit of some firms. Equilibrium is restored at a lower price with fewer firms in each individual country but more firms in total. Exit of the redundant firms frees up the resources that had been devoted to fixed costs and shifts the production frontier of each country out to TFT''. No trade, or more correctly, no net trade, need occur, because both countries are identical and both attain consumption point C in Fig. 12.7.

The movement from A to C in Fig. 12.7 is a combination of a pro-competitive effect and an exit effect. We can decompose the movement from A to C by considering point B. At B, output per firm must be the same as at C, because the average cost of producing at C is the same as at B (recall from Eq. (12.1) that average cost falls continuously in firm output). Points A and B involve the same number of firms because the same resources are devoted to total fixed costs. Thus, the movement from A to B is a pure expansion in

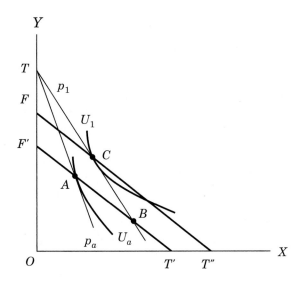

FIGURE 12.7

Exit of redundant firms.

firm outputs, holding the number of firms constant. A to B is therefore the pro-competitive gain from trade. The movement from B to C is a reduction in the number of firms, holding the outputs of surviving firms constant, and therefore shows the firm-exit effect.

Increased Product Diversity

A recent series of papers has emphasized increased product diversity as a form of gains from trade. This emphasis is usually referred to as the *monopolistic competition model* of trade because it draws on a model of the same name used in microeconomics and industrial organization theory. The idea is that an industry is "competitive" in that there are a large number of firms, but it is also "monopolistic" in that each firm is producing a somewhat unique product. The latter assumption implies that these firms do individually face downward-sloping demand curves.

The situation is shown in Fig. 12.8, where we now assume that both X and Y are produced with increasing returns to scale. Production functions for X and Y are identical, and the goods are symmetric but imperfect substitutes in consumption. This last assumption means that consumers are indifferent between one unit of X and one unit of Y, but that they would like to have some of both rather than more of just one. The consumer is, for example, indifferent between a stereo and a television, but would rather have one stereo and one television than either two stereos or two televisions. This model, which reflects consumer preference for diversity, is called the *love of variety* approach.

In autarky, each of the identical countries in Fig. 12.8 could attain consumption point A. But this is now not the best choice, even in autarky. Because of the large fixed costs, it is in a country's interest in autarky to produce only one good, specializing in either Y at point T or in X at point

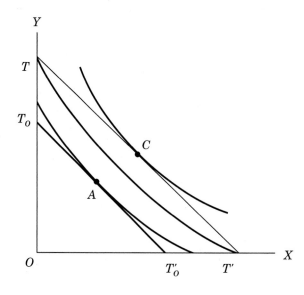

Y

O

X

FIGURE 12.8
Increasing product diversity: "love of variety."

T' in Fig. 12.8. This puts the country on an indifference curve through T and T', which is higher than the indifference curve through A. The benefits of product diversity are outweighed by the high fixed costs of starting production of the second good. With trade, each country could specialize in one of the goods and trade half of its output for half of the output of the other country's good, thereby attaining consumption point C (again, this is unlikely to be the actual equilibrium). In this situation, there is no change in the average cost of a good, nor are there any procompetitive gains. Instead, where scale economies were limiting the number of goods consumed before trade, consumers "decided" to take the gains from trade in the form of having more products rather than having lower costs for their existing products.

Gains from trade through product differentiation can be looked at in a second way. For example, although consumers may buy only one automobile each, each would choose a different "ideal" automobile, depending on tastes and income level. This approach to product diversity is labeled the *ideal variety* approach. Because of scale economies, no country can afford to produce a unique automobile for each consumer. Germany produces Volkswagens and Mercedes-Benzes, and France produces Renaults and Peugeots, all of which have somewhat differing characteristics. Trade in automobiles occurs between France and Germany because some Germans prefer Renaults or Peugeots and some Frenchmen prefer Volkswagens or Mercedes-Benzes.

This situation is shown in Fig. 12.9. Suppose that automobiles have only two characteristics, size and fuel efficiency. There is a tradeoff between these two characteristics: buying a bigger car means sacrificing some fuel efficiency. Figure 12.9 shows three possible combinations of size and efficiency, denoted X, Y, and Z, corresponding to three different types of cars. Suppose that all three models could be produced at the same average cost for the same volume of production. But because of scale economies, the average cost rises steeply as sales fall. Assume finally that societies consist of only

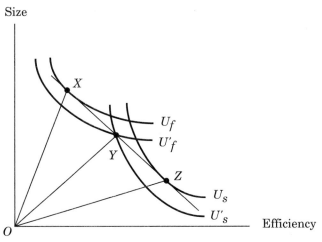

FIGURE 12.9
Increasing product diversity: "ideal variety."

two groups, students and faculty, and that the former have a relatively high preference for efficiency and the latter a relatively high preference for size. Their indifference curves are U_s and U_f in Fig. 12.9, respectively.

Even though the three models cost the same at the same level of production, scale economies force a choice. If the country produces both X and Y, giving both students and faculty their "ideal" cars, the volume of sales of each model will be much lower and the average cost much higher than if only the single compromise model Y were produced. Thus, an entirely possible outcome is that only model Y is produced. It sells for a modest cost, but faculty are cramped and students are poor from buying gas. In Fig. 12.9, these groups attain indifference curves U_f' and U_s', respectively. Now if we add a second, identical country through trade, one country could produce model X and the other model Z, each exporting half its output for half the foreign output of the other model. Each country would be producing the same number of cars as in autarky, and consequently, the cars would have the same average cost. Assuming X and Z sell for the same price that Y did in autarky, consumers pay the same for cars but attain the higher indifference curves U_f and U_s. As in the example of Fig. 12.8, consumers take the gains from trade in terms of increased product diversity rather than in the form of lower prices.

Specialized Plants and Inputs

Increases in market size due to trade may also permit firms to build plants specialized to fewer product lines and to create specialized inputs. Two of many possible examples are machinery that is highly specialized to certain products and consultants who specialize in certain business or engineering problems. Little theoretical work has been done on the former, although empirical analysis in Canada has emphasized plant specialization as an important source of gains from trade liberalization. The U.S.-Canada Auto Pact of 1965 was partly motivated by the fact that Canadian plants were producing too many models in small production runs.

Figure 12.8 can be used to depict the gains from specialized inputs with indifference curves now interpreted as isoquants for final output. Creation of specialized inputs requires an initial fixed cost of TT_0. In autarky, each country creates only one such input in the simple example of Fig. 12.8. An output level corresponding to the isoquant through T and T' is attained in each country from the amount of resources devoted to producing this good. When the countries are combined through trade, the creation of two specialized inputs is profitable because the output level at C can be attained if each country trades half of the output of its specialized input for half of the other country's product.

Before moving on, recall the point about factor returns discussed briefly at the end of Section 12.2. When there is more than one factor, scale economies, whether resulting in lower prices for existing goods or in more goods, make it more likely that all factors will gain from trade. While relative factor prices may change as in the Heckscher-Ohlin model, lower prices for existing goods relative to factor prices or the benefits of having a more diverse consumption bundle, may mean gains from all factors. In the case of increased product diversity, for example, the wage rate could fall in the production of one of the differentiated products, but this decrease in welfare could be outweighed by the utility gain that results from having more products. This effect generates even more political support for free trade.

12.5 AN EXTENSION OF THE COURNOT MODEL TO FREE ENTRY AND EXIT

Suppose we take the Cournot model of the previous chapter and add free entry and exit by firms until profits are zero. Now we will have two equilibrium conditions, $MR_x = MC_x$ as in Chapter 11, and the zero-profit condition $p_x = AC_x$. Suppose all firms are identical so that we can deal with a representative firm i. We can use our cost function from Eq. (12.1) to write the second condition as marginal cost plus F/X_i, where X_i is the output of the representative firm.

$$p_x(1 - s_i/e) = MC_x \qquad p_x = MC_x + F/X_i \qquad (12.7)$$

where s_i is the market share of the representative firm. Divide the second equation by the first.

$$\frac{1}{1 - s_i/e} = 1 + \frac{F}{(MC_x)X_i} \qquad (12.8)$$

Assume that fixed costs (F), marginal costs (MC_i), and the market elasticity of demand (e) are all constants. Now assume that we take two identical countries and combine them in trade. This is equivalent to doubling the size of a single country. Under the assumptions noted, only one result is possible: s_i *must fall and X_i must increase.* They cannot both stay constant; with the market growing, a constant output per firm must mean that the individual firm's market share is falling. s_i and X_i cannot increase or decrease together; that would mean that Eq. (12.8) is no longer satisfied. The equation can be satisfied if s_i increases and X_i falls, but this is impossible in the growing market; a firm's market share cannot grow in a growing market if its output is falling (this can be seen more formally by replacing s_i with X_i/X, where X is total sales).

We have now determined that the larger market induced by trade leads to an expansion in output per firm. This by itself is a sufficient condition for gains from trade. But we can carry the model a bit further. If all firms are identical as we have assumed, then the market share of a representative firm, s_i, is just $1/N$ where N is the number of firms. The fact that s_i falls when we combine two identical economies means that the total N must rise. But the number of firms cannot in the end be double (that is, each country cannot continue to support the same number of firms as in autarky) if we place some simple restrictions on the form of demand functions.[3] Suppose that the number of firms did double (the number of firms in each country stayed constant). Because each firm increases its output due to an increased perceived marginal revenue (s_i falls), profits of the existing firms will fall below zero, leading some firms to exit. In this case, we get the result shown in Fig. 12.7. Trade leads to an exit of some firms in each country but leaves the total number of firms in the expanded economy larger than in either country in autarky. The market is more competitive, surviving firms have lower average costs and higher outputs per firm, and the two identical countries necessarily gain from trade.

12.6 AN ALGEBRAIC VERSION OF THE MONOPOLISTIC-COMPETITION MODEL*

In this section we will take a more formal look at increased product diversity in a monopolistic-competition model. The purpose of the section is to show more rigorously how the number of products is determined and to demonstrate that we can indeed construct a case in which all gains from trade are in the form of increased diversity. The model we will use corresponds very closely to the situation shown in Fig. 12.8. Suppose that the X sector is actually composed of many firms producing somewhat different products. Suppose that the utility functions of identical consumers are given by

$$U = \sum_{i-1}^{n} X_i^{\alpha}, \qquad 0 < \alpha < 1 \qquad (12.9)$$

where the number of products produced, n, is *endogenously determined*. Each product that is produced yields diminishing marginal utility, and so the consumer would always rather have one each of two products, say X_1 and X_2, rather than two units of either. Labor is the only factor of production. We will assume free entry of firms such that profits are driven to zero. The economy's budget constraint is thus that labor income is spent on X.

$$\overline{L} = \sum_{i=1}^{n} p_{xi} X_i \qquad (12.10)$$

More advanced treatments will show that the demand function for X_i is given by the following rather complicated formula.

$$X_i = \frac{\overline{L}}{p_{xi}^{\sigma} \left[\sum_{j} p_{xj}^{-\alpha\sigma} \right]} \qquad \text{where} \quad \sigma = \frac{1}{1-\alpha} \qquad (12.11)$$

---

*The analysis in this section is considerably more difficult. You can skip it without losing continuity and refer to Fig. 12.8 for a grasp of the basic ideas behind the monopolistic-competition approach.

If there are many X producers, we can safely assume that each producer treats the term in square brackets as a constant. Students with calculus can find the elasticity of demand for X_i as p_{xi}/X_i times the derivative of Eq. (12.11) with respect to p_{xi}. The elasticity of demand is given by

$$e_i = -\frac{dX_i/X_i}{dp_{xi}/p_{xi}} = \sigma = \frac{1}{1-\alpha} \qquad (12.12)$$

The X producers have the same technology that we described in Eq. (12.1). Let labor be numeraire, so that $w = 1$. p_{xi} is the price of X_i in terms of labor. Producer maximization then requires that the firm set marginal revenue equal to marginal cost, MC_x.

$$p_{xi}\left[1 - \frac{1}{e_i}\right] = p_{xi}[1 - (1-\alpha)] = p_{xi}\,\alpha = \mathrm{MC}_x \qquad (12.13)$$

Freedom of entry and exit requires that equilibrium is characterized by price equals average cost.

$$p_{xi} = \mathrm{MC}_x + F/X_i \qquad (12.14)$$

If we combine Eqs. (12.13) and (12.14), we can solve out for the equilibrium level of X_i, which is the same for all X_i that are produced (i.e., all X_i that are produced are produced in the same amount).

$$X = \frac{\alpha F}{\mathrm{MC}_x(1-\alpha)} \qquad (12.15)$$

Goods are produced in a fixed amount independent of other factors such as the size of the economy, measured by the labor endowment. So suppose that we double the labor endowment, which we can again think of as combining two identical economies. The labor endowment must equal the total labor used in the n goods that are produced.

$$\overline{L} = n(MC_x X_i + F) = n\left[\frac{\alpha F}{1-\alpha} + F\right] = n\left[\frac{F}{1-\alpha}\right] \qquad (12.16)$$

With goods produced in fixed amounts, the economy expands entirely by expanding the number of goods (an increase in $\overline{L}$ increases n in the same proportion). This is the situation shown in Fig. 12.8. Doubling the size of the economy through trade allows each consumer to purchase a more diverse consumption bundle, thereby capturing the welfare benefit from increased diversity shown in Fig. 12.8. Trade does not increase the scale of production of any good, yet it is scale economies that are responsible for the gain from trade. Scale economies are what limit the number of goods produced (degree of product diversity) initially.

Since any good continues to be produced in the same amount, as shown in Eq. (12.15), we can denote the production of a representative good simply as X. The utility function in Eq. (12.9) can then be written as

$$U = nX^\alpha \qquad (12.17)$$

If we combine two identical economies, and if the output of any particular good remains fixed, consumers in each country will have twice as many goods from which to choose and will consume half as much of each good as they did in autarky (the fixed amount of a good must now be shared among consumers in both countries). Treating n and X as the autarky values, denote free trade utility by U^f and autarky utility by U^a.

$$U^f = (2n)(X/2)^\alpha = 2^{1-\alpha}nX^\alpha > nX^\alpha = U^a \qquad \text{given that} \quad 2^{1-\alpha} > 1$$
$$(12.18)$$

Consumers gain through increased diversity. As suggested earlier, it is better to have one stereo and one television than to have two of either.

12.7   CONCLUDING REMARKS

Our analysis of scale economies has produced a number of results that differ in very basic ways from those of the more traditional Ricardian and Heckscher-Ohlin models. First, there is the question of the direction of trade. In the traditional models, the direction of trade is related to underlying characteristics of the economy. In the Heckscher-Ohlin model, for example, we saw that a country exported the goods that intensively used the country's relatively abundant factors. With scale economies, however, there may be some inherent arbitrariness in the pattern of specialization. This was illustrated in Fig. 12.1 and in subsequent diagrams, where we noted that with scale economies, trade can arise between two identical economies, or rather, between two economies for which there exists no pattern of comparative advantage. Of course, in reality the gains from scale economies occur in *addition* to gains due to comparative advantage. The methodology of the no-trade model is not to present *alternative* theories but rather to focus on individual determinants of trade and gains from trade one at a time. The theories are in fact *complementary* in that generally all of them have simultaneous and important roles in actual trade.

Countries typically specialize when there are increasing returns, but the welfare effects of trade may depend on which country specializes in which good. One implication of this result is that the observed pattern of trade in goods produced with returns to scale may often be determined by historical factors, such as which country entered an industry first. The first entrant gains an advantage (sometimes called *first mover advantage*) by achieving low costs and perhaps technical expertise early; this may discourage foreign entrants who might have to enter at an initial high cost.

Second, returns to scale have implications for the gains from trade, implications that differ in a number of ways from the more traditional results. On the one hand, scale economies offer more possibilities for gains, whereas on the other hand, there are possible complicating factors. As we showed earlier, scale economies may mean that there will be gains from trade even for two identical economies. Alternatively, gains from trade exist independent of any pattern of comparative advantage. The lower costs and increased product diversity achieved through the capture of scale economies are thus an additional source of gains that complement the gains achieved from other bases for trade, such as differences in factor endowments.

Strong conclusions about gains from trade are, however, impossible to draw because scale economies are generally associated with distortions, for reasons noted earlier. The result is that a country's prices may not accurately reflect the underlying costs and the pattern of comparative advantage. When this happens, a country can end up specializing in the wrong goods to the point of experiencing welfare losses from trade.

Many economists are finding empirical evidence that scale economies are a very important determinant of trade and the gains from trade for countries the size of Canada and many of the Western European nations. Empirical estimates of the gains from trade liberalization in both of these regions suggest that an important source of gains has been a rationalization of the manufacturing and certain service industries. Some would assert that these rationalization effects constitute a major source of gains from the formation of the EEC, outweighing factors having to do with comparative advantage. There is also an increasing acceptance of the view that issues involving scale economies and imperfect competition are important for a country as large as the United States. Finally, with the increased mobility of factors of production (especially capital) and technology across international borders, there is some reason to suggest that the Heckscher-Ohlin and Ricardian bases for trade may be relatively less important in explaining trade among the industrialized countries than they were even a few decades ago. The very large volume of trade among the very similar economies of North America, the EEC, and Japan seems to constitute prima facie evidence that scale economies, imperfect competition, and product differentiation are important determinants of trade.

The principal points of the chapter are summarized as follows.

1. With increasing-returns-to-scale technologies, trade and gains from trade can arise even between two identical economies. We could refer to this as *non-comparative-advantage trade* in contrast to trade generated by underlying differences among countries. We also showed that the gains from trade are not necessarily distributed evenly, even between identical countries.

2. There are several sources of gains from trade in the presence of scale economies, although they are often hard to disentangle in practice. Expansion of an increasing returns sector through trade generates a benefit equal to the excess of price over marginal cost on incremental output. This pro-competitive gain can be broken down into the excess of price over average cost (the profit effect) and the fall in the average cost of producing existing output (the decreasing-average-cost effect). Gains may also be captured as a result of the exit of some firms, which frees up the resources that were used in fixed costs for other uses.

3. Gains from trade may be captured from increased product or input diversity instead of from lower average costs for a fixed range of products. In other words, gains may be captured by having either the same range of products at lower costs or a larger range of products at the same costs.

Of course, these two extremes will generally be mixed in practice. The final sections of the chapter modeled the two extreme cases. Section 12.5 gave an extension of the Cournot model of the previous chapter, showing that combining two identical economies leads surviving firms to increase production (resulting in a decrease in the average production cost) of a fixed range of products. Section 12.6 used a version of the monopolistic-competition model, in which any good that is produced is produced in a fixed amount, to show that trade between two identical countries leads to gains from increased product diversity.

4. The chapter focused largely on a one-factor model in order to concentrate on the essence of scale economies. However, two points that are important in a multi-factor context were briefly noted. First, trade based on scale economies between similar economies may drive factor prices farther apart in the two countries. We will explore this further in Chapter 21. Second, scale economies make it more likely that all factors will gain from trade, contrary to the Heckscher-Ohlin model. While trade may change *relative* factor prices, the increased factor productivities due to the capture of scale economies may mean that the *absolute* or real returns to all factors rise. In the case of increased product diversity, a factor's return may fall in terms of a representative good, but this negative effect may be outweighed by the availability of a more diverse consumption bundle.

PROBLEMS

1. Show that if both countries want to consume at E in Fig. 12.1, there will be excess demand for X and excess supply of Y.
2. Show by redrawing Fig. 12.2 that the relative price of Y could drop so low that Country H would lose from trade.
3. Show that if a firm's price is less than its average cost, its profits must be negative.
4. What is the largest output that the firm could produce in Fig. 12.3 and still break even?
5. Using Fig. 12.7, show that point C could not be attained by the two countries if some firms did not exit from the industry.
6. Redraw Fig. 12.8 with different indifference curves such that autarky equilibrium at A is preferred to an equilibrium at either T or T'.
7. In the discussion of product diversity and monopolistic competition, we consider two different situations: (a) consumers have identical tastes but prefer diversity (*love of variety*, Fig. 11.8) and (b) consumers have heterogeneous tastes (*ideal variety*, Fig. 11.9). Determine which approach is likely to be more useful in each of the following situations: (1) choosing groceries in a supermarket, (2) buying a house, (3) shopping for clothing, (4) choosing a new stereo.

NOTES

1. Equilibrium is generally not given by a tangency between an indifference curve and the production frontier. The slope of the production frontier incorporates the externality effects

that one producer has on another, while private firms do not take these effects into consideration in making their input and output decisions. If, for example, there are external economies in the X sector, then the "social" marginal cost of producing an additional unit of X is less than the private marginal cost, which is equal to the price of X, p_x. In equilibrium, we would have $p = p_x/p_y > \text{MRT}$. The price line would cut the production frontier as in Fig. 11.1 of the previous chapter. Figure 12.1 could be generated by an economy in which the external economies are equally strong in both sectors (not very likely, but it helps make the simple point we wish to show).

2. Students with calculus will recognize the second equation in Eq. (12.4) as the rule for differentiation of a product. Strictly speaking, it is valid only when Δ approaches zero.

3. A sufficient condition is that demand is not "too convex." A linear demand curve is sufficient for the result that some firms in each country must exit. The difficulty is that, if demand is very convex, the price fall caused by the pro-competitive effect causes consumers to spend much more on X in total. Holding the initial number of firms at the combined autarky total, if this effect is sufficiently strong, the markup revenue received by a firm may increase even though that firm is cutting its markup *rate* in half. Basically, if combining the two economies does not at least double revenues for each firm (causing markup revenues to fall), then some firms will exit the market.

REFERENCES

Ethier, W. (1979). "Internationally Decreasing Costs and World Trade." *Journal of International Economics* 9: 1–24.

Ethier, W. (1982). "National and International Returns to Scale in the Modern Theory of International Trade." *American Economic Review* 72: 389–406.

Grossman, G. (1992). *Imperfect Competition and International Trade.* Cambridge: MIT Press.

Helpman, E. (1981). "International Trade in the Presence of Product Differentiation, Economies of Scale and Monopolistic Competition. A Chamberlinian, Heckscher-Ohlin Approach." *Journal of International Economics* II: 304–340.

Helpman, E., and Krugman, P. (1985). *Market Structure and Foreign Trade.* Cambridge: MIT Press.

Horstmann, I., and Markusen, J. R. (1986). "Up the Average Cost Curve: Inefficient Entry and the New Protectionism." *Journal of International Economics* 20: 225–248.

Harris, R. G., and Cox, D. (1984a). *Trade, Industrial Policy, and Canadian Manufacturing.* Toronto: University of Toronto Press.

Harris, R. G. (1984b). "Applied General Equilibrium Analysis of Small Open Economies with Scale Economies and Imperfect Competition." *American Economic Review* 74: 1016–1032.

Kemp, M. C. (1969). *The Pure Theory of International Trade and Investment.* Englewood Cliffs, N. J.: Prentice-Hall.

Krugman, P. (1979). "Increasing Returns, Monopolistic Competition, and International Trade." *Journal of International Economics* 9: 469–479.

——. (1981). "Intraindustry Specialization and the Gains from Trade." *Journal of Political Economy* 89: 469–479.

Lancaster, K. (1980). "Intra-Industry Trade Under Perfect Monopolistic Competition." *Journal of International Economics* 10: 151–175.

Markusen, J. R. (1981). "Trade and the Gains from Trade with Imperfect Competition." *Journal of International Economics* 11: 531–551.

——. (1989). "Trade in Producer Services and in Other Specialized Intermediate Inputs." *American Economic Review* 79: 85–95.

Melvin, J. R. (1969). "Increasing Returns to Scale as a Determinant of Trade." *Canadian Journal of Economics* 2: 389–402.

Wonnacott, R. J., and Wonnacott, P. (1967). *Free Trade Between the United States and Canada.* Cambridge, Mass.: Harvard University Press.

CHAPTER
13

TASTES, PER CAPITA INCOME, AND TECHNOLOGICAL CHANGE AS DETERMINANTS OF TRADE

13.1 INTRODUCTION

Our models to this point have focused on the production side of the general equilibrium structure of economies to describe the causes of trade and the sources of gains from trade. This focus is representative of trade theory in general, which has devoted the overwhelming share of its attention to production, neglecting consumption almost entirely. Many models assume that consumers have identical and homogeneous utility functions, regardless of where they are located. This means that if commodity prices were equalized by trade, consumers everywhere would demand goods in the same proportions. All trade would then be due to various differences in production among countries. As students have realized by now, this emphasis generates a markedly diverse and sophisticated set of predictions about the supply-side determinants of comparative advantage, such as differences in factor endowments, policy-based market distortions, and imperfect competition associated with increasing returns to scale.

There has been much less theoretical attention paid to demand-based determinants of trade. Neither has there been much empirical examination of the apparent presumption by trade economists that production differences are more important than consumption differences for explaining trade patterns.[1] This phenomenon is curious in that the assumption of identical and homogeneous preferences across countries is easily shown to be questionable. For example, in 1991, 59 percent of household consumption in Bangladesh was estimated to have been devoted to food. The corresponding shares of food in household budgets in other countries were: Indonesia 48 percent, Argentina 35 percent, Greece 30 percent, Japan 17 percent, and United States 10 percent.[2] In contrast, budget shares allocated to medical care were: Bangladesh 2 percent, Indonesia 2 percent, Argentina 4 percent, Greece 6 percent, Japan 10 percent, and United States 14 percent. In part, these differences reflect variations in relative prices due to trade barriers and government policies. However, they clearly indicate that preferences are not homogeneous, in that the relative share spent on food declines and that of medical care rises as the level of economic development rises. They might suggest as well that tastes are also not identical, though this cannot be conclusively inferred from share data alone. However, an obvious national difference that would affect preferences is that the industrialized countries tend to have larger percentages of their populations at advanced ages, increasing the demand for health care. Accordingly, one purpose of this chapter is to bring together some strands of literature in order to examine the possible ways in which international differences in consumption patterns can influence trade flows.

A second shortcoming of our production-based models to this point is that they are entirely static in nature. They investigate the effects of differences in important supply characteristics on trade flows. However, most people will recognize that international trade bears important relationships to dynamic changes in the world economy, such as shifts in technology and new product innovation. These models are also not as fully developed as the standard trade theories, but it is important to bring them into our discussion of trade determinants. Thus, the second purpose of this chapter is to analyze some relatively simple aspects of the influence of technological change on international trade.[3]

We should place these newer theories in some historical context. Interest in developing trade models that could serve as alternatives to the Ricardian and Heckscher-Ohlin concepts emerged largely in the 1960s and 1970s after several empirical studies raised questions about the practical validity of these traditional models. We review these studies in the next chapter. However, most models based on demand variations, scale economies, and technological differences are relatively recent and are still under active theoretical development. This helps explain why there are many disparate views of what determines trade in these terms and why the models vary in complexity and rigor. However, these influences on trade are clearly important and deserve separate treatment here.

13.2 INTERNATIONAL CONSUMPTION BEHAVIOR AND TRADE

In this section we analyze the implications of allowing consumption patterns to vary between countries in two ways. First, we take national utility functions to be homogeneous but not identical. Second, we consider the case of identical but nonhomogeneous preferences.

Different Tastes

We begin with the most simple specification of international differences in preferences. Following our previous methodology, we assume that the only difference that exists between two countries is in demand conditions, for only in this way can we be sure that the results derived depend entirely on differences in demand. In particular, we assume that endowments in the two countries are identical, that production functions are identical between countries, and that production takes place with constant returns and perfect competition. These assumptions imply that the production possibility curves for the two countries will be identical. Thus, in Fig. 13.1, TT' represents the production possibility curve for both Country H and Country F. In this section we also assume that there are no distortions in either economy and that the utility functions of the two countries, while differing, are both homogeneous. The case of nonhomogeneous demand is considered in Section 13.3. The autarky equilibrium is the point where the highest indifference curve for each country is tangent to the production possibility curve. If we assume that tastes in Country H are biased toward commodity Y relative to tastes in Country F, then U_h and U_f could be representative indifference curves for the utility functions of H and F, respectively.

The autarky positions for countries H and F are A_h and A_f, respectively, and the autarky price lines are p_h and p_f in Fig. 13.1. Therefore, in autarky,

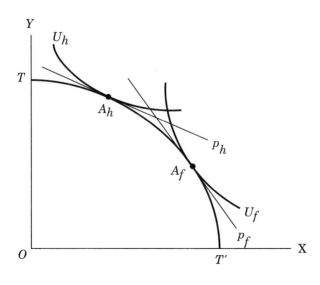

FIGURE 13.1
International differences in tastes.

commodity Y is relatively expensive in Country H, whereas commodity X is relatively expensive in Country F. The reason for this outcome is simply that have a stronger preference for good Y, driving up its price in comparison with X, with the opposite situation prevailing in F. When trade is permitted, the residents of Country H, observing that Y is relatively less expensive in the foreign country, will shift their purchases from the home country to Country F. Similarly, residents of the foreign country, observing that commodity X can be purchased more cheaply in Country H, will shift some of their purchases to that country. The results of these shifts in demand will be that the production point for the home country will move down the production possibility curve, whereas the production point for the foreign country will move up toward the Y axis. These adjustments will continue until there is no longer any incentive for residents of one country to increase their purchases in the other, or in other words, until commodity trade has succeeded in equalizing commodity prices. Such a situation is shown in Fig. 13.2, where the common world price ratio is p_w and where the common production point is Q. Figure 13.2 is drawn so that trade is balanced, or so that the triangles $C_h B_h Q$ and $Q B_f C_f$ are identical.

From the analysis of Fig. 13.2 we can conclude that Country H, the country whose tastes are biased toward commodity Y, will import commodity Y and export commodity X, while Country F, where tastes are biased toward commodity X, will import X and export Y. Thus, we conclude that when trade is caused by taste differences, the country will import the commodity toward which its tastes are biased. Another way of stating this result is simply that nations tend to import the goods that are most preferred in consumption when differences in tastes are the predominant source of comparative advantage.

In the specific example given in Fig. 13.2, both countries enjoy gains from trade. The gains-from-trade theorem does apply to this particular

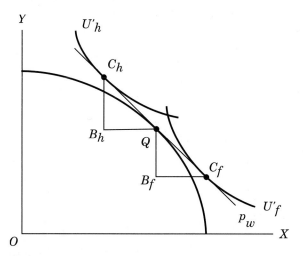

FIGURE 13.2
Trade based on differences in tastes.

model because none of the assumptions required for the theorem is violated. Similarly, we can see that factor prices will be equalized by trade, for at the international trade equilibrium, both countries produce at exactly the same point. Because they share the same production functions, the two countries will have precisely the same efficiency locus, and the equilibrium production same point on this locus. As a result, relative and absolute factor prices must be the same in the two countries. The Stolper-Samuelson theorem also holds in this model. In Country F, for example, trade results in a relative reduction in the price of *X*. If *X* is labor-intensive, the wage-rental ratio will fall, the real return to labor will fall, and the real return to capital will rise. The opposite changes will occur in Country H. Thus, the primary results from Chapter 8 apply to a model in which trade is due to taste differences.

Nonhomogeneous Tastes

An alternative possibility, which also generates differences in international consumption patterns, is that tastes are nonhomogeneous but are nevertheless identical in both nations. This nonhomogeneity will help explain the fact that budget shares for food and other consumption items vary widely across countries at different levels of income per capita.

Recall that in Chapter 3 we discussed a situation in which, although tastes were nonhomogeneous, aggregation of the individual curves into community indifference curves was possible. This occurred when income-consumption curves were linear but did not go through the origin. We use this type of "quasi-homogeneous" preferences in Fig. 13.3 to illustrate how differences in per capita income lead to differences in consumption patterns, which in turn lead to trade. Assume that we have two countries with identical populations but that Country F has uniformly superior technologies for producing both goods *X* and *Y*. In Fig. 13.3 the production possibility curve of Country F ($T_f T'_f$) is a "radial blowup" of Country H's production

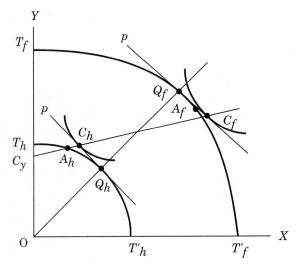

FIGURE 13.3
Trade based on nonhomogeneous tastes.

possibility curve $(T_h T_h')$. That is, along any ray from the origin, the slopes of the two production possibility curves are the same. Assume also that tastes are nonhomogeneous in that there is a "minimum consumption requirement" of Y of the type discussed in Chapter 3. The origin for a system of indifference curves is then point C_y. All consumers in both countries are assumed to have the same (nonhomogeneous) preferences.

Given that the populations are identical by assumption, the larger national product associated with the higher production possibility frontier implies that Country F has higher per capita income than does Country H. The lower income per person in Country H implies a relatively high demand for Y in that country in autarky and vice versa for Country F. The autarky equilibria will be at points like A_h and A_f in Fig. 13.3, where because of the similar production structure, there is a relatively high autarky price of Y in Country H and a relatively high autarky price of X in Country F. As in the previous section, each country will have a comparatively high price for its "most preferred good," except now, "preference" derives from differences in per capita income. Underlying preferences or tastes are assumed to be the same for all consumers.

The autarky price differences lead to a trading equilibrium as shown in Fig. 13.3. The production points of countries H and F are Q_h and Q_f, respectively. These lie along the same ray from the origin because of our "radial blowup" assumption made earlier and the equalization of commodity prices by trade. Consumption points are C_h and C_f for countries H and F, respectively, at the free trade price ratio p. These consumption points lie on a ray through C_y. Country H, low in per capita income, imports Y, and Country F, high in per capita income, imports X. As in the case of the taste differences shown in Fig. 13.2, trade is due to differences in demand. In both examples, the countries produce goods in the same proportions, but they consume them in different proportions at the same set of prices.

Notice an important implication of this analyis. With quasi-homogeneous preferences of this kind, the proportion of income spent on good Y (the good with the minimum consumption requirement) falls and the proportion spent on good X rises as per capita income increases. Another way of stating this is that demand for Y is income-inelastic (elasticity is less than unity) and demand for X is income-elastic (elasticity is greater than unity). Comparing this to the trade pattern established previously, we see that the poorer country imports the good with the low income elasticity. Strictly in terms of demand patterns, then, we would expect that poorer countries would tend to import food to satisfy their relatively greater demand for it.

The models in this section have demonstrated that variations in tastes, embedded in a standard trade model, cause nations to import the goods they most prefer. Trade in this view is still inter-industry in nature, as it was in the Heckscher-Ohlin model. However, this outcome is at odds with two observations about trade in the real world. First, some countries tend also to export goods for which there is a sizeable domestic demand. Second, international trade in manufactures often is more intra-industry in nature. We can use other ideas about demand patterns to build toward an understanding of these facts.

13.3 THE LINDER HYPOTHESIS

This analysis of the possible role of per capita income in determining trade leads naturally to a discussion of the ideas of Swedish economist Staffan Linder (1961). Linder argued that the principles governing trade in manufacturing goods are not the same as those governing trade in primary products. He was quite prepared to support the idea that trade in primary products is determined by factor endowments. However, he argued against the notion that differences in factor endowments are the major determinants of trade in manufactured products. He chose instead to highlight the role of demand, beginning his argument with an observation similar to the one we made in our chapter on increasing returns to scale: a large volume of trade exists between the developed countries. These countries have very similar factor endowments and thus, according to the Heckscher-Ohlin theory, we might not expect a large volume of trade between them. We must, therefore, look for a cause of trade other than factor endowments.

Linder contended that a manufactured good is created by an innovative entrepreneur in response to a perceived demand. A new manufactured good is, in other words, introduced only when an entrepreneur believes there is sufficient potential demand to warrant production. It is this perception of potential demand, rather than considerations of factor endowments, that triggers production. The second assertion in the argument is that an entrepreneur is most familiar with the home market. Barriers of distance, language, and culture mean that entrepreneurs are much less likely to be able to perceive what kinds of new products could be successfully introduced into foreign markets.

The third assertion follows from the first two. For a manufactured product to be produced in (and therefore potentially exported from) a country, there must exist significant home demand for the product. The range of manufactured goods produced in a country is therefore determined by domestic demand as much as by production considerations such as factor endowments.

Suppose that an entrepreneur perceives a home demand for a product and begins production. Where will this entrepreneur find export opportunities for additional sales? Linder argued that the best opportunities will be found in countries that have very similar demand patterns to the entrepreneur's home country. Thus, if an American invents a new communications device, such as a modem or telefax machine, and produces it for the home market, the best export opportunities for this device will be found in Canada, Western Europe, and Japan. Similarly, entrepreneurs in Canada, Western Europe, and Japan will find that their best foreign markets will be in the United States and in one another's countries.

The final assertion in Linder's argument is implicitly contained in this last statement. The countries with the most similar demand patterns for manufactured goods will tend to be those with similar per capita incomes. People in countries with lower per capita incomes may wish to buy relatively simple products. However, people in countries with much higher per capita incomes may want more sophisticated devices, such as coffee makers with flashing lights, digital readout, and remote control. Thus, the volume of trade in manufactured goods will be highest among countries of similar per capita incomes, such as the United States, Canada, Western Europe, and Japan. For obvious reasons, Linder's hypothesis is also referred to as the *overlapping demand hypothesis* or the *preference similarity hypothesis*. Predictions about which specific products each country might export are difficult to make, because such exports depend on the history of entrepreneurial activity in each market. Overall, however, international patterns of income and demand determine the extent of trade in manufactured goods. In particular, it is possible to export goods for which there is a strong domestic demand.

13.4 EXPLAINING THE EXISTENCE OF INTER-INDUSTRY TRADE AND INTRA-INDUSTRY TRADE: COMBINING DEMAND AND SUPPLY INFLUENCES

So far, we have made a number of references in the text to the concepts of *inter-industry trade* and *intra-industry trade*. We begin this section by discussing these concepts more fully before going on to consider a model in which important determinants of these kinds of trade can be combined into a unified general equilibrium trade theory.

As we have suggested, *inter-industry trade* refers to international exchange of widely dissimilar goods, such as the exportation of automobiles in return for imported clothing. It should be evident that such trade stems from differences in countries that produce rankings of sectoral comparative advantage. In the Ricardian model, for instance, international differences in labor productivity (associated with different technologies) in distinctive types of goods generate a particular trade pattern. More fundamentally, however, economists associate inter-industry trade with the Heckscher-Ohlin model, in which variations in factor endowments by country and in factor intensities by commodity determine comparative advantage. Thus, labor-abundant countries tend to export labor-intensive goods, such as clothing, and capital-abundant countries tend to export capital-intensive goods, such as automobiles. Land endowments are also quite important in determining trade. As noted previously, it follows that inter-industry trade should be prevalent in trade between countries with disparate endowments, such as labor-abundant, developing countries on the one hand and capital-abundant, developed countries on the other. Except in cases of peculiar endowment structures, such as the acute scarcity of natural resources and land in Japan, we would not expect to see much trade among the developed economies as a group.

It should be clear that this last prediction is false. As we discuss in Chapter 14, trade among developed nations accounted for 57.0 percent of world exports in 1990. Most of that trade was in manufactures involving *intra-industry trade* (IIT), or the simultaneous importing and exporting of similar products. There is substantial IIT among the industrialized nations both in manufactured inputs, such as machinery, high-technology electronics, and specialized chemicals, and in manufactured final goods, such as automobiles, consumer durables, cosmetics, and alcoholic beverages. The United States, for example, is a significant importer and exporter of both wines and beers. It is difficult to reconcile this fact with theories of trade based on differences in factor endowments.

Explanations for Intra-Industry Trade

There are numerous possible sources of IIT. We limit ourselves here to four explanations that are seen as the most important.[4]

Industrial classification. Some trade flows are misleadingly measured as IIT because of the industrial classification system. For example, the United States exports fruits and vegetables during the summer, when they ripen, and imports produce in the winter from countries in the southern hemisphere. This trade, based on *seasonal growing variations,* could easily be explained in a Heckscher-Ohlin framework by considering climate as a factor of production. However, trade flows are typically reported on a calendar-year basis, so both imports and exports of identical goods exist within these trade categories. A second and more significant example lies in the common phenomenon of high-wage nations' producing sophisticated components of electronics products, exporting them to low-wage nations for assembly into final goods, then importing the final products. A prominent case of this *mid-product processing* occurs in United States trade with Mexico, wherein several American firms ship components to *maquiladora* plants in Mexico along the border for assembly into automobile parts, televisions, and the like.[5] Similar processes happen in trade between the high-income countries of the European Community and the Mediterranean nations and between Japan and developing nations in Asia. The point here is that such trade is largely based on differences in wage costs, suggesting that it is generated by Ricardian or Heckscher-Ohlin factors. Nonetheless, both the exports of components and the imports of final goods tend to be counted in the same trade categories, resulting in IIT.

Transport costs. For many products, shipping costs are high in relation to their market value. The prototypical examples are heavy and inexpensive goods, such as cement, bricks, and lumber, though we could also mention electricity and certain tradeable services like construction. High transport costs imply that markets for such goods are limited geographically. It is quite possible that localized markets exist across national borders, generating two-way trade. For example, it may well be that lumber is exported from British Columbia in Canada to the state of Washington in the United States and simultaneously exported from Maine in the United States to Quebec in Canada. There are numerous examples in Western Europe of cities that lie across a national border from each other, meaning that these cities form an integrated market. Two-way trade associated with transport costs is common as different localized binational markets engage in ordinary commerce.[6] In this sense, IIT can be a result of political and geographic decisions on where to draw national borders.

Product differentiation. One of the strongest assumptions in traditional trade theories is that imported and domestic goods are completely homogeneous, or perfect substitutes in consumption. However, many commodities, especially manufactured goods, are differentiated by style and quality. It is obvious that automobile models vary in size, horsepower, comfort, performance, and appearance. Similarly, wines, beer, furniture, and other goods are differentiated by quality and variety. Manufactured inputs, such as machinery, electronic components, and software are also differentiated in significant ways. If preferences are heterogeneous, so that imported goods and similar domestic goods are seen by consumers as imperfect substitutes, the products can command different prices and profit markups in various markets. This is because each variety of a product will face a distinct demand curve in each market, allowing its producer to act with some market power. Thus, firms will compete not only on the basis of price, but also on the bases of performance, quality, service, and other dimensions of product differentiation.

As we discussed in Chapter 12, these simple observations carry crucial implications for international trade. It is evident that consumers and firms prefer to have many choices of which car or wine or machine to purchase. When either the *love of variety* idea or the *ideal product* idea is incorporated into models of monopolistic competition and product differentiation, it follows that international trade is simply an extension across borders of tastes for diversity. Thus, there are consumers in the United States who prefer German beer and consumers in Germany who prefer American beer, resulting in two-way trade. Similarly, there are homeowners in Canada who enjoy Scandinavian furniture and homeowners in Sweden who prefer Canadian furniture. Trade in differentiated inputs is also prevalent. Thus, tastes for variety and the ability to differentiate products provide a powerful explanation for IIT.

Increasing returns to scale. IIT associated with product differentiation is considerably reinforced by the existence of scale economies. We developed numerous perspectives on scale economies and trade in Chapter 12. For our present purposes, we simply reiterate the fact that if industries in each country tend to produce a relatively small range of differentiated goods, each subject to increasing returns, the result will be substantial two-way trade at lower costs. It is inefficient for each country to produce an entire set of models of automobiles and trucks, for example, if some models can be obtained from other countries. Thus, each automobile industry in the United States, Canada, Germany, France, the United Kingdom, Japan, and Korea produces a subset of differentiated models at relatively low cost. Indeed, in nearly any manufactured product for which scale economies are potentially important, the combination of increasing returns and product differentiation leads to significant IIT.[7] Finally, note that increasing returns clearly expand the likelihood that a nation will export goods for which it has strong domestic demand.

A Unified Model of Trade

Many of the various elements that we have analyzed in this and the preceding chapter can easily be combined into a model that helps explain the stylized facts that motivated our discussion: the apparently large volume of trade among the industrialized countries relative to trade between the industrialized countries and the developing countries, and the existence of IIT in manufactured goods.[8]

Suppose that there are two goods, food and manufactures, and that food is labor-intensive while manufactures are capital-intensive. Assume that food has a high minimum-consumption requirement (implying a low income elasticity of demand), whereas manufactures have no minimum-consumption requirement (implying a high income elasticity of demand). Let there be two blocks of countries, a capital-abundant "North" and a labor-abundant "South." (These titles, which are used commonly in international economics, are meant to distinguish the industrialized, higher-income nations from the developing, lower-income nations.) The North will be relatively specialized in producing manufactures because of its capital abundance, as suggested by the factor-proportions theory. Suppose also that the countries of the North have higher per capita incomes, which is the result when ownership of capital is spread uniformly over laborers. Countries of the North will therefore consume relatively more manufactures because of their higher incomes. In contrast, the labor-abundant South will be relatively specialized in both producing food, because it is labor-intensive, and consuming food, because of the lower per capita incomes. If there were no taste biases, the South would export food and the North would export manufactures exactly as predicted by the Heckscher-Ohlin theorem. However, the consumption biases mean that the level of North-South trade in food for manufactures will be reduced below what it would be in a Heckscher-Ohlin world. The consumption bias in each region toward its own export good reduces both imports and exports.

Assume finally that manufactures are not a homogeneous good but a collection of differentiated manufactured goods, as discussed earlier. With increasing returns in each product, each manufacturing firm will produce a somewhat unique good and sell it to consumers in all the countries that make up the industrial North. This is intra-industry trade because these countries are simultaneously importing and exporting similar manufactured goods to one another. In the North, the taste bias toward manufactures due to the high per capita income now actually increases the amount of intra-industry trade among the northern countries. Relative to a Heckscher-Ohlin world with homogeneous tastes, the northern manufacturing firms switch exports from the South, where demand is low due to low per capita incomes, to other northern countries where demand is conversely high. Thus, nonhomogeneous demand leads to a decrease in North-South trade and to an increase in IIT among the northern industrialized countries. These are the stylized facts that were to be explained. We should note that while this model is most useful from the standpoint of economic realism, it makes the assumption that there is a strong positive correlation between capital intensity in production and a high income elasticity of demand in consumption. This assumption, which seems reasonable on some grounds, has not yet been supported by conclusive, empirical evidence.

13.5   THEORIES OF TRADE BASED ON DYNAMIC CYCLES

We turn next to issues of dynamic changes in trade patterns. During the 1960s and perhaps earlier, some international trade economists observed that the pattern of trade in the world had undergone a gradual shift during the 20th century. The change seemed to be particularly pronounced with respect to the manufactured exports of some developed countries. It was noted that while numerous goods were originally developed and produced in the United States, the location of their production often shifted subsequently to Europe and then to developing countries, only to be replaced by a new generation of products in the United States. This gradual and systematic pattern of change seemed to call for a new theory of international trade that could account for the dynamic introduction of new goods and the movement over time in comparative advantage toward the developing countries as the new goods advanced in age.

The Life Cycle for New Products

Several economists developed informal theories of this process as related to new products, though they attempted to relate it to notions of underlying comparative advantage.[9] Raymond Vernon was the first to construct an explicit *product cycle* hypothesis.[10] In this view, a product goes through a full life cycle from innovation to standardization. Vernon's conception of the *innovative stage* of the cycle borrowed ideas from the Linder hypothesis, though there is nothing particularly dynamic (having to do with changes over time) in Linder's analysis. Consider a product such as a personal computer (PC). At some point, entrepreneurs in some high-income country, such as the United States, Germany, or Japan, decide that potential demand has risen to the point where PCs can be profitably introduced. High incomes are again important to the extent that new products are income-elastic in demand. It is also important for demand in the innovating country to be fairly price-inelastic for the new good, in order for the firm to be able to earn some (at least temporary) profits as it refines the production technique. Thus, demand patterns are again central to the theory.

Production of the computers initially occurs in the home market where there is easy communication between factory managers and sales person-nel. This localized production, according to Linder and Vernon, is necessary in order to facilitate critical revisions of the PC and of the technology for producing it. Such revisions to the innovative product can benefit from cus-tomer comments, while providing repair services is easier in local markets. Exports to other high-income countries are expected to begin within a rela-tively short time as consumers in those countries recognize the existence of the PC. An increasing proportion of domestic output will likely be exported to other countries as their incomes grow.

The second phase, often called the *maturing stage* of a product cycle, occurs when the technology for producing the good has become fairly stable, and demand in other high-income and middle-income countries has risen to the point where entrepreneurs there find it profitable to begin production themselves. After all, they have the advantages of lower transport costs and local communication, while the limited need for additional technical change in the personal computer has diminished. Such production could come about through several mechanisms. First, the firm that innovated the PC could undertake foreign direct investment in factories in Western Europe and countries such as Canada, Australia, and even South Korea or Taiwan. Indeed, the product cycle model provides one hypothesis about why firms engage in foreign direct investment. Second, local firms in these countries could begin production of the new good under licensing arrangements with the innovating firm. Finally, firms in these other countries might develop a competing product with similar characteristics, such as a PC with more memory or improved graphics capabilities. After some time it might well be that these firms begin exporting the PC and its substitutes back to the original innovating country. One reason is that they might have lower costs of production because of the lower wage rates in their economies, an explanation of particular relevance to, say, Taiwan. These producers might also gain scale economies and production expertise as they penetrate markets in the innovating nation. Also important is that firms in the innovating country will have moved on to develop newer versions of the good and will have begun scaling back production of the older PC model.

The third phase of the product cycle, often called the *standardized stage,* occurs when production of the original PC becomes routine and labor-intensive. Note that by this stage, demand for the product is likely to have become much less price-inelastic because consumers have come to understand how the product works and numerous competing products have been introduced. In this final phase, production is likely to move to the low-wage developing countries through foreign direct investment, as there is relatively little local ability in those countries to develop competing products. Such production is capable of servicing markets in North America, Japan, and Western Europe so that the original producers are now in the position of import competitors. The process could even continue to the point where the original producers are driven out of the market entirely.

However, disappearance of the innovating firms is unlikely. As the last phase of the product cycle approaches, our example PC firm has been developing and exporting newer products such as work stations or super-computers. There is a continuous introduction of new products, each of which may be expected to go through a similar life cycle. As a second example, color television receivers were first developed decades ago by American firms. However, Japanese and European televisions began soon thereafter to compete with North American firms and eventually dominated the North American market. Currently, most television sets sold in the United States are produced in developing countries, such as Mexico, under license to U.S., Japanese, and European firms. However, North American electronics firms have moved on to other products and are competing with firms in Japan to be the first to introduce commercially successful high-definition television receivers.

Another example might be textile production. During the early nineteenth century, Great Britain had a large share of the world export market in high-quality woven textiles. As the century progressed, many of Britain's export markets were lost to new producers in North America and Europe. By the middle of the twentieth century, these countries were in turn losing sales to producers in Japan. The Japanese began to experience cost increases in the 1960s, and production began to shift to countries such as Korea, Taiwan, and Mexico. By this time the Europeans, North Americans, and Japanese were beginning to specialize in new products, such as sophisticated textile materials, that may someday also be produced largely by developing countries.

The Life Cycle for New Technologies

It seems useful to distinguish between new products, on the one hand, and new technologies as embodied in production processes (such as steelmaking) or new producers' goods (such as machinery) on the other hand. The product cycle previously described tends to focus on final consumption goods. Yet it seems likely that there is a closely related phenomenon with respect to production technology, which we might call the *technology cycle*. Techniques of production and various types of machinery often seem to follow a cycle from development and use in the advanced countries to eventual use in developing countries. Such a phenomenon is of interest because production technologies and producers' goods are important exports of the industrialized nations.

A simple theory of a technology cycle begins with the observation that the industrialized nations are high-income and high-wage countries.

High wages create a strong incentive to invest in labor-saving production technology, because the payoff to a new innovation is the number of worker hours saved, times the wage rate. The industrialized nations are thus the leaders in the development of new technology. This new technology improves productivity and tends to lead to further wage increases. Indeed, it would be very difficult to decide whether the development of new technology stimulates wage increases or vice versa. Presumably the causality runs both ways.

In any case, beginning with the observation of continuous technological development and wage increases, we can postulate a technology cycle similar to the product cycle. In the first phase, a new technology, such as a piece of textile machinery, is developed in an industrialized country. This machine is used for production in the innovating country or in other high-wage developed nations. It is not exported to developing countries because its use would make production there inappropriately capital-intensive. As time passes, wages rise in the developed countries to the point where the textile machine no longer permits profitable production. Simultaneously, incomes in some developing nations rise to the point where use of the machine is justified for foreign production. The machine becomes an export of the industrialized country. In later stages of the cycle the machine may, in fact, be produced abroad.

To the best of our knowledge, this phenomenon is not well-researched and should thus be regarded as somewhat speculative at this point. Yet it does seem to offer a potentially important hypothesis about the direction of trade in technology and production equipment. As noted, however, a satisfactory theory must deal with the simultaneous causality between technical change and high per capita income.

Some Implications of Cycle Models

It is important to understand the implications of this continuous process of product and technology development and production relocation. There are basically two forces in operation here: the innovation of new goods and technologies and the international diffusion of information about how to produce them. As demonstrated in theoretical analyses by Paul Krugman and David Dollar, these forces set up a potential conflict between the interests of the advanced, innovative countries (the "North" in our earlier terminology) and those of the developing nations (the "South").[11] The introduction of new goods helps satisfy the tastes for variety that consumers in all countries share in these models. However, production of these new goods is at first feasible only in the North because only firms in that region have the technical knowledge required. This gives Northern firms a temporary monopoly, which is translated into higher wages for northern workers. Thus, new products raise welfare for northern workers through higher wages and more consumption variety. The faster the rate of innovation, the greater the gain in utility for the North. In these models, new products also raise welfare for southern workers because the variety gains outweigh the higher costs of new goods associated with the premium wages. In general, of course, this may not be true, and the monopoly costs could be larger.

The existence of lower wages in the South sets up an incentive to transfer technological information about production to the South, where production costs would be reduced. However, when technology is diffused in this fashion, the Northern monopoly disappears. Thus, technology transfer raises the welfare of southern workers through higher wages but lowers the welfare of northern workers by reducing their wages (though prices also decline). If rates of technology transfer are quite rapid in comparison with rates of new product development, relative wages may converge. In this sense, Northern countries may have an incentive to enact barriers, such as patents, to free transfer of technology.

While these models are highly stylized, they do point out important features of the world economy. Advanced countries like the United States, Canada, and Japan have high wages due in part to their highly innovative economies. An important component of maintaining high incomes is the need for continuous product and technology innovation through research and development expenditures, assisted by the maintenance of a technically skilled labor force. At the same time, the transfer of new technologies is crucial for raising incomes in the developing countries. Indeed, some countries may find themselves rapidly climbing a "technology ladder" from the production of standardized goods to product innovation. Japan has passed through this process, and Korea, Taiwan, Singapore, and Hong Kong appear to be doing the same now. Other countries, such as Thailand and Indonesia, quickly take their places at the lower end of the ladder. These dynamic processes are a key determinant of global economic growth, but they do put a burden on the wealthy countries to engage in continuous innovation. Failing this, the developed countries could be tempted to erect barriers to imports from the poorer countries, an observation that seems to be increasingly consistent with actual trade policies.

13.6 CYCLE MODELS AND COMPARATIVE ADVANTAGE

At first glance, these dynamic theories seem to stand in stark contrast to our earlier discussions about the determinants of trade. Although the earlier discussions suggested a stable pattern of trade based on patterns of comparative advantage, returns to scale, and so on, the dynamic theories seem to suggest a continuously shifting pattern of trade, at least for manufactured goods. Are we forced to choose between two irreconcilable approaches?

Much of the apparent conflict disappears if we think of goods as being composed of a number of characteristics. For new goods, the standard Heckscher-Ohlin effects of labor or capital intensity are relatively unimportant in comparison with issues such as engineering inputs, shifting technical specifications, and experimentation in use. As products mature, however, we usually observe a relatively stable pattern of trade emerging in product characteristics associated with more traditional factors. Indeed, whether a mature product is produced with stable technologies that are labor-intensive (say, television production) or capital-intensive (say, steel plate production) determines the type of countries that will export back to the innovating nations.

Similarly, even though the particular goods being produced in a country may continually change, the underlying characteristic of goods exported from a particular country will remain largely the same, as long as that country remains in a similar position relative to others in terms of its wages and its capacity for product and technology innovation. The product-cycle theory suggests that we should find the wealthiest nations specializing in new consumer goods that cater to high-income tastes. These nations should be observed to produce and export new capital-intensive, or labor-saving, equipment and technologies. If the types of product characteristics embodied in a nation's exports are in turn systematically related to the determinants of trade discussed earlier, including factor endowments, scale economies, and nonhomogeneous tastes, then the product-cycle approach may not, in fact, be that different after all.

Several reservations can be expressed about the cycle theories. As we have just mentioned, it may be that the cycle theories are actually not very distinctive after all, if we think of countries as trading the characteristics embodied in goods rather than the goods themselves. Instead of viewing the United States as having moved from exporting radios to televisions to home computers, perhaps we should think of the United States as exporting sophisticated electronic goods, "sophisticated" being defined relative to the period in question.

Second, although incentives for product innovation and imitation remain as strong as ever, changes in the world economy may have shrunk the *length* of typical product and technology cycles so much that the model has limited empirical validity. This is largely because the product cycle theory as developed in the 1960s significantly underestimated the ability of multinational enterprises to move production abroad at little cost. As we noted earlier, the theory relies on the assumption that a new product must initially be produced at home in order to allow easy communication among engineers, plant managers, and sales personnel. In an era of increasingly sophisticated multinational firms, this communication problem has become less of a constraint. Firms may quickly transfer the production of a new product to the location that offers the most attractive factor prices. But in this case, production is determined by the traditional determinants of comparative advantage. We should also point out that in recent years, changes in global production techniques have tended to deemphasize traditional mass-production techniques in many high-technology sectors in favor of more flexible manufacturing methods pioneered by Japanese firms. Where such techniques are prevalent, we would expect to see much less shifting of production and comparative advantage to low-wage countries than we saw in the 1970s.

A final reservation about the cycle theories is that they are largely partial-equilibrium explanations of trade and are stated in such a way that it is difficult to understand the nature of causality. They seem to assert that high per capita incomes cause the development of new products and technologies. But, as we noted previously, it would be equally valid to assert that new technologies cause high incomes. Until this type of problem can be fully worked out, the cycle models will have to be regarded as incomplete. A satisfactory model should give a complete or general equilibrium description of the economy, rather than treating the level of income as exogenous. In the last ten years, economists have begun to develop such models, in which growth in income levels and incentives for product innovation are endogenously determined as a result of variables such as initial factor endowments, tax and tariff rates, and economies of scale.[12] Interestingly, in these so-called "new growth models," international trade is as much a spur to further innovation as it is the result of underlying demand and supply factors in static models.

13.7   CONCLUDING REMARKS

In this chapter we have examined several ways in which demand influences international trade, and we have considered simple theories of dynamic technical change and trade. Our main conclusions may be stated as follows.

1. Demand differs across countries both because people have different tastes and because demands depend on per capita income when tastes are identical but nonhomogeneous. Empirical studies of demand tend to strongly reject the hypothesis of homogeneity, as we will discuss again in the next chapter. In these relatively simple specifications of demand patterns, countries tend to import the goods for which they have the strongest preferences.

2. Differences in demand caused by differences in per capita income are a cornerstone of the Linder hypothesis. This model has other elements, such as the role of entrepreneurs in developing new products, but per capita income is central to the implications of the models for international trade questions. A country can export only those products for which an entrepreneur has perceived and filled a domestic demand. Thus, trade in manufactures is most prevalent among developed countries, which have similar tastes because of similar per capita incomes.

3. The existence of some intra-industry trade is due to the categorization of industries for purposes of reporting trade data. Some of it is due to transport costs in conjunction with localized markets that spill over national borders. Most importantly, however, IIT is the result of preferences for product variety in conjunction with economies of scale.

4. These factors may be combined with the notion of nonhomogeneous preferences and factor endowments into a unified model that explains the prevalence of trade in differentiated manufactures among developed countries and the prevalence of inter-industry trade between developed countries and developing countries.

5. The product-cycle model also depends heavily on differences in demand associated with per capita income. Fundamentally, the cycle models

are useful in understanding the importance of product and technology innovation and international diffusion. These processes have important influences on incomes in different nations.

6. The cycle models may be criticized on numerous grounds. A more satisfactory dynamic theory of trade awaits further development of models that capture the mutual dependence of technical change and per capita income.

PROBLEMS

1. Suppose in Fig. 13.2 that over time, tastes in Country H shift toward commodity X. How will this affect welfare in the two countries? How will relative and real factor rewards be affected?

2. In Fig. 13.2, how is the volume of trade affected by the degree of differences in tastes between the two countries?

3. In Fig. 13.3, show that trade disappears as the minimum consumption requirement for Y goes to zero.

4. Try to think of several products that have undergone cycles. What are the underlying characteristics of the products in question?

5. Using the Linder hypothesis as applied to the product cycle, explain why the United States was a leader in the development and export of automobiles. Explain why high-quality hockey skates were first produced in Canada.

6. In which ways is the product-cycle model inconsistent with the Heckscher-Ohlin model? In which ways are the two consistent?

7. How would you use the product-cycle model to help explain the existence of IIT?

NOTES

1. Our review in the next chapter of empirical work in trade considers one such study, the results of which suggest that demand differences do indeed play an important role.
2. The source for these data is World Bank, *World Development Report,* 1993.
3. Deeper analysis of trade and economic growth will be presented in Part Four.
4. Interested readers are referred to Greenaway and Milner (1986). We also provide further commentary on the empirical importance of IIT in the next chapter.
5. In fact, this process is encouraged by certain provisions of U.S. and Mexican trade policy. Under U.S. law, only the value added by workers in Mexico is subject to import taxes when the final goods are shipped back. These policies will be phased out under the terms of the North American Free Trade Agreement.
6. Readers should not infer from this that increases in transport costs would expand IIT. Rather, higher transport costs tend to diminish all trade flows. However, we do observe two-way trade in particular products with significant shipping costs.
7. It is also possible to develop models of IIT in homogeneous products manufactured under increasing returns. Recall from Chapter 12, for example, that if two identical firms produce the same good monopolistically in autarky in two countries, the introduction of free trade would lower prices in a Cournot-Nash equilibrium through the *threat* of two-way trade or cross-penetration of each other's markets. However, in the equilibrium, there could be IIT if there were no transport costs. Such "cross-hauling" is possible even in the presence of transport costs if the firms engage in "reciprocal dumping" or charging lower prices in export markets than at home, as shown by Brander and Krugman (1983).
8. This model is based on the formal theory developed by Markusen (1986). Important elements of this theory were also advanced by Krugman (1980).

9. See Posner (1961) and Hirsch (1967).
10. See Vernon (1966).
11. See Krugman (1979) and Dollar (1986).
12. Grossman and Helpman (1991) provide a series of such models and a review of the literature.

REFERENCES

Brander, J. A., and Krugman, P. R. (1983). "A 'Reciprocal Dumping' Model of International Trade." *Journal of International Economics* 15: 313–323.

Dollar, D. (1986). "Technological Innovation, Capital Mobility, and the Product Cycle in North-South Trade." *American Economic Review* 76: 177–190.

Greenaway, D., and Milner, C. (1986). *The Economics of Intra-Industry Trade.* London: Basil Blackwell.

Grossman, G. M., and Helpman, E. (1991). *Innovation and Growth in the Global Economy.* Cambridge: MIT Press.

Helpman, E., and Krugman, P. R. (1985). *Market Structure and Foreign Trade.* Cambridge: MIT Press.

Hirsch, S. (1967). *Location of Industry and International Competitiveness.* Oxford: Clarendon Press.

Linder, S. B. (1961). *An Essay on Trade and Transformation.* Stockholm: Almqvist & Wiksell.

Krugman, P. R. (1979). "A Model of Innovation, Technology Transfer, and the World Distribution of Income." *Journal of Political Economy* 87: 253–265.

———. (1980). "Scale Economics, Product Differentiation, and the Pattern of Trade." *American Economic Review* 70: 950–959.

———. (1981). "Intra-Industry Specialization and the Gains from Trade." *Journal of Political Economy* 89: 959–973.

Markusen, J. R. (1986). "Explaining the Volume of Trade: An Eclectic Approach." *American Economic Review* 76: 1002–1011.

Posner, M. V. (1961). "International Trade and Technical Change." *Oxford Economic Papers* 13: 323–341.

Vernon, R. (1966). "International Investment and International Trade in the Product Cycle." *Quarterly Journal of Economics* 80: 190–207.

———, ed. (1970). *The Technology Factor in International Trade.* New York: Columbia University Press.

CHAPTER
14

EMPIRICAL STUDIES OF COMPARATIVE ADVANTAGE MODELS

14.1 INTRODUCTION

The preceding chapters demonstrate that economists have developed numerous models to explain why international trade takes place. These models make assumptions that, in large measure, embody strong abstractions from reality in order to isolate the particular influence of some important variable on the pattern and volume of trade. These theoretical abstractions allow analysts to investigate the implications of different circumstances for trade flows and economic welfare. Undertaking an analysis in the real-world environment of imperfect competition, numerous factors, commodities, and trade restrictions would be most difficult. Nonetheless, it is natural for analysts to wonder how well their theoretical predictions correlate with actual empirical data on international trade. Accordingly, a large body of literature has appeared in which economists attempt to test various aspects of the theory of comparative advantage or to assess the importance of different explanations for trade. In this chapter we review only a small subset of the most important studies.[1]

We first discuss some complications that should be kept in mind in considering this body of empirical work. One problem is that it is difficult, even in principle, to test theories of comparative advantage directly because they rely on statements about differences in autarky relative costs and prices across countries. Autarky, or the absence of any trade, is virtually an unobservable situation, and available data would be influenced by international trade. Thus, economists resorted to indirect means of testing trade theories based on observable variables.

A second problem is that to establish theoretical statements about trade, economists make numerous simplifying assumptions that cannot be true under all realistic circumstances. Thus, even in cases where it is possible to translate our theories into equations that embody observable variables, these equations cannot be expected to hold literally or without error. Accordingly, because they cannot fully test trade theories, empirical trade analysts must pose a simpler question: "How closely do actual trade data correspond to the levels predicted by various trade theories?" Given this constraint, empirical work consists largely of measurement and judgment rather than precise testing.[2]

A third point is that our various international trade theories should not be seen as competing hypotheses. Rather, each theory tends to focus on a particular aspect of national economies that is expected to induce trade. In principle, each of these influences operates simultaneously, both alone and in conjunction with the others, to explain the pattern and volume of trade. The task for empirical economists, therefore, is to assess the relative importance of various trade determinants.

Despite these problems, economists have made great progress in studying the effects of various influences on the patterns of international trade. It is well worth examining some of the important work on the determinants of comparative advantage. One reason for considering this work is that it has caused some trade theorists to reconsider their models in light of new empirical regularities discovered in trade data. A second reason is that, whatever their methodological shortcomings, our empirical studies have resulted in a large body of evidence that is highly suggestive of the importance of varying determinants of trade. Finally, as our theories have suggested, understanding the sources of international trade is critically important in evaluating the relationships between trade and such significant issues as income distribution, market structure, and technology. In turn, empirical work can be used to inform the decisions of governments making trade policy.

14.2 THE GAINS FROM TRADE

With few exceptions, our models point strongly to the conclusion that a country in a state of free trade likely enjoys substantially higher welfare than it would in isolation. This view was perhaps most apparent in the Classical and Heckscher-Ohlin models, in which the ability to trade at world prices allowed nations to specialize their resources along the lines of comparative advantage and allowed consumers to avail themselves of cheaper import prices. Additional gains from trade came from rationalization of industry, greater economies of scale, improved quality, and enhanced competition.

As mentioned earlier, it is difficult to test for the existence of gains from trade because of the absence of autarky data. Economists often appeal to an obvious point in claiming that there are such gains: countries could presumably refuse to trade if engaging in trade made them worse off. Thus, from the standpoint of *revealed preference,* countries consider themselves to be better off in a regime of open trade than in isolation, which was the basic point of Chapter 5. Of course, we must recall that free trade may well redistribute income, making some individuals worse off and some better off, so that some scheme of compensatory payments to the losers must be potentially available.

In practical terms, it is not difficult to see the wisdom in the view that free trade is superior to autarky, because a policy of self-sufficiency is generally no more sensible for a country than it is for an individual. If a small economy, such as that in Hong Kong or Switzerland, attempted to meet all its needs for food, machinery, steel, and the like through domestic production alone, success would come only at high costs, tending to impoverish the nation.

This powerful statement is supported by historical evidence in a fascinating study by Richard Huber.[3] Japan moved from a position of virtual autarky in 1858 (the end of its feudal period) to one of nearly free trade in the 1870s after the Meiji Restoration. The effects on the Japanese economy were dramatic. In this period, foreign trade rose from a negligible percentage of national income to perhaps 7 percent. In autarky Japan needed to produce both primary goods and manufactures. Japan was especially inefficient in the production of the latter; in order to sustain production of iron bars, for example, the price of that commodity relative to tea was some 9 times the corresponding relative price in London. Once trade began, the prices of tea and silk, Japan's primary export goods, rose dramatically toward world levels. Similarly, the relative prices of import goods fell sharply as Japanese consumers and firms took advantage of lower foreign costs. Overall, Huber calculated that by the 1870s, Japan's terms of trade had improved by 340 percent. This change, in conjunction with access to better foreign technologies, expanded Japanese real national income by as much as 65 percent in 15 years.

The Japanese example is unique perhaps only in providing an opportunity to study a transition from autarky to open trade.[4] Economists point to a more recent body of evidence, however, that suggests that developing economies that are more open to trade undergo economic transformation and growth more rapidly than those developing countries that are relatively inward-looking and protectionist. Numerous studies have shown that, since the 1960s, the export-oriented economies of Asia, such as Korea, Hong Kong, Taiwan, and Singapore, have performed markedly better than countries in Latin America and Africa. The key difference is that the former countries have generally exposed their industries to competition at world relative price levels, while the latter nations have sustained relative prices that do not correlate well with comparative advantage. Substantial debate continues among economists over the conclusiveness of such comparisons.[5] However, there seems little question that the more open economies have raised their levels of per-capita income relative to the other countries. This fact suggests that the existence of pervasive barriers to trade tends to prevent nations from achieving full gains from trade.

14.3 TESTS OF THE RICARDIAN MODEL

Most empirical work has focused on the predictions of particular models rather than on the broader question of the gains from trade. The Ricardian model, for example, rests on the assumption of different technologies in different countries, generating varying labor productivities. These labor productivities determine comparative advantage. Tests of the model attempt to find relationships between relative labor productivity and international trade flows.

Note that the sharpest prediction of the theory, that countries are specialized in the goods they export, may be rejected in practice. With few exceptions, countries also produce the goods they import and a host of nontraded goods.[6] Nonetheless, it is interesting to examine how strongly differences in labor efficiency correlate with exports. The pioneering work was done in the 1950s by G. MacDougall, who computed simple measures of average labor productivity in the United States and the United Kingdom for the year 1937.[7] He hypothesized that, given that the American wage rate at that time was approximately twice that in Britain, U.S. firms should have an export advantage in manufacturing sectors for which U.S. labor productivity exceeded twice the level in the U.K. He tested this notion by calculating the ratios of U.S. exports to U.K. exports of 25 products to countries other than themselves. MacDougall considered only trade with third countries because trade barriers greatly influenced bilateral trade between the United States and the United Kingdom. However, exporters in both countries faced largely equivalent market conditions in other countries and could compete on an equal footing. MacDougall's test results were supportive of the Ricardian model. Twenty of the 25 products satisfied the simple prediction that, in cases where U.S. productivity exceeded twice the U.K. level, the ratio of U.S. exports to U.K. exports exceeded one, while in other cases the ratio was less than unity.

A fuller examination along these lines was performed by Robert Stern, who compared American and British trade in 1950 and 1959.[8] By 1950, average U.S. wages were approximately 3.4 times the average U.K. wages, suggesting that the ratio of American to British exports would be greater than unity in sectors where the ratio of outputs per worker exceeded 3.4 and less than unity in other cases. Of the 39 sectors considered, 33 conformed to this prediction in 1950, with the relationship becoming somewhat weaker by 1959. The results for the 1950 data suggested that a 1-percent increase in the ratio of labor productivities was associated with a 1.27 percent percent rise in the export ratio.

These two studies seemed to provide encouraging support for the Ricardian model. In fact, it is surprising that economists have not devoted much additional effort to such analysis in order to verify more conclusively that labor productivity differences constitute an important determinant of international trade. However, in interpreting these results, we must keep two important caveats in mind. First, the empirical specifications were exceedingly simple and did not control for the potential effects of other determinants of trade, such as transport costs, imperfect competition, and product differentiation. Second, the results found by MacDougall and Stern are consistent with other trade theories as well. For example, it is easy to show that in a world where trade is caused by differences in factor endowments but where factor prices are not equalized, the relative productivity of labor will tend to be higher in capital-abundant countries. Accordingly, the results may have simply captured the effects on trade of American capital abundance and British labor abundance in that period.

14.4   TESTS OF THE HECKSCHER-OHLIN MODEL

Recall that the Heckscher-Ohlin model makes a series of strong assumptions in order to isolate the effects of different relative factor endowments on trade between two countries. These assumptions include identical technologies with constant returns to scale, perfect competition, the absence of factor-intensity reversals, identical and homogeneous preferences, the absence of international factor migration, and the absence of impediments to trade. Again, it is obvious that this set of assumptions does not hold in reality and that the predictions of the model cannot be expected to hold literally. The task is to assess the significance of endowment differences in explaining trade patterns. This complicated subject occupies our discussion in this section.

The Leontief Paradox

As we mentioned in Chapter 8, the Heckscher-Ohlin model is incapable of predicting that any country will export a particular good when there are more goods than factors. For example, the more capital-abundant country may not export the most capital-intensive good when there are three commodities. However, the implicit international trade in factor services must obey the Heckscher-Ohlin theorem. That is, with two factors and two or more goods, the capital-abundant country will find that its bundle of exports is more capital-intensive than its bundle of imports.

This theorem on the factor content of trade was first examined by Wassily Leontief in perhaps the most famous empirical study in economics.[9] Leontief had greatly aided the American planning efforts in World War II by developing a technique of accounting for all the inputs required in the production of GNP. This technique, called input-output analysis, recognizes that the production of, say, an automobile requires *primary* inputs, such as capital and labor, in addition to *intermediate* inputs, such as steel, paint, glass, and the like. The prior production of these latter inputs also requires capital and labor in addition to other intermediate inputs, which in turn require capital and labor, and so on. Leontief developed a method for assembling these various inputs into an input-output table that could be used to compute the total labor and capital embodied in production of any bundle of goods.

An obvious application was to discover how much capital and labor were required to produce U.S. exports in comparison with U.S. imports. Note that an immediate methodological problem arises. While it is sensible to use an American input-output table to compute the factor contents of U.S. exports, a computation of the factor contents of U.S. imports would require detailed and consistent data on production techniques in all foreign trading partners. This was not feasible for Leontief, so he calculated the capital and labor required to produce U.S. goods that are similar to (or compete with) American imports. This procedure is theoretically valid under either of two conditions. First, if the factor-endowments model holds and international factor prices are equalized, each country shares the same techniques of production, and using the U.S. table will not bias the import computations. Second, if production functions exhibit fixed coefficients, or a constant ratio of capital to labor regardless of the factor-price ratio, use of the U.S. techniques similarly captures foreign production methods adequately. Leontief chose the latter condition.

Leontief calculated the capital and labor requirements in the production of a representative bundle of $1 million worth of both exports and import-competing goods in 1947. In that year the United States was unquestionably the most capital-abundant nation in the world and was certainly capital-abundant and labor-scarce relative to the rest of the world. Thus, the expectation was that exports were capital-intensive. Nevertheless, Leontief discovered that the capital-labor ratio in U.S. imports exceeded that in U.S. exports by some 23 percent. This unexpected outcome has been termed the *Leontief paradox.*

Leontief's famous result caused great surprise among economists schooled in the Heckscher-Ohlin tradition. Leontief himself was puzzled by the finding and asserted that the issue was really one of measurement. In particular, his belief was that, because of superior education and training in conjunction with better management techniques, American labor was perhaps three times more productive than foreign labor. Thus, in effective labor units, the United States was really labor-abundant. While this view anticipated later thinking about labor skills, it was ad hoc and unconvincing of the time. The three-to-one ratio suggested by Leontief was not predicated on a careful evaluation of labor efficiency throughout the world; it was simply the ratio required to get the "expected" result. In fact, there is little evidence that this huge superiority in U.S. labor ever existed, even in the early 1950s. Moreover, to the extent that labor was enhanced by better American management or entrepreneurship, we would expect the relative productivity of capital to be enhanced as well.

Numerous attempts have been made to verify Leontief's results, with mixed results. Because the United States may have been an unusual country, similar computations have been made for other countries with all manner of endowments, incomes, and market structures. In some cases, the results of these studies were consistent with expectations under the endowment model. For example, Peter Heller demonstrated that Japan's international trade in the 1960s followed an interesting dual structure.[10] Japan's exports to less-developed nations were capital-intensive, and its imports were labor-intensive, while its exports to more-developed nations were relatively labor-intensive in comparison with imports. In many other studies, however, the results seemed to contradict the Heckscher-Ohlin theorem. Geographically, then, the Leontief paradox is not an isolated event.

A more compelling objection was that 1947 was not a very appropriate year for testing the endowment theory. The model relies on the specification of a long-run equilibrium without market distortions. It can hardly be argued that the economies of Europe and Japan were in an equilibrium in 1947; rather, they were beginning a process of rapid dynamic adjustment in production and factor supplies. Robert Baldwin recomputed Leontief's ratios for the United States using the 1958 input-output table and 1962 international trade data, with the result that the paradox was still strongly in evidence. However, the analysis by Robert Stern and Keith Maskus showed that by 1972, American exports had become capital-intensive relative to imports. Thus, the paradox may have been reversed by the 1970s. Even so, there remains the puzzling fact noted by Harry Bowen that in the post-War period, American relative capital abundance seems to have declined.[11] It is unclear how the relative capital intensity of exports could have risen in that context.

Alternative Explanations for the Paradox

A more revealing line of objections to Leontief's finding has come from noting that the assumptions of the Heckscher-Ohlin model are too strict to be believed. Indeed, the most enduring and valuable outcome of the debate over the Leontief paradox is that it stimulated trade theorists to think more fully about the implications of departures from those assumptions.

For example, it is possible that the international structure of trade barriers could partially explain Leontief's result. Our analysis of the endowment model showed that free trade would lower the real incomes of each country's scarce factor, providing an incentive for that factor to lobby for import protection. Thus, the United States might be expected to have high trade barriers to labor-intensive imports, and some foreign countries might erect restrictions on capital-intensive imports. These policies could reduce the levels of trade below those expected from endowment-based comparative advantage. (Recall that trade restrictions cannot overturn comparative advantage altogether unless there are significant subsidies paid to exporting and importing the "wrong" commodities.) While this possibility is surely important, it has proved most difficult to test conclusively because tariffs have complicated effects across sectors in general equilibrium.[12]

Another possibility is that preferences across countries differ rather than being identical and homogeneous. Certainly, if there are significant *taste biases* in the sense that some countries have strong preferences for goods in which they would otherwise have a comparative advantage, the pattern of trade could be reversed. We noted in the last chapter that consumption patterns do vary markedly across nations. As we discuss later, this fact seems to help explain a significant share of world trade.

Another important possibility is that countries do not share access to identical technologies. This observation is at the core of the product-cycle model and related ideas about trade in a more dynamic context. The issue here is that trade data for a particular year may not reflect a long-run, static equilibrium so much as a short-run, dynamic transition under varying technologies. In the product cycle, for example, American exports of new goods may seem to be labor-intensive when, in reality, they make relatively heavy use of new technological information through the employment of highly skilled, technical labor inputs such as engineers and scientists.

The most substantive objection to Leontief's procedure is simply that it is inadequate to suppose that there are only two primary factors of production, capital, and labor, in the world. Various forms of land and natural resources also serve as sources of comparative advantage. Indeed, these may be the most relevant factors for the Heckscher-Ohlin model because they are internationally immobile. Further, physical capital and labor exist in different forms. We should not expect the average worker in higher-income countries to share identical productivity characteristics with the average worker in lower-income countries. Rather, national labor forces consist of different endowments of laborers of various skills, with skills being higher in countries that invest more in education and training. Because acquiring new skills often involves a lengthy investment process, it is reasonable to suppose that laborers of widely varying skills do constitute different endowments. For this reason, laborers are often distinguished by their *human capital,* or accumulated investments in education and training.

Regarding natural resources, Jaroslav Vanek made the observation that the Leontief paradox is consistent with the possibility that the United States was abundant in capital and labor but scarce in natural resources, such as oil, the extraction of which is quite capital-intensive, as we indicated in Chapter 8.[13] Thus, in the act of importing scarce natural-resource services, the United States was implicitly importing the services of capital as well. Some empirical economists accounted for this possibility in their work by excluding certain natural-resource-intensive products from their computations. In the study by Stern and Maskus, for example, this exclusion reinforced their finding that the Leontief paradox was reversed in 1972. In general, relative supplies of land and natural resources clearly affect world trade patterns. The United States and Canada are both large net exporters of agricultural commodities, while Canada also exports the services of energy and minerals. In contrast, Japan, Hong Kong, and Singapore are extremely scarce in such resources, and their imports are dominated by oil, raw materials, and food.

With respect to labor skills, Donald Keesing was the first to show that a disaggregation of U.S. labor by skill type was important in explaining the factor contents of trade.[14] American net exports were clearly intensive in highly skilled laborers, such as professional workers. This finding has proved to hold strongly in examinations of other data sets and definitions of human capital. Most trade economists agree that a fundamental determinant of U.S. comparative advantage is a relatively abundant supply of highly-skilled labor. This finding explains the fact that average wages in American export sectors are markedly higher than average wages in import-competing sectors. This is true of other developed nations as well.

These observations were important in spurring additional theoretical research, especially in terms of the product cycle and related ideas. However, the role of additional factors is properly incorporated into the factor-endowments model only through the factor-content (or HOV) theorem, which we discussed in Chapter 8. We simply state the mathematical result here, because it is useful in motivating subsequent discussion, and we refer interested readers to an article by Edward Leamer for a formal proof.[15] Retain all assumptions of the Heckscher-Ohlin theorem, except allow there to be m factors and n goods, with $n \geq m$. For any country j, let s^j be its proportion of world income. Finally, let F_i^j and F_i^w denote the endowments of factor i for country j and the world, respectively. Let us define a ranking of factor abundance and scarcity for country j by virtue of its share of world endowments of each factor:

$$(F_1^j/F_1^w) > (F_2^j/F_2^w) > \cdots > (F_i^j/F_i^w) > s^j > (F_{i+1}^j/F_{i+1}^w) > \cdots > (F_m^j/F_m^w)$$

$$(14.1)$$

Under the HOV theorem, country j's consumption share lies somewhere in the middle of this chain, as we have written. It also follows that country j's net exports of the services of any factor are positive if its abundance ranking for that factor lies above the consumption share, and its net exports are negative if its ranking lies below that share. That is, a country exports the services of its abundant factors and imports the services of its scarce factors when factor abundance is measured relative to a global standard. This is the essence of the factor-content theorem.

The practical importance of this theorem is that it can be used to rank a country's factor endowments in terms of their relative abundance as revealed by trade. Indeed, Leamer used Leontief's own data to show that the United States had in fact been revealed to be relatively abundant in capital and scarce in labor with the allowance of more than two factors. Thus, there may never have been a Leontief paradox. Moreover, once these rankings are compiled, they may be compared to actual data on national and world factor endowments as a full test of the HOV theorem. Such tests have been performed for the United States by Keith Maskus and for a collection of countries by Harry Bowen, Edward Leamer, and Leo Sveikauskas.[16] The results of these tests indicate that the rankings of factor abundance revealed by trade data do not convincingly replicate actual endowment rankings, suggesting that the theorem does not hold literally in real-world situations.

Judging the Importance of Factor Endowments in Explaining Trade

Of course, we should not be surprised by the inability of actual data to conform to the rigorous assumptions of the HOV model. These assumptions are made simply to study the theoretical effects of endowment differences on trade in factor services. No one would be surprised to learn that the world is not perfectly competitive and that there exist market distortions, such as taxes and trade barriers. Rather than testing the truth of a theory based on unrealistic assumptions, it is more illuminating to measure how strongly factor endowments seem to affect actual trade flows.

Two statistical approaches to this question have been employed. The first technique is to relate measures of U.S. net exports across manufacturing industries to factor intensities in production. Two studies worth mentioning are one by Robert Baldwin and one by Robert Stern and Keith Maskus.[17] Baldwin found that capital intensity was negatively related to net exports, another version of the Leontief paradox, but that human capital was positively associated with net exports. Stern and Maskus demonstrated that over the last few decades, U.S. comparative disadvantage became more strongly associated with lower-skilled labor inputs. They further showed the importance of human capital and technological inputs, such as research and development spending, in explaining the structure of U.S. trade. In general, the results from studies of this nature are consistent with economists' beliefs about underlying relative endowments across countries, providing indirect support for the Heckscher-Ohlin theory.

A second approach, developed by Edward Leamer in an important book, is quite close to the spirit of the Heckscher-Ohlin-Vanek model.[18] In that model, if we assume that the numbers of factors and goods are equal, that factors are fully employed and homogeneous in all countries, and that factor prices are equalized internationally, the net exports of any commodity are a (complicated) linear function of the difference between a country's vector of factor supplies and its vector of factor demands. Assuming identical and homothetic tastes, the demand for factors is simply the product of the country's global income share and global factor endowments.

TABLE 14.1
Relative factor endowments, 1975 (percent of world endowments)

Factor*	Canada	Fed. Rep. Germany	India	Japan	Mexico	South Korea	U.K.	U.S.
GNP	3.46	9.22	1.99	11.14	1.00	0.47	5.10	32.94
Capital	3.65	10.28	1.18	14.92	0.70	0.37	4.87	29.36
Prof. Labor	2.37	6.11	13.47	8.03	1.64	0.70	6.00	24.53
Lit. Labor	1.74	5.19	14.29	11.05	2.35	1.86	4.77	17.11
Illit. Labor	0.02	0.07	65.24	0.20	1.30	1.41	0.06	0.15
Trop. Land	0.00	0.00	9.11	0.00	4.02	0.00	0.00	0.14
Dry Land	2.38	0.00	5.68	0.00	6.24	0.00	0.00	32.44
Temp. Land	38.03	1.27	3.77	1.91	0.00	0.51	1.25	18.47
Coal	1.96	10.80	8.49	1.67	0.32	1.35	11.13	50.87
Minerals	19.06	1.79	3.43	1.89	3.09	0.31	0.98	27.58
Oil	9.76	1.25	0.73	0.16	2.18	0.00	1.63	58.04

Source: E. E. Leamer, *Sources of International Comparative Advantage: Theory and Evidence.*

*Prof. Labor: professional and technical workers; Lit. Labor: literate, nonprofessional workers; Illit. Labor: illiterate workers; Trop. Land: land in tropical rainy climate; Dry Land: land in dry climate; Temp. Land: land in humid, temperate climate.

It is possible to use a statistical procedure termed *regression analysis* to estimate this linear relationship. Regression analysis involves finding the linear equation that most closely fits a set of data that has observations on a dependent variable (here, net exports in each commodity) and one or more explanatory variables (here, national endowments of factors). For each of ten broadly defined commodities, such as raw materials and labor-intensive manufactures, Leamer estimated this relationship using a sample of 47 countries (defined to make up the "world,' this sample did cover most of the major trading nations) with measures of 10 factor endowments in 1975. The regression estimates were then taken as measures of the link between endowments and trade.

It is worth mentioning some basic results. Table 14.1 shows computations of relative factor endowments, or shares of each country in the world supply of factors, for selected nations. The entries in the first row are national shares in world GNP, or the s^j-terms in our earlier analysis. The remaining rows show each country's share in the world supply of factor endowments. In theory, these may be compared to the GNP shares to measure relative factor abundance. For example, in 1975 Japan had 14.92 percent of the world capital stock, which exceeded its GNP share of 11.14 percent, suggesting that Japan was capital-abundant. Japan was clearly very scarce in land and natural resources. The United States was abundant in dry land, coal, and oil and scarce in lower-skilled labor and tropical land. In fact, the United States was a large net importer of oil, suggesting that its tastes are biased heavily toward oil consumption in comparison with other countries.[19] Canada was abundant in temperate land, minerals, and capital.

India seemed to be scarce in capital and oil but relatively abundant in other factors. The fact that India was well-endowed with so many factors but had a small share of world GNP reflects the very low productivity of inputs there. This suggests that production functions in India were significantly inferior to those in other countries in 1975, in contrast to the Heckscher-Ohlin assumption of identical technologies.

The interesting question is how these endowments relate to trade flows. Leamer's preferred regression estimates of the trade equations are shown in Table 14.2 for selected groupings of commodities. Each entry in the table indicates the change in net exports, in thousands of U.S. dollars, that is estimated to result from a unit increase in the associated endowment. Thus, a $1 million increase in the capital stock of the average country would reduce net exports (or raise net imports) of raw materials by $8,800 and of cereals by $4,300. However, it would increase net exports (or lower net imports) of animal products by $40, of labor-intensive products by $1,000, of capital-intensive products by $16,500, of chemicals by $3,800, and of machinery by $29,100. Readers may verify that the results make good sense. Increases in land and resource supplies tend to expand exports of raw materials and agricultural goods while reducing exports of manufactured goods. Expansions of the stock of literate labor (essentially educated, blue-collar workers) raise net exports of most manufactured goods but reduce net exports of materials and agricultural commodities. Professional labor is a source of comparative advantage for chemicals. Overall, the equations fit the data well; each equation typically explains as much as 50 to 60 percent of the observed trade patterns. The conclusion from this analysis is that

TABLE 14.2
Estimates of the effects of factor endowments on trade, 1975

	Commodity group*						
Factor	Raw Mtls	Animal	Cereals	Labor-Int.	Capital-Int.	Chemicals	Machinery
Capital	−8.8	0.04	−4.3	1.0	16.5	3.8	29.1
Prof. labor	303.1	−279.4	946.3	−699.7	−1947.9	481.7	−1177.4
Lit. labor	−59.4	−17.3	−97.4	78.9	126.7	−53.4	77.7
Illit. labor	2.5	17.9	−18.8	4.8	39.1	−4.4	8.3
Trop. land	−0.1	−0.3	2.3	−0.5	−0.8	−0.8	−0.7
Dry land	−0.3	0.7	1.0	−0.3	−0.3	−0.2	−0.3
Temp. land	0.6	7.4	20.6	−3.8	−11.8	−8.5	−19.2
Coal	0.4	−0.05	0.03	−0.07	−0.08	0.03	−0.05
Minerals	1.1	−0.03	−0.01	−0.05	−0.07	−0.05	−0.08
Oil	0.04	0.03	0.24	−0.04	−0.2	−0.04	−0.2

Source: E. E. Leamer, *Sources of International Comparative Advantage: Theory and Evidence.*

*Raw mtls.: raw materials; Animal: animal products; Labor-int.: labor-intensive manufactures; Capital-int.: capital-intensive manufactures. The unit of measurement for each commodity group is $1000. The unit for each type of labor is 1000 workers; for each type of land 1000 hectares; for coal, minerals, and oil $1000; and for capital $1 million.

factor endowments are an extremely important influence on comparative advantage in world trade.[20]

14.5 PREFERENCES, TECHNOLOGY, AND SCALE ECONOMIES: THE IMPORTANCE OF INTRA-INDUSTRY TRADE

As we have emphasized in this book, there are other theoretical determinants of trade than Ricardian technological differences and variations in factor endowments. Prominent in this discussion have been differences in tastes as in the Linder Hypothesis, dynamic evolution of comparative advantage as in the product-cycle model, and increasing returns to scale and imperfect competition. These views have been subject to considerably less empirical testing than the endowment model. Again, rigorous tests of these ideas are difficult to execute. Nonetheless, we can gain some insights from a brief review of the major studies available. We proceed by considering work that is focused on each issue separately. However, one feature these theoretical notions have in common is that each can serve as an explanation for the existence of intra-industry trade (IIT). We discuss the empirical significance of IIT in the final subsection.

International Preferences

Casual consideration of international trade data would suggest that the Linder hypothesis provides a powerful explanation of trade patterns. As we show later, the bulk of international trade in manufacturing goods takes place among the developed countries, which have similar per capita incomes. Thus, it seems that a regression in which bilateral trade flows are explained by differences in per capita incomes (with the amount of trade rising as incomes grow more similar) should be successful. Indeed, early exercises of this sort consistently found such a correlation. However, countries with similar per capita incomes also tend to be geographically concentrated, such as those in Western Europe. Thus, trade among these countries may be accounted for simply by lower transportation costs. For example, this view is consistent with one explanation of the failure of Japan to engage in as much IIT as other developed countries: Japan is far-removed from other industrial markets. One test of this hypothesis is to relate *changes* in bilateral trade and per capita incomes over time, which holds geographical proximity (and relative transport costs) fixed. Several efforts along these lines have found no clear evidence for the Linder hypothesis.[21]

One problem with the Linder hypothesis is that it places relatively little theoretical structure on the determinants of trade and therefore provides little guidance to the empirical analyst. A more recent and very promising line of research makes assumptions about the form in which tastes are allowed to differ. As we discussed in Chapter 13, if tastes are quasi-homogeneous, a model may be developed to help explain the observed international variations in the shares of consumption of different goods. We noted earlier that the proportion of income spent on food declines rapidly with the level of per capita income, falling from an average of 50 percent for the poorest countries to 17 percent for the richest countries. Thus, food is clearly a *necessity good* in economic terms. In contrast, relative expenditures on medical care, transport and communication, and education tend to rise sharply with incomes. Linda Hunter has explored the implications of quasi-homogeneity for trade patterns.[22] She estimated demand functions for 11 commodity groups across a sample of 34 countries in 1975 based on a particular utility function that implies quasi-homogeneous demand functions. She then "neutralized" the effects of demand differences by forecasting what trade would be if preferences were homogeneous and all markets continued to clear. The difference in these estimates suggests the importance of nonhomogeneity in explaining world trade. Her results suggest that as much of 29 percent of world trade may be caused by nonhomogeneous preferences, with this effect being stronger for higher-income countries. Hunter's approach has been criticized because of the special nature of the underlying utility functions, and her results should not be considered definitive. Nevertheless, the evidence is most intriguing and suggests that empirical analysts should devote more effort to the issue of tastes and trade.

The Product Cycle

The product cycle is an intuitively appealing notion that is supported by substantial anecdotal evidence. For example, virtually any product in the consumer electronics industry, such as color televisions, video recorders, and semiconductors, seems to obey the prescriptions of the model. New innovations in the technologies underlying these products are predominantly developed in the industrial nations while, with little delay, mass production is located in the developing economies. Similar processes seem to characterize chemicals, textiles, and some other goods. Indeed, a number of industry case studies, now rather out of date, have yielded results that support the model.

Despite this fact, generalized testing of the product cycle has been frustrated by contradictory results. Again, a primary difficulty is distinguishing this theory from other possible explanations of trade. One clear example is that in numerous studies of American trade structure, there is a strongly positive correlation between net export strength by industry and the industry's investment in research and development (R&D). This seems to constitute strong indirect evidence for the product-cycle model, except that it is quite possible that R&D spending is simply a surrogate measure for the relative abundance in the United States of technically skilled labor inputs. The latter factor may well be the ultimate source of American comparative advantage. Further, there always remains an issue of underlying causality—is high R&D spending a determinant of trade or the result of profitable trading opportunities based on other sources of comparative advantage? This question has yet to be answered definitively.

One direct approach to measuring the product-cycle model, pioneered by Gary Hufbauer, is the practice of identifying the first date at which a particular product entered world trade. Countries like the United States might be expected to have strong net export positions in newer goods. This proposition has received only weak support in the literature. More recently, David Audretsch argued that it should be possible to characterize the newness of goods in terms of their underlying production profiles, with global production of a good rising at an increasing rate for innovative goods and remaining fairly stable for standardized goods.[23] His correlations concurred somewhat with this hypothesis, suggesting that innovativeness may be a measurable concept in world trade.

The product-cycle model inherently concerns the dynamics of trade. It helps explain theoretically the existence of multinational enterprises (MNEs), among other things. As we discussed in the last chapter, the practice by MNEs of trading inputs and outputs within the firm and rapidly relocating production has probably reduced the length of the product cycle to an indistinguishable length. In this sense, a proper test of the model would take into account the existence and growth of MNEs, attempting to explain the reasons for their existence across industries. To date, this task has not been adequately performed. Further, we noted the importance to the model of understanding how rapidly new technological information diffuses among countries through technology transfer, product copying, and the like. This process also has not yet been studied in a satisfactory way.

We must conclude that adequate formal testing of the product-cycle model has yet to be designed and performed. The model certainly helps explain some features of the world economy that most economists believe are important, such as the need to invest in product development and quality and the desire to shift production location over time. Further, it may be that the very existence of MNEs is indirect validation of the model.[24] At this time, however, we remain fairly skeptical of the model's applicability to the major proportion of world trade.

Scale Economies and Imperfect Competition

Most economists would regard economies of scale as a significant factor influencing international trade. An obvious point to make in this context is that international trade is dominated by transactions among very large firms, rather than by the perfectly competitive, atomistic firms of standard trade theory. Indeed, recent research has demonstrated that a significant proportion of global trade in manufactures takes place as internal transactions within multinational enterprises.[25] These facts would be of little theoretical interest if such firms existed simply to conduct trade based on traditional notions of comparative advantage. However, our earlier discussion pointed out that the existence of increasing returns can have important and distinctive effects on trade and the gains from trade. This issue has commanded surprisingly little empirical work despite its obvious importance.

That increasing returns exist at the level of individual plants in manufacturing is clear.[26] However, direct evidence that scale economies affect trade tends to be contradictory.[27] Many studies in numerous countries have detected a positive correlation between the size of industrial plants and production for exports, strongly suggesting that scale economies facilitate the achievement of lower costs for exporting. However, when analysts add a variable measuring economies of scale to statistical studies of trade flows based on theoretical models, the results provide only weak evidence that economies of scale contribute to international trade. It should be noted that measuring scale economies in a consistent way across industries has proven an elusive task. For example, standard measures of how concentrated an industry is, such as the percentage of industry sales accounted for by the largest four firms, are not necessarily related to significant scale economies or to barriers to entry. More fundamentally, we have pointed out that increasing returns may occur in a variety of important ways. Besides plant size are issues of geographical concentration, cost-reducing innovations in intermediate inputs, diffusion of technological information, and learning economies from repeated production. Indeed, evidence is emerging that the use of new intermediate goods, such as computers and advanced machinery, significantly improves the productivity of manufacturing firms and helps expand exports. However, most of these impacts—arguably the most important influences on scale economies and trade—have not been measured particularly well.

Such problems have pushed economists toward two alternative and more revealing approaches. One body of research is termed *numerical general equilibrium analysis.* In this approach, economists develop models of an entire economy (or, say, several economies linked together in a regional trade agreement), taking account of various market structures in different industries. A key feature of these models is that they are capable of incorporating important economy-wide constraints, such as a fixed supply of labor and capital in the short run, that would have significant influences on the degree to which sectoral outputs can change in response to a shift in government policy. Another feature is that they can provide estimates, or even well-informed guesses, about the values of important parameters in each industry, such as the ease of technical substitution among inputs for production functions, elasticities of demand for outputs and inputs, and the extent of differentiation of products coming from different countries. Typically these estimates are taken from other published studies and combined with a set of data on outputs, consumption, and trade for a particular year, assuming the available data represent a general equilibrium for the economy. If the model can be combined with the data in a way that does not violate any economic constraints and that is consistent with fundamental economic behavior (that is, consumers maximize utility, producers maximize profits or minimize costs, and the government attempts to provide public services in an efficient way), it can be used for policy analysis. Specifically, the effects of changes in trade policy (such as tariff reductions or entrance into a free trade area) on industry outputs, trade, and consumer welfare may be simulated under the given set of parameters. It is critical that various ranges of key parameters be used to see how sensitive the results are to particular assumptions about their values.

For our purposes, a key set of parameters is the importance of scale economies in various sectors. Models in which economies of scale are presumed to exist in manufacturing industries tend to show significant interrelationships between trade and returns to scale. For example, Richard Harris constructed a numerical general equilibrium model in which the manufacturing sector was characterized by increasing returns to scale in order to examine the issue of how trade liberalization would affect the Canadian economy.[28] In this model, the bilateral removal of tariff and nontariff barriers in the context of a free trade area with the United States should allow Canadian industries to take advantage of scale economies as they sell in the larger U.S. market. The Canadian economy should also become more efficient because of industry rationalization, gains in productivity, shifts in resources among sectors, and price competition, as we have discussed in earlier chapters on imperfect competition. Harris' model predicts that, in the long run, the effects of the Canada-United States Free Trade Area should include a rise of 9 percent in Canadian real wages, 3.2 percent in Canadian real GNP, 8 percent in Canadian labor productivity, and 30 percent in real trade volumes. While these estimates are subject to some uncertainty, they clearly point out the large potential effects of trade liberalization in the presence of increasing returns. In contrast, regression estimates in static models with constant returns rarely discover a potential gain in real GNP from tariff cuts of more than 1 percent. This work has helped stimulate a large body of numerical general equilibrium models of various economies. These models have consistently pointed to the key role that scale economies play in shaping trade patterns and in achieving efficiency gains from trade.

A second approach has been to incorporate imperfect competition, presumably based on increasing returns, directly into trade models and to estimate or simulate its effects. An excellent review of this literature was provided by David Richardson.[29] Many of these studies have been concerned with oligopolistic competition in a particular industry and therefore, they say little about the general determinants of trade. Nonetheless, imperfect competition clearly plays a significant and perhaps dominant role in explaining trade in automobiles, aircraft, semiconductors, and computers, among other sectors.

Intra-Industry Trade

The three types of models just examined share an important characteristic. Each is capable, in theory, of explaining the prevalence of intra-industry trade (IIT) in the world economy. As we discussed in Chapter 13, this phenomenon is the simultaneous import and export by a country of very similar types of products. For example, the Linder hypothesis and related notions about trade among nations with similar per capita incomes is consistent with the observation that many slightly differentiated consumer goods are traded internationally. If trade takes place to satisfy tastes for variety in consumption, we can understand the fact that the United States and Canada have extensive two-way trade in beers, that French, Italian, and German wines are traded simultaneously with American wines, and that high-fashion clothing of different brands and styles is exchanged among high-income economies. Countries might also simultaneously import and export similar products that embody different levels of technological sophistication, as suggested by the product cycle models. Finally, scale economies allow firms in different nations to produce at lower cost by specializing in similar types of goods or inputs, with international trade among the countries serving as the incentive for that specialization. This process is characteristic of automobiles, machinery, chemicals, and other industrial commodities.

Intra-industry trade is important enough to warrant consideration of some details on its measurement. Some central facts about world trade in goods are presented in Table 14.3. In 1990, total world merchandise exports amounted to $3.188 trillion. It is interesting that the high-income, developed economies accounted for 74.6 percent of this trade. This is hardly surprising because these economies also produced 71.7 percent of world GDP. More striking is the fact that the developed countries traded extensively among themselves, accounting for $1.816 trillion or 57.0 percent of world exports.

TABLE 14.3

The composition of world merchandise exports by country group, 1990

Country group	Exports ($billions)	Share of world exports (%)	Export share in GDP (%)	Exports per capita
World	3188	100.0	14.3	$603
High-income developed	2379	74.6	14.9	$3062
Intra-HID	1816	57.0	11.4	$2337
Other high income	177	5.5	54.7	$4414
Upper middle income	307	9.6	20.2	$670
Lower middle income	184	5.8	19.8	$293
Low income	141	4.4	15.4	$46

Sources: World Bank, *World Development Report, 1992* and International Monetary Fund, *Direction of Trade Statistics Yearbook, 1993.*

Exports are also scaled in the table by GDP and population in order to help neutralize the effects of country size on these comparisons. Thus, the high-income, developed economies tend to have somewhat lower export-to-GDP ratios (though there are marked exceptions; for example the Swiss ratio is 28.4 percent). At the same time, their populations are highly productive in exports, with over $2000 per person exported among them. Poor countries engage in far fewer exports per capita and claim a far smaller share of world trade.

The dominance of world trade by exchange among the developed economies is difficult to reconcile with standard Heckscher-Ohlin and Ricardian trade models. The Heckscher-Ohlin model, for example, predicts that trade should transpire largely between countries with markedly different relative factor endowments. Thus, we would expect *inter-industry* trade in very different products to dominate world trade. To be sure, such trade is important in several commodities and for several countries. Japan must import a disproportionate share of the world's natural resources because of its scarcity of land and minerals. Developing countries in Asia export labor-intensive manufactures, such as clothing, in return for machinery and specialized inputs. We suggested earlier in this chapter that the factor-content theorem provides a credible explanation for an important component of world trade.

Nonetheless, the significant degree of trade among the developed economies, which have relatively similar factor endowments and technologies, must be caused primarily by other economic factors. Our answer lies in extensive amounts of IIT that take advantage of economies of scale and differentiation of products. Table 14.4 provides some simple statistics on IIT for certain countries and products. The formula for computing these IIT indexes is the following:

$$\text{IIT} = 100[1 - (|e_j - i_j|)/(e_j + i_j)] \tag{14.2}$$

TABLE 14.4
Intra-industry trade by commodity and country, 1990

Commodity	Canada	Fed. Rep. Germany	Japan	South Korea	U.K.	U.S.
Fuels	73.1	31.8	4.7	11.9	99.9	30.7
Chemicals	92.8	75.8	99.0	50.6	89.9	75.0
Special industrial machinery	62.5	45.6	35.5	26.9	89.7	91.8
Computers	46.3	74.7	39.0	68.4	95.3	99.8
Automobiles	79.7	58.7	26.0	10.1	62.3	37.5
Clothing	24.1	52.1	0.2	0.2	60.7	17.3
Precision instruments	48.9	71.6	70.4	37.6	91.6	67.7

Source: Computed from United Nations, *Yearbook of International Trade Statistics, 1990.*

This index, originally developed by Herbert Grubel and Peter Lloyd, can range from zero, indicating complete inter-industry trade in industry j (that is, either exports or imports are zero) to 100, indicating complete intra-industry trade (exports equal imports).[30] One significant problem exists with these computations. When IIT indexes are calculated for aggregated commodity groups, as in Table 14.4, they tend to overstate the true amount of IIT by lumping together goods that really are not very similar. It is more appropriate to compute them for highly detailed and disaggregated commodities, which would have the effect of considerably reducing the figures in Table 14.4. Nonetheless, studies that have done this consistently find that IIT is an important phenomenon across a wide range of goods and countries.

Note in Table 14.4 that Germany and the United Kingdom tend to have especially high IIT measures. This reflects their membership in the European Economic Community, where proximity and common trade practices act to encourage considerable trading of similar commodities across borders. In particular, notice the high percentages of IIT in clothing trade for these countries. There is a great deal of cross-border trade in fashion in Western Europe. Similarly, Canada has high indexes reflecting its overwhelming trade relationship with the United States. Japan, however, tends to have smaller IIT figures, which, as we suggested earlier, reflects both its peculiar land scarcity and its long distances from other developed countries. In this regard, Japan is more like Korea than it is like the United States.

At the same time, however, IIT varies across commodities. Chemicals, computers, industrial machinery, and precision instruments tend to have a high percentage of IIT in the industrial economies. All of these products are subject to technological differentiation and scale economies. Canada has a very high IIT figure in automobiles, which is caused by substantial two-way trade with the United States. These two countries share largely free trade in automobiles as a result of The United States-Canada Automotive Agreement of 1965. Again, IIT in automobiles is prevalent in Western Europe. For most countries IIT is relatively small in clothing, which is an indication that trade in that sector is largely driven by comparative advantage (Korea) and disadvantage (Canada, Japan, and the United States) in labor-intensive goods. Fuels are also largely governed by inter-industry forces.

These highly aggregated figures are crude, yet they suggest important phenomena in world trade. Numerous economists have attempted to use statistical techniques to explain the structure of IIT across commodities and countries. One classic reference is the study by Bela Balassa.[31] Balassa demonstrated that trade in manufactures increased rapidly in Western Europe after the formation of the European Common Market, indicating that forces such as product differentiation, scale economies, and industrial rationalization tend to accompany economic integration activities among similar countries. Similarly, in their book, Grubel and Lloyd were the first to carefully document the existence of IIT. They used their findings to make a series of hypotheses about the sources of IIT. It is interesting to note that IIT is one economic phenomenon that was measured empirically before it was explained theoretically. In this sense, the Grubel and Lloyd study is one of the most important empirical efforts in international trade because it stimulated substantial theoretical inquiries into the relationships among imperfect competition, demand, and trade.

In a recent study, Balassa attempted to capture basic determinants of IIT indirectly by measuring certain *national* characteristics rather than *commodity* and *industrial* characteristics, such as product differentiation and scale economies.[32] He hypothesized that IIT would rise with the level of per capita GNP (a measure of economic development and also an indirect indicator of product differentiation) and the level of GNP itself (a measure of market size and scale economies). He also expected IIT to fall as geographic distance between trading partners became larger and as trade restrictions became more significant. Finally, he made allowance for the fact that some countries share borders and some countries are members of economically integrated areas, such as the European Community. These latter variables would be positively correlated with IIT to the extent that they allowed for greater information flows about differentiated products and allowed for rationalized industrial structures. Balassa analyzed 38 developed and developing countries in 1971, using disaggregated trade data to compute an IIT index for each country. His results seemed to support his hypotheses, as each variable performed in the expected direction and was statistically significant. Particularly important factors seemed to be membership in the European Community, the existence of common borders, and the level of economic development.

Studies such as Balassa's clearly suggest that IIT is an important phenomenon and that it is caused by identifiable factors. Nevertheless, these studies attract criticism of the kind we discussed earlier. For example, no one has yet specified a fully integrated theory of IIT that would allow us to determine appropriate equations for use in these studies. In that sense, the results are difficult to interpret, and indeed, they seem to change considerably depending on the equations used and the variables included. Also, the use of broad aggregate variables as loose and indirect measures of important characteristics underlying IIT is questionable. It cannot be stated with confidence that per capita GNP measures product differentation and tastes as opposed to, say, relative capital and labor endowments. In fact, per capita GNP has often been used as a variable measuring factor endowments in studies of the Heckscher-Ohlin model. Accordingly, the status of empirical work on the endowment model is generally equivalent to the status of empirical work on models of IIT. Both are considered important determinants of actual trade flows and should be viewed as complementary explanations of international commerce.

14.6 CONCLUDING REMARKS

Active research continues to be done on empirical testing of international trade theory. It has proven difficult to observe practical versions of our complicated general equilibrium trade theories. Because of these difficulties, economists have had more success in measuring the contributions of various determinants of trade flows. Economists generally agree that relative labor productivity, factor endowments, tastes, and product differentiation with scale economies all seem to provide important sources of comparative advantage. While it is not possible to determine the exact contribution of each influence, our conclusion is that there are numerous important variables that clearly induce countries to trade among themselves.

The main points for review from this chapter include the following.

1. There is substantial evidence that economies garner significant gains from trade. One study of Japan in the 19th century actually demonstrated such gains in a comparison of autarky with liberalized trade. Indirect evidence of this point is also strong, as it is clear that relatively open economies have grown more rapidly than relatively closed economies in the post-war period.

2. Relative labor productivities are correlated with relative export performances of nations, as suggested by the Ricardian model. However, these results are difficult to interpret in light of the fact that other theories predict similar outcomes.

3. The Leontief paradox was the unexpected finding that American exports were labor-intensive and imports were capital-intensive in 1947. This result was tremendously important in stimulating further thinking about the determinants of trade. Attempts to explain the finding through relaxing certain assumptions of the Heckscher-Ohlin model have met with mixed success. More importantly, economists now believe that numerous factor endowments, including capital, types of labor, and natural resources provide sources of comparative advantage. This perspective has led to the development of the factor-content trade theorem, which is true under very general circumstances.

4. The rigorous assumptions of the factor-endowments model have forced economists to attempt to measure the contribution of endowments to trade rather than test the theorem literally. This effort has proved largely successful, pointing to the importance of factor endowment differences in actual trade flows. Generally, differences in natural resources and land supplies provide important sources of comparative advantage, as do differences in labor skills.

5. Differences in tastes seem to have a significant influence on world trade flows, though research into this question is still relatively new. Broad empirical evidence in favor of the product-cycle model has not yet been found.

6. Models of IIT point toward other influences on trade, including product differentiation, imperfect competition, and scale economies. While IIT is certainly a measurable and important phenomenon, no full "test" of its theoretical predictions yet exists. However, economists have tried, with substantial success, to measure the contribution of its underlying determinants to the extent of IIT. Factor endowments as well as characteristics of IIT provide important explanations for the structure of international trade, with the former being more closely associated with trade in primary goods and labor-intensive manufactures and the latter being more closely associated with trade in differentiated manufacturing goods.

PROBLEMS

1. Explain why Leontief's result was considered to be paradoxical. Why do economists consider his approach to have been only an incomplete "test" of the Heckscher-Ohlin model?

2. Criticize the various theoretical attempts to reconcile or explain the Leontief paradox. Further, explain how other theories of trade could help explain the paradox.

3. Why do countries engage in intra-industry trade? List several consumer commodities for which both domestic and imported varieties are available for purchase. Do you think that trade in such goods can be reconciled with the notion that trade is determined by differences in factor endowments? Differences in technologies? Why or why not?

4. The following data represents hypothetical trade in four commodities for some country. Compute the IIT index for each commodity. Which commodities are more characterized by inter-industry trade and which by intra-industry trade? How would you suggest using these data to calculate an IIT index for the country as a whole?

	Exports	Imports
Commodity 1	$0	$5000
Commodity 2	$3000	$2500
Commodity 3	$10000	$1000
Commodity 4	$4500	$7000

5. Below are actual trade data (in millions of dollars) for the United States in 1989 for a broad category of machinery and some detailed subcategories. Compute the IIT indexes at each level. Why do you suppose the indexes for the more detailed

	Exports	Imports
General industrial machinery	$13095	$14974
Certain fuel pumps	$115	$345
Ball bearings	$106	$574
Pressure-reducing valves	$48	$26
Forklift trucks	$315	$737

categories are lower? What would you conclude about the accuracy of computing IIT indexes directly from aggregate categories as opposed to taking an average of the indexes from the subcategories that comprise them?

NOTES

1. Interested readers are referred to the excellent survey by Deardorff (1984).
2. Note that this is a common problem in the social sciences, in which it is largely impossible to isolate the effects of a particular variable on some system as may be done in a chemistry laboratory. Recently, economists have begun constructing laboratory experiments with human and animal subjects to investigate relatively simple questions in economic theory. However, this approach is virtually absent from the testing of international trade theories.
3. See J. Richard Huber (1971).
4. We may currently be witnessing a similar transformation as the economies of Eastern and Central Europe and China reorient themselves toward greater trade with the Western market economies.
5. See the paper by Sebastian Edwards (1993) for a review.
6. The exceptions are countries for which economic activity is dominated by the production of a primary commodity, such as oil or cocoa, for export. Notice, however, that comparative advantage in such goods is surely related more to endowments of natural resources than to labor-productivity advantages.
7. See the study by G.D.A. MacDougall (1951).
8. See Robert M. Stern (1962).
9. See W. Leontief (1953).
10. See P. Heller (1976).
11. See R. E. Baldwin (1971), R. M. Stern and K. E. Maskus (1981), and H. P. Bowen (1983).
12. Interested readers are referred to the article by Edward Leamer (1988).
13. See J. Vanek (1963).
14. See the article by D. B. Keesing (1965).
15. See E. E. Leamer (1980).
16. See K. E. Maskus (1985) and H. P. Bowen, E. E. Leamer, and L. Sveikauskas (1987).
17. See R. E. Baldwin (1971) and R. M. Stern and K. E. Maskus (1981).
18. See E. E. Leamer (1984).
19. In reality, the U.S. share of the world's oil is not this large because the data sample excludes many nations with large stocks of petroleum, such as those of the Middle East.
20. For more recent estimates of world endowments and trade equations, see the paper by K. E. Maskus (1991).
21. However, in his 1990 article, Jeffrey Bergstrand has provided firmer evidence for the role of preference similarity in explaining bilateral trade flows.
22. See the article by L. Hunter (1991).
23. See the papers by G. C. Hufbauer (1970) and D. B. Audretsch (1987).
24. There are numerous possible explanations for MNEs, as we discuss in Chapter 22.
25. For example, in a study of U.S. trade flows with 27 countries in 1989, S. Lael Brainard (1993) found that the share of both U.S. imports and exports accounted for by intra-firm transfers was around 25 percent.
26. See, for example, the review in F. M. Scherer (1980).
27. An excellent review is provided by James R. Tybout (1993).
28. See R. G. Harris (1991). The structure of the model is explained by D. Cox and R. Harris (1985).
29. See the article by J. D. Richardson (1989).
30. See H. G. Grubel and P. J. Lloyd (1975).
31. See B. Balassa (1966).
32. See B. Balassa (1986). There are now hundreds of such studies in the literature.

REFERENCES

Audretsch, D. B. (1987). "An Empirical Test of the Industry Life Cycle." *Weltwirtschaftliches Archiv* 123: 297–308.

Balassa, B. (1966). "Tariff Reductions and Trade in Manufactures among Industrial Countries." *American Economic Review* 56: 466–473.

————.(1986). "Intra-Industry Specialization: A Cross-Country Analysis." *European Economic Review* 30: 27–42.

Baldwin, R. E. (1971). "Determinants of the Commodity Structure of U.S. Trade." *American Economic Review* 61: 126–146.

Bergstrand, J. (1990). "The Heckscher-Ohlin-Samuelson Model, the Linder Hypothesis and the Determinants of Bilateral Intra-Industry Trade." *Economic Journal* 100: 850–868.

Bowen H. P. (1983). "Changes in the International Distribution of Resources and Their Impact on U.S. Comparative Advantage," *Review of Economics and Statistics* 65: 402–414.

Bowen, H. P., Leamer, E. E., and Sveikauskas, L. (1987). "Multicountry, Multifactor Tests of the Factor Abundance Theory." *American Economic Review* 77: 791–809.

Brainard, S. L. (1993), "An Empirical Assessment of the Factor Proportions Explanation of Multinational Sales," National Bureau of Economic Research working paper.

Cox, D., and Harris, R. (1985). "Trade Liberalization and Industrial Organization: Some Estimates for Canada." *Journal of Political Economy* 93: 115–145.

Deardorff, A. V. (1984). "Testing Trade Theories and Predicting Trade Flows." In R. Jones and P. Kenen, eds., *Handbook of International Economics: Volume I.* Amsterdam: North-Holland, 467–518.

Edwards, S. (1993). "Openness, Trade Liberalization, and Growth in Developing Countries." *Journal of Economic Literature* 31: 1358–1393.

Grubel, H. G., and Lloyd, P. J. (1975). *Intra-Industry Trade: The Theory and Measurement of International Trade in Differentiated Products.* New York: John Wiley.

Harris, R. G. (1991). "Symposium—The Canada-U.S. FTA: Economic Impact and Transition Effects." *Journal of Policy Modelling* 13: 421–434.

Heller, P. S. (1976). "Factor Endowment Changes and Comparative Advantage: The Case of Japan, 1959–1969." *Review of Economics and Statistics* 58: 283–292.

Huber, J. R. (1971). "Effect on Prices of Japan's Entry into World Commerce after 1858." *Journal of Political Economy* 79: 614–628.

Hufbauer, G. C. (1970). "The Impact of National Characteristics and Technology on the Commodity Composition of Trade in Manufactured Goods." In R. Vernon, ed., *The Technology Factor in International Trade.* New York: Columbia University Press, 145–231.

Hunter, L. (1991). "The Contribution of Nonhomothetic Preferences to Trade." *Journal of International Economics* 30: 345–358.

Keesing, D. B. (1965). "Labor Skills and International Trade: Evaluating Many Trade Flows with a Single Measuring Device." *Review of Economics and Statistics* 47: 287–294.

Leamer, E. E. (1980). "The Leontief Paradox, Reconsidered." *Journal of Political Economy* 88: 495–503.

————.(1984). *Sources of International Comparative Advantage: Theory and Evidence.* Cambridge: MIT Press.

————.(1988). "Measures of Openness." In R.E. Baldwin, ed., *Trade Policy Issues and Empirical Analysis.* Chicago: University of Chicago Press, 147–200.

Leontief, W. W. (1953). "Domestic Production and Foreign Trade: The American Capital Position Re-examined." *Proceedings of the American Philosophical Society* 20: 332–349.

MacDougall, G. D. A. (1951). "British and American Exports: A Study Suggested by the Theory of Comparative Costs, Part I." *Economic Journal* 61: 697–724.

Maskus, K. E. (1985). "A Test of the Heckscher-Ohlin-Vanek Theorem: The Leontief Commonplace." *Journal of International Economics* 19: 201–212.

————(1991). "Comparing International Trade Data and Product and National Characteristics Data for the Analysis of Trade Models." In P. Hooper and J. D. Richardson, eds., *International Economic Transactions: Issues in Measurement and Empirical Research.* Chicago: University of Chicago Press, 17–56.

Melvin, J. R. (1968). "Production and Trade with Two Factors and Three Goods." *American Economic Review* 63: 1249–1268.

Richardson, J. D. (1989). "Empirical Research on Trade Liberalization with Imperfect Competition: a Survey." *OECD Economic Studies* 12: 47–65.

Scherer, F. M. (1980). *Industrial Market Structure and Economic Performance.* Chicago: Rand McNally.

Stern, R. M. (1962). "British and American Productivity and Comparative Costs in International Trade." *Oxford Economic Papers* 14: 275–304.

Stern, R. M., and Maskus, K. E. (1981). "Determinants of the Structure of U.S. Foreign Trade, 1958-76." *Journal of International Economics* 11: 207–224.

Tybout, J. R. (1993). "Internal Returns to Scale as a Source of Comparative Advantage: The Evidence." *American Economic Review: Papers and Proceedings,* 83: 440–444.

Vanek, J. (1963). *The Natural Resource Content of United States Foreign Trade, 1870–1955.* Cambridge: MIT Press.

————.(1968). "The Factor Proportions Theory: The n–Factor Case." *Kyklos* 4: 749–756.

PART
III

TRADE POLICY

CHAPTER
15

TARIFFS

15.1 INTRODUCTION

In Chapter 5 we contrasted a free trade equilibrium with an autarky equilibrium, in which a country does not trade at all. Both these extremes are virtually unheard of in practice. Instead, when a country does engage in trade, the government of that country will erect various barriers to restrict trade. The most common of these barriers are taxes levied on the importation of foreign goods. These taxes, commonly referred to as *tariffs,* are simply a form of commodity taxation. Tariffs are sometimes levied on exports as well as on imports. This is the case, for example, with Canadian exports of natural gas to the United States. While there are other forms of trade restriction, this chapter will concentrate on tariffs. Other barriers, such as import quotas, will be discussed in the following chapter, and we will defer until Chapter 19 a detailed discussion of why such policies are put into use by governments.

For now, we establish the two essential reasons that governments may choose to levy taxes on trade. The more important objective is to protect the operations of domestic industries that compete with imports. Taking a Heckscher-Ohlin framework, for example, we would expect import restrictions to be more severe in sectors that intensively use an economy's scarce factors. The most extreme form of protective tariff would be a tax that eliminates imports. We refer to this as a *prohibitive tariff.* The second objective would be to raise revenues for the government. This practice is common in many developing countries, where it is easier to tax international trade at the border than to establish broad-based income taxes. Indeed, many exporters of primary products tax their foreign sales for revenue purposes. However, trade taxes are relatively unimportant as sources of revenue for developed economies.[1]

15.2 THE WELFARE LOSS FROM TARIFFS

In this section we focus on a small economy facing fixed world prices. That is, the country can trade as little or as much as it wants at a fixed world price ratio p^*. In this case, tariffs will affect the equilibrium price ratio facing domestic producers and consumers, but they will not affect p^*. Assume also that the pattern of comparative advantage is such that this country exports Y and imports X. Its government then places an *ad valorem* tax of t on each unit of X imported into the country.[2] Because p^* is fixed, the domestic price of X will rise by the full amount of the tax. Let $p = p_x/p_y$ be the domestic price ratio. Because exports are not taxed, the domestic and world prices will be related by $p_x = p_x^*(1 + t)$ and $p_y = p_y^*$ or $p = p^*(1 + t)$. Because of the import tariff on X, the domestic price ratio will be greater than the world price ratio $(p > p^*)$.

It is tariff-distorted domestic prices, rather than world prices, that consumers pay and producers receive. Of course, trade must still be balanced at the world price ratio, because p^* remains the price ratio at which the country does business with the rest of the world. These facts give us equilibrium conditions that can be summarized as follows:

$$\text{MRS} = \text{MRT} = p = p^*(1 + t) > p^* \tag{15.1}$$

$$p_x^*(X_c - X_p) + p_y^*(Y_c - Y_p) = 0 \quad \text{or} \quad p^* = \frac{(Y_c - Y_p)}{(X_p - X_c)} \tag{15.2}$$

where subscripts p and c again denote the amounts of a good produced and consumed, respectively. Equation (15.1) notes that domestic consumers and producers will equate the domestic MRS in consumption and MRT in production to the domestic price ratio, which is in turn greater than the world price ratio. Thus, at the post-tariff equilibrium, the slopes of the community indifference curve and the production frontier will be equal to each other but greater than the slope of the world price ratio. Equation (15.2) requires that the domestic production and consumption points be linked by the world price ratio.

These equilibrium conditions imply that the post-tariff equilibrium must be as shown in Fig. 15.1. In that diagram, A refers to the autarky equilibrium, whereas C_f and Q_f refer to the free-trade consumption and

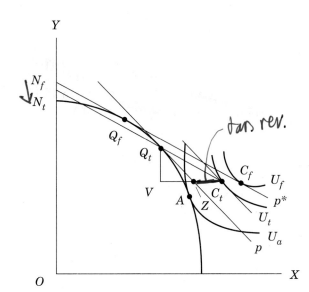

tar rev.

Imp↓ → lend to ↓
m eaps. also

FIGURE 15.1
Effects of an import tariff.

production points, respectively. A tariff on imports of X will result in production at a point like Q_t and consumption at a point like C_t. Points Q_t and C_t are linked by the world price ratio as required by the balance-of-payments constraint (Eq. (15.2)). Points Q_t and C_t also satisfy Eq. (15.1) in that we have MRS = MRT > p^*.

Several characteristics of the post-tariff equilibrium are clear from Fig. 15.1. First, the post-tariff level of welfare (U_t) is lower than the free-trade level (U_f) but higher than the autarky level (U_a). Therefore, the tariff leads to a welfare loss relative to free trade but certainly not relative to autarky. Second, the tariff causes production to move from the free-trade point (Q_f) back toward the autarky point (A). Third, the reduction in imports caused by the tariff also induces a decline in the volume of exports, which must be true in the absence of any change in the world price ratio. The new trade triangle is $Q_t V C_t$. Thus, tariffs penalize both imports and exports in general equilibrium. Advocates of their use often fail to recognize that the resource shifts caused by tariffs must reduce production for exports. Finally, because exports of $V Q_t$ units of Y are worth $V Z$ units of X at domestic prices but $V C_t$ at world prices, the quantity $Z C_t$ depicts the tariff revenue, measured in units of the import good X. We implicitly assume that the government rebates this revenue to citizens in a lump-sum fashion, allowing them to reach the consumption equilibrium at point C_t.

These effects on welfare, production, and trade reveal the essential effect of tariffs, which is to move the country back from free trade in the direction of autarky. The country specializes less in the good in which it has a comparative advantage and thus sacrifices some of the gains from trade. Indeed, real national income is reduced from ON_f to ON_t. If the tariff

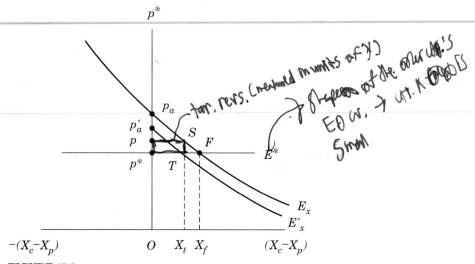

FIGURE 15.2
Effects of a tariff on excess demand curves.

were continually raised, the country would eventually find it unprofitable to import any X in Fig. 15.1 and would be driven all the way back to the autarky equilibrium at A. As we mentioned, such a tariff is called a prohibitive tariff.

Tariffs accomplish this movement toward autarky by distorting domestic prices, and, because domestic producers and consumers respond to domestic prices, by distorting domestic decision making. By raising the price of X, the tariff makes it seem that X is more valuable than it actually is and thereby encourages domestic producers to produce more of it. Resources are diverted from the true pattern of comparative advantage by this misrepresentation, so gains from specialization are lost. Consumer prices are similarly distorted, so gains from exchange are also lost.

Now examine the effects of tariffs by using an excess demand curve like those developed in Chapter 4. In Fig. 15.2, the excess demand curve for the small country crosses the price axis at p_a, showing that at lower relative prices, the economy would choose to import good X. The fact that this is a small economy is depicted by the existence of a perfectly elastic foreign excess demand curve E^* at free-trade price ratio p^*. The free-trade equilibrium involves a level of imports equal to X_f at that price. An ad valorem import tariff on X imposed at rate t will shift down the import demand section of good X's excess demand curve by t percent. That is, in Figure 15.2, E'_x is defined by the relationship $p'(1 + t) = p$, where p gives price along the original excess demand curve. Note that this tariff would be prohibitive if the world price p^* were between p'_a and p_a. At the world price of p^* in Fig.

15.2, the tariff reduces imports from X_f to X_t, with exports correspondingly reduced to p^*X_t units of good Y, whether the tax is imposed on imports or exports. The domestic relative price ratio in the small importer becomes $p = p^*(1 + t)$, while tariff revenues are the rectangle pp^*TS, which is measured in units of Y.

An additional important point is that in addition to reducing overall income, tariffs redistribute income. In Fig. 15.1, the tariff raises the domestic price of X and shifts production from Q_f to Q_t. We know from our earlier analysis that this shift will generally change factor prices. In the Heckscher-Ohlin model, the increase in the price and production of X will increase the real income of the factor used intensively in the production of that good and decrease the real income of the other factor (the Stolper-Samuelson theorem). Thus, in this case, the losses shown in Fig. 15.1 are shared unevenly, and one factor is actually made better off. Because overall welfare in the economy falls with the tariff, it follows that the other factor suffers a welfare loss in excess of the entire welfare loss. These distributional consequences of protection help to explain why we have protectionist policies. Chapter 19 will focus on this issue.

15.3 TARIFFS, TAXES, AND DISTORTIONS[3]

tar. = tax on cons. + Subs. to prods.

As we noted earlier, tariffs are simply a special kind of tax. The purpose of this section is to expand on the notion of tariffs as taxes and to analyze the relationship of tariffs to other types of taxes. Recall from Fig. 15.1 that an import tariff on X has the effect of raising both the price charged to the consumers and the price received by the producers. This hurts the consumer of X and helps its producers. The tariff acts like a tax on consumers and a subsidy to producers. In fact, a tariff has the equivalent effect of a consumption tax combined with a production subsidy. From the information in Fig. 15.1 alone, we would find it impossible to tell whether the equilibrium at C_t was caused by an import tariff or by a combined consumption-tax/production-subsidy on X.

Import Tariffs and Export Taxes

It is somewhat more difficult to grasp the point that an import tariff on X is exactly equivalent to some export tax on Y.[4] As we indicated earlier, restricting imports is equivalent to restricting exports. Recall that an import tariff on X raises the domestic price of X above the world price ($p_x > p_x^*$) while leaving the domestic price of Y equal to the world price ($p_y = p_y^*$). The effect of the tariff on relative prices is to set $p > p^*$. For its part, an export tax establishes the following relationship between the domestic price of Y and the world price: $p_y = p_y^*(1 - t)$. (Note that for this small country, the tax would reduce the domestic price received by producers of the export good by the full amount of the tax, because exports must be sold at the fixed world price.) Thus, the tax drives a wedge between the domestic and world prices of $Y (p_y < p_y^*)$ while leaving the domestic price of X equal to the world price $(p_x = p_x^*)$. The effect of the export tax is also to set $p > p^*$. Thus, an import tariff and an export tax have the same effect on the domestic price ratio, and since it is only the ratio that matters, both have the same effect on production and consumption. Again looking only at the information in Fig. 15.1, we would find it impossible to tell whether the equilibrium at C_t was generated by an import tariff or by an export tax.

Export taxes and import tariffs are equivalent in that they tend to raise the relative domestic price of imports and lower the relative domestic price of exports. Both tend to shift resources out of export industries into import-competing industries. Many observers have argued that countries should restrict imports by tariffs and simultaneously encourage exports by subsidies. This contention is wrong on two accounts. First, we should not do either in a small economy, where free trade is optimal, and second, the two proposed policies have exactly opposite effects and would therefore tend to cancel each other.

Export Subsidies

It is interesting to consider the effects of subsidizing exports in a small open economy. This policy is analyzed in Fig. 15.3. Suppose that s is an ad valorem subsidy rate on exports of Y. Then $p_y = p_y^*(1 + s)$ and $p = p^*/(1 + s) < p^*$. Equation (15.1) must be replaced by

$$\text{MRS} = \text{MRT} = p = \frac{p^*}{1 + s} < p^* \tag{15.3}$$

The balance-of-payments constraint in Eq. (15.2) must, of course, continue to hold.

Figure 15.3 shows that the export subsidy causes the country to produce more Y and less X (point Q_s) than at the free trade equilibrium (point Q_f). Thus, real national income of ON_s is smaller than in free trade, as was the case with the tariff. Both policies distort resource allocation. The difference is that the subsidy generates excessive production of Y, while the tariff generates excessive production of X. Consumption occurs at C_s where the MRS in consumption equals the distorted domestic price ratio. The country trades more with the rest of the world (both exports and imports increase), but welfare is reduced from U_f to U_s. Observe the implication that artificially increasing trade by subsidizing exports will not make an economy better off in general. Indeed, export subsidies are usually more welfare-decreasing than tariffs because they require taxpayers to fund them, rather than generating tax revenues.

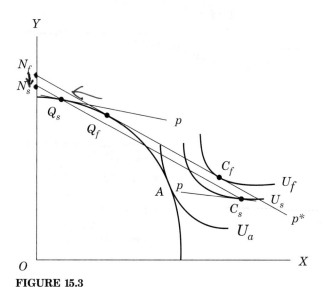

FIGURE 15.3
Export subsidies.

In fact, an export (or import) subsidy could actually make an economy worse off than in autarky, as we prove later in Section 15.7. It is possible to see this, however, by considering Fig. 15.3 again. If the production distortion induced by the subsidy is so large that the world price line emanating from point Q_s actually passes below indifference curve U_a, the country would be better off not trading than subsidizing exports.

Consumption Taxes and Production Subsidies

Now let us return to the notion that an import tariff (or export tax) is equivalent to a consumption tax and a production subsidy. Suppose that for some political reason the government is determined to increase production in the import-competing sector relative to the level it attains in free trade. One reason the government might wish to do this is that some minimum level of production in the import-competing sector is viewed as important for national security reasons, as might be the case with steel, oil, or semiconductors. Given this objective, the important economic question is, what is the least-cost method of achieving it? The problem with an import tariff is that it acts as a tax on consumption, in addition to serving as a subsidy to production. Might it not be better to use a direct output subsidy instead? The answer is definitely yes, as is shown in Fig. 15.4. If the government uses an import tariff to shift production from Q_f to Q_t, consumption will move to C_t, resulting in a welfare level of U_t.

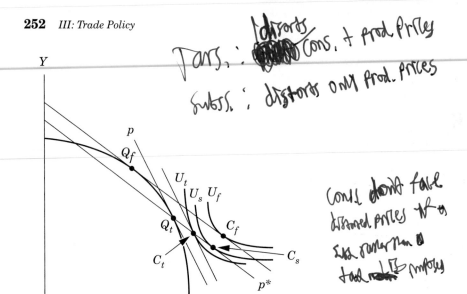

Tars, : *distorts* ~~Cons~~ *Cons. + prod Prices*

Subss : *distorts only prod. Prices*

Const don't face
distorted prices the
Sub rather than a
tax reduces imports

FIGURE 15.4
Consumption taxes and production subsidies.

Suppose instead that the government simply subsidizes production of X in such a way that the producer receipts per unit are the same as with the tariff. In this case output will still shift to Q_t, but consumers will not face distorted prices and will instead be allowed to trade at world prices. This will allow consumers to attain consumption bundle C_s and utility level U_s in Fig. 15.4. This result can be explained by using the terminology of gains from exchange and gains from specialization developed in Chapter 5. The tariff in Fig. 15.4 distorts both consumer and producer prices, thereby causing a loss of gains from exchange as well as gains from specialization. The subsidy distorts only producer prices and thereby causes a loss only of gains from specialization. Curiously, despite the logic in Fig. 15.4, politicians and the general public appear to find tariffs more acceptable than subsidies because tariffs are the more common method of protection. More will be said about the politics underlying such choices in Chapter 19.

Tariffs and Distortions

A final point concerning tariffs and taxes is explored in Fig. 15.5. As we noted earlier in this chapter, the result that tariffs are harmful for a small open economy relies on the assumption that there are no distortions in the economy. If there are distortions, it may be the case that tariffs could be used to offset these distortions and thereby increase welfare. This possibility is an application of what is known in economics as the *theory*

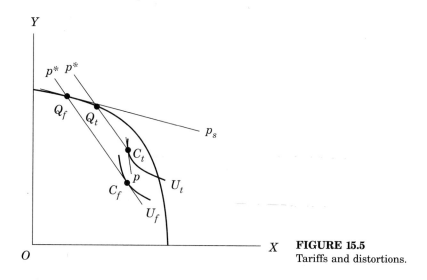

FIGURE 15.5
Tariffs and distortions.

of the second best. This theory states that in the presence of multiple distortions (such as domestic taxes or monopoly), welfare is not necessarily improved by removing a single distortion (such as an import tariff). An equivalent statement is that in the presence of distortions, adding an additional distortion may improve welfare.

An application of the latter form of the theory of the second best is shown in Fig. 15.5. Suppose that for some political reason, the producers of Y have managed to obtain a subsidy from the government and that the government is unwilling to take the political risk of removing the subsidy. Free trade production will take place at a point like Q_f in Fig. 15.5, where the domestic producer price ratio p_s (the slope of the production frontier) is flatter than the world price ratio. Consumers can trade at world prices, and so consumption is given by point C_f. Even though the government cannot remove the subsidy, it can improve welfare by introducing an additional distortion, namely, an import tariff on X. This will raise the domestic price of X and, with the rate of subsidy on Y unchanged, encourage the production of X, moving the output mix from Q_f to Q_t. The consumer prices will then be distorted by the tariff on X ($p > p^*$), so consumption will occur at a point like C_t. Welfare is thus improved by the tariff, even though the country trades at fixed world prices. The tariff accomplishes this result by influencing production in a direction opposite to the influence of the distortionary subsidy. The effect of the tariff is to push the economy back in the direction of its efficient pattern of specialization. Of course, as our earlier analysis pointed out, imposition of the tariff could also lower welfare if the tariff-inclusive domestic price ratio does not induce much change in production but substantially worsens the consumption distortion. Such an equilibrium would occur on an indifference curve below the one giving the original consumption choice.[5]

*Remark the mon. (Hy invisible)
to trade,
the worse to
terms of trade
become*

15.4   MONOPOLY POWER

Thus far we have assumed that the country is small and faces fixed world prices (i.e., the country is essentially a perfect competitor on world markets). Suppose now that the country is large enough that world prices will be influenced by what the country wishes to buy and sell. More specifically, the world price of our export good will fall as we export more, and the world price of our import good will rise as we import more. The more we wish to trade, the worse our terms of trade become.[6]

Figure 15.6 depicts two countries in a trading situation in which E_x^h is the home country's excess demand curve for good X and E_x^f is the foreign country's excess demand for X. An equilibrium would be established in free trade at p_f^* (see point F). Home imports are X_h^0, which coincide with foreign exports of X_f^0. Notice the effect, however, when the home country imposes a tariff (either as an import tariff on X or an export tariff on Y). The resulting downward shift in the home country's excess demand curve to $E_x^{h'}$ causes the equilibrium world price ratio to fall to p_t^* (point T) at the same time that it drives up the domestic price ratio in the home country to p (point S; recall that $p = p_t^*(1 + t)$). The resulting restriction of imports in the home country to level X_h^1 (and of foreign exports to X_f^1) is a move toward autarky. This comes about because of the higher domestic price that distorts

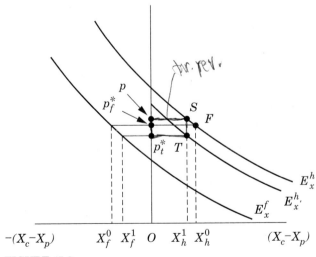

FIGURE 15.6
Terms of trade effects from tariffs.

production and consumption decisions and that would lower welfare in the home country. However, the fall in the relative equilibrium world price of the home country's import good from p_f^* to p_t^* represents a gain in the home country's terms of trade. The welfare benefits from this would, to some extent, offset the welfare losses from reduced trade. Tariff revenue is the area $pp_t^* TS$.

Figure 15.7 illustrates the possibility that the improvement in the terms of trade is so strong that Country H is actually made better off by the tariff. The tariff lowers the world price ratio from p_f^* to p_t^*, resulting in post-tariff production and consumption at Q_t and C_t, respectively. Home welfare increases from U_f to U_t following the imposition of the tariff.

The economic explanation of this possibility is fairly simple. While a country would like its firms to behave competitively when selling at home, it would be beneficial for the country to behave as a monopolist when selling abroad. Because we have assumed that individual firms are competitive, they cannot behave in this way. Therefore, the government can act to make the country behave as a monopolist. The tariff causes the country to restrict its "output" (exports) like a monopolist and also to restrict its "demand" (imports) like a monopsonist, thereby moving prices in the country's favor. At the same time, however, this action clearly worsens the other country's economic welfare. Country F suffers both a terms-of-trade loss and distortionary losses from the fact that the altered relative price pushes resources out of its export sector and changes consumption decisions. Accordingly, we might expect F to retaliate against

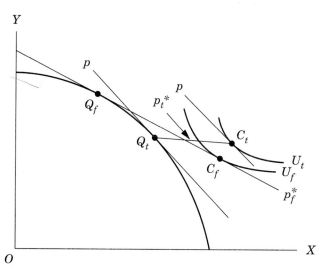

FIGURE 15.7
Welfare improvement from tariffs.

H with its own tariff on H exports. This process of tariff imposition and retaliation—a "trade war" in popular terminology—is harmful to global welfare and is likely to leave both H and F worse off than in free trade. We discuss this possibility more fully in the next section.

15.5 THE OPTIMUM TARIFF AND RETALIATION

When a country can gain by imposing a tariff, we might ask what the best possible tariff level is. This is known as the *optimal tariff* issue. The key to deriving the optimal tariff was contained in our preceding discussion, where we noted that a tariff could allow a country to exert its monopoly power in the supply of its export good or to exert its monopsony power in purchases of its import good.

Since most of our discussion has concerned tariffs on imports, let us take the latter approach and think of the country as exercising its monopsony power in the purchase of imports. Figure 15.8 depicts the situation for Country H, which is again assumed to import good X. E_x^f is the partial-equilibrium foreign supply curve (technically, the excess supply curve) and I_x^h is the home country's (excess) demand curve for X. Free trade equilibrium would be given by the intersection of the two, establishing a free trade price of p_{xf}^* and setting imports equal to I_{xf}.

But this free trade equilibrium is not a welfare optimum for Country H. An optimum requires that Country H equate the domestic price of X to

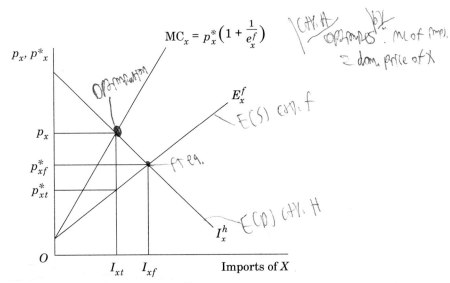

FIGURE 15.8
The optimum tariff.

the marginal cost of imports. The foreign supply curve gives the price of imports for each quantity of imports, and price is simply the average cost. Let C_x denote the total cost of imports. We have

$$C_x = p_x^* I_x; \qquad \text{AC}_x = \frac{C_x}{I_x} = p_x^*; \qquad I_x = X_c - X_p \qquad (15.4)$$

where AC_x is the average cost of imports. Free trade thus equates the domestic price of X to the average cost of X ($p_x = p_x^*$).

Marginal cost is defined as the change in cost (ΔC_x) in response to a change in the quantity of imports (ΔI_x). ΔC_x can be approximated as follows.

$$\Delta C_x = p_x^* \Delta I_x + I_x \Delta p_x^* \qquad (15.5)$$

Dividing Eq. (15.5) by ΔI_x, we have

$$\frac{\Delta C_x}{\Delta I_x} = p_x^* + I_x \frac{\Delta p_x^*}{\Delta I_x} = p_x^* \left[1 + \frac{I_x}{p_x^*} \frac{\Delta p_x^*}{\Delta I_x} \right] \qquad (15.6)$$

Let e_x^f be defined as Country F's elasticity of supply of exports. Since $\Delta C_x / \Delta I_x = \text{MC}_x$, Eq. (15.6) can be rewritten as

$$\text{MC}_x = p_x^* \left(1 + \frac{1}{e_x^f} \right); \qquad e_x^f = \frac{p_x^* \Delta I_x}{I_x \Delta p_x^*} \qquad (15.7)$$

Since the supply curve slopes upward, e_x^f is positive, and marginal cost is greater than average cost ($\text{MC}_x > \text{AC}_x = p_x^*$). The marginal cost curve is shown by MC_x in Fig. 15.8. The economic reason that marginal cost of imports exceeds average cost is straightforward. Let the home country choose to import another unit of X, which would cost p_{xf}^* at the free-trade price. However, because the home country is large, its decision to import another unit would raise the world price, increasing the cost on *all* units imported. Thus, full marginal costs consist of the price of another unit of imports plus the extra inframarginal costs generated on existing imports.

Country H maximizes its welfare by equating p_x to MC_x. Thus in Fig. 15.8 the country should import quantity I_{xt}, requiring a domestic price of p_x. This restriction on imports drives down the world price of X from p_{xf}^* to p_{xt}^* and results in a welfare gain for Country H, as discussed in the previous section. We also know that an import tariff will lead to the relationship $p_x = p_x^*(1 + t)$, where t is the ad valorem tariff rate. Thus, the optimal tariff rate will be the rate that solves the equation

$$p_x = p_x^*(1 + t) = p_x^* \left(1 + \frac{1}{e_x^f} \right); \qquad t = \frac{1}{e_x^f} \qquad (15.8)$$

The optimum tariff is thus equal to the inverse elasticity of foreign export supply. The more inelastic foreign excess supply is, the larger the optimum tariff will thus be (i.e., t will be large when e_x^f is small).

It is easy to see that the optimum tariff formula covers the special case of a small open economy. If a country can trade as much or as little as it wishes at fixed world prices, this means that the supply curve facing the country is horizontal, or infinitely elastic. In this situation, e_x^f is infinite and $1/e_x^f$ is zero. Thus, the optimal tariff for a small economy is zero, and free trade is indeed the optimal policy, as discussed in section 15.2.

Two qualifications of this discussion should be noted. First, the optimal tariff formula is deceptively simple in that it seems to tell us exactly what the tariff should be. But in fact, e_x^f is generally a variable that changes its value as we move along the foreign excess supply curve. The equation $t = 1/e_x^f$ is unfortunately no more than an equilibrium condition and does not by itself tell us what the numerical value of t should be. The optimal value of t must be found by first estimating E_x^f and I_x^h and then using E_x^f to construct MC_x or e_x^f. It is only after this has been done that the *formula* can be applied to find the optimal *value* of t. Note especially in this regard that t will depend on domestic factors, even though the optimal tariff formula seems to rely only on the foreign elasticity. The optimal tariff t will equal $1/e_x^f$ evaluated at the point where the domestic excess demand curve crosses MC_x. Because e_x^f generally varies along MC_x, the actual value of e_x^f and therefore t will depend on where I_x^h crosses MC_x. Thus, domestic factors do indeed help determine the value of the optimum tariff, and the simple formula does not, in fact, provide a shortcut to finding this value.

The second qualification is a much more important one. The optimal tariff discussed here is based on the assumption that the government in Country F will not retaliate when Country H institutes the tariff. However, H's optimal tariff clearly reduces F's welfare by reducing F's trade volume and worsening terms of trade (that is, it reduces the relative price of F's export good). Suppose, then, that the foreign government will exactly match any tariff that H imposes with a tariff on H's exports. From our earlier analysis we know that this tariff is equivalent to Country F imposing a tax on its exports. Thus, in Fig. 15.6, this retaliatory move will cause the export-supply portion of E_x^f (i.e., the portion to the left of the vertical axis) to shift up, which will further restrict trade and move the terms of trade back against Country H. Indeed, it is quite possible to end up with exactly the same world price ratio that prevailed with free trade. The volume of trade will be lower, and therefore, since neither country has succeeded in improving its terms of trade, both countries will be unambiguously worse off.[7]

Because of the high probability of foreign retaliation, the term "optimal tariff" is very misleading. It is optimal only under the special assumption of no retaliation. If all countries pursue this so-called "optimal" strategy simultaneously, it is likely that every country will be worse off—hardly an optimal outcome. If countries cooperate instead of myopically pursuing their self-interests, they may find that relatively free trade constitutes the optimal policy.

15.6   EFFECTIVE PROTECTION

One fundamental implication of our discussion thus far is that a tariff provides protection from imports, allowing expanded domestic production of the protected commodity. This prediction assumes that the tariff is the only tax that directly affects costs and prices of the good in question. Such an assumption is reasonable for goods that are produced solely by untraded primary inputs, such as capital and labor, and for goods that require intermediate inputs that are freely traded internationally. However, most commodities are produced with the use of intermediate goods that are themselves subject to trade taxes. Thus, a tariff on imported steel, for example, would raise costs and lower output in the automobile sector even if there were a protective tariff on cars. In general, manufacturers are better off as tariffs rise on imports that compete with their outputs and worse off as tariffs rise on their imported inputs. The term *effective protection* refers to the fact that all such tariffs need to be taken into account in computing the net protective effect of the tariff structure.

Because our goal is to isolate the costs of intermediate inputs, the notion of effective protection actually refers to the positive or negative stimulus to *value added* in production of a commodity. Value added per unit of output, v, is the difference between the price of a final good and the cost of purchasing intermediate inputs. As such, it measures the portion of the value of output that is available for payments to primary inputs. For example, if the price of an automobile is $15,000 and the cost of acquiring the steel, leather, glass, rubber, and so on needed to produce the car is $10,000, there remain $5,000 to pay for wages, the costs of capital (e.g., profits and interest), and the costs of land (e.g., rents). Value added thus captures the costs of primary inputs. In this case, value added makes up 33 percent of the gross value of the car. If the tariff structure combines to expand value added relative to free trade, it effectively raises payments to these primary factors.

In this sense, the effective rate of protection, t_e, is defined as the percentage change in a sector's value added per unit of output to a situation in which tariffs have been, v', in moving from free trade with no tariffs imposed.

$$t_e = \frac{1}{v}(v' - v) \tag{15.9}$$

Continuing with this example, suppose for simplicity that steel is the only intermediate input in cars and that the prices given exist in free trade. We choose units so that one unit of steel is required per automobile. Now suppose that a 20-percent tariff is imposed on imported cars and that the domestic producers of cars respond to the tariff by raising their price by 20 percent, to $18,000.[8] With no tariff on steel, domestic value added thus rises to $8,000 per car, and the effective rate of protection becomes $t_e = (\$8,000 - \$5,000)/\$5,000 = 0.6$, or 60 percent. Interestingly, the 20 percent *nominal* tariff on the final good raises the *effective* tariff from zero to 60 percent. Of course, this result simply reflects the fact that value added is a portion of gross output, so the nominal tariff has a magnified effect on value added. Thus, the share of primary inputs in cars (measured at free trade prices) rises by 60 percent, the effective protection provided them.

Suppose now that a 20-percent tariff is imposed on imported steel, raising its domestic price to $12,000, while the tariff on cars remains. The effective protection afforded to cars is now $t_e = (\$6,000 - \$5,000)/\$5,000 = 0.2$, or 20 percent. In this case, the effective rate of protection equals the nominal rate. Finally, if we raise the steel tariff to 50 percent, our computation becomes $t_e = (\$3,000 - \$5,000)/\$5,000 = -0.4$, or -40 percent. Thus, it is possible for the tariff on inputs to be high enough to reduce effective protection for the final good relative to free trade. Thus, despite the existence of the 20 percent nominal tariff on automobiles, production of cars will probably fall as the sector is forced to shed labor and other primary inputs.

From these examples we can draw certain conclusions.

1. If the tariff on the output exceeds the tariff on the input, the effective rate of protection is higher than the nominal tariff.
2. If the tariffs are equal, the effective rate of protection is equal to the nominal tariff.
3. If the output tariff is lower than the tariff on the input, the effective rate of protection is less than the nominal tariff and may even be negative.[9]

A further point to note is that tariffs are not the only determinants of effective protection. Trade taxes, domestic taxes, subsidies, quotas, and other nontariff barriers on outputs and inputs must be considered. One inference we can make is that any tariff system will be a serious disadvantage to export industries, which must sell at world prices. For an export industry, input tariffs will raise costs that may not be offset by export subsidies. Thus, we can expect that a general reduction in tariffs will be a substantial impetus to exports by improving their competitive position.

While the concept of effective protection provides important insights, it should be noted that it relies on several restrictive assumptions. Perhaps the most crucial is that all production functions exhibit constant returns to scale with fixed input coefficients. The first characteristic allows us to compute value added per unit of output without regard to the actual level of output. If constant returns to scale were not assumed, computations of value added would become more complicated. For example, suppose the automobile tariff just discussed would, by itself, double domestic output of cars. Unless steel inputs also doubled, which would not happen except under constant returns, the impact on the share of primary inputs would depend on the tariff and on returns to scale. Because we wish to isolate the changes due to tariffs, it is convenient to focus on the constant-returns case. Similarly, the assumption of fixed coefficients implies that inputs are always combined in the same proportions, regardless of factor prices or output scale. In theoretical terms, this notion means that isoquants are right-angled, or that elasticities of substitution among inputs are zero. If, however, production functions allow for substitution in production, then any change in factor prices would be expected to change the production coefficients. Like the problem with returns to scale, such changes would affect observed value-added shifts, making computations more difficult.

Removing the assumption of fixed coefficients causes two major effects. First, allowing input substitution tends to reduce calculated effective rates of protection. Second, it may alter the ranking of effective rates across sectors. However, evidence suggests that such shifts in rankings are not great even when substitution elasticities as high as 2 are assumed. Thus, it seems practical to use effective rates of protection as indicators of how the full tariff structure will influence resource allocation across industries.

A further assumption is that production and trade take place in the protected industries both before and after the tariffs are imposed. This assumption is necessary to ensure that the calculated rates actually do measure changes in value added relative to free trade levels. A final assumption is that the elasticities of foreign demand for exports, foreign supply of imports, and domestic supply of nontraded inputs are infinite. These assumptions eliminate the possibility of price changes other than those associated with the imposition of tariffs. Thus, changes in the terms of trade associated with the tariff structure are ignored. This is a major limitation on studies of effective protection because accounting for finite elasticities would change the computations significantly. Unfortunately, relatively little reliable information exists on the values of the requisite elasticities. In general it has been found that relaxing the assumption of perfectly elastic supplies of domestic, nontraded inputs tends to lower the effective rates of protection.

We should also note that allowing for more complex production processes with many required inputs complicates the process of calculating effective rates of protection, although not excessively. In particular, the importance of the various intermediate inputs must be weighted in the calculation process, and the data requirements for these calculations increase in proportion to the number of inputs.[10]

We conclude this section with two notes on the practical relevance of effective rates of protection. First, developed countries often have a structure of *escalating tariffs,* meaning that raw materials are allowed to be imported largely duty-free, while processed intermediates have higher tariffs, and finished goods have yet higher import taxes. As suggested earlier, this structure means that the effective protection provided to finished products is higher than nominal rates would suggest. In general, estimates suggest that in the industrialized countries, effective rates of protection on final goods are approximately twice the nominal tariff rates. This is especially true in certain labor-intensive products, suggesting that the tariff structure may be used to achieve substantial implicit protection. Tariff escalation continues to be a significant issue of contention between developed-country importers and developing-country exporters in multilateral trade negotiations.

TABLE 15.1
**Nominal and effective rates of protection in selected industries,
United States, Japan, and Republic of Korea**

Industry	United States[a]		Japan[a]		Republic of Korea[b]	
	NRP (%)	ERP (%)	NRP (%)	ERP (%)	NRP (%)	ERP (%)
Agriculture	1.80	1.91	18.40	21.40	72.3	85.7
Food products	4.70	10.16	25.40	50.31	11.7	−27.6
Wearing apparel	22.70	43.30	13.80	42.20	29.0	93.8
Wood products	1.70	1.72	0.30	−30.59	8.6	6.5
Chemicals	2.40	3.66	4.80	6.39	28.5	50.9
Iron and steel	3.60	6.18	2.80	4.34	12.9	31.5
Electrical machinery	4.40	6.34	4.30	6.73	26.2	44.8
Transport equipment	2.50	1.94	1.50	0.03	31.9	12.4

Source: A. V. Deardorff and R. M. Stern (1984) and J. Yoo, (1993, 22).

[a] Nominal tariff rates and effective rates of protection to be phased in by 1986 following the Tokyo Round of tariff negotiations.

[b] Nominal tariff rates and effective rates of protection in 1982.

A second observation is that many developing countries have arranged their protective structures so that effective tariffs are far higher than published tariffs. In part, this is an attempt to foster growth in domestic manufacturing through a regime of *import-substituting industrialization.* Again, the goal is to promote domestic output of final goods by escalating tariffs on the inputs. This policy is often accompanied by a deliberate overvaluation of the domestic currency, done in part to discourage exports of primary products in favor of keeping primary goods at home for use in manufacturing import-competing goods. On occasion, these protection levels can be extraordinary. For example, it was estimated that in 1969, Argentina had nominal tariff rates of 63 percent on finished textiles and 76 percent on woodworking industries. However, the associated effective rates of protection, accounting for trade barriers, taxes, and the exchange-rate regime, amounted to 832 percent and 1,308 percent, respectively.[11]

To provide further perspective, Table 15.1 presents recent nominal tariff rates and estimates of effective protection rates in the United States, Japan, and the Republic of Korea. It can be seen that all countries heavily protect wearing apparel, while Japan and Korea strongly protect their agricultural sectors. Indeed, the costs of agricultural protection in Korea are so high that the food products industry is effectively taxed, despite an 11.7 percent nominal tariff.

15.7   GAINS FROM TRADE WITH MANY GOODS, TRADE TAXES, AND SUBSIDIES

Up to this point, we have focused mainly on a simple model in which there are only two goods. Results of the analysis suggest that an import tariff reduces welfare relative to free trade but still leaves welfare greater than or equal to the autarky level. An import or export subsidy, however, has the potential of making the country worse off relative to autarky.

Can we say anything about a country that trades many goods, some of which are taxed and some of which are subsidized? It turns out that there is in fact a very simple condition for gains from trade: if net trade tax revenue (the sum of all import and export tax revenues minus trade subsidy payments) is positive, then the country is better off than in autarky. Another way of saying this is that if trade is, on average, taxed more than it is subsidized, then there are still gains from trade.

Suppose that there are n goods, $(X_1 \ldots X_n)$, with fixed world prices $(p_1^* \ldots p_n^*)$ (although the argument easily generalizes to a large economy) and corresponding domestic prices $(p_1 \ldots p_n)$. Domestic and world prices are related by $p_i = p_i^*(1 + t_i)$. If good i is imported, then a positive t_i is an import tariff and a negative t_i is an import subsidy. If good i is exported, then a positive t_i is an export subsidy and a negative t_i is an export tax (e.g., if the world price is higher than the domestic price $(t_i < 0)$, then t_i is an export tax).

Domestic producers optimize with respect to domestic prices. In a competitive economy, this means that the value of production at *domestic* prices in (distorted) trade is greater than or equal to the value of autarky production at these same prices. Let superscript d denote quantities in tax/subsidy distorted trade and superscript a denote autarky quantities. Subscripts p and c denote production and consumption quantities as before. Competitive equilibrium is characterized by

$$\sum_i^n p_i^*(1 + t_i)X_{ip}^d \geq \sum_i^n p_i^*(1 + t_i)X_{ip}^a \tag{15.10}$$

Equation (15.10) can be rearranged as

$$\sum_i^N p_i^* X_{ip}^d \geq \sum_i^n p_i^* X_{ip}^a + \sum_i^n p_i^* t_i (X_{ip}^a - X_{ip}^d) \tag{15.11}$$

The balance-of-trade condition and the autarky market-clearing condition are given by

$$\sum_i^n p_i^* X_{ip}^d = \sum_i^n p_i^* X_{ic}^d \qquad X_{ip}^a = X_{ic}^a \tag{15.12}$$

Substituting Eq. (15.12) into Eq. (15.11), the latter becomes

$$\sum_i^n p_i^* X_{ic}^d \geq \sum_i^n p_i^* X_{ic}^a + \sum_i^n p_i^* t_i (X_{ip}^a - X_{ip}^d) \tag{15.13}$$

A welfare comparison of distorted-trade versus autarky consumption must, however, be done at domestic prices. By adding and subtracting several terms to both sides of the equation, Eq. (15.13) becomes

$$\sum_I^n p_i^*(1 + t_i)X_{ic}^d \geq \sum_i^n p_i^*(1 + t_i)X_{ic}^a + \sum_i^n p_i^* t_i \left[(X_{ic}^d - X_{ip}^d) - (X_{ic}^a - X_{ip}^a) \right] \tag{15.14}$$

Consider the term in square brackets on the right-hand side of Eq. (15.14). Let $M_i = X_{ic} - X_{ip}$ be the imports of good i. In autarky, these are zero. Thus, the term in square brackets on the right-hand side of Eq. (15.14) reduces to M_i^d. Using the relationship between world and domestic prices, Eq. (15.14) then reduces to a relatively simple expression.

$$\sum_i^n p_i X_{ic}^d \geq \sum_i^n p_i X_{ic}^a + \sum_i^n p_i^* t_i M_i^d \qquad (15.15)$$

The second summation on the right-hand side of Eq. (15.15) gives the total net value of trade tax revenue. Equation (15.15) gives us the welfare comparison we are seeking. The value of domestic consumption in the distorted trade equilibrium is greater than or equal to the value of autarky consumption (evaluated at distorted-trade, domestic prices) if net trade tax revenue is positive. Again, recall that if X_i is imported ($M_i > 0$), $t_i > 0$ is an import tariff, and if X_i is exported ($M_i < 0$), $t_i < 0$ is an export tax. A country whose taxes on trade exceed its subsidies cannot be worse off than in autarky, but a country whose subsidies exceed its taxes on trade can be worse off.

15.8 CONCLUDING REMARKS

Tariffs, which are taxes on imports, are the most common form of government interference with international trade. They exist largely to protect domestic firms that compete with imports, though tariffs are sometimes levied for purposes of raising government revenues. We have analyzed tariffs and other trade taxes and subsidies in our general equilibrium framework, making the following major points.

1. Tariffs, like other forms of commodity taxes, alter relative prices and change quantities transacted. Import tariffs raise the domestic price of imports and so reduce their quantity. If a country is small and thus faces fixed world prices, this reduction causes a reduction in the gains from trade, thereby reducing national welfare. Tariffs simply move the country back in the direction of autarky.

2. The effects of tariffs, as policy distortions, on consumers and producers can be examined in terms of both the import-competing and export sectors. Specifically, an import tariff is equivalent to a combination of a tax on consumption of the import good combined with a subsidy on production of the import-competing good. Furthermore, an import tax is equivalent to an export tax (in a two-sector model), and an import tariff can be offset by an export subsidy.

3. While tariffs are almost surely welfare-reducing for a small country,[12] a large country may be able to exploit its monopoly power on world markets by using a tariff to gain a favorable terms-of-trade effect for itself. However, this power is greatly undermined by the likelihood that

other countries will retaliate against the country imposing the tariff. The noncooperative scenario of tariff imposition and retaliation is unlikely to benefit any country. The probable outcome is that the volume of world trade will be reduced without a significant gain for any country in terms-of-trade advantage. Gains from trade are lost with the reduction in world trade. Stated in other terms, all countries suffer efficiency losses in terms of distorted consumption and production decisions with no offsetting advantages in international relative prices. However, in a cooperative scenario, countries are likely to find that the so-called "optimal" tariffs are not, in fact, optimal at all. By cooperatively reducing their tariffs, countries can expand trade without suffering adverse terms-of-trade effects and can thereby increase their welfare.

4. Tariffs frequently fall upon imported intermediate goods in the production process. The effect of these tariffs is to generate a pattern of distortions in the use of intermediate goods in the production process. The real extent of tariff protection in such cases is hidden by the layering of tariffs, and effective protection on final goods may be much greater or smaller than nominal tariff rates would indicate. It is important to account for these intersectoral effects of the tax structure in order to understand the nature of resource allocation pressures.

PROBLEMS

1. Is it possible for a tariff to make a country worse off than in free trade?

2. Redraw Fig. 15.1 for the case in which the country exports X and imports Y.

3. Suppose a country produces two goods, X and Y, along a linear production transformation curve where X is the imported good and production is specialized in Y. Show the welfare losses from the imposition of a tariff on X and decompose these losses into production losses and consumption losses.

4. The government of the Republic of Korea at one time followed an aggressive policy of import protection with tariffs and export promotion with subsidies. Contrast this policy with one of free trade.

5. For the past several years, the United States has been subsidizing exports of grain. Analyze the welfare effects of this policy.

6. Suppose that instead of instituting an optimal import tariff, the government decides to use an optimal export tax. Using a methodology similar to that of Fig. 15.8, can you derive the optimal export tax formula? (Hint: in this case the home country would act as a monopolist in its export good).

7. Suppose a commodity is produced only after the introduction of a tariff on imports with which it competes. Will the usual effective-protection calculation be correct in this case?

8. Assume that yarn is the only input into cloth and that the proportion of yarn in the unit cost of cloth is 0.4 (that is, $a_{yc} = 0.4$). Let the nominal tariff rate on cloth be 25%. Compute the effective rates of protection to cloth when the yarn tariff is: (a) 0%, (b) 10%, (c) 25%, (d) 50%. Solve for the tariff rate on yarn that would make the effective rate on cloth zero.

9. Consider an industry X_1 with two intermediate inputs, X_{21} and X_{31}, and suppose that $a_{21} = 0.2$ and $a_{31} = 0.5$. Tariff rates are $t_1 = 30\%$, $t_2 = 20\%$, and $t_3 = 10\%$. Calculate the effective rate of protection on X_1.

10. Suppose that a small country exports both goods X_1 and X_{21}, where X_{21} is an input into X_1. Let $a_{21} = 0.3$ and suppose that the export tax rates are $t_1 = 25\%$ and $t_2 = 10\%$. Can you compute the effective rate of tax on X_1?

NOTES

1. For example, tariff revenue amounts to only 0.01 percent of total government revenue in the United Kingdom, 0.02 percent in Germany, and 1.56 percent in the United States. On the other hand, tariffs provide the government of Argentina with 13.31 percent of total revenue and the government of Ghana with 40.90 percent of all revenues. The source for these figures is International Monetary Fund (1986).

2. An *ad valorem* tax is one that is levied as a percentage of the value of the taxed goods, like a sales or excise tax. Not all tariffs are of this form. Some tariffs are specific tariffs, levied per unit of quantity, as in so many dollars per ton of fish. Frequently, specific and ad valorem tariffs are combined into compound tariffs.

3. A comprehensive treatment of the effects of various taxes on trade and welfare is given by Melvin (1975).

4. This point is credited to Lerner (1936), who assumed competitive markets in its proof. See also Kaempfer and Tower (1982) for extensions of numerous complications to the simple model.

5. Certain aspects of trade policy in the presence of domestic distortions are discussed in Bhagwati (1967, 1971), Johnson (1965), and Melvin (1975).

6. The original argument was made by Bickerdike (1906) and was formalized and generalized by a number of authors, including Graaff (1949).

7. See Johnson (1954) for a full discussion of the tariff war outcome and Markusen (1981) for an analysis of the opposite problem of cooperative tariff reduction. Note that the *threat* of retaliation by F might be sufficient to deter the initial decision by H to impose its optimal tariff, so there is a strategic element to this analysis as well.

8. Thus, we assume that the price of cars goes up by 20 percent, whether they are produced domestically or imported. Implicitly, this means that the importing country is small and that imported and domestic cars are perfect substitutes. We retain these assumptions with respect to intermediate inputs as well.

9. A further possibility is the existence of *negative value added,* which refers to the unusual situation in which an inefficient domestic activity is so heavily protected that it is induced to produce a certain output, despite the fact that at world prices, the value of that output is less than the value of the intermediate inputs. For example, heavily distorted economies produce some products, such as cars, that cannot be sold on world markets for a price that would cover input costs.

10. In the presence of multiple inputs into the production of some good j, the value added of j with protection on inputs will be

$$v_j' = (1 + t_j) - \sum_{i=1}^{n} a_{ij}(1 + t_i)$$

Here, a_{ij} denotes input-output coefficients, and t refers to the tariff rate on the output and on the inputs. To derive value added in free trade, this equation can be recalculated with all tariff rates set to zero. The resulting v_j' and v_j can then be substituted into Eq. (15.9) in order to calculate the effective rate.

11. See the paper by J. Berlinski and D. M. Schydlowsky (1982).

12. Recall the possibility that a tariff could raise welfare in the face of some other domestic distortion.

REFERENCES

Berlinski, J., and Schydlowsky, D. M. (1982). "Argentina." In B. Balassa, ed., *Development Strategies in Semi-industrial Economies,* Washington, DC: The World Bank.

Bhagwati, J. N. (1967). "Non-Economic Objectives and the Efficiency Properties of Trade." *Journal of Political Economy* 75: 738–742.

———. (1971). "The Generalized Theory of Distortions and Welfare." In J. Bhagwati et al., eds., *Trade, Balance of Payments and Growth: Essays in Honor of Charles P. Kindleberger,* Amsterdam: North-Holland.

Bickerdike, D. F. (1906). "The Theory of Incipient Taxes." *Economic Journal* 16: 529–535.

Corden, W. M. (1974). *Trade Policy and Economic Welfare.* Oxford: Clarendon Press.

Deardorff, A. V., and Stern, R. M. (1984). "The Effects of the Tokyo Round on the Structure of Protection." In R. E. Baldwin and A. O. Krueger, eds., *The Structure and Evolution of Recent U.S. Trade Policy.* Chicago: University of Chicago Press.

Graaff, J. de V. (1949). "On Optimal Tariff Structures." *Review of Economic Studies* 16: 47–59.

Johnson, H. G. (1954). "Optimal Tariffs and Retaliation." *Review of Economic Studies* 21: 142–153.

———. (1965). "Optimal Trade Intervention in the Presence of Domestic Distortions." In R. Caves et al., eds., *Trade, Growth and the Balance of Payments. Essays in Honor of G. Haberler.* New York: Rand McNally.

Kaempfer, W. H., and Tower, E. (1982). "The Balance of Payments Approach to Trade Tax Symmetry Theorems." *Weltwirtschafliches Archiv.* 118:148–165.

Lerner, A. (1936). "The Symmetry between Import and Export Taxes." *Economica* 11: 306–313.

Markusen, J. R. (1981). "The Distribution of Gains from Bilateral Tariff Reduction." *Journal of International Economics* 11: 553–572.

Melvin, J. R. (1975). *The Tax Structure and Canadian Trade.* Ottawa: Economic Council of Canada.

Yoo, Jung-ho. (1993). "The Political Economy of Protection Structure in Korea." In A. O. Krueger and T. Ito, eds., *Trade and Protectionism.* Chicago: University of Chicago Press.

CHAPTER
16

QUOTAS AND OTHER NONTARIFF BARRIERS

16.1 INTRODUCTION

We noted in Chapter 15 that import tariffs are the most common form of trade restriction and that they are simply a specific form of taxation. Tariffs impose no restrictions on the amount of a good that can be imported; consumers may acquire as much of the good as they are willing to pay for. Thus, tariffs directly affect the price of imports and only indirectly affect the quantity of imports via the effect of price increases on consumer and producer decisions.

While tariffs are the most widespread form of protection, a type of trade restriction in increasing use is the quantitative restriction, or *quota*. Quotas are ceilings on the quantities of imports allowed for particular goods. For example, a quota might state that no more than 500,000 cotton shirts or no more than 100,000 automobiles can be imported during some specific time period. Quantitative restrictions are widely used in many kinds of trade, including trade in agricultural goods and textiles. Where they are used, quotas are probably much more restrictive than tariffs. From 1966 to 1986, quota coverage ratios, or the percentage of goods for which imports are restricted by quotas, doubled in developed countries, and quotas are probably used even more widely by less-developed countries.

Quotas are, in a sense, the opposite of tariffs, in that quotas directly restrict the quantities of imports and only indirectly affect prices through the artificial scarcity that the quantity restriction creates. Yet, tariffs and quotas are fundamentally similar in that they both ultimately restrict the quantity of imports and raise their domestic prices. However, only under certain circumstances, which we will discuss later, do tariffs and quotas have identical effects on the importing economy.

16.2 EFFECTS OF QUOTA PROTECTION

In Fig. 16.1, the home country, which is assumed here to be too small to affect world prices, imports $C_x - Q_x$ units of X at the fixed world price ratio of p^* in free trade. Suppose a quota is imposed by the home country that restricts imports to only QR units of X per period. This quantitative restriction on imports of X leads to an artificial scarcity of X in H that, in turn, raises the price of X to both consumers and producers. Because the cost of QR units of X on the world market is still given by p^*, a new equilibrium following the imposition of the quota can be found by locating a trade triangle that is QR units long on the X side but still has a hypotenuse with a slope of p^*. One endpoint of the hypotenuse of the trade triangle will be a point along the production possibilities curve, and the other will be a point on a community indifference curve, such that the slopes of these two curves are the same. This new trade triangle shows the restricted level of imports of X allowed under the quota and the amount of exports of Y that must be used to purchase these imports at world prices. The common slope of the production frontier and the community indifference curve at the endpoints of the trade triangle is the new domestic price ratio, p = MRT = MRS, brought about by the artificial scarcity of X caused by the quota.

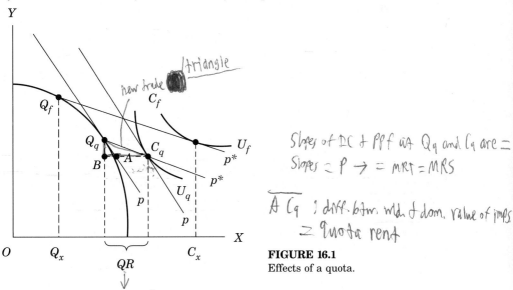

FIGURE 16.1
Effects of a quota.

Notice the similarity of this restricted-trade equilibrium to that shown in Fig. 15.1, where trade was restricted by an import tariff. Just as with the tariff, the quota lowers aggregate domestic welfare, in this case from U_f to U_q. We can similarly infer that this quota-induced movement toward autarky will actually benefit the scarce factor in the economy, according to the Stolper-Samuelson Theorem. Finally, the distance AC_q, which is the gap between the world price line p^* and the domestic price ratio p, represents the difference in the value of imports at world and domestic prices.

This gap between prices in the home and foreign countries was easily explained as the result of a tax when we analyzed tariffs in Chapter 15. In the case of a quota, however, there is no tax to compensate for the difference between foreign and domestic prices. Instead, some lucky group of importers is allowed to buy X very cheaply in Country F and sell it at a significant premium in Country H. A quota is simply a permit to import some good into a certain country during a specified time period. If the quota is actually restrictive, that is, if it actually creates an artificial scarcity in the importing country, it is said to be *binding*. Any binding quota has associated with it some value stemming from the artificial scarcity that the quota creates. This scarcity value of the quota is called a quota *rent.* In Fig. 16.1, export quantity BQ_q is worth BC_q units of imports at world prices but is worth only BA units of good X at domestic prices, indicating that the domestic price of the import good is indeed higher under the quota. Thus, the rent from quota QR, when measured in units of good X, is exactly the line segment AC_q. Referring again to Fig. 15.1, we have assumed that this rent is used for consumption purposes, achieving a final equilibrium at point C_q.

How does a group get to be lucky enough to earn these quota rents? The allocation of rents from import quotas depends on the method by which the quota rights are distributed by the government of the importing country. One simple allocative mechanism is to grant the import permits to firms currently importing the good according to the share of the import market that each firm has already captured. This mechanism will, to some extent, *offset* the losses incurred by importers from the restriction in the volume of trade by returning to them valuable quota rents. An alternative mechanism, frequently discussed by economists, but only rarely used by policy makers, is to auction the quota rights off to the highest bidder. Because the maximum bid that an importer would be willing to make for the right to import in the presence of a binding quota is exactly the difference between the home and foreign prices, auctioning the quota rights will allow the government to collect all of the quota rents as auction revenue.[1] Unfortunately, a much more common means of allocating import quota permits is to grant them to friends of the government as political favors, or with bribes of governmental officials. Because these quota-induced scarcity rents are economically valuable, firms may well expend real resources in trying to acquire them. This activity, which economists label *rent-seeking,* could come in many forms, including constructing lobbying headquarters in the capital city where quota decisions are made, building excessive importation or production capacity in anticipation of getting a larger share of a future import quota, and bribery. To the extent that rent-seeking results in a diversion of economic resources from their most efficient uses (as opposed to transfers of these rents among domestic citizens), the economy suffers further losses in national income.[2] Typically, analysts have found that this kind of resource waste is more pronounced in the presence of quotas than tariffs, which is why many economists believe that tariffs are a less costly means of import protection.

A final mechanism for establishing a quota is for the importing country to request that the exporting country voluntarily restrict its exports. Such a practice, known as a *voluntarily export restraint* (VER), leads to an allocation of quota rents among exporters in F rather than importers in H. However, when a VER is used as a protectionist barrier, the welfare implications for the home country are worse than those demonstrated in Fig. 16.1. Because the VER allows the foreign country to collect and benefit from any quota rents, domestic welfare falls to a level below U_q, which welfare level included the supplement to national income gained by collecting quota rents.

The effects of an import quota can also be analyzed by examining the excess-demand curve for imported good X. Figure 16.2 shows the excess demand curve for the home country, E_x. In an initial free trade equilibrium facing a perfectly elastic foreign excess demand curve E^*, the home country imports X_f units of good X at the world price of p^*. However, when a quota of QR is imposed on imports, the home excess demand curve is distorted to E_{xq} because QR is the maximum level of imports allowed by the quota at any price. This causes the price of X in H to rise to p.

We can also use an excess-demand graph to examine the impacts of quotas when the country imposing the quota is a large country, that is when it does not face fixed world prices. Figure 16.3 shows excess-demand curves for good X: E_x^h for H and E_x^f for F. The initial equilibrium has imports of X into H of X_h at price p^* being equal to exports of X_f from F. A binding quota,

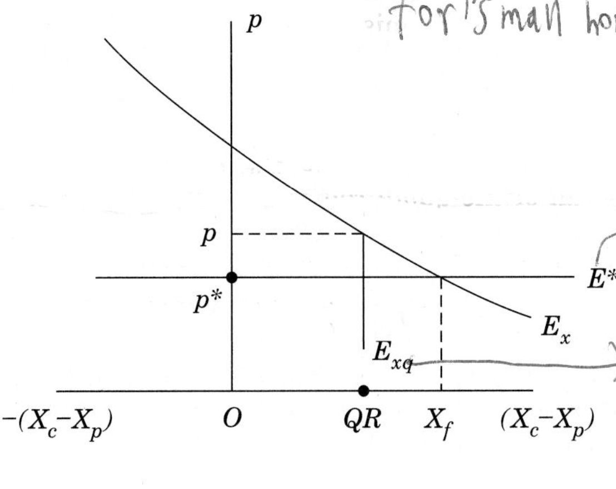

FIGURE 16.2
Quotas and excess demand.

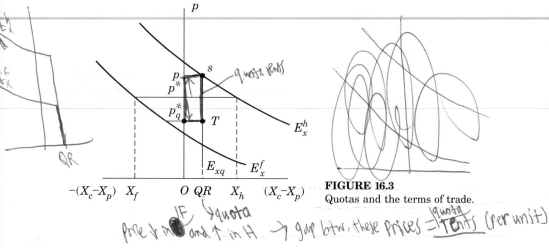

FIGURE 16.3
Quotas and the terms of trade.

QR, on imports of X by Country H creates a disequilibrium situation that leads to price and quantity changes for both countries. The first implication of the quota is that trade between H and F is now undertaken with respect to an excess demand curve in H that has been truncated at QR, E_{xq}. The quota allows a maximum of only QR units of X into H and, as we have only two countries in this illustration, only QR units of X out of F. At the initial, free trade equilibrium price of p^* there is now a surplus of X in F, which drives the price of X down to p_q^*. Meanwhile, in the home country, a shortage of X is created by the quota, and the relative price of X is raised to p.

In the new equilibrium, trade has been restricted to QR units of X, while the price of X has fallen in F and risen in H. The gap between these two prices, again, signifies the rents that accrue to those who possess the right to import X into H. Here, quota rents are given by the rectangle $pp_q^* TS$. Note that because H is a large country, the quota actually bestows a terms-of-trade effect. If the home country keeps the quota rents for itself, say in the form of an auctioned quota, then welfare in the home country can actually rise following imposition of the quota, as long the terms-of-trade effect from forcing the price of X down in F offsets the losses from the reduced volume-of-trade effect. At the other extreme, if the quota is imposed as a VER, then it is F that benefits from the terms-of-trade effect. However, welfare in H suffers from both a negative volume-of-trade effect and a negative terms-of-trade effect.

In light of this, why would a country ever ask its trading partners to voluntarily restrict their exports? The answer has three parts. First, as will be seen in Chapter 19, restrictions of trade are policy actions that redistribute income toward politically successful interest groups. Second, however, such policies may backfire if foreign countries retaliate when significant losses result from the policies of their trading partners. Third, as VERs are voluntary, they lie beyond the restrictions on trade policy imposed by the General Agreement on Tariffs and Trade.[3] Thus, a VER represents a way in which protection can be established for some important interest group at home, while mollifying foreign interests as well. As an example, during the 1980s, the United States asked Japan to make significant voluntary reductions of automobile exports to the United States. This request was in response to political pressure on the U.S. government from automobile workers and manufacturers for protection against imports. The result of the quota was a significant rise in vehicle prices in the United States. In the late 1980s, the United States rescinded its request to Japan for restricted automobile exports, but Japan, enjoying the benefits of the favorable terms-of-trade effects of the VER, did not immediately increase its exports.

16.3 COMPARING THE EFFECTS OF QUOTAS AND TARIFFS

Quotas and tariffs are not always interchangeable means of protecting producers from import competition. Depending on economic conditions, their impacts on an economy can differ substantially. In this section we will examine some of the many ways in which the effects of quotas and tariffs diverge. First, however, we will examine the conditions under which quotas and tariffs will have identical effects.

In Fig. 16.1, we noted that a quota restricting imports of good X to QR units per time period causes a new equilibrium trade triangle to emerge between the new consumption point C_q and the new production point Q_q. Domestic relative prices in this new equilibrium are p. Notice, however, that an ad valorem tariff on X imports equal to $p/p^* - 1$ will bring about the same equilibrium by causing domestic prices to diverge from world prices so that $p = p^*(1 + t)$. Such a tariff is almost identical in effect to the quota QR. The only difference is that QR generates quota rents of AC_q, while the tariff generates the same amount through government revenues. This last difference can be accounted for if the quota is distributed by governmental auction of the quota rights, or if the tariff revenue is distributed not by lump-sum transfer to the general public, but in exactly the same way as the quota rents would have been allocated (e.g., by parceling out the revenues to domestic importers who would have received the quota rights.)

This potential equivalence between a tariff and a quota can also been seen in the context of an excess-demand diagram. Figure 16.4 redraws Fig. 16.2 with the addition of E_{xt}, which is a tariff-distorted excess-demand curve for X in H. A quota of QR units of X per period of time will distort the domestic equilibrium to point E with Country H importing QR units at the fixed world price of p^*, while the domestic price ratio rises to p. If a tariff of rate $t = p/p^* - 1$ is imposed instead, the home excess-demand curve for Y shifts down to E_{xt}, but again we arrive at the distorted equilibrium point E. As long as the tariff revenue and quota rents are distributed in an identical fashion, the tariff and quota will have the same economic effects.

If this equivalence proposition is valid, one might wonder why both tariffs and quotas exist in importing nations. We now consider important

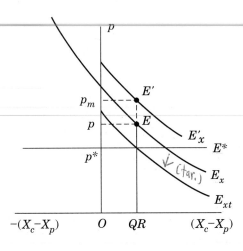

FIGURE 16.4
Quotas versus tariffs.

instances under which tariffs and quotas do not have identical effects on the economy.

Economic Growth

The equilibrium reached by both a tariff and a quota illustrated in Fig. 16.4 shows just how precarious the equivalence between both policies is. Any perturbation to the world price or to the domestic excess-demand curve will throw the equilibrium out of line and leave us with non-equivalent policy instruments. To illustrate the effects of such perturbations, we will first examine the case of economic growth and then the case of price fluctuations as caused by seasonal conditions, for example.

As considered here, economic growth is associated with increases in the resource endowments of Country H.[4] Suppose that the scarce factor in economy H grows larger. Invoking the Rybczynski theorem, the implication is that resources will be moved toward the import-competing sector as the country's economy becomes more like the world economy. This will have the effect of moving Country H's excess-demand curve down as the home autarky price moves toward the world price p^*.

Figure 16.5 shows how the economy will react to such an adjustment under quota or tariff protection. Initially, a quota of QR units is established. As the excess-demand curve shifts down from E_x to E'_x, the quota-distorted domestic price will gradually fall from p to p'. This happens because the same level of imports continues to arrive in H, but their relative scarcity falls as growth in the scarce factor allows Country H to produce more of its own X. On the other hand, suppose that an initially equivalent tariff is used to achieve a domestic price of p_q and import quantity of QR in H. As scarce-factor growth pushes down the excess-demand curve, the tariff-distorted excess demand curve will also fall from E_{xt} to E'_{xt} because it is the constant tariff *rate* that causes the excess-demand curve to adjust. The tariff will leave price in Country H the same at p because $p = p^*(1 + t)$ still holds, but the level of imports will shrink to X_t. In this case of growth in the scarce

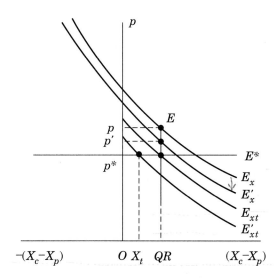

FIGURE 16.5
Quotas, tariffs and growth.

factor, the quota is actually preferable in welfare terms to the tariff because as growth proceeds, the quota becomes less binding (price adjusts toward p^*, which is the true opportunity cost of this good through imports from the rest of the world), while the tariff prevents price from falling. On the other hand, if the source of economic growth had been in the abundant factor, the quota would have become increasingly binding and domestic price would steadily rise. Under an initially equivalent tariff, this kind of growth would result in rising imports at an unchanged domestic price. Thus, welfare losses under the quota would become increasingly large relative to those under the tariff. A problem at the end of the chapter will demonstrate this case.

Price Fluctuations

The argument that tariffs and quotas are nonequivalent in the presence of growth generalizes to trade under any sort of changing economic conditions. Quotas are rigid with respect to import quantities, so all changes must be absorbed by price changes. (Of course, some changes, such as declining income during an economic recession, could cause the demand for imports to fall so far that the quota becomes nonbinding, resulting in changes in the quantities of imports.) Tariffs permit quantities of imports to change so that adjustment will occur in quantities (and also in prices as well if the importing nation is large). It is tempting to conjecture that economic changes will, therefore, lead to larger domestic price fluctuations under quotas than under tariffs. This is true with respect to domestic price responses to domestic changes (as in Fig. 16.5) but not with respect to changes that are foreign in origin. The argument is as follows.[5]

In general, the domestic and foreign price ratios are related by

$$p = p^*(1 + t) \qquad t > 0 \qquad (16.1)$$

If there is an import tariff, t is the fixed ad valorem rate of the tariff. If there is an import quota, however, we consider t be an "implicit tariff" rate that gives the difference between the foreign price and the price domestic consumers are willing to pay. In other words, t is the percentage difference between the world and domestic relative prices induced by the quota.

Suppose that a small open economy facing a perfectly elastic foreign excess-demand curve can choose between a tariff and a quota. Suppose also that the foreign excess-demand curve shifts up and down randomly. Under a tariff, the domestic price ratio will fluctuate in proportion to the foreign price fluctuation because t is fixed in Eq. (16.1). But under a quota, t varies inversely with the world price. That is, an increase in the foreign price p^* will narrow the gap between the world and domestic price ratios. Alternatively, a decrease in p^* will mean that domestic importers are willing to bid more for the import licenses, and thus the "implicit tariff" t is increased in value. The effect of this can be seen from Eq. (16.1). If any increase in p^* causes a fall in t, these changes will be partially or totally offsetting, with the result that the domestic price ratio fluctuates less than the world price ratio. Thus, the quota provides better insulation from foreign price fluctuations, whereas the tariff provides better insulation from fluctuations that are domestic in origin. This result should, however, be interpreted with care insofar as the stabilization of domestic prices does not necessarily constitute a welfare criterion that the government should pursue.

Domestic Monopoly

In Chapter 11 we discussed the importance of free international trade as an effective anti-monopoly policy. Because of the presence of economies of scale, and fixed costs in particular, many economies face the problem of being large enough to support only one or a few producers of some goods efficiently. However, opening up the economy to free international trade allows these countries to enjoy the benefits of competition among the firms of many nations. The key element here is referred to as the *contestable market hypothesis* by economists. A firm, even when it is the only producer of a certain good in a given jurisdiction, will behave more competitively than otherwise if its market is contestable. That is, a monopolist will avoid price increases if those increases are likely to attract new sellers onto the market.

Applying the contestable market hypothesis to trade policy analysis shows that monopolists will behave quite differently under tariffs and quotas. The simple reason is that a tariff leaves the domestic market contestable, albeit at the higher tariff-distorted price, while a quota, as a restriction on the quantity of sales onto a market, destroys the contestability of that market. Suppose a monopolistic producer in the domestic economy is protected by an import tariff. Any movement by that monopolist to restrict output and raise price above the current, tariff-distorted level will be offset by increasing amounts of imports from foreign competitors. If, on the other hand, the protection is rendered by binding import quota, the domestic monopolist can reduce output and raise prices without fear that additional imports will flood the domestic market and force price back down. In the context of Fig. 16.4, a domestic monopolist protected by a quota is able to restrict output, forcing the importing country's excess-demand curve (which reflects consumption minus production) to rise. Suppose the extent of monopoly power allows a shift up of E_x to E_x' in Fig. 16.4.[6] In this domestically monopolized market, import prices will rise to p_m when imports are artificially scarce due to a quota of QR, but prices remain at p with a tariff.

There are some additional problems with this analysis, however. First, how might we expect import quota permits to be distributed when there is a single domestic firm producing competing goods for the domestic market? The quota rights are more valuable to the competing domestic firm—because they increase that firm's market power—than they would be to non-producing importers. Consequently, if quota rights were auctioned by the government, a domestic monopolist might be expected to outbid all rivals for those rights and then pass the high cost of the quota permits on to consumers with higher prices of both the imported goods and the monopolist's own domestically produced goods.

Second, we are dealing with what gets called the *double-distortion problem* in the case of protection and imperfect competition. That is, the domestic economy is distorted not only by the protection of a tariff or quota but also by the presence of monopoly. Monopoly imposes welfare costs on an economy by inducing too little domestic output, but protection imposes welfare costs by inducing too much output. If a country switches from tariff protection to quota protection, it is giving license to domestic monopolists to cut output and raise prices. However, the lower levels of monopoly output may simply offset the distorted over-production arising from protection, and the economy may see an overall improvement in welfare.[7]

An interesting application of this problem arises in current attempts by numerous countries to liberalize their economies by relaxing trade barriers. The principles of the GATT have attempted to move nations in the direction of freer trade by having them convert quantitative restrictions to tariffs. This *tariffication* process allows countries to impose temporary tariffs that maintain domestic price levels. However, if the quotas were protecting domestic monopolies, they may have led those monopolistic firms to produce less output in exchange for a higher domestic price under the quota. Then, with the switch to tariffs at the same price levels, these firms may be induced to expand output, contrary to the underlying pattern of comparative advantage. This process may lead to the paradoxical outcome of liberalized trade policies' causing the volume of trade to shrink.[8]

16.4 OTHER NONTARIFF BARRIERS

Quotas are not the only nontariff method of restricting trade. There are many other policies, included with quotas in a category economists call *nontariff barriers* (NTBs), that can act directly or indirectly to restrict imports. There are corresponding measures that artificially restrict or promote exports in a way that tends to lower aggregate welfare for the export-promoting country (but, of course, raises welfare for certain groups within that country). However, in order to limit our discussion, we will focus on import restrictions. This should be sufficient to give an understanding of the issues involved.[9]

Quantitative Restrictions

This chapter has been devoted to an analysis of quantitative restrictions, but only two specific types, global quotas and VERs, have been examined. There are a number of other ways in which imports can be restricted using explicit quantitative restrictions (as opposed to some of the other implicit restrictions we will discuss). However, these other types of restrictions may differ from global quotas, they have many of the same general impacts, such as creating artificial shortages on domestic markets that drive up consumer prices and lead to a reallocation of resources.

While a global quota establishes a limit on imports of a certain good during some period of time, regardless of the country of origin of the good, many countries employ country-specific quotas. A country-specific quota is similar to a VER, but with the importing country retaining the quota rents. Country-specific quotas are commonly used in two ways. First, they may be imposed on a type of commodity. The United States, for instance, imposes limitations on imports of sugar on a country-by-country basis, with each specific exporting country having its own quota allotment of sugar exports. Trade in textiles and apparel is managed in much the same way; importing nations negotiate country-specific import targets with each significant exporter. One damaging outcome of such tightly managed trade is that the importer does not necessarily import from the least-cost source— that is, the source with the greatest comparative advantage. Another way in which country-specific quotas are used is to prohibit trade of several or all categories of goods with some specific country. This kind of trade embargo is called an *economic sanction* and is used for political and diplomatic ends, although it does cause the same kinds of domestic market disruptions that other trade barriers cause.[10]

Quantitative restrictions can interfere with trade even when they are not binding. It is often the case, particularly in developing countries, that importers must obtain licenses to import certain goods. These licenses require the importer to spend time filling out forms and waiting for official permission. Such activities represent very real costs even though they do not appear in any official accounting figures. These costs include the opportunity costs of the importer's time, interest costs due to time delays, the cost of uncertainty over whether or not a license will be granted, the resource costs of additional bureaucrats, and so on. Import licenses, whether from binding quotas or not, also present the opportunity for bureaucrats to engage in arbitrary and unfair practices in issuing licenses (e.g., bureaucrats could discriminate in favor of friends or those willing to pay bribes).

Price and Earnings Restrictions

There are many ways besides the use of ad valorem tariffs in which government regulations can directly affect the price of imports. Another kind of tariff restriction is a specific tariff charged per unit of a good rather than per unit of value of the good. Specific tariffs have the effect of taxing lower-quality items more heavily than higher-quality items. Suppose a $1,000 levy is imposed on all motorized, wheeled vehicles. The price to consumers of a simple motorcycle import might rise from $2,000 to $3,000 as a result of the specific tax (a 50-percent rise), while an imported luxury car might rise in price from $50,000 to $51,000 (a 2-percent rise). Such a taxation policy heavily distorts consumer choices governing the quality of goods imported.

When tariffs are not employed, there are other methods a government can use to raise the costs of importing. Importers may be required to post bonds or make advance deposits against taxes that they will have to pay in the process of selling their goods in some importing country. For instance, suppose there is a 10-percent tariff against bicycle imports and that importers are required to pay that amount in advance of shipping goods. This requirement raises the effective penalty of the tax, for importers must now finance the advance as well as the purchase of foreign-made goods in order to sell on the domestic market. This kind of practice is used when an anti-dumping duty is being considered against exporters suspected of unfairly dumping goods on the domestic market. While the anti-dumping charge is pending (under investigation), the importer must pay a deposit against the eventuality that a negative ruling will come about.

In general, domestic tax laws can be applied to foreign firms in a way that is highly discriminatory against imports. Anyone who has had no involvement with tax laws other than filling out a yearly income tax return is unaware of the complexity of domestic tax policies. There are many ways to use these laws to discriminate against foreign goods and firms, and all countries avail themselves of these opportunities to some degree. There was, for example, a great deal of controversy between Canada and the United States in the early 1980s when Canada introduced highly discriminatory taxation laws dealing with oil and natural gas. A slightly different version of this problem arises with government-owned corporations, which are often given implicit or explicit competitive advantages over foreign firms. A common example of this in recent decades might be the favorable treatments given to government-owned airlines.

Another way to restrict imports is to regulate the earnings from importing by means of *exchange controls*. With exchange control, importers face restrictions not on imports per se, but on their ability either to buy the foreign currency needed to pay for imports or to turn earnings in domestic currency into foreign currency to pay the exporting country. Exchange control, which is very common in developing countries, suffers the same problems as import licensing and generally discourages the development of new markets by exporters.

Trade-Restricting Regulations

Many common forms of import restrictions come in the form of government regulations that may directly or indirectly inhibit the volume of trade. For example, governments have the right to issue regulations governing technical and safety standards for products. A government standard regulating pesticide use in food production could limit imports from nations that do not observe this standard. Such standards should be adopted to protect consumer health and safety, not to discriminate against imports, though the latter is often the case.[11]

To amplify this point, note the importance to consumers of knowing what is in the goods they buy. Consequently, packaging, labeling, and advertising regulations, as well as health, safety, sanitary, and quality specifications, are important elements of the government's regulatory structure designed to promote consumer welfare. Much of this regulatory structure is designed to correct possible problems, such as misleading advertising, in an otherwise unregulated market place. However, in the presence of international trade, there is the possibility for discriminatory application of such regulations against imports. In many cases, regulatory requirements do make good economic sense because they correct market externalities and do not discriminate against foreign goods per se. An example might be the U.S. requirements concerning safety and emission controls for automobiles. But in other cases there would seem to be little purpose in the regulations other than to harass importers. For instance, if meat products require government grading at the time of processing, the absence of grading inspectors in foreign countries could make most meat imports illegal.

Another example is the frequent use of government procurement regulations, in which nations provide strong preferences to domestic suppliers of various products, such as military items. Governments are often required by law to do this. This is, in fact, not a trivial issue, for in many countries, spending by the various levels of government adds up to a sizable proportion of GNP. Purchasing more expensive domestic goods instead of cheaper foreign goods raises costs to taxpayers and consumers and distorts the allocation of resources, just as tariffs do.

Another common form of trade-inhibiting regulation is the domestic content requirement. In the contemporary, complex world of international trade, final goods often contain many levels of intermediate inputs that have been traded back and forth between countries before final consumption takes place. Automobiles might be assembled in Mexico with an engine made in the United States that has an engine block milled in Mexico made of American steel. A domestic content provision forces importers to import goods that are made of a certain percentage of domestically produced components. If the domestic content provision is high enough, this amounts to an actual prohibition of trade, even though there might be no tariff or quota on the imported good per se. In fact, such restrictions are far more common when placed on the domestic operations of foreign firms that engage in foreign direct investment in production facilities in the regulating country. In many countries, governments place trade-related requirements on the operations of multinational enterprises within their borders, including minimum amounts of domestic components to be used in production or maximum amounts of imports to be brought in for production.[12]

16.5 ESTIMATES OF THE COST OF PROTECTION

Our analysis of tariffs and quotas has demonstrated that they have potentially important effects on prices, production, consumption, and economic welfare. It is natural for economists to wonder about how significant these effects are in practice. The potential welfare impacts have attracted considerable attention from analysts who apply some of these theoretical notions to real-world data in the presence of trade restrictions.

Before discussing some of these studies, we make an important point about measuring these effects. For now, let country H be a small importer. Figure 16.6 reproduces some of the welfare effects we have already discussed. Recall that if country H imposes a tariff, consumption moves from C_f to C_t. We decomposed this loss in utility into a loss from inefficient specialization (the economy's production point moves from Q_f to Q_t) and a loss from inefficient consumption (the change in domestic prices causes consumers to move from point C_s to point C_t). We would like to compute these changes in utility directly, but doing so is virtually impossible because utility indexes are not readily measurable. In principle, however, we can calculate these changes in terms of national income sacrificed because of these inefficiencies. Suppose

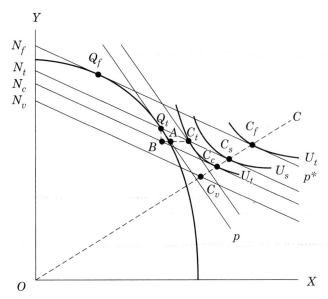

FIGURE 16.6
National income losses from trade restrictions.

we measure national income in terms of good Y, using world relative prices p^*. The loss in national income associated with inefficient production is clearly the distance $N_f - N_t$. The further reduction in national income associated with the loss on the consumption side would depend on where some p^* line is tangent to indifference curve U_t. To simplify matters, we make the assumption that preferences are homothetic, so that indifference curves will be tangent to world price lines along ray OC. Thus, at point C_c, the economy is equally well off as at point C_t, and the associated loss in national income associated with the inefficient consumption is the distance $N_t - N_c$. The total inefficiency loss, which economists term the *deadweight loss* from the tariff, is then the distance $N_f - N_c$. It measures the sacrifice in real national income that the economy absorbs in order to have the tariff in place. An alternative explanation is that this is the quantity of good Y that would have to be paid to consumers in order for them to agree to have the tariff imposed. The fact that such compensation is not often paid suggests that there must be a number of political and noneconomic explanations for the fairly common existence of import barriers, which is an issue we treat analytically in Chapter 19.

If the trade restriction is a quota, the same analysis applies, so long as there is no distortionary rent-seeking and so long as the quota rents are spent in the same manner as the tariff revenue. However, an additional cost emerges if the restriction is a VER. In this case, the quota rents, distance AC_t, are ceded to the foreign country. This would induce some change in the final consumption equilibrium to a point on an indifference curve lower than U_t.[13] In turn, domestic utility would be represented by point C_v, where this lower indifference curve would be tangent to the world price line. The additional loss in national income for Country H is then the distance $N_c - N_v$.

Finally, if Country H were large, we would need to account for any changes in the terms of trade that would ensue from a trade restriction. In this case, as we know, there will be offsetting gains in national income from these price changes, which could even leave the importing nation better off.

As the reader might imagine, actually calculating these measures of utility loss is quite difficult, and very few economists have attempted to do so. Rather, most analysts have relied on various approximations based on simplified assumptions. The most common approach is to assume that the import commodity on which a barrier is placed represents such a small proportion of the domestic economy that it can be treated with partial-equilibrium analysis (an assumption that is clearly at odds with standard trade theory). Clearly, such approaches tend to underestimate the welfare effects of protection because they ignore the impacts on consumption and production of other goods.

The basic partial-equilibrium analysis is presented in Figs. 16.7 and 16.8. In Fig. 16.7, the curves S and D represent the supply and demand curves for good X within Country H. At the initial free trade equilibrium, the economy imports quantity Q_1Q_2 of good X at price p_x^* (for now we ignore foreign supply behavior). A standard assumption is that the utility level

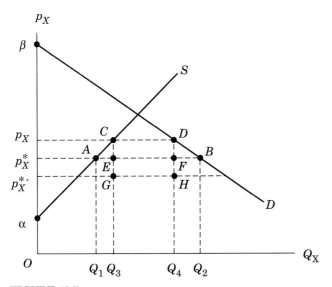

FIGURE 16.7
Partial-equilibrium effects of an import restriction.

consumers attain at point B may be measured by the concept of *consumer surplus,* which in this simple diagram is the area $\beta p_x^* B$. The notion is simply that the area under the demand curve but above market price measures all of the excess utility inframarginal consumers gain from being able to purchase all units at the common price.[14] A second assumption is that the excess benefits that domestic firms experience at point A may be measured by the concept of *producer surplus,* which is area $\alpha p_x^* A$. The idea here is that producers are willing to supply good X along the supply curve, so there are

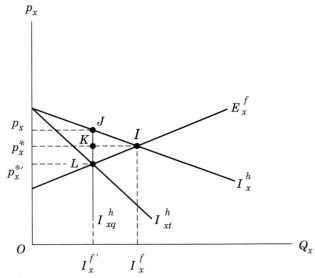

FIGURE 16.8
Partial-equilibrium trade effects of an import restriction.

inframarginal benefits associated with selling all units of domestic output at the common market price.[15]

Now allow Country H to impose a tariff or quota that raises the domestic price to p_x and reduces the foreign price to $p_x^{*'}$ (that is, we assume that H is large). Of interest here are the resulting welfare changes. It is clear that consumer surplus in H falls by the area $p_x p_x^* BD$. Part of this loss in consumer utility represents an income transfer to domestic firms in the form of higher producer surplus, area $p_x p_x^* AC$. Unless we have some reason to weight the dollar losses to consumers differently than the gains to producers, this transfer has no net effect in welfare. Similarly, part of the consumer loss represents a transfer from consumers to the recipients of the tariff revenue or quota rents. This transfer is the area $CEFD$. To sum up these effects, Country H experiences deadweight efficiency losses of CAE and DFB. These are the partial-equilibrium counterparts to the losses discussed earlier. However, notice that because foreign price is forced down, the full amount of tariff revenue or quota rents is area $CGHD$. The lower rectangle $EGHF$ represents a gain to Country H from the terms-of-trade improvement. Thus, the overall welfare effect in H is $EGHF - CAE - DFB$. Country F, on the other hand, is worse off because its volume of trade is reduced and it suffers a deterioration in its terms of trade. If, however, the restriction had been a VER for which F earned the rents, the analysis would be somewhat different.

A more convenient representation of these effects is given in Fig. 16.8, which is a partial-equilibrium diagram of international trade in good X. The line I_x^h is the import-demand curve in H (that is, it is the horizontal difference between S and D in the import region in Fig. 16.7), and the line E_x^f is the export-supply curve for Country F. The free trade equilibrium is at point I, with imports equal to OI_{xf} (equal to $Q_1 Q_2$ in Fig. 16.7). When Country H imposes a tariff, its tariff-distorted import-demand curve becomes I_{xt}^h (it would be I_{xq}^h if an import-equivalent quota were introduced). Trade volume shrinks to OI'_{xf}, domestic price in H rises to p_x, and foreign price falls to $p_x^{*'}$. The higher price in H generates the following welfare effects: deadweight efficiency losses of area JKI (the sum of ACE and DFB in Fig. 16.7) and tariff revenue or quota rents of $p_x p_x^{*'} LJ$, which consist of a transfer from consumers (area $p_x p_x^* KJ$) to revenue receipts and a terms-of-trade gain (area $p_x^* p_x^{*'} LK$). Thus, Country H experiences a net gain or loss from the trade barrier of area $p_x^* p_x^{*'} LK - JKI$.[16] On the other hand, Country F experiences a terms-of-trade loss equal to H's terms-of-trade gain (this is simply an income transfer between nations) and a further efficiency loss of area KLI. However, note that if the restriction were a VER, so that Country F achieved a terms-of-trade gain by selling good X at price p_x, the welfare effect in H would be a loss of $p_x p_x^* IJ$, and the effect in F would be a net gain or loss of $p_x p_x^* KJ - KLI$. In any case, the global net welfare loss is JLI.

Many economists have used these principles to calculate estimates of the welfare effects of various trade barriers. Of course, the actual approaches are more sophisticated than these diagrams would suggest. Notice that the results of such exercises depend critically on the elasticities of supply and demand that are assumed to exist, so there is a wide range of estimates available of the effects of major trade barriers. We review a small subset of studies of U.S. trade protection here, presenting average estimates.[17]

In Table 16.1 we show recent estimates of the costs of some major U.S. trade actions. For example, the United States has had long-standing import quotas on dairy products (cheese, ice cream, and so on). Available estimates suggest that, per year, the dairy quotas cost U.S. consumers some $5.5 billion per year, while transferring nearly $4 billion to dairy farmers and processors.[18] Quota rents are perhaps $250 million per year and are earned by U.S. dairy importers. If we suppose that around half of that represents a transfer from U.S. consumers to quota recipients, the net deadweight efficiency loss to the United States (areas *CAE* and *DFB* in Fig. 16.7) amount to $1.4 billion. The remaining rents are a gain for the United States, generating an overall welfare loss of $1.28 billion per year. Foreign exporters are estimated to lose $140 million per year because of U.S. dairy quotas. The United States also has quotas on imported sugar, except that U.S. law allows foreign exporters to charge the American price for sugar, thereby earning the quota rents. American welfare is harmed by perhaps $460 million per year, while foreign welfare is reduced by $950 million per year because the deadweight efficiency losses from producing less sugar far outweigh the terms-of-trade gains from the quota rents.

We have mentioned the automobile VERs before. These were negotiated with Japan in the early 1980s and by 1985 were estimated to cost U.S. consumers some $5.8 billion per year in higher car prices. In total, welfare was reduced by perhaps $3.2 billion per year. However, the VER rents earned by Japanese automobile firms (and the rents earned by European firms because they could also raise their prices in the U.S. market) actually resulted in a welfare gain for foreign countries. The most costly import barriers are the bilateral VERs imposed on textiles and apparel by the United States under the terms of the Multifiber Arrangement (MFA). These restrictions are estimated to cost American consumers $27 billion per year in higher clothing prices. Quota rents are earned by foreign countries so that the United States suffers a large overall welfare loss. However, the quota rents are insufficient to compensate for the large deadweight efficiency losses in the exporting nations from the VERs, and those nations annually lose some $5.5 billion. Because similar VERs are imposed under the MFA by most other developed nations, the global welfare losses from textiles protection are quite large indeed.

Finally we mention the interesting case of a small "trade war" between the United States and Canada. In 1986 the United States imposed a 15 percent tariff on imports of construction lumber from Canada, charging that because Canadian provinces charged their loggers very low fees to harvest trees, the resulting lumber exports were effectively subsidized.[19] The effect of this tariff was actually to raise U.S. welfare by virtue of large terms-of-trade gains. After all, the United States is Canada's largest market

TABLE 16.1
Average estimates of the annual costs of U.S. import protection, mid- to late-1980s ($billions)

Product	Barrier	Consumer loss	Producer gain	U.S. DW loss	Revenues or rents	Foreign DW loss	U.S. welfare	Foreign welfare
Dairy products	Quotas	-5.50	+3.97	-1.40	+0.25(US)	-0.02	-1.28	-0.14
Sugar	Quotas	-1.30	+0.84	-0.30	+0.31(F)	-1.11	-0.46	-0.95
Automobiles	VERs	-5.80	+2.60	-0.70	+5.00(F)	-1.50	-3.20	+1.00
Machine tools	VERs	-0.54	+0.16	-0.20	+0.35(F)	na	-0.38	na
Carbon steel	VERs	-6.80	+3.80	-2.00	+2.00(F)	na	-3.00	na
Textiles and apparel	VERs	-27.00	+19.00	-5.50	+5.00(F)	-8.00	-8.00	-5.50
Lumber part 1	Tariff	-0.57	+0.41	-0.03	+0.34(US)	-0.05	+0.18	-0.26
Lumber part 2	Export tax*	-0.57	+0.41	-0.03	+0.34(F)	-0.05	-0.16	+0.08

Sources: G. Haufbauer, D. Berliner, and K. Elliot (1986), G. Hufbauer and K. Elliot (1994), J. de Melo and D. Tarr (1992), K. Maskus (1989), R. Feenstra (1992), and J. Kalt (1988).

Note: For purposes of calculating deadweight losses, estimated revenues or rents were divided equally between a higher U.S. price and a lower foreign price, except in the case of lumber. The export tax in "Lumber Part 2" refers to a Canadian tax on its exports of lumber to the United States.

by far and therefore has significant price-setting power. Canada's welfare declined, of course, because of the inefficiencies imposed on the economy and because of the terms-of-trade loss. After intense negotiations, the two countries agreed to replace the American import tariff with a Canadian *export tax,* which had the same effect on prices and efficiency losses in both countries but which served to shift the tax revenues from the United States to Canada. Accordingly, the net welfare effect seems to have been negative for the United States and positive for Canada, at least in this simple framework.[20] Note the interesting implication of this case and the fact that most of the quantitative trade barriers allow the foreign countries to earn quota rents; as a matter of policy, the United States often seems to prefer transferring trade-policy revenues or rents to exporting partners. Presumably, this is done in order to maintain good foreign relations.

We close this section with some important observations on these cost estimates. First, many have pointed out that these welfare costs of protection are quite small in relation to economic activity. For example, the sum of the U.S. deadweight losses in Table 16.1 is $10.13 billion, while overall welfare losses add up to $16.48 billion. In 1986, however, American GNP was $4.3 trillion. Thus, the net welfare costs of these barriers, the most visible of U.S. import restrictions, were around 0.3 percent of GNP. This may seem too small a price to warrant much concern about the effects of trade protection or to warrant complicated international negotiations over trade liberalization.

However, there are other costs to consider. First, even if net costs are low, consumer costs are substantially higher. They amount to some $47.5 billion in Table 16.1, or 1.1 percent of GNP. Moreover, this represents a particularly costly means of taxing individuals to achieve some goal associated with trade protection. For example, it is estimated that the auto VERs protected perhaps 55,000 U.S. manufacturing jobs from destruction by imports, suggesting that consumers were implicitly taxed around $105,000 per job. In principle, it would have been far cheaper to establish a direct tax in order to pay retraining and relocation subsidies to U.S. autoworkers or even simply to pay them their prior wages. Second, we have pointed out that most of the estimates available are based on partial equilibrium calculations. Studies based on general equilibrium models tend to find higher net costs of protection. Third, the estimates in Table 16.1 do not attempt to measure the resource wastes from rent-seeking activity as firms try to convince the U.S. government to adopt and maintain these trade barriers. Fourth, it is surely the case that the imposition of VERs on autos, machine tools, and other manufactured goods has expanded the domestic market power of U.S. firms, inducing further price increases and consumer costs that are not accounted for in those figures.

Perhaps most significantly, however, the estimates we have discussed present results based generally on *static* models with constant returns to scale. If we also try to account for the costs imposed by trade protection on the economy from having smaller economies of scale and limited industry rationalization, the apparent welfare costs can be larger. For example, in the study by R. Harris that we reviewed in Chapter 14, the elimination of tariffs on trade between the United States and Canada was expected to expand scale economies and raise worker productivity in Canadian industries, thereby substantially raising the expected welfare gains to Canada from the free trade agreement. Moreover, there may well be significant *dynamic* gains from trade liberalization associated with technological improvement and improved resource allocation over time. To date, such effects have not been measured very satisfactorily.

16.6   CONCLUDING REMARKS

Nontariff barriers are similar to tariffs in a very basic sense. Nontariff barriers restrict trade, raise import prices, and redistribute income just as tariffs do. The most common NTBs are probably quotas, which impose quantitative restrictions on imports. We also discussed voluntary export restraints and other forms of quantitative trade restrictions. The main conclusions from our analysis include the following.

1. There are circumstances under which quotas and tariffs have identical effects. Major circumstances in which quotas and tariffs are *not* equivalent include: (a) the issuing of quotas by methods other than license auction, (b) domestic growth and preference shifts, (c) domestic or foreign price fluctuations, and (d) domestic monopoly power.

2. The welfare effects of tariffs are easier to measure than those of nontariff barriers, for several reasons. First, tariffs are direct and measurable, while many NTBs, such as discriminatory taxes or regulations and import licensing, are indirect and hard to measure. It is interesting to note that economists generally try to convert nontariff barriers to tariff equivalents when trying to assess the impact of NTBs on various domestic variables. Second, tariffs are a visible form of taxation, at least to the affected businesses, whereas NTBs tend to be less apparent in their operations and effects. The visibility and measurability of tariffs is important in helping to simplify trade liberalization negotiations. Third, revenues created by tariffs are earned by the government treasury, while the rents from many NTBs (except in the rare case of auctioned quotas) generally end up in the hands of private companies and individuals, often in a highly arbitrary manner. This fact inevitably provides incentives for rent-seeking behavior that wastes economic resources. Fourth, tariffs probably cost less to administrate, largely because the red tape associated with numerous quantitative import barriers tends to lead to a waste of time and effort on the part of importers working their way through the bureaucratic process. Finally, as we discussed earlier, quantitative import barriers tend to reduce the contestability of domestic markets far more than do tariffs, suggesting that NTBs are more costly in domestic welfare terms. Of course, this very fact helps explain why domestic firms

typically prefer to be protected by quantitative restrictions rather than trade taxes.

3. There are many numerical estimates of the welfare costs and benefits of tariffs and NTBs, though most are of a partial-equilibrium nature. These studies typically find that the static net welfare effects, including deadweight losses and international rent transfers, are quite small as a percentage of national output. However, such estimates tend to miss important effects on welfare arising from the fact that trade barriers may well inhibit the attainment of scale economies, industry rationalization, and dynamic competition and growth.

PROBLEMS

1. Suppose that a small country reaches an agreement with its trade partners to limit its imports by use of a VER. Show the welfare effects of this trade restriction for the importing country.
2. Draw a diagram such as Fig. 16.3 in which one country has an import quota and the other an export quota. What are the equilibrium terms of trade?
3. Suppose the domestic excess demand for some good grows. Show what happens if the domestic market is protected by a quota or an initially equivalent tariff. Which instrument leads to the better welfare outcome for the country?
4. We know from earlier chapters that domestic factor prices depend on domestic commodity prices and outputs. Suppose X is labor-intensive. Compare the effects on the real wage under tariffs and quotas as the economy grows, as in Fig. 16.5.
5. In light of our analysis of monopoly, discuss the use of auction quotas with respect to the resulting price and quantity decisions of a domestic monopolist. If the monopolist gains control of the entire import quota allotment, how much will the monopolist produce domestically?

NOTES

1. Strictly speaking, this is true only if the auction takes place among perfectly competitive bidders. Alternatively, if only a few importing firms bid for the important licenses, there would emerge some sharing of the quota rents between the firms and the government.
2. Rent-seeking was initially analyzed by A. Krueger (1974), who also showed that the implied welfare costs from this activity in highly distorted economies can be significant. Rent-seeking is a specific version of the general process called *directly-unproductive-profit-seeking,* as analyzed by J. Bhagwati (1982).
3. The General Agreement of Tariffs and Trade is typically referred to as the GATT. See Chapter 20 for a detailed treatment.
4. Alternatively, we could analyze the effects of shifts in preferences for good X, which exercise we leave to the reader.
5. See Fishelson and Flatters (1975) and Young (1979).
6. Determining exactly how this excess-demand curve would shift is problematic because the extent of the shift depends on the cost curves of the domestic monopolist.
7. See Bhagwati (1968) and Kaempfer, McClure and Willet (1989).
8. See Kaempfer and Marks (1993).

9. In Chapter 20, *Administered Protection,* we go into much more detail discussing the actual practice of protection, including such measures as countervailing duties and anti-dumping tariffs and safeguards. Baldwin (1974) also presents a good general discussion of various measures of protection.
10. See Kaempfer and Lowenberg (1988) for an analysis of the political economy of the use of international economic sanctions.
11. We discuss issues of regulation and trade more fully in Chapter 20.
12. One common example of such provision is in trade in advanced military weaponry. Sweden, for instance, will import U.S. fighter planes only if a considerable part of the plane is actually built in Sweden or is made of Swedish components.
13. The precise equilibrium would depend on preferences and the production frontier in country H, which we do not consider further.
14. Strictly speaking, this makes sense only if D is an income-compensated demand curve or if changes in income do not affect the demand for good X. Otherwise, as price changes, so will real national income, shifting this demand curve and complicating the computation of consumer surplus. This qualification is rarely considered in applied work.
15. Producer surplus is most appropriately considered rents to the specific factors in the domestic X industry.
16. An appropriate way of considering JKI as a deadweight loss is to note that the economy could import $I'_{xf}I_{xf}$ units of X at the free trade price and enjoy net gains (consumer surplus gains minus producer surplus losses) of $JI'_{xf}I_{xf}I$.
17. R. Feenstra (1992) provides a useful review of recent work on U.S. trade barriers.
18. It is interesting to note that the monetary benefits of trade protection are often embedded (or "capitalized") in the prices of the assets they protect, such as farmland or cows. It has been estimated that these producer benefits amount to $450 per dairy cow.
19. This is an example of a *countervailing duty,* which we consider in detail in Chapter 20.
20. Canada removed its tax in late 1993, arguing that its extraction fees and other charges were sufficiently raised to avoid any export subsidization. As of mid-1994, however, the United States was threatening to reimpose its tariff.

REFERENCES

Baldwin, R. E. (1974). "Nontariff Distortions of International Trade." In R. E. Baldwin and J. D. Richardson, eds., *International Trade and Finance.* Boston: Little, Brown.

Bhagwati, J. N. (1968). "More on the Equivalence of Tariffs and Quotas." *American Economic Review* 58: 142–146.

———.(1982). "Directly-unproductive Profit-seeking (DUP) Activities." *Journal of Political Economy* 90: 988–1002.

Feenstra, R. C. (1992). "How Costly Is Protectionism?" *Journal of Economic Perspectives* 6: 159–178.

Hufbauer, G. C., Berliner, D. T., and Elliot, K. A. (1986). *Trade Protection in the United States: 31 Case Studies.* Washington: Institute for International Economics.

Hufbauer, G. C., and Elliot, K. A. (1994). *Measuring the Costs of Protection in the United States.* Washington: Institute for International Economics.

Kaempfer, W. H., and Lowenberg, A. D. (1988). "The Theory of International Economic Sanctions: A Public Choice Approach." *American Economic Review* 78: 786–793.

Kaempfer, W. H., and Marks, S. V. (1994). "The Possibility of Inefficient Liberalization through Tariffication." *Review of International Economics* 2:123–130.

Kaempfer, W. H., McClure, H., and Willett, T. D. (1989). "Incremental Protection and Efficient Political Choice between Tariffs and Quotas." *Canadian Journal of Economics* 22: 228–236.

Kalt, J. P. (1988). "The Political Economy of Protectionism: Tariffs and Retaliation in the Timber Industry." In R. E. Baldwin, ed., *Trade Policy Issues and Empirical Analysis.* Chicago: University of Chicago Press, 339–364.

Krueger, A. O. (1974). "The Political Economy of the Rent-Seeking Society." *American Economic Review* 69: 291–303.

Maskus, K. E. (1989). "Large Costs and Small Benefits of the American Sugar Programme." *The World Economy* 12: 85–104.

de Melo, J., and Tarr, D. (1992). *A General Equilibrium Analysis of U.S. Foreign Trade Policy.* Cambridge: MIT Press.

Young, L. (1979). "Ranking Optimal Tariffs and Quotas for a Large Country under Uncertainty." *Journal of International Economics* 9: 249–264.

IMPERFECT COMPETITION, INCREASING RETURNS, AND STRATEGIC TRADE POLICY

17.1 INTRODUCTION

An interesting and important phenomenon occurs when governments are observed to act as agents in support of large domestic firms in the international marketplace. Certain governmental actions are designed to give domestic firms strong advantages over foreign rivals in competing for international business. These actions often involve some direct or indirect form of subsidy that lowers the production costs of the domestic firms relative to their competitors' costs.

Although such subsidies or other forms of support may increase profits for the national firms, analysis in previous chapters (e.g., Chapter 10) should warn us that this in no way implies that these subsidies are welfare-improving for the country. On the other hand, knowing that large, imperfectly competitive firms are "under-producing" (producing outputs for which price exceeds marginal cost) might make us suspect that measures to stimulate the production and sales of large domestic firms are welfare-improving.

During the decade of the 1980s, numerous scientific papers were produced that examined trade policies such as tariffs and quotas under conditions of imperfect competition and increasing returns to scale. This body of work has become known as the "strategic trade policy literature," however inapt the apellation. Many interesting models in the literature produced non-traditional results, such as a finding that a production subsidy or an export subsidy can improve welfare. This result never holds in a competitive, distortion-free environment. Other authors changed the basic assumptions of some models in seemingly harmless ways, thereby completely reversing the findings.

The resulting literature is full of special cases, models, and results that do not generalize in any simple fashion. The strategic trade policy literature is not a useful guide to government policy at this time. Yet, taken together, this collection of special cases may help us better understand how our global economy's trade is increasingly dominated by large, multinational firms. In this chapter, we will examine a number of special cases in order to get a sense of the strategic trade policy literature and to become familiar with some differing economic environments and the results they produce. In particular, we will consider the degree of competitiveness and whether or not firms can enter or exit an industry in response to changing profits. The final sections of the chapter consider a few other important dimensions of strategic trade policy.

17.2   EXPORT RIVALRY I: COURNOT COMPETITION[1]

In this section and the next, we will consider the simplest possible model. There are two countries, Home and Foreign, each having a single firm that produces a similar product. We will assume that there are no domestic sales and that each firm sells its product only to a third country. The result of this unlikely assumption is that changes in profits of one nation's firm are equivalent to changes in national welfare. There is no conflict between a profit increase from higher prices and a reduction in domestic consumers' welfare. The job of a government in this model is very simple: help the domestic firm earn the highest possible profit in the international marketplace.[2]

Here we will present a diagrammatic analysis; a formal algebraic analysis appears in Section 17.4 for those who are interested. A Cournot model, in which a firm can be thought of as choosing its best output given the output of the other firm, is characterized by a construction called a *reaction curve,* which gives the firm's optimal output for every possible output of its rival.

The reaction curve for the Home firm is shown in Fig. 17.1 as RC_h. The reaction curve is downward-sloping: as X_f increases, the market remaining for the Home firm essentially shrinks, making it optimal for the Home firm

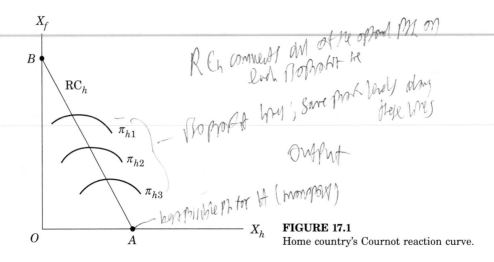

[handwritten annotations:]
RC_h connects all of the optimal P/L on each Isoprofit he

Isoprofit line; Same profit level along these lines

Output

highest possible P/L for H (monopoly)

FIGURE 17.1
Home country's Cournot reaction curve.

to reduce its output, X_h. Point A in Fig. 17.1 is the output the Home firm would produce if the Foreign firm produced nothing, and point B is the level of X_f at which the Home firm quits producing entirely.

With some further analysis, we could derive a set of iso-profit curves for the Home firm, shown as $\pi_{h1} < \pi_{h2} < \pi_{h3}$. Each point on one iso-profit curve yields the same level of profits for the Home firm. The Home firm's profits improve as its rival's output, X_f, decreases, so the Home firm moves to higher iso-profit curves as it moves down the reaction curve. The reaction curve is in fact the locus of points where the Home firm's profits are maximized for given levels of X_f. Thus, RC_h connects all of the "top" points on the iso-profit curves. The best possible point for the Home firm in Fig. 17.1 is point A, where it is a monopolist.

A similar reaction curve for the Foreign firm is shown as RC_f in Fig. 17.2. RC_h and RC_f are in fact mirror images of each other under assumptions used in Section 17.4 (including the assumption that the firms have equal marginal costs). The Cournot equilibrium for the Home and Foreign is given by point C, where the two reaction curves intersect: each firm is choosing its optimal output given the output of the other firm. The Foreign firm has iso-profit curves corresponding to those of the Home firm, with these curves being vertical on RC_f; RC_f is the locus of optimal choices of X_f for given levels of X_h. The iso-profit curves at the Cournot equilibrium for the Home and Foreign firms are shown as π_{hc} and π_{fc} respectively. These iso-profit curves are perpendicular to each other at the Cournot equilibrium, indicating that each firm is choosing its optimal output given the output of the other firm. The hatched area between these two iso-profit curves gives a region in which both firms could be better off by agreeing to reduce outputs.

Now consider an activist government in Country H. The Foreign firm's reaction curve RC_f could be thought of as a constraint: any profit-maximizing output that the Home government can help the Home firm attain must lie

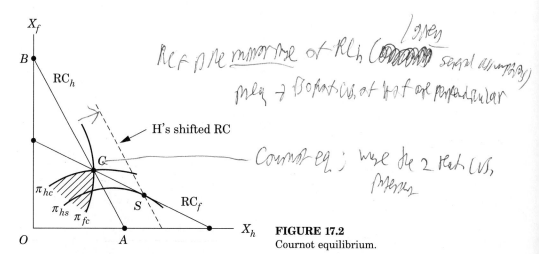

FIGURE 17.2
Cournot equilibrium.

on the Foreign reaction curve RC_f. In Fig. 17.2, we see that the best possible point for the Home firm is point S, where iso-profit curve π_{hs} is just tangent to the foreign reaction function RC_f. How can the Home government influence the situation so that the Cournot equilibrium will shift to S in Fig. 17.2? One way would be to give the Home firm an output subsidy. This would reduce the Home's firm's marginal cost, making it willing to supply a larger quantity of X_h for any given level of X_f. In other words, the output subsidy would shift the Home firm's reaction curve to the right in Fig. 17.2. If the Home government chooses the most effective subsidy, the Home firm's reaction curve will shift just enough to pass through point S in Fig. 17.2. This new reaction curve is shown by the dashed line. The Home firm earns higher profits in international markets, and these profits are a component of Home's national income.[3]

Note that the Foreign firm is worse off after the Home subsidy. The Foreign firm is on a lower iso-profit curve than π_{fc} in Fig. 17.2, so Foreign national income is reduced. The subsidy's effect of making Home better off and Foreign worse off is generally called *rent shifting*; oligopolistic rents in this market are shifted from the Foreign firm to the Home firm.[4]

This argument, as illustrated in Fig. 17.2, establishes a case in which active government support for a domestic firm in the international marketplace can increase national welfare. But it is a fragile argument, as we shall show in the next section.

17.3 EXPORT RIVALRY II: BERTRAND COMPETITION[5]

A plausible alternative to the Cournot assumption that firms pick quantities is that firms pick prices. Each firm picks its optimal price given the price of its rival. This is known as Bertrand competition. This difference might seem insignificant, but it actually reverses the result of the previous section. The Home government's optimal policy is to *tax* the Home firm, not subsidize it.

The difference arises because Bertrand competition is inherently more competitive than Cournot competition. Bertrand competitors produce more than Cournot competitors; indeed, there is a sense in which the Bertrand competitors are producing "too much" and Cournot competitors "too little." A tax by the Home government can restrain Bertrand competition and thereby reduce profits of the Home firm by less than the resulting tax revenue. Home welfare therefore increases.

In a Cournot situation, the Home firm behaves as if increasing its output will not lead the Foreign firm to alter its output when in fact, Foreign *will* lower its output. In a sense, the Home firm behaves as if the market is *more* competitive than it actually is and produces too little. In a Bertrand situation, the Home firm behaves as if decreasing its price (increasing its output) will not lead the Foreign firm to change its price. This must mean that Home behaves as if Foreign will respond by reducing its output (Foreign must reduce its output to hold its price constant because demand shifts to Home when Home reduces its price). But in fact, Foreign will respond by lowering its price (increasing its output). In a sense, the Home firm behaves as if the market is *less* competitive than it actually is and thus produces too much.

If two firms in Cournot equilibrium were suddenly changed into Bertrand competitors, each firm would feel an incentive to increase its output, believing that the other firm would respond by reducing its output rather than by holding it constant as under Cournot behavior. In Bertrand equilibrium, the outputs of the two firms will be higher and their profits lower than under Cournot competition. Thus, Home's "conjecture" about how Foreign will respond to a change in its output (and vice versa) is crucial to determining the equilibrium.

Figure 17.3 shows a Bertrand reaction function for the Home firm, labeled RC_h. In the Bertrand case, the axis shows prices rather than quantities. If the Foreign firm raises its price p_f, the demand for X_f decreases and the demand for X_h increases. Because of the increased demand, it is optimal for the Home firm to increase its price p_h (generally by less than the increase in p_f), giving the Bertrand reaction curve an upward slope. A set of iso-profit curves for the Home firm can be derived here in the same fashion as in Fig. 17.1. Profits of the Home firm increase as the Foreign firm increases its price, because when p_f increases, more demand is shifted to the Home firm. Figure 17.3 shows three iso-profit curves with $\pi_{h3} > \pi_{h2} > \pi_{h1}$. The reaction curve RC_h is the locus of "bottom" points on the iso-profit curves; that is, the reaction curve gives the optimal (profit-maximizing) level of p_h for each level of p_f.

Figure 17.4 adds the corresponding reaction curve for the Foreign firm, RC_f. Bertrand equilibrium is given by the intersection of the reaction curves at point B. At the Bertrand equilibrium, the two iso-profit curves π_{hb} and π_{fb} are perpendicular: each firm is choosing its optimal price given the price

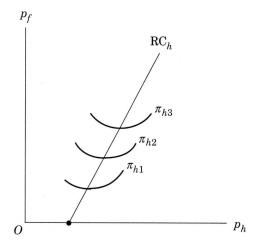

FIGURE 17.3
Home country's Bertrand reaction curve.

of the other firm. The hatched area between the two iso-profit curves is a set of mutually preferred points at which both firms could achieve higher profits if they cooperated to increase prices.

Now consider an activist Home government as we did in the previous section. The Foreign reaction curve RC_f can be thought of as a constraint, and the Home government's task is to help guide its firm to the highest profit level consistent with this constraint. The best point for Home on RC_f is point T, with corresponding profit level π_{ht} in Fig. 17.4. The appropriate policy for the Home government is to shift the Home firm's reaction curve to the right, to the position of the dashed line through T. But the appropriate policy is now an output tax, the reverse of the optimal policy in the Cournot case. When the reaction curve is shifted to the right, the Home firm wishes to charge a higher price p_h for any given level of p_f. This is consistent with

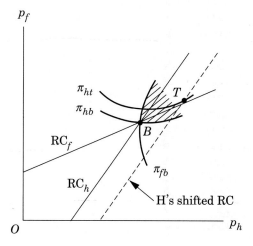

FIGURE 17.4
Bertrand equilibrium.

a higher level of marginal cost for the Home firm and is accomplished by a tax rather than a subsidy.

It is interesting to note that H's tax also serves to raise the profits of the Foreign firm, whereas the optimal subsidy in the Cournot case lowered the profits of the Foreign firm. As indicated above, we can think of Bertrand equilibrium as characterized by each firm's belief that there is less competition then there actually is; hence, the firms are producing "too much." The tax imposed by the Home government acts to restrain competition, benefiting the Foreign firm as well as the Home country.[6]

The contrast between this result and that of the previous section serves to illustrate the caveat offered in the introduction to this chapter. The theory of strategic trade policy is very sensitive to the underlying assumptions and cannot be taken as a reliable guide to government policy at this time.

17.4   THE FORMAL MODEL[7]

The results derived in the previous two sections are not always valid, and they depend in particular on the shape of the demand functions and the firms' cost functions. One simple, underlying model that does produce the results shown in Figs. 17.1–17.4 (including the linear reaction functions) assumes that the consumer's demand curve is linear and that the Home and Foreign firms have constant marginal costs. We will assume for a reason noted presently that the Home and Foreign firms produce imperfect substitutes Let p_h and p_f denote the prices of the Home and Foreign goods, respectively. The consumer's (inverse) demand functions for the two goods are given by

$$p_h = a - bX_h - cX_f \qquad p_f = a - bX_f - cX_h \qquad b > c \qquad (17.1)$$

The assumption that $b > c$ implies that the goods are imperfect substitutes. The revenue for each firm is price times output.

$$R_h = p_h X_h = aX_h - bX_h^2 - cX_f X_h$$
$$R_f = p_f X_f = aX_f - bX_f^2 - cX_h X_f \qquad (17.2)$$

A firm's marginal revenue is the change in revenue associated with a small change in output. We first make the Cournot assumption that each firm regards its rival's output as fixed. The firms optimize by setting marginal revenue equal to marginal cost (here we employ mathematical derivatives).

$$\text{MR}_h = \frac{dR_h}{dX_h} = a - 2bX_h - cX_f = m_h$$

$$\text{MR}_f = \frac{dR_f}{dX_f} = a - 2bX_f - cX_h = m_f \qquad (17.3)$$

where m_h and m_f are the marginal costs of the Home and Foreign firms, respectively. The marginal-revenue-equals-marginal-cost conditions can be solved to give each firm's optimal output as a function of the other firm's output.

$$X_h = \left[\frac{a - m_h}{2b}\right] - \frac{c}{2b}X_f \qquad X_f = \left[\frac{a - m_f}{2b}\right] - \frac{c}{2b}X_h \qquad (17.4)$$

These two equations are the Cournot reaction functions of section 17.2. The horizonal intercept of Home's reaction curve RC_h is $(a - m)/(2b)$, the amount the Home firm would produce if $X_f = 0$. The slope of RC_h is $dX_f/dX_h = -(2b)/c$. The corresponding comments apply to the Foreign firm's reaction curve RC_f. The Cournot equilibrium is given by the solution to the two simultaneous equations in Eq. (17.4), the intersection of the two reaction functions. In the case where the marginal costs of the two firms are equal, this is given very simply by

$$X_h = X_f = \frac{a - m}{2b + c} \qquad \text{when} \quad m_h = m_f = m \qquad (17.5)$$

Now we turn to the Bertrand case. We can use the inverse demand functions in Eq. (17.1) to solve for the demands for X_h and X_f as functions of p_h and p_f. These are given by

$$X_h = \frac{(ab - ac) - bp_h + cp_f}{b^2 - c^2}$$

$$X_f = \frac{(ab - ac) - bp_f + cp_h}{b^2 - c^2} \qquad (17.6)$$

Note that the demands are not well defined if $b = c$, the case in which the two goods are perfect substitutes. If the goods are perfect substitutes, then X_h gets all the market if p_h is only barely below p_f, and vice versa. The model has a *bang-bang property* (flipping from one extreme to the other) if the goods are perfect substitutes, which is why we have modeled them as imperfect substitutes. Profits for the two firms are given by price minus marginal cost times the output levels, given in Eq. (17.6).

$$\pi_h = \frac{(p_h - m_h)((ab - ac) - bp_h + cp_f)}{b^2 - c^2}$$

$$\pi_f = \frac{(p_f - m_f)((ab - ac) - bp_f + cp_h)}{b^2 - c^2} \qquad (17.7)$$

The Bertrand assumption is that each firm picks its optimal price given the level of the other firm's price. To find each firm's optimal price given the price of the other firm, we must first set the derivative of their respective profit equations in Eq. (17.7) equal to zero.

$$\frac{d\pi_h}{dp_h} = \frac{ab - ac - 2bp_h + cp_f + bm}{b^2 - c^2} = 0$$

$$\frac{d\pi_f}{dp_f} = \frac{ab - ac - 2bp_f + cp_h + bm}{b^2 - c^2} = 0 \qquad (17.8)$$

These equations can now be solved to show each firm's optimal price given the price charged by the other firm.

$$p_h = \left[\frac{ab - ac + bm}{2b}\right] + \frac{c}{2b}p_f \qquad p_f = \left[\frac{ab - ac + bm}{2b}\right] + \frac{c}{2b}p_h \qquad (17.9)$$

The first equation is the Bertrand reaction curve of the Home firm, RC_h in Fig. 17.4, and the second equation is the Bertrand reaction curve of the Foreign firm, RC_f. The slope of the Home firm's reaction curve is $dp_f/dp_h = 2b/c$, and the slope of the Foreign firm's reaction curve is $dp_f/dp_h = c/(2b)$.

For comparison purposes, we can solve the two reaction functions for the Bertrand equilibrium, assuming equal marginal costs in the two countries ($m_h = m_f$), and then work backward to get the (identical) Bertrand outputs of the two firms. These are given by

$$X_h = X_f = \frac{a - m}{2b + c - c^2/b} > \frac{a - m}{2b + c} \qquad m = m_h = m_f \qquad (17.10)$$

where the right-hand side of the inequality is the Cournot output level given in Eq. (17.5). In this case, we see that the Bertrand equilibrium is more competitive than the Cournot equilibrium, as we asserted in the previous section of the chapter. Outputs of both firms are higher in the Bertrand equilibrium, and this higher level of competition gives rise to the result in the previous section that a tax actually helps a country's welfare by "restraining" competition.

17.5 ADDING DOMESTIC CONSUMPTION TO THE COURNOT MODEL

In this section, we return to the Cournot model of Chapter 11, in which there are just two countries, Home and Foreign. Each country's domestic firm produces X, the goods produced in both countries are identical, and each country consumes X. Home and Foreign are assumed to be identical countries. For a reminder, Fig. 17.5 reconsiders the case of a production subsidy in a competitive model discussed in Chapter 11. In free trade, the country exports X, producing at Q and consuming at C, with the world price ratio given by p^*. Now suppose that the government puts a production subsidy on X, which implies that the producer price ratio now exceeds the consumer price ratio. Producers will now increase the production of X to a point like Q', with consumption occurring at C'. Exports increase, but this is at the expense of a deterioration in welfare.

The effects of this subsidy may be even farther-reaching. Note in Fig. 17.5 that the country has increased both its imports and its exports at the price ratio p^*. If the country has some influence over world prices, this will force up the price of Y and force down the price of X. A new equilibrium might occur at a price ratio p', with production and consumption at Q'' and C'', respectively. There has been a further deterioration in welfare due to the deterioration in the terms of trade.

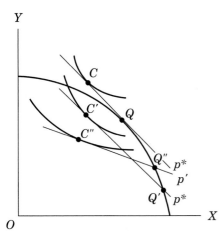

FIGURE 17.5
Production subsidy in a competitive model.

Figure 17.5 thus gives us the standard view of a production subsidy, and similar results hold for an export subsidy, as we noted in Chapter 15. In the standard competitive trade model, neither production subsidies nor export subsidies are optimal. Note further that the deterioration in the terms of trade for the country imposing the subsidy must constitute an improvement in the terms of trade for the other country. Foreign's welfare improves as a consequence of Home's subsidy. The apparent reason for this is that Home is now selling its export good more cheaply to Foreign. In this model, Home should oppose a production subsidy on the export good, while Foreign should welcome it.

These results can be reversed in a simple Cournot model of the type developed in this chapter and in Chapter 11. The situation is shown in Fig. 17.6. Y is a competitive good produced with constant returns to scale, while X is produced with increasing returns in the form of a fixed cost, $\overline{Y}F_x$, and a constant marginal cost. This marginal cost in terms of good Y is given by the slope of $F_x\overline{X}$ in Fig. 17.6.

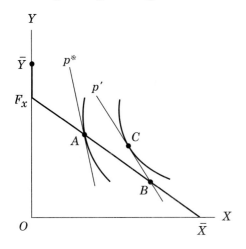

FIGURE 17.6
Production subsidy in a Cournot model.

Suppose that we initially have two identical countries and that a single X producer in each country is engaged in Cournot competition with the X producer in the other country (see Chapter 11, Section 11.5). Because of the scale economies, the price must exceed marginal cost (Chapter 12), and so equilibrium in each country could be at a point like A in Fig. 17.6 with a price ratio p^*. Because the countries are identical, no net trade takes place, so each country consumes at A and produces at A in Fig. 17.6.

Under reasonable demand assumptions (such as those of the previous section), a small production subsidy to the Home firm will have the effect on the Home country shown in Fig. 17.6 and the effect on the Foreign country shown in Fig. 17.7. In the Home country, the production subsidy stimulates production to point B in Fig. 17.6 and causes the Home country to export X. The increased production of X also causes the world price of X to fall to a new level, shown by p' in Fig. 17.6. Consumption occurs at point C, which constitutes a welfare improvement over A.

Note the contrast between Figs. 17.5 and 17.6. The reason for the welfare improvement in Fig. 17.6 is that the initial price ratio exceeds marginal cost. With price (the value of X to consumers) greater than marginal cost, there is a welfare gain in stimulating the production of X. It does not follow that an even larger subsidy will continue to improve welfare, and in fact, it can be shown that the deteriorating terms of trade will eventually outweigh the favorable production expansion effect. Nevertheless, Fig. 17.6 makes it clear that there does exist a case for a small production subsidy when there are scale economies and/or imperfect competition and when initial exports are zero.

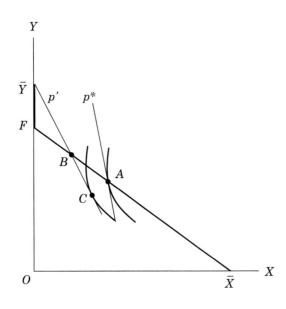

FIGURE 17.7
Effect of Home's production subsidy on Foreign.

Welfare effects on Foreign are shown in Fig. 17.7. The increased production by Home means that it captures a larger share of the world market, or alternatively, that the demand curve facing the Foreign firm shifts left at each price of X. The Foreign firm will reduce production, moving to a point like B in Fig. 17.7. The price ratio has fallen to p' here as in Home so consumers in F import X to arrive at the consumption bundle C in Fig. 17.7. Foreign welfare has deteriorated. This last result is not inevitable. We could have drawn Fig. 17.7 so that the price ratio p' would cut through the indifference curve passing through A, achieving a higher utility level in F. But the point is that the subsidy in H could make Foreign worse off; this contrasts with the result in the constant returns, perfect competition model that the subsidy in H must make Foreign better off.

17.6 FREE ENTRY AND EXIT

The argument that a country can gain through the use of a production subsidy when there are scale economies and/or imperfect competition turns out to be fragile. Different assumptions from those used to produce the case in Fig. 17.6 can reverse the conclusion. We saw one example of this in Section 17.3: Bertrand behavior (choosing prices as strategic variables) can lead to conclusions about policy that are opposite to those obtained under Cournot behavior (choosing quantities as strategic variables). In this section, we present another important modification of the basic Cournot model. Instead of using a model with only one firm in each country, let us now assume free entry of firms in each country up to the point where profits are zero. This is certainly a realistic assumption for many if not most manufacturing industries.

Figures 17.8 and 17.9 show a special case from Horstmann and Markusen (1986). In addition to assuming free entry, they assume that firms behave in a Cournot fashion (as in Chapter 11) and that consumers have linear demand curves as in Section 17.4. The technology of production in the X sector is characterized by the same assumptions we have used in this chapter: fixed cost plus constant marginal cost, and a single factor of production. Given these assumptions, *a specific production subsidy in H results in the entry of additional firms, and each firm continues to produce the same output at the same average cost as before the subsidy.*

The equilibrium is shown in Fig. 17.8, where point A is the initial equilibrium and p^* is the initial price ratio. Figure 17.8 is similar to Figs. 17.6 and 17.7, except that the initial equilibrium involves average-cost pricing as a consequence of the free-entry assumption (p^* equals the slope of the chord connecting A with $\overline{Y}$). The production subsidy creates profits that lead to the entry of new firms. These firms use additional resources for fixed costs, so the production frontier shifts inward to $\overline{Y}F'\overline{X}'$ in Figure 17.8. In the new equilibrium, each firm produces the pre-subsidy output at pre-subsidy average cost, and so the new production point is B. (The average cost of production is the same at A and B.)

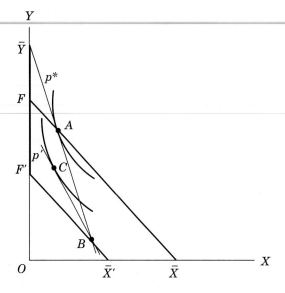

FIGURE 17.8
Production subsidy with free entry and exit.

However, the subsidy does imply that the consumer price ratio is less than the producer average cost, and so the consumer price ratio is shown by p' in Fig. 17.8. H will export X to arrive at consumption bundle C. Production of X has increased, but welfare has deteriorated. The reason is that the increased production of X has not resulted in the capture of scale economies but has come from the inefficient entry of new firms, each producing at the old scale. The possible gains that we saw in Fig. 17.6 are

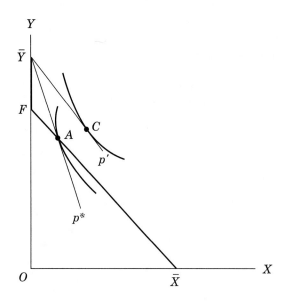

FIGURE 17.9
Effect of Home's production subsidy on Foreign with free entry and exit.

now dissipated by entry and the use of scarce resources to finance fixed costs.

The situation for Country F is shown in Fig. 17.9. The initial equilibrium at point A and price ratio p^* is identical to the equilibrium for Country H at A in Fig. 17.8. The Home subsidy forces down the price of X, and so the Foreign firms now make negative profits. Because the firms in each country have identical costs and because trade is free, the unsubsidized firms in F cannot compete against the subsidized firms in H (remember that the latter make zero profits). All the Foreign producers of X are driven out of business, and Country F specializes in Y. Production occurs at $\overline{Y}$, and consumers import X to reach the consumption bundle C. The trade vector $\overline{Y}C$ in Fig. 17.9 is equal but opposite to the trade vector CB in Fig. 17.8, so that trade balances as is required for an equilibrium.

Figure 17.9 shows that country F is better off as a consequence of the subsidy in H. Country H is worse off, so this combined result is much like the one obtained from a constant returns, perfect competition model. The comparison is appropriate. In the case of free entry (at least under the specific assumptions used here), scale economies are not captured as a consequence of the subsidy, but rather, new firms are added at constant scale almost as if the industry had constant returns. It is also true that no rents are transferred to Country H because, with free entry, there are no rents being earned (profits are always zero in equilibrium).

For the ambitious reader, we can use the model of section 17.4 to give a brief demonstration of how a production subsidy leads only to entry and not to changes in individual firm outputs.[8] Suppose that there are n identical firms in total, and consider firm i, whose output is denoted by X_i. The output of a representative "other" firm is denoted X_j. The price of the good (all firms produce the same good) and the revenue of firm i are given by

$$p = a - b(X_i + (n-1)X_j) \qquad R_i = pX_i = aX_i - bX_i^2 - (n-1)X_jX_i \quad (17.11)$$

Firm i's optimization condition that marginal revenue equals marginal cost (m) is given by

$$\text{MR}_i = \frac{dR_i}{dX_i} = a - 2bX_i - b(n-1)X_j = m \qquad (17.12)$$

Free entry and exit occur until profits are zero. This can be expressed as the condition that price equals average cost $(m + F/X)$.

$$p = a - bX_i - b(n-1)X_j = m + \frac{F}{X_i} \qquad (17.13)$$

If we solve Eqs. (17.12) and (17.13) for X_i, we get $bX_i = F/X_i$, or

$$X_i = \left(\frac{F}{b}\right)^{1/2} \qquad (17.14)$$

The output of an individual firm is independent of marginal cost. Thus, a government tax or subsidy on output, which changes the firm's marginal cost, has no effect on the output per firm in general equilibrium. A subsidy leads only to the inefficient entry of additional firms, as shown in Fig. 17.8.

17.7   IMPORT PROTECTION AS EXPORT PROMOTION

Another interesting example of the strategic use of export subsidies occurs when the marginal costs of production are decreasing.[9] Suppose that a U.S. firm and a Japanese rival are both selling in their own markets, exporting to the other's market, and perhaps selling in third countries. Assume that marginal cost decreases with the amount produced. Now assume that the Japanese erect a trade barrier (a tariff or quota) to imports of the American product.

The effect of the Japanese trade barrier is to restrict the Japanese home market to the domestic firm, or at least to give that firm a larger share of the domestic market. Output of the Japanese firm increases, and that of the U.S. firm falls, given constant levels of sales by each firm in other markets. This change in output levels implies a decrease in the marginal cost of production for the Japanese and an increase in marginal cost for the U.S. firm. Thus, there will be further ramifications of the Japanese trade barrier in that the Japanese firm will now be more competitive in the U.S. market and in third-country markets. Conversely, the U.S. firm will be less competitive in its home and third-country markets.

The equilibrium condition that marginal revenue equals marginal cost now implies that the Japanese firm will expand sales in the United States and in third countries and that U.S. sales will shrink. Rents in these markets will be shifted to the Japanese firm, an effect described in an earlier section, and the prices charged could even fall in the Japanese market, providing a benefit to consumers in that country. Import protection by the Japanese thus becomes export promotion.

This argument also holds when the scale economies are in the form of dynamic *learning-by-doing,* in which marginal costs of production fall with accumulated sales experience. Protecting or reserving the home market for the domestic firm allows that firm to lower its costs more quickly and therefore to compete more effectively in export markets. Some analysts have suggested that this is exactly what the Japanese did with their domestic semiconductor industry. By reserving their domestic market for domestic firms, the Japanese developed a semiconductor industry that could not have existed independently. On the basis of accumulated experience, the Japanese are now leading exporters of semiconductors.

More recent analysis has made a similar point in a model with constant marginal cost but significant fixed costs.[10] Suppose that by closing its domestic market to imports and reserving it for domestic producers, the Japanese forced a U.S. firm into exiting from the market. The exit of the U.S. firm then has effects similar to those in the decreasing-marginal-cost model. The exit is very costly to U.S. consumers, leaving the Japanese firms (collectively) in a monopoly position, extracting high monopoly rents from U.S. consumers in the U.S. market. The Japanese firms benefit considerably from their new monopoly status in the U.S. market. As in the earlier model, import protection becomes export promotion.

As in the case of the production subsidy discussed earlier, these argument may be weakened by the inefficient entry of new domestic firms in response to the introduction of protection. Nevertheless, it again illustrates why the existence of scale economies and imperfect competition may imply radically different policies from those suggested by traditional theory.

17.8 QUOTAS AND VERs AS "FACILITATING PRACTICES"

Two recent articles raise interesting points about how non-tariff instruments of trade policy can lead to some unexpected outcomes in the presence of imperfect competition and scale economies.[11] Both of the authors raise the possibility that a voluntary export restraint imposed by Home on the Foreign exporter competing in a duopoly with a Home firm may lead to an increase in the profits of both firms. A Bertrand duopoly model is used, much like that developed in Sections 17.3 and 17.4. The voluntary export restraint puts a check on the amount the Foreign firm can export to the Home country, but leaves the rents generated by the supply restriction in the hands of the Foreign firm. Both authors show that the VER can lead to an increase in the profits of both firms by restraining the "excessive" competition associated with Bertrand pricing. In essence, the VER facilitates collusion. In fact, this is what makes the export restraint voluntary.

With countries turning more to nontariff barriers to trade, this type of phenomenon needs further investigation. Contingent trade policies and domestic-content restrictions are two types of policies that deserve more study.[12] Economists have done some work on domestic-content restrictions, which specify the minimum domestic content a product must have to qualify for free trade within a regional trade block.[13] Their findings suggest that these content restrictions have anti-competitive effects similar to the effects of VERs.

17.9 TRADE POLICY IN MONOPOLISTIC-COMPETITION MODELS

Strategic trade policy questions have also been examined in monopolistic-competition models of the type introduced in Chapter 12. It has been shown that a tariff on imported, differentiated goods improves welfare, both because of the usual optimal-tariff argument (the tariff improves the terms of trade) and because consumer expenditure is shifted to domestic substitute products produced with increasing returns to scale.[14] This leads to a beneficial expansion in the domestic increasing-returns sector.

It was later shown that this result depends on the domestic and imported differentiated products' being substitutes for each other.[15] While it may be reasonable to assume that differentiated consumer goods are generally substitutes, this is not so obvious with differentiated producer goods. An imported machine and a domestic computer may be complements in production, for example. Markusen (1989, 1990) showed that if the imported and domestic differentiated products are general equilibrium complements, then an import tariff may reduce welfare. The tariff generates a favorable terms-of-trade effect, but the increased prices of the imported (producer) goods may generate a fall in demand for and production of the domestic inputs produced with increasing returns to scale. In the terminology of Chapter 12, this can generate a negative "production expansion effect" that outweighs the favorable terms-of-trade effect. Once again, we see that appropriate policy depends heavily on the underlying structure of the economy.

17.10   CONCLUDING REMARKS

This chapter has presented some examples of why scale economies and imperfect competition may give governments an incentive to provide strategic assistance to their domestic firms in international markets. By "assistance" we mean policies such as direct or indirect subsidies that lower the costs to domestic firms of doing business abroad.

We noted that such subsidies are not optimal in models based on constant returns to scale and perfect competition. Domestic welfare deteriorates as a consequence of production or export subsidies, and the only beneficiaries are foreign consumers who can buy cheaper imports. But scale economies and imperfect competition imply an excess of price (the value of a good to consumers) over marginal cost (the value of resources needed to produce an additional unit). In such a situation, there is an incentive for governments to stimulate production. Furthermore, the existence of monopoly profits or rents in world markets may imply that a government can transfer more of those rents to domestic firms by subsidizing domestic production.

These are important findings, but it must be remembered that their validity rests on fairly specific assumptions. We demonstrated two cases, Bertrand competition and free entry and exit, in which pro-subsidy arguments are not valid. Arguments in favor of subsidies must, therefore, be very carefully evaluated in light of industry structure and other variables. At the present time, the theory offers little support for a comprehensive government program of support to domestic firms in the international marketplace. Some specific findings are as follows.

1. When a Home firm is competing with a Foreign rival for sales to third markets, the Home government can shift oligopoly rents in favor of the

Home firm by a production or export subsidy. This increases welfare in H if the Home and Foreign firms are Cournot competitors. But such a subsidy would reduce Home welfare if the firms are Bertrand competitors. Bertrand behavior, in which the two firms are exporting "too much," is in a sense more competitive than Cournot competition. The optimal policy is actually a production or export tax, which, although it increases the profits of the Foreign firm, also increases Home welfare.

2. Section 17.5 added domestic consumption to the basic Cournot model and exploited the type of diagrammatic analysis introduced in Chapter 12. Here we see quite clearly why the traditional argument against production or export subsidies following from a competitive model may be reversed. With price in excess of marginal cost, an expansion in the output of the imperfectly competitive, increasing-returns sector is beneficial, and conversely, a contraction is harmful. A small production or export subsidy can improve domestic welfare.

3. The reversal of the conventional competitive result can be reversed back again if firms are allowed to enter or exit in response to policy changes. Under special assumptions (linear demand, constant marginal cost), it can be shown that a production subsidy leads only to the entry of new firms, not to an expansion in the output of the existing firms. No beneficial capture of scale economies occurs and, as in the case of the competitive model, the production subsidy hurts the subsidizing country and helps the other country.

4. In some cases, domestic and foreign markets are linked in a way that produces interesting implications for strategic trade policy. If marginal costs are declining or if firms are initially operating near zero profits, then the imposition of import protection in the Foreign country can lead to ramifications in the Home country. This protection reserves the Foreign market for Foreign firms, giving them advantages in terms of lower marginal costs or forcing the exit of Home firms from the market. In either case, the Home country can suffer losses both through the loss of sales in the Foreign market and through loss of sales and/or higher prices in its domestic market.

5. It has been shown that some policies, notably voluntary export restraints, can facilitate reduced competition between domestic and foreign firms. It is possible that such policies can lead eventually to increased profits for both domestic and foreign firms. Consumers are, of course, the losers.

6. There is generally some presumption that tariffs are beneficial in monopolistically competitive industries. They generate a favorable terms-of-trade effect and lead to a beneficial expansion by domestic, increasing-returns firms. But this conclusion can be reversed if the imported goods are general equilibrium complements for the domestic increasing-returns goods. In such a case, the higher import prices may lead to reduced production of the domestic goods, generating a welfare-reducing contraction in domestic, increasing-returns production.

PROBLEMS

1. If both governments in Fig. 17.2 were to cooperate to extract the maximum possible rents from the third country (e.g., the United State and the EC cooperate with respect to Boeing and Airbus), should both governments levy a tax or a subsidy? Explain your answer.

2. Answer the same question with respect to Bertrand competition in Fig. 17.4.

3. In Fig. 17.6, convince yourself that as long as production of X increases, the production subsidy must lead to a welfare improvement.

4. Given that there is domestic consumption in each country as in Figs. 17.6 and 17.7, reconsider your answers to questions 1 and 2. Should two cooperating governments tax or subsidize their X producers? Explain your answer.

5. Redraw Fig. 17.7 to show that the Home country subsidy could make the Foreign country better off.

6. With reference to Fig. 17.8, is it valid to suggest that the subsidy makes the Home country worse off by causing the Home firm to sell its export good for less than it costs to produce it?

NOTES

1. Much of the analysis of this section (and the more technical presentation in Section 17.4) is drawn from a series of papers by James Brander and Barbara Spencer, including Spencer and Brander (1983), and Brander and Spencer (1985). See also Dixit (1984).

2. This is a point for more advanced students. If markets are segmented and marginal costs are constant, then the domestic and foreign markets can be treated independently. The government's job in the international marketplace is to assist its firm in earning the maximum profits, just as is the case here. If there are domestic sales, then the government may wish to intervene in the domestic market, but that intervention is independent of its international policy.

3. When the subsidy is applied, the Home firm's actual profits at S in Fig. 17.2 will be higher than π_{hs} by the amount of the subsidy payment sX_h if s is the specific (per unit) subsidy rate. But this amount of higher profits is completely offset from a welfare point of view by the fact that consumers (taxpayers) pay the subsidy sX_h. Thus, the *net* contribution of the subsidy to increased national income in the Home country is indeed the difference between π_{hc} and π_{hs} in Fig. 17.2. An alternative way of saying the same thing is that π_{hs} in Fig. 17.2 equals the firm's profits minus the value of subsidy payments.

4. The term *rent shifting* is a bit of a misnomer, or rather, the phenomenon is more general. For example, the same result is found in a model of external economies in which there are no monopoly rents. The result arises from the fact that price exceeds marginal cost (and not necessarily from the existence of profits), and thus, the country whose firm expands production captures the excess of price over marginal cost on added output, while the country whose firm contracts suffers the loss of price over marginal cost on reduced output.

5. Much of this section (and the more technical analysis of Bertrand competition in Section 17.4) is drawn from Eaton and Grossman (1985).

6. Similar to our discussion in the previous section, the Home firm's actual profits after the tax are not given by π_{ht} in Fig. 17.4; they are reduced below that amount by the tax. But this reduction is completely offset from a welfare point of view by the tax collection, so the difference between π_{ht} and π_{hb} is the *net* benefit of the tax to the Home country. The tax increases the Home Country's welfare, not the private profits of the Home firm.

7. This section presents a formal derivation of the results in the previous two sections. It can be skipped without loss of continuity.

8. As this suggests, the less ambitious reader can exit the section at this point.

9. This section is based on the article by Krugman (1984).
10. See Cronshaw and Markusen (1994).
11. See Harris (1985) and Krishna (1989).
12. Articles by Deardoff (1987) and Kaempfer and Willet (1989) consider the general preference by governments for nontariff barriers.
13. See Krishna and Itoh (1988) and Lopez-de-Silanes, Markusen, and Rutherford (1994).
14. See Flam and Helpman (1987).
15. See Markusen (1989, 1990).

REFERENCES

Baldwin, R.E., and Krugman, P. R. (1988). "Market Access and International Competition: A Simulation Study of 16K Random Access Memories." In Robert Feenstra, ed., *Empirical Methods for International Trade*. Cambridge: MIT Press.

Brander, J. A., and Spencer, B. J. (1985). "Export Subsidies and International Market Share Rivalry." *Journal of International Economics* 18:227–242.

Cronshaw, M., and Markusen, J. R. (1994). "The Theory and Consequences of Results-Oriented Trade Policy." In R. Stern, ed., *New Directions in International Trade Theory*. Ann Arbor: University of Michigan Press, forthcoming.

Deardorff, A. (1987). "Why Do Governments Prefer Nontariff Barriers?" *Carnegie-Rochester Conference Series on Public Policy* 26m:191–216.

Dixit, A. K. (1984) "International Trade Policy for Oligopolistic Industries." *Economic Journal* Supplement:1–16.

Dixit, A. K., and Grossman, G. M. (1986). "Targeted Export Promotion with Several Oligopolistic Industries." *Journal of International Economics* 21:233–250.

Eaton, J., and Grossman, G. M. (1985). "Optimal Trade and Industrial Policy under Oligopoly." *Quarterly Journal of Economics* 101:383–406.

Flam, H., and Helpman, E. (1987). "Industrial Policy under Monopolistic Competition." *Journal of International Economics* 22:79–102.

Harris, R. (1985). "Why Voluntary Export Restraints Are 'Voluntary.'" *Canadian Journal of Economics* 18:799–809.

Helpman, E., and Krugman, P. R. (1989). *Trade Policy and Market Structure*. Cambridge: MIT Press.

Horstmann, I., and Markusen, J. R. (1986). "Up the Average Cost Curve: Inefficient Entry and the New Protectionism." *Journal of International Economics* 20:225–248.

Kaempfer, W. H., and Willett, T. D. (1989). "Combining Rent Seeking and Public Choice Theory in the Analysis of Tariffs versus Quotas." *Public Choice* 63:79–86.

Krishna, K. (1989). "Trade Restrictions as Facilitating Practices." *Journal of International Economics* 26:251–270.

Krishna K., and Itoh, M. (1988). "Content Protection and Oligopolistic Interactions." *Review of Economic Studies* 55:107–125.

Krugman, P. R. (1984). "Import Protection as Export Promotion: International Competition in the Presence of Oligopoly and Economies of Scale." In H. Kierzkowski, ed., *Monopolistic Competition in International Trade*. Oxford: Oxford University Press.

Lopez-de-Silanes, F., Markusen, J. R., and Rutherford, T. F. (1994). "Trade Policy with Multi-national Firms" NBER and University of Colorado working paper.

Markusen, J. R. (1989). "Trade in Producer Services and in Other Specialized, Intermediate Inputs." *American Economic Review* 79:85–95.

Markusen, J. R. (1990). "Derationalizing Tariffs with Specialized Intermediate Inputs and Differentiated Final Goods." *Journal of International Economics* 28:375–384.

Spencer, B. J., and Brander, J. A., (1983). "International R&D Rivalry and Industrial Strategy." *Review of Economics Studies* 50:707–722.

Venables, A. J. (1975). "Trade and Trade Policy with Imperfect Competition: The Case of Identical Products and Free Entry." *Journal of International Economics* 19:1–20.

CHAPTER
18

PREFERENTIAL TRADE AREAS

18.1   INTRODUCTION

The discussion of trade policies contained in the previous three chapters leaves us with a number of questions about these policies. One is why these welfare-worsening policies are used. This question is addressed explicitly in the next chapter on the political economy of trade policy. Another interesting question is how to eliminate or reduce the use of welfare-worsening policies. Efforts to do so are called trade liberalization and can take several forms. The simplest path to liberalization is for a country to cut tariffs unilaterally, but the politics of that are similar to the politics of establishing tariffs in the first place, as discussed in Chapter 19. More often, countries lower their import barriers at the same time as their trade partners do. Such liberalization can be in the form of a multilateral agreement, such as the various General Agreement on Tariffs and Trade (GATT) rounds, or an agreement among a smaller set of countries, typically with some geographical proximity. This latter type of agreement, called a *preferential trade agreement,* is the topic of this chapter, while multilateral negotiations are included in the discussion of the practice of trade policy in Chapter 20.

The principles of the GATT include the ideal of Most Favored Nation status for the many trade partners of a given country. The MFN principle of the GATT is designed to prevent the development of bilateral, preferential trade treatment, under which the pattern of trade could become distorted and less than optimal. However, the GATT does allow countries to vary from the MFN principles and treat one another's imports preferentially under one exemption, the creation of a preferential trade area. These preferential trade areas are allowed by the GATT only under certain circumstances—for instance, if "almost all" trade among the parties to the agreement is covered.

In this chapter we investigate the theory that preferential cooperation among countries makes them better off. Typically, this has been referred to as the *theory of customs unions,* although cooperative trading agreements can take many forms. This body of theory investigates whether some sort of geographically discriminatory change in trade barriers is of benefit to those countries that are party to the cooperation. This question is increasingly important as the trading world seems to be evolving from a multilateral system to a system in which many countries belong to regional trade blocks. (This is sometimes referred to as a "minilateral" trading system.) Recent examples of this evolution include the extension in coverage and comprehensiveness of the European Community, the North American Free Trade Agreement (NAFTA) among Mexico, Canada and the United States, side agreements between Mexico and Chile on one hand and Israel and the United States on the other, and a 1991 agreement known as Mercosur among the South American nations of Argentina, Brazil, Paraguay, and Uruguay.[1]

Of the many forms of preferential trade cooperation, the least restrictive is a *free-trade area,* in which a number of countries agree to eliminate all trade barriers among themselves while maintaining their own tariffs against outside countries. A slightly stronger form of cooperation, a *customs union,* eliminates all trade barriers among nations who are members of the union but imposes a common tariff against nonmember countries. When the cooperation extends beyond the elimination of trade barriers to the movements of factors, the cooperation is called a *common market.*

Of course, cooperation can exceed agreements on free trade and factor movements. In the European Economic Community, for example, member nations have agreed to coordinate tax policies, monetary and fiscal policies, and various other domestic regulations. Taking this sort of cooperation to its logical conclusion would result in complete integration and the institution of a single government to determine policy for all member nations. Theoretically, this latter alternative would be equivalent to a redefinition of the member nations as a single new country.

The discussion of trade models presented in Section 18.2 will show that the benefits enjoyed from the establishment of free trade areas can be attributed to a number of possible sources. First, there could be gains from trade associated with specialization that takes advantage of intercountry differences in endowments or tastes. Second, a free trade area may allow its members to attain increasing returns to scale. Third, domestic industries in a free trade area will face increased competition, so losses due to the existence of monopolies may be eliminated. Fourth, by forming a customs union, a group of countries may be able to affect the terms of trade between themselves and the rest of the world and reap benefits associated with a common optimum tariff. There is no way to predict the order of importance of these effects for a particular case, and any complete analysis of preferential trade theory should take all of them into account. Traditionally, however, the economic literature on customs unions has concentrated almost entirely on the first source of benefits, giving limited attention to the fourth. The discussion in this chapter will begin with the first point and will then briefly discuss some of the other potential sources of benefits from preferential trade areas.

The classical presumption in the theory of preferential trade is that, because free trade areas or customs unions reduce tariffs and therefore move countries toward free trade, such cooperation is welfare-improving. However, previous chapters in this book have presented examples of situations in which this presumption is not necessarily true. As one example, consider the case of a country that has imposed both tariffs and domestic commodity taxes. In this case we established that the removal of the tariff alone does not necessarily improve welfare. This was an application of the theory of the second best, which states that in a system with several distortions the removal of any single distortion cannot be presumed to be welfare-improving. Furthermore, even in a world in which tariffs are the only distortion, if tariffs have improved the terms of trade and if something like an optimum tariff is being levied, then certainly the removal of this tariff will make the economy worse off. It is at best simplistic to say that tariff removal, by moving a country toward free trade, makes the economy better off. The development of the free trade area literature can be seen as an attempt to identify particular circumstances in which the formation of a free trade area will necessarily increase welfare.

18.2 TRADE CREATION AND TRADE DIVERSION

The simplest model of preferential trade considers a single commodity X whose money price in three countries A, B, and C (adjustment having been made for exchange rates) is as shown in the first line of Table 18.1. Country A, with a price of 35, is the high-cost producer and in free trade would clearly import from Country C. Now suppose that Country A imposes a 100-percent tariff, implying that imports from Country B would now cost 52 and imports

TABLE 18.1
Trade creation and diversion in a simple, three-country model

Country	A	B	C
Price	35	26	20
100% tariff		52	40
50% tariff		39	30

from C would cost 40. Clearly this tariff is prohibitive, for, faced with these alternatives, the domestic economy finds it cheaper to produce commodity X at home. If Country A were to form a free trade area with either B or C, welfare would be improved, for commodity X could be obtained at a price of 20 or 26 as opposed to the cost of 35 under domestic production. The formation of a free trade area with either B or C results in new trade relative to the prior protection. This situation is referred to as *trade creation.*

Alternatively, suppose that Country A has been imposing a 50-percent tariff, which has given rise to the relative costs shown in the third line of Table 18.1. With this tariff rate, Country A finds it cheaper to buy commodity X from Country C than to produce it at home, and the tariff is, therefore, not prohibitive. Furthermore, even though domestic consumers must pay a price of 30, the economy as a whole is paying only 20, the difference being the amount collected by the domestic government as tariff revenue. Now suppose Country A forms a free trade area with B. Domestic consumers will face a price of 26 in B and a price of 30 in C and will therefore divert their purchases from C to B. This situation is referred to as *trade diversion,* which in the simple case shown reduces domestic welfare: consumers must pay 26 units, whereas formerly they effectively paid only 20.

The simple case represented by Table 18.1 suggests that preferential trade agreements resulting in trade creation are welfare-increasing, whereas trade-diverting preferential trade is welfare-reducing. It is easy to show, however, that these results depend on some very special assumptions. In particular, it is implicit in the argument that there is no substitution in consumption (in other words, the indifference curves are rectangular) and that the production possibility curve is linear. We will now consider the effects of relaxing these two assumptions.

18.3 SUBSTITUTION IN CONSUMPTION

The implications of the highly specific assumption of zero substitutability between goods are demonstrated in Figs. 18.1 and 18.2, where the costs of commodity X are now measured relative to commodity Y. In order to simplify the analysis, we now assume that Country A cannot produce commodity X at all but must import it from B or C. Thus, for Country C, the relative cost of X in terms of Y is represented by the line AC, and for Country B it is represented by the line AB. Suppose preferences for consumers in Country A are represented by isoquants such as I_0, implying that consumption must always be along the line OZ. With free trade, Country A would purchase commodity X from Country C and would consume at point E.

Any tariff on X rotates the price lines AC and AB around A toward the horizontal axis as the relative price consumers pay for imports from either B or C increases. (Only the tariff-inclusive price line of C, AC', is shown.) After the tariff is imposed, consumers will import X at the tariff-distorted price of AC'. However, imports will lead to tariff revenues, which will shift

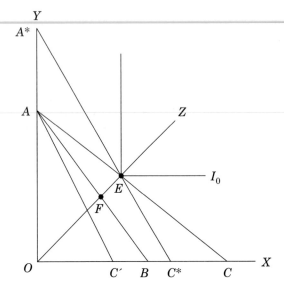

FIGURE 18.1
Trade diversion with no substitution in consumption.

out A's relative cost of importing X to A^*C^*. In other words, following the imposition of a tariff, consumption remains at point E in Fig. 18.1 because imports from C remain cheaper than those from B, and the supplement to income of tariff revenue allows consumers to continue choosing E.[2]

Now suppose Country A forms a free trade area with Country B while maintaining its tariff on Country C. This causes consumption to shift to point F in Fig. 18.1 because consumers can now buy imports more cheaply from B than they can from C. The free trade area has led trade to be diverted from C to B, and this trade diversion has resulted in a welfare loss. Note that if the initial tariff had been small enough to leave the distorted price line for imports from C to the right of AB, forming the free trade area would not have changed the pattern of trade.

The result of Fig. 18.1 depends on the fact that the indifference curves are rectangular, or in other words, that they exhibit zero elasticity of substitution. Fig. 18.2 proves this by representing the same situation except with indifference curves that illustrate substitution in consumption. With free trade, consumption will take place at E. The imposition of a tariff that increases the domestic price ratio to p will move consumers to point H, where there is a tangency between this new domestic price line and the highest indifference curve along the terms-of-trade line AC. Now consider the formation of a free trade area between countries A and B. With the tariff still imposed on C, domestic consumers will buy X from B at the price ratio line AB and will thus consume at point K. Point K, because it is on the same indifference curve as point H, implies that the formation of a free trade area has neither reduced nor improved welfare, even though the free trade area has been trade-diverting. Of course, this is a very special case, but the point is that the relative cost ratio for Country B could lie either

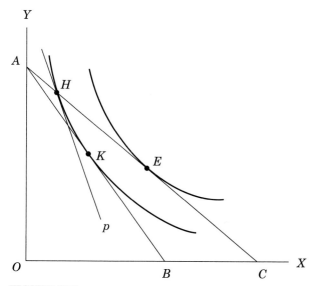

FIGURE 18.2
Substitution in consumption.

above or below AB. Therefore, there is no clear presumption that trade diversion is either welfare-improving or welfare-reducing. With substitution in consumption, a country in a free trade area that diverts trade to a less efficient producer could actually increase its welfare. Note, however, that the optimum scenario in terms of this model is free trade, moving consumption back to point E. A free trade area with B represents a second-best solution in this example, whether the trade diversion increases or reduces welfare relative to point H.

18.4 A HECKSCHER-OHLIN APPROACH

In the last section, we relaxed the assumption that there was no substitution in consumption but retained the assumption that the production possibility curve was linear. We now examine the effects of trade creation and trade diversion in the traditional Heckscher-Ohlin-type model with a production possibility curve illustrated by TAT' in Fig. 18.3. With free trade, production is at A and consumption at C_0, so that the price line p represents the terms of trade with Country C. With a tariff, production would move to Q with consumption at C_1. The question now is whether a free trade area with Country B, with a relatively higher price of X than exists in Country C, could make the domestic economy better off than the tariff-ridden situation of C_1. The answer clearly depends on the price line in B. Suppose the domestic economy could buy from B at the price ratio p'. This price line passes above C_1 and thus necessarily intersects the indifference curve tangent to p_1 at C_1. The equilibrium consumption point for p' must, therefore, be on a higher

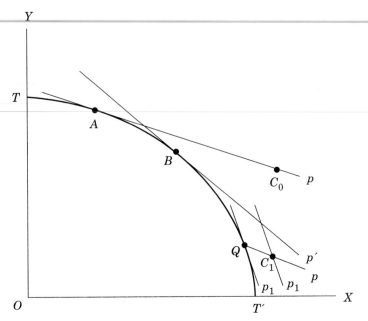

FIGURE 18.3
Welfare improvements with trade diversion.

community indifference curve. The switch from trading with Country C to trading with Country B at prices p' is an example of trade diversion; thus it is again clear that trade diversion may be welfare-improving.

It is interesting to note in Fig. 18.3 that trade diversion may improve welfare whether or not there is substitution in consumption, the very situation that allowed trade diversion to improve welfare in Fig. 18.2. This can easily be seen by supposing, in Fig. 18.3, that community indifference curves are rectangular as in Fig. 18.1. Even in this case, as long as the terms of trade p' with partner B pass above point C_1, the establishment of the free trade area will be welfare-improving. Thus, it is clear that predicting a welfare loss from trade diversion depends on the conditions of no substitution in consumption and a linear production possibility curve.

Fig. 18.4 represents the same free trade situation of Fig. 18.3, but it assumes that when a tariff is imposed, the terms of trade with the rest of the world are improved to p'' with consumption point C_1. This situation, in which a tariff increases welfare by improving the terms of trade, is an example of the optimum tariff discussed in Chapter 15. Again it is assumed that, in the initial tariff situation, trade takes place with Country C.

We now ask whether a free trade area with Country B could be welfare-improving. The answer is clearly no. Indeed, if the situation of Fig. 18.4 represents the optimum tariff, then no alternative trade agreement of any kind, including free trade, could make the country better off. In other words, if we are already pursuing the optimum policy, then no change, whether

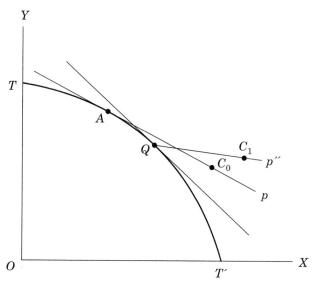

FIGURE 18.4
Including terms of trade effects.

trade-diverting or trade-creating, could possibly make us better off. The only exception to this is if *A* and *B* join together in a customs union with a common external tariff against the rest of the world. In such a case, there is the potential that the joint market power of *A* and *B* could lead to an even greater, shared welfare gain from the imposition of a joint tariff. This is essentially what the Oil Producing Exporting Countries (OPEC) managed to do in the early 1970s by raising the world price of oil.

Kemp and Wan (1976) provide a convincing argument that any sort of customs union, if properly defined, can be welfare-improving. Their argument runs as follows. Consider a situation in which any number of countries in a group, *M,* produce and exchange any number of commodities, *N,* and in which each country is allowed to have any kinds of tariffs, domestic taxes, or other distortionary policies. Now consider the possibility that some subgroup of these countries, *S,* forms a customs union. Suppose it is actually possible to combine this subgroup *S* into a single economy whose resources are equal to the sum of those of the individual subgroup members. Suppose further that this fictitious single country is now faced with the same excess demands and supplies that faced subgroup *S* before the union. The question now is whether this new economy can organize itself in such a manner that individual consumers are better off than they were before the union. Unless the initial situation happened to have been the optimum, the answer is yes. After all, given the same excess demands and supplies from foreigners, and given that the initial situation contained distortions, a preferred equilibrium position will clearly exist. Note finally that to ensure that the same excess demands and supplies face the new union, a system of external taxes, subsidies, and so on can be defined that maintains the initial world terms of trade for all commodities.

The situation described earlier would almost certainly involve redistributions of income among consumers and, more importantly, would probably involve redistributions among countries. Thus, ensuring that this customs union will be welfare-improving would almost certainly involve international transfers, transfers that might well be difficult to implement in practice. It is also clear that the conditions facing the customs union among the S countries described previously must also apply to $S + 1$ countries, and so by logical extension, we would end up with free trade. It is interesting to note that this argument leads back to the classical proposition that a customs union, because it moves us closer to free trade, is presumed to be welfare-improving. We have seen that while this is not generally true, the appropriate kinds of redistributions, some of them international in nature, can give any customs union the potential to improve the welfare of member nations.

18.5   OTHER ISSUES

As was suggested in our introduction, the gains associated with any form of economic cooperation can come from a variety of sources. The analysis conducted so far has concentrated almost entirely on production differences and is thus an incomplete analysis of possible gains associated with preferential trade. Most discussion in the literature has focused on the question of whether free trade areas are trade-creating or trade-diverting, and on circumstances under which trade diversion may make a country better or worse off. However, a successful, complete analysis may well reveal that these issues are not the fundamentally important ones.

Let us first consider the welfare implications of forming a preferential trade area when scale economies or imperfect competition are present. In either case, the advantages of a trade area arise from the internal advantages of a larger market rather than from the trade diversion or trade creation that results from trading with a partner in the absence of tariffs. For instance, an industry can capitalize on scale economies more easily in the larger market of a free trade area. Within this larger market, firms can rationalize production, produce larger runs, and effectively lower average costs, simply because a larger market without protective barriers is available. Perhaps the major impetus behind the establishment of the Canada-United States Free Trade Agreement in the 1980s was to allow Canadian industry to take advantage of the potential economies of scale in a larger North American market.[3]

In a similar fashion, the formation of preferential trade areas will generally be welfare-improving when extensive imperfect competition is present in the initially protected economy. As explained in Chapter 11, the establishment of free trade when some domestic sector is imperfectly competitive will force that sector to compete with possible imports. Thus, free trade leads not only to regular gains from trade but also to procompetitive gains from trade. In the second-best world of preferential trade areas, these procompetitive gains are at least partially available. Suppose a monopolist produces in the import competing sector. As long as this monopolist chooses to produce at a price less than or equal to the tariff-inclusive price of imports, monopoly inefficiency is present. With the free trade area, the domestic monopolist must behave competitively at the price of imports from the partner, even when the partner's industry might otherwise cause trade diversion. This reduces the scope of potential monopolistic inefficiency.

One interesting question that remains involves the current policy dynamics of preferential trade agreements. In recent years, the world has seen an expansion of the amount of trade taking place under preferential agreements with the extension of membership in the European Economic Community, the creation of the Canada-United States Free Trade Agreement of 1988, and the expansion of the latter to the North American Free Trade Agreement of 1994. What might be leading to this renewed policy interest in preferential trade among nations? We will discuss two of the many possible explanations.

First, over the past twenty-five years, international trade has become increasingly restricted by quotas and other nontariff barriers as the levels of tariffs have fallen. However, when a preferential trade agreement is implemented in the presence of quota-restricted trade, the welfare consequences can be quite different from those outlined in Sections 18.2, 18.3, and 18.4. Consider how an equilibrium would be depicted in Fig. 18.3 if trade were restricted by a VER rather than a tariff. First, as explained in Chapter 16, the VER would generate no rents for the importing country. Consequently, consumption would take place somewhere along p_1 rather than at C_1. Second, because the quota restricts the quantity of the imports but does not directly raise their price, importers holding the quota licenses could still continue to import from the least-cost source in Country C, even after the formation of a free trade area with B. Given thes two outcomes, it is probable that preferential trade with some nations will improve welfare when trade is generally restricted by quotas.

Second, preferential trade agreements generally take the form of treaties between nations, and this can have significant implications for the flow of trade as compared to trade governed by Most Favored Nation status. In general, an exporting firm always faces the possibility that its exports could suddenly be restricted by a large increase in the level of protection in the importing country. However, when a preferential trade agreement is in place between two countries, exporting firms in both nations can make plans with a greater degree of certainty that future trade will not be disrupted. This is because it is easier for protectionist interests to politically implement changes in the tariff and quota code for a nation than it is for them to alter the structure of a treaty establishing a free trade area or some other form of preferential trade. For instance, under NAFTA, U.S. firms will be able to relocate production facilities in Mexico with less fear of a disruption in exports back to the United States by some sort of specific trade action, even if tariff rates were zero before the agreement. Thus, a preferential trade agreement, because it might be seen as having more permanence than regulated trade, can lead to dynamic, long-run gains that simple tariff reductions fail to attain.

18.6 CONCLUDING REMARKS

This chapter has focused on preferential trade areas, which represent a second-best movement toward free trade. Other important methods of moving toward free trade are unilateral tariff reductions and multilateral, negotiated trade liberalization agreements. Unfortunately, these partial movements toward free trade contain the potential for welfare losses precisely because they are second-best policies that fail to correct all distortions.

The general literature on preferential trade has focused on the issue of trade diversion, in which imports from nonmembers are replaced with imports from members, and trade creation, in which imports from members replace inefficient domestic production. In spite of the terminology, however, trade diversion is not necessarily welfare-reducing. In particular, imports coming from a lower-priced member of a free trade area, even if they replace imports from the least-cost nonmember. may increase welfare by helping to rationalize domestic consumption and production patterns.

There are several other sources of potential gains from the establishment of a free trade area. Scale economies and diminished market power on the part of imperfectly competitive firms can lead to more efficient domestic production following the establishment of a free trade area. Furthermore, when trade is protected by nontariff barriers, the traditional analysis of trade diversion and creation no longer applies. Finally, the establishment of a free trade area among countries may provide more certainty to firms about the permanence of tariff reductions and might consequently lead to more dynamic, long-run adjustment on the part of those firms.

PROBLEMS

1. In Table 18.1, suppose that the cost of production in A is 29. What will be the effect of a 50-percent tariff?
2. Draw Fig. 18.2 to illustrate the case in which trade diversion is welfare-improving.
3. In Fig. 18.2, it is not always reasonable to suppose that the terms of trade (slope of line AB) are unchanged after A begins to buy goods from B. How can you account for this? How would this change the conclusions concerning the welfare effects of trade diversion?
4. In Fig. 18.4, if C_1 were moved far enough to the right on p'', could it be on a lower community indifference curve than C_0?
5. Redraw Fig. 18.3 to show the case in which trade diversion reduces welfare.

NOTES

1. A significant problem with the development of free trade areas is that they may actually be lessening the extent to which multilateral agreements are depended upon to liberalize trade. Countries may put more effort into negotiating bilateral accords rather than new GATT agreements. This might lead the overall pace of international trade liberalization to slow or even reverse.
2. Consumers can still afford E because all of the tariff revenue that is taxed away from them is assumed to be rebated right back to them.
3. The importance of scale economies in the economic effects of the Canada-United States trade agreement is discussed in detail in Harris (1991).

REFERENCES

Harris, R. G. (1991). "Symposium—The Canada–U.S. FTA: Economic Impacts and Transition Effects." *Journal of Policy Modelling* 13:421–434.

Kemp, M. C., and Wan, H. Y. (1976). "An Elementary Proposition Concerning the Formation of Customs Unions." *Journal of International Economics* 6:95–97.

Krauss, M. B. (1972). "Recent Developments in Customs Union Theory: An Interpretive Survey." *Journal of Economic Literature* 10:413–436.

Lipsey, R. G. (1960). "The Theory of Customs Unions—A General Survey." *Economic Journal* 70:496–513.

Lipsey, R. G., and Lancaster, K. (1956–57). "The General Theory of the Second Best." *Review of Economic Studies* 24:11–32.

Melvin, J. R. (1969). "Comments on the Theory of Customs Unions." *Manchester School of Economic and Social Studies* 36:161–168.

Michaely, M. (1963). "On Customs Unions and the Gains from Trade." *Economic Journal* 75:577–583.

Schott, J. J., ed. (1989). *Free Trade Areas and U.S. Trade Policy.* Institute for International Economics: Washington, D.C.

CHAPTER
19

THE POLITICAL ECONOMY OF TRADE POLICY

19.1 INTRODUCTION

So far in this text, policy analysis has been normative in nature. That is, the policy choices discussed have been examined from the perspective of what is "optimal" given the aggregate utility structure of the assumptions in place. In fact, given the presumptions of the theory discussed so far, the only way to explain why we do not always see optimal policies in use is that policy makers might not be aware of what the optimal policy is or of what kinds of distortions arise from the policies actually in place. This suggests that the better we understand the behavior of the economic world, the closer we will be to policy optimality. In this chapter, however, we move from this normative analysis of what policies are "best" given an assumed social welfare function to a positive analysis of policy. In other words, in this chapter we will develop a theory of why countries impose the types of policies that they do, even if those policies are sub-optimal.

Public choice economics is the study of governmental decision-making behavior using economic models. This means that decision makers in the public sector are modeled to be utility maximizers who optimize in the face of constraints on their behavior in the same way as we have modeled decision makers in the private sector. Throughout this part of the book, the repeated conclusion of the analysis has been that direct trade interventions in the form of tariffs or quotas are rarely optimal policies. This might lead inquisitive students to wonder, then, just why we have so many direct trade intervention policies in place worldwide. The analysis developed in this chapter, however, may lead students to wonder why we do not see an even more pervasive use of trade policy.

There are decision makers at many levels of government: members of the executive branch, legislators and other elected officials, bureaucrats, independent commissioners, and more. What informs the decisions they reach? Public choice analysis makes the simple assumption that these individuals behave just like the head of a household who attempts to maximize household utility subject to various constraints on income and time and the like, or like the manager of a firm who attempts to maximize profits for that firm subject to cost, technology, and various market constraints. A governmental decision maker—a legislator, for instance—is ultimately self-interested, aiming to maximize his or her own utility before attaining some socially optimal set of policies.

What things are we likely to find in a policy maker's utility function? When we considered consumption behavior in Chapter 3, consumers were assumed to have a utility function:

$$U = U(X, Y).\tag{19.1}$$

Clearly, other things matter to an individual's level of satisfaction besides the consumption level of goods X and Y. For instance, upholding certain values or norms might be important, or the individual might have altruistic motives regarding the consumption levels of others. However, the conclusions based on the simple model of utility as a function of consumption of X and Y greatly simplified the process and allowed us to draw very clear conclusions. In this fashion, there is undoubtedly a variety of things that are important to a governmental policy maker's level of utility: political ideology, personal wealth (acquired in the form of bribes), the decision maker's place in history, and so forth. However, to simplify the set of important utility-enhancing elements we will assume that elected officials desire to be reelected and will behave in a manner consistent with maximizing the likelihood of this event.

An immediate implication of assuming that governmental officials enact policies in order to maximize their chances of staying in office is that, to a large extent, the public's desires will be served by these officials. However, a number of decision-making problems arise in public choice analysis that create policy distortions—that is, failure of a government to enact socially optimal policies. Thus, the conclusions of this chapter will include the acknowledgement that governmental failure to enact socially optimal policies results not from simple ignorance of what those policies might be but from systematic governmental failure.

19.2   THE MEDIAN-VOTER MODEL

The median-voter model is one way of examining the behavior of governmental decision makers in an indirect fashion. If we begin by assuming that legislators are self-interested and desire to stay in office, then their behavior will be to enact those policies into law that satisfy the voter who lies at the median of a distribution of individual voter preferences on some issue. In satisfying the median voter's interests, a legislator will maximize the likelihood of reelection because a majority of voters, as represented by the interests of the median voter, will favor the policies put forward by that official. This allows us to model behavior in the policy-making process indirectly by looking at the preferences of voters.

Figure 19.1 is a model of median-voter preferences with respect to some specific policy action under consideration by the government. International trade policies are a natural subject for consideration in the median-voter model because, as the Stolper-Samuelson Theorem of Chapter 8 and the Specific-Factor model of Chapter 9 showed us, trade policies that change relative prices on domestic markets from their world levels create differential welfare effects on easily isolated groups in an economy. The Stolper-Samuelson Theorem, for instance, demonstrates that a tariff that raises the domestic price of the labor-intensive, imported good will raise the real return to labor and lower the real return to capital, regardless of the sector in which these factors are employed.[1]

Suppose our median-voter model is being used to explain the preferences of individuals regarding a piece of legislation that would raise the domestic price of some imported good through an import tariff. In Fig. 19.1, an array of voter preferences on this issue is presented from 0 to 1 on the horizontal axis. Each individual member of the electorate is assigned a position along this array based on the change in utility that he or she will experience if the import tariff is put into place. All those who lose from this tariff are lumped first, followed by those who gain. The preference of the median voter is at 0.5 on the distribution. The actual utility loss or gain is then measured as a negative or positive amount along the vertical axis. In this example, 60 percent of the voters will lose if this tariff is enacted into law.

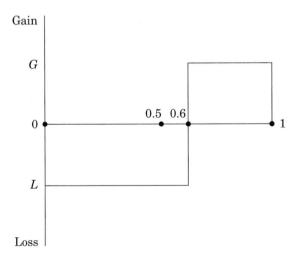

FIGURE 19.1
Median voter choice.

Figure 19.1 clearly makes the simplifying assumption that all winners from the proposed tariff gain an equal amount per individual, G, while all losers are penalized by an amount of L per individual. A more general approach might simply array individual voters along a positively sloped locus from the most harmed to the most benefited. However, such a generalization really adds little to the analysis, and the assumption that all winners gain G and all losers lose L is consistent with previous assumptions regarding factor homogeneity and identical and homothetic tastes. That is, if we assume that labor and capital factors of production are homogeneous and that each individual has identical and homothetic preferences, then individuals should either all gain or all lose from the tariff by equal amounts within their respective groups.[2]

The median voter in Fig. 19.1 loses if this tariff is passed and is thus likely to vote against a legislator who attempts to pass it. This leads us to conclude that a legislator interested in reelection who represents a district like the one in Fig. 19.1 would vote against this measure. If the majority of the legislators voting on this tariff represented constituencies that have individual preferences like those in Fig. 19.1, this tariff would be voted down.

Whether it can be characterized as protectionist (i.e. raising trade barriers) or liberalizing (lowering trade barriers), trade policy is almost always redistributive in nature. That is, it causes some members of a society to gain while others lose. The median voter model, as presented so far, insures that the position of the majority will be followed, which would seem to be a positive outcome except to those who find themselves in the minority group on issue after issue. However, there are several problems that arise from depending upon the preferences of the median voter to decide political outcomes.

19.3 PUBLIC CHOICE PROBLEMS WITH MEDIAN VOTER DECISIONS

Even when the dictates of the median voter are followed, policy decisions are likely to be suboptimal because of the many problems involved in the process of aggregating individual preferences and turning them into political decisions. In this section, we will apply public choice analysis to the median-voter model in order to illustrate some of these policy-making failures. We will begin with one serious flaw inherent to median-voter decisions in particular: the fact that median voter choices fail to register intensity of preferences.

Figure 19.2 examines voter preferences with respect to a second issue. Suppose a trade liberalization issue is under consideration by a policy-making board.[3] Once again, 60 percent of voters will be harmed by the liberalization, while only 40 percent will benefit. However, in this case, the extent of each individual gain or loss is quite different. Each individual who

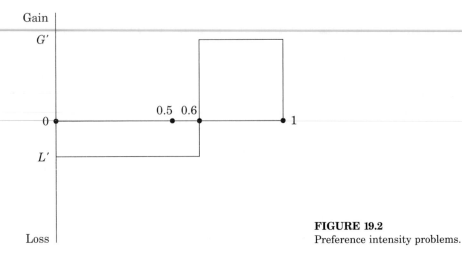

FIGURE 19.2
Preference intensity problems.

benefits from this policy will gain G' from its passage, while each loser will lose L'. Figure 19.2 has been constructed so that $0.4G'$ clearly is greater than $0.6L'$; therefore, the net effect of the liberalization measure on the whole of society is positive. Nevertheless, because the median voter belongs to the group opposed to the measure, the median voter model predicts that the liberalization measure will fail.

Consideration of the implications of the Stolper-Samuelson Theorem in combination with the failure of a median-voter decision-making process to register preference intensity is important for trade policy. In general, in the absence of any other distortion, import protection will lower social welfare for an economy. However, the Stolper-Samuelson Theorem demonstrates that a tariff policy that raises the price of the imported good will raise the absolute return to the scarce factor while lowering the absolute return to the abundant factor. From a median-voter perspective, though, the question is not whether the tariff will be beneficial on the whole (which it would not be), but how many votes these two factors will command in the political system. In most economies, the distribution of factor ownership is skewed so that almost all members of the economy own one unit of labor, while some individuals own many units of capital and none. This suggests that labor interests would tend to have their way in most median-voter decisions. In other words, even in an economy where labor is relatively scarce in economic terms, labor is likely to be the politically abundant factor—that is, in the majority. The empirical implication of this, in accordance with the Stolper-Samuelson Theorem, is that, other things held constant, labor-scarce countries are likely to have higher tariff rates on average than labor-abundant countries.

Studies of welfare economics must grapple with the problem that social welfare redistributions pose for a political entity. The policy measures suggested by Figs. 19.1 and 19.2 are redistributive policies that allow one segment of society to gain only at the expense of some other group. By the *Pareto criterion* of welfare economics, neither policy choice is "optimal" because only by harming some can there be a gain for others. An alternative way of judging the issue, however, is called the *compensation criterion.* According to this welfare judgement, a policy is socially wise if those who gain from the policy can fully compensate those who lose, even if no compensation is made. Notice that the measure considered in Fig. 19.1 is a poor social choice because the gainers could never fully compensate losers. The measure considered in Fig. 19.2, however, is good social policy because compensation is possible.

While the median voter would vote down the issue considered in Fig. 19.2, there are ways for the minority to prevail. Notice that a market-based election in which voters "buy" votes would allow passage of this issue because the minority's willingness to pay in order to pass the liberalization exceeds the majority's willingness to pay in order to maintain the status quo. Some voting schemes have been used in which intensities of preference are explicitly weighted into the election using this kind of market allocative device. Actually, undertaking compensation is another way of ensuring the outcome with the greatest net benefit to society. A transfer from the benefited group to some or all of the losers may cancel their opposition.

While such compensation schemes may seem impractical, illegal, or perhaps even immoral, they actually take place in the political system all the time under the name of *logrolling,* the colorful name given to vote trading. In Table 19.1, we consider the welfare effects of a pair of simultaneous policy decisions. Three individuals, A, B, and C will gain or lose the dollar amounts shown in the table from issues 1 and 2. Issue 1 benefits A by $20 at a cost of $5 each to B and C. The net social gain of the measure is $10, but of course B and C would vote it down two-to-one in a majority election. Similarly, issue 2 would be defeated by a coalition between A and C, even though it has an identical net social benefit of $10. However, if A and B are able to arrange a vote on a package of issues 1 and 2, the issue will pass by a two-to-one vote because the personal benefit to each is $15, while only C will vote against it.

While in this case logrolling solves the compensation problem and allows both A and B to secure enough votes to enact the policies that are beneficial not only to them but also to society as a whole, logrolling can also lead to nonoptimal policy decisions. Table 19.2 changes the payoffs to

TABLE 19.1
Gains from logrolling

	Gain or loss to individual			
	A	B	C	Net
Issue 1	+20	−5	−5	+10
Issue 2	−5	+20	−5	+10
Issue 1&2	+15	+15	−10	+20

the gainers and losers in such a way that, although issues 1 and 2 are both socially detrimental, a logrolling coalition between A and B to pass a legislative package of issues 1 and 2 is still possible.

One of the most damaging tariffs in U.S. tariff history, the Smoot-Hawley tariff of 1930, was actually a package of tariff bills for different sectors of the economy rolled into a single package. The political strategy employed in passing the Smoot-Hawley tariff is almost a textbook example of the possibility of welfare losses from logrolling. Legislators, all seeking to gain protection for industries that were politically important to them, agreed to vote for high tariffs for other industries in order to "buy" more votes for their own favored sectors. The result was an increase of average protective tariffs in the United States to more than 50 percent of the value of imports. This level compares unfavorably to current levels of less than 5 percent.

So far, two underlying assumptions have been made in the median-voter model in order to obtain the result that self-interested political decision makers will follow the wishes of the median voter. First, we have assumed that the median voter has full knowledge of the gains or losses that he or she will receive from political measures. Second, we have assumed that individuals actually vote their preferences. In practice, neither of these conditions will hold fully, and as a result, the preferences of the median voter might not win out in political decisions.

It may be rational for members of a political system to maintain ignorance of the issues at stake in the system and the payoffs to them as individuals as well as to abstain from participating in the system. Coming to understand the potential payoffs of a political decision is costly in that resources must be expended to gather and evaluate information. Voting, either directly for an issue in a referendum or indirectly for a set of issues by voting for a political candidate, is also costly to an individual in that time and resources are lost by going to the polls and waiting to vote. While the costs of collecting information on political issues and then voting are undoubtedly small for most individuals, these costs must be compared to the benefits of political participation.

The benefit to an individual from political participation is the likelihood that his or her efforts will actually swing an election to a positive outcome

TABLE 19.2
Losses from logrolling

	Gain or loss to individual			
	A	**B**	**C**	**Net**
Issue 1	+20	−15	−15	−10
Issue 2	−15	+20	−15	−10
Issue 1&2	+5	+5	−30	−20

from a negative outcome for that individual. However, political outcomes are public goods because they affect all members of a political system regardless of whether one specific member participated in the decision or not. This allows individuals to engage in what the public choice literature calls *free riding*—that is, deciding to accept the outcome without engaging in the political process.

In addition, the likelihood that an individual voter will cast the vote that swings an election is effectively zero. Even in local elections where only hundreds or thousands of votes are cast, it is highly unlikely that an election will end up in a tie where the marginal voter seals the outcome. In a larger election with millions of potential voters in the electorate, the likelihood of a tied outcome vanishes. As a result, the benefits to an individual from voting—the result that that person's vote changes an outcome in his or her favor—are quite different from the benefits that accrue to the individual from the election itself. Because individuals can rely on benefiting (or losing) from a political decision whether or not they vote, and because the costs of participation, however slight, are likely to exceed the direct benefits of participation, it is rational to remain ignorant and abstain.[4]

Rational ignorance and rational abstention would not cause any variance from the outcomes predicted by the median voter model if every voter had an equal probability of not participating in an election. However, in this case we cannot make the assumption of identical individuals. In most cases, there are strong asymmetric influences against free-riding by voters. The asymmetric gains and losses shared by many individuals from political outcomes suggest that interest groups of individuals will form. In many cases, these interest groups will be successful in at least partially overcoming free-riding by members of the group. This may allow interest groups to have disproportional influence on political decisions.

Consider a political issue in which a small segment of the electorate gains immensely at the expense of the rest of the voting public if some issue is enacted. In the context of international trade policy, such an issue might be a protective tariff for a specific industry, the redistributional gains and losses from which are interpreted from the perspective of the specific-factor model of Chapter 9. A tariff on some good will probably raise consumer prices of that protected good by only a small percentage at most. Consequently, members of the group losing from this protection will have very small per capita losses. However, to the factors of production that are specific to the protected industry, and to close substitutes for the mobile factors used in the protected industry or goods produced by that industry, the benefits per individual are likely to be very significant.

In Figure 19.3 we examine the political decision to protect an industry. Consumers of the good, shown here as 95 percent of the electorate, will each lose a small amount of L if the tariff is passed. However, specific factors in the protected industry, who comprise the remaining 5 percent of the electorate, will each gain the large amount G from the tariff. The

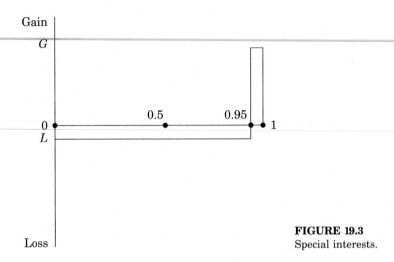

FIGURE 19.3
Special interests.

figure is constructed so that the net social welfare effect of the tariff is negative; that is $0.95L > 0.05G$. This is consistent with the net losses associated with reducing the gains from trade for some good. Furthermore, the median voter is clearly worse off, even if only by a small margin, if the tariff is passed. Nevertheless, special interests in favor of protection often get their way in the political system.

The reason that a tariff can be enacted in spite of the fact that it diminishes total social welfare and is against the best interests of the median voter lies in the differing abilities of interest groups to effect political decisions. Small, well-organized special interests like producer groups are likely to have significant advantages in organization over large but diffuse consumer interests. Special interests in an industry seeking protection will be much more aware of the potential benefits from protection than most consumers will be of the costs of protection. Furthermore, well-organized special interests will be much more successful at controlling free-riding by their members.

An additional factor likely to move political decisions in favor of the interests of small special interests and against the interests of the median voter is the ability of special interest groups to provide funding for political campaigns. So far, we have not included funding in our analysis of political decisions; however, where members of a political system are making rational decisions to remain ignorant and to abstain from voting, funding of political campaigns can provide low-cost information (or misinformation) to potential voters to motivate them toward greater participation. However, well-organized special interests have a comparative advantage in raising political contributions because of their ability to control free-riding by members, and such funding can even be financed out of the benefits expected to accrue to the special interest if the tariff it seeks is imposed.

Political contributions of this kind are called *rent seeking* because the group seeking protection is willing to share its benefits from protection, which are called rents, with the political decision makers in order to affect the political outcome. Of course, rent-seeking expenditures can go far beyond contributions to political campaigns to include bribes and other means of influencing political decisions. The resources expended in rent-seeking activities are sometimes referred to as *directly unproductive activity* because they are exhausted not in producing more goods for society but in merely redirecting the allocations of other goods. Engaging in this unproductive activity wastes resources and may cause policies to be enacted that fail to meet the compensation criterion discussed earlier.[5]

The analysis of tariffs and quotas developed in Chapters 15 and 16 demonstrated that these alternatives to free trade are welfare-improving only in unusual cases and optimal in only extraordinary situations. This might lead a student to ask why trade protection is so widely used. In this section we have examined some of the problems inherent in political decision making that lead to the enactment of policies that are at variance with the interests of the median voter and/or the net social welfare. This understanding allows us to explain the use of tariffs and quotas as well as distortive taxes and subsidies like those examined in Chapter 10. In fact, from a public choice perspective, a frequently asked question is not why tariffs and quotas are so widely used but why they do not get used even more extensively.

19.4 MEDIAN-VOTER DECISIONS UNDER UNCERTAINTY

While the median voter model must be subject to some of the modifications suggested in the previous section for it to satisfactorily describe the policy-making process, it is still a useful starting point for explaining political decisions. In this section we continue to employ it in order to examine political decisions under uncertainty. Our assumption so far has been that the outcomes of political decisions could be predicted with certainty, even if some affected by the decisions did not go to the expense of discovering what their payoff would be. In this section, however, we relax that assumption and allow for some uncertainty as to what the economic results of a political decision might be.

Suppose a decision to move toward free trade is certain to benefit 60 percent of the electorate while harming the remaining 40 percent. Assume that all exporting industries will expand and that all import-competing industries will shrink. However, some industries not currently exporting will begin to do so, perhaps because of mutual liberalization by trade partners. If factors are specific to industries, then factors employed in export industries and newly exporting industries will be better off following liberalization, but factors that remain in those sectors producing import-competing goods will be worse off. However, factors currently employed in the import-competing

sectors are uncertain whether they will be able to switch to the export
sector or whether they will be stuck with lower welfare in the shrinking
import-competing sector.

If we suppose that all individuals will gain or lose an identical amount,
P, then the total net payoff to society of the liberalization is equal to
$0.6P - 0.4P$, or $0.2P$. However, as shown by Fig. 19.4, only those factors
currently employed in the export sector (40 percent of all factors) are
certain of their welfare after the liberalization policies are implemented.
The remaining 60 percent of the electorate is uncertain as to whether they
will end up better off (a $\frac{1}{3}$ chance) or worse off (a $\frac{2}{3}$ chance). For this entire
group, the *expected* payoff from liberalization is a loss of $\frac{1}{3}P$ for each member.
Consequently, in the absence of any additional compensation from the 40
percent of the population that is confident of their gains, the median-voter
result suggests that this country will vote down liberalization.

While the numbers in this example are arbitrary, they suggest what
has been referred to as a *status quo bias* against liberalizing trade policy.
Liberalization policies toward freer trade tend to have the promise of
improving aggregate welfare, and they definitely will favor certain groups
in a nation; however, large portions of the rest of the electorate are unsure
whether they will be among the winners or the losers from the move toward
free trade. This uncertainty lends itself to a bias toward staying with the
status quo rather than adopting the policy change toward liberalization.

Status quo bias can help explain not only resistance to tariff liberalization but also increased protection in many circumstances. Suppose certain
sectors, like the steel industry or sugar-producing farmers, are subject to
increased pressure from imports because world capacity is rising and world
production costs are falling relative to domestic costs. The changing trade
equilibrium from these adjustments threatens the standard of living enjoyed

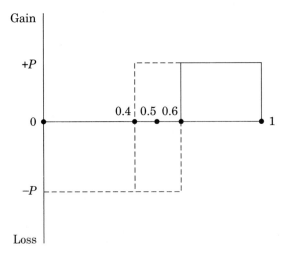

FIGURE 19.4
Uneven distribution of uncertainty.

by specific factors in steel and sugar unless tariffs or quotas are imposed to protect the status quo. It is quite possible that factors in other sectors, say textiles and automobiles, will be willing to support protection for steel and sugar, even if doing so lowers their own standard of living slightly, in an implicit insurance arrangement to protect themselves if they should find themselves in the same position. This type of protectionism is explained by what is called a *conservative welfare function* on the part of society, by which trade policies are formulated in attempts to maintain the existing income distribution among sectors. Each sector buys into the implicit agreement with the understanding that its position will also be protected should it come under a similar threat from increased imports.

19.5 THE FORM OF PROTECTION

The analysis in the previous sections applies to the questions of whether or not protection should exist for some sector of the economy and at what level the protection should be. A somewhat different issue is the decision of what form the protection should take. Chapters 15 and 16 examined tariffs and quotas. The many other policy instruments available for transfering resources to some specific sector of the economy include discriminatory exchange rates, production subsidies, factor-use subsidies, and other types of barriers to free trade such as technical specifications. In this section we will discuss some of the political economy issues involved in choosing instruments of protection by focusing on the choice from among tariffs, quotas, and production subsidies.

Let us assume that there are three interest groups in an economy: consumers, producers of import-competing goods, and a group that benefits by government expenditures of revenue upon their interests. We begin with the consumer group whose interests are easily detailed: consumers gain from eliminating unnecessary distortions in the economy. The analyses of Chapters 15 and 16 help us rank the abilities of these three policies to minimize economic distortions. Assuming perfect competition and constant returns to scale, it is easy to show that production subsidies are the least damaging. Production subsidies distort only the production side of the economy and cause smaller welfare losses than do tariffs and quotas, which distort both producer and consumer prices from their world levels (refer to Fig. 15.4). However, as shown by the analysis in Chapter 16, the welfare losses from quota distortions generally exceed those from tariff distortions. Thus, consumer preferences rank production subsidies as preferred to tariffs, which are in turn preferred to quotas: or $S > T > Q$.

Even though all three instruments of protection will increase output, producers of import-competing goods also have a distinct ranking of the three policy options. The foremost consideration for them is a higher output price for their products on the domestic market. This is attained by all of the policies because in each case, home producers are protected from the price-reducing effects of imports. Consequently, we will call this group *protection seekers.* For several reasons, protection seekers prefer quotas to the other two options. First, quotas might allow domestic producers and foreign exporters to collude on a division of market share. With a quota there is a restriction on the quantity of imports that foreign firms can deliver to the domestic market, so further price competition is supplanted by cooperation. Second, where products might be slightly differentiated in some larger product class—for instance, different truck-bed sizes—quotas can be finely tailored to different product categories in a way that helps a producer interest group enforce against free-riding among members of the group. In other words, a larger contribution to the lobbying effort by some firm might be rewarded by a tightening of the portion of the quota that benefits that producer the most. Finally, quotas are thought to be less politically visible instruments of protection than tariffs, so the political efficiency of a protection-seeking group is enhanced by quotas.

The political effectiveness of protection-seeking may be greater for subsidies than for tariffs. As explained earlier, subsidies cause a smaller welfare loss to the economy than tariffs. These smaller welfare losses associated with direct subsidies might mitigate political opposition to them based on the rational ignorance argument. Furthermore, direct production subsidies are likely to be firm-specific benefits, whereas tariffs are public goods, a benefit available to any new firm that decides to produce in the protected industry. Consequently, subsidies might be preferred to tariffs by existing members of a protected industry because subsidies help to control free-riding by members of an industry and are unlikely to be shared with newcomers. All of this allows us to presume that protection seekers will rank their policy choices as $Q > S > T$.

The final group consists of interests that benefit from government expenditures on their behalf. For example, in the presence of effective constraints on deficit spending by the government, government pensioners may act to ensure that more revenues are available to be spent on larger pensions. This kind of activity, known as *revenue seeking,* includes the pursuit of government research grants by college professors and other such noble endeavors. While both tariffs and quotas can be used to enhance government revenues, subsidies are an additional drain on revenues and are thus least preferred by revenue seekers. Tariffs will be the most-preferred policy by this group because, while quotas can be used for revenue purposes when the quota rights are auctioned off, these rights are usually distributed in a way that does not add to revenue.[6] This gives us a policy ranking for revenue seekers of $T > Q > S$.

The policy preferences of the three groups are summarized in Table 19.3. Having already decided to grant protection to the protection seekers, the government now attempts to select a policy instrument for the job. Assuming that the groups are of roughly equal size, subsidies are preferred to tariffs by a 2-1 margin (consumers and protection seekers over revenue seekers). Tariffs are preferred to quotas also by a 2-1 margin (consumers and revenue seekers over protection seekers). However, by an equivalent

TABLE 19.3
Policy preferences of interest groups

Group	Policies		
Consumers	Subsidies	>Tariffs	>Quotas
Protection Seekers	Quotas	>Subsidies	>Tariffs
Revenue Seekers	Tarrifs	>Quotas	>Subsidies

2-1 margin, quotas are seen as superior to subsidies (revenue and protection seekers over consumers). This gives us a nontransitive political ordering of the policies:

$$\text{Subsidies} > \text{Tariffs} > \text{Quotas} > \text{Subsidies.}^{7}$$

The solution to this policy paradox comes from considering the order in which the issues are considered or voted on. Thus, if tariffs and quotas are compared first, with the preferred choice of that pair (tariffs) being subsequently compared to subsidies, subsidies will prevail. Order of consideration is determined by the institutional structure used to decide issues of protection. In the United States, for instance, the Constitution dictates that matters of protection will be considered by the House Ways and Means Committee. This committee is responsible for budgetary issues in general. As such, it gives strong consideration to revenue seekers' concern that subsidies not be used for import protection, and as a result, they rarely are. Furthermore, the GATT has established strong multilateral rules on lowering tariff rates while having only weak rules on the use of quotas. Consequently, while tariffs were the most important protective device until recent decades, quantitative restrictions of various types are now more widely used. This shift in policy is due not to any change in the ordering of policy preferences by the various interest groups but rather to a change in the institutional structure of protection decision making. In the next chapter, the importance of the institutions under which protection is administered will be explained in detail.

19.6   EMPIRICAL EVIDENCE

Studies of the political economy of trade policy have focused on the endogeneity of the level and form of protection (Baldwin, 1985). Tariffs and other forms of protection are the results of interactions in the political arena among various interest groups. So, an industry group in an import-competing sector is likely to have strong protectionist interests, while consumers of the import, or other industries that use the import as an intermediate input, would have free trade interests. In this context, political market failures like free-riding and optimal voter ignorance lead to policy outcomes that would not be described as optimal in the sense of maximizing the public interest.

Tests of the political economy of trade policy have taken several forms: case studies of specific protectionist legislation, microlevel examinations of relative protection, and time-series analysis of the level of protection. Magee (1980) essentially undertook a case study of the Trade Reform Act of 1973 and used the political economy of trade policy to compare different strands of more general trade policy. Magee examined the positions on the Trade Reform Act of 1973 taken by lobbying groups from labor and management in various industries. He found that labor and capital groups from specific industries almost always took the same position before Congress. From this he inferred that the specific-factor model was supported vis-a-vis the Stolper-Samuelson theory as a determinant of the income-distribution effects of trade policy. Several other authors have studied other specific protectionist legislation or the protectionist history of selected industries. For instance, Coughlin (1985) and McArthur and Marks (1988) examined interest-group interactions during Congressional consideration of the Automobile Domestic Content Bill of 1982, and Tosini and Tower (1987) examined the Textile Bill of 1985. Maskus (1988), on the other hand, has examined the history of protection received by the sugar industry in the United States.

The variance in degree of protection across industries, or *relative protection,* has also been investigated in several studies, including Lavergne (1983) and Ray (1981). Because protection is not universal across sectors, cross-sectional studies generate some understanding of the factors that make certain interest groups more successful than others. Typically, the factors considered that might aid an interest group in its lobbying efforts include, among others, size distribution or concentration ratios of firms, labor intensity, and geographical dispersion of the industry.

Time-series analysis of the political economy of protection rests upon the presumption that over time, the strength, size, or political effectiveness of a given interest group active in trade policy creation will vary. In general, these time-series analyses have been aggregative in nature, and therefore, macroeconomic variables like unemployment, inflation, and real GNP are modeled as being the factors that determine an interest group's effectiveness in gaining protection. For instance, in periods of high unemployment, protectionist interest groups gain political strength by invoking the image of "unfair foreign competition stealing away domestic jobs." Time-series analysis thus posits a "tariff cycle" in which protection ebbs and flows in a manner consistent with the conservative social welfare function (Bohara and Kaempfer, 1991).

19.7   CONCLUDING REMARKS

In this chapter we have examined governmental policy-making behavior from the perspective of public choice analysis. Critical to this approach is the presumption that decision makers attempt to maximize their own utility by selecting policies that maximize their chances of staying in office. Such behavior on the part of policy makers does serve the public interest to some extent in that decisions that favor the majority of voters will be selected. However, several "decision-making failures" are likely to arise that will lead to suboptimal policies. The principal findings of this chapter can be summarized as follows.

1. The median-voter model can be used as an indirect model of the utility-maximizing behavior of policy makers because policy makers interested in reelection must respect the preferences of the majority of voters in their constituencies.

2. Political decisions based on the preferences of the median voter fail to directly register the intensity of preferences held by those voters. As a result, it is possible that policies can be enacted that are favored by a majority of voters but that decrease the net social welfare. If individuals who gain from some policy can compensate those who lose, the socially optimal policy might be achieved, and logrolling is one mechanism that allows such compensation. However, logrolling is just as likely to result in legislation that reduces net social welfare.

3. Rational ignorance and rational abstention on the part of voters will increase the influence of special interest groups on political outcomes. It is rational for individual voters to remain ignorant of issues and how those issues affect them and to then abstain from voting because the expected benefits to that individual of casting a vote are likely to be so small that even the small costs involved in voting will exceed these benefits. Special interest groups, however, are likely to have organizational advantages in political action.

4. A status quo bias is likely to allow protectionist policies to persist in spite of the fact that they can clearly be shown to be welfare-reducing. The explanation for this may lie in the fact that a policy change will force some individuals to change sectors in the economy, leaving them unsure as to whether they will be winners or losers from liberalization.

5. Preferences of the members of various interest groups can be examined to gain insights into the form that protection is most likely to take. Tariffs, quotas, and production subsidies have all been discussed as policy options for protecting a domestic industry in competition with imports. Which policy option is selected will depend upon the institutional structure used in making the decision to protect.

PROBLEMS

1. Suppose labor and capital are the only factors of production. According to the Stolper-Samuelson Theorem, how would these groups benefit or lose from import protection in a labor–abundant country? How would they benefit or lose according to the specific-factor approach if capital were sector-specific, but labor were mobile between sectors?

2. Suppose the liberalization bill considered in Fig. 19.4 has the same division of benefits but that all members of the electorate are uncertain whether they will gain or lose from the liberalization. What policy decision will be made?

3. Suppose a domestic monopolist is granted a quota of Q units rather than a price-equivalent import tariff. Suppose further that the quota is auctioned off to the highest bidder for government revenue. Explain whether revenue-seeking groups would prefer the tariff or the quota.

NOTES

1. Of course, the distributional conclusions of the sector-specific factor analysis of Chapter 9 are quite different from the conclusions of the Stolper-Samuelson Theorem. One thing that a public choice analysis of trade policy allows us to do is compare these two theories in a policy-making framework to see which one forms a more accurate picture of the policy process. This is the question addressed by Magee (1980).
2. One exception to this would be if individual capital owners own different amounts of capital. Then each would gain or lose from a piece of legislation according to the amount of capital owned.
3. Notice that in this case, the policy is a liberalization (i.e., tariff-reducing) issue rather than a protectionist issue. As explained in Chapter 18, liberalization is as much of a political economy issue as is protection.
4. Using this kind of marginal-cost/marginal-benefit analysis to examine voting might lead one to question why voter turnouts are so high rather than to ask why they are so low. However, there are other utility-enhancing factors, like civic pride, and other costs of not voting, like group or social pressure, that make it rational for many individuals to vote in spite of the minimal direct economic benefits.
5. Another type of directly unproductive activity is the use of resources to smuggle goods into a country in an attempt to avoid tariffs. In the case of smuggling, resources are used up not to produce any direct benefits but simply to avoid the tariff.
6. In the United States, most quotas are given to foreign exporters or foreign countries so that they may determine the allocations and profit by the quotas.
7. This nontransitive ranking is a result that we previously avoided on the individual level by showing that indifference curves could not cross.

REFERENCES

Baldwin, R. E. (1985). *The Political Economy of U.S. Trade Policy*. Cambridge: MIT Press.

Bohara, A. K., and Kaempfer, W. H. (1991). "A Test of Tariff Endogeneity in the United States." *American Economic Review* 81: 952–960.

Coughlin, C. C. (1985). "Domestic Content Legislation: House Voting and the Economic Theory of Regulation." *Economic Inquiry* 23: 437–448.

Fernandez, R., and Rodrik, D. (1991). "Resistance to Reform: Status Quo Bias in the Presence of Individual-Specific Uncertainty." *American Economic Review* 81: 1146–1155.

Hillman, A. L. (1989). *The Political Economy of Protection*. Chur, Switzerland: Harwood Academic Publishers.

Lavergne, R. P. (1983). *The Political Economy of U.S. Tariffs: An Empirical Analysis*. Toronto: Academic Press.

Magee, S. P. (1980). "Three Simple Tests of the Stolper-Samuelson Theorem." In P. Oppenheimer, ed., *Issues in International Economics*. London: Oriel Press, 138–153.

Magee, S. P., Brock, W. A., and Young, L. (1989). *Black Hole Tariffs and Endogenous Policy Theory: Political Economy in General Equilibrium*. Cambridge, Mass.: MIT Press.

Maskus, K. E. (1989). "Large Costs and Small Benefits of the American Sugar Programme." *The World Economy* 12: 85–104.

Ray, E. J. (1981). "The Determinants of Tariff and Nontariff Restrictions in the United States." *Journal of Political Economy* 89: 105–121.

Tosini, S. C. and Tower, E. (1987). "The Textile Bill of 1985: The Determinants of Congressional Voting Patterns." *Public Choice* 54: 19–25.

CHAPTER
20

ADMINISTERED PROTECTION

20.1 INTRODUCTION

The preceding chapters have discussed the major tools of trade protection, their effects in different markets, and the political reasons they exist. We turn now to a discussion of how trade policy is formulated and implemented. It is important to understand the institutional framework within which various countries attempt to regulate international trade. This framework is considerably more complicated than what might be suggested by a straightforward consideration of tariffs and quotas. There are important multilateral institutions, such as the General Agreement on Tariffs and Trade, or GATT, that attempt to set rules governing the behavior of international trading partners. Also significant are agreements among groups of countries, such as the European Community, on their mutual rules of exchange. Finally, unilateral actions taken by certain countries, particularly the United States, attempt to induce foreign trading partners to change their policies. The 1980s and 1990s have been periods of considerable activity and change in these arrangements, which are the subject of the next section of the chapter.

A number of particular features of these rules, or abrogations of them, are worth discussing. In the third section we consider various forms of *contingent protection,* or tariffs levied to offset the domestic effects of rapid import surges and imports generated by allegedly unfair foreign trade practices. While such policies make sense in principle, in operation their effects can often be harmful. A final perspective on trade protection is provided in the fourth section, where we illustrate the role of trade policy within a framework of domestic business regulation. The trade implications of regulatory policies for *environmental protection* are considered. Several interesting analytical features are noted, including the fact that different countries may have decidedly different interests in pursuing strong protection for the environment. Thus, we will place trade policy into this broader international economic context.

20.2   INTERNATIONAL TRADE INSTITUTIONS AND RULES

In the period since World War II, an increasing number of countries have bound themselves to a set of rules governing the conditions under which their trade policies are set. The initial impetus for establishing such rules came from the recognition prior to World War II that a world in which countries were free to set unilateral tariffs in a noncooperative fashion carried substantial risks of damaging protectionism.

A dramatic illustration of this danger came with the passage by the U.S. Congress of the highly restrictive *Tariff Act of 1930,* also known as the *Smoot-Hawley Tariff,* named for its two senate sponsors. Amid growing concern about slumping business growth and stagnant employment, doubts were raised about the benefits of a liberal trade policy. While the congressional discussions were originally devoted to raising tariffs on agricultural imports, they quickly spread under lobbying pressure to protection against manufacturing imports. Indeed, the formulation of this law provided a classic example of the process of logrolling discussed in the previous chapter. Despite formal warnings of impending retaliation from numerous trading partners, President Hoover signed the bill in June, 1930, raising average tariff rates to over 60 percent on thousands of products, the most restrictive tariff law ever enacted by the United States. Retaliation came quickly in the form of restrictive quotas and higher tariffs on U.S. products by over 40 countries, including most of the largest trading nations. Following the initial retaliation, even broader restrictions were enacted against imports from all sources in numerous countries. The result of these changes in trade laws, in conjunction with declining spending during the Great Depression, was severely impaired trade. The volume of world commerce fell by 67 percent from 1929 to 1933 and did not return to its 1929 level until the early 1940s. Most scholars of international trade history consider the Smoot-Hawley Tariff and subsequent retaliatory episodes to have been a major contributor to the worldwide depression of the time.[1]

Since that stark lesson, many nations have preferred to act in a cooperative manner to reduce tariffs. This process began with the enactment by the United States of the *Reciprocal Trade Agreements Act of 1934,* which empowered the President to negotiate bilateral tariff-reduction treaties with major trading partners. A key feature of these agreements was their negotiation under the principle of the *Most Favored Nation* (MFN) designation. Under MFN, any country to which the U.S. authorities had granted such status would immediately and unconditionally receive the most favorable treatment (i.e., lowest tariffs) applied by the United States to the imports of any other country. As noted below, this principle is now a cornerstone of the international trading system.

Multilateralism: The General Agreement on Tariffs and Trade

At the end of World War II the United States and other major countries were vitally interested in developing a set of multilateral economic and political institutions that would assist in the process of global economic reconstruction. The major institutions included the United Nations, which is a forum for resolution of political disputes, the International Monetary Fund, which is designed to assist nations with macroeconomic and financial difficulties, and the International Bank for Reconstruction and Development (the World Bank), which provides development loans and policy advice to developing countries.

Discussions were held on the establishment of a fourth major institution, the International Trade Organization (ITO). The principles and obligations set out in the Havana Charter, the governing document for the ITO, were quite ambitious, specifying a framework of rules covering not only tariffs on merchandise trade but also certain domestic regulatory policies in services, intellectual property rights, and related areas. As a recognized multilateral organization, the ITO also would have retained certain mechanisms for enforcement of these rules. In fact, the ITO was overly ambitious in the sense that agricultural and certain business interests in the United States and other nations found it unacceptably constraining and lobbied against its adoption. The U.S. Congress has never ratified the Havana Charter, and the ITO has not come into being.

In its place, the United States and 22 other nations agreed to implement, over a period of several years beginning in 1948, two less ambitious components of the ITO negotiations. One component was a multilateral agreement to negotiate reciprocal reductions in tariffs, and the second part was a series of articles setting out general obligations relating to trade policy. These components together were known as the General Agreement on Tariffs and Trade, or GATT.[2] Because the GATT placed far fewer restrictions on national governments than the ITO would have, and because it embodied no real enforcement procedures, it was easier for countries to accept. Interestingly, the initial contracting parties adopted the GATT on a provisional and temporary basis, pending the adoption of the ITO, which has never happened. Thus, the GATT has survived for 45 years as an interim arrangement, which gives it an unusual position among major international institutions. In fact, it has thrived, as the great majority of countries have seen fit to join it. The current number of members has reached 116, with numerous other countries having agreed to abide by the rules of the GATT in anticipation of their admission.[3] The late 1980s and early 1990s have been a period of particularly rapid accession as countries undergoing structural reforms in their economies have found it important to align themselves closely with the international trading system.

In essence, the GATT has two primary functions. It specifies certain general obligations that all signatories must observe in setting their trade policies, and it provides a forum for periodic negotiations on multilateral tariff reductions. The general obligations form the guiding principles of GATT. Chief among these is the principle of *nondiscrimination,* which embodies two features. First is the obligation of *national treatment,* by which each country must give imports that have cleared the border equivalent treatment to that given domestic, competing goods. Thus, in principle, domestic taxes and regulations cannot be biased against foreign goods. Second, each GATT member is to accord all other members unconditional MFN status, meaning that imports from all member nations are charged the lowest tariffs without discrimination. Countries are also obliged to attempt to allocate, on a nondiscriminatory basis, import shares of goods that are limited by quotas.

The MFN principle is thought by most economists to carry strong advantages over a policy of bilateral discrimination. It allows comparative advantage to be the primary determinant of trade patterns, which contributes to global efficiency. It makes negotiations on lower tariffs easier because it requires the establishment of a single schedule of import taxes per country rather than a series of bilateral tax rates. It contributes directly to the advancement of multilateralism by allowing national tariff concessions to be spread broadly across trading partners, thereby easing the conclusion of reciprocal agreements on lower taxes. And it provides a mechanism whereby exporters from small, developing countries, which individually have little or no bargaining leverage, can enjoy enhanced access to markets in large nations. Without the MFN principle, countries would be free to negotiate bilateral tax rates and to exercise their market power with some impunity, resulting in less liberalized and more fragmented world trade.

There are three important exceptions to the MFN rule. First, procedures are set out under which groups of countries are allowed to form regional trading arrangements, such as free trade areas and customs unions. Such arrangements are explicitly discriminatory in their treatment of goods from countries within the region versus goods from outside the region. Second, developed nations are encouraged to provide preferential tariff treatment of goods from developing countries by instituting a *Generalized System of Preferences* (GSP). Finally, as agreed to during the Tokyo Round of GATT trade negotiations in the late 1970s, groups of countries may negotiate side agreements among themselves, commonly called Codes, which obligate only the Code signatories to treat one another without discrimination. For example, there is a Code on Government Procurement, most of the signatories to which are developed economies, which sets out rules under which governments accept bids from domestic and foreign firms for various contracts. Its provisions apply only to those countries that have signed it, providing an example of *conditional MFN* treatment.

The GATT also obliges members to bind their tariff rates, meaning that once an agreement has been reached on lower trade barriers, no country can unilaterally raise them again or replace them with new tariffs. This requirement is thought to be most beneficial in fostering an environment of certainty about trade policies, which is important for firms engaged in trade. However, another key feature of the GATT provides an important exception to this rule. Countries are allowed to invoke the right to use *safeguards policies,* or temporary trade barriers imposed on imports that expand more rapidly than expected and that harm domestic industries. To use such safeguards, a government must demonstrate that substantial economic injury has occurred to a domestic industry. In imposing a temporary tariff to help alleviate this injury and, in principle, to assist the adjustment of labor and capital into other industries, a country must agree to pay compensation to the affected foreign exporting countries. Such compensation can come either in the form of lower import tariffs in other industries, which is most unlikely for political reasons, or through inviting the foreign governments to retaliate with temporary tariffs on exports of the tax-imposing nation.

A further general obligation of the GATT is that countries are to avoid the use of quantitative trade barriers, such as quotas, and to forgo the payment of export subsidies. There are, however, well-known exceptions to this provision. Developing economies are largely exempt from this requirement and can use quantitative restrictions for a variety of reasons without fear of retaliation. The *Multi-Fiber Arrangement* (MFA), which is a series of bilateral trade quotas covering textiles and apparel, has been negotiated outside the GATT. Many countries have kept their programs of support for agriculture apart from GATT rules. The United States, for example, negotiated a special GATT waiver in 1955 that states that it can utilize import quotas to support domestic farm prices, which is a common policy in most countries. Similarly, the European Community supports its farmers with its *Common Agricultural Policy,* which relies on a series of variable tariffs that act very much like quotas, to maintain high domestic prices that are uniform throughout the region. Moreover, the United States and the EC have followed a policy of subsidizing exports of their grains for some time. Indeed, trade in textiles and apparel and agricultural commodities has been largely exempt from GATT disciplines for decades. Finally, nations are permitted to impose import quotas in order to safeguard their balance of payments, promote national security objectives, and protect the health and safety of their citizens. It is permissible, for example, to exclude imports of foods that are thought to have been produced in an unsafe manner, provided the exclusion is based on adequate scientific testing.

The agreement also sets out guidelines under which countries may develop and enforce laws designed to protect domestic industries from imports they allege are unfairly priced. Unfair pricing results when foreign firms "dump" their goods onto a market at a price below average cost or when foreign firms sell their goods cheaply as a result of an output or export subsidy paid by their governments. Governments are empowered to impose *antidumping duties* and *countervailing duties* against such imports in order to offset their harmful effects on domestic firms. We consider these policies in detail later in this chapter.

Finally, a key function of the GATT is to provide a forum for *dispute settlement* between member countries. An elaborate mechanism exists whereby if one country believes that its due benefits under GATT rules have been nullified or impaired by another country's policy, the first country can request consultation and arbitration on the matter. Failing a resolution by these procedures, a panel of experts may be convened to investigate the merits of the complaint according to GATT rules. Once the panel issues a ruling, the disputants are expected to modify their policies accordingly, to grant compensation, or to invite retaliation.

The GATT's second primary function is to facilitate periodic multilateral trade negotiations (MTN) among member nations. In this capacity, GATT has achieved its greatest success by inducing global reductions in tariffs. Including the just-completed Uruguay Round, there have been eight so-called "GATT Rounds." The first five were devoted to reciprocal tariff cuts among a relatively small number of nations. The Kennedy Round, from 1964-67, was the first to enjoy fairly wide multilateral participation, and it resulted in substantial tariff reductions among the industrialized nations. Tariffs on manufactured goods were cut by approximately one-third. Large numbers of developing countries were induced to join the GATT after the Kennedy Round because the agreement was expanded to recognize their special problems. In particular, developed countries agreed not to expect substantial reciprocity in trade policies from developing countries and committed themselves to providing preferential market access to the products of those nations. These provisions introduced the notion of *special and differential treatment* for the poorer countries. Overall, the Kennedy Round effected significant global trade liberalization.

The seventh MTN was the Tokyo Round, from 1974-79. The Tokyo Round Agreement further slashed tariffs on manufactures, again by about one-third. For the first time, the developing countries participated in the tariff reductions, though other contentious issues regarding trade of developing nations remained unresolved. The most notable aspect of the Tokyo Round was its effort to apply GATT disciplines to a range of nontariff barriers (NTBs). Several codes were negotiated among subsets of countries on policies covering government subsidies, safeguards, antidumping, government procurement, customs procedures, and technical standards for protecting health, safety and so on, along with special arrangements for specific products, such as civil aircraft.[4] Perhaps the most controversial of these has been the antidumping code, which has been accused by some observers of validating abuses of procedural protectionism in the United States, the European Community, and elsewhere. The Tokyo Round also clarified the participatory role of developing countries in the GATT and expanded the notion that those nations should be afforded special treatment.

The GATT negotiations have clearly succeeded in bringing down global tariffs. By 1986, the end of the period in which the Tokyo-Round tariff commitments were phased in, import taxes in the industrialized nations had been cut to an average of 5.8 percent on manufactures. To provide an idea of the level of tariffs, Table 20.1 shows average tariff rates for numerous

TABLE 20.1
Estimates of post-Tokyo Round (1987) average tariff rates by selected country and industry

Developed Countries	Tariff Rate (%)*	Developing Countries	Tariff Rate (%)*
Australia	14.8	Argentina	13.0
Austria	11.3	Brazil	20.8
Belgium-Luxembourg	5.4	Chile	10.5
Canada	4.6	Colombia	15.0
Denmark	6.4	Greece	46.4
Finland	6.2	Hong Kong	0.0
France	4.9	India	47.0
West Germany	5.7	Israel	5.7
Ireland	6.6	South Korea	10.8
Italy	4.4	Mexico	10.6
Japan	6.2	Portugal	4.4
Netherlands	5.7	Singapore	0.9
New Zealand	13.8	Taiwan	13.4
Norway	4.5	Turkey	16.5
Spain	13.1		
Sweden	3.9		
Switzerland	3.5		
United Kingdom	4.9		
United States	3.3		

Industry	Tariff Rate (%)*	Industry	Tariff Rate (%)*
Agriculture	8.7	Food Products	11.8
Wearing Apparel	17.3	Wood Products	4.0
Chemicals	8.8	Iron and Steel	7.3
Electrical Machinery	8.0	Transport Equipment	7.1

Source: Deardorff and Stern (1989).

Notes: *Tariff rates for individual countries are weighted by the shares of 22 industries in total imports, and tariff rates for individual industries are weighted by the shares of 33 countries in total imports.

developed and developing countries and for major industry groups in 1987.[5] In general, developing nations place higher tariffs on imports than do developed nations. Notable exceptions include Hong Kong and Singapore, which place very few restrictions on their trade activities. It should also be noted that many of the nations with higher tariffs have undertaken significant unilateral cuts in their trade taxes since 1987, including New Zealand, Spain, India, Mexico, Portugal, and Turkey. Among industrial groups, wearing apparel and food products are subject to the highest average tariffs across countries.

An accompanying effect that detracts from this trend toward tariff liberalization is that the use of nontariff barriers to restrict trade has proliferated at the same time. One indication of this growth in NTBs, at least in the developed countries, is given in Table 20.2, which reports percentages of imports in particular product categories that are subject to certain restrictions. The NTBs included in this analysis involve a broad set of policies that are designed both directly and indirectly to reduce imports.[6] Common

TABLE 20.2
Percentage of imports affected by nontariff barriers in selected developed countries, 1966 and 1986

Country	All Foods 1966	All Foods 1986	Agricultural Raw Materials 1966	Agricultural Raw Materials 1986	Fuels 1966	Fuels 1986	Manufactures 1966	Manufactures 1986	Textiles & Clothing 1966	Textiles & Clothing 1986	Transport Equipment 1966	Transport Equipment 1986	All Goods 1966	All Goods 1986
EC	61	100	4	28	11	37	10	56	20	100	39	31	21	54
France	56	99	4	37	22	100	6	61	0	94	59	84	16	82
West Germany	71	99	9	20	7	0	12	59	22	96	70	39	24	41
Italy	72	96	0	53	0	0	9	66	15	95	65	53	27	30
U.K.	42	96	0	0	0	0	9	44	24	95	39	27	16	38
Switzerland	53	90	4	55	0	99	15	39	58	80	68	85	19	50
Japan	73	99	0	59	33	28	48	50	39	43	65	38	31	43
U.S.	32	74	14	45	92	0	39	71	55	98	73	87	36	45
All Countries	56	92	4	41	27	27	19	58	30	89	56	65	25	48

Source: Laird and Yeats (1990).

Note: Figures represent imports within categories restricted by NTBs as a percentage of total imports of that product type.

examples of these NTBs include quotas, import and export licensing, VERS, government procurement policies, domestic content laws, antidumping duties, commodity agreements, advertising restrictions, sanitary regulations, packaging requirements, customs valuation procedures, foreign exchange restrictions, and subsidies for import-competing industries. The figures in the table suggest, for example, that 61 percent of food imports into the EC were covered by NTBs in 1966, while 100 percent were covered in 1986. Several facts are evident from Table 20.2. The use of NTBs by developed nations grew markedly over the 20-year period, except in fuels. Imports of foods and manufactures are heavily regulated, with textiles and clothing being especially subject to NTBs as a result of the MFA. France subjected 82 percent of its total merchandise imports to some form of NTB regulations in 1986, the highest level among the developed countries reported in the analysis. Japan and the United States had similar NTB coverage, with just below 50 percent of imports subject to restrictions.

Thus, despite its success in reducing tariffs, the GATT has been unable to prevent the proliferation of NTBs. Indeed, for several reasons it had come under substantial and widespread criticism by the mid-1980s. Governments of several members had become increasingly dissatisfied with its operation, both because of certain structural difficulties and because of the GATT's limited sectoral coverage. Regarding GATT's structure and procedures, complaints were voiced about safeguards and dispute settlement. Many observers consider GATT's safeguards provisions deficient in that the requirements for countries to raise tariffs on an MFN basis and to pay compensation or allow foreign retaliatory tariffs has encouraged governments to negotiate bilateral market-sharing arrangements that lie outside the GATT's rules. For example, the recent proliferation of bilateral voluntary export restraints, which were discussed in Chapter 16, can be explained largely by the fact that they transfer the implicit quota rents from the importing-country market to exporting firms or governments, inducing their cooperation in protecting firms in the importer. Unfortunately, such policies tend to fragment world trade, in addition to conferring welfare costs, and they represent a marked retreat from multilateralism.

The GATT's dispute-resolution processes are often criticized as ineffective and needlessly lengthy.[7] A primary difficulty is that GATT panel rulings have no legal force. A country that is found to be in violation of its GATT commitments can unilaterally block the publication of such a determination simply by not agreeing to it. Even when these rulings are issued, countries violating their GATT obligations need not modify or eliminate the offending trade policy because GATT can enforce no such changes. Rather, the GATT system relies on the voluntary compliance of its members to maintain its integrity and credibility. Overall, this system has worked reasonably well; most nations do modify their policies as requested. Nonetheless, in some instances panel rulings have gone largely unheeded, leading to impatience with the processes for settling trade disputes.

At least as important as these structural problems has been the absence of effective GATT rules in broad areas of economic activity. For example, we noted that the GATT Articles place relatively few obligations on developing nations for reciprocity in tariff cuts and avoidance of the use of NTBs and subsidies. In the last two decades labor-intensive manufacturing exports from many developing countries, particularly from the so-called *newly industrializing countries* (NICs) of East Asia, into the industrialized countries grew rapidly and came to be regarded by some observers as a significant source of downward pressure on the real wages of lower-skilled workers in the United States, the European Community, and elsewhere. Thus, many policymakers have expressed concerns that the apparently laudatory effort to promote economic development through special and differential treatment had generated *free-riding behavior* by the more successful developing-country exporters.[8]

A more contentious problem has been that agriculture and textiles, two major components of merchandise trade, are substantially exempt from GATT rules and tariff reductions. With few effective restraints, countries are permitted to employ quotas, variable levies, and export subsidies to support their domestic agricultural sectors. Over time these policies have become quite common, as suggested in Table 20.2, and they have become markedly disruptive in international markets.[9] And, as we mentioned, world trade in clothing and textiles is largely governed by a system of bilateral quotas under the MFA. Many developing countries view the MFA as inimical to their interests in industrial development.

A final major shortcoming of GATT is that its Articles virtually ignore policies that are not direct restrictions on trade in merchandise but that may indirectly affect such trade. Most countries have regulations that encourage or discourage foreign direct investment (FDI) by multinational enterprises in their markets.[10] Common examples include requirements that products contain some minimum content of domestic inputs, that some proportion of the output from the FDI be exported, and that the multinational enterprise export a value of goods at least as large as the value of its imported inputs. Thus, the global pattern of FDI and resulting trade flows could be inefficient and costly as a consequence of these *trade-related investment measures,* or TRIMs. A related issue is that nations provide markedly different levels of intellectual property rights. It is possible that widely varying policies on patents, for example, could affect the decisions of firms to engage in research and product development, invest in foreign facilities, and transfer technologies abroad. If so, world trade and competition is also affected by *trade-related intellectual property rights,* or TRIPs. Finally, countries have extensive regulations covering the provision of services in their markets by foreign firms. Important services that could be traded directly include transportation, tourism, professional consulting, and information. Services that are tradeable through establishing facilities in overseas markets include financial, business, legal, and medical services as well as construction and telecommunications. These so-called "new issues"—TRIMs, TRIPs, and regulations on trade in services—have become quite contentious among countries because they set conditions for increasingly important forms of international competition.

With this background, in 1986 GATT members began the most ambitious set of trade negotiations to date, the Uruguay Round.[11] Negotiating groups were established in each of the areas just mentioned and in numerous other areas of concern. Provisional agreement on a final text was reached by all member nations in December, 1993, though as of mid-1994 this text remains subject to legislative approval in each country. Although the text does not proceed as far toward trade liberalization and policy harmonization as some advocates had hoped, it does represent a signal achievement in extending GATT coverage to numerous problems. If this text is adopted, tariffs will be cut again by about one third. Countries will be obligated to scale back their agricultural supports to some extent and to begin converting NTBs to tariffs in anticipation of future cuts. The MFA will be phased out over ten years and replaced by tariffs. Directly trade-distorting TRIMs will be gradually abolished, and nations will move toward a common set of TRIPs policies. Relatively little progress was made in services though a framework for future negotiations has been established. Rules on permissible government subsidies and the use of antidumping duties will be tightened and clarified. Dispute settlement procedures will be made more enforceable by a limitation on the ability of nations to block panel reports, while the GATT itself will be replaced by a body called the World Trade Organization, which will have more authority to consult with governments on their trade practices. Greater expectations will be placed on developing countries regarding reciprocity and observation of GATT principles.

We finish this discussion with some perspective on the GATT as an institution for promoting trade liberalization. In principle, the GATT represents two fundamental approaches to this objective. These are *multilateralism,* wherein many (or most) countries agree collectively to reduce trade barriers, and reliance on *rules-based trade policy,* by which each country commits itself to obeying certain international norms in setting its trade regulations. We alluded earlier to some of the benefits of multilateralism, as enshrined in the MFN requirement. Chief among these benefits is its promotion of cooperative efforts in trade liberalization. Left to their own devices, countries would rarely engage in unilateral reductions in trade barriers, even if it were in their economic interests to do so, because domestic political opposition by import-competing firms and workers would likely prevent their doing so. By sharing multilateral tariff cuts, however, GATT members can point to the need for opening domestic markets in exchange for greater market access elsewhere. The more nations that are involved in this process, the greater is the force of the argument and the larger is the trend toward global liberalization. In this view, the GATT may be considered a valuable cooperative device. Without such a device, it would typically be very difficult for individual countries to mount the political will to move toward freer trade. Of course, coordinating the interests of many countries across many industries is an immensely difficult problem, which explains why the GATT rounds have become increasingly complicated and lengthy. In fact, this tradeoff between cooperation advantages and coordination difficulties helps explain the recent emergence of great interest in policies of regional economic integration, which we discussed in Chapter 18.

Many economists also prefer the GATT approach because it is based on setting rules of behavior. For example, once a nation has agreed to a set of tariff rates within GATT, it is bound not to raise those rates except under specific and publicized conditions. Further, a set of rules provides international businesses with greater certainty that nations will not act arbitrarily in changing their trade policies. Thus, the GATT also serves as a commitment device, by which countries are committed to observe certain norms. However, other economists view this approach as an undesirable constraint on policy choice. They argue that a *discretionary trade policy,* or *results-oriented trade policy,* wherein trade negotiations and trade barriers can be targeted to achieve certain specific goals, is more effective. Such goals might include taking advantage of scale economies and technological innovation through strategic trade policy to reserve particular market shares for home firms. More likely, larger nations may see discretion as a means of opening foreign markets on a bilateral basis in particular sectors. There is a substantial element of this latter philosophy in current U.S. trade policy, as we will discuss.[12]

It seems clear that, while multilateralism has an important role to play in the world economy, the GATT as traditionally constituted cannot meet all the needs of its member nations. Thus, a broader World Trade Organization that is simultaneously more inclusive of various sectoral interests and less insistent on strict nondiscrimination seems to provide a valid compromise solution to many of the problems we have noted. Further, regional trading blocs and a certain amount of unilateralism in trade policy have become inevitable supplements to this fundamentally multilateral approach.

Unilateralism: Section 301 in U.S. Trade Law

A key objective of multilateralism is to open markets to greater import competition on a cooperative basis, but the GATT process has been rather slow and ineffective at this task, at least with respect to nontariff barriers. Further, apparent violations of GATT obligations or of commitments made under other international agreements are common in many nations. Finally, we have noted that in the past, the GATT has had little effective discipline over large sectors of economic activity such as agriculture, services, and regulations covering foreign investment. For example, it is often alleged that Japan maintains a tight web of domestic regulations covering distribution of goods and services that keeps out foreign competition, despite the low levels of formal trade barriers on nonagricultural commodities.

Impatience with this situation has led a few countries, most notably the United States, to undertake unilateral measures to open foreign markets.

The U.S. *Section 301* of the Trade Act of 1974 (and subsequent revisions) gives the President legal authority to negotiate with foreign governments over removing or modifying commercial practices designated as unfair by the Unites States Trade Representative (USTR). The USTR is the official empowered to negotiate bilateral and multilateral trade agreements and to advise the President on international trade matters. Under Section 301, the President can enforce the protection of U.S. rights that have been impaired by "unjustifiable" foreign violations of trade obligations and can push for greater market access by negotiating the removal of "unreasonable" restrictions on business activity. This latter interpretation of the law allows wide application of Section 301 procedures to numerous foreign practices, including not only explicit trade barriers but also restrictions on foreign service providers, lack of reciprocity in investment regulations, discriminatory government procurement, and the like. Especially targeted for action have been foreign failures to provide effective patents, copyrights, and trademarks for U.S. owners of intellectual property. For example, in 1991 the USTR administered cases involving China (market access and intellectual property), Canada (lumber subsidies, prohibitions on fish exports, and provincial import restrictions on beer), India (intellectual property), Thailand (intellectual property), the EC (meat inspection practices, canned fruit subsidies, oilseeds support, and operation of U.S. benefits under the terms of Spanish and Portuguese accession to the Community), Norway (procurement of toll equipment), Japan (construction contracts and the operation of a bilateral agreement on trade in semiconductors), and Brazil (intellectual property).[13]

Upon identification of a foreign practice of significant concern, negotiations begin between the USTR and the foreign government enforcing that practice. If the alleged violation is covered by the terms of the GATT, the negotiations could take place under the auspices of GATT. However, because most complaints are about non-GATT business restrictions, the talks are usually bilateral in nature. If agreement is not reached in these discussions, the USTR is given one year to recommend some action, such as dropping the case, continuing the discussions if progress seems imminent, or imposing retaliatory import barriers against the country in question. Retaliatory actions are chosen and enacted by the President.

Use by the United States of Section 301 is one of the most controversial issues in global trade relations. To its credit, the procedure has registered a substantial number of successes in accelerating the liberalization of particular markets. Over 90 cases were undertaken from 1975 to 1992, with approximately 70 percent of these resulting in the elimination or modification of the targeted practice. Moreover, with few exceptions, the United States has asked that the targeted policy be changed on an MFN basis, allowing firms from all foreign countries to benefit rather than discriminating in favor of U.S. firms. In this sense, the United States has successfully liberalized certain aspects of global trade by threatening particular governments with restricted access to its enormous market.

However, many economists are wary of the process for several reasons. First, it does at times result in trade retaliation (and possibly subsequent re-retaliation by the targeted government), which represents a failure that is costly to both sides of the dispute.[14] Second, the number of successes is rather misleading because they have tended to come in cases in which the United States has "identif(ied) barriers that the foreign government could dismantle without risking crippling local opposition."[15] Pursuing difficult cases involving significant potential displacement costs from foreign liberalization has been less successful; such cases seem more amenable to multilateral and cooperative negotiations.

A more fundamental concern is that, if not handled properly, this decided departure from multilateralism poses significant risks for the cohesion of the world trading system. For example, much about the operation of Section 301 has prima facie inconsistencies with the GATT system because its actions often target foreign policies that are acceptable under GATT rules. Some observers worry that this situation could erode confidence in the GATT system and ultimately contribute greatly to fragmentation of global trade. Moreover, Section 301 is highly resented in nations against which it has been applied, which may contribute to general intransigence against trade liberalization. Finally, the greatest concern is that the United States will ultimately choose to resort primarily to bilateral agreements that commit governments to managing their trade volumes and patterns according to negotiated targets. For example, in recent bilateral discussions with Japan, the United States has insisted that its share of Japanese imports of semi-conductors and automobile parts rise to specified minimum levels within a certain period of years. If these quantitative targets fail to be met, U.S. retaliation is likely. Quite apart from the apparent difficulty of achieving a government-mandated increase in foreign market share, such *managed trade* policies tend to be decidedly anticompetitive and may risk significant trade diversion.

20.3 CONTINGENT PROTECTION

One form of administered protection that has become increasingly prevalent in recent years is the use of tariffs to raise the domestic prices of imported goods that are seen to be artificially low in price. These low prices are considered to be the result of unfair pricing practices, stemming either from dumping by foreign firms or from advantages afforded by foreign governments through production or export subsidies. The GATT allows importing countries to offset these low prices by imposing import duties on the products of specific firms that can be shown to be dumping or to have benefited from subsidies and whose actions cause potential injury to domestic firms. We consider here some of the analytical issues involved in enforcing an antidumping (AD) policy and in setting countervailing duties (CVDs) against foreign subsidies. The use of such policies is labelled *contingent protection* because it is triggered by price and injury contingencies.

Dumping and Antidumping

Dumping has two legal definitions. The first is the practice by a firm of selling a product in an export market at a price below that at which it sells the product in its home market. Such pricing behavior may seem bizarre in that foreign sales would be expected to incorporate a price sufficient to cover the additional transport costs. Nonetheless, examples of such pricing are not uncommon. The second definition is the practice of selling a product in an export market at a price below the average cost of producing it. In U.S. legal terminology, the average cost is termed the *fair value* of the product, and dumping constitutes sales at *less than fair value* (LFV).

Consider the possible reasons for a firm to engage in dumping. First, it is possible that the normal course of business cycles could, on occasion, cause demand for the firm's product in its home market to fall below its production capacity. Rather than reduce price or lay off workers, the firm might choose to export the excess production to foreign markets and charge a low price to ensure the sales. We might term this behavior *sporadic dumping,* because it is related to fluctuations in economic activity. To the extent that such sales induce lower production and employment in the importing country, that country may well wish to offset them with temporary tariffs in order to avoid absorbing the negative effects of foreign recessions. There are good reasons to suspect, however, that sporadic dumping is limited in scope. Exports typically require the establishment of customer relations and a marketing and distribution system. Few firms would go to the expense of maintaining such systems merely to have access to a residual market in the event of lower home demand.

A second possibility is that a foreign firm may choose to engage in *predatory dumping,* whereby it sells its goods in an export market at a price low enough to drive domestic competing firms out of business or, perhaps more likely, to deter entry by other firms. This would require setting a price so low that a domestic competitor could not cover variable costs at any level of production and would choose to leave the market. The predatory foreign firm would accept current losses in anticipation of future monopoly profits once the market is reserved in its favor. In light of the many potential strategic interactions among international oligopolistic firms that we have discussed elsewhere, behavior of this kind could be considered conceivable. Indeed, fears of predatory pricing are used to justify domestic firms' lobbying efforts for strong antidumping laws. If it occurs, predatory dumping is surely harmful to the importing country and calls for an offsetting import tax. However, there is little evidence of its existence, again for practical reasons. First, once a foreign firm has established its monopoly and raised its price, the old firms will almost certainly be enticed back into the market and new firms will enter, a fact that the foreign firm must take into account prior to dumping. Thus, to sustain its monopoly, the foreign firm would have to continue charging a price low enough to deter entry forever, which is unlikely to be a profitable strategy. Second, predatory behavior is illegal under domestic antitrust laws in many importing nations, including the United States, and would be unlikely to escape prosecution by the antitrust authorities, especially because domestic competing firms would lobby heavily for such action.

The fact that firms have market power does suggest the most likely reason for dumping. Suppose that firms produce differentiated products so that each firm has some monopoly power (that is, it faces a downward-sloping demand curve) in every market in which it chooses to sell. Recall from Chapter 11 that a monopolist would choose to set price in each market according to the following profit-maximizing rule:

$$p_j = \mathrm{MC}_j/[1 - 1/e_j] \qquad (20.1)$$

Here, the subscript j refers to import market j. If we assume that the marginal costs of exporting to each country are similar, we see that a firm would certainly choose to set different prices in different markets. In particular, the more elastic the demand is for a good in a particular market, the lower will be the price charged there because the profit-maximizing markup over marginal cost will be lower. This practice is called *international price discrimination* and is quite likely to characterize many products and markets. Note that this practice requires that different markets be segmented, (that is, isolated from one another) so that consumers in one country will not buy the good at a low price and resell it in other markets at higher prices. In particular, if a firm charges a lower price in an export market than at home, it may need to lobby its government for a tariff to avoid such re-imports.

Why, then, would a firm charge a low price abroad and a high price at home? It must be that demand for the good is more elastic in foreign markets than at home. This is the case when a good in its home market is familiar to customers and commands their loyalty, while in foreign markets it must compete with domestic products and other imports. Indeed, such bias in preferences toward home goods seems to be common in actual practice. Thus, in the face of differential demand elasticities, profit-maximizing pricing that constitutes dumping is quite likely to occur. Perhaps the best term for it is *equilibrium dumping,* in recognition of its source. Note that because such pricing reflects demand parameters, the logical justification for a tariff to offset this dumping is not that the dumping harms domestic firms. However, because the foreign firm makes profits in the importing country, it may be appropriate to impose a tariff to shift those profits to the domestic treasury. Under some circumstances this form of strategic trade policy makes sense.[16]

Having analyzed the circumstances that may lead to dumping, we now turn to the structure and effects of antidumping law, with emphasis on the United States.[17] In the United States, legislation against dumping has existed since at least 1916, though the current law is based on the Tariff Act of 1930, with numerous subsequent revisions to tighten its provisions. Note that these laws are designed to prevent dumping by foreign firms in the American market; there is no U.S. law prohibiting U.S. firms from dumping abroad. As noted, dumping is found to exist either if a foreign firm sells in the American market at a price below that in its home market or if the firm sells the product at a price below average cost of production. In either case, if dumping is found to have occurred, an AD tariff is imposed to equal the *dumping margin,* or the difference between the import price and the fair value of the product. These duties are imposed until the dumping ceases.

While this process seems unobjectionable, except to consumers who may enjoy the low price of imported goods, it embodies numerous features that make trade economists leery of its operation. First, note from the earlier discussion that international price discrimination is likely to be a common phenomenon and does not, in itself, justify AD duties. Thus, the cost standard seems the more sensible foundation for defining potentially harmful dumping. However, as we have noted often in this book, a condition for economic efficiency is that a firm charge a price equal to its *marginal cost,* rather than its *average cost.* Economists would argue against an average-cost standard in defining dumping because there are potential circumstances under which a firm would price at less-than-average cost because of its low marginal cost. One example would be the pricing of the first several units of output of a product, such as computer chips, that is subject to significant scale economies. In computer chips, a heavy fixed cost is required in terms of research and development for each new semiconductor generation. Once the device is developed, however, the marginal cost of producing each unit is quite small. Thus, the expected pricing behavior would involve a low price on the initial units, despite a high cost per unit, in order to sell a sufficient volume over time to recoup the R&D costs.

Economists' preference for marginal-cost pricing may be too rigorous a criterion to be of much practical use, given the difficulties of estimating marginal costs. Therefore, unit costs have become the legal standard. In this regard, it is noteworthy that U.S. law contains a clear bias toward affirmative findings of dumping by specifying inflated standards for the composition of costs in determing fair market value. When a domestic firm, industry association, or trade union alleges dumping by a specific foreign firm, an office in the U.S. Department of Commerce undertakes an investigation of the complaint. Commerce officials may compare domestic price of the imported good with either its price in the exporter's market or its price in third-country markets, assuming these prices are above unit costs. If such prices are difficult to obtain, Commerce officials are empowered to compute a fair value for the product based on the foreign firm's production costs. The unusual aspect of this latter procedure is that Commerce is obliged to add to production costs a margin of at least ten percent for general expenses and at least eight percent for profits. The latter margin is remarkable in the sense that few international firms average as much as an eight percent profit in any year. For products from socialist (or "nonmarket") economies, where it is quite difficult to obtain reliable cost data, Commerce is empowered to compare import price with either prices or constructed costs of firms in third-country markets, often in countries where costs may be expected to be signficantly higher. Overall, the use of constructed cost standards in determining whether a product has been sold at LFV tends to generate frequent findings of remarkably large dumping margins. Note in particular that the eight-percent markup minimum makes it illegal for foreign firms to use pricing practices that are quite common for domestic firms, such as sales and rebates, that imply short-term losses in order to defend market shares.

It is important to note that an affirmative dumping finding by Commerce results in a lasting AD duty only if another government agency, the International Trade Commission (ITC), finds that the dumping has resulted in or threatens to result in material injury to a domestic industry. The ITC is a quasijudicial agency that recommends or discourages the imposition of tariffs or other remedies to offset injuries caused by dumping, export subsidies, and import surges. (Discussion of the latter two issues will follow.) In considering the potential for injury, the ITC looks at such indicators as prices, profits, sales, and employment of domestic firms in the face of import competition. The ITC has a reputation for fair (that is, non-politicized) investigations and recommendations, though it should be noted that over time, the U.S. Congress has continually reduced the standards for showing the existence of injury to the point where a finding of injury is now the expected outcome.

The institutional bias in these procedures toward imposing AD tariffs has had some marked effects. First, there is no doubt that the AD process has become the favored route of domestic firms that wish to benefit from import protection in all countries that employ these procedures. In the United States, 411 AD investigations were undertaken over the period from 1980 to 1988 (many of these in the steel industry), with another 332 investigations under the CVD statutes, which work in a similar manner. In contrast, only 71 investigations based on safeguards procedures were launched. Related figures for other countries include 364 AD and CVD cases in the EC versus 39 safeguards cases, 500 versus one in Australia, 470 versus two in Canada, and 75 versus zero in developing countries, where such procedures have been instituted only quite recently.[18] Second, the mere *expectation* of losing such a case seems to have altered the behavior of foreign firms subject to AD investigations. Under U.S. law, a foreign firm can avoid legal costs and the need to surrender its confidential cost data by agreeing with the Commerce Department to either raise its prices or stop selling in the American market. These agreements, called *price undertakings,* have become common, and they serve to place a minimum on prices or a limit on competition in the U.S. market.[19] Indeed, AD cases may well act as a device for facilitating collusion among oligopolistic firms, as explained in Chapter 17. For these reasons, trade economists now tend to view AD actions as a substantial nontariff barrier to trade.

Subsidies and Countervailing Duties

As interesting as AD actions is the practice whereby countries impose CVDs to offset the price-reducing effects of foreign export or production subsidies. To understand CVD's, it is useful to begin by considering the analytical justification for them. Figure 20.1 shows a situation in which markets are competitive and in which Country F exports good X. Free trade equilibrium involves a relative price of p^*, while Country H imports quantity OX_h^0. Suppose the exporting country pays an ad valorem subsidy to firms for exporting X.[20] This policy would expand F's excess-supply curve to $E_x^{f'}$, inducing an expansion of exports to quantity OX_f^1 (equal to H's higher imports at point S). The effect is a deterioration in F's terms of trade: world price falls to p_s^*, while the domestic relative price in F rises to $p'(p' = p_s^*[1 + s])$ as greater exports cause additional scarcity of good X in the exporting country's market. The resulting production and consumption distortions in F, combined with its worsened terms of trade, necessarily imply a decline in its economic welfare when it pays an export subsidy. Note the substantial subsidy cost of area WVp_s^*p', as the subsidy must be paid on all exports. This welfare loss demonstrates our point in Chapter 15 that a country can make itself worse off by artificially expanding trade and generating negative trade-policy revenues. In contrast, the importing country enjoys a welfare gain from this subsidy because of the decline in the relative price of its import good. This gain in H's terms of trade will outweigh the distortionary effects of the lower relative price in its market. In effect, this policy represents an election by the exporting nation to transfer income to the importing nation.[21] Overall, global welfare declines because of the departure from free trade.

Consider the impacts of a tariff imposed by H to offset, or countervail, the price-reducing effect of F's subsidy. Country H may choose to do this, despite its welfare gain from the subsidy, because domestic firms

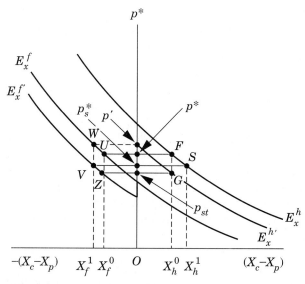

FIGURE 20.1
A countervailing duty.

that have been hurt by the additional imports could lobby for such a response. The objective is to return the relative price in H to its free trade level, which would be accomplished through a tariff that shifts the excess demand curve down to E_x'. The post-tariff equilibrium involves a return to the free trade quantity of imports but yet a *further* improvement in H's terms of trade, as world price falls to p_{st}. Of course, this represents an additional deterioration in F's terms of trade. Note the interesting implication of this solution: because outputs and domestic prices have returned to their old levels, there is no remaining distortionary impact of the subsidy; it has been completely offset by the tariff. Global welfare returns to its free trade level. The only effect is a transfer of income from taxpayers in Country F to the government in Country H (that is, the subsidy is paid to exporters who then surrender its proceeds to H in the form of tariff revenue) in the amount $UZGF/2$ (measured in units of good Y). Of course, if taxpayers in F were to recognize this fact, they would lobby for an end to the export subsidy or oppose its institution in the first place. Thus, the essential justification for CVDs is that they can restore global optimality and deter the introduction of export subsidies.

As might be expected, the situation is somewhat more complicated in markets that are not perfectly competitive, as our earlier discussion on strategic trade policy demonstrated. In such a case, it is no longer necessary that the exporting nation lose and the importing nation gain from an export subsidy. Moreover, there may be subsidies coming from third countries as well that would need to be considered in making welfare calculations. Nevertheless, in most cases there is a clear presumption that export subsidies interfere with global efficiency and that the levying of CVDs to deter them, or better still, international agreements to avoid using them, are in the public interest.

With that background, consider the GATT approach to disciplining the use of subsidies. The GATT Articles have long pledged member nations to forgo the use of explicit export subsidies except in agriculture, which, as we have noted, has traditionally lain substantially outside the purview of the Agreement. Thus, most trade conflicts over explicit export subsidies have involved the European Community and the United States, whose governments grant the largest such subsidies for grain exports. In both cases, these governments find it difficult to scale back on their subsidies because of political opposition by domestic farming groups. However, it seems that an agreement to move in that direction has emerged from the Uruguay Round. Other export subsidies are granted in a more hidden fashion, through concessional loans to foreign nations wishing to buy high-technology manufactured goods from the United States, Japan, the European Community, and other industrial nations.[22] Periodically, these nations have agreed among themselves to cut back on such activities.

A more difficult issue for international relations involves setting rules for domestic production subsidies that tend to expand exports indirectly. It is clear that governments may wish to subsidize certain activities for a variety of social and economic reasons. Common examples include output subsidies in defense industries, regional subsidies paid to expand employment and attract investment in depressed areas, subsidies to labor training or quality improvements in other inputs, subsidies for environmental cleanup, subsidies to research and development, and subsidies to the production of high-technology commodities that may have cost-reducing spillovers in other sectors. Indeed, as our discussion in Chapter 15 noted, economists recognize the superiority of subsidies to tariffs in achieving virtually all such goals. Nonetheless, each policy has the potential to expand domestic production, thereby reducing imports or raising exports, to the detriment of foreign competitors. Thus, it is by no means clear which of these kinds of programs, if any, should be avoided in the interests of international trade relations.

Recognizing this fact, the GATT approach has been to categorize various subsidies in terms of their apparent trade intent or impact for purposes of deciding whether to enact rules against their use. In general terms, subsidies cannot be disputed if they are clearly granted for purposes of socioeconomic development (such as regional assistance), if they are granted widely without favoring specific industries or firms, or if they support activities at the "pre-competitive" stage (such as R&D assistance, especially for basic research). At the other extreme, countries may take action against foreign subsidies if they have a clear trade-distorting intent, such as direct export assistance or input-purchase subsidies that discriminate in favor of domestic input suppliers. Most often, however, the intent of a government subsidy policy lies between these clear extremes, in which case nations may complain and request GATT dispute-resolution panels. This large, ill-defined area in allowable subsidy policies has led to increasing numbers of bilateral disputes in recent years and remains a significant source of controversy within the GATT.

GATT rules allow member nations to use CVD statutes to act against some foreign subsidies, which we can illustrate with U.S. practice. As with AD cases, if a domestic firm feels that its operations have been harmed by imports that have been priced unfairly as a result of a foreign export, output, or input subsidy, it can request an investigation by Commerce of the extent of the subsidization and an examination by the ITC of the resulting injury. If these investigations find in favor of the complainant, a CVD equivalent to the extent of the subsidization is imposed in order to raise the import price until the subsidy is removed. The adminstrative procedures are virtually identical to the AD procedures, the principal difference being that the target of the investigation is action by foreign governments rather than by foreign private firms. In this context, CVD cases are more likely to result in negotiated agreements to cease or modify the subsidy because governments may be more capable than individual firms of seeing some joint advantage in doing so. Nevertheless, the procedures are again biased in favor of the domestic firms in these quasijudicial proceedings, and the U.S. authorities have at times been accused of abusing them to harass foreign governments and firms. In fact, a major motivation of the Canadian government in agreeing to a Free Trade Agreement with the United States seems to have been to shield its firms from arbitrary and harsh application of U.S. AD and CVD laws. Canada insisted on the establishment of binational judicial panels for overseeing the operation of such laws in both countries, a novel process that will be extended to trinational panels among the United States, Canada, and Mexico under the terms of the North American Free Trade Agreement.

Safeguards

We finish our discussion of contingent protection by noting that GATT rules also allow countries to protect their industries temporarily from fairly traded imports (that is, imports that have not been dumped or subsidized) under certain circumstances. Policies that do so are called *safeguards*. When a country believes that it has experienced a rapid surge of imports that threatens serious injury to a domestic industry, it can impose offsetting protection, typically through nondiscriminatory increases in tariffs.[23] Two features are most relevant here. First, the GATT rules explicity state that such protection is to be temporary. A country may impose the higher tariff for no longer than five years, with the tariff rate declining over time. This protection is designed to help the besieged industry adjust to the new competition, either by allowing resources to move out as it contracts in an orderly fashion, or by adopting new technologies to raise efficiency. As might be guessed, the difficulty of making such adjustments has often resulted in the protection's lasting far longer than originally intended.

A second important feature of safeguards is that under GATT procedures, a country that invokes its right to raise its tariffs beyond their bound levels is required to pay some compensation to foreign countries that stand to lose business as a result. This may come either through an agreement to lower tariffs on other industries—clearly a politically unpopular option—or by allowing foreign governments to retaliate with higher tariffs of their own. From the standpoint of international relations, neither option is very palatable, and countries have increasingly resorted to protecting their industries through bilateral quantitative restrictions on trade such as VERs. As we have noted previously, VERs have the advantage of transferring some economic rents to foreign exporters, making their use less objectionable to foreign governments than the use of tariffs or import quotas. However, proliferation of such measures has worried many observers about potential frictions imposed on the multilateral trading system. Thus, reform of safeguards policies was an important issue in the Uruguay Round.

In the United States, safeguards are enacted through Section 201 of the Tariff Act of 1930 (subsequently revised). Section 201 is popularly referred to as the *escape clause*. Under this law, a representative of a domestic industry may petition for relief by asking the ITC to investigate whether imports have become a source or threat of serious injury. If the ITC finds that injury has occurred or is likely to occur, it recommends some form of relief to the U.S. President. The relief typically takes the form of temporary tariffs or quotas, though an additional option is to award *trade adjustment assistance,* or supplementary unemployment compensation to workers who might lose their jobs. The President may reject or accept the recommendation and may also develop different policies for import relief. The United States has seldom used the escape clause in recent years, largely because of the preferences of firms to avail themselves of easier routes to protection.

20.4   TRADE POLICY AND ENVIRONMENTAL REGULATIONS

A major source of stress on the international trading system is that global competition is affected not only by explicit trade barriers but also by numerous aspects of domestic regulations. Regulations governing product-safety rules, environmental protection requirements, anticompetitive business practices, intellectual property rights, foreign direct investments, and prudential financial practices may exist for reasons other than to restrict international trade but may have that effect anyway. For example, many countries have *domestic content laws,* which require that a foreign firm wishing to invest in a domestic production facility must purchase some minimum percentage of its inputs, such as materials, labor, and capital, from domestic sources. The evident intent is to expand employment in a particular sector, but the requirement could easily result in an artificial restriction on imports of materials and machinery. Similarly, a weak or unenforced antitrust law could result in interlocking business practices among domestic firms, in turn limiting market access for foreign firms that might otherwise be competitive suppliers of products or inputs.[24] It is also conceivable that differences in the costs of environmental regulations in various countries could influence decisions by multinational enterprises about production location and trade. Thus, in many contexts, it is possible to view domestic regulations as indirect nontariff barriers to trade.

Traditional GATT rules have imposed few effective disciplines on such practices, largely because issues of domestic regulation have lain outside the realm of the GATT, which is primarily focused on tariffs. However, as international competition has intensified because of growth, innovation, and the operation of MNEs, conflicts between domestic regulations and trade interests have inevitably become more frequent. For this reason, the industrialized nations at the Uruguay Round prominently introduced the question of trade-related regulations of investment, intellectual property rights, and services. Further, issues of environmental regulation and its impact on investment and trade figured importantly in the negotiation of NAFTA. It seems likely that these kinds of questions will dominate trade-policy discussions for the foreseeable future.

In this section we focus on environmental regulation to discuss the interactions between trade policy and regulatory policy from an economic standpoint. Before doing so, however, we make some general observations. First, as our discussion in Chapter 15 pointed out, it makes little sense to use trade barriers to correct underlying market distortions. The clearest example lies in the generous income and price supports for farming in the European Community, which have stimulated massive amounts of surplus agricultural production. In most cases, rather than scaling back on the supports, the European Community has chosen to dispose of some of the surplus by paying export subsidies, which has surely worsened economic welfare. More generally, there are likely to be numerous interactions between trade policies and regulations, such as the combination of high tariffs and regulations on FDI, which together have frequently induced inefficient investments in developing economies. Thus, trade policy exists in a second-best world, and proper analysis would consider the merits of deregulation with careful regard for its effects on welfare in light of the operation of other policies and distortions.

A related point is that the use of retaliatory trade barriers to change offending foreign regulations is also questionable. Suppose, for example, that the United States determines under Section 301 that a country such as Thailand is not providing sufficient copyright protection for American books and movies. A tariff imposed on Thai exports in retaliation will not remove the source of the distortion and may, in fact, have little deterrent impact. As always, a better approach is a direct attack on the problem, which in this case would be to negotiate with Thailand over a modification of its copyright law. The problem here, of course, is that, because international trade is the most common interface between the two countries, the only way to enforce any agreements made in such negotiations might be to threaten trade sanctions. Again, an interesting second-best problem emerges.

A fundamentally important difficulty in using trade policies to induce changes in foreign business regulations is that different countries naturally have varying preferences about the structure of their regulations. For example, many economists suggest that environmental cleanliness is a commodity with a high income elasticity of demand, so that as nations get richer, they prefer less pollution.[25] Developing countries may prefer to limit environmental protections that discourage fast economic growth. This might be particularly true for countries with large geographical areas for, in a Heckscher-Ohlin sense, they would have a large relative endowment of "environmental space" (air, land, and water) that would be used intensively in production. Put differently, such nations would have relatively larger abilities to absorb environmental effluents. Given these static and dynamic differences in views about appropriate domestic regulations, it seems unreasonable for all countries to harmonize all their policies to common, international standards. Thus, multilateral agreements on regulatory standards may be especially difficult to achieve unless those nations preferring the strongest standards stand ready to provide offsetting compensation to those with the lowest standards. Note how strongly this situation contrasts to the general indication in economic theory that global free trade in goods provides an acceptable standard of optimality. Of course, this difference reflects the theoretical presumption of the absence of distortions that necessitate regulatory actions in the first place.

What is the ultimate market distortion with respect to the environment, as seen by many economists? It is that countries fail to deal adequately with the overriding feature of air, land, and water, which is that in some measure these are *common-resource inputs,* meaning that many users take advantage of them simultaneously. It is then difficult to assign a dollar cost to the act of despoiling one unit of such an input and to determine appropriate taxes on its use. In simplest economic terms, countries with heavy environmental damage fail to encourage appropriate conservation because the prices they place on their environmental inputs are insufficient to equalize at the margin, the economic benefit of developing natural resources and the environmental cost of exploiting them. In this light, trade policy has little role to play in a sound and sensible regime of environmental regulations.

Trade and the Environment

It is not difficult to understand the potential conflicts between environmental regulations and trade policy.[26] There are three types of problems that carry an international economic dimension. First, a country might use trade policies to complement or enforce its domestic environmental policies. For example, if a country is worried that some domestic industry produces excessive amounts of pollution, it can subsidize imports of the pollution-generating commodity in order to reduce domestic output. Similarly, a potential advantage of lower import barriers to agricultural goods in the developed economies is that some agricultural production will shift to developing economies, which tend to use chemical inputs less intensively, given their relatively greater abundance of land and labor. More commonly, a nation might restrict exports of some natural resource in the belief that free trade will result in excessive exploitation of the resource. Canada, for instance, insists on the right to ban the export of logs under certain conditions. Numerous developing countries have also instituted bans on the export of tropical hardwood logs, claiming that such quotas limit the exploitation of rainforests.

By now it should be clear how most economists would view such policies. Because they do not directly address the problem, management of environmental resources, trade policies are likely to be ineffective approaches. This ineffectiveness is well-established in many cases. Moreover, given the second-best nature of the approach, layering a trade barrier onto an existing environmental distortion could well make the situation worse. Indeed, many developing countries, such as Indonesia, have found their tropical forests being cut down *faster* after the imposition of an export ban than before. The primary reason is that the export restriction markedly reduces the market value of the trees, diminishing incentives for economic forest management. Rather, farmers and developers have a greater incentive to cut the trees down in order to open up new land areas. An additional reason for the rapid harvest is that the export ban makes the lumber very cheap domestically, inducing an artificial expansion of production of wood products, such as tropical plywoods, which are then exported excessively under the implicit subsidy. Thus, rather than employing export policy to regulate timber harvest, it would be more sensible to allow unrestricted exports combined with sensible land-management policies, such as development zoning, harvesting taxes, and replanting requirements. Toward this end, the trees should be accorded an economic value that induces their harvest according to forward-looking optimization.

A second general problem is that countries have different environmental standards, which may influence trade. For example, nations employ import barriers to protect their domestic environmental standards from the effects of more-limited foreign standards. This is most common in requiring that imported plants and animals be examined for pests and that food imports be inspected for sanitary problems. Such imports may be excluded if they present a health risk for domestic farmers and consumers. These regulations are perfectly allowable under GATT rules. They make sense economically because the source of the potential health problem is imports, so that banning them is the most direct solution. The difficulty, of course, is that inspection authorities may abuse the system and eliminate or delay imports of uncontaminated foods that compete with domestic products. This "red tape" should be viewed as a nontariff trade barrier. The GATT tries to discourage this implicit protectionism by requiring that such inspections be based on accepted scientific testing principles and completed in a timely fashion. In practice, the GATT has been relatively lenient in allowing nations to define and enforce their safety and health standards subject to this testing requirement. There is little indication that multilateral trade rules would ever seriously restrain legitimate efforts to protect public safety.

A more complicated issue of environmental policy emerges when foreign production practices themselves offend the spirit of domestic environmental law, even if there is no concern over consumer safety. A stark example of this issue emerged in the United States in 1990. Under pressure from environmental groups, the United States acted under the provisions of its Marine Mammal Protection Act (MMPA) to exclude imports of tuna caught by Mexican fishermen. Mexican fishing techniques involved using large drift nets that capture and destroy numerous dolphins as they harvest tuna. The "kill rates" for dolphins with this technique exceeded the norms allowed the U.S. fishing fleet under the MMPA. Mexico objected to the import ban as an unwarranted extension of American law to another sovereign nation and filed a GATT complaint. The GATT panel agreed with Mexico, stating that the U.S. import ban represented an improper use of *extraterritoriality;* the United States had no right to use trade policy to impose its environmental regulations on another nation. Environmentalists in the United States were understandably upset by this ruling, which continues to serve as a rallying cry for opposition to, or substantial modification of, GATT rules. It may be worth noting that, in the end, the United States did not have to alter its implementation of the law, because Mexico joined the United States in signing a multilateral pact with several other Latin American nations committing themselves to changing their fishing techniques. Further, public preferences in the United States shifted strongly in favor of tuna that could be advertised as "dolphin friendly," generating a market response toward new techniques on the part of the Mexican fleet.

Perhaps an even more controversial extension of this issue is that differing national environmental standards are thought by many observers to influence the decisions of MNEs on where to produce. Some countries might choose to adopt low-cost, limited environmental regulations in order to attract FDI and expand employment, effectively trading environmental degradation for growth. In turn, the country from which investment leaves would suffer employment losses, inducing it to lower its environmental standards to match those of its competitor. This possibility was featured prominently in the debate over NAFTA. Opponents of the agreement argued that U.S. firms would move large parts of their operations to Mexico to take advantage of its limited and poorly enforced standards. While this must be admitted as a theoretical possibility, available evidence strongly suggests that differences in environmental costs rarely provide an important motivation for FDI.[27] Neither is there any evidence that environmental standards converge on the lowest level in the presence of freer trade. Indeed, the experience of the European Community suggests just the opposite, that standards tend to ratchet upward toward the highest levels among countries at similar levels of development.

For our purposes, however, the relevant question is again whether it is sensible to deal with these potential problems by imposing restrictions on trade (and perhaps outward flows of FDI). For standard reasons that by now should be clear, the answer is no. However, the issue is somewhat deeper. Many people argue that limited environmental standards are tantamount to *social dumping* through implicit government production subsidies and that importing countries should impose *social countervailing duty protection,* or tariffs that equalize the resulting cost differences. This proposal has also been raised with respect to differences in labor rights, educational attainment, intellectual property rights, and public infrastructural investments. The idea is reminiscent of a long-discredited notion known as the *scientific tariff,* wherein each country would impose tariffs that would just offset any cost differences between imports and domestic goods, effectively eliminating trade and its associated gains. Similar problems exist with the social dumping idea, which refuses to recognize that nations have legitimately different interests in social policy. To countervail such differences would both ignore the benefits of comparative advantage and impose a punitive kind of extraterritoriality.

A final general issue emerges when the environmental damage itself, created in one country, crosses into another country. Prominent examples of such *cross-border externalities* include unsanitary water supplies on the U.S.-Mexico border, acid precipitation in Canada, airborne pollutants in Eastern Europe, diminution of the ozone layer, and global warming. The last two problems are perhaps most interesting in that they present threats to all nations, rather than being localized, cross-border problems. Whatever the scientific evidence on the extent of those threats, the problems raise interesting international economic questions.

How should countries respond to international environmental externalities? Again, it is clear that trade restrictions are likely to be crude instruments for changing foreign behavior. While they could induce lower production by a polluting industry, they do not force that industry to pay for its damages, or to "internalize" the problem. Indeed, if the polluting industry does not export its product to the offended nation, that nation would be able to impose trade barriers only on other products from the polluting firm's nation, an even less effective tactic. This problem is worsened as the externality becomes more multilateral in nature, as with global warming. In that case it would be nearly impossible to calculate the damages suffered by various nations and to assign those damages to the polluting nations. The resulting tariffs would be virtually meaningless.

These observations point directly to the negotiation of bilateral and multilateral governmental agreements over the terms of environmental cleanup and allowable pollutant discharges. One current example is the Montreal Protocol, which sets limits for the emission of chloroflourocarbons (chemicals that deplete ozone) among the signatories, most of which are developed countries. Such negotiations can presumably recognize each nation's particular size, endowment structure, level of economic and technological development, and other characteristics relevant to assessing appropriate levels of emissions. They might also involve commitments by wealthier nations to pay compensation to poorer nations in return for lower levels of pollutant releases. Such "side payments" are generally efficient in an economic sense in that they transfer income from those who are willing to pay for a cleaner environment to those who may otherwise be unwilling to undertake it. In this context, it is worth noting that such compensation may come in the form of greater market access for products of developing countries in developed countries, as is available through major trade agreements. At the same time, nations must have means of enforcing the commitments made in environmental treaties. Because trade is the primary interface among countries, commercial sanctions against national violators likely represents the most efficient form of deterrent. Here, then, is a justification for marrying trade policy to international environmental policy.

Overall, however, there is a general presumption on the part of economists of little logical connection between trade policy and environmental regulations. Despite this, growing conflicts are inevitable between advocates of open trade and those who view trade barriers as a means of supporting domestic environmental laws and even extending their reach abroad. By now, economists have become strongly skeptical about the benefits of activist trade policy for nearly any purpose, including strategic industrial policy, income distribution, and environmental protection. Beyond the fundamental crudity of trade barriers for these purposes, history amply suggests that arguments for trade restrictions tend ultimately to reflect narrow protectionist interests rather than well-designed social objectives.

Nonetheless, the issues described in this section seem likely to loom large in the evolution of global trade policies over the foreseeable future. Thus, numerous observers have suggested that the next major round of trade negotiations at the GATT should be devoted to international environmental concerns; indeed, some have taken to calling it the "Green Round" in recognition of the environmental interests underlying its purpose.

20.5 CONCLUDING REMARKS

In this chapter we have reviewed some of the major practical issues pertaining to international trade rules and institutions. The international trading system has functioned quite well in fostering an expansion of global trade and income but has come under increasing strain in recent years. Our discussion has suggested some summary conclusions.

1. In the period since World War II, the global trading system has been governed loosely by the mutually agreed-upon rules that constitute the GATT. The guiding principle of the GATT is nondiscrimination, as embodied in MFN, which has assisted greatly in bringing down world tariff barriers to their currently low levels. However, there are numerous exceptions to nondiscrimination, and whole sectors of economic activity lie substantially outside the GATT's realm. Further, the use of quantitative trade restrictions has proliferated recently. The just-completed Uruguay Round attempted to gain control over many of these problems.

2. The United States has become quite active in attempting to remove "unfair" foreign trade practices unilaterally through Section 301 of its trade law. While application of this law has been largely successful, it poses significant risks for the system of world trade.

3. Contingent protection, as embodied especially in AD and CVD actions, has become the favored route of industries to import relief in the developed countries. There are economic arguments in favor of these policies, but the arguments are weak, especially in the case of dumping. Current practice seems to use these procedures, in part, to facilitate collusion through import protection.

4. Growing conflicts between trade policy and domestic regulatory environments pose perhaps the greatest challenge for the world trading system in the near future. Countries vary markedly in their regulatory policies for a variety of reasons, but these differences may have important trade impacts.

5. Trade policy has a relatively small role to play in the context of environmental regulation, at least as a matter of economic logic. Nonetheless, the temptations to use trade sanctions for this purpose seem likely to grow over time. Placing this issue into some multilateral context will be an important task for the next major round of trade negotiations.

NOTES

1. See C. P. Kindleberger (1973) for an analysis of the depression and the role of trade barriers in fostering it. Readers interested in a history of earlier U.S. trade policy may consult the classic volume by F. Taussig (1892). For a history of Canadian trade policy, see J. H. Dales (1966) and R. E. Caves (1976).
2. For an authoritative discussion of these negotiations and an analysis of the body of international trade rules that has emerged since then, see John Jackson (1989).
3. Because the GATT is an "agreement" among contracting parties and not an "organization," it has no members per se. Nonetheless, we will use the terms "members" to refer to contracting parties.
4. See R. M. Stern, J. H. Jackson, and B. Hoekman (1988) for a full discussion of the economics of these agreements and J. H. Jackson (1989) for a treatment of their legal ramifications.
5. Not all of the developing countries in this table were GATT members at that time.
6. See S. Laird and A. Yeats (1990) for a complete description.
7. For example, the GATT is often derided in the popular media as the "General Agreement to Talk and Talk."
8. Partly in recognition of the rapid economic growth in Singapore, Hong Kong, South Korea, and Taiwan, these countries have largely been removed from the GSP. Concern remains, however, over rapid export growth from a new generation of industrializing nations, such as Malaysia, Thailand, and Mexico.
9. See Organization for Economic Cooperation and Development (1987) for a description of agricultural NTBs in the developed nations and an attempt to quantify the effects of these distortions.
10. We analyze motivations for FDI and its effects in Chapter 23.
11. As the names of the Tokyo Round and the Uruguay Round suggest, most MTN rounds are named for the places at which they are initiated. However, the negotiations actually take place at the GATT building in Geneva, Switzerland. The papers in J. Schott (1990) provide a comprehensive analysis of the various negotiating issues and proposed resolutions.
12. See J. Bhagwati (1991) for a defense of multilateralism and L. D. Tyson (1992) for proposals for an activist U.S. trade policy.
13. For information on all aspects of U.S. trade laws, see United States International Trade Commission.
14. Several cases of retaliation are discussed by Robert Hudec in his paper in J. Bhagwati and H. T. Patrick (1990). The contributions in that volume provide a strong indictment of Section 301.
15. This statement was made by K. E. Maskus (1987), p. 417.
16. E. Helpman and P. Krugman (1989) spell out this theory in detail.
17. See R. Boltuck and R. Litan (1991) for a detailed treatment. The administrative processes are similar in the EC, Canada, and Japan.
18. See P. Messerlin (1990).
19. T. Prusa (1992) analyzes the incentives for foreign and domestic firms to come to such agreements.
20. A production subsidy to the export good could be analyzed separately, with due recognition for differences between consumer and producer prices in F.
21. This explains why many economists joke that the appropriate response by the importer is simply to write a thank-you note.

22. For example, in the United States, such assistance is available through the Export-Import Bank.
23. The astute reader will have noticed that AD and CVD laws require the demonstration of "material injury," while safeguards require showing "serious injury." This difference is more than semantic; "material" is a considerably weaker standard in legal terms. This fact helps explain the far greater resort of firms to AD and CVD remedies for protection.
24. This is a common complaint leveled at Japan by the United States and is one focus of ongoing bilateral talks on structural reform in Japan.
25. G. Grossman and A. Krueger (1993) discuss the economics of this phenomenon and provide estimates of the relevant income elasticities.
26. For full discussions see Anderson and Blackhurst (1992) and Low (1992).
27. On the theory of FDI under differential regulations, see Markusen, Morey, and Olewiler (1993), while on the empirical evidence see Pastor (1992).

REFERENCES

Anderson, K., and Blackhurst, R., eds. (1992). *The Greening of World Trade Issues*. London: Harvester Wheatsheaf.

Bhagwati, J. (1991). *The World Trading System at Risk*. Princeton: Princeton University Press.

Bhagwati, J., and Patrick, H. T., eds. (1990). *Aggressive Unilateralism: America's 301 Trade Policy and the World Trading System*. Ann Arbor: University of Michigan Press.

Boltuck, R., and Litan, R. E., eds. (1991). *Down in the Dumps: Administration of the Unfair Trade Laws*. Washington: Brookings Institution.

Caves, R. E. (1976). "Economic Models of Political Choice: Canada's Tariff Structure." *Canadian Journal of Economics* 9:278–300.

Dales, J. H. (1966). *The Protective Tariff in Canada's Economic Development*. Toronto: University of Toronto Press.

Deardorff, A. V., and Stern, R. M., (1989). *A Computational Analysis of Alternative Scenarios for Multilateral Trade Liberalization*. Ottawa: Economic Council of Canada.

Grossman G. M., and Krueger, A. B. (1991). "Environmental Impacts of a North American Free Trade Agreement," in P. M. Garber, ed., *The Mexico-U.S. Free Trade Agreement*. Cambridge, Mass.: MIT Press, 13–56.

Helpman, E., and Krugman, P. R. (1989). *Trade Policy and Market Structure*. Cambridge, Mass.: MIT Press.

Jackson, J. H. (1989). *The World Trading System: Law and Policy of International Economic Relations*. Cambridge, Mass.: MIT Press.

Kindleberger, C. P. (1973). *The World in Depression, 1929–1939*. Berkeley: University of California Press.

Kowalczyk, C. (1989). "Trade Negotiations and World Welfare." *American Economic Review* 79:552–559.

Laird, S., and Yeats, A. (1990). "Trends in Nontariff Barriers of Developed Countries, 1966–1986." *Weltwirtschaftliches Archiv*, 126:299–325.

Low, P., ed. (1992). *International Trade and the Environment*. Washington: World Bank.

Markusen, J. R., Morey, E., and Olewiler, N. (1993). "Environmental Policy When Market Structure and Plant Locations Are Endogenous." *Journal of Environmental Economics and Management* 24:69–86.

Maskus, K. E. (1987). "The View of Trade Problems from Washington's Capitol Hill." *The World Economy* 10:409–423.

Messerlin, P. A. (1990). "Antidumping," In Schott, 108–129.

Organization for Economic Cooperation and Development (1987). *National Policies and Agricultural Trade*. Paris: OECD.

Pastor, R. A. (1992). "NAFTA as the Center of an Integration Process: The Non-Trade Issues." In N. Lustig, B. P. Bosworth, and R. Z. Lawrence, eds., *Assessing the Impact: North American Free Trade*. Washington: Brookings Institution, 176–209.

Prusa, T. J. (1992). "Why Are So Many Antidumping Petitions Withdrawn?" *Journal of International Economics* 33:1–20.

Schott, J. J., ed. (1990). *Completing the Uruguay Round: A Results-Oriented Approach to the GATT Trade Negotiations.* Washington: Institute for International Economics.

Stern, R. M., Jackson, J. H., and Hoekman, B. (1988). *An Assessment of the GATT Codes on Non-Tariff Measures.* Brookfield, V.: Gower.

Taussig, F. (1892). *The Tariff History of the United States.* New York: G. P. Putnam's Sons.

Tyson, L. D. (1992). *Who's Bashing Whom? Trade Conflict in High-Technology Industries.* Washington: Institute for International Economics.

United States International Trade Commission, annual. *The Year in Trade: Operation of the Trade Agreements Program.* Washington: Government Printing Office.

FACTOR TRADE, GROWTH, AND THE THEORY OF DIRECT FOREIGN INVESTMENT

CHAPTER
21

TRADE
IN FACTORS
OF PRODUCTION

21.1 TRADE IN FACTORS

Up to this point, we have assumed that countries may trade commodities but that factors of production are immobile among countries. We noted in the Introduction that it is this immobility of factors that has traditionally distinguished the study of international trade from interregional trade. Yet anyone who has read history is aware of many examples of human migrations, such as those from Europe to North America in the nineteenth century. Those familiar with more contemporary business events are aware of the high level of capital movements and foreign investment that have characterized the world economy since World War II.

It is thus apparent that some factors of production are mobile. What are the effects of such factor movements on world trade and welfare? This question is of particular interest in countries that are the sources of foreign investment as well as countries that are the recipients of investment. Some arguments seem to suggest that both source and host countries are worse off.

International trade economists generally identify three types of factor movements: direct foreign investment, portfolio investment, and labor migration. A direct foreign investment is defined as an investment in which the investor acquires a substantial controlling interest in a foreign firm or sets up a subsidiary in the foreign country. Direct foreign investment thus involves ownership and/or control of a business enterprise abroad. Companies that engage in direct foreign investment are known as multinational enterprises or transnational corporations. (Direct foreign investment will be the subject of the following chapter.)

This chapter will be confined to the discussion of portfolio investment and labor migration. Portfolio investment occurs when an individual or company buys foreign bonds or purchases foreign stocks in quantities too small to gain control of a foreign firm. We will assume throughout the chapter that portfolio investment and labor migration occur in response to differences in wage and rental rates between two countries. Of course, portfolio investment and labor migration actually occur for reasons other than differences in factor prices. These reasons might include escape from war or repression in the case of labor migration or uncertainty over future economic conditions in the case of capital mobility. With this qualification in mind, we restrict our discussion to factor movements motivated by factor price differences.

Portfolio capital movements and labor migration have very similar effects on production and trade. Thus, we analyze the two together, generally referring arbitrarily to capital as the mobile factor. The two may differ with respect to the repatriation of earnings. Capital owners generally tend to remain in their home countries, repatriating their foreign earnings and consuming at home. Migrants generally spend most of their earnings in their new countries. Yet migrants often repatriate substantial sums (e.g., guest workers in Europe or Mexican and West Indian farm workers in the United States) and capital owners sometimes move with their funds (e.g., Canadians retiring to Florida or employees working abroad on a company investment project). Thus, we treat capital and labor movements as being essentially similar.

The preceding chapters have shown a number of cases in which trade does not equalize factor prices. We emphasized in Chapter 8 that the conditions under which trade in commodities leads to the equalization of factor prices are very restrictive, and thus equalization should, in fact, be regarded as the exception rather than the rule. The following situations can result in unequal factor prices between countries, thus providing incentives for factors to migrate. (1) If production technology differs between countries (Chapter 7), it is unlikely that trade will equalize factor prices even if it equalizes commodity prices. (2) If some goods are produced with increasing returns to scale (Chapter 12), then trade will not equalize factor prices. (3) If tariffs or transport costs prevent trade from equalizing commodity prices, factor prices will differ between countries. (4) If imperfect competition or production taxes exist in some sectors, marginal costs and therefore factor prices will not be equal between countries. (5) If there are more factors of production than traded goods, then trade in goods alone is generally not sufficient to equalize factor prices.

This last point might seem puzzling, but in fact, we saw a perfect case of this type in the specific-factors model of Chapter 9. With three factors and two goods, trade in two goods generally cannot equalize the prices of the three factors. Think of trying to solve two equations (making the unit cost of producing each good equal its price) for three unknowns (the three factor prices).

We will use this idea in an even simpler model in this section to explore the benefits of trade in factors in addition to trade in goods. Suppose that there is only a single produced good, X, with two factors of production, L and K. Suppose that countries H and F can trade only goods. It is clear in this very simple model that there is no way to capture any gains from trade: the countries must have at least two goods between them to trade.

The situation is shown in the Edgeworth-Bowley box of Fig. 21.1. The dimensions of the box represent the total "world" endowments of capital and labor, the combined endowments of the two countries. The lower left-hand corner is the origin for Country H, and the upper right-hand corner is the origin for Country F. Isoquants are drawn for the production of X in each country. If the two countries have identical technologies, then the contract curve is the diagonal of the box, but identical technologies are in no way necessary for the argument.

Suppose that the endowment point for the two countries is at E in Fig. 21.1. Thus, the Home country is relatively well-endowed with capital, and the Foreign country is relatively well-endowed with labor. At E, the X isoquants of the two countries are not tangent (not drawn). The X isoquant for Home is steeper than that for foreign, indicating that w/r is higher in Home than in Foreign at the endowment point. This makes sense because labor is the relatively scarce factor in H, and capital is the relatively abundant factor in H. The fact that factor prices are not the same in the two countries indicates that there are unexploited gains from trade, just as earlier in the book we showed that the inequality of commodity prices indicates unexploited gains from trade.

Free trade in factors of production starting at point E leads to an equilibrium at point A, where the factor-price ratios of the two countries are equalized at $(w/r)^*$. Country H exports capital, its abundant factor, and

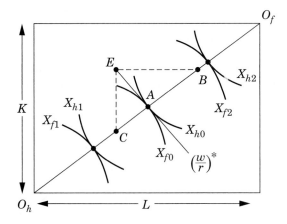

FIGURE 21.1
Factor trade.

imports labor to reach point A. Country F exports labor, its abundant factor, and imports capital. The isoquants X_{h0} and X_{f0} are the free trade production levels of X in the two countries, and because X is not traded, they are also the free trade consumption levels. Both countries gain mutually from trade.

It is interesting and important to point out that the exchange of capital for labor is not the only possible way of moving from E to A in Fig. 21.1. Suppose, for example, that capital and X can be traded but that labor is immobile. Then Home can export capital in the amount EC to Foreign. Point C then becomes the production point for the two countries. But Foreign must pay Home for the capital, and hence, Foreign exports X in the amount CA. Point A continues to be the consumption point of the two countries, while C is the production point.[1]

This last result is interesting in light of controversies over the export of capital in countries like the United States. As in the case just mentioned, the United States loses production of X (jobs in manufacturing?), and imports X instead. But this is in no way "bad." We end up at the same consumption point A in either case. Of course, factor price changes redistribute income, but these price changes are the same regardless of how we move from E to A.

To make the point more strongly, note that Home could arrive at A by importing labor from Foreign to arrive at B, which now becomes the production point. Home is now producing a lot of X, which will make the critics happy. But Home must pay for the imported labor, exporting X to Foreign (or giving the additional production to the foreign labor) to arrive again at the consumption point A. The level of production of X (jobs in manufacturing) does not have direct welfare consequences. As we have noted several times in the book, production must not be confused with consumption as a measure of the gains from trade.

21.2 A GAINS-FROM-TRADE THEOREM

In this section, we show how the gains-from-trade theorem of Section 5.2 of chapter 5 can be extended to take factor trade into consideration. But we need to prepare this explanation by considering Fig. 21.2. An isoquant for producing X is shown in the diagram. Let point A be the point where the free trade factor price ratio $(w/r)^*$ is tangent to the X isoquant. Thus, point A in Fig. 21.2 is analogous to point A in Fig. 21.1. We can think of the tangent line through A in Fig. 21.2 as an isocost line, giving the cost of producing X at factor prices $(w/r)^*$. Suppose instead that we produce X using the autarky factor proportions E. Putting a line with factor-price ratio $(w/r)^*$ through point E, we see that the cost of producing X using autarky factor proportions E at free trade factor-price ratio $(w/r)^*$ exceeds the cost of producing X using the optimal (free trade) factor proportions at A. It then follows that if profits to the competitive firm from using the optimal factor proportions A to produce in free trade are zero, then using the autarky

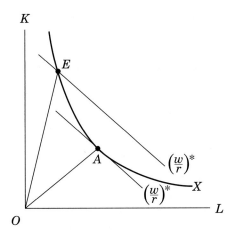

FIGURE 21.2
Optimal input combinations at free trade factor prices.

factor proportions E to produce at free trade factor prices must lead to losses (negative profits).

The following analysis can pertain to either country, so we shall drop the use of subscripts to refer to a particular country. Let $\overline{L}$ and $\overline{K}$ denote the country's endowments of capital and labor, and let L^m and K^m denote imports of capital and labor, respectively. A negative value for L^m or K^m denotes an export of that factor. L^f and K^f denote the amounts of L and K actually used in production in free trade, so

$$L^f = \overline{L} + L^m \qquad K^f = \overline{K} + K^m \qquad (21.1)$$

The profit from producing the free trade output level X_p^f from inputs (L^f, K^f) at free trade prices (p^*, w^*, r^*) is zero, while the profit that would result from producing the autarky output X_p^a from $(\overline{L}, \overline{K})$ at the free trade prices must be negative, which is the result we established in the previous paragraph and in Fig. 21.2. Thus, we have the following inequality.

$$p^* X_p^f - w^* L^f - r^* K^f = 0 \geq p^* X_p^a - w^* \overline{L} - r^* \overline{K} \qquad (21.2)$$

In autarky, the production of X equals the consumption of X: $X_p^a = X_c^a$. In free trade, exports of X (which could be negative, indicating that X is imported), equal the value of imports of factors (which could also be negative, indicating that the country exports factors). This equation is given by

$$p^* (X_p^f - X_c^f) = w^* L^m + r^* K^m \qquad or \qquad p^* X_c^f = p^* X_p^f - w^* L^m - r^* K^m \qquad (21.3)$$

If Eq. (21.1) is substituted into Eq. (21.2), the latter can be written as

$$p^* X_p^f - w^* L^m - r^* K^m \geq p^* X_p^a \qquad (21.4)$$

Now substitute the right-hand side of Eq. (21.3) for the left-hand side of Eq. (21.4). The latter equation now becomes

$$p^* X_c^f \geq p^* X_c^a \qquad (21.5)$$

This says that with free trade in goods and factors, the free trade consumption bundle is revealed preferred to the autarky consumption bundle.

This analysis establishes that free trade in goods and factors is superior to autarky. Although we applied the analysis to the special case of only one good and two factors, the technique is very general and is easily extended to the case of many goods and factors. The gains-from-trade result also holds if only a subset of the goods and factors are traded.

21.3 TRADE IN FACTORS INDUCED BY DISTORTIONS*

We have emphasized several times that trade induced by distortions is not necessarily beneficial trade. Production taxes and subsidies can generate trade that is not necessarily welfare-improving. The same is true for factor trade, as we will show in this section. The points made in this section are important for policy, insofar as some governments have deliberately erected barriers to trade in goods in order to induce foreign firms to invest inside their countries. We now show that, once barriers to goods have been erected, permitting factors to flow may reduce welfare. Using trade barriers to attract foreign investment into a country is not likely to improve welfare.

The basic idea is as follows. Suppose that a country erects a tariff barrier to the import of a capital-intensive good. The domestic price of the good, equal to the domestic cost of producing a unit of the good, is greater than the price paid to the foreigner for the good. (Of course, the domestic consumer faces the higher, distorted domestic price.) The tariff on the capital-intensive good raises the domestic return to capital (the Stolper-Samuelson theorem). Now suppose that capital flows into the country to produce the good "behind the tariff wall." What happens is that costly domestic production will now displace cheap imports, and for each unit of imports displaced by domestic production, the country will incur a loss equal to the difference between the high, domestic price and the low, foreign price. The initial tariff must be harmful for a small country, as we showed in our chapter on tariffs, and the capital import now adds an additional harmful effect. This could be called the "secondary burden" of the tariff. When the domestic price of capital-intensive goods and the return to capital are artificially increased by a tariff, the factor trade thereby generated is not beneficial.

This may seem to be an abstract point, but in fact, many countries have from time to time deliberately erected import barriers as an import-substitution policy, hoping to attract foreign capital. Our recent analysis

---

*Material in this section is technically more difficult, although it uses the same technique developed in earlier chapters. We try to develop the argument in the first few paragraphs, so the rest of the section may be skipped without loss of continuity. The section draws very heavily on an important paper by Brecher and Alejandro (1977).

suggests that this is a particularly unwise policy, unless it can be proven that the policy will counteract some other domestic distortion.

Now we turn to a more formal analysis. Consider the basic two-factor, two-good Heckscher-Ohlin model. We assume that the country imports X, the capital-intensive good, and places an import tariff on X. We assume that the country is small and hence faces fixed world prices, p^*. If we hold the tariff fixed, then domestic prices are held fixed, and domestic factor prices will also be held fixed if the country produces both goods (recall from Chapter 8 that the goods prices determine factor prices). The relationships between domestic and world prices are given by

$$p_x = p_x^*(1+t) \qquad p_y = p_y^* \qquad\qquad (21.6)$$

Let superscript r (restricted) denote quantities when trade in goods, but not factors, is permitted under the tariff. Let superscript s denote trade when a small amount of trade in factors is also permitted.[2] Similar to the previous section but using s instead of f, L^s and K^s will denote the amounts of L and K actually used in production, equal to endowments $\overline{L}$ and $\overline{K}$ plus imports L^m and K^m (which will be exports if their values are negative). If domestic factor prices were equal to foreign factor prices before the tariff, as we shall assume, the tariff on the capital-intensive good raises the domestic return to capital above the world return and lowers the domestic return to labor below the world return.

In this competitive model, the value of profits from producing the restricted (commodity trade only) outputs equals zero. Because permitting a small amount of factor trade does not change either commodity or factor prices by assumption, the profits from producing in the presence of factor trade at these prices is also zero. This gives us

$$p_x X_p^r + p_y Y_p^r - w\overline{L} - r\overline{K} = p_x X_p^s + p_y Y_p^s - wL^s - rK^s = 0 \qquad (21.7)$$

Using the relationships in Eq. (21.1) (with superscript s replacing superscript f), Eq. (21.7) can be rewritten as

$$p_x X_p^r + p_y Y_p^r = p_x X_p^s + p_y Y_p^s - wL^m - rK^m \qquad (21.8)$$

Using Eq. (21.6), Eq. (21.8) can be rewritten in terms of world prices.

$$\left[p_x^* X_p^r + p_y^* Y_p^r\right] = \left[p_x^* X_p^s + p_y^* Y_p^s - wL^m - rK^m\right] + p_x^* t(X_p^s - X_p^r) \qquad (21.9)$$

The term in square brackets on the left-hand side of Eq. (21.9) is the value of production at world prices when there is no factor trade, which must equal the value of consumption in this equilibrium. The term in square brackets on the right-hand side of Eq. (21.9) is the value of production minus the payments (or receipts) for imported factors, which must, by the balance of trade constraint (similar to Eq. 21.3), equal the value of consumption at this equilibrium. Thus, Eq. (21.9) can be written in terms of consumption quantities.

$$\left[p_x^* X_c^r + p_y^* Y_c^r\right] = \left[p_x^* X_c^s + p_y^* Y_c^s\right] + p_x^* t(X_p^s - X_p^r) \qquad (21.10)$$

For welfare purposes, consumption must be evaluated at domestic prices. Thus, we need to replace world prices in Eq. (21.10) with domestic prices from Eq. (21.6).

$$[p_x X_c^r + p_y Y_c^r] = [p_x X_c^s + p_y Y_c^s] + p_x^* t [(X_c^r - X_p^r) - (X_c^s - X_p^s)] \quad (21.11)$$

The left-hand side of Eq. (21.11) is the value of consumption when only trade in goods is permitted, while the first quantity in square brackets on the right-hand side is the value of consumption when a small amount of factor trade is permitted. The second term on the right-hand side in square brackets is imports of X with goods trade only, minus the imports of X with factor trade. We expect this second term to be positive. The import tariff on X raises the return to the factor used intensively in X, which is capital in this case, and so capital should flow into the country and/or labor should flow out. This generates a Rybczynski effect (Chapter 8), in which the country specializes further in the production of the capital-intensive good, and hence reduces its imports of X.

Allowing factor trade leads to a replacement of imports by domestic production. The tariff raises the cost of the import good, thereby raising the return to the factor used intensively in its production, thereby generating an inflow of this factor, thereby replacing imports with domestic production. But this factor trade is welfare-worsening according to Eq. (21.11). If the second bracketed term on the right-hand side is positive, then consumption without factor trade (the left-hand side of Eq. (21.11) is greater than the value of consumption with factor trade (the first bracketed term on the right-hand side). As indicated at the beginning of this section, the economy is using costly domestic production to replace *apparently* costly imports. But the price of imports has been distorted by the tariff; imports are actually cheap compared to domestic production. On each unit of imports displaced, the economy loses the difference between the domestic price p_x (the cost of producing a unit domestically) and the world price p_x^* (the cost of obtaining the good from abroad). But, as seen from Eq. (21.6), this difference is $p_x^* t$, "which, times the change in imports (the second bracketed term on the right-hand side of Eq. (21.11)), equals the loss in welfare.

21.4 TRADE POLICY IN THE PRESENCE OF FOREIGN-OWNED FACTORS OF PRODUCTION

In this section, we briefly make an important point about tariffs that was noted by Bhagwati and Brecher (1980). We have noted a number of times that while a tariff may reduce aggregate income in a small economy, it also has strong redistribution effects among groups of factor owners. Consider then a situation in which the Home country, prior to the adoption of an import tariff, already has a sizable stock of foreign investment. Further, suppose that this investment is sunk in fixed plant and equipment; that is, the investment cannot be "liquidated" and moved back to the Foreign country. Assume finally that this foreign investment constitutes a significant proportion of the domestic capital stock.

In such a situation, the effects of a tariff on the total income of the *domestically-owned* factors of production may be either better or worse than the effects predicted earlier in this book. If the import good is capital-intensive, then the tariff boosts the return to capital while making labor worse off. But because capital has a significant share of foreign ownership, the gain to capital is captured largely by foreigners. Domestically owned factors are even worse off than the standard analysis (no foreign ownership) suggests. On the other hand, suppose that the import good is labor-intensive, in which case the tariff increases the real income of labor. This is outweighed by the aggregate losses to capital, but in this case, most of those losses are absorbed by the Foreign country. Thus, the gain to domestic labor may well exceed the loss to domestic capital, and Home's aggregate income may increase.

In this last case, while the tariff has an aggregate negative effect on income, its redistribution effect in favor of domestically owned factors of production may outweigh the overall efficiency loss such that domestic welfare rises. This is an important theoretical result, but a country should be cautioned against using trade policy to redistribute income away from foreign capital: in the long run, that capital can be withdrawn, through depreciation if nothing else.

21.5 TERMS-OF-TRADE EFFECTS, THE TRANSFER PROBLEM, AND GLOBAL WELFARE

The simple models in the previous sections have been constructed such that factor trade has no effect on equilibrium commodity prices. In this section, we briefly explore the consequences of relaxing that assumption. Terms-of-trade effects (changes in commodity prices) influence the division of gains from trade between countries, as we have noted several times in this book, particularly in the chapter on technology as a basis for trade and in the chapter on tariffs. Terms-of-trade (TOT) effects will always help one country and harm the other. Thus, changes in the terms-of-trade induced by a factor flow or by other changes imply a "secondary" burden or benefit in addition to the primary change.

The analysis of this terms-of-trade change has often been called the "transfer problem" and is usually conducted with respect to a unilateral gift or transfer of money or commodities from one country to another, although the principle is exactly the same as in the case of factor movements. (The problem was originally discussed with regard to war reparation payments following World War I.)

Suppose that Country F makes a gift of money or commodities to Country H, or that some factors leave F to take up residence in H. Country H now has greater purchasing power and Country F less purchasing power.

Assume further that Country H imports Y and exports X. The effect of this transfer on the terms of trade turns out to depend on the consumption response of citizens in each country (in addition to the production response in the case of a factor movement). Suppose that the residents of H use their added purchasing power exclusively for the purchase of X, their export good. The demand for X will rise relative to the demand for Y in Country H. Suppose also that residents of F react to their reduced purchasing power by decreasing consumption of Y, their export good, while holding consumption of X relatively constant. The demand for Y will fall relative to the demand for X in Country F. If we put these two effects together we will see that the world demand for X has risen relative to Y following the transfer. The price of X will rise relative to Y, and Country H will receive a secondary benefit from the positive TOT effect.

The result is that if each country has a relatively high propensity to spend on its own export good, the TOT tends to move in favor of the country receiving the transfer. The receiving country thus ends up gaining more than the amount of the transfer, and the sending country ends up losing more than the amount of the transfer. The receiving country receives a secondary benefit and the sending country a secondary burden. If each country has a high propensity to spend on its own import good, the opposite conclusion applies.[3]

From the point of view of the world as a whole, it turns out that the negative TOT effect experienced by one country balances the positive TOT effect of the other country. Thus, world real income is not changed by terms-of-trade effects. The TOT effect can be expressed in terms of either imports or exports, so let us express it in terms of X. It can be shown that the TOT effect is approximately equal to the country's excess supply for X times the change in the price of X, $(X_p - X_c)\Delta p^*$, where X_c and X_p are the quantities of X consumed and produced, respectively. If X is exported, $(X_p - X_c) > 0$, and a rise in the relative price of X, Δp^*, improves welfare. If X is imported, $(X_p - X_c) < 0$, and a rise in p^* decreases welfare.

In a two-country world, the exports of one country must match the imports of the other country. Thus, if we add the TOT effects together for H and F, we will have a world TOT effect of zero:

$$(X_p^h - X_c^h)\Delta p^* + (X_p^f - X_c^f)\Delta p^* = 0 \qquad (21.12)$$

because $(X_p^h - X_c^h) = -(X_p^f - X_c^f)$. The consequence of this is that we can ignore the TOT when talking about the effects of factor mobility for the world as a whole.

From the point of view of the world as a whole, the welfare effects are the same as those discussed in earlier sections. If countries do not have distortionary tariffs or other taxes, factor movements are guaranteed to increase total world income by creating gains for both countries. If, on the other hand, factor movements are prompted by distortionary taxation, then one country may experience negative primary effects as discussed in the previous section, and world real income may decrease. As we have seen several times in this book, not only do distortions cause welfare losses in their own right, but they may also lead to further losses when combined with what would otherwise be welfare-improving policies (free trade in goods and factors).

21.6 FACTOR TRADE AND COMMODITY TRADE AS SUBSTITUTES

The previous several sections have focused on the welfare effects of factor mobility. In this section and the next we will focus on the ways in which factor movements influence the amount of world trade in commodities. If factor trade leads to a *reduction* in the amount of commodity trade, we say that factor trade and commodity trade are substitutes (i.e., the exchange of factors can substitute for the role usually played by commodity exchange). If factor movements lead to an *increase* in the volume of commodity trade, we say that factor trade and commodity trade are complements.

Consider the basic Heckscher-Ohlin model, with two goods (X and Y) produced by two countries (H and F) using identical technologies and factors K and L. Suppose that initially there is free trade (and no transport costs) in commodities but that factors cannot be traded. Assume that the factor endowments of the two countries are similar enough that both countries produce both goods in free trade.

In this situation, free trade will equalize factor prices between countries, as we noted in Chapter 8 (Fig. 8.8). This situation is shown in Fig. 21.3. With identical technologies and with commodity prices equalized by trade, the unit-value isoquants for X and Y are in the same position for both countries. Each country adopts the factor proportions A for Y and B for X at

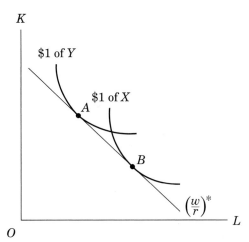

FIGURE 21.3
Factor-price equalization.

the common factor-price ratio $(w/r)^*$. In this case, there is no incentive to trade factors; all gains from trade are captured through commodity trade.

Suppose that Country H has been importing Y (i.e., H is relatively capital-scarce) and that H now places an import tariff on Y. This raises the price of Y in H relative to its price in F: $(p_x/p_y)_h < (p_x/p_y)_f$. This shifts inward the unit-value isoquant for Y in H: with the price of Y higher, fewer physical units of K and L are needed to produce one dollar's worth of X. This is shown in Fig. 21.4. H has equilibrium factor-price ratio $(w/r)_h$ while F has equilibrium factor-price ratio $(w/r)_f$. H's tariff on the capital-intensive good has raised the return to capital and lowered the return to labor in H relative to F.

Now suppose that we allow trade in factors. H will import capital and/or export labor. This causes the factor ratios used in the countries to converge and reduces commodity trade as the scarce factor in each country becomes less scarce and the abundant factor becomes less abundant. But factor prices in the two countries cannot begin to converge as long as there is commodity trade because the tariff maintains the commodity-price differences, which in turn determine the factor-price differences. Factor trade will continue until all commodity trade is eliminated. Once trade in commodities is eliminated, equilibrium commodity prices will be determined within each country independently and will depend on the relative supplies of capital and labor. The continued gain of capital and loss of labor in H leads to a fall in the relative price of the capital-intensive good Y and an increase in the relative price of the labor-intensive good X. Because the opposite is occurring in F, the commodity price ratios converge in the two countries. As indicated in Fig. 21.3, factor prices converge in the two countries at exactly the same point as their commodity prices converge. When factor trade fully equalizes factor prices, it equalizes commodity prices as well.

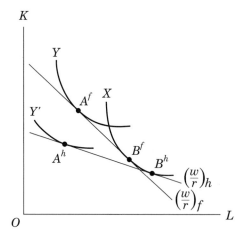

FIGURE 21.4
Factor prices unequal due to a tariff on Y in country H.

Mundell (1957) pointed out that the resulting free factor-trade equilibrium is *exactly* the same as the free commodity-trade equilibrium in all important respects. Commodity and factor prices must be the same in each case. With factor and commodity prices the same, the income and utility of all agents must be the same. The value of trade in commodities (or alternatively, the value of the factors embodied in that commodity trade) must be the same as the value of factor trade in the free factor-trade equilibrium. In this sense, trade in goods and factors are substitutes.

The Mundell conclusion is somewhat extreme, but it points to a very general result. In many other situations, gains from trade cannot be fully exhausted by trading only goods or only factors. For example, in the two-good, three-factor, specific-factors model, trade in two goods cannot equalize the prices of the three factors. Thus, there are additional gains to be captured from factor trade. Yet, we usually get the Mundell result that trade in goods and factors are substitutes in the sense that permitting trade in factors reduces trade in goods. Suppose, for example, that two countries had the same supplies of labor but that one had more X-sector capital and one had more Y-sector capital. In Chapter 9, we demonstrated that in this case, each country would have a relatively low price for the type of capital that is in abundant supply. If factor trade in capital were now permitted, each type of capital would move from where it is abundant to where it is scarce. Trade in factors would then reduce (substitute for) commodity trade.

21.7 FACTOR MOVEMENTS AND COMMODITY TRADE AS COMPLEMENTS

Now consider a very different situation in which trade is caused by differences in production technologies.[4] Assume two countries, H and F, with identical factor endowments. Assume also that H and F have identical technologies for producing Y but that Country H has superior technology for producing X. It is assumed that Country H's X isoquants have the same shape as the X isoquants for Country F, but that the former are renumbered so that more output is produced from the same inputs (this is called "Hicks-neutral" technical superiority, named after John Hicks).

The situation is shown in Figs. 21.5 and 21.6. The first two assumptions together imply that the countries have identical Edgeworth-Bowley boxes and identical contract curves in Fig. 21.6. But their production frontiers differ, as shown in Fig. 21.5. $\overline{Y}\,\overline{X}^f$ gives the production frontier for F. Country H can produce the same maximum amount of Y but more X, so H's frontier is given by $\overline{Y}\,\overline{X}^h$.

Suppose that Q^f in Figs. 21.5 and 21.6 gives F's production point in free-trade equilibrium. If H allocated factors in the same way in Fig. 21.6 (point Q^f), H would be at point A in Fig. 21.5, producing the same amount of Y but more X. This cannot be an equilibrium for H because the marginal cost of producing X will be less in H relative to that in F. This is because, beginning at Q^f in Figure 21.6, fewer factors are needed for an additional

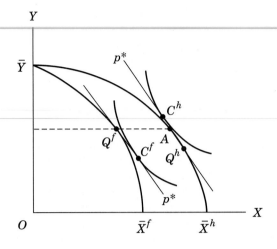

FIGURE 21.5
Country H with technical superiority
in X.

unit of X in Country H than in Country F because of H's superior technology. Thus, if $p_x^f = \mathrm{MC}_x^*$ in Fig. 21.6, then we must have $p_x^h > \mathrm{MC}_x^*$ at Q^f. The equilibrium for H must be at a point like Q^h in Figs. 21.5 and 21.6.

   If the countries are producing at Q^f and Q^h in Figs. 21.5 and 21.6, we can conclude two things. First, Country H must be exporting X and importing Y (Fig. 21.5). Second, the wage-rental ratio must be higher in H (Fig. 21.6) because the capital-labor ratios there are higher. This case differs from the one considered in the previous section in that here, each country will have a relatively high price for the factor used intensively in its

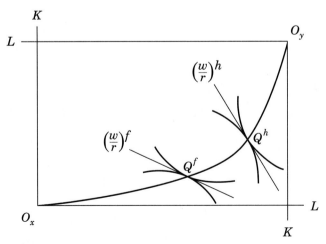

FIGURE 21.6
Equilibrium without factor trade.

export industry. If we permit factors to migrate, labor will flow into Country H and/or capital will be exported to country F, as long as we retain our assumption that X is labor-intensive. The corresponding situation holds, of course, in Country F.

The result of this factor mobility is that each country becomes relatively better-endowed with the factor used intensively in its export industry. This adds a Heckscher-Ohlin, or factor-proportions, basis for trade, which tends to reinforce the basis for trade caused by the difference in technology. Factor mobility can then lead to an increase in the volume of commodity trade. Country H will now export X not only because it has superior technology but also because it is now relatively well-endowed with labor.

In this simple model of trade based on differences in production technology, factor movements and commodity trade turn out to be complements. Although this may seem to be a very special case, it is in fact true that the complementary relationship holds for a wide variety of models in which the basis for trade is something other than differences in factor endowments.

As a second example of complementarity, consider the simple, symmetrical model of external economies of scale introduced in Chapter 12. Assume that scale economies are strong enough to outweigh factor-intensity effects such that the production set is nonconvex. Figure 21.7 draws the identical production frontiers for two identical economies, $\overline{Y}\,\overline{X}$. One country specializes in Y and one in X, each trading half of its output for half of the other's output so that they both reach the consumption point C in Fig. 21.7. Figure 21.8 shows the factor market, with each country having the identical factor endowment E. Country H produces output $\overline{X}$ with factor-price ratio $(w/r)_h$ and Country F produces $\overline{Y}$ with factor-price ratio $(w/r)_f$.

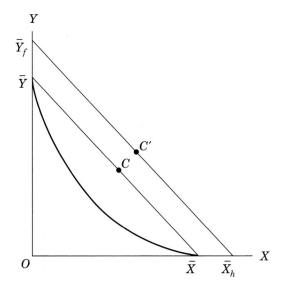

FIGURE 21.7
Specialization for two identical countries with increasing returns.

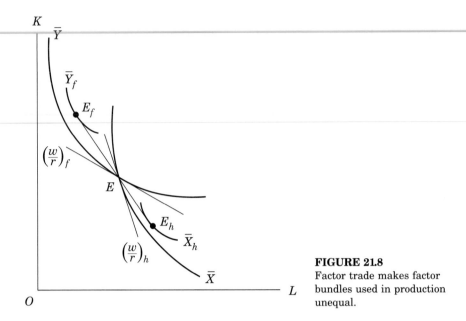

FIGURE 21.8
Factor trade makes factor bundles used in production unequal.

Now suppose that the two countries can trade factors. Country H should import L and export K; vice versa for Country F. Factor prices are equalized once H reaches point E_h, producing $\overline{X}_h$, and F reaches point E_f, producing $\overline{Y}_f$ in Fig. 21.8. The output of both goods has increased, and these new production levels correspond to points $\overline{Y}_f$ and $\overline{X}_h$ in Fig. 21.7. Both countries will now trade to reach consumption point C' in Fig. 21.7. Factor trade has led to an increase in the volume of commodity trade and has caused a difference between the two countries' endowments.

21.8   CONCLUDING REMARKS

While international trade theory has traditionally focused on trade in commodities while assuming that factors of production are immobile, factor movements are actually of considerable importance to many countries. For example, Canada and the United States were developed with foreign labor and capital. In the latter half of the twentieth century, North American capital has in turn been exported. Major issues in recent Canadian international policy have revolved more around factor movements (foreign investment) than around commodity trade. The following points summarize the principal results of the chapter.

1. Countries can gain mutually by trading factors of production just as they can by trading commodities. If the price of a factor is not equalized between countries, then its marginal product is high where it is expensive and low where it is cheap. Owners of the factor in the country where it

is cheap should be willing to supply it to the other country, and complete free trade will equalize the price of that factor at a point between the two countries' no-factor-trade prices. Both countries gain.

2. There may be some indeterminacy in the trade pattern as we noted in connection with Fig. 21.1. The capital-abundant, labor-scarce country can export capital and import goods, export capital and import labor, or export goods and import labor, arriving in each case at the same equilibrium in terms of income, consumption, and welfare. Although theoretically equivalent in many cases, these alternative ways of exploiting the gains from trade are often treated differently in practice. Some countries object to the importation of foreign capital, while others object to labor immigration, the latter being particularly intrusive on the indigenous society.

3. However, a country does not necessarily gain from trade induced by distortions. We gave an example in which a tariff raised the domestic price of the capital-intensive good and hence the return to capital. If the country then permits capital imports, the imported capital generates costly domestic production of the protected good that displaces cheap imports of the good. This capital inflow, generated by the distortionary tariff, is welfare-reducing.

4. Some standard results about trade and protection need to be modified if there are substantial, fixed stocks of foreign-owned factors of production in the domestic economy. A tariff on the imports of capital-intensive goods affects national income negatively (at least for a small economy), but there is also a significant redistribution effect in favor of capital and against labor. In this case, however, it is foreign owners of capital who capture much of the benefit, and hence, domestically owned factors of production are much worse off than an examination of aggregate income would suggest.

5. In many cases, factor trade generates a change in the commodity terms of trade, producing a secondary benefit for the country whose terms of trade improve and a secondary cost for the country whose terms of trade deteriorate. This is known as the *transfer problem,* a term coined during the analysis of World War I reparations payments.

6. Trade in factors and trade in goods are substitutes in many models, including the Heckscher-Ohlin model. By this we mean that allowing trade in factors leads to a reduction in the volume of trade in goods. The term *substitutes* is also used in a welfare sense when the gains from trade can be captured through trade in either goods or factors. In practice (as is the case in our example of the specific-factors model), trade in goods alone rarely equalizes factor prices, indicating that there are further unexploited gains from trade in factors. Allowing trade in factors then adds to the welfare gains but may also reduce the volume of commodity trade.

7. Many examples can be constructed in which trade in goods and trade in factors are complements in terms of the volume of trade. If, for example,

countries have identical relative factor endowments but Hicks-neutral differences in technologies, then each country should import the factor used intensively in the industry in which it has a technological advantage. This makes relative factor endowments unequal and leads to an increase in the volume of commodity trade. Another example can be found in the increasing-returns example of Figs. 21.7 and 21.8. If the countries are specialized and have identical relative factor endowments, then each country will have a relatively high price for the factor used in its export industry. Allowing factor trade will lead to a divergence of factor ratios and an increase in the volume of trade.

PROBLEMS

1. In the Heckscher-Ohlin model, each country's abundant factor loses as a consequence of trade. Does this effect occur for the two countries in Fig. 21.1?

2. Gross domestic product (GDP) is defined as the total value of production in a country, whereas gross national product (GNP) is the income of domestic citizens. GNP thus equals GDP minus the repatriated profits of foreign investors plus the repatriated profits from investments by domestic citizens abroad. For the three possible trades discussed in connection with Fig. 21.1, discuss how GNP and GDP differ.

3. If the current account is defined as the sum of merchandise (goods) trade and trade in factor services, discuss the merchandise surplus or deficit in the three possible trades of Problem 2.

4. For a small economy that imports a labor-intensive good and in which the entire capital stock is foreign-owned, what is the welfare effect of a tariff on the income of the domestic factor owners?

5. Suppose that the domestic economy exports a capital-intensive good but that most of the domestic capital stock is foreign-owned. With reference to the Stolper-Samuelson theorem, discuss the possibility that an improvement in the terms of trade could reduce the welfare of domestic citizens.

NOTES

1. A country's GNP (gross national product) refers to the income of its citizens, while GDP (gross domestic product) is the value of production in the country. In the presence of factor trade, the two are not the same. In the case just mentioned, point C in Fig. 21.1 gives the two countries' GDPs (production). Point A gives their GNPs (consumption). For Country H, GNP equals GDP plus the earnings of its capital now located in Country F. Conversely, GDP exceeds GNP for Country F because some of the value of production accrues to factors owned by H.

2. Because commodity prices determine factor prices and are fixed, factors would continue to flow in this model until the country specialized in only one good. Hence, we will consider permitting only a small movement of factors such that the country continues to produce both goods after the factor flow. Allowing factors to move freely until the country specializes is discussed with respect to a different issue in Section 21.5.

3. See Samuelson (1952, 1954) for a formal treatment.

4. This analysis relies on the work of Purvis (1972) and Markusen (1983).

REFERENCES

Bhagwati, J. N., and Brecher, R. A. (1980). "National Welfare in the Open Economy in the Presence of Foreign-Owned Factors of Production." *Journal of International Economics* 10:103–115.

Brecher, R. A., and Diaz-Alejandro, C. (1977). "Tariffs, Foreign Capital, and Immiserizing Growth." *Journal of International Economics* 7:317–322.

Jones, R. W. (1967). "International Capital Movements and the Theory of Tariffs." *Quarterly Journal of Economics* 81:1–38.

Jones, R. W., Coelho, I., and Easton, S. (1986). "The Theory of International Factor Flows: The Basic Model." *Journal of International Economics* 20:313–327.

Markusen, J. R. (1983). "Factor Movements and Commodity Trade as Complements." *Journal of International Economics* 13:341–356.

Markusen, J. R., and Melvin, J. R. (1979). "Tariffs, Capital Mobility, and Foreign Ownership." *Journal of International Economics* 9:395–410.

Mundell, R. A. (1957). "International Trade and Factor Mobility." *American Economic Review* 47:321–335.

Purvis, D. D. (1972). "Technology, Trade, and Factor Mobility." *Economic Journal* 82:991–999.

Samuelson, P. A. (1952). "The Transfer Problem and Transportation Costs: The Terms of Trade When Impediments Are Absent." *Economic Journal* 62:278–304.

———.(1954). "The Transfer Problem and Transportation Costs II: Analysis of Effects of Trade Impediments." *Economic Journal* 64:264–289.

CHAPTER
22

DIRECT FOREIGN INVESTMENT AND MULTINATIONAL FIRMS

22.1 DIRECT FOREIGN INVESTMENT IN THE OLI FRAMEWORK

Direct foreign investment is defined as an investment in which the investor acquires a substantial controlling interest in a foreign firm or sets up a subsidiary in a foreign country. Direct foreign investment involves ownership and/or control of a business enterprise abroad. For the remainder of this chapter, we refer to companies that engage in direct foreign investment as multinational enterprises (MNE), although they are also sometimes referred to as transnational corporations. The study of multinational enterprises (MNEs) is becoming much more important in international economics because these firms now account for a considerable proportion of international trade. It is estimated that multinationals now account for foreign sales worth some U.S.$5.5 trillion, compared to a value of world exports of goods and nonfactor services of around U.S.$4 trillion. Of this latter amount, around one third is intrafirm trade between parents and foreign affiliates. In short, international business is increasingly carried out on an intrafirm basis rather than through the use of arm's-length export markets, the latter of which has been our assumption up to this point.

Most international trade economists believe that there are important differences between direct and portfolio investments, although they disagree in their interpretations of the consequences of these differences. One relevant observation is that MNEs seldom move substantial amounts of capital between countries (which portfolio investments do); rather, they frequently provide for many of their needs from the foreign capital markets. Thus, the U.S. manufacturer moving into Canada may borrow funds for plant and equipment from Canadian banks or issue stocks or bonds on Canadian securities markets. Canadian land developers operating in Texas or Florida may mortgage their properties with U.S. banks. The implication of these observations is that direct foreign investments are generally not caused by the difference in the general return to capital that prompts portfolio capital movements. The MNE is formed to take advantage of specific business opportunities rather than the secondary benefits of general levels of interest rates and returns to capital. To make a domestic analogy, U.S. land developers in Denver who make investments in the Houston market do so because they see profitable business opportunities there, not because interest rates differ between Denver and Houston. These same business factors would lead the developers to enter the Australian land market.

A second important difference between direct and portfolio investments proceeds from the fact that foreign firms are at an inherent disadvantage in the domestic market. Thus, if foreign firms are identical to domestic firms, they will not find it profitable to enter the domestic market. Therefore, the MNE must possess some special advantage such as superior technology or lower costs due to scale economies. This point also helps to explain the previous observation that MNE investments are often not primarily motivated by differences in returns to capital. They seem instead to be motivated by such advantages as the ability to exploit superior technical knowledge.

The inherent disadvantages of setting up MNE operations abroad are numerous, a point we can make by providing a few convincing examples. (1) Maintaining branch plants or subsidiaries in foreign countries necessitates costs in communication and transportation not faced by domestic firms. These include direct costs such as overseas phone calls and travel expenses for executives as well as time costs due to mail delays and so on. (2) Language and cultural differences between the home country and the foreign ("host") countries inevitably create costs for the MNE that are not faced by domestic firms. (3) Similarly, the MNE, at least initially, does not have a close familiarity with the host country's business community, tax laws, and other government procedures. Local laws often, in fact, tend to discriminate actively against the MNE. (4) The MNE faces risks such as exchange rate changes, expropriation, or other capricious government actions that are not as important to domestic firms. Thus, if the firms and their owners are risk-averse, the uncertainty faced by the MNE constitutes a true business cost. (5) The MNE frequently must station managers and technicians abroad. Often, only substantially higher wages can induce these personnel to live abroad.

The point is perhaps clear. Because of these disadvantages, the MNE will enter a foreign market only if it has some compensating advantages over local firms. These advantages (e.g., superior technology) are thereby transferred to the foreign country and thus constitute an important potential gain for the host country. There may, however, be offsetting costs such as increased monopoly power.

Any analysis of direct foreign investment must identify the advantageous conditions that can outweigh the inherent disadvantages of foreign production. One organizing framework was proposed by Dunning (1977, 1981), who suggested that three conditions are necessary for a firm to undertake direct investment. This has become known as the OLI framework. First, a firm must have an *ownership advantage* (the "O" in OLI). This could be a product or a production process to which other firms do not have access, such as a patent, blueprint, or trade secret. But the advantage could also be as intangible as a trademark or a reputation for quality. The ownership advantage is anything that gives the firm enough valuable market power to outweigh the disadvantages of doing business abroad.

Second, the foreign market must offer a *location advantage* (the "L" in OLI) that makes it more profitable to produce in the foreign country than to produce at home and export to the foreign market. Tariffs, quotas, transport costs, and cheap factor prices are the most obvious sources of location advantages. But more intangible factors, such as customer access, can also be important. Indeed, many multinationals are in service industries (e.g., hotels) in which on-site provision of the services is an inherent part of the companies' business (of course, we could simply think of services as being characterized by very high transport costs).

Third, the MNE must have an *internalization advantage* (the "I" in OLI). This is the most abstract of the three conditions, but the advantage can be highlighted by considering alternatives to direct investment. Even if a company has the advantage of a proprietary product or production process, and even if tariffs and transport costs make it advantageous to produce abroad rather than to export, it is still not certain that the company should set up a foreign subsidiary. One fairly simple alternative would be to license a foreign firm to produce the product or use the production process. Why not just sell the blueprints to a foreign firm rather than go through the costly and difficult process of setting up a foreign production facility? Reasons for wishing to do so are referred to as *internalization advantages;* that is to say that the product or process is better exploited internally within the firm rather than at arm's length through markets. Further discussion of internalization is postponed until later in the chapter.

22.2 OWNERSHIP ADVANTAGES ARISING FROM KNOWLEDGE-BASED ASSETS

In this section, we will discuss one important source of ownership advantages that leads firms to establish plants in multiple countries. Important differences in the degree of multinational activity across industries have long been observed. In some industries, MNEs account for a major share of total output, while in others this share is minor. It has also been consistently shown that the degree of multinationality in an industry is closely related to such variables as R&D, marketing expenditures, number of scientific and technical workers, product newness and complexity, and product differentiation (e.g., Caves, 1982).

These explanatory variables give rise to the concept of knowledge-based, firm-specific assets (FSAs). These are proprietary assets of the firm that are embodied in such things as the human capital of the employees, patents or other exclusive technical knowledge, copyrights or trademarks, or even more intangible assets such as management skill or the reputation of the firm. There are two good reasons why these knowledge-based assets are more likely to give rise to direct foreign investment (DFI) than are physical capital assets. First, knowledge-based assets can easily be transferred among locations. For example, an engineer or manager can visit many separate production facilities at relatively low cost. Further, knowledge often has a joint, or "public-goods," character in that it can be supplied to additional production facilities at very low cost.

Blueprints for new products or production processes (knowledge-based assets) can be provided to additional plants without reducing the value of the blueprints to the initial plants. Blueprints are thus a joint input (or "public good") into all plants. Chemical formulae and pharmaceuticals have similar properties. Trademarks and other marketing devices also have this characteristic. Assets based on physical capital such as machinery tend not to have this characteristic. That is, physical capital usually cannot yield a flow of services in one location without reducing its productivity in others.

The joint-input characteristic of knowledge-based assets has important implications for the efficiency of the firm and for market structure. These implications are encapsulated in the concept of economies of multi-plant production. Such economies arise because a single, two-plant firm has a cost efficiency over two independent, single-plant firms. The multi-plant firm (i.e., the MNE) need make only a single investment in R&D, for example, while two independent firms must each make the investment. The latter industry structure therefore involves the duplication of FSAs. Cost efficiency would then dictate the establishment of MNEs (multi-plant firms) as the equilibrium market structure in industries where FSAs are important; indeed, the empirical evidence bears out this assumption.

The converse proposition should also be emphasized. Scale economies based on physical capital intensity do not by themselves lead to DFI. This type of scale economy implies the cost efficiency of centralized production rather than geographically dispersed production. Of course, some industries with high physical capital intensity may also be industries in which FSAs are important (e.g., automobiles).

What, then, is being traded in cases of multinational production? Basically, MNEs in this framework are exporters of the services of FSAs. These include management, engineering, marketing, and financial services, many of which are based on human capital. They also include the "services" of patents and trademarks, which are other knowledge-based assets.

Subsidiaries import these services in exchange for repatriated profits, royalties, fees, or often the final product itself. Note that this can lead to some misconceptions. For example, this chapter was first typed on a Compaq computer "made" in Singapore. Does importing this kind of "high-tech" product from a developing country threaten the welfare of the United States? Not at all. The bulk of the design and engineering work, in addition to the production of complex components, was done in the United States. The final product was produced abroad by this multinational using cheap assembly labor in Singapore and highly skilled human-capital services from the United States. The work that makes the product "high-tech" was done in the United States.

22.3 THE TRANSFER OF KNOWLEDGE CAPITAL THROUGH DIRECT FOREIGN INVESTMENT

We can adapt the imperfect-competition model of Chapter 12 to an analysis of the economies of multi-plant production arising from knowledge-based assets. Two goods (X and Y) are produced from a single factor, labor (L), which is in fixed supply ($\overline{L} = L_x + L_y$) and is internationally immobile. Y is produced with constant returns by a competitive industry, with the simple production function $Y = L_y$. We will measure values in terms of labor; that is, the price of labor is 1, which in turn means that p_y also equals 1 (1 unit of labor produces 1 unit of Y). To begin producing X, a firm must first incur the initial sunk costs of F (firm-specific cost) and G (plant-specific cost) in terms of Y or L. Additional plants may be opened for the cost of G only. F is thus intended to represent the knowledge-based capital that is a joint input ("public good") within the firm. F could be thought of as an R&D investment necessary to design a product or a production process. Once the design is produced, it can be costlessly incorporated into additional plants. This leads to multi-plant economies of scale in that a two-plant firm incurs F only once, while two one-plant firms must each incur F. The fact that the services of F can be costlessly extended to additional plants does not, of course, imply that these services are of no value to the additional plants.

An economy is represented in Fig. 22.1 for which $\overline{Y}GF\overline{X}$ is the country's production frontier. $\overline{Y}$ is the maximum feasible production of Y. In order to begin production of X, a firm must invest the fixed costs G (given by the distance $\overline{Y}G$) and F (given by the distance GF). After investing the fixed costs, the company can produce X at constant marginal cost in terms of Y, which gives the linear segment $F\overline{X}$. This linear segment has slope $-m$ if m is the marginal cost of X in terms of Y.

Because of the fixed costs, average cost exceeds marginal cost, and hence, the price of X must exceed the marginal cost m if the firm is to make nonnegative profits. The average cost of producing X in terms of Y is given by the simple formula

$$\text{AC}_x = \frac{L_x}{X} = \frac{\overline{L} - L_y}{X} = \frac{\overline{Y} - Y}{X} \qquad (22.1)$$

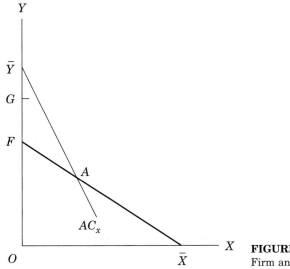

FIGURE 22.1
Firm and plant specific fixed costs.

Consider point A in Fig. 22.1. Calculated from Eq. (22.1), the average cost of producing this amount of X_i is simply the slope of a line passing through $\overline{Y}$ and A. Average cost is everywhere decreasing in X. The non-negative profit constraint requires that the price ratio at a point like A be at least as steep as the average-cost line $\overline{Y}A$.

Figure 22.2 shows an equilibrium in which the firm producing X is making positive profits. Equilibrium production is at A, and the equilibrium price ratio is p. An indifference curve is shown tangent to p at A. Point I gives total income or GNP in terms of good Y. But total labor income in terms of Y is simply $L_x + L_y = \overline{L} = \overline{Y}$. Total income ($IO$) is thus comprised of profits ($I\overline{Y}$) plus labor income ($\overline{Y}O$). The budget line for labor is the line through $\overline{Y}$ with slope p. The indifference curve tangent at B thus represents the consumption bundle and welfare level of labor, with the difference between B and A being consumption from profits. The division of total output between labor income and profits is simply a distributional issue in the closed economy, but it becomes an issue of GDP (gross domestic output: the value of domestic output) versus GNP (gross national product: the income of domestic citizens) if a foreign-owned MNE is producing X and repatriating the profits.

Figure 22.3 shows outcomes when the country (call it Foreign) is host to an MNE enterprise. Because this firm has already invested F, production in the host country does not require this initial investment. Thus, the production frontier is now $\overline{Y}G\overline{X}'$, which is similar to a technical improvement over the autarkic frontier $\overline{Y}F\overline{X}$. The value of the imported services, measured in terms of opportunity cost, is the distance GF. In Fig. 22.3, it is assumed that the MNE maximizes profits by producing at point B at price ratio p^m. Point I is total GDP, but the amount $I\overline{Y}$ is

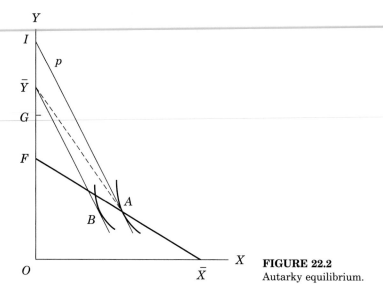

FIGURE 22.2
Autarky equilibrium.

repatriated as profits by the MNE, leaving labor income $\overline{Y}O$ as the GNP of the domestic citizens. This allows the latter to reach consumption bundle C. The multinational provides Foreign with the services of its firm-specific asset (so Foreign does not have to invest in creating such an asset) and repatriates profits.

The basic tension for the host country is between the benefits from this "technology transfer" and the cost of profit repatriation. Foreign gains or losses depend on the location of autarky consumption point A relative to C. Two possibilities are illustrated in Fig. 22.3. If autarky consumption was at point A, the country gains from hosting the multinational. If autarky consumption was at point A', the country loses. If we think about extending a line from $\overline{Y}$ through A or A', the slope of that line is the average cost of producing the autarky bundle, AC_x^a. Therefore, the condition for multinational investment to improve the welfare of the host country is that $p^m < AC_x^a$. The multinational must sell X for less than the average cost of producing it in autarky.

The explanation of this result is as follows. If a domestic firm is producing X in autarky at price p^a, the Foreign economy is capturing the profits $(p^a - AC_x^a)$ for foreign nationals. When the multinational displaces Foreign's firm because of the former's lower cost, Foreign loses this profit income. But if the multinational charges a price less than the autarky average cost, Foreign will still be better off because that average cost represents the true resource (opportunity) cost of producing the good. If Foreign can obtain X for a price less than the resource cost of producing it in autarky, then Foreign is better off.

This argument is easily extended to the case in which the foreign country does not produce the good in the absence of the multinational.

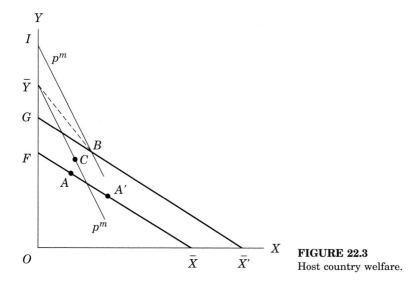

FIGURE 22.3
Host country welfare.

Suppose that Foreign initially imports X at price p^*. Wherever A (now representing consumption, but not production, which is at $\overline{Y}$) might lie in Fig. 22.3, the line connecting A and $\overline{Y}$ is the price ratio p^*. The condition for gains when the multinational replaces imports of X with local production is then that $p^m < p^*$.

It seems that this condition for the host country to gain is likely to be met in practice. The multinational can produce X at a lower cost than Foreign's firm can, and competition among multinationals for entry into Foreign's market may, for example, be a sufficient condition for gains for Foreign. In the case where Foreign initially imports rather than produces the good, Foreign seems certain to gain. The multinational will not incur the fixed cost G of producing in Foreign unless the marginal cost of producing there is less than the marginal cost of serving Foreign by exports. A lower marginal cost would typically mean a lower equilibrium price.

However, it is possible to construct cases in which Foreign does not gain. Suppose that either the MNE or one of Foreign's firms could make profits in Foreign if that firm were a monopolist. But suppose that Foreign's market is too small to support two firms without causing losses to one firm. The MNE has an advantage in that it has already incurred F in Home's market. Thus, if the MNE competes with one of Foreign's firms, it might result that the MNE makes profits while Foreign's firm incurs losses and exits the market. This leaves the MNE as a monopolist, and the MNE might then charge a price roughly equal to that which would be charged by an indigenous monopolist. Consumers in Foreign pay the same price as with an indigenous firm, but Foreign loses the profit income that it would have earned with a domestically-owned firm. Foreign is worse off with the MNE in this case.

In general, the home country benefits from the foreign investment by its MNE. The MNE will move production abroad only if doing so increases its profits, which are part of the domestic income stream (a formal proof is given in the next section). But, as in many trade situations, this does not necessarily imply that every group within the home country is better off. Clearly, owners of factors used intensively in certain industries that are moved abroad may be worse off as the demand for their factor services falls. As with all determinants of trade, we need to remember the distinction between the total income of a country and the distribution of income among various subgroups within society. *

22.4   WELFARE ANALYSIS*

In this section, we will employ the same type of "revealed preference" analysis that we have used a number of times before in order to assess the effect of a direct foreign investment in which a home firm builds a plant in a foreign country (and may indeed transfer production to that country, serving its own market by imports from the foreign plant). This will be contrasted to autarky for both countries, and will thus be quite similar to the case considered in the diagrammatic exposition of the previous section. The model can easily be extended to consider the case in which the MNE initially serves the foreign country by exports and then switches to direct investment.

Consider first the effects on the foreign country. We use superscripts a and m to represent autarky and multinational direct investment, respectively. Subscripts p and c represent production and consumption. In this case, we reverse the procedure that we employed several times before and begin by *assuming* that Foreign gains from the inward direct investment to see what conditions this implies. For Foreign to gain from the direct investment, consumption with the MNE must be revealed preferred to consumption in autarky.

$$p_x^m X_c^m + p_y^m Y_c^m \geq p_x^m X_c^a + p_y^m Y_c^a \qquad (22.2)$$

With the MNE, the balance-of-payments constraint is that the value of production minus repatriated profits (π) is equal to the value of consumption. In autarky, production quantities must equal consumption quantities.

$$p_x^m X_p^m + p_y^m Y_p^m - \pi = p_x^m X_c^m + p_y^m Y_c^m \qquad X_p^a = X_c^a \qquad Y_p^a = Y_c^a \quad (22.3)$$

Substituting these equations into the inequality in Eq. (22.2), we have

$$p_x^m X_p^m + p_y^m Y_p^m - \pi \geq p_x^m X_p^a + p_y^m Y_p^a \qquad (22.4)$$

---

*This section is more difficult and may be skipped without loss of continuity.

Now subtract the economy's total labor endowment $\overline{L}$ from both sides of Eq. (22.4) and break $\overline{L}$ down into the labor allocated to X and that allocated to Y.

$$(p_x^m X_p^m - L_x^m) + (p_y^m Y_p^m - L_y^m) - \pi \geq (p_x^m X_p^a - L_x^a) + (p_y^m Y_p^a - L_y^a) \quad (22.5)$$

Y is assumed to be a competitive, constant-returns industry, so profits are zero in that industry either with or without the MNE (note that $p_y^a = p_y^m = 1$ in this model).

$$(p_y^m Y_p^m - L_y^m) = (p_y^m Y_p^a - L_y^a) = 0 \quad (22.6)$$

Equation (22.6) greatly simplifies Eq. (22.5), which can now be written as

$$(p_x^m X_p^m - L_x^m) - \pi \geq (p_x^m X_p^a - L_x^a) \quad (22.7)$$

But this can be simplified further, by noting that the first term in parentheses represents the profits the MNE earns in Foreign. Assuming that the MNE repatriates all profits, this term is equal to π, and so the left-hand side of Eq. (22.7) is equal to zero. (Even if the MNE does not repatriate the profits, it still owns them, and they do not enter into the welfare of Foreign's residents.) Equation (22.7) then simplifies to

$$(p_x^m X_p^a - L_x^a) = \left[p_x^m - \frac{L_x^a}{X_p^a} \right] X_p^a = [p_x^m - AC_x^a] X_p^a \leq 0 \quad (22.8)$$

The bracketed terms of Eq. (22.8) factor out autarky production of X, leaving the sign of the left side of the inequality to depend on a very simple expression, the price charged by the multinational minus the average cost of producing the good in autarky. Thus, a sufficient condition for Foreign to benefit from the inward direct investment (for the inequality in Eq. (22.2) to hold) is that the multinational charge a price that is less than the average cost of producing X in autarky. This is the same condition discussed in the previous section.

The condition for Home to gain follows the same derivation, except that the sign of π is reversed, because these gains are in addition to Home income, which equals the value of production plus repatriated profits, π. All we need to do is reverse the sign of π in Eq. (22.7).

$$(p_x^m X_p^m - L_x^m) + \pi \geq (p_x^m X_p^a - L_x^a) \quad (22.9)$$

The term in parentheses on the left-hand side of Eq. (22.9) is the profits the MNE earns in Home's market, while the second term π is the profits it earns in Foreign. Thus, the left-hand side is its total profits in multinational operation, which we can denote π^m. The right-hand side is the profits it earns in autarky evaluated at the multinational prices, which we can denote π^a. The condition in Eq. (22.9) can then be written as

$$\pi^m \geq \pi^a \quad (22.10)$$

Home gains if the MNE's profits are revealed preferred to its autarky profits. This must be the case because the MNE would otherwise have declined to make the foreign investment. In this case, the maximization of profits by the home firm is consistent with the interest of welfare in the home country.

22.5   INTERNALIZATION

As noted in the introduction, internalization involves the question of why an MNE would want to exploit its assets abroad by opening or acquiring a subsidiary versus simply selling or licensing the rights to exploit those assets to a foreign firm. This is a somewhat complicated question, but international business economists believe the basic reason to be the variety of transaction costs involved in using arm's-length markets. Although the transaction costs of opening a foreign subsidiary are high, the costs of licensing or other forms of arm's-length transfers can be even higher.

One source of internalization advantages (reasons to transfer assets internally) is that the same joint, or "public-goods," property that promotes efficient foreign production also implies that the value of the firm's FSAs can be dissipated easily. If engineers can supply technology to a branch plant at almost zero cost, so can licensees who can "defect" from the MNE and start their own firms once they learn the technology (of course, the same problem may happen within a subsidiary). The licensee can also peddle the technology to third parties. This potential for licensees to dissipate knowledge-based assets leads the firm to internalize the problem through DFI. This problem does not occur with physical capital assets, and thus we have a second reason why MNE activity tends to be concentrated in industries in which knowledge-based assets are important. This directly implies that MNEs are heavily involved in trade in the services of such assets.

Many examples of internalization advantages can be found in the literature on multinational firms. Rather than trying to be comprehensive here, we will mention just a few in order to give you the flavor of this interesting subject. (1) As just noted, because of the "public-goods" nature of knowledge capital, the value of knowledge assets can be easily dissipated if these secrets are not carefully guarded within the firm. Thus, knowledge-capital assets are transferred internally rather than at arm's length. (2) An important asset of an MNE is its reputation for product quality. If the innovating firm licenses a foreign firm, the foreign firm has an incentive to skimp on quality in order to realize short-run profits on the cost savings. But this destroys the MNE's reputation in the long run.

Our next examples of internalization advantages are related to the frequency of multinationals' specialization in technically new or complex products. (3) The nature of the MNE's knowledge capital (new and/or complex technology) is not known to a potential buyer or licensee. Therefore, it is difficult for the firm to convince that buyer or licensee of the exact value of the product or process without giving away the secrets themselves. (4) The MNE might not have a good idea about how a product will sell in a new market, whereas a local firm (potential licensee) has a much better idea.

Although the MNE might like to use the local firm rather than making a costly, up-front investment, that firm can use its informational advantage to extract rents from the MNE and can even withhold the information that the market is indeed very good. (5) The novel and complex nature of the technology may mean that, while it is very familiar to the employees of the firm, it cannot be transferred simply by selling the blueprints to a foreign licensee. In this case, the necessary training of foreign technical and managerial personnel may be very costly. Thus, it is better to open a subsidiary, stationing the firm's own engineers, technicians, and managers abroad for some period of time. (6) Because of the newness and complexity of the technology, there is considerable uncertainty on the part of the MNE as well as on the part of the subsidiary (point 3) as to how easily the technology can be transferred and what significant start-up problems and costs might be encountered. These informational uncertainities make writing complete licensing contracts difficult for the firm as well as for the potential licensee.

22.6   CONCLUDING REMARKS

In this chapter, we consider direct investment and the multinational firm. This is a complex topic because multinationals are a complex collection of heterogeneous enterprises. Each firm has different reasons for international expansion and different ways of operating in the international marketplace. This chapter takes a unifying approach to direct investment and attempts to present a conceptual framework applicable to many types of enterprises with seemingly disparate modes of operation. In this process of generalization, many real-world features of multinationals and the considerable differences among them are glossed over. The principal points of the chapter are summarized as follows.

1. The determinants of DFI are quite different from those of portfolio invest-ment, which was discussed in the previous chapter. Portfolio investments seem to be motivated basically by international factor-price differences and can therefore be analyzed using the traditional tools of international trade theory. DFI seems to be determined more by the characteristics of individual firms, and thus the traditional microeconomic theory of the firm seems to provide more appropriate methods of analysis.

2. The basic notion is that firms are at a certain disadvantage in competing with the indigenous firms in a foreign country. Thus, for a firm to become a multinational, it must have certain compensating advantages over foreign firms. Dunning's OLI framework identifies three conditions under which a firm will undertake DFI given the inherent disadvantages it faces. First, it must possess an *ownership advantage* in a product or production process. Second, it must have a *location advantage* which leads the firm to want to produce abroad rather than serve the foreign country by exports. Third, the firm must have an *internalization advantage* which makes it choose to exploit its ownership advantage abroad by creating or purchasing a subsidiary rather than through arm's-length markets.

3. Empirical literature associates multinationals with variables such as R&D, technical and professional workforces, product differentiation, new and technically complex products, and marketing expenditures. Multinationality thus seems to be associated with *knowledge-capital intensity*. This makes sense for two reasons. First, the services of knowledge capital can be easily transported among distant production facilities, whereas the services of physical capital, for example, cannot be. Second, the services of knowledge capital such as blueprints and chemical formulae often have a joint-input property in that they can be supplied to additional plants without reducing their services in existing plants. This joint-input property creates multi-plant economies of scale, giving multi-plant firms (multinationals) advantages over single-plant firms in that the former can spread the fixed costs of knowledge capital over many plants (average production costs for the entire firm are lower).

4. The welfare effects of MNEs on host countries seem to involve a complicated tradeoff between increased technical efficiency (exploiting the MNE's knowledge capital rather than recreating it) and the possibility of increased monopoly power. Profits that might have gone to indigenous firms and entered the host country's income may now be repatriated by the multinational. Competition among multinationals that keeps prices near average costs is a sufficient condition to ensure that the host country gains.

5. The multinational's home country gains from its firms' investments abroad because any profits enter the home country's income. But we cautioned that, as in all instances of trade, this does not necessarily mean that all groups within the home country are better off. If the multinational transfers production abroad, owners in the home country of factors used intensively in the production of the good may find themselves worse off. This type of distribution problem is common to trade originating from a variety of causes.

6. Internalization advantages often result from the same joint-input, or "public goods," property of knowledge capital that leads to ownership advantages. The same characteristics that make knowledge capital easy to transfer to a new plant make its value easily dissipated outside the firm if it is not carefully controlled. Blueprints, formulae, and reputations are just a few examples of knowledge capital that can easily be lost to competitors without careful monitoring. In other cases, particularly those involving new and/or complex products, the knowledge capital is embodied in the employees of the firm and is not at all easy to transfer at arm's length. The problem is compounded by the difficulties of writing contracts with potential buyers or licensees of the technology when the product is new and production costs are uncertain. In many of these cases, the costs of opening a subsidiary are high, but the costs of arm's-length arrangements may be even higher.

PROBLEMS

1. "U.S. multinationals are bad for Canada because they transfer profits out of Canada." Evaluate this argument.

2. With reference to the previous question, if all multinationals do is transfer profits (i.e., they offer no efficiency advantages), how can they exist in the face of free entry by domestic competitors in host countries?

3. "U.S. multinationals are bad for Canada because they undermine economic independence." In what sense might direct investment create more dependence than trade in goods?

4. "U.S. multinationals are bad for the United States because they transfer jobs abroad." Evaluate this argument. What types of jobs in the United States might be lost by the movement of plants to Mexico and what types of jobs might be created in the United States?

5. Section 22.3 noted that multi-plant economies imply that the MNE may improve welfare by avoiding the duplication of R&D and other activities. Yet in some regard, the (possibly) lower level of R&D in Canada due to MNEs is welfare-reducing rather than cost-saving. Try to evaluate the argument that reduced R&D is a harmful effect of the MNE. (Suggestion: it might rely on externalities or spillovers of domestic R&D to other sectors of the economy.)

REFERENCES

Brainard, S. Lael (1993a). "An Empirical Assessment of the Proximity/Concentration Tradeoff between Multinational Sales and Trade." MIT and NBER working paper.

Brainard, S. Lael (1993b). "An Empirical Assessment of the Factor Proportions Explanation of Multinational Sales." MIT and NBER working paper.

Casson, M. (1987). *The Firm and the Market: Studies on Transactions Costs and the Strategy of the Firm.* Cambridge, Mass.: MIT Press.

Caves, R. E. (1982). *Multinational Enterprise and Economic Analysis.* Cambridge, Mass.: Harvard University Press.

Caves, R. E., Porter, M. E., and Spence, M. (1980). *Competition in the Open Economy—A Model Applied to Canada.* Cambridge, Mass.: Harvard University Press.

Davidson, W. H., and McFetridge, D. (1984). "International Technology Transaction and the Theory of the Firm." *Journal of Industrial Economics* 32:253–264.

Dunning, J. (1977). "Trade, Location of Economic Activity and MNE: A Search for an Eclectic Approach." In Ohlin, Hesselborn, and Wijkman, eds., *The International Allocation of Economic Activity.* London: Macmillan.

———. (1981). *International Production and the Multinational Enterprise.* London: George Allen and Unwin.

Eastman, H. C., and Stykolt, S. (1967). *The Tariff and Competition in Canada.* Toronto: Macmillan.

Ethier, W. J. (1986). "The Multinational Firm." *Quarterly Journal of Economics* 80:805–833.

———. (1993). "Multinational Firms in the Theory of International Trade." In E. Bacha, ed., *Development, Trade and the Environment.* London: Macmillan.

Gorecke, P. K. (1976). "The Determinants of Entry by Domestic and Foreign Enterprises in Canadian Manufacturing." *Review of Economics and Statistics* 58:485–488.

Horstmann, I., and Markusen, J. R. (1987). "Strategic Investments and the Development of Multinationals." *International Economic Review* 28:109–121.

Horstmann, I., and Markusen, J. R. (1987). "Licensing versus Direct Investment: A Model of Internalization by the Multinational Enterprise." *Canadian Journal of Economics* 20:464–481.

——. (1992). "Endogenous Market Structures in International Trade." *Journal of International Economics* 32:109–129.

Lipsey, R. E. (1994). "Outward Direct Investment and the U.S. Economy." National Bureau of Economic Research Working Paper 4691.

——. (1993). "Foreign Direct Investment in the United States: Changes over Three Decades." In K. Froot, ed., *Foreign Direct Investment.* Chicago: University of Chicago Press for the NBER, 113–170.

Magee, S. P. (1977). "Applications of the Dynamic Limit Pricing Model to the Price of Technology and International Technology Transfer." In K. Brunner and A. Meltzer, eds., *Optimal Policies, Control Theory, and Technology Exports.* Amsterdam: North-Holland, 203–224.

Markusen, J. R. (1984). "Multinationals, Multi-Plant Economies, and the Gains from Trade." *Journal of International Economics* 16:205–226.

Mansfield, E., and Romeo, A. (1980). "Technology Transfer to Overseas Subsidiaries by U.S. Based Firms." *Quarterly Journal of Economics* 94:737–750.

Rugman, A. (1981). *Inside the Multinationals: The Economics of Internal Markets.* New York: Croom Helm and Columbia University Press.

Scherer, F. M., et al. (1975). *The Economics of Multi-Plant Operation: An International Comparisons Study.* Cambridge, Mass.: Harvard University Press.

Teece, D. (1986). *The Multinational Corporation and the Resource Cost of International Technology Transfer.* Cambridge, Mass.: Ballinger.

UNCTAD. *World Investment Report 1993: Transnational Corporations and Integrated International Production.* New York: United Nations.

Wilson, R. (1977). "The Effect of Technological Environment and Product Rivalry on R&D Effort and Licensing." *Review of Economics and Statistics* 59:171–178.

CHAPTER
23

FACTOR ACCUMULATION AND INTERTEMPORAL TRADE

23.1 INTERTEMPORAL GAINS FROM TRADE AND FOREIGN INVESTMENT

Preceding chapters have viewed trade as taking place in a timeless or static environment. Yet many important issues such as growth and foreign investment arise in a dynamic or intertemporal context. These issues are traditionally the province of international finance and growth theory, and as such we will not devote a great deal of analysis to them in this book. However, a few points are considered important in the analysis of international trade. Several of these connect the study of international trade to the study of international finance and growth.

In previous chapters, we have considered trade across different goods and subsequently across factors of production. But trade can also occur across time (intertemporal trade); that is, we can exchange a good or factor today for the same good or factor tomorrow. Alternatively, we can say that goods today can be exchanged for *assets,* which are simply claims on goods in the future. Thus, intertemporal trade in goods is accompanied by international trade in assets, the subject matter of international finance.

Consider a very simple situation, in which there is one commodity (corn) and two time periods. To simplify matters further, assume that initially we get a fixed endowment of corn each period so that there is no production or investment. This situation is shown in Fig. 23.1, where C_0 and C_1 are current and future consumption levels of corn, respectively, and E is the endowment point.

Individuals in the economy have identical preferences between current and future consumption, as represented by the indifference curves in Fig.

409

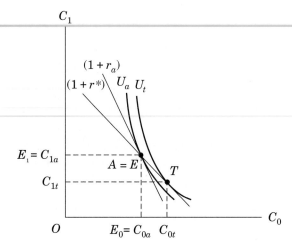

FIGURE 23.1
Intertemporal trade with fixed endowments.

23.1. In the absence of the ability to trade, the economy's consumption in each period must equal the endowment; thus, autarky consumption is C_{0a} and C_{1a} in the two time periods. The economy attains welfare level U_a in autarky. The important point is that the slope of U_a at the equilibrium E is a type of price ratio involving people's willingness to substitute between current and future consumption. The slope of U_a is simply the consumer's marginal rate of substitution between C_0 and C_1, which in equilibrium will be equal to the market "price ratio" of C_1 in terms of C_0. While this price ratio involves the rate of interest, it is not actually equal to the rate of interest. Suppose that the rate of interest is 10 percent. If one person lends a unit of corn to someone else today, then in the next period the lender will get back one unit of corn plus 10 percent. A unit of consumption forgone today gives the lender $(1 + .10) = 1.10$ tomorrow. More generally, the return on forgone consumption is $(1 + r)$, where r is the rate of interest. Algebraically, we have

$$\Delta C_1 = (1 + r)(-\Delta C_0) \quad \text{or} \quad -\frac{\Delta C_1}{\Delta C_0} = (1 + r) \tag{23.1}$$

The equilibrium price ratio tangent to U_a at $E = A$ in Fig. 23.1 is thus $(1 + r_a)$, where r_a denotes the autarky rate of interest.

Now suppose we can trade at a world rate of interest r^*, which differs from our autarky rate. r^* is arbitrarily assumed to be less than r_a in Fig. 23.1 As in the static case, this difference in intertemporal prices is a source of gains from trade. In Fig. 23.1 the economy can now attain point T and utility level U_t. It does so by borrowing an amount $(C_{0t} - E_0)$ (which is like an import) in the current period and paying back an amount $(E_1 - C_{1t})$ (which is like an export) in the future period. If instead r^* were greater than r_a, the country would be a net lender in the first period. The difference between r^* and r_a thus determines the direction of intertemporal trade, just as the difference between autarky and world commodity prices determines the direction of commodity trade in the static model.

Typically, an intertemporal trade involves the exchange of an asset, which is a claim on future production as noted above. Thus, the country shown in Fig. 23.1 will give the foreign country some sort of bond in period 0, stating a promise to repay in period 1 the borrowed corn plus interest. In the terminology of balance-of-payments accounting, we say that the country runs a *current account deficit* in period 0, meaning that its current consumption exceeds its current production. This is matched by a *capital account surplus,* meaning that the country has sold an asset to the foreign country to pay the current account deficit.

Figure 23.1 shows that the country attains a higher welfare level through foreign borrowing, but it must be pointed out that this may be misleading. Just as trade may significantly redistribute income among factor owners in the static model, borrowing can cause significant redistribution and even welfare losses for some groups in this case. Suppose, for example, that the two time periods are very long, so that a significantly different set of individuals is alive in each time period. The first generation in Fig. 23.1 greatly increases its consumption and welfare by foreign borrowing. The future generation must, however, pay back the loans, and so it has lower levels of consumption and welfare than it would have had in autarky. Moreover, the future generation is powerless to prevent the current generation (or its government) from spending so freely at the future generation's expense.

The situation shown in Fig. 23.1 does not allow for the possibility of productive investment. Figure 23.2 adds a transformation curve IE , which

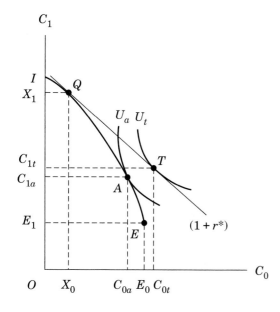

FIGURE 23.2
Intertemporal trade with productive real investment.

shows the country's ability to transform current output into future output through investment. In our example, corn can be planted instead of consumed, thereby yielding higher future output and consumption by sacrificing current consumption. Again, point E represents the endowment point, whereas the curve IE shows the transformation curve or investment opportunities.

The autarky equilibrium is given by point A, where U_a is tangent to IE. At A, an amount $(E_0 - C_{0a})$ is invested in the initial period. The payoff from this investment is the increased consumption $(C_{1a} - E_1)$ in the future period. Investment opportunities thus allow the country to increase future consumption by sacrificing current consumption.

Now suppose that the country can borrow or lend at the world interest rate r^*. This means that the country faces a world "price ratio" $(1 + r^*)$ as shown in Fig. 23.2. The production optimum for the country is to invest (plant corn) up to the point where the marginal return is just equal to the world rate of interest (the return from lending the corn to foreigners). This production optimum is given by point Q where $(1 + r^*)$ is just tangent to IE. X_0 can be thought of as the corn left over after planting (investment) in period 0, and X_1 is the harvest in period 1. An initial-period investment of $(E_0 - X_0)$ returns an amount $(X_1 - E_1)$ in the future period.

The country's consumption optimum is given by point T. The country borrows an amount $(C_{0t} - X_0)$ in the initial period and repays $(X_1 - C_{1t})$ in the future period. The ability to invest and borrow internationally raises welfare to U_t.

Note a very important difference between Figs. 23.1 and 23.2. In Fig. 23.1, current consumption can be increased only via foreign borrowing at the expense of future consumption. But when productive investment opportunities exist (Fig. 23.2), foreign borrowing used to finance investment can lead to increased consumption in both periods and thus to an unambiguous welfare gain for both "generations."

The policy implication is that foreign borrowing per se does not jeopardize future consumption (or future generations). The question is, however, whether the borrowed funds are squandered on current consumption or invested productively. In the latter case, the ability to borrow from abroad may raise both current and future consumption. Many capital-scarce, developing countries or fast-growing countries (such as Canada in the 20th century) can benefit from foreign borrowing by using the funds as shown in Fig. 23.2.

23.2 ADJUSTMENT OF CAPITAL STOCKS TO INTERNATIONAL PRICE CHANGES

Economic systems are often characterized by significant lags in responding to changes. These lags may be of some importance for economic policy in some cases. In this section, we will present a relatively informal analysis of lags due to the time taken to transform capital from one sector to another or to change the total stock of capital. The general point of the section is that long-run changes tend to reinforce short-run changes, or alternatively that long-run responses are more elastic than short-run responses.

Consider a sector-specific factors model of the type discussed in Chapter 9, in which labor is mobile between X and Y but the capital stock (machines) in X is useless in producing Y, and similarly, the Y-sector capital stock is useless in producing X. In Fig. 23.3, the country's "short-run" production frontier with sector-specific capital is shown by SS'. Equilibrium is at point A with international price ratio p^0. Now suppose that the world price ratio changes permanently to p^1. The short-run response of the economy is to move to point B. But, as we know from Chapter 9, this raises the return to X-sector capital and lowers the return to Y-sector capital. In order to simplify the point, suppose that the total number of machines (the total capital stock) is fixed but that over time, we can change the composition of machines: when Y-sector machines wear out, we replace them with X-sector machines. The change in the terms of trade makes it optimal to do exactly this type of capital transformation. But we know from Chapter 9 that increasing X-sector capital and/or decreasing Y-sector capital at constant prices must generate an increase in the output of X and a decrease in the output of Y. Over the long run, production moves from B to C in Fig. 23.3.

Point C in Fig. 23.3 is on the "long-run" production frontier for the economy; LL' is defined as a set of points in which the returns to capital are equal in the two sectors, holding the total stock of capital constant. We could think of this long-run frontier as a Heckscher-Ohlin-type production frontier in which both factors are mobile between sectors. The long-run production frontier can be thought of as the "outer envelope" of a series of short-run (specific-factors) production frontiers, such as SS' in Fig. 23.3, each of which lies inside of LL' except at one point, such as the coincidence of SS' and LL'

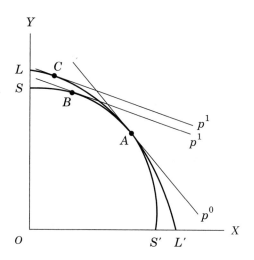

FIGURE 23.3
Long-run versus short-run responses to price changes: sector-specific capital.

at A. The result shown in Fig. 23.3 is a fairly general one: beginning in a position of equilibrium, a permanent change in the terms of trade generates a long-run change in production that reinforces or exaggerates the short-run change.

Similar results occur when the total stock of capital is endogenously determined. Consider a very simple case of the same specific-factors model, in which the specific factor in the X sector is land, which is in fixed supply. But the specific factor in Y is capital, K, which can be adjusted over time. In order to determine the long-run equilibrium level of the capital stock, a dynamic optimizing model needs to be developed, a task that is beyond the scope of this book. However, one common result derived from such a model is relatively easy to understand. Let q denote the price of a new unit of capital, such as a machine. Assume that machines are produced from some combination of X, Y, and L. Let δ denote the rate of depreciation on a machine (e.g., 10 percent per year) and ρ denote the consumer's "rate of time preference," the degree to which a consumer prefers one unit of corn this year instead of next year (sort of like a psychic rate of interest). A consumer is indifferent between one unit this year and one unit next year if the ratio of this year's price to next year's price is $(1 + \rho)$. The basic result derived from dynamic models is that the stock of capital is adjusted until the rental rate on capital, r, is equal to

$$r = (\rho + \delta)q \qquad (23.2)$$

The term $(\rho + \delta)q$ is basically the marginal cost of owning a machine for a year: the "time cost" of forgone consumption, ρ, plus the depreciation on the machine, δ, times the price of the machine. In long-run equilibrium, this is equal to the return (revenue) from the machine, r. In simple terms, Eq. (23.2) requires that marginal revenue (r) equal marginal cost, $(\rho + \delta)q$.

Suppose that point A in Fig. 23.4 is a long-run equilibrium in which Eq. (23.2) is satisfied at world price ratio p^0. SS' gives the short-run production

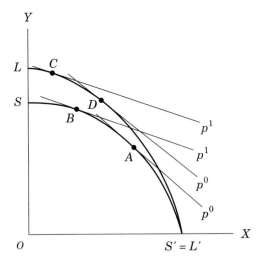

FIGURE 23.4
Long-run versus short-run responses to price changes: endogenous capital accumulation.

frontier over which the stock of capital is fixed at its initial equilibrium level. Now suppose that the world price ratio shifts permanently to p^1. In the short run, the production moves to point B. But the results of Chapter 9 tell us that the return to capital in Y has risen relative to the price of Y, X, and L, and so r has risen relative to q in Eq. (23.2). Consumers will now accumulate more capital until equality in Eq. (23.2) is restored. We illustrate the new equilibrium as point C on production frontier LL' in Fig. 23.4. Results from Chapter 9 will also tell us that the production point, at price ratio p^1, moves from B to a point like C in which more Y and less X is produced. As in the case of Fig. 23.3, we find that the long-run change, in which the capital stock is allowed to adjust, reinforces the short-run change.

The argument also holds in reverse. Suppose that point C in Fig. 23.4 is the initial equilibrium at world price ratio p^1. Now suppose that the price ratio changes to p^0, leading production to shift in the short run to point D on production frontier LL'. But now the return to capital in Y falls, leading to a reduction in the capital stock until Eq. (23.2) is again satisfied. In the long run, the production frontier shifts to SS', and the production point shifts from D to A. Adjustment of the capital stock in the long run leads to changes in production that reinforce the short-run changes. In the case of Fig. 23.4, the long-run change leads to a reduction in (per year) consumption, but this is in fact optimal. It must be remembered that maintaining a high capital stock is costly, because consumption must be given up in order to replace depreciating capital. When the rate of return to capital falls, it is no longer optimal to maintain such a large capital stock.

23.3 ADJUSTMENT OF CAPITAL STOCKS TO TECHNOLOGY CHANGES

Technology changes generate responses within an economy that lead to similar long-run versus short-run effects. Of course, technology is itself endogenously determined in part, and we can think of "technical change" as a factor of production (knowledge capital) that is created by a particular type of investment (research and development expenditures). In this section, however, we will consider a simple case of an exogenous discovery.

Consider the same sector-specific-factors model that we used in the previous section, in which labor is mobile between the X and Y sectors, land is a fixed factor in the X sector, and an endogenous capital stock is used in Y production. Figure 23.5 shows the case of an exogenous improvement in Y-sector technology. We assume that this technology improvement simply multiplies the old output of Y by a constant α greater than 1. The initial equilibrium is at point A on production frontier SS'. The technology improvement shifts the production frontier to TS', and production shifts to point B at constant prices.

This technology change must increase the return to capital in Y for two reasons. First, the marginal product of capital is now higher at the same capital-labor ratio by the multiple α. But because the marginal product of

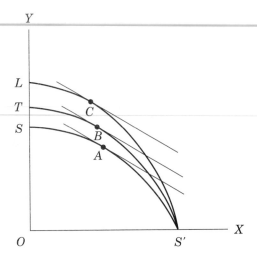

FIGURE 23.5
Long-run versus short-run responses to
an improvement in Y technology.

labor is higher by the same amount, labor will now move from the X sector
to the Y sector until the marginal products are again equalized (which is
why point B in Fig. 23.5 involves a lower level of X production than does
point A). With the capital-labor ratio in Y now lower, the marginal product
of capital increases further.

Capital will then accumulate until the long-run equilibrium condition
in Eq. (23.2) is again satisfied. The production frontier shifts further to
LS' and production shifts to point C at constant prices. Production of Y
increases further and production of X decreases further as more labor is
shifted to the Y sector to combine with the increased capital stock.

Figure 23.6 considers the case of technical change in the X sector in
the same model. Production is initially at point A on production frontier SS'.

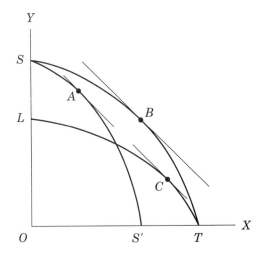

FIGURE 23.6
Long-run versus short-run responses to
an improvement in X technology.

The technology improvement in X shifts the production frontier to ST at constant prices and shifts production to B. Because labor is now shifted out of Y and into X (because of its increased marginal product in X), the capital-labor ratio in Y increases, leading to a reduction in the marginal product of capital in Y and a fall in r, the return to capital. Capital will now diminish until Eq. (23.2) is again restored to an equality. The production frontier shifts to LT and production shifts to point C. (With the decreased capital stock in Y, labor will shift to X to maintain the equality of marginal products in the two sectors.) In the long run, the changes in production reinforce the short-run changes.

As a final point, it is important to note that we can get the same results shown in Figs., 23.4, 23.5, and 23.6 if capital is internationally traded instead of (or in addition to) being adjusted through domestic capital formation. Changes in technology or in international prices that lead to an expansion of the capital-intensive sector (sector Y in this case) and to an increase in the return to capital generate secondary changes in which capital is drawn into the country, reinforcing the initial changes in outputs. Thus, with either endogenous, internal capital formation or international capital mobility, the long-run responses to parameter changes (e.g., prices, technologies) tend to be larger or more elastic than short-run changes in which the stock of capital is held fixed.

23.4 DYNAMIC SCALE ECONOMIES AND THE ACCUMULATION OF KNOWLEDGE CAPITAL

There has been a great deal of interest in recent years in dynamic scale economies and their consequences for diverging growth rates among countries. Particular interest has been attached to learning and the accumulation of knowledge capital. In the chapter on multinationals, we noted that knowledge often has a "public good," or joint-input, property, in that it can be used in additional plants at little or even zero cost. The same property of knowledge has been adopted in the *new growth theory* literature, with respect to time as well as to additional users (e.g., Lucas (1988), Romer (1987), Grossman and Helpman (1993a)). Knowledge capital is modeled as equally accessible to all users in not only the current time period but also all future time periods. Once a chemical formula is discovered, for example, it is available forever. Furthermore, knowledge capital is modeled as nondepreciating: the chemical formula does not wear out, although a superior product might be discovered. These models also typically treat new knowledge as nonexclusionary; that is, once something is discovered, it becomes public knowledge, and no potential user can be excluded. The creation of knowledge is thus an externality in that its benefits cannot be captured by any one individual.

Figure 23.7 illustrates some of the principal ideas and their consequences for comparative growth rates between two countries. Assume that,

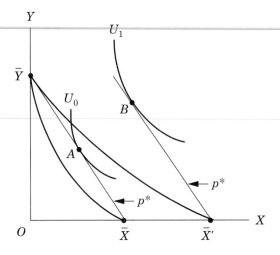

FIGURE 23.7
Dynamic external economies.

with no externalities, Y is produced with constant returns by a competitive industry. But the production of X, while also competitive, produces new knowledge as a by-product of production that is freely available to all firms in this sector. This new knowledge, a positive externality in current production, is also inherited in the next period. That is, current production of X increases productivity in the subsequent period. However, we also assume that the knowledge externality is country-specific and accrues to the country only in proportion to its own X production.

In Fig. 23.7, we have drawn the production frontier, $\overline{Y}\,\overline{X}$, as nonconvex so that countries will specialize. Suppose for the sake of argument that the (fixed) world price ratio happens to be p^*, connecting the ends of the production frontier. Assume that in the initial period, this is the production frontier of two absolutely identical countries. Assume that the home country arbitrarily specializes in Y, producing at $\overline{Y}$, while the foreign country arbitrarily specializes in X, producing at $\overline{X}$. Both countries consume at point A, reaching utility level U_0. The countries are equally well-off, and they are indifferent as to the pattern of specialization in the current period. Because new knowledge becomes a public good within the country, no single firm in Home has an incentive to invest in its development (the firm cannot appropriate the rents), and hence, there is no market force that would tend to move Home away from specializing in Y.

In the second period, nothing has happened from Home's point of view, and so it continues to specialize in Y and consume at A. But Foreign inherits a larger stock of knowledge capital in the second period, and its production frontier is shown as shifting to $\overline{Y}\,\overline{X}'$. Foreign continues to specialize in X in the second period, producing at $\overline{X}'$, consuming at B, and enjoying utility level U_1. The income and welfare levels of the two countries diverge in the second period because of the dynamic externality connected with the production of X. Furthermore, given the assumption that knowledge does not depreciate, the income growth in Foreign can continue indefinitely into the future.

This example gives us a flavor of the *new growth theory*, in which concepts such as increasing returns, learning, and non-depreciating knowledge capital are introduced into dynamic models of growth and trade. The important property exhibited in these models is the absence of diminishing returns to investment activities which, in traditional constant-returns models, tends to level the growth among countries. In the newer models, countries' growth rates can diverge, with some growth surges attributable to specialization in particular sectors or to a first-mover advantage. Other countries, such as Home in our example, are left behind in a low-level "development trap."

23.5 INCOME ELASTICITIES AND LONG-RUN CHANGES IN THE TERMS OF TRADE

In this section, we will briefly discuss another factor which may be a determinant of uneven growth rates between countries. This factor pertains to demand for goods and services as a function of income and was of particular concern to development economists in the 1950s and 1960s. For most of this book we have assumed that utility functions are homogeneous. It is a property of such utility functions that income elasticities of demand for all goods equal 1. That is, a 1 percent increase in income results in a 1 percent increase in the demand for every good. Graphically, this means that an increase in income leads consumers to move out along a ray from the origin.

A different assumption is illustrated in Fig. 23.8. Suppose that Y is food and X is manufactures. Suppose also that the production frontier shifts

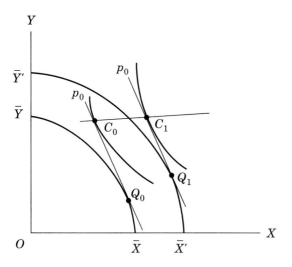

FIGURE 23.8
Nonunitary income elasticities of demand.

out in a neutral fashion from $\overline{X}\,\overline{Y}$ to $\overline{X}'\overline{Y}'$ in response to technical change. The number of people is thus constant and per capita income increases. Assume finally that the income-elasticity of demand is very low for food and very high for manufactures. Most of the increased income per capita will thus be spent on manufactures at constant prices. This last assumption is illustrated in Fig. 23.8 by the fact that consumption shifts in a biased fashion from C_0 to C_1 at constant prices p_0.

This biased growth in demand will have terms-of-trade effects. Fig. 23.8 has been drawn such that the country actually decreases its trade offer after growth ($C_o Q_o$ exceeds $C_1 Q_1$), despite neutral change on the production side. Demand is channeled to the country's own export good (X), while few additional imports (Y) are demanded. The increased production of Y actually exceeds the increased home consumption demand, whereas the increased production of X falls short of the increased home demand. Export supply and import demand both decrease with growth.

The opposite conclusions would apply to a country that had a comparative advantage in Y. Neutral growth on the production side would lead to increased export supply (because increased home demand for Y is low) and increased import demand (because increased home demand for X is high). If you then put these two countries together, it must be the case that the terms of trade improve over time for the country exporting X (the high-income-elasticity good) and deteriorate for the country exporting Y. Neutral and equal growth in production for the two countries would translate into unequal growth in per capita incomes. The country exporting X would experience a higher rate of growth in per capita income due to the terms-of-trade effects.

This simple idea has been applied to the analysis of economic development, where it has been asserted that highly developed countries export the high-income-elasticity goods (manufactures in our example) and less-developed countries export the low-income-elasticity goods. The consequence of this is that the developed countries' terms of trade improve with time, and less-developed countries' terms of trade deteriorate. Thus, the rich get richer and the poor fall farther behind. Early empirical tests were somewhat supportive of this assertion (Prebisch 1964, Singer 1950). Because of strong productivity growth over time in manufactures, the prices of many products have in fact fallen significantly, to the extent that countries specializing in primary products have fared much better than the dismal case presented by the Prebisch-Singer hypothesis.

23.6 TERMS-OF-TRADE EFFECTS, DISTORTIONS, AND IMMISERIZING GROWTH

If a country's growth results in an increased desire to trade (e.g., growth is concentrated in the export sector), then growth will lead to a deterioration in the country's terms of trade unless the rest of the world is growing at the same rate or faster. This raises the question of whether the resulting deterioration in the terms of trade could be so severe that the country is actually made worse off by growth. The answer is that this can indeed happen, a phenomenon referred to as *immiserizing growth*.

An example of immiserizing growth is shown in Fig. 23.9. A technical improvement in the export sector shifts the production frontier from $\overline{Y}\,\overline{X}$ to $\overline{Y}\,\overline{X}'$. At the initial prices p_0, the country wishes to trade more, supplying more exports of X and demanding more imports of Y. This causes the country's terms of trade to deteriorate (the relative price of X to fall), and this deterioration can be so large that welfare is reduced. This effect is illustrated in Fig. 23.9 by a fall in consumption from C_0 to C_1 and a reduction in welfare from U_0 to U_1 at the new price ratio p_1.

This possibility of being made worse off by a technical improvement seems paradoxical. The important fact to consider about the situation shown in Fig. 23.9 is that the country obviously has monopoly power in trade. The country's increased export supply and increased import demand affect prices in a substantial way. We also know from our discussions in Chapter 15 that when a country has monopoly power in trade, free trade is not the optimal policy. A tariff should be instituted to move the terms of trade in the country's favor.

The welfare loss in Fig. 23.9 results from the fact that the country with monopoly power is engaging in free trade rather than optimizing its trade with a tariff. This absence of an optimizing policy means that as growth occurs, trade policy is not being adjusted in an optimal way. This results in the possibility of immiserizing growth as shown.

Immiserizing growth cannot occur if a country follows an optimal trade policy. When growth occurs, the country can always increase its import tariff

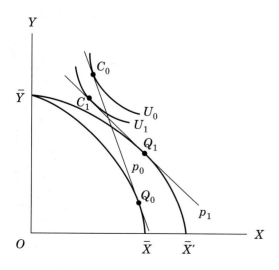

FIGURE 23.9
Immiserizing growth.

(or export tax) so as to leave the country's trade offer unchanged at the old prices. There will then be no deterioration in the terms of trade and thus no welfare losses.

The failure to have an optimal trade policy is a distortion in a certain sense, and it is this distortion that leads to the possibility of immiserizing growth. There are other types of distortions that can also lead to welfare losses from growth. Fig. 23.10 shows a small economy faced with the fixed world price ratio p_0. Production is distorted by a production tax on X (or a production subsidy on Y), which raises the price ratio above the marginal rate of transformation. Initial production and consumption points are Q_0 and C_0, respectively. Suppose now that growth is heavily biased toward the export sector Y. Production must shift to a point on the new production frontier $\overline{X}'\overline{Y}'$ that has the same slope as point Q_0. This may be a point such as Q_1, which results in lower consumption at C_1 and thus immiserizing growth.

The economic reasoning behind the result in Fig. 23.10 is as follows. Because of the distortion, the economy is initially overproducing Y at Q_0. Biased growth in favor of Y causes the economy to produce even more Y, effectively increasing the degree of distortion. Another diagram could be drawn to show that biased growth in favor of X would effectively decrease the distortion and thus lead to an unambiguous increase in welfare.

As a final point, it cannot be emphasized strongly enough that the theoretical possibilities raised in this section should not be taken as support for import-substitution possibilities. This is especially true for smaller, developing countries. History has shown that smaller countries, such as Taiwan, Singapore, Hong Kong, and Korea have grown much faster by adopting open-economy, export-oriented policies than have countries which have adopted import-substitution strategies. Many of the latter countries,

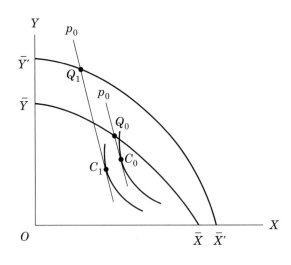

FIGURE 23.10
Growth in the presence of a production distortion.

especially in Latin America, have now abandoned these policies in favor of open-economy strategies.

It is beyond the scope of this book to conduct a detailed analysis of the determinants of growth, but we can briefly mention several possibilities as to why the open-economy export orientation leads to faster growth. First, industries are characterized by (static) scale economies, and import substitution policies lead small, inefficient plants to produce too many goods, an additional burden to the income losses from not following comparative advantage. Higher incomes in the short run from the capture of comparative advantage and scale economies in an export-oriented approach may translate into higher long-run savings and investment. Second, many industries are subject to dynamic scale economies such as learning-by-doing and the accumulation of knowledge capital that we discussed earlier in this chapter. Import substitution policies lead to diversified production in many final and intermediate goods, while export orientation tends to lead to higher concentration in fewer industries and goods. Learning and productivity growth may be far greater when production is concentrated in this fashion.

23.7 CONCLUDING REMARKS

Although issues of intertemporal trade and growth are more the domain of international finance and growth theory, this chapter, especially its first section, has briefly touched on a few issues that have been of particular interest to the study of international trade and that serve as bridges between these two subjects. The principal points of the chapter can be summarized as follows.

1. In addition to trading across goods and factors, countries can gain from trading across time–that is, by trading currently produced goods and services for future goods and services. A country that imports currently produced goods and services (i.e., consumes more than it produces in the current period) is said to run a current-account deficit. The terms *current-account deficit* and *surplus* indicate the direction of intertemporal trade. A country pays for a current-account deficit by selling assets (creating a capital-account surplus), which are claims to the future production of the country.

2. Although there are intertemporal gains from trade, these gains fall unequally to different groups (e.g., generations), and some groups may actually be made worse off. But this is not a new problem; we have noted many instances throughout the book in which the aggregate gains from trade are accompanied by strong redistributive effects. The welfare effects of a current-account deficit on future generations depend on whether the borrowing is used simply to finance increased current consumption or whether it is productively invested. In the latter case, current-period international borrowing may increase both current and future consumption.

3. Sections 23.2 and 23.3 analyzed the impacts of price and technology changes on countries' capital stocks. The general result is that price and technology changes lead to factor price changes and hence to factor supply changes that tend to reinforce the initial change. For example, an increase in the price of a capital-intensive good leads to an increase in the return to capital, which leads the country to accumulate more capital in the long run. The increase in capital stock then leads to a Rybczynski-type effect, which is a further expansion in the production of the capital-intensive good. Long-run responses of production to underlying changes thus reinforce short-run changes; put differently, long-run responses are more elastic. This result generally applies to both the situation in which capital stocks are adjusted through internal accumulation and depreciation and the situation in which capital is adjusted through international factor flows.

4. Section 23.4 discussed some aspects of dynamic scale economies that have been the focus of recent work on growth theory. This literature adopts an idea similar to that presented in our chapter on multinationals: that certain activities generate knowledge capital that has a "public good" characteristic. The *new growth theory* extends this idea to an intertemporal dimension, assuming that new knowledge is not only freely available to all within a time period, but nondepreciating over time. A new chemical formula does not "wear out" with the passage of time. This property of knowledge capital leads to the existence of dynamic scale economies, and because of the assumption that no one can appropriate this knowledge (it is freely available to all), the scale economies are externalities for the economy. An economy that somehow specializes in a sector with dynamic external economies will grow faster than an economy which initially specializes in a sector without such externalities. Growth in incomes may diverge, with one economy caught in a "development trap."

5. A related idea about "development traps" is contained in literature that emphasizes the demand side of the general equilibrium model. If some goods have high income elasticities of demand while others have low income elasticities, then the terms of trade will tend to shift in favor of the former countries as per capita incomes in the world grow over time (demand shifts toward the high-income-elasticity goods). The fear has been that production in developing countries is concentrated in low-income-elasticity goods, and hence, these countries will fall farther behind the developed countries that produce high-income-elasticity goods and services. Support for this argument is mixed at best. Strong productivity growth in manufacturing has led to significant price falls for these products, much to the benefit of developing countries.

6. The final section considered distortions and growth and noted first that strong growth in a country might generate a terms-of-trade change so adverse that the country loses despite the productivity growth. This possibility is known as *immiserizing growth*. We noted that this is simply

an example of how an otherwise favorable change (growth) can, in the presence of a distortion (no optimal tariff), have an unfavorable effect, and we presented a second example of how a distortion can generate such a result.

7. We emphasized that the argument about immiserizing growth should not be used to justify an import-substitution strategy for economic development. History has shown that countries that adopt open-economy, export-oriented strategies generally grow much faster than countries that adopt import-substitution strategies. Terms-of-trade arguments notwithstanding, export orientation allows the capture of the short-run gains from focusing on comparative advantage and the capture of scale economies through specialization, which can translate into higher savings and investment in the long run. Export orientation may also allow faster learning- by-doing and the accumulation of knowledge capital by concentrating on a small range of production, but there is little clear, empirical evidence to support these points at this time.

PROBLEMS

1. In light of Section 23.1, contrast the effects on future generations of two types of borrowing by the United States: (a) The U.S. government borrows to finance current expenditures on public goods. (b) General Motors borrows to finance construction of a new plant.

2. Consider the case in Fig. 23.6 in which technical change occurs in the land-intensive sector X, thereby reducing the return to capital (used only in Y production). We showed that in the long run, the diminishing of capital reduces consumption in the future once the adjustment is complete. Does this mean that allowing capital to adjust reduces welfare? (Hint: Welfare is determined by consumption in all time periods and may increase in the short run as depreciating capital is not replaced.)

3. Consider the case in which either all factor supplies grow in the same proportion or technical change occurs in both sectors at the same rate. (a) Show the effect on the production possibility curve. (b) If the rest of the world does not grow, is it likely that the country's terms of trade will deteriorate?

4. In Fig. 23.7, why don't the firms in the home country simply switch to producing X in the first period, knowing that income will then be higher in the second period?

5. Draw a diagram corresponding to Fig. 23.8 for a country that exports Y. Putting your diagram together with Fig. 23.8, try to show that equal growth in both countries must cause a rise in p_x/p_y.

6. With reference to Fig. 23.10, show that if growth leads instead to an increase in the production of X, then welfare must increase.

REFERENCES

Bhagwati, J. N. (1958). "Immiserizing Growth: *A Geometric Note." Review of Economic Studies* 25: 201–205.

——. (1968). "Distortions and Immiserizing Growth: A Generalization." *Review of Economic Studies* 35: 481–485.

Chacholiades, M. (1973). *The Pure Theory of International Trade*. Chicago: Aldine.

Dales, J. H. (1966). *The Protective Tariff in Canada's Development*. Toronto: University of Toronto Press.

Findlay, R. (1984). "Growth and Development in Trade Models." In P. B. Kenen and R. W. Jones, eds., *Handbook of International Economics*. Amsterdam: North–Holland.

Grossman, G. M., and Helpman, E.(1993a). *Innovation and Growth in the Global Economy*. Cambridge, Mass.: MIT Press.

——. (1993b). "Hysteresis in the Trade Pattern," In Either, Helpman, and Neary, eds., *Theory, Policy and Dynamics in International Trade: Essays in Honor of Ronald W. Jones*. London: Cambridge University Press.

Isard, W. (1960). *Methods of Regional Analysis*. Cambridge, Mass.: MIT Press.

Johnson, H. G. (1967). "The Possibility of Income Losses from Increased Efficiency or Factor Accumulation in the Presence of Tariffs." *Economic Journal:* 77: 151–154.

Lucas, R. E. Jr. (1988). "On the Mechanics of Economic Development." *Journal of Monetary Economics* 22: 3–42.

Manning, R. A., and Markusen, J. R. (1991). "National Product Functions in Comparative Steady-State Analysis." *International Economic Review* 32: 613–624.

Markusen, J. R., and Svensson, L. E. O. (1985). "Trade in Goods and Factors with International Differences in Technology." *International Economic Review* 26: 175–192.

Markusen, J. R. (1990). "First–Mover Advantages, Blockaded Entry, and the Economics of Uneven Development." In E. Helpman and A. Razin, eds., *International Trade and Trade Policy*. Cambridge, Mass.: MIT Press.

Prebisch, R. (1964). *Towards a New Trade Policy for Development, Report by the Secretary General of UNCTAD*. New York: United Nations.

Romer, P. M. (1987). "Growth Based on Increasing Returns Due to Specialization." *American Economic Review, Papers and Proceedings* 77: 56–62.

Singer, H. (1950). "The Distribution of Gains between Investing and Borrowing Countries." *American Economic Review* 40: 473–485.

APPENDIX
1

MORE ON COMMUNITY INDIFFERENCE CURVES

A1.1   INTRODUCTION

Chapter 3 discussed, in relatively informal terms, the problem of the aggregation of individual consumer's tastes into community indifference curves. We noted that strong assumptions are required in order to show that community indifference curves exist and possess the properties of individual indifference curves discussed earlier in that chapter. Appendix 1 presents a more advanced discussion of this problem.

A1.2   THE DERIVATION OF COMMUNITY INDIFFERENCE CURVES

One simple example of a situation in which a well-defined community indifference curve does exist is the Robinson Crusoe economy, in which it is assumed that there is only one consumer. Utility maximization for this simple community would proceed in the same way as maximization for a single individual, except that the constraints would differ. Under the assumption that the community possesses the capacity to produce commodities using different production functions, and assuming that these production functions exhibit constant returns to scale, then instead of the linear budget constraint of Fig. 3.3, the individual would be faced with a production constraint of the kind derived in Chapter 2. Thus our Robinson Crusoe economy will maximize utilities subject to the production possibility curve. In terms of Fig. A1.1, where TAT' represents the production possibility curve and three representative indifference curves have been included, by an argument completely analogous to that used to demonstrate the condition necessary for the maximization of individual welfare, it can be shown that utility is maximized where the highest indifference curve is tangent to the production possibility curve. Thus in an economy in which no trade is allowed, the equilibrium production and consumption points will be point A in Fig. A1.1.

This Robinson Crusoe economy is too simple to warrant further consideration. What we seek are conditions under which preferences for a group of individuals can be represented by indifference curves such as those of Fig. A1.1. To facilitate our understanding of what such conditions are, we now construct a set of community indifference curves under quite general conditions and compare the characteristics of these with the indifference curves for individual consumers. We begin with the case in which there are only two consumers, but it will become clear as we proceed that any number of consumers could be included.

An indifference curve for an individual consumer is defined as the locus of all those bundles of commodities for which utility is some constant. To be consistent with this definition, the aggregate indifference curves for two individuals must be the locus of all bundles of commodities whose levels of utility for both individuals are constant. We thus choose a specific indifference curve for each individual and seek a method of aggregating these two indifference curves. For the first individual we choose the indifference curve shown in Fig. A1.2. We now choose some point on that indifference curve and call it O_2, the origin for the indifference curve map of the second individual. The indifference curve chosen for the second individual is as shown in the figure. To determine which point on the indifference curve for the second individual is the relevant one, we recall from the discussions surrounding Fig. 3.4 of Chapter 3 that, in equilibrium, the indifference curves for the two individuals must have the same slope. We thus determine

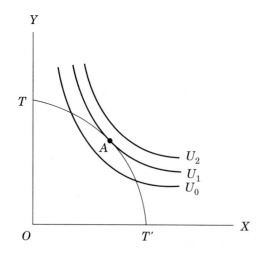

FIGURE A1.1
Equilibrium in a Robinson Crusoe economy.

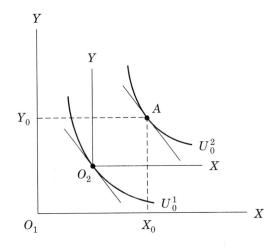

2 ways to add
2 indiff crvs.

FIGURE A1.2
Summation of two individual
indifference curves.

the slope of the indifference curve for the first individual at O_2, and then search along the indifference curve for the second individual until we find a point that has the same slope. Suppose this is point A in Fig. A1.2. Point A, a bundle of commodities containing Y_0 of Y and X_0 of X, is clearly a point in outputs space that allows the individuals to have utilities associated with the indifference curves U_0^1 and U_0^2, and it is therefore a point on a community indifference curve for these two individuals. By placing O_2 at other points on the indifference curve U_0^1 of the first individual and repeating the same procedure, other points on the community indifference curve can be found. The locus of all such points could be considered as a type of community indifference curve for these two individuals. Note that point A is a point on the community indifference curve and that the price ratio at this point is the same as that at O_2, suggesting that the slope of the community indifference curve will be the same as the slopes of the individual indifference curves from which that point was derived.

An alternative way of demonstrating the addition of the two indifference curves to arrive at the point A is to plot the indifference curves for the second individual not from O_2 but from A. This gives rise to the box diagram shown in Fig. A1.3 (similar to that of Fig. 3.4). Note that this figure gives precisely the same information as Fig. A1.2, the only difference being that we are plotting the indifference curves for the second individual down from the aggregate commodity bundle, rather than up from point A, as was done in Fig. A1.2. In this diagram the community indifference curve can be traced out by sliding the indifference curve for the second individual along that of the first and allowing the origin O_2 to trace out the community indifference curve. Thus the indifference curve for the first individual remains fixed, and we find other points along this curve where the indifference curve U_0^2 is tangent to it. Another such point would be B, and the origin for the second individual's indifference curve map would now be O_2'. The point O_2'

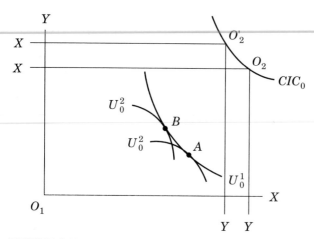

FIGURE A1.3
Construction of a CIC using the factor-box diagram.

is another point on the community indifference curve, and by repeating this procedure, we can find an entire locus of points such as CIC_0 of Fig. A1.3. Note that for all points on CIC_0, the utility levels for the two individuals are constant.

A1.3   PROPERTIES OF COMMUNITY INDIFFERENCE CURVES

Since curve CIC_0 in Fig. A1.3 is a locus of commodity bundles of which the levels of utility for both individuals are constant, it must be a community indifference curve. But what properties does this community indifference curve have? In particular, does it have the same characteristics as the indifference curves for individual consumers discussed in Section 2 of Chapter 3? Specifically, we wish to establish whether or not these community indifference curves can intersect. To consider this question, we have redrawn in Fig. A1.4 the initial situation of Fig. A1.3 and have included the contract curve.

Another way of asking the question of whether community indifference curves such as CIC_0 intersect is to ask whether there could be through point O_2 another community indifference curve having a different slope. Two points are relevant for this question. First, as we previously observed, the slope of the community indifference curve at O_2 is equal to the slope of the two indifference curves at point A. Second, the choice of the two indifference curves tangent at A was entirely arbitrary, and any other pair of indifference curves could have been chosen. Suppose, for example, that instead of fixing the level of utility for the two individuals equal to that associated with the indifference curves tangent at point A we had instead chosen the two indifference curves U_1^1 and U_1^2 tangent at point B. It is clear

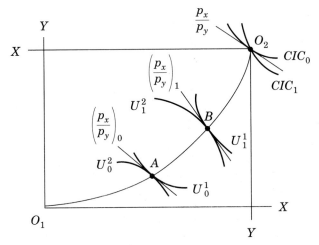

FIGURE A1.4
Illustration of intersecting community indifference curves.

that exactly the same procedure as described in Fig. A1.3 for point A could now be carried out for point B and that a new community indifference curve could be constructed. The question now is whether this new indifference curve would be exactly the same as indifference curve CIC_0, the one derived from point A. That this need not be the case can easily be seen by observing that this new indifference curve must have the same slope at O_2 as the two individual indifference curves have at point B. But there is no reason that the slope of the indifference curves at point B need be the same as the slope of the indifference curves at point A. As the diagram has been drawn, the price line at point B is steeper than the price line at point A, and thus the community indifference curve associated with B must be steeper than that associated with A, and we would have a curve such as CIC_1. Furthermore, any point on the contract curve O_1AO_2 could have been chosen to derive a community indifference curve through point O_2, and in general, all such points would lead to a community indifference curve through point O_2, each with a slope different from that of CIC_0. There are, then, an infinite number of such community indifference curves through point O_2, all having different slopes.

Although it is certainly possible to define the curves such as CIC_0 and CIC_1 derived in Fig. A1.4 as community indifference curves, they would not be very useful for illustrating the international trade propositions that we will subsequently derive. To give one simple example, suppose that in Fig. A1.1, instead of the set of nonintersecting indifference curves shown, we had a set of community indifference curves of the kind derived in Fig. A1.4. In this case there would be a whole set of indifference curves through point A, all having different slopes, and there would be other indifference curves tangent to the transformation TAT' at points other than point A. In such a case it would not be at all obvious which of these particular tangency points would be the appropriate equilibrium position.

Our next question is whether conditions could be imposed on the utility functions of the two individuals such that the community indifference curves would not intersect. It is obvious from Fig. A1.4 that only if the equilibrium price ratio line has the same slope at all points on the contract curve will there be a single community indifference curve through point O_2. Is there any reason to expect such a condition to hold? Certainly not in general, and as long as the utility functions for the two individuals differ, we would expect the slopes of the equilibrium price lines along the contract curve to differ. This suggests that one criterion to be imposed is that the utility functions of the two individuals be the same.

But identical tastes are not sufficient for the existence of nonintersecting community indifference curves, as was seen from Fig. 3.5 of Chapter 3. Indeed, it is clear that only if the sets of indifference curves for the two individuals have the same slope along a ray from the origin will this condition necessarily be fulfilled. This condition is a familiar one, for it is precisely the characteristic that homogeneous production functions were found to have in Chapter 2. Thus the second condition that must be imposed on the utility functions of the two individuals is that they be homogeneous.

With tastes identical and homogeneous, the equilibrium price lines at all points on the linear contract curve of Fig. A1.5 will have identical slopes. It then makes no difference which point on the contract curve is chosen to derive the community indifference curves, for in all cases the slope will be the same at point O_2. Furthermore, the same argument applies for different initial aggregate bundles of commodities X and Y. Suppose, for example, that $\overline{X'}$ and $\overline{Y'}$ were available for distribution between the two individuals. In Fig. A1.5, O_2' will be the origin for the indifference curve map of the second individual. The same procedure outlined earlier could be used to derive an indifference curve through O_2', and again it is obvious that there

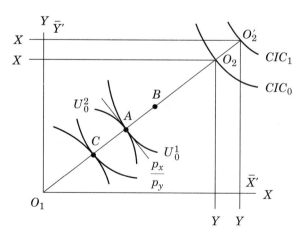

FIGURE A1.5
Community indifference curves with identical and homothetic preferences.

will only be one such curve through this point, regardless of which initial point on the contract curve O_1O_2' is chosen. Thus a whole set of community indifference curves can be derived by choosing different aggregate bundles of commodities to be distributed between the two individuals. Note that the community indifference curve through O_2' in Fig. A1.5 will have the same slope as the community indifference curve through O_2, demonstrating that the set of community indifference curves will also be homogeneous.

It has been shown that a set of nonintersecting community indifference curves will exist if the utilty functions for the two individuals are (1) identical and (2) homogeneous. It has been shown that identical tastes alone are not sufficient for the existence of nonintersecting community indifference curves. It is equally clear that homogeneity by itself is not sufficient, and indeed, the utility functions assumed in Fig. A1.4, while not the same for the two individuals, could easily have been derived from homogeneous utility functions. A question that naturally occurs is whether any other sets of conditions would give rise to nonintersecting indifference curves. To illustrate another possibility, in Fig. A1.6 we have assumed that the utility functions for two individuals, while homogeneous, are not identical, so that the contract curve would be O_1AO_2. The slope of the equilibrium price line will generally vary along the contract curve in Fig. A1.6 just as it did in Fig. A1.4. But suppose our choice of points along this contract curve is in some way constrained. In particular, suppose the initial endowment of X and Y received by the two individuals is represented by point E, the point at which both individuals receive equal quantities of the two commodities.

Because the two individuals have different tastes, E is not an equilibrium point and the two individuals trade with one another to reach point A. Indeed, it can be shown that for any endowment point there will be a unique

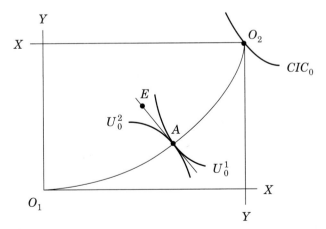

FIGURE A1.6
Community indifference curves when there is a given distribution of income.

equilibrium point on the contract curve, as long as the utility functions for the two individuals are homogeneous. Thus, with endowment point E, a single point on the contract curve results in equilibrium for the two individuals, and thus only one community indifference curve can be constructed through point O_2. In this case, we have restricted the possible equilibrium positions to the single point A by specifying the initial endowment point rather than by insisting that the slope of the equilibrium price line be the same at all points on the contract curve.

A1.4 CONCLUDING REMARKS

It has been shown that a set of nonintersecting community indifference curves can be assumed to exist if the utility functions for the individuals are homogeneous and if either (1) the utility functions are identical or (2) the distribution of income is fixed. For the case of identical and homogeneous utility functions, community indifference curves give unambiguous welfare comparisons only if the distribution of income is also fixed. While these conditions may seem somewhat severe, it should be noted that the conditions required for aggregation in any area of economics are very restrictive. Indeed, it can be shown that exactly the same conditions required for the existence of community indifference curves are required for the existence of aggregate consumption functions, so that from a theoretical point of view the aggregate consumption function used so widely in macroeconomics is as unrealistic as the community indifference curves that will be employed in this analysis.

It should also be noted that community indifference curves are for the most part used only for illustrative purposes, and that most of the conclusions we reach can be derived even if community indifference curves do not exist. Community indifference curves are employed mainly because of their heuristic value.

Although our discussion has been restricted to the two-individual case, our conclusions will be true for any number of individuals. Thus in the discussion of Fig. A1.5. any number of individuals could have been assumed and the community indifference curve CIC_0 derived as long as *all* were identical with homogeneous preferences.

PROBLEMS

1. Show that if community indifference curves intersect, there could be many equilibrium positions in Fig. A1.1.
2. In Fig. 3.3 of Chapter 3 trace out a locus of consumption points as the price of X falls.
3. The construction of nonintersecting community indifference curves in Fig. A1.5 was illustrated for two individuals. Show that the procedure applies equally well for three or more individuals.

APPENDIX
2

THE OFFER CURVE

A2.1 INTRODUCTION

Chapter 4 discussed the determination of general equilibrium for the closed and open economy models using the notion of excess demand functions. A closely related approach with a long history in international trade is the use of offer curves. As with excess demand functions, offer curves are derived directly from the production possibility curve and the community indifference curves discussed in Chapters 2 and 3 and Appendix 1.

A2.2 CONSTRUCTION OF THE OFFER CURVE

We begin by recalling the closed economy equilibrium described in Fig. 4.1 of Chapter 4. It is clear from Fig. 4.1 that even if the model were expanded to include other countries, no international trade would take place if the price ratio remained at p_a. This price ratio precisely equates the quantities of X and Y that the industries wish to produce and the quantities of X and Y that the consumers wish to consume. It is intuitively clear, however, that international trade can take place if the world price ratio differs from p_a. We now turn to an examination of how domestic producers and consumers behave when faced with price ratios that differ from the autarky price ratio of Fig. 4.1.

In Fig. A2.1 the point A reproduces the initial equilibrium shown in Fig. 4.1. Price $p_0 X_0$ and Y_0, is equivalent to the autarky price p_a of Fig. 4.1. (To avoid confusion, the indifference curve tangent to p_0 at A has not been included.)

We now suppose that producers and consumers in this country are faced with a new price line p_1, implying a relatively higher price for commodity Y.

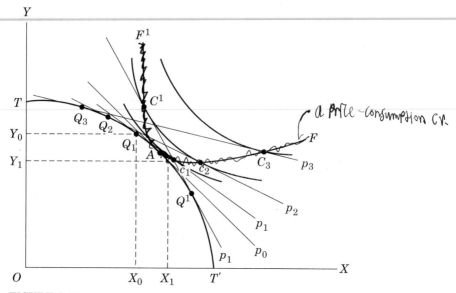

FIGURE A2.1
Construction of the reciprocal demand curve.

Both producers and consumers are assumed to maximize (output and utility, respectively) subject to this constraint, so that production moves to Q_1 and consumption moves to point C_1. Note that both Q_1 and C_1 must lie on the price line p_1, for although we no longer insist that the same quantities of the two goods be consumed as are produced, we do insist that the value of the consumption bundle be equal to the value of the production bundle. Consumption at C_1 would be possible if this country could find some other economy that was willing to accept the quantity of Y, $Y_0 - Y_1$, in exchange for the amount $X_1 - X_0$ of commodity X. For the moment, however, we are not concerned with the question of whether p_1 will be an equilibrium price line, but only with the question of how producers and consumers in this country would react when faced with a variety of different commodity price ratios.

Suppose the economy were faced with the price ratio line p_2. In this situation consumption would take place at point C_2 with production Q_2, and for a price ratio line p_3, consumption would be at C_3 and production at Q_3. Note that in all these cases consumers maximize utility by moving to the point where this price line is tangent to the highest community indifference curve. If this procedure were carried out for a large number of such price lines, the equilibrium consumption points would trace out the line $AC_1C_2C_3F$. This is a type of *price-consumption curve*.

The points along the price-consumption curve AF in Fig. A2.1 were derived by considering the price ratio lines whose slopes became progressively less steep. It is clear, however, that exactly the same procedure could be used for price lines that are steeper than p_0. In Fig. A2.1 only one such price line, p^1, implying production at Q^1 and consumption at C^1, has been included.

If a variety of such price lines were used, then the curve AC^1F^1 could be traced out. It is important to note that if attention is restricted to situations in which domestic consumers and producers face the same relative prices, the locus FAF^1 shows all possible equilibrium points that could exist for this economy.

In most circumstances it is more convenient to show the relationship depicted by FAF^1 of Fig. A2.1 without specifically including the production possibility curve and the indifference curves. In Fig. A2.2 we have reproduced the relevant information from Fig. A2.1 but have left out the indifference curves in order to avoid clutter. Initially we consider only price lines that are less steep than the autarky price line tangent at point A. For the three price lines illustrated we have drawn in the *trade triangles*. Thus, if price p_1 prevailed, the economy would wish to export B_1Q_1 of commodity Y and import B_1C_1 of commodity X. Similarly, B_2Q_2 and B_2C_2 would be the desired exports and imports of commodities Y and X, respectively, if the price were p_2. Note that these quantities of X and Y are just the excess demands and excess supplies that would prevail in the economy at these various price lines.

To illustrate more clearly the way in which the trade bundles vary as prices change, in Fig. A2.3 we have plotted only the exports and imports associated with the various price lines of Fig. A2.2. In other words, we have plotted the trade triangles from Fig. A2.2 all from the common origin in Fig. A2.3, so that B_1Q_1 and B_1C_1 of Fig. A2.2 become OQ_1 and OC_1 of Fig. A2.3, giving point E_1. The trade triangles for p_2 and p_3 are plotted in exactly the same fashion, producing E_2 and E_3 in Fig. A2.3. If other price lines were considered, other points in Fig. A2.3 could be found, and these

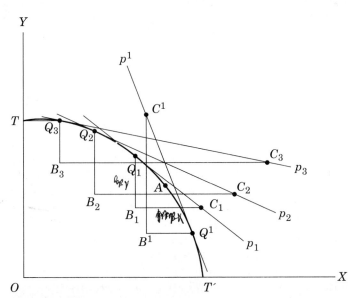

FIGURE A2.2
Trade triangles at various price ratios.

Y (exports)

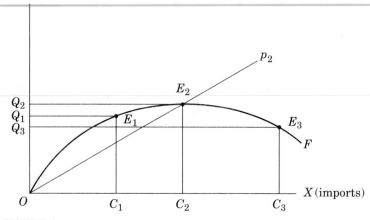

FIGURE A2.3
Offer curve for a country importing X.

would result in the locus OF. It is this locus that is commonly referred to as the *offer curve*.

While the axes in Fig. A2.3 are the same as in Fig. A2.2, the quantities being measured are not total production and total consumption, but rather excess demands and excess supplies. In other words, we are plotting the desired exports and the desired imports for various possible commodity price lines. Note that in Fig. A2.3, the line from the origin to any point E on the offer curve represents the commodity price line that was used to derive that point. Thus for the point E_2 the price line p_2 is precisely the same as p_2 in Fig. A2.2, except that as drawn it has the opposite slope. That the price lines are identical is easily verified by noting that the triangle OC_2E_2 of Fig. A2.3 is precisely the same as the triangle $C_2B_2Q_2$ of Fig. A2.2.

In Fig. A2.3 we considered only price lines whose slopes are less steep than the autarky price line through point A of Fig. A2.2. We now wish to consider price lines that are steeper than p_0. The first thing to observe is that for any such price line, the excess demand and supply conditions are the reverse of those of Fig. A2.2. Thus, instead of exporting commodity Y and importing X, the economy wants to import commodity Y and export commodity X. One such trade triangle, for prices p^1, is shown in Fig. A2.2. It is clear that since consumers want to consume at C^1 and producers want to produce at point Q^1, there is an excess supply of commodity X equal to the amount B^1Q^1 and an excess demand for commodity Y equal to B^1C^1. These points can now be depicted in Fig. A2.4 by noting that negative exports of Y are imports of Y and that negative imports of X are exports of X. Thus the points C^1 and Q^1 can be plotted in the third quadrant of Fig. A2.4, giving rise to point E^1. Other such points could be found in a similar fashion, and the locus of all such points would give OF^1, the other branch of the offer curve. Note that the curve FOF^1 of Fig. A2.4 gives exactly the same information about trade as the curve FAF^1 of Fig. A2.1. Of course, Fig. A2.1 gives other information as well, for it shows us precisely where production

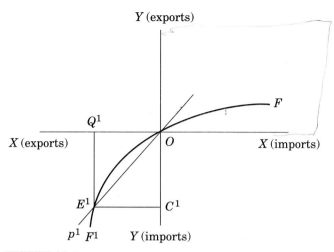

FIGURE A2.4
Offer curve for all possible prices.

and consumption take place for each of the equilibrium positions. Such information is not included in Fig. A2.4.

From Fig. A2.4 it can be seen that the offer curve is always concave toward the import axis. The reason for this shape can be found by examining Fig. A2.2, the diagram from which this information was obtained. We note first of all that at the price line p_0 (not shown in the diagram A2.4) excess demands and supplies for both commodities are zero, giving rise to the origin in the excess demand and supply diagram of Fig. A2.3. It is also clear that as the price ratio declines, excess demand for X increases monotonically, as can be seen by comparing B_1C_1, B_2C_2, and B_3C_3 in Fig. A2.2. In fact, we note that for every reduction in p, the desired consumption of X rises and the amount of X produced falls. Both changes act to increase imports. Thus we can say that the desired imports of X increase as p (the relative price of X) decreases. Now consider the changes in the desired exports of commodity Y associated with these price ratios. At p_0 (not shown) excess supplies of Y are zero, and at p_1 excess supplies of Y are B_1Q_1. As the price ratio continues to fall, the production of Y continues to rise, but we note that at least after some point the consumption of Y will begin to rise as well. This is because of the positive income effect associated with the fall in the relative price of X. Therefore, as the price ratio falls, the excess supplies of Y initially rise, reach some maximum, and thereafter decline. This behavior gives an offer curve of the shape shown in Fig. A2.4. It should be noted, however, that this argument about the shape of the offer curve depends crucially on the existence of homogeneous community indifference curves.

When we began the derivation of the offer curve, we arbitrarily considered price ratio lines that resulted in exports of Y and imports of X; that is, we chose price lines that were less steep than p_0. Just as appropriately we could have started by increasing the slope of the price line and then considered prices such as p^1 of Fig. A2.2, implying imports of Y and exports

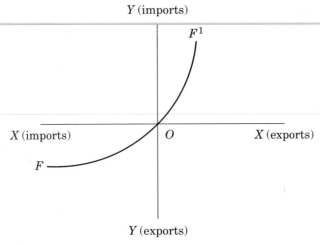

FIGURE A2.5
Offer curve for a country importing Y.

of X. If the various excess demand and supply bundles for such price lines had been plotted in the first quadrant, the offer curve would have been concave to the Y axis rather than to the X axis, resulting in Fig. A2.5. It should be noted that Fig. A2.4 and Fig. A2.5 provide the same information and differ only in the initial choice of the commodity to be exported. All that is required to convert Fig. A2.4 to Fig. A2.5 is to interchange the first and third quadrants.

A2.3 EQUILIBRIUM WITH TWO COUNTRIES

It is often convenient to use offer curve diagrams to illustrate the determination of equilibrium prices in different circumstances and to show how prices change when various parameters of the model change. To facilitate such an analysis, in this section we show how the equilibrium terms of trade are established for a world in which there are two countries that trade exclusively with one another. To simplify the analysis, we assume that we know in advance which country will export which commodity.

We assume that there are two countries, a home country, which we designate H, and a foreign country, which we designate F. As before, we have two goods, X and Y, and we assume that in the final equilibrium Country H imports X and exports Y and that Country F exports X and imports Y. Because Country H is an importer of X, we need to consider only price lines such as p_1, p_2 and p_3 of Fig. A2.2. These produce an offer curve having the shape shown in Fig. A2.3 and shown as OH in Fig. A2.6. We note again that the offer curve is concave to the import axis. For Country F, which imports Y, we have an offer curve with the shape shown in quadrant I of Fig. A2.5 and reproduced as OF in Fig. A2.6. Again, the offer curve is concave to the import axis, which in this case is commodity Y.

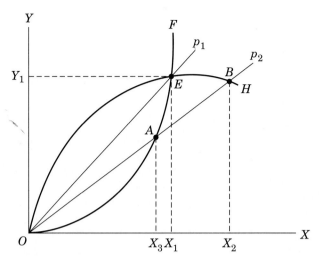

FIGURE A2.6
Offer curve equilibrium for two countries.

As drawn, the two offer curves of Fig. A2.6 intersect only once, at point E. Through this point we have drawn price line p_1, and this will be the equilibrium free trade price line for this simple two-country model. To demonstrate that this is indeed an equilibrium, we need only consider how the offer curves were constructed. Recall that all points on the offer curve show the quantities of one good that the country is willing to exchange for a quantity of the other. Furthermore, we saw that the price line relevant to any point on the offer curve is a line from the origin through that point. Thus the offer curve OH of Fig. A2.6 shows us that at price line p_1 the home country desires to import a quantity of X equal to X_1 and to export an amount of Y equal to Y_1. The offer curve OF indicates that the foreign country wishes to import an amount of Y equal to Y_1 and to export X_1 of commodity X. Clearly, at price p_1 the exports of one country are exactly equal to the imports of the other, and thus the point E of Fig. A2.6 is an equilibrium.

A2.4 STABILITY AND UNIQUENESS

We have seen that the intersection of the two offer curves OH and OF in Fig. A2.6 produces an equilibrium at E with price line p_1. These two offer curves clearly intersect only once, and therefore this equilibrium is unique. It is easy, however, to construct situations in which more than one equilibrium exists, but before doing so, we find it useful to examine the question of when an equilibrium such as E is stable.

An equilibrium is said to be stable if, after a slight displacement from the initial equilibrium position, there is a tendency for the original equilibrium to be reestablished. To investigate whether or not p_1 of Fig. A2.6 is stable, we consider price line p_2, which is clearly not an equilibrium price line, and ask whether there are market forces that would tend to reestablish

p_1. The price line p_2 intersects the home country's offer curve at point B, meaning that at those prices Country H wishes to import X_2 of commodity X. Price line p_2 intersects the foreign country's offer curve at point A, thus indicating that Country F wishes to export X_3 of commodity X. Because Country H wishes to import more than Country F wants to export, there is clearly an excess demand for commodity X. Turning to commodity Y, we can similarly show that Country H wishes to export more Y than Country F wishes to import, and there is therefore an excess supply of commodity Y. The excess demand for commodity X and the excess supply of commodity Y imply that the relative price of X will rise and the price line will rotate counterclockwise through point O. Note that the excess demand for X and the excess supply of Y will continue to exist until the price line passes through E, the original equilibrium point. It can also be shown that for price lines steeper than p_1 there will be an excess demand for Y and an excess supply of X, and again, there will be a tendency for price line p_1 to be reestablished. Since there are market forces that tend to reestablish price line p_1 after any small perturbation of prices, equilibrium E is stable.

Now consider Fig. A2.7, where the offer curves have been drawn to intersect three times so that we have a case of multiple equilibria. Points E_1, E_2, and E_3 are all equilibria, and to each point there corresponds a commodity price line. We now wish to determine whether all three of these equilibria are stable. Beginning at equilibrium E_1 with price line p_1, we consider price line p' and ask whether market forces will tend to reestablish the equilibrium price p_1. The price line p' intersects the home country's offer curve at B, and thus quantity X_2 is the home country's desired amount of imports of commodity X. Note that we have labelled Fig. A2.7 to correspond to Fig. A2.6. The intersection of price line p' with the foreign country's offer curve is at point A, just as it was in Fig. A2.6, and this leads to X_3 as the desired quantity of exports for Country F. But whereas the desired imports of commodity X are greater than the desired exports of commodity X in

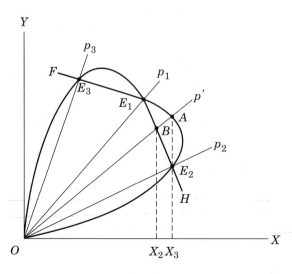

FIGURE A2.7
Multiple equilibria where E_1 is unstable.

Fig. A2.6, the situation is reversed in Fig. A2.7. The amount X_3 is larger than X_2, and thus the foreign country wishes to export a larger quantity of commodity X than Country H wants to import. It can similarly be shown that at price line p' in Fig. A2.7 there is excess demand for commodity Y, and this combined with the excess supply of commodity X means that the relative price of Y will rise. An increase in the relative price of Y implies that the price line will rotate clockwise through O, and thus the price will move away from the equilibrium E_1. Indeed, the relative price of X will continue to fall until price p_2 is reached.

It can similarly be shown that a price line slightly steeper than p_1 results in excess demand for X and excess supply of Y and results in prices moving toward p_3. Clearly, price p_1 is unstable, since any small perturbation of prices moves the equilibrium point away from E_1.

A consideration of points E_2 and E_3 would show that both these equilibria are stable. Indeed, a close examination of Fig. A2.7 would show that E_2 and E_3 are both similar to equilibrium E of Fig. A2.6 in terms of the excess demands and supplies that would exist at prices close to p_2 and p_3. Thus in Fig. A2.7 the middle equilibrium E_1 is unstable, but stable equilibria exist on either side of E_1. This property can be shown to carry forward to other more complex situations. When there are many equilibria, the equilibrium points alternate between being stable and unstable, and each unstable equilibrium has a stable equilibrium on either side.

A2.5 CONCLUDING REMARKS

As we have seen, the offer curve is a representation of the excess demands and supplies for the two commodities that will exist at various commodity price ratios. Given the offer curve and the equilibrium price line, the imports and exports can be immediately derived. The offer curve can be an important tool in the determination of equilibrium prices when more than one country is assumed.

The offer curves that have been derived in this chapter have assumed the existence of community indifference curves. It should be noted, however, that offer curves will exist whether or not community indifference curves exist, as long as, for any given price line, the equilibrium consumption bundles can be found. Thus in Fig. A2.1 suppose community indifference curves did not exist but the consumption points C_1, C_2, and C_3 could nevertheless be found. It is obvious that in this case the offer curve of Fig. A2.3 could be derived in precisely the same fashion. The only complication that arises if community indifference curves do not exist is that the consumption points of Fig. A2.1 need not necessarily lie along a smooth line such as AF. If they do not, the offer curve of Fig. A2.3 will not necessarily have the shape shown. Variations from this shape can significantly complicate the analysis, and thus smooth offer curves concave to the import axis are assumed for simplicity. The important point, however, is that this assumption is largely a matter of convenience; offer curves can generally be assumed to exist, regardless of whether community indifference curves exist.

PROBLEMS

1. With a single factor of production, the production possibility curve will be linear. Using the techniques of Fig. A2.1 and Fig. A2.2, show how the offer curve can be constructed in this case.
2. Show that if the offer curves of Fig. A2.4 and Fig. A2.5 were superimposed on one another they would be tangent at the origin.
3. Suppose that in Fig. A2.1 the maximum producible quantity of Y (that is, T) were larger and the maximum producible quantity of X (that is, T') were smaller. Show how this would change the position of the offer curve.
4. Show how changes in taste could affect the position of the offer curve.
5. Show that E_2 of Fig. A2.7 is stable.
6. Draw a pair of smooth, concave offer curves that intersect five times. Which equilibria are stable?

REFERENCES

Chipman, J. S. (1965). "A Survey of the Theory of International Trade: Part 2, The Neo-Classical Theory." *Econometrica* 33:685–760.
Johnson, H. G. (1959). "International Trade, Income Distribution and the Offer Curve." *Manchester School* 27:241–260.
Lerner, A. P. (1953). *Essays in Economic Analysis*. London: Macmillan.
Meade, J. E. (1952). *A Geometry of International Trade*. London: Allen & Unwin.
Melvin, J. R. (1985). "Domestic Taste Differences, Transportation Costs and International Trade." *Journal of International Economics* 18:65–82.

APPENDIX
3

EXTENSIONS OF THE HECKSCHER-OHLIN MODEL

A3.1 INTRODUCTION

In Appendix 3 we extend and amplify some of the results from Chapter 8. In Section A3.2 we expand on the relation between prices and outputs, and in Section A3.3 we take up the question of factor-intensity reversal.

A3.2 ENDOWMENTS, OUTPUTS, AND PRICES

This section continues the discussion of the relation among factor endowments, commodity outputs, factor prices, and commodity prices, and it expands on the results of Sections 8.3, 8.4, and 8.5. We make use of the unit-value isoquant diagram and the factor-box diagram, beginning by showing that these two figures are really just different versions of the same basic figure and that one can be derived from the other. This can be illustrated by reference to Fig. A3.1, which depicts the factor-box diagram that would correspond to the isoquant diagram in Fig. A3.2. The basic difference between the two diagrams is that in Fig. A3.2, the two sets of isoquants have been plotted from the same origin rather than from different corners of the factor box. The overall endowment *ratio*, that is, the line $O_x O_y$ in Fig. A3.1, is shown as the overall endowment ray k_0 in Fig. A3.2. The tangency between the two isoquants (not shown) at the point A of Fig. A3.1 gives the same wage-rental ratio ω_0 that is shown in Fig. A3.2.

To illustrate further the relation between Fig. A3.1 and Fig. A3.2, we have assumed that in Fig. A3.2 the overall endowment point is E_0, which thus corresponds to point O_y of Fig. A3.1. The overall endowment E_0 is of

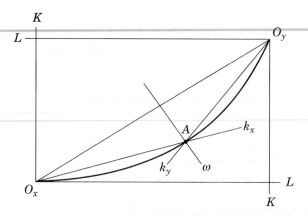

FIGURE A3.1
Equilibrium in the factor-box
diagram.

course just the sum of the amounts of capital and labor used to produce the equilibrium quantities of X and Y. Furthermore, we know that commodity Y must be produced by using capital and labor according to the ratio k_y and that X is produced by using capital and labor in the ratio k_x. Thus, OE_0, the overall endowment vector, is a weighted sum of the two vectors k_y and k_x. To find the lengths of the two vectors k_y and k_x that sum to the vector OE_0, we can draw from E_0 a line A_0E_0 having slope equal to that of k_y and intersecting the vector k_x at point A_0. The X isoquant through A_0 gives the amount of X that would be produced given the capital-labor ratios of the two

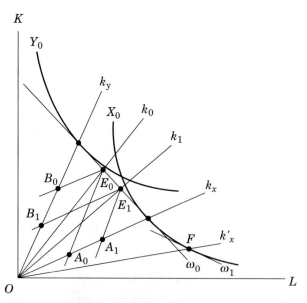

FIGURE A3.2
The effects on relative outputs of changes in the overall K-L ratio.

industries and the overall endowment E_0. Note that the point A_0 of Fig. A3.2 corresponds exactly to point A of Fig. A3.1 and that the triangle OE_0A_0 of Fig. A3.2 is similar to the triangle O_xO_yA of Fig. A3.1. The efficiency locus OA_0E_0 could be drawn in Fig. A3.2, and thus we have constructed Fig. A3.1 from Fig. A3.2.

An alternative approach would have been to draw from E_0 a line parallel to k_x and intersecting k_y at point B_0. The Y isoquant through B_0 would give the output of commodity Y measured from the origin O. The distance E_0A_0 equals the distance OB_0 since $OB_0E_0A_0$ is a parallelogram. Points A_0 and B_0 of Fig. A3.2 give the amounts of capital and labor used in the two industries, and the two vectors OB_0 and OA_0 sum to the endowment point OE_0.

Figure A3.2 also shows how a change in the overall capital-labor ratio affects the output of the two commodities. For the overall capital-labor ratio k_0, the output of Y is B_0 and the output of X is A_0. For a lower overall capital-labor ratio, as illustrated by k_1, the output of Y is B_1 whereas the output of X is A_1. It can be seen that $B_1 < B_0$ and that $A_1 > A_0$, and thus a reduction in the overall capital-labor ratio leads to a reduction in the output of Y and an increase in the output of X. It is important to note that the preceding comparison has been made under the assumption that commodity prices have not changed, which in turn implies that the unit-value isoquants have not changed. The Rybczynski theorem is just a special case of this proposition, the case in which a reduction in the capital-labor ratio is accomplished by increasing the quantity of labor without changing the amount of capital.

A continuation of this argument demonstrates that as we consider lower and lower overall capital-labor endowment ratios, we find that the output of Y, the capital-intensive commodity, continues to fall, whereas the output of X, the labor-intensive commodity, continues to rise. Indeed, when the overall capital-labor ratio becomes equal to k_x, the output of Y becomes zero and all resources are used in the production of commodity X. Similarly, an increase in the capital-labor ratio results in an increase in the output of Y and a reduction in the output of X, and when the overall capital-labor ratio becomes equal to k_y, the output of X is zero and all factors are used in the production of Y. Note that for all capital-labor ratios between k_y and k_x the wage-rental ratio, ω_0 from Fig. A3.2, is a constant. This assumes that commodity prices are unchanged, which in turn implies that the unit-value isoquants are unchanged.

Now suppose we continue to reduce the capital-labor ratio beyond the point where specialization in commodity X has taken place. In particular, assume that the overall capital-labor ratio becomes k_x'. There will be specialization in X, and, with cost-minimization by firms, the wage-rental ratio must be tangent to the isoquant at F, the point where the wage-rental ratio ω_1 is tangent to the isoquant X_0. Note that for this wage-rental ratio it will not be profitable to produce commodity Y, for the tangency between Y_0 and an isocost line with slope ω_1 would imply a much higher cost than is associated with the isocost line through point F.

A similar argument would demonstrate that for overall capital-labor ratios higher than k_y there is specialization in commodity Y and the wage-rental ratio is equal to the slope of the isoquant Y_0 at the relevant production point. Thus in the area between the K axis and k_y we will have specialization in commodity Y, with the wage-rental ratio being equal to the slope of the isoquant Y_0. Throughout the range from k_y to k_x, both commodities are produced and the wage-rental ratio is equal to ω_0. Between the ray k_x and the L axis we have specialization in X and the wage-rental ratio equal to the slope of X_0. The cone formed by k_y and k_x is referred to as the *cone of diversification*, because, if the overall capital-labor ratio lies within this cone, production is diversified in the sense that some of both commodities are produced. Outside this cone of diversification, that is, between the capital axis and k_y or between k_x and the L axis, variations in the overall capital-labor ratio result in changes in the wage-rental ratio. Inside the cone of diversification, variations in the overall capital-labor ratio leave the wage-rental ratio unchanged, but result in a change in the levels of output of the two commodities.

A3.3   THE FACTOR-INTENSITY-REVERSAL CASE

In Sections 8.3 and 8.4 it was argued that the proofs of both the Heckscher-Ohlin and factor-price-equalization theorems require the assumption that no factor-intensity reversals be present. In this section it will be shown why such reversals can result in the failure of these two theorems. We begin by defining factor-intensity reversals.

Factor-intensity reversal refers to the situation where, at one set of relative factor prices, commodity X is capital-intensive relative to commodity Y, and where at another set of factor prices, commodity X is labor-intensive relative to commodity Y. This phenomenon is illustrated in Fig. A3.3, where X_0 and Y_0 are representative isoquants for the two commodities. We see that at wage-rental ratios such as ω_0 we have $k_x > k_y$, whereas at factor-price ratios such as ω' we have $k_y > k_x$. It can thus be seen that, since for some factor-price ratios $k_x > k_y$ and for other factor-price ratios $k_y > k_x$, there must be some wage-rental ratio that results in the same capital-labor ratios in both industries. This is represented by k_r in Fig. A3.3 and is referred to as the *factor-intensity-reversal ray*.

Now imagine a situation where the endowment point for one of the countries lies on the factor-intensity-reversal ray. If the factor-box diagram were now constructed, it would be found that the efficiency locus would be the diagonal of the box, implying that the production possibility curve would be linear. Of course, it would be very unusual if the endowment point for any country were precisely on the factor-intensity-reversal ray, and the important conclusion to be drawn from this special case is that for capital-labor ratios close to the factor-intensity-reversal ray, the production frontier is almost linear. For capital-labor ratios that differ significantly from the factor-intensity-reversal ray, the production possibility curve will

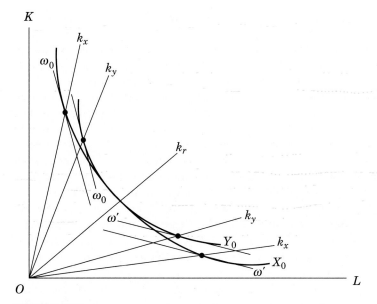

FIGURE A3.3
The factor-intensity-reversal case.

have the usual bowed-out shape. We thus could have the situation shown in Fig. A3.4, where the production frontier for Country H is almost linear and the production frontier for Country F is more bowed out. This could result in a situation where the production possibility curves for the two countries intersect more than once, and then trade patterns would depend crucially on the nature of demand conditions. This can be illustrated by supposing that, in autarky, the highest community indifference curve for Country F is tangent at A_f, whereas the autarky point for Country H is A_h. If we now ignore all of the diagram below Y_0 we see that when trade is

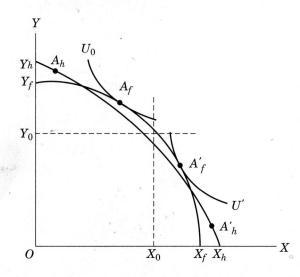

FIGURE A3.4
Possible effects of factor-intensity reversal on the production possibility curves.

allowed, Country H would export commodity Y and Country F would export commodity X.

But suppose that, instead of the tastes represented by indifference curve U_0, we had assumed that preferences in both countries were much more biased toward commodity X, resulting in indifference curves such as U'. This indifference curve is tangent to the production frontier for Country F at A'_f, and an indifference curve from this family would be tangent to the production frontier for Country H at A'_h. Now, ignoring all of the diagram to the left of X_0, it is clear that the pattern of trade that would result is exactly opposite to what it was for the initial tangency at A_f. Here Country F exports Y while Country H exports X, and thus the pattern of trade is reversed. It is thus obvious that if the Heckscher-Ohlin theorem holds for one of these situations, it cannot hold for the other so that, in general, the Heckscher-Ohlin theorem cannot be proved unless factor-intensity reversals are excluded.

A factor-intensity reversal can result in more than one cone of diversification. This can be seen in Fig. A3.5, where rather than the two isoquants being drawn tangent to one another, the Y isoquant has been pulled toward the origin so that the two isoquants intersect twice. In Fig. A3.5 there are two cones of diversification, or in other words, there are two isocost lines tangent to both isoquants that allow the production of both commodities. If the overall endowment ratio for Country H is k_h in the cone defined by k_x and k_y, then the wage-rental ratio in Country H will be ω_h. If the capital-labor ratio for Country F is k_f, lying in the cone of diversification

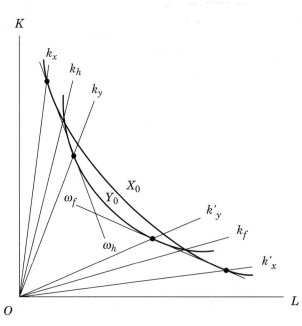

FIGURE A3.5
Factor-intensity reversal with two cones of diversification.

defined by k_y' and k_x', then the wage-rental ratio in F will be ω_f. In this example both countries produce both commodities, but since production takes place in different cones of diversification, the wage-rental ratios are not the same, and thus factor prices are not equalized. Thus, a complete proof of the factor-price-equalization theorem must preclude the possibility of factor-intensity reversals.

Figure A3.5 also illustrates why the Heckscher-Ohlin theorem need not hold when there are factor-intensity reversals. Recall that the production of two commodities for each country depends on the location of the overall endowment ratio within the cone of diversification. Thus if k_h were close to k_x, Country H would be producing a relatively large quantity of commodity X. Similarly, if k_f were close to k_y', Country F would be producing a relatively large amount of commodity Y. With identical tastes in the two countries, this implies that H exports X and F exports Y. But we could just as easily have assumed that k_h was close to k_y and k_f close to k_x', in which case the opposite trade pattern would have been observed. Note that in both cases Country H is relatively well endowed with K, since $k_h > k_f$. Thus, predictions of trade patterns cannot be made from knowledge of relative endowments if factor-intensity reversals are present.

A3.4 CONCLUDING REMARKS

It was shown that while the unit-value-isoquant diagram and the factor-box diagram provide essentially the same information, each diagram is useful for illustrating different phenomena. For example, the unit-value-isoquant diagram clearly indicates how changing factor supplies change equilibrium outputs at constant commodity prices. Unit-value isoquants are also useful for illustrating the case of factor-intensity reversal. It was shown that neither the Heckscher-Ohlin theorem nor the factor-price-equalization theorem can be proved when factor-intensity reversals exist.

PROBLEMS

1. Suppose the isoquants in Fig. A3.5 intersect three times. How will this affect the production possibility curves?
2. Show that free trade may actually cause relative factor prices to become more unequal between countries than in autarky when a factor-intensity reversal exists.
3. Show that, with a factor-intensity reversal, both countries can export their labor-intensive commodities.
4. Use Fig. A3.2 to prove the magnification effect described in Chapter 8.

APPENDIX
4

THE SPECIFIC-FACTORS MODEL: AN ALTERNATIVE APPROACH

A4.1 INTRODUCTION

In Chapter 9 we provided a traditional analysis of the specific-factors model. In Appendix 4 we provide an alternative approach that some readers may find helpful in understanding this model and, in particular, in allowing a comparison with the Heckscher-Ohlin model. We begin in Section A4.2 by showing how the production possibility curve is constructed. In subsequent sections we illustrate the effects of endowment changes and commodity price changes. Specific comparisons with the results from the Heckscher-Ohlin model are provided.

A4.2 THE PRODUCTION POSSIBILITY CURVE

The model is the same as in Chapter 9 and is described by Eqs. (A4.1)–(A4.5), which reproduce the set of equations in (9.1) and (9.2) in Chapter 9. Equations (A4.1) and (A4.2) are the production functions, assumed to exhibit constant returns to scale, while Eqs. (A4.3), (A4.4), and (A4.5) are the factor constraints.

$$X = F_x(R_x, L_x) \tag{A4.1}$$

$$Y = F_y(S_y, L_y) \tag{A4.2}$$

$$\overline{R} = R_x \tag{A4.3}$$

$$\overline{S} = S_y \tag{A4.4}$$

$$\overline{L} = L_x + L_y \tag{A4.5}$$

Equations (A4.3) and (A4.4) show that the entire available stock of factor R is used to produce commodity X and that the entire endowment of factor S is used to produce commodity Y. All factors of production are fully employed. The wage rate is defined to be w, and the returns to R and S are r and s, respectively.

The fact that both production functions use the entire available endowment of the specific factor makes the construction of the production possibility curve somewhat easier than was the case for the Heckscher-Ohlin model of Chapter 8. Recall from Chapter 2 that one representation of a production function such as (A4.1) is the total product curve, which fixes the input of one of the factors and shows total output as a function of varying quantities of the other factor. In the present model, with S_y fixed at $\overline{S}$ for industry Y, the total product curve provides a complete description of production conditions in the Y industry. Such a total product curve is shown as F_y in quadrant II of Fig. A4.1, where the vertical axis measures the output of Y and the horizontal axis measures the input of L_y, which is measured leftward from the origin. For the moment, ignore curve F'_y. The total available supply of labor is shown by $\overline{L}$ on the L_y axis and the use of $\overline{L}$ by the Y industry would result in an output of $\overline{Y}$. The total product curve for industry X is shown as F_x in quadrant IV, where the output of X is plotted

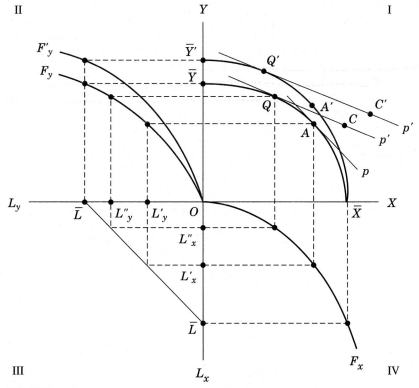

FIGURE A4.1
Production possibility curve for the specific-factors model.

as a function of labor input L_x. Here $\overline{X}$ is the maximum amount of X that could be produced by using the entire endowment of labor in the X industry.

The 45° line $\overline{LL}$ in quadrant III provides a convenient method of illustrating all possible ways that the total endowment of labor can be divided between the two industries. Thus, if L'_y of labor is used in the Y industry, then L'_x is available for use in industry X. This allocation of labor would result in the outputs of X and Y shown by point A in quadrant I. Other allocations of labor between the two industries would give other points on $\overline{LL}$, and these would produce other points on the production possibility curve. Thus, the production frontier will be $\overline{Y}A\overline{X}$, as shown in quadrant I.

It is now easy to see how changes in the endowments of either the specific factors or labor would change the production possibility curve. First, consider an increase in the amount of S used in industry Y. With more S available for all allocations of labor to the Y industry, the total product curve would shift to F'_y in quadrant II. Now the entire allocation of labor to the Y industry produces point $\overline{Y}'$, and the allocation of labor between the two industries that originally produced point A now gives point A'. We note that the production frontier $\overline{Y}'A'\overline{X}$ is entirely above the original production possibility curve except at the endpoint $\overline{X}$. For an increase in the endowment of R the argument is similar. The total product curve F_x would shift out and the production possibility curve would shift out everywhere except at point $\overline{Y}$. An increase in the available endowment of labor could be illustrated by shifting the $\overline{LL}$ 45° line in quadrant III farther away from the origin. This shift would increase the maximum producible quantities of both Y and X and would therefore result in a shift outward of the production possibility curve over its entire length. Of course, this expansion of output need not be uniform along the production frontier, for the outward shift will depend on the shapes of the total product curves for the two industries.

The production frontiers of Fig. A4.1 can now be used to illustrate trading equilibrium in exactly the same way as was shown for the Heckscher-Ohlin model. Thus suppose A is the initial autarky equilibrium and p is the domestic price ratio. Assume for the moment that the world price ratio is given and equal to p'. When trade is allowed, production moves from A to Q and consumption from A to point C, where C represents a tangency between a community indifference curve (not shown) and the price line p'. In this situation Y is exported and X is imported. If we now assume that an increase occurs in the amount of the specific factor S, the production possibility curve shifts out to $\overline{Y}'A'\overline{X}$, and the new production and consumption points become Q' and C'.

A4.3   FACTOR RETURNS

In Chapter 8 we were able to derive relations between factor prices and commodity prices and between endowment changes and output changes. In Sections A4.4 and A4.5 of this Appendix we examine these issues in terms of the specific-factors model. To facilitate such a discussion we now illustrate how factor returns are determined. This is most easily done through the use of Fig. A4.2, which presents a slightly different characterization of the specific-factors model. Quadrant III in Fig. A4.2 is exactly the same as quadrant III in Fig. A4.1 and shows the total quantity of labor available to the two industries. In quadrants II and IV, however, we now show the marginal product curves rather than the total product curves. The marginal product curve is simply the slope of the total product curve, and since both F_y and F_x are concave to the labor axes (that is, they exhibit diminishing returns), the marginal product curves both slope downward. In Fig. A4.2 the curve MP_y in quadrant II is derived directly from F_y of quadrant II of Fig. A4.1. At all points on the labor axis, such as L'_y, the curve MP_y is a measure of the slope of F_y for that particular labor allocation to the Y industry. Note that while the axes of quadrant I in Fig. A4.2 are in units of Y and X, just as they are in Fig. A4.1, the scales in the two diagrams are quite different. Figure A4.1 shows the total outputs of X and Y, while Fig. A4.2 shows the payments to labor measured in terms of X and Y.

In a perfectly competitive industry, in equilibrium factor owners receive their marginal product in payment for their services, and therefore in the Y industry we have $MP_y = w/p_y$. Thus, in Fig. A4.2 the distance OM,

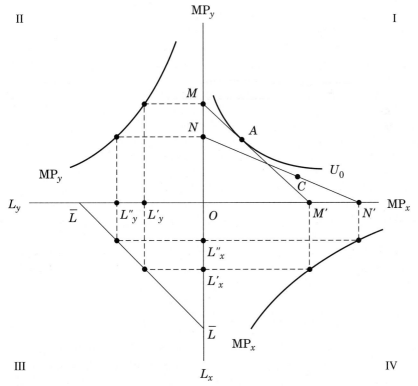

FIGURE A4.2
Marginal product curves showing factor incomes.

which is the marginal product of labor in Y, gives the real return to labor for workers in the Y industry. Similarly, OM' is the marginal product, or the real return to labor, in the X industry. Note also that since $MP_y = w/p_y$ and $MP_x = w/p_x$, the slope of line MM' in Fig. A4.2 is $p_x/p_y = p$, which is the price ratio associated with point A of Fig. A4.1. Further, since OM is the return to labor for workers in the Y industry and OM' is the return to labor for workers in the X industry, the line MM' is simply the budget constraint for a representative worker. Thus point A, the tangency between an indifference curve and the budget constraint, represents the equilibrium consumption point for a representative worker. Furthermore, because all consumers in the economy have been assumed to have identical and homogeneous preferences, point A in Fig. A4.2 represents the same Y/X consumption ratio as point A of Fig. A4.1 does. Of course, point A in Fig. A4.1 represents aggregate consumption, while point A in Fig. A4.2 represents the individual worker's consumption point.

We can use Fig. A4.2 to show the relations between changes in commodity prices and factor prices and to illustrate how outputs change when endowments change, but before we do so, we will review some of the properties of production functions that exhibit constant returns to scale. In Chapter 2 we noted that for such production functions, the marginal products are constant for any capital-labor ratio (along any ray from the origin). Therefore, in Fig. A4.3 the marginal products of both L and R are constant along the capital-labor ratio k_x. This property was used in the proof of the Stolper-Samuelson theorem in Chapter 8, where it was shown that the changes in the marginal products of both inputs depend only on the change in the capital-labor ratios. Thus, if the capital-labor ratio in Fig. A4.3 changes from k_x to k_x', the direction of change in the marginal product for R can be found by comparing points A and B, while the direction of change in the marginal product for L can be found by comparing points A and C. The movement from A to C, for example, keeps R fixed at $\overline{R}$ and reduces the input of L_x. This is equivalent to moving along the curve F_x toward the origin in Fig. A4.1. As we move toward the origin, the slope of F_x increases, or in other words, the marginal product increases. Thus, the marginal product of L is an increasing function of the capital-labor ratio. In exactly the same way we can show that the marginal product of R is a decreasing function of the capital-labor ratio.

We have seen that the marginal products, or in other words, the real returns to the factors, depend on the capital-labor ratios, and thus changes in the real returns to factors are known as soon as changes in capital-labor ratios are known. Of even more importance for our present discussion is the fact that since the marginal products are functions *only* of the capital-labor ratios, if we know how one marginal product changes we immediately know that the other marginal product has changed in the opposite direction. Thus, an increase in the marginal product of labor implies a decrease in the marginal product of R, or in other words, if we find that w/p_x increases, we know that r/p_x must fall. Note that these relations hold regardless of what is happening to output or to endowments.

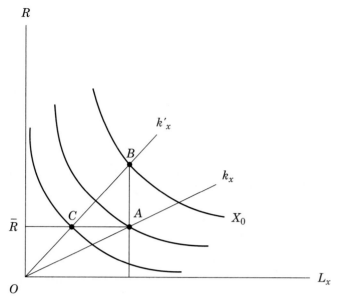

FIGURE A4.3
The relation between marginal products and capital-labor ratios.

A4.4 COMMODITY PRICES AND FACTOR PRICES

We are now in a position to consider how price changes affect factor payments. In Fig. A4.1 it was assumed that point A was the autarky equilibrium and that with trade, production moved to Q and consumption to C on price line p'. This change resulted in a movement of labor out of the X industry and into the Y industry, and the new labor allocation is given by points L_y'' and L_x'' in Fig. A4.1. This same allocation of labor is shown in Fig. A4.2 and gives the new budget constraint for labor shown by the line NN'. Note that NN' is the price line p' in Fig. A4.1.

How have the factors of production been affected by this price change? We note that the marginal product of labor has fallen from OM to ON in the Y industry and risen from OM' to ON' in the X industry. Thus, the welfare of a representative worker will depend on consumption patterns. In the situation shown in Fig. A4.2 the new budget line NN' is below the indifference curve U_0 tangent to MM' at point A, so labor has been made worse off by the relative increase in the price of Y. But this result obviously depends on the position of the indifference curve. Had preferences been biased toward commodity X, labor would have been able to benefit by this price change. In general, then, the effect of a price change on the welfare of labor is uncertain, for workers may be made better off or worse off depending on their preferences for the two commodities, a result that we earlier called the *neoclassical ambiguity*. Note that this conclusion is in sharp contrast to the findings of the Heckscher-Ohlin model, in which it was shown that commodity price increases have unambiguous effects on factor prices. Specifically, it was shown that the factor used intensively in the industry whose price has risen will benefit.

How have the returns of the specific factors been affected by the relative increase in the price of Y? We have noted that the marginal product of labor has fallen from OM to ON in the Y industry, implying, from our previous discussion, that the marginal product of S has necessarily increased. Then since $\text{MP}_S = s/p_y$, where s is the return to S, it is clear that the return to S has increased. In the X industry the marginal product of labor has risen from OM' to ON'. Therefore, the marginal product of R has fallen, and r/p_x, the real return to owners of factor R, has been reduced. Thus, a relative increase in the price of commodity Y produces a gain for the specific factor used to produce Y but reduces the income of the specific factor used in industry X. We therefore have the following proposition:

Commodity price and factor prices. A relative price increase is beneficial to the specific factor used in that industry, reduces the income of the other specific factor, and has an ambiguous effect on labor.

Again note the contrast of these results with the results of the Stolper-Samuelson theorem of Chapter 8.

A4.5   ENDOWMENT CHANGES AND FACTOR PRICE EQUALIZATION

The effects of endowment changes are shown in Fig. A4.4, which takes as the initial situation the trading equilibrium of Fig. A4.2 with consumption at point C on budget constraint NN'. We now consider the increase in S that resulted in the shift of the total product curve from F_y to F_y' in Fig. A4.1. Because of the assumption of constant returns to scale, the total product curves of Fig. A4.1 all have the same slope along any ray from the origin. Thus, the upward shift in the total product curve results in an upward shift of the marginal product curve, as shown in quadrant II of Fig. A4.4. For a small open economy with fixed p, the increase in the endowment of S shifts out the production possibility curve in Fig. A4.1 to $\overline{Y}'A'\overline{X}$ and shifts the production point from Q to Q'. With commodity prices unchanged, the new budget constraint for workers has the same slope as NN' and is shown as VV' in Fig. A4.4.

The effects of an increase in the endowment of S are now clear from Fig. A4.4. The marginal product of labor has increased from ON to OV in industry Y and from ON' to OV' in industry X. Consumption is now at point C', which lies on a higher indifference curve than C, and thus labor is unambiguously better off. Because the marginal product of labor has increased in Y, the marginal product of S in the Y industry has necessarily fallen and therefore owners of S have been made worse off by the increase in the endowment of S. Similarly, because the marginal product of labor has

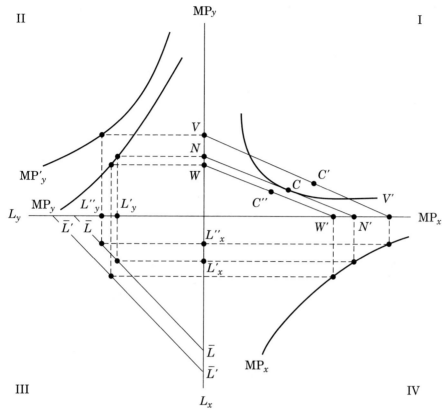

FIGURE A4.4
Effects of changes in $\bar{L}$ and changes in $\bar{S}$.

increased in the X industry, the returns to R, the factor specific to the X industry, have also fallen. Thus an increase in the endowment of S reduces the return to both specific factors and increases labor's real income. It is easily seen that exactly the same result holds for an increase in the supply of R, for the effects of increases in the specific factors are symmetrical. Thus, an increase in R with constant commodity prices lowers the return to both specific factors and increases the return to labor. In general, then, any increase in the endowment of a specific factor at constant commodity prices lowers the real return to both specific factors and increases the return to labor. These results are in sharp contrast to the results derived in Chapter 8, where it was shown that endowment changes with given commodity prices do not affect factor prices if both commodities continue to be produced.

Now, returning to the original marginal product curve MP_y in Fig. A4.4, consider an increase in the endowment of labor. This shifts the labor endowment curve in quadrant III to $\bar{L}'\bar{L}'$, and with the same commodity prices, this shift generates the new budget constraint WW' with consumption at point C''. The increase in the endowment of labor has lowered the marginal product of labor in both industries and unambiguously makes labor worse off. At the same time, because both marginal products of labor have fallen, the marginal products of both the specific factors have increased, and consequently the returns to both specific factors have risen. Therefore, an increase in the endowment of labor is beneficial to both specific factors and harmful to workers. We have the following proposition:

Endowment changes and factor prices. At constant factor prices any increase in the endowment of a specific factor increases the return to labor and lowers the return to both specific factors. An increase in the endowment of labor reduces the return to labor and increases the return to both specific factors.

The output effects of changes in endowments can also be seen in Fig. A4.4. First, consider the increase in S that resulted in the upward shift of the total product curve for commodity Y shown in Fig. A4.1. In Fig. A4.4 the shift in the budget line from NN' to VV' was accomplished by a reduction in the labor force in industry X from L'_x to L''_x. With a reduction in the labor input, and because the input of R is fixed, output of commodity X must necessarily have been reduced. We note that in industry Y labor has increased from L'_y to L''_y and that since the input of S has also increased, the output of Y has clearly increased. Thus, the increase in S results in a production shift from Q to Q' in Fig. A4.1, resulting in more Y and less X at the new equilibrium. Symmetric results can be shown for industry X, and thus we have demonstrated that an increase in the specific factor increases the output of the commodity that uses that factor and reduces the output of the other commodity.

At fixed commodity prices, an increase in the endowment of L results in the allocation of more labor to both industries, as is shown in Fig. A4.4. An increase in the endowment of labor therefore shifts out the production frontier throughout its entire length and, with fixed commodities prices, increases the output of both commodities X and Y. Thus we can state the following proposition:

Endowment changes and outputs. An increase in one specific factor increases the output of the commodity that uses that factor and reduces the output of the other industry. An increase in the supply of labor increases both outputs.

Note the contrast to the Rybczynski theorem from Chapter 8. In the endowment model an increase in a factor increases the output of the commodity that uses that factor intensively and reduces the output of the other industry.

A principal result of the Heckscher-Ohlin model was the factor-price-equalization theorem, which showed that under certain conditions the equalization of commodity prices between two trading countries results in the equalization of factor prices. That such a theorem does not apply to the specific-factors model can easily be seen from Fig. A4.4. We reinterpret

Fig. A4.4 as representing two countries with identical endowments of L and R, but such that the foreign country has a larger supply of S. Therefore in Fig. A4.1 the two production possibility curves represent the two countries. Although it is not shown, it is clear that in a trading equilibrium Country F would export commodity Y and import commodity X. In Fig. A4.4 $\overline{LL}$ represents the common labor supply for the two countries and MP_x the common marginal product of labor curve for the X industry. The marginal product curves for the Y industry in H and F are shown in quadrant II as MP_y and MP'_y, respectively. If trade equalizes commodity prices, then VV' could represent the price line in Country F and NN' the price line in Country H. But although relative commodity prices have been equalized by trade, it is clear that factor prices have not. It follows from our earlier discussion that the real wage will be higher in Country F than in H, whereas the returns to both specific factors will be higher in H than in F. Thus the factor-price-equalization theorem does not hold for the specific-factors model, and we have the following proposition:

Trade and factor prices. The equalization of commodity prices by international trade does not equalize factor prices.

A4.6   THE PATTERN OF TRADE

One of the principal results of the Heckscher-Ohlin theorem described in Chapter 8 is that we can predict trade patterns from the knowledge of factor endowments alone. In particular, we found that a country will export the commodity that uses its abundant factor most intensively. We now want to investigate whether a similar property holds for the specific-factors model. To facilitate comparison we begin, as we have done in the past, by assuming that our two countries, H and F, have identical endowments of labor and *total* capital in the long run. We know from our earlier discussion that in such a case, with preferences assumed to be identical in both countries, the two economies are identical in every respect and there is no possibility of international trade.

We now retain the assumption of identical long-run endowments, but we assume that in the short run the capital in the two countries has been allocated differently between the two industries. In particular, we will assume that in Country H there is more capital in the Y industry and that in Country F more capital has initially been allocated to the X industry. In Fig. A4.5 F'_y and F'_x represent the total product curves for F, and F_y and F_x represent the total product curves for H. With the assumption of an identical endowment of labor in the two economies, these total product curves result in the production possibility curves $\overline{Y}_h Q_h \overline{X}_h$ and $\overline{Y}_f Q_f \overline{X}_f$ for H and F, respectively. Obviously, the two countries are not identical and trade will take place. The pattern of trade is easily seen from Fig. A4.5, and indeed this figure is similar to Fig. 8.4. of Chapter 8. We note that Country H will export commodity Y and Country F will export commodity X. The production points will be Q_h and Q_f for countries H and F, respectively,

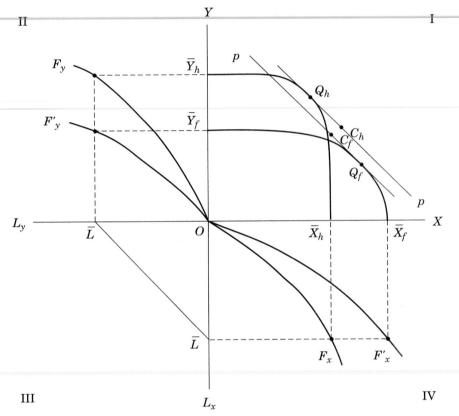

FIGURE A4.5
Pattern of trade in two-country world.

with consumption at C_h and C_f. Thus, in the short run each country will export the commodity that is produced with the relatively abundant specific factor.

Suppose we now consider an increase in the labor supply in Country F. In Fig. A4.5 this would result in a new labor constraint curve in quadrant IV farther from the origin (not shown). As we have already seen, an increase in the labor supply shifts out the production possibility curve and increases Country H's production of both X and Y. At the new equilibrium commodity prices would differ, but there is no reason to expect that the pattern of trade would change. From the long-run point of view we have now created a situation where Country H is relatively well endowed with labor, and by the Heckscher-Ohlin theorem Country H would export the labor-intensive commodity. In the short-run model, however, we do not obtain this result. Trading patterns depend principally on how capital is allocated between the two industries and is much less sensitive to the overall endowments of capital and labor in the economies as a whole. Thus, a relative abundance of labor in one country does not imply that that country necessarily exports the labor-intensive commodity. We have the following proposition:

Pattern of trade. In the specific-factors model, trade patterns cannot be predicted from knowledge of the factor endowments alone, but depend on the nature of the production functions and on the allocation of capital between the two industries.

A4.7 CONCLUDING REMARKS

The specific-factors model provides an interesting contrast to the results of the Heckscher-Ohlin model. In particular, we have seen that the theorems associated with the endowment model do not carry over to the specific-factors framework. Trade does not equalize factor prices, and trade patterns cannot be predicted from knowledge of endowments alone. In the endowment model, factor prices were uniquely determined by commodity prices and real factor rewards responded in a predictable way when commodity prices changed. In the specific-factors model, although the returns to the specific factors are unambiguously related to commodity price changes, such is not the case for the return to labor. Whether labor loses or gains from a price change depends on the consumption pattern of the representative worker. Changes in endowments also have somewhat different effects in the specific-factors model. Whereas an increase in a specific factor necessarily increases the output of the commodity using it, an increase in labor increases the output of both commodities, and which output increases most depends on the nature of the production functions.

PROBLEMS

1. Draw a diagram that illustrates how an increase in the labor supply shifts the production possibility curve.
2. If commodity prices are fixed, what determines how the relative outputs of X and Y are affected by an increase in the labor supply?
3. (*a*) Draw a diagram similar to Fig. A4.2 that shows labor gaining from an increase in the relative price of Y. (*b*) Show that the diagram of part (*a*) can be drawn by assuming either different production functions or different tastes.
4. Use the definition of constant returns to scale to show that the total product curves derived for different amounts of the specific factor all have the same slope along a ray from the origin.
5. Show that if, after trade, the real return to labor is relatively higher in Country H, the real return to both specific factors must be relatively higher in Country F.

INDEX